Team for the preparation of the Human Development Report 2009

Director

Jeni Klugman

Research

Led by Francisco R. Rodríguez, comprising Ginette Azcona, Matthew Cummins, Ricardo Fuentes Nieva, Mamaye Gebretsadik, Wei Ha, Marieke Kleemans, Emmanuel Letouzé, Roshni Menon, Daniel Ortega, Isabel Medalho Pereira, Mark Purser and Cecilia Ugaz (Deputy Director until October 2008).

Statistics

Led by Alison Kennedy, comprising Liliana Carvajal, Amie Gaye, Shreyasi Jha, Papa Seck and Andrew Thornton.

National HDR and network

Eva Jespersen (Deputy Director HDRO), Mary Ann Mwangi, Paola Pagliani and Timothy Scott.

Outreach and communications

Led by Marisol Sanjines, comprising Wynne Boelt, Jean-Yves Hamel, Melissa Hernandez, Pedro Manuel Moreno and Yolanda Polo.

Production, translation, budget and operations, administration

Carlotta Aiello (production coordinator), Sarantuya Mend (operations manager), Fe Juarez-Shanahan and Oscar Bernal.

Foreword

Migration not infrequently gets a bad press. Negative stereotypes portraying migrants as 'stealing our jobs' or 'scrounging off the taxpayer' abound in sections of the media and public opinion, especially in times of recession. For others, the word 'migrant' may evoke images of people at their most vulnerable. This year's Human Development Report, *Overcoming Barriers: Human Mobility and Development*, challenges such stereotypes. It seeks to broaden and rebalance perceptions of migration to reflect a more complex and highly variable reality.

This report breaks new ground in applying a human development approach to the study of migration. It discusses who migrants are, where they come from and go to, and why they move. It looks at the multiple impacts of migration for all who are affected by it—not just those who move, but also those who stay.

In so doing, the report's findings cast new light on some common misconceptions. For example, migration from developing to developed countries accounts for only a minor fraction of human movement. Migration from one developing economy to another is much more common. Most migrants do not go abroad at all, but instead move within their own country.

Next, the majority of migrants, far from being victims, tend to be successful, both before they leave their original home and on arrival in their new one. Outcomes in all aspects of human development, not only income but also education and health, are for the most part positive—some immensely so, with people from the poorest places gaining the most.

Reviewing an extensive literature, the report finds that fears about migrants taking the jobs or lowering the wages of local people, placing an unwelcome burden on local services, or costing the taxpayer money, are generally exaggerated. When migrants' skills complement those of local people, both groups benefit. Societies as a whole may also benefit in many ways—ranging from rising levels of technical innovation to increasingly diverse cuisine to which migrants contribute.

The report suggests that the policy response to migration can be wanting. Many governments institute increasingly repressive entry regimes, turn a blind eye to health and safety violations by employers, or fail to take a lead in educating the public on the benefits of immigration.

By examining policies with a view to expanding people's freedoms rather than controlling or restricting human movement, this report proposes a bold set of reforms. It argues that, when tailored to country-specific contexts, these changes can amplify human mobility's already substantial contributions to human development.

The principal reforms proposed centre around six areas, each of which has important and complementary contributions to make to human development: opening up existing entry channels so that more workers can emigrate; ensuring basic rights for migrants; lowering the transaction costs of migration; finding solutions that benefit both destination communities and the migrants they receive; making it easier for people to move within their own countries; and mainstreaming migration into national development strategies.

The report argues that while many of these reforms are more feasible than at first thought, they nonetheless require political courage. There may also be limits to governments' ability to make swift policy changes while the recession persists.

Foreword

This is the first Human Development Report for which as Administrator I am writing the foreword. Like all such reports, this is an independent study intended to stimulate debate and discussion on an important issue. It is not a statement of either United Nations or UNDP policy.

At the same time, by highlighting human mobility as a core component of the human development agenda, it is UNDP's hope that the following insights will add value to ongoing discourse on migration and inform the work of development practitioners and policy makers around the world.

Helen Clark
Administrator
United Nations Development Programme

The analysis and policy recommendations of this report do not necessarily reflect the views of the United Nations Development Programme, its Executive Board or its Member States.

The report is an independent publication commissioned by UNDP. It is the fruit of a collaborative effort by a team of eminent advisers and the Human Development Report team.

Jeni Klugman, Director of the Human Development Report Office, led the effort.

Acknowledgements

This report is the fruit of the efforts, contributions and support of many people and organizations. I would like to thank Kemal Derviş for the opportunity to take on the daunting task of Director of the Human Development Report, and the new UNDP Administrator, Helen Clark, for advice and support. Coming back to the office after its 20 years of growth and success has been a tremendously rewarding experience, and I would like to especially thank my family, Ema, Josh and Billy, for their patience and support throughout. The dedication and hard work of the whole HDR team, listed earlier, was critical. Among those who provided important strategic advice and suggestions, which were especially critical in pulling the report together, were Oliver Bakewell, Martin Bell, Stephen Castles, Joseph Chamie, Samuel Choritz, Michael Clemens, Simon Commander, Sakiko Fukuda-Parr, Hein de Haas, Frank Laczko, Loren Landau, Manjula Luthria, Gregory Maniatis, Philip Martin, Douglas Massey, Saraswathi Menon, Frances Stewart, Michael Walton and Kevin Watkins.

Background studies were commissioned on a range of thematic issues and published online in our Human Development Research Papers series, launched in April 2009, and are listed in the bibliography. A series of 27 seminars that were held between August 2008 and April 2009 likewise provided important stimulus to our thinking and the development of ideas, and we would again thank those presenters for sharing their research and insights. We would also like to acknowledge the contribution of the national experts who participated in our migration policy assessment.

The data and statistics used in this report draw significantly upon the databases of other organizations to which we were allowed generous access: Andean Development Corporation; Development Research Centre on Migration, University of Sussex; ECLAC; International Migration Institute, Oxford; Inter-Parliamentary Union; Internal Displacement Monitoring Centre; the Department of Statistics and the International Migration Programme of the ILO; IOM; Luxembourg Income Study; OECD; UNICEF; UNDESA, Statistics Division and Population Division; UNESCO Institute for Statistics; UNHCR; Treaty Section, United Nations Office of Legal Affairs; UNRWA; the World Bank; and WHO.

The report benefited greatly from intellectual advice and guidance provided by an academic advisory panel. The panel comprised Maruja Asis, Richard Black, Caroline Brettell, Stephen Castles, Simon Commander, Jeff Crisp, Priya Deshingkar, Cai Fang, Elizabeth Ferris, Bill Frelick, Sergei Guriev, Gordon Hanson, Ricardo Hausmann, Michele Klein-Solomon, Kishore Mahbubani, Andrew Norman Mold, Kathleen Newland, Yaw Nyarko, José Antonio Ocampo, Gustav Ranis, Bonaventure Rutinwa, Javier Santiso, Maurice Schiff, Frances Stewart, Elizabeth Thomas-Hope, Jeffrey Williamson, Ngaire Woods and Hania Zlotnik.

From the outset, the process involved a range of participatory consultations designed to draw on the expertise of researchers, civil society advocates, development practitioners and policy makers from around the globe. This included 11 informal stakeholder consultations held between August 2008 and April 2009 in Nairobi, New Delhi, Amman, Bratislava, Manila, Sydney, Dakar, Rio de Janeiro, Geneva, Turin and Johannesburg, involving almost 300 experts and practitioners in total. The support of UNDP country and regional offices and local partners was critical in enabling these consultations. Several events were hosted by key partners, including the IOM, the ILO and the Migration Policy Institute. Additional academic consultations took place in Washington D.C. and Princeton, and HDRO staff participated in various other regional and global fora, including the Global Forum on Migration and Development (GFMD) in Manila, preparatory meetings for the Athens GFMD, and many conferences and seminars organized by other UN agencies (e.g. ILO, UNDESA and UNITAR), universities, think-tanks and non-governmental organizations. Participants in a series of Human Development Network discussions provided wide-ranging insights and observations on the linkages between migration and human development. More details on the process are available at http://hdr.undp.org/en/nhdr.

A UNDP Readers Group, comprising representatives of all the regional and policy bureaux, provided many useful inputs and suggestions on the concept note and report drafts, as did a number of other colleagues who provided inputs and advice. We would especially thank Amat Alsoswa, Carolina Azevedo, Barbara Barungi, Tony Bislimi, Kim Bolduc, Winifred Byanyima, Ajay Chhibber, Samuel Choritz, Pedro Conceição, Awa Dabo, Georgina Fekete, Priya Gajraj, Enrique Ganuza, Tegegnework Gettu, Rebeca Grynspan, Sultan Hajiyev, Mona Hammam, Mette Bloch Hansen, Mari Huseby, Selim Jahan, Bruce Jenks, Arun Kashyap, Olav Kjoren, Paul Ladd, Luis Felipe López-Calva, Tanni Mukhopadhyay, B. Murali, Theodore Murphy, Mihail Peleah, Amin Sharkawi, Kori Udovicki, Mourad Wahba and Caitlin Wiesen for comments.

A team at Green Ink, led by Simon Chater, provided editing services. The design work was carried out by Zago. Guoping Huang developed some of the maps. The production, translation, distribution and promotion of the report benefited from the help and support of the UNDP Office of Communications, and particularly of Maureen Lynch. Translations were reviewed by Luc Gregoire, Madi Musa, Uladzimir Shcherbau and Oscar Yujnovsky. Margaret Chi and Solaiman Al-Rifai of the United Nations Office for Project Services provided critical administrative support and management services.

The report also benefited from the dedicated work of a number of interns, namely Shreya Basu, Vanessa Alicia Chee, Delphine De Quina, Rebecca Lee Funk, Chloe Yuk Ting Heung, Abid Raza Khan, Alastair Mackay, Grace Parker, Clare Potter, Limon B. Rodriguez, Nicolas Roy, Kristina Shapiro and David Stubbs.

We thank all of those involved directly or indirectly in guiding our efforts, while acknowledging sole responsibility for errors of commission and omission.

Jeni Klugman
Director
Human Development Report 2009

Acronyms

CEDAW	United Nations Convention on the Elimination of All Forms of Discrimination against Women
CMW	United Nations International Convention on the Protection of the Rights of All Migrant Workers and Members of their Families
CRC	United Nations Convention on the Rights of the Child
ECD	Early childhood development
ECLAC	Economic Commission for Latin America and the Caribbean
ECOWAS	Economic Community of West African States
EIU	Economist Intelligence Unit
EU	European Union
GATS	General Agreement on Trade in Services
GDP	Gross domestic product
GCC	Gulf Cooperation Council
HDI	Human Development Index
HDR	Human Development Report
HDRO	Human Development Report Office
ILO	International Labour Organization
IOM	International Organization for Migration
MERCOSUR	Mercado Común del Sur (Southern Common Market)
MIPEX	Migrant Integration Policy Index
NGO	Non-governmental organization
OECD	Organisation for Economic Co-operation and Development
PRS	Poverty Reduction Strategy
PRSP	Poverty Reduction Strategy Paper
TMBs	Treaty Monitoring Bodies
UNDESA	United Nations Department of Economic and Social Affairs
UNDP	United Nations Development Programme
UNESCO	United Nations Educational, Scientific and Cultural Organization
UNHCR	Office of the United Nations High Commissioner for Refugees
UNICEF	United Nations Children's Fund
UNODC	United Nations Office on Drugs and Crime
UNRWA	United Nations Relief and Works Agency for Palestine Refugees in the Near East
USSR	Union of Soviet Socialist Republics
WHO	World Health Organization
WTO	World Trade Organization

Contents

Contents

Contents

BOXES

FIGURES

Contents

Overview

Consider Juan. Born into a poor family in rural Mexico, his family struggled to pay for his health care and education. At the age of 12, he dropped out of school to help support his family. Six years later, Juan followed his uncle to Canada in pursuit of higher wages and better opportunities.

Life expectancy in Canada is five years higher than in Mexico and incomes are three times greater. Juan was selected to work temporarily in Canada, earned the right to stay and eventually became an entrepreneur whose business now employs native-born Canadians. This is just one case out of millions of people every year who find new opportunities and freedoms by migrating, benefiting themselves as well as their areas of origin and destination.

Now consider Bhagyawati. She is a member of a lower caste and lives in rural Andhra Pradesh, India. She travels to Bangalore city with her children to work on construction sites for six months each year, earning Rs 60 (US$1.20) per day. While away from home, her children do not attend school because it is too far from the construction site and they do not know the local language. Bhagyawati is not entitled to subsidized food or health care, nor does she vote, because she is living outside her registered district. Like millions of other internal migrants, she has few options for improving her life other than to move to a different city in search of better opportunities.

Our world is very unequal. The huge differences in human development across and within countries have been a recurring theme of the Human Development Report (HDR) since it was first published in 1990. In this year's report, we explore for the first time the topic of migration. For many people in developing countries moving away from their home town or village can be the best—sometimes the only—option open to improve their life chances. Human mobility can be hugely effective in raising a person's income, health and education prospects. But its value is more than that: being able to decide where to live is a key element of human freedom.

When people move they embark on a journey of hope and uncertainty whether within or across international borders. Most people move in search of better opportunities, hoping to combine their own talents with resources in the destination country so as to benefit themselves and their immediate family, who often accompany or follow them. If they succeed, their initiative and efforts can also benefit those left behind and the society in which they make their new home. But not all do succeed. Migrants who leave friends and family may face loneliness, may feel unwelcome among people who fear or resent newcomers, may lose their jobs or fall ill and thus be unable to access the support services they need in order to prosper.

The 2009 HDR explores how better policies towards human mobility can enhance human development. It lays out the case for governments to reduce restrictions on movement within and across their borders, so as to expand human choices and freedoms. It argues for practical measures that can improve prospects on arrival, which in turn will have large benefits both for destination communities and for places of origin.

How and why people move

Discussions about migration typically start from the perspective of flows from developing countries into the rich countries of Europe, North America and Australasia. Yet most movement in the world does not take place between developing and developed countries; it does not even take place between countries. The overwhelming majority of people who move do so inside their own country. Using a conservative definition, we estimate that approximately 740 million people are internal migrants—almost four times as many as those who have moved internationally. Among people who have moved across national borders,

1

Most migrants, internal and international, reap gains in the form of higher incomes, better access to education and health, and improved prospects for their children

just over a third moved from a developing to a developed country—fewer than 70 million people. Most of the world's 200 million international migrants moved from one developing country to another or between developed countries.

Most migrants, internal and international, reap gains in the form of higher incomes, better access to education and health, and improved prospects for their children. Surveys of migrants report that most are happy in their destination, despite the range of adjustments and obstacles typically involved in moving. Once established, migrants are often more likely than local residents to join unions or religious and other groups. Yet there are trade-offs and the gains from mobility are unequally distributed.

People displaced by insecurity and conflict face special challenges. There are an estimated 14 million refugees living outside their country of citizenship, representing about 7 percent of the world's migrants. Most remain near the country they fled, typically living in camps until conditions at home allow their return, but around half a million per year travel to developed countries and seek asylum there. A much larger number, some 26 million, have been internally displaced. They have crossed no frontiers, but may face special difficulties away from home in a country riven by conflict or racked by natural disasters. Another vulnerable group consists of people—mainly young women—who have been trafficked. Often duped with promises of a better life, their movement is not one of free will but of duress, sometimes accompanied by violence and sexual abuse.

In general, however, people move of their own volition, to better-off places. More than three quarters of international migrants go to a country with a higher level of human development than their country of origin. Yet they are significantly constrained, both by policies that impose barriers to entry and by the resources they have available to enable their move. People in poor countries are the least mobile: for example, fewer than 1 percent of Africans have moved to Europe. Indeed, history and contemporary evidence suggest that development and migration go hand in hand: the median emigration rate in a country with low human development is below 4 percent, compared to more than 8 percent from countries with high levels of human development.

Barriers to movement

The share of international migrants in the world's population has remained remarkably stable at around 3 percent over the past 50 years, despite factors that could have been expected to increase flows. Demographic trends—an aging population in developed countries and young, still-rising populations in developing countries—and growing employment opportunities, combined with cheaper communications and transport, have increased the 'demand' for migration. However, those wishing to migrate have increasingly come up against government-imposed barriers to movement. Over the past century, the number of nation states has quadrupled to almost 200, creating more borders to cross, while policy changes have further limited the scale of migration even as barriers to trade fell.

Barriers to mobility are especially high for people with low skills, despite the demand for their labour in many rich countries. Policies generally favour the admission of the better educated, for instance by allowing students to stay after graduation and inviting professionals to settle with their families. But governments tend to be far more ambivalent with respect to low-skilled workers, whose status and treatment often leave much to be desired. In many countries, agriculture, construction, manufacturing and service sectors have jobs that are filled by such migrants. Yet governments often try to rotate less educated people in and out of the country, sometimes treating temporary and irregular workers like water from a tap that can be turned on and off at will. An estimated 50 million people today are living and working abroad with irregular status. Some countries, such as Thailand and the United States, tolerate large numbers of unauthorized workers. This may allow those individuals to access better paying jobs than at home, but although they often do the same work and pay the same taxes as local residents, they may lack access to basic services and face the risk of being deported. Some governments, such as those of Italy and Spain, have recognized that unskilled migrants contribute to their societies and have regularized the status of those in work, while other countries, such as Canada and New Zealand, have well designed seasonal migrant programmes for sectors such as agriculture.

While there is broad consensus about the value of skilled migration to destination countries, low-skilled migrant workers generate much controversy. It is widely believed that, while these migrants fill vacant jobs, they also displace local workers and reduce wages. Other concerns posed by migrant inflows include heightened risk of crime, added burdens on local services and the fear of losing social and cultural cohesion. But these concerns are often exaggerated. While research has found that migration can, in certain circumstances, have negative effects on locally born workers with comparable skills, the body of evidence suggests that these effects are generally small and may, in some contexts, be entirely absent.

The case for mobility

This report argues that migrants boost economic output, at little or no cost to locals. Indeed, there may be broader positive effects, for instance when the availability of migrants for childcare allows resident mothers to work outside the home. As migrants acquire the language and other skills needed to move up the income ladder, many integrate quite naturally, making fears about inassimilable foreigners—similar to those expressed early in the 20th century in America about the Irish, for example—seem equally unwarranted with respect to newcomers today. Yet it is also true that many migrants face systemic disadvantages, making it difficult or impossible for them to access local services on equal terms with local people. And these problems are especially severe for temporary and irregular workers.

In migrants' countries of origin, the impacts of movement are felt in higher incomes and consumption, better education and improved health, as well as at a broader cultural and social level. Moving generally brings benefits, most directly in the form of remittances sent to immediate family members. However, the benefits are also spread more broadly as remittances are spent—thereby generating jobs for local workers—and as behaviour changes in response to ideas from abroad. Women, in particular, may be liberated from traditional roles.

The nature and extent of these impacts depend on who moves, how they fare abroad and whether they stay connected to their roots through flows of money, knowledge and ideas. Because migrants tend to come in large numbers from specific places—for example, Kerala in India or Fujian Province in China—community-level effects can typically be larger than national ones. However, over the longer term, the flow of ideas from human movement can have far-reaching effects on social norms and class structures across a whole country. The outflow of skills is sometimes seen as negative, particularly for the delivery of services such as education or health. Yet, even when this is the case, the best response is policies that address underlying structural problems, such as low pay, inadequate financing and weak institutions. Blaming the loss of skilled workers on the workers themselves largely misses the point, and restraints on their mobility are likely to be counter-productive—not to mention the fact that they deny the basic human right to leave one's own country.

However, international migration, even if well managed, does not amount to a national human development strategy. With few exceptions (mainly small island states where more than 40 percent of inhabitants move abroad), emigration is unlikely to shape the development prospects of an entire nation. Migration is at best an avenue that complements broader local and national efforts to reduce poverty and improve human development. These efforts remain as critical as ever.

At the time of writing, the world is undergoing the most severe economic crisis in over half a century. Shrinking economies and layoffs are affecting millions of workers, including migrants. We believe that the current downturn should be seized as an opportunity to institute a new deal for migrants—one that will benefit workers at home and abroad while guarding against a protectionist backlash. With recovery, many of the same underlying trends that have been driving movement during the past half-century will resurface, attracting more people to move. It is vital that governments put in place the necessary measures to prepare for this.

Our proposal

Large gains to human development can be achieved by lowering the barriers to movement and improving the treatment of movers. A bold vision is needed to realize these gains. This

Large gains to human development can be achieved by lowering the barriers to movement and improving the treatment of movers

The two most important dimensions of the mobility agenda that offer scope for better policies are admissions and treatment

report sets out a case for a comprehensive set of reforms that can provide major benefits to migrants, communities and countries.

Our proposal addresses the two most important dimensions of the mobility agenda that offer scope for better policies: admissions and treatment. The reforms laid out in our proposed core package have medium- to long-term pay-offs. They speak not only to destination governments but also to governments of origin, to other key actors—in particular the private sector, unions and non-governmental organizations—and to individual migrants themselves. While policy makers face common challenges, they will of course need to design and implement different migration policies in their respective countries, according to national and local circumstances. Certain good practices nevertheless stand out and can be more widely adopted.

We highlight six major directions for reform that can be adopted individually but that, if used together in an integrated approach, can magnify their positive effects on human development. Opening up existing entry channels so that more workers can emigrate, ensuring basic rights for migrants, lowering the transaction costs of migration, finding solutions that benefit both destination communities and the migrants they receive, making it easier for people to move within their own countries, and mainstreaming migration into national development strategies—all have important and complementary contributions to make to human development.

The core package highlights two avenues for opening up regular existing entry channels:
- We recommend expanding schemes for truly seasonal work in sectors such as agriculture and tourism. Such schemes have already proved successful in various countries. Good practice suggests that this intervention should involve unions and employers, together with the destination and source country governments, particularly in designing and implementing basic wage guarantees, health and safety standards and provisions for repeat visits as in the case of New Zealand, for example.
- We also propose increasing the number of visas for low-skilled people, making this

conditional on local demand. Experience suggests that good practices here include: ensuring immigrants have the right to change employers (known as *employer portability*), offering immigrants the right to apply to extend their stay and outlining pathways to eventual permanent residence, making provisions that facilitate return trips during the visa period, and allowing the transfer of accumulated social security benefits, as adopted in Sweden's recent reform.

Destination countries should decide on the desired numbers of entrants through political processes that permit public discussion and the balancing of different interests. Transparent mechanisms to determine the number of entrants should be based on employer demand, with quotas according to economic conditions.

At destination, immigrants are often treated in ways that infringe on their basic human rights. Even if governments do not ratify the international conventions that protect migrant workers, they should ensure that migrants have full rights in the workplace—to equal pay for equal work, decent working conditions and collective organization, for example. They may need to act quickly to stamp out discrimination. Governments at origin and destination can collaborate to ease the recognition of credentials earned abroad.

The current recession has made migrants particularly vulnerable. Some destination country governments have stepped up the enforcement of migration laws in ways that can infringe on migrants' rights. Giving laid-off migrants the opportunity to search for another employer (or at least time to wrap up their affairs before departing), publicizing employment outlooks—including downturns in source countries—are all measures that can mitigate the disproportionate costs of the recession borne by both current and prospective migrants.

For international movement, the transaction costs of acquiring the necessary papers and meeting the administrative requirements to cross national borders are often high, tend to be regressive (proportionately higher for unskilled people and those on short-term contracts) and can also have the unintended effect of encouraging irregular movement and smuggling. One in ten countries have passport costs that exceed 10 percent of per capita income; not surprisingly, these costs are negatively correlated with emigration rates. Both origin and destination governments can simplify procedures and reduce document costs, while the two sides can also work together to improve and regulate intermediation services.

It is vital to ensure that individual migrants settle in well on arrival, but it is also vital that the communities they join should not feel unfairly burdened by the additional demands they place on key services. Where this poses challenges to local authorities, additional fiscal transfers may be needed. Ensuring that migrant children have equal access to education and, where needed, support to catch up and integrate, can improve their prospects and avoid a future underclass. Language training is key—for children at schools, but also for adults, both through the workplace and through special efforts to reach women who do not work outside the home. Some situations will need more active efforts than others to combat discrimination, address social tensions and, where relevant, prevent outbreaks of violence against immigrants. Civil society and governments have a wide range of positive experience in tackling discrimination through, for example, awareness-raising campaigns.

Despite the demise of most centrally planned systems around the world, a surprising number of governments—around a third—maintain *de facto* barriers to internal movement. Restrictions typically take the form of reduced basic service provisions and entitlements for those not registered in the local area, thereby discriminating against internal migrants, as is still the case in China. Ensuring equity of basic service provision is a key recommendation of the report as regards internal migrants. Equal treatment is important for temporary and seasonal workers and their families, for the regions where they go to work, and also to ensure decent service provision back home so that they are not compelled to move in order to access schools and health care.

While not a substitute for broader development efforts, migration can be a vital strategy for households and families seeking to diversify and improve their livelihoods, especially in developing countries. Governments need to recognize

this potential and to integrate migration with other aspects of national development policy. A critical point that emerges from experience is the importance of national economic conditions and strong public-sector institutions in enabling the broader benefits of mobility to be reaped.

The way forward

Advancing this agenda will require strong, enlightened leadership coupled with a more determined effort to engage with the public and raise their awareness about the facts around migration.

For origin countries, more systematic consideration of the profile of migration and its benefits, costs and risks would provide a better basis for integrating movement into national development strategies. Emigration is not an alternative to accelerated development efforts at home, but mobility can facilitate access to ideas, knowledge and resources that can complement and in some cases enhance progress.

For destination countries, the 'how and when' of reforms will depend on a realistic look at economic and social conditions, taking into account public opinion and political constraints at local and national levels.

International cooperation, especially through bilateral or regional agreements, can lead to better migration management, improved protection of migrants' rights and enhanced contributions of migrants to both origin and destination countries. Some regions are creating free-movement zones to promote freer trade while enhancing the benefits of migration—such as West Africa and the Southern Cone of Latin America. The expanded labour markets created in these regions can deliver substantial benefits to migrants, their families and their communities.

There are calls to create a new global regime to improve the management of migration: over 150 countries now participate in the Global Forum on Migration and Development. Governments, faced with common challenges, develop common responses—a trend we saw emerge while preparing this report.

Overcoming Barriers fixes human development firmly on the agenda of policy makers who seek the best outcomes from increasingly complex patterns of human movement worldwide.

While not a substitute for broader development efforts, migration can be a vital strategy for households and families seeking to diversify and improve their livelihoods

Freedom and movement: how mobility can foster human development

The world distribution of opportunities is extremely unequal. This inequality is a key driver of human movement and thus implies that movement has a huge potential for improving human development. Yet movement is not a pure expression of choice—people often move under constraints that can be severe, while the gains they reap from moving are very unequally distributed. Our vision of development as promoting people's freedom to lead the lives they choose recognizes mobility as an essential component of that freedom. However, movement involves trade-offs for both movers and stayers, and the understanding and analysis of those trade-offs is key to formulating appropriate policies.

Freedom and movement: how mobility can foster human development

Every year, more than 5 million people cross international borders to go and live in a developed country.[1] The number of people who move to a developing nation or within their country is much greater, although precise estimates are hard to come by.[2] Even larger numbers of people in both destination and source places are affected by the movement of others through flows of money, knowledge and ideas.

For people who move, the journey almost always entails sacrifices and uncertainty. The possible costs range from the emotional cost of separation from families and friends to high monetary fees. The risks can include the physical dangers of working in dangerous occupations. In some cases, such as those of illegal border crossings, movers face a risk of death. Nevertheless, millions of people are willing to incur these costs or risks in order to improve their living standards and those of their families.

A person's opportunities to lead a long and healthy life, to have access to education, health care and material goods, to enjoy political freedoms and to be protected from violence are all strongly influenced by where they live. Someone born in Thailand can expect to live seven more years, to have almost three times as many years of education, and to spend and save eight times as much as someone born in neighbouring Myanmar.[3] These differences in opportunity create immense pressures to move.

1.1 Mobility matters

Witness for example the way in which human development outcomes are distributed near national boundaries. Map 1.1 compares human development on either side of the United States–Mexico border. For this illustration, we use the Human Development Index (HDI)—a summary measure of development used throughout this report to rank and compare countries. A pattern that jumps out is the strong correlation between the side of the border that a place is on

and its HDI. The lowest HDI in a United States border county (Starr County, Texas) is above even the highest on the Mexican side (Mexicali Municipality, Baja California).[4] This pattern suggests that moving across national borders can greatly expand the opportunities available for improved well-being. Alternatively, consider the direction of human movements when restrictions on mobility are lifted. Between 1984 and 1995, the People's Republic of China progressively liberalized its strict regime of internal restrictions, allowing people to move from one region to another. Massive flows followed, largely towards regions with higher levels of human development. In this case the patterns again suggest that opportunities for improved well-being were a key driving factor (map 1.2).[5]

These spatial impressions are supported by more rigorous research that has estimated the effect of changing one's residence on well-being. These comparisons are inherently difficult because people who move tend to have different characteristics and circumstances from those who do not move (box 1.1). Recent academic studies that carefully disentangle these complex relations have nonetheless confirmed very large gains from moving across international borders. For example, individuals with only moderate levels of formal education who move from a typical developing country to the United States can reap an annual income gain of approximately US$10,000— roughly double the average level of per capita income in a developing country.[6] Background research commissioned for this report found that

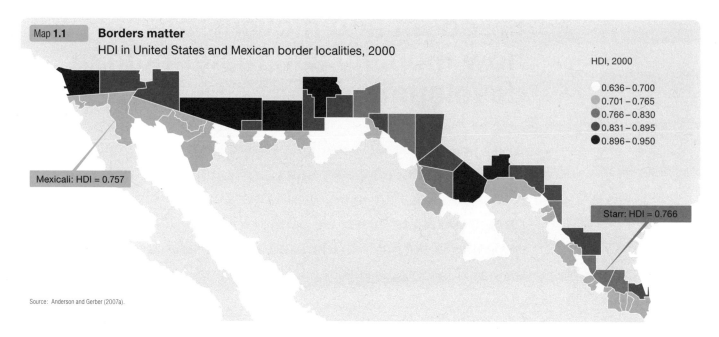

Map **1.1** **Borders matter**
HDI in United States and Mexican border localities, 2000

HDI, 2000

- 0.636 – 0.700
- 0.701 – 0.765
- 0.766 – 0.830
- 0.831 – 0.895
- 0.896 – 0.950

Mexicali: HDI = 0.757

Starr: HDI = 0.766

Source: Anderson and Gerber (2007a).

a family who migrates from Nicaragua to Costa Rica increases the probability that their child will be enrolled in primary school by 22 percent.[7]

These disparities do not explain all movement. An important part of movement occurs in response to armed conflict. Some people emigrate to avoid political repression by authoritarian states. Moving can provide opportunities for people to escape the traditional roles that they were expected to fulfil in their society of origin. Young people often move in search of education and broader horizons, intending to return home eventually. As we discuss in more detail in the next section, there are multiple drivers of, and constraints on, movement that account for vastly different motives and experiences among movers. Nevertheless, opportunity and aspiration are frequently recurring themes.

Movement does not always lead to better human development outcomes. A point that we emphasize throughout this report is that vast inequalities characterize not only the freedom to move but also the distribution of gains from movement. When the poorest migrate, they often do so under conditions of vulnerability that reflect their limited resources and choices. The prior information they have may be limited or misleading. Abuse of migrant female domestic workers occurs in many cities and countries around the world, from Washington and London to Singapore and the Gulf Cooperation Council (GCC) states. Recent research in the Arab states found that the abusive and

exploitative working conditions sometimes associated with domestic work and the lack of redress mechanisms can trap migrant women in a vicious circle of poverty and HIV vulnerability.[8] The same study found that many countries test migrants for HIV and deport those found to carry the virus; few source countries have re-integration programs for migrants who are forced to return as a result of their HIV status.[9]

Movement across national borders is only part of the story. Movement within national borders is actually larger in magnitude and has enormous potential to enhance human development. This is partly because relocating to another country is costly. Moving abroad not only involves substantial monetary costs for fees and travel (which tend to be regressive—see chapter 3), but may also mean living in a very different culture and leaving behind your network of friends and relations, which can impose a heavy if unquantifiable psychological burden. The lifting of what were often severe barriers to internal movement in a number of countries (including but not limited to China) has benefited many of the world's poorest people—an impact on human development that would be missed if we were to adopt an exclusive focus on international migration.

The potential of enhanced national and international mobility to increase human well-being leads us to expect that it should be a major focus of attention among development policy makers and researchers. This is not the case. The academic literature dealing with the effects of migration is dwarfed by research on the consequences of international trade and macroeconomic policies, to name just two examples.[10] While the international community boasts an established institutional architecture for governing trade and financial relations among countries, the governance of mobility has been well characterized as a non-regime (with the important exception of refugees).[11] This report is part of ongoing efforts to redress this imbalance. Building on the recent work of organizations such as the International Organization for Migration (IOM), the International Labour Organization (ILO), the World Bank and the Office of the United Nations High Commissioner for

Refugees (UNHCR), and on discussions in such arenas as the Global Forum on Migration and Development, we argue that migration deserves greater attention from governments, international organizations and civil society.[12] This is not only because of the large potential gains to the world as a whole from enhanced movement, but also because of the substantial risks faced by many who move—risks that could be at least partly offset by better policies.

1.2 Choice and context: understanding why people move

There is huge variation in the circumstances surrounding human movement. Thousands of Chin have emigrated to Malaysia in recent years to escape persecution by Myanmar's security forces,

Map **1.2** **Migrants are moving to places with greater opportunities**
Human development and inter-provincial migration flows in China, 1995–2000

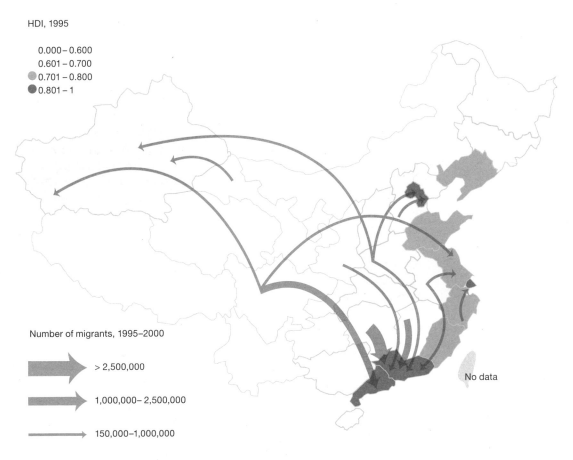

HDI, 1995

0.000 – 0.600
0.601 – 0.700
0.701 – 0.800
0.801 – 1

Number of migrants, 1995–2000

> 2,500,000

1,000,000 – 2,500,000

150,000 – 1,000,000

No data

Source: UNDP (2008a) and He (2004).

Box **1.1**   **Estimating the impact of movement**

Key methodological considerations affect the measurement of both returns to individuals and effects on places reported in the extensive literature on migration. Obtaining a precise measure of impacts requires a comparison between the well-being of someone who migrates and their well-being had they stayed in their original place. The latter is an unknown counterfactual and may not be adequately proxied by the status of non-migrants. Those who move internationally tend to be better educated and to have higher levels of initial income than those who do not, and so can be expected to be better off than those who stay behind. There is evidence that this phenomenon—known technically as migrant selectivity—is also present in internal migration (see chapter 2). Comparisons of groups with similar observable characteristics (gender, education, experience, etc.) can be more accurate but still omit potentially important characteristics, such as attitudes towards risk.

There are a host of other methodological problems. Difficulties in identifying causality plague estimates of the impact of remittances on household consumption. Understanding how migration affects labour markets in the destination place is also problematic. Most studies have tried to look at the impact on wages at the regional level or on particular skill groups. These may still be subject to selection bias associated with individual choices of location. A key issue, discussed in chapter 4, is whether the migrants' skills substitute for or complement those of local people; determining this requires accurate measures of these skills.

One increasingly popular approach seeks to exploit quasi- or manufactured randomization to estimate impacts. For example, New Zealand's Pacific Access Category allocated a set of visas randomly, allowing the impact of migration to be assessed by comparing lottery winners with unsuccessful applicants.

There is also an important temporal dimension. Migration has high upfront costs and the gains may take time to accrue. For example, returns in the labour market tend to improve significantly over time as country-specific skills are learned and recognized. A migrant's decision to return is an additional complication, affecting the period over which impacts should be measured.

Finally, as we discuss in more detail in the next chapter, migration analysis faces major data constraints. Even in the case of rich countries, comparisons are often difficult to make for very basic reasons, such as differences in the definition of migrants.

Source: Clemens, Montenegro and Pritchett (2008), McKenzie, Gibson and Stillman (2006).

but live under constant fear of detection by civilian paramilitary groups.[13] More than 3,000 people are believed to have drowned between 1997 and 2005 in the Straits of Gibraltar while trying to enter Europe illegally on makeshift boats.[14] These experiences contrast with those of hundreds of poor Tongans who have won a lottery to settle in New Zealand, or of the hundreds of thousands of Poles who moved to better paid jobs in the United Kingdom under the free mobility regime of the European Union introduced in 2004.

Our report deals with various types of movement, including internal and international, temporary and permanent, and conflict-induced. The usefulness of casting a broad net over all of these cases might be questioned. Are we not talking about disparate phenomena, with widely different causes and inherently dissimilar outcomes? Wouldn't our purpose be better served if we limited our focus to one type of migration and studied in detail its causes, consequences and implications?

We don't think so. While broad types of human movement do vary significantly in their drivers and outcomes, this is also true of more specific cases within each type. International labour migration, to take one example, covers cases ranging from Tajik workers in the Russian Federation construction industry, impelled to migrate by harsh economic conditions in a country where most people live on less than US$2 a day, to highly coveted East Asian computer engineers recruited by the likes of Motorola and Microsoft.

Conventional approaches to migration tend to suffer from compartmentalization. Distinctions are commonly drawn between migrants according to whether their movement is classed as forced or voluntary, internal or international, temporary or permanent, or economic or non-economic. Categories originally designated to establish legal distinctions for the purpose of governing entry and treatment can end up playing a dominant role in conceptual and policy thinking. Over the past decade, scholars and policy makers have begun to question these distinctions, and there is growing recognition that their proliferation obscures rather than illuminates the processes underlying the decision to move, with potentially harmful effects on policy-making.[15]

In nearly all instances of human movement we can see the interaction of two basic forces, which vary in the degree of their influence. On the one hand we have individuals, families and sometimes communities, who decide to move of their own free will in order to radically alter their circumstances. Indeed, even when people are impelled to move by very adverse conditions, the choices they make almost always play a vital role. Research among Angolan refugees settling in northwest Zambia, for example, has shown that many were motivated by the same aspirations that impel those who are commonly classified as economic migrants.[16] Similarly, Afghans fleeing conflict go to Pakistan or Iran via the same routes and trading networks established decades ago for the purposes of seasonal labour migration.[17]

On the other hand, choices are rarely, if ever, unconstrained. This is evident for those who move to escape political persecution or economic deprivation, but it is also vital for understanding decisions where there is less compulsion. Major factors relating to the structure of the economy and of society, which are context-specific but also change over time, frame decisions to move as well as to stay. This dynamic interaction between individual decisions and the socio-economic context in which they are taken—sometimes labelled in sociological parlance the 'agency–structure interaction'—is vital for understanding what shapes human behaviour. The evolution over time of key structural factors is dealt with in chapter 2.

Consider the case of the tens of thousands of Indonesian immigrants who enter Malaysia every year. These flows are driven largely by the wide income differentials between these countries. But the scale of movement has also grown steadily since the 1980s, whereas the income gap between the two countries has alternately widened and narrowed over the same period.[18] Broader socio-economic processes have clearly played a part. Malaysian industrialization in the 1970s and 1980s generated a massive movement of Malays from the countryside to the cities, creating acute labour scarcity in the agricultural sector at a time when the commercialization of farming and rapid population growth were producing a surplus of agricultural labour in Indonesia. The fact that most Indonesians are of similar ethnic, linguistic and religious backgrounds to Malays doubtless facilitated the flows.[19]

Recognition of the role of structural factors in determining human movement has had a deep impact on migration studies. While early attempts to conceptualize migration flows focused on differences in living standards, in recent years there has been growing understanding that these differences only partly explain movement patterns.[20] In particular, if movement responds only to income differentials, it is hard to explain why many successful migrants choose to return to their country of origin after several years abroad. Furthermore, if migration were purely determined by wage differences, then we would expect to see large movements from poor to rich countries and very little movement among rich countries—but neither of these patterns holds in practice (chapter 2).

These observed patterns led to several strands of research. Some scholars recognized that a focus on the individual distracts from what is typically a family decision and indeed strategy (as when some family members move while others stay at home).[21] The need to go beyond the assumption of perfectly competitive markets also became increasingly evident. In particular, credit markets in developing countries are highly imperfect, while household livelihoods often depend on such volatile sectors as agriculture. Sending a family member elsewhere allows the family to diversify against the risk of bad outcomes at home.[22] Other researchers emphasized how structural characteristics and long-run trends in both origin and destination places—often labelled 'push' and 'pull' factors—shape the context in which movement occurs. Movement, for example, can result from growing concentration in the ownership of assets such as land, making it difficult for people to subsist through their traditional modes of production.[23] It was also recognized that the opportunities available to migrants are constrained by barriers to entry, as we discuss in chapters 2 and 3, and by the way in which labour markets function, as shown by the considerable evidence that both international and internal migrants are channelled into lower-status and worse-paid occupations.

Most importantly, theories that emphasize purely economic factors fail to capture the broader social framework in which decisions are taken. For example, young men among the lower caste Kolas in the Central Gujarat region of India commonly seek factory jobs outside their village in order to break away from subordinate caste relations. This occurs despite the fact that factory wages are not higher, and in some cases are

Theories that emphasize purely economic factors fail to capture the broader social framework in which decisions to migrate are taken

lower, than what they would earn as agricultural day labourers at home.[24] Escaping traditional hierarchies can be an important factor motivating migration (chapter 3).

Moreover, the relationship between movement and economics is far from unidirectional. Large-scale movements of people can have profound economic consequences for origin and destination places, as we will discuss in detail in chapter 4. Even the way in which we think about basic economic concepts is affected by the movement of people, as can be illustrated by the issues raised for the measurement of per capita incomes and economic growth (box 1.2).

1.3 Development, freedom and human mobility

Our attempt to understand the implications of human movement for human development begins with an idea that is central to the approach of this report. This is the concept of human development as the expansion of people's freedoms to live their lives as they choose. This concept—inspired by the path-breaking work of Nobel laureate Amartya Sen and the leadership of Mahbub ul Haq and also known as the 'capabilities approach' because of its emphasis on freedom to achieve vital 'beings and doings'—has been at the core of our thinking since the first Human Development Report in 1990, and is as relevant as ever to the design of effective policies to combat poverty and deprivation.[25] The capabilities approach has proved powerful in reshaping thinking about topics as diverse as gender, human security and climate change.

Using the expansion of human freedoms and capabilities as a lens has significant implications for how we think about human movement. This is because, even before we start asking whether the freedom to move has significant effects on incomes, education or health, for example, we recognize that movement is one of the basic actions

---

Box **1.2**   **How movement matters to the measurement of progress**

Attempts to measure the level of development of a country rely on various indicators designed to capture the average level of well-being. While a traditional approach uses per capita income as a proxy for economic development, this report has promoted a more comprehensive measure: the Human Development Index (HDI). However, both of these approaches are based on the idea of evaluating the well-being of those who reside in a given territory.

As researchers at the Center for Global Development and Harvard University have recently pointed out, these approaches to measuring development prioritize geographical location over people in the evaluation of a society's progress. Thus, if a Fijian moves to New Zealand and her living standards improve as a result, traditional measures of development will not count that improvement as an increase in the development of Fiji. Rather, that person's well-being will now be counted in the calculation of New Zealand's indicator.

In background research carried out for this report, we dealt with this problem by proposing an alternative measure of human development. We refer to this as the *human development of peoples* (as opposed to the human development of countries), as it captures the level of human development of all people born in a particular country. For instance, instead of measuring the average level of human development of people who live in the Philippines, we measure the average level of human development of all individuals who were born in the Philippines, regardless of where they now live. This new measure has a significant impact on our understanding of human well-being. In 13 of the 100 nations for which we can calculate this measure, the HDI of their people is at least 10 percent higher than the HDI of their country; for an additional nine populations, the difference is between 5 and 10 percent. For 11 of the 90 populations for which we could calculate trends over time, the change in HDI during the 1990–2000 period differed by more than 5 percentage points from the average change for their country. For example, the HDI of Ugandans went up by nearly three times as much as the HDI of Uganda.

Throughout the rest of this report, we will continue to adopt the conventional approach for reasons of analytical tractability and comparability with the existing literature. We also view these two measures as complements rather than substitutes: one captures the living standards of people living in a particular place, the other of people born in a particular place. For example, when we analyse human development as a cause of human movement, as we do throughout most of this report, then the country measure will be more appropriate because it will serve as an indicator of how living standards differ across places. For the purposes of evaluating the success of different policies and institutions in generating well-being for the members of a society, however, there is a strong case for adopting the new measure.

Source: Ortega (2009) and Clemens and Pritchett (2008).

that individuals can choose to take in order to realize their life plans. In other words, the ability to move is a dimension of freedom that is part of development—with intrinsic as well as potential instrumental value.

The notion that the ability to change one's place of residence is a fundamental component of human freedom has been traced back to classical philosophy in several intellectual traditions. Confucius wrote that "good government obtains when those who are near are made happy, and those who are far off are attracted to come,"[26] while Socrates argued that "anyone who does not like us and the city, and who wants to emigrate to a colony or to any other city, may go where he likes, retaining his property."[27] In 1215, England's Magna Carta guaranteed the freedom "to go out of our Kingdom, and to return safely and securely, by land or water." More recently, American philosopher Martha Nussbaum argued that mobility is one of a set of basic human functional capabilities that can be used to assess the effective freedom that individuals have to carry out their life plans.[28]

Yet world history is replete with the experiences of societies that severely limited human development by restricting movement. Both feudalism and slavery were predicated on the physical restriction of movement. Several repressive regimes in the 20th century relied on the control of internal movement, including the Pass Laws of South African *apartheid* and the *propiska* system of internal passports in Soviet Russia. The subsequent demise of such restrictions contributed to dramatic expansions in the freedoms enjoyed by these countries' peoples.

Our report seeks to capture and examine the full set of conditions that affect whether individuals, families or communities decide to stay or to move. These conditions include people's resources or entitlements as well as the way in which different constraints—including those associated with policies, markets, security, culture and values—determine whether movement is an option for them. People's ability to choose the place they call home is a dimension of human freedom that we refer to as *human mobility*. Box 1.3 defines this and other basic terms used in this report.

The distinction between freedoms and actions is central to the capabilities approach. By referring to the capability to decide where to

live as well as the act of movement itself, we recognize the importance of the conditions under which people are, or are not, able to choose their place of residence. Much conventional analysis of migration centres on studying the effect of movement on well-being. Our concern, however, is not only with movement in itself but also with the freedom that people have to decide whether to move. Mobility is a freedom—movement is the exercise of that freedom.[29]

We understand human mobility as a positive and not only a negative freedom. In other words, the absence of formal restrictions on the movement of people across or within borders does not in itself make people free to move if

---

Box **1.3**	**Basic terms used in this report**

Human Development Index (HDI) A composite index measuring average achievement in three basic dimensions of human development: a long and healthy life, access to knowledge and a decent standard of living.

Developed/developing We call countries that have achieved an HDI of 0.9 or higher developed, and those that have not developing.

Low/medium/high/very high HD A classification of countries based on the value of the HDI according to the most recent data. The ranges are 0–0.499 for low HDI, 0.500–0.799 for medium HDI, 0.800–0.899 for high HDI and greater than 0.900 for very high HDI.

Internal migration Human movement within the borders of a country, usually measured across regional, district or municipal boundaries.

International migration Human movement across international borders, resulting in a change of country of residence.

Migrant An individual who has changed her place of residence either by crossing an international border or by moving within her country of origin to another region, district or municipality. An emigrant is a migrant viewed from the perspective of the origin country, while an immigrant is a migrant viewed from the perspective of the destination country. While sometimes the term 'migrant' (as opposed to 'immigrant') has been reserved for temporary migration, we do not adopt such a distinction in this report.

Human mobility The ability of individuals, families or groups of people to choose their place of residence.

Human movement The act of changing one's place of residence.

they lack the economic resources, security and networks necessary to enjoy a decent life in their new home, or if informal constraints such as discrimination significantly impede the prospects of moving successfully.

Let us illustrate the implications of this approach with a couple of examples. In the case of human trafficking, movement comes together with brutal and degrading types of exploitation. By definition, trafficking is an instance of movement in which freedoms become restricted by means of force, deception and/or coercion. Commonly, a trafficked individual is not free to choose to abort the trip, to seek alternative employment once she gets to her destination, or to return home. A trafficked person is physically moving, but doing so as a result of a restriction on her ability to decide where to live. From a capabilities perspective, she is less, not more, mobile.

Alternatively, consider the case of someone who has to move because of the threat of political persecution or because of degraded environmental conditions. In these cases external circumstances have made it more difficult,

perhaps impossible, for her to remain at home. These circumstances restrict the scope of her choices, reducing her freedom to choose where to live. The induced movement may very well coincide with a further deterioration in her living conditions, but this does not mean that the movement is the cause of that deterioration. In fact, if she were not able to move, the outcome would probably be much worse.

If it is tempting to view the distinction between mobility and movement as somewhat academic, we should take this opportunity to emphasize that freedom to choose where to live emerged as an important theme in research to find out what poor people think about migration (box 1.4). In the end, their views matter more than those of the experts, since it is they who must take the difficult decision as to whether or not to risk a move.

1.4 What we bring to the table

Putting people and their freedom at the centre of development has implications for the study of human movement. In the first place, it requires

---

Box **1.4**   **How do the poor view migration?**

In recent years there has been growing interest in the use of qualitative methods to understand how people living in poverty view their situation, as indicated by the landmark World Bank study *Voices of the Poor*, published in 2000. In preparing the current report we commissioned research to investigate relevant findings of Participatory Poverty Assessments—large-scale studies that combine qualitative and quantitative research methods to study poverty from the point of view of the poor. What emerged is that moving is commonly described by the poor as both a *necessity*—part of a coping strategy for families experiencing extreme hardship—and an *opportunity*—a means of expanding a household's livelihoods and ability to accumulate assets.

In Niger, two thirds of respondents indicated that in order to cope with lack of food, clothing or income they had left their homes and looked for livelihoods elsewhere. Some households reported members leaving in search of paid work, particularly to reduce pressures on dwindling food supplies in times of scarcity. In the villages of Ban Na Pieng and Ban Kaew Pad, Thailand, participants described migration as one of the ways in which a family's socio-economic status could be enhanced. For these communities, remittances from abroad enabled those left behind to invest in commercial fishing and thus expand the family's standing and influence.

Seasonal internal migration was the most common type of migration discussed in focus groups with the poor. When international migration was discussed, it was described as something for the better off. For instance, participants in the Jamaica study said that the better off, unlike the poor, have influential contacts that help them acquire the necessary visas to travel and work abroad. Similarly, in Montserrat participants described how the more educated and financially better off were able to leave the country after the 1995 volcano eruption, while the less well off stayed on despite the devastation.

Participatory Poverty Assessments give us a good picture of how poor people see movement but may be uninformative about how others have managed to move out of poverty, as these assessments are by design limited to people who are still poor. A more recent study of 15 countries carried out by the World Bank examines pathways out of poverty. In these studies, the ability to move evolved as a common theme in conversations about freedom. In Morocco, young women expressed frustration with traditional restrictions that limit women's ability to travel without a male escort or search for employment outside the home. Men described the ability to migrate as both a freedom and a responsibility, because with the freedom to move comes the responsibility to remit.

Source: Azcona (2009), Narayan, Pritchett, and Kapoor (2009), World Bank (2000), World Bank (2003), and ActionAid International (2004).

us to understand what makes people less or more mobile. This means considering why people choose to move and what constraints encourage them or deter them from making that choice. In chapter 2, we look at both choices and constraints by studying the macro patterns of human movement over space and time. We find that these patterns are broadly consistent with the idea that people move to enhance their opportunities, but that their movement is strongly constrained by policies—both in their place of origin and at their destinations—and by the resources at their disposal. Since different people face different constraints, the end result is a process characterized by significant inequalities in opportunities to move and returns from movement.

We explore how these inequalities interact with policies in chapter 3. While, as we have emphasized in this introductory chapter, there is considerable intrinsic value to mobility, its instrumental value for furthering other dimensions of human development can also be of enormous significance. But while people can and do expand other freedoms by moving, the extent to which they are able to do so depends greatly on the conditions under which they move. In chapter 3 we look at the outcomes of migration in different dimensions of human development, including incomes and livelihoods, health, education and empowerment. We also review the cases in which people experience deteriorations in their well-being during movement—when this is induced by trafficking or conflict, for example—and argue that these cases can often be traced back to constraints on the freedom of individuals to choose where they live.

A key point that emerges in chapter 3 is that human movement can be associated with trade-offs—people may gain in some and lose in other dimensions of freedom. Millions of Asian and Middle Eastern workers in the GCC states accept severe limitations on their rights as a condition for permission to work. They earn higher pay than at home, but cannot be with their families, obtain permanent residence or change employers. Many cannot even leave, as their passports are confiscated on entry. For many people around the world the decision to move involves leaving their children behind. In India, seasonal workers are in practice excluded from voting in elections when these are scheduled during the peak period of

internal movements.[30] People living and working with irregular status are often denied a whole host of basic entitlements and services and lead their lives in constant fear of arrest and deportation. Understanding the effects of movement requires the systematic analysis of these multiple dimensions of human development in order to gain a better sense of the nature and extent of these trade-offs, as well as the associated policy implications.

More complex trade-offs occur when movers have an effect on the well-being of non-movers. Indeed, the perception that migration generates losses for those in destination countries has been the source of numerous debates among policy makers and academics. Chapter 4 focuses on these debates. The evidence we present strongly suggests that fears about the negative effects of movement on stayers (both at source and destination) are frequently overstated. However, sometimes these concerns are real and this has significant implications for the design of policy.

If movement is constrained by policies and resources, yet enhanced mobility can significantly increase the well-being of movers while often also having positive effects on stayers, what should policy towards human movement look like? In chapter 5, we argue that it should look very different from what we see today. In particular, it should be redesigned to open up more opportunities for movement among low-skilled workers and to improve the treatment of movers at their destinations.

We do not advocate wholesale liberalization of international mobility. This is because we recognize that people at destination places have a right to shape their societies, and that borders are one way in which people delimit the sphere of their obligations to those whom they see as members of their community. But we also believe that people relate to each other in myriad ways and that their moral obligations can operate at different levels. This is primarily because individuals don't belong to just one society or group. Rather than being uniquely or solely defined by their religion, race, ethnicity or gender, individuals commonly see themselves through the multiple prisms of a set of identities. As Amartya Sen has powerfully put it, "A Hutu labourer from Kigali… is not only a Hutu, but also a Kigalian, a Rwandan, an African, a labourer and a human being."[31]

While there is considerable intrinsic value to mobility, its instrumental value for furthering other dimensions of human development can also be of enormous significance

We see mobility
as vital to human
development and
movement as a natural
expression of people's
desire to choose how
and where to lead
their lives

The responsibilities of distributive justice are overlapping and naturally intersect national boundaries; as such, there is no contradiction between the idea that societies may design institutions with the primary purpose of generating just outcomes among their members, and the idea that the members of that same society will share an obligation to create a just world with and for their fellow humans outside that society. There are many ways in which these obligations are articulated: the creation of charities and foundations, the provision of development aid, assistance in building national institutions, and the reform of international institutions so as to make them more responsive to the needs of poor countries are just some of them. However, our analysis, which informs the recommendations in chapter 5, suggests that reducing restrictions on the entry of people—in particular of low-skilled workers and their families—into better-off developed and developing countries is one relatively effective way of discharging these obligations.

Our report's policy recommendations are not only based on our view of how the world should be. We recognize that the formulation of policies towards human movement must contend with what can at times look like formidable political opposition to greater openness. However, having considered issues of political feasibility, we argue that a properly designed programme of liberalization—designed so as to respond to labour market needs in destination places while also addressing issues of equity and non-discrimination—could generate significant support among voters and interest groups.

Our analysis builds on the contributions to thinking about human development that have been made since the concept was introduced in the 1990 HDR. That report devoted a full chapter to urbanization and human development, reviewing the failed experiences of policies designed to reduce internal migration and concluding: "[A]s long as differences exist between rural and urban areas, people will move to try to take advantage of better schools and social services, higher income opportunities, cultural amenities, new modes of living, technological innovations and links to the world."[32] Like other HDRs, this one begins with the observation that

the distribution of opportunities in our world is highly unequal. We go on to argue that this fact has significant implications for understanding why and how people move and how we should reshape policies towards human movement. Our critique of existing policies towards migration is directed at the way in which they reinforce those inequalities. As noted in the 1997 HDR, it is precisely because "the principles of free global markets are applied selectively" that "the global market for unskilled labour is not as free as the market for industrial country exports or capital".[33] Our emphasis on how migration enhances cultural diversity and enriches people's lives by moving skills, labour and ideas builds on the analysis of the 2004 HDR, which dealt with the role of cultural liberty in today's diverse world.[34]

At the same time, the agenda of human development is evolving, so it is natural for the treatment of particular topics to change over time. This report strongly contests the view—held by some policy makers and at times echoed in past reports—that the movement of people should be seen as a problem requiring corrective action.[35] In contrast, we see mobility as vital to human development and movement as a natural expression of people's desire to choose how and where to lead their lives.

While the potential of increased mobility for increasing the well-being of millions of people around the world is the key theme of this report, it is important to stress at the outset that enhanced mobility is only one component of a strategy for improving human development. We do not argue that it should be the central one, nor are we arguing that it should be placed at the same level in the hierarchy of capabilities as, say, adequate nourishment or shelter. Neither do we believe mobility to be a replacement for national development strategies directed toward investing in people and creating conditions for people to flourish at home. Indeed, the potential of mobility to improve the well-being of disadvantaged groups is limited, because these groups are often least likely to move. Yet while human mobility is not a panacea, its largely positive effects both for movers and stayers suggest that it should be an important component of any strategy to generate sustained improvements in human development around the world.

People in motion:
who moves where,
when and why

2

This chapter examines human movement across the world and over time. The patterns are consistent with the idea that people move to seek better opportunities, but also that their movement is strongly constrained by barriers—most importantly, by policies at home and at destination and by lack of resources. Overall, the share of people going to developed countries has increased markedly during the past 50 years, a trend associated with growing gaps in opportunities. Although these flows of people are likely to slow temporarily during the current economic crisis, underlying structural trends will persist once growth resumes and are likely to generate increased pressures for movement in the coming decades.

People in motion: who moves where, when and why

The aim of this chapter is to characterize human movement generally—to give an overview of who moves, how, why, where and when. The picture is complex and our broad brushstrokes will inevitably fail to capture specifics. Nevertheless, the similarities and commonalities that emerge are striking, and help us understand the forces that shape and constrain migration.

We start by examining the key features of movement—its magnitude, composition and directions—in section 2.1. Section 2.2 considers how movement today resembles or differs from movement in the past. Our examination suggests that movement is largely shaped by policy constraints, an issue that we discuss in detail in the third section (2.3). In the last section (2.4), we turn to the future and try to understand how movement will evolve in the medium to longer term, once the economic crisis that started in 2008 is over.

2.1 Human movement today

Discussions about migration commonly start with a description of flows between developing and developed countries, or what sometimes are loosely—and inaccurately—called 'South–North' flows. However, most movement in the world does not take place between developing and developed countries. Indeed, it does not even take place between countries. The overwhelming majority of people who move do so within the borders of their own country.

One of the reasons why this basic reality of human movement is not better known lies in severe data limitations. Background research conducted for this report sought to overcome this knowledge gap by using national censuses to calculate the number of internal migrants on a consistent basis for 24 countries covering 57 percent of the world's population (figure 2.1).[1] Even with a conservative definition of internal migration, which counts movement across only the largest zonal demarcations in a country, the number of people who move internally in our sample is six

times greater than those who emigrate.[2] Using the regional patterns found in these data, we estimate that there are about 740 million internal migrants in the world—almost four times as many as those who have moved internationally.

By comparison, the contemporary figure for international migrants (214 million, or 3.1 percent of the world's population) looks small. Of course this global estimate is dogged by a number of methodological and comparability issues, but there are good reasons to believe that the order of magnitude is right.[3] Box 2.1 deals with one of the most frequently voiced concerns about the international data on migration, namely the extent to which they capture irregular migration is discussed below.

Even if we restrict attention to international movements, the bulk of these do not occur between countries with very different levels of development. Only 37 percent of migration in the world is from developing to developed countries. Most migration occurs *within* countries in the same category of development: about 60 percent of migrants move either between developing or between developed countries (the remaining 3 percent move from developed to developing countries).[4]

This comparison relies on what is inevitably a somewhat arbitrary distinction between countries that have achieved higher levels of development and those that have not. We have classified countries that have attained an HDI greater than or equal to 0.9 (on a scale of 0 to 1) as *developed* and those that have not as *developing* (see box 1.3). We use this demarcation throughout this report, without intending any judgement of the merits of any particular economic or political

Figure **2.1** **Many more people move within borders than across them**
Internal movement and emigration rates, 2000–2002

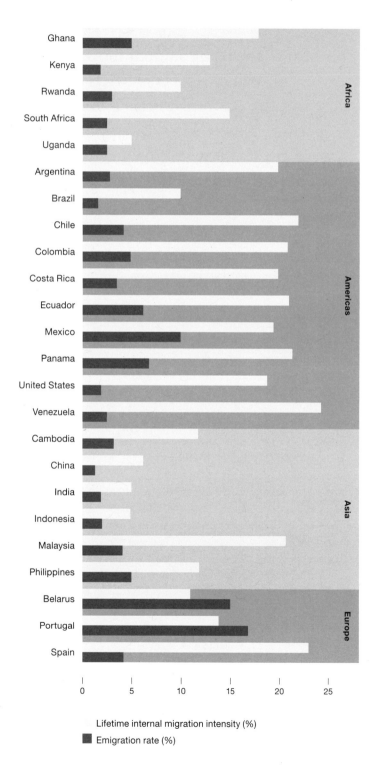

Lifetime internal migration intensity (%)
■ Emigration rate (%)

Source: Bell and Muhidin (2009) and HDR team estimates based on Migration DRC (2007) database.
Note: All emigration data are from the Migration DRC (2007) database and cover 2000–2002. The internal migration rates are based on census data from 2000 to 2002, except for Belarus (1999), Cambodia (1998), Colombia (2005), Kenya (1999) and the Philippines (1990).

system or seeking to obscure the complex interactions involved in increasing and sustaining human well-being. The countries and territories thereby classified as developed feature many that would normally be included in such a list (all Western European countries, Australia, Canada, Japan, New Zealand and the United States), but also several that are less frequently labelled as developed (Hong Kong (China), Singapore and the Republic of Korea, in East Asia; Kuwait, Qatar and the United Arab Emirates, in the Gulf region). However, most Eastern European economies, with the exception of the Czech Republic and Slovenia, are not in the top HDI category (see Statistical Table H).

One obvious reason why there is not more movement from developing to developed countries is that moving is costly, and moving long distances is costlier than undertaking short journeys. The higher expense of international movement comes not only from transport costs but also from the policy-based restrictions on crossing international borders, which can be overcome only by those who have enough resources, possess skills that are sought after in the new host country, or are willing to run very high risks. Nearly half of all international migrants move within their region of origin and about 40 percent move to a neighbouring country. The proximity between source and destination countries, however, is not solely geographical: nearly 6 out of 10 migrants move to a country where the major religion is the same as in their country of birth, and 4 out of 10 to a country where the dominant language is the same.[5]

The pattern of these inter- and intra-regional movements is presented in map 2.1, where the absolute magnitudes are illustrated by the thickness of the arrows, the size of each region has been represented in proportion to its population, and the colouring of each country represents its HDI category. Intra-regional movement dominates. To take one striking example, intra-Asian migration accounts for nearly 20 percent of all international migration and exceeds the sum total of movements that Europe receives from all other regions.

The fact that flows from developing to developed countries account for only a minority of international movement does not mean that differences in living standards are unimportant. Quite the contrary: three quarters of

Box **2.1** Counting irregular migrants

The only comprehensive estimates of the number of foreign-born people in the world come from the United Nations Department of Economic and Social Affairs (UNDESA) and cover approximately 150 United Nations (UN) member states. These estimates are primarily based on national censuses, which attempt to count the number of people residing in a particular country at a given moment, where a resident is defined as a person who "has a place to live where he or she normally spends the daily period of rest." In other words, national censuses attempt to count all residents, regardless of whether they are regular or irregular.

However, there are good reasons to suspect that censuses significantly undercount irregular migrants, who may avoid census interviewers for fear that they will share information with other government authorities. House owners may conceal the fact that they have illegal units rented to irregular migrants. Migrants may also be more mobile and thus harder to count.

Studies have used a variety of demographic and statistical methods to assess the magnitude of the undercount. In the United States, the Pew Hispanic Center has developed a set of assumptions consistent with census-based studies and historical demographic data from Mexico that estimate the undercount to be approximately 12

percent. Other researchers estimated under-coverage rates in Los Angeles during the 2000 Census at 10–15 percent. Thus it appears that the official count in the United States misses 1–1.5 million irregular migrants, or 0.5 percent of the country's population.

Few studies of the undercount of migrants have been conducted in developing countries. One exception is Argentina, where a recent study found an underestimation of the migrant stock equivalent to 1.3 percent of the total population. In other developing countries, the undercount rates could be much higher. Estimates of the number of irregular migrants for a number of countries—including the Russian Federation, South Africa and Thailand—range from 25 to 55 percent of the population. However, there is huge uncertainty about the true number. According to the migration experts surveyed by the HDR team, irregular migration was estimated to average around one third of all migration for developing countries. An upper bound for the number of migrants omitted from international statistics can be obtained by assuming that none of these migrants are captured by country censuses (that is, an undercount of 100 percent); in that case, the resulting underestimation in the global statistics for developing countries would be around 30 million migrants.

Source: UN (1998), Passel and Cohn (2008), Marcelli and Ong (2002), Comelatto, Lattes, and Levit (2003). See Andrienko and Guriev (2005) for the Russian Federation, and Sabates-Wheeler (2009) for South Africa and Martin (2009b) for Thailand.

international movers move to a country with a higher HDI than their country of origin; among those from developing countries, this share exceeds 80 percent. However, their destinations are often not developed countries but rather other developing countries with higher living standards and/or more jobs.

The difference between human development at origin and destination can be substantial. Figure 2.2 illustrates this difference—a magnitude that we loosely call the human development 'gains' from migration—plotted against the origin country's HDI.[6] If migrants were on average emigrating to countries with the same level of human development as their origin countries, this magnitude would be zero. In contrast, the difference is positive and generally large for all but the most developed countries. The fact that the average gain diminishes as human development increases shows that it is people from the poorest countries who, on average, gain the most from moving across borders.

That movers from low-HDI countries have the most to gain from moving internationally is confirmed by more systematic studies. Background research commissioned for this

report compared the HDI of migrants at home and destination and found that the differences—in both relative and absolute terms—are inversely related to the HDI of the country of origin.[7]

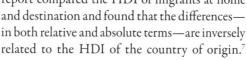

Figure **2.2** **The poorest have the most to gain from moving...**
Differences between destination and origin country HDI, 2000–2002

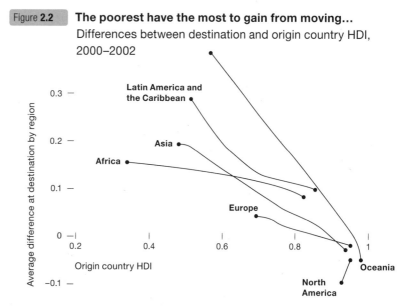

Source: HDR team estimates based on Migration DRC (2007) database.
Note: Averages estimated using Kernel density regressions.

Map **2.1** **Most movement occurs within regions**

Origin and destination of international migrants, circa 2000

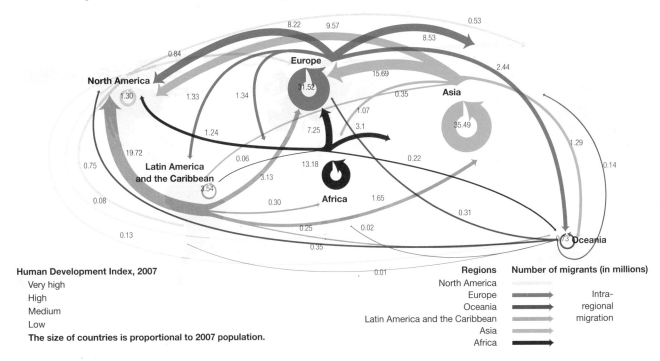

Human Development Index, 2007
  Very high
  High
  Medium
  Low
The size of countries is proportional to 2007 population.

Regions
North America
Europe
Oceania
Latin America and the Caribbean
Asia
Africa

Number of migrants (in millions)

Intra-
regional
migration

Source: HDR team estimates based on Migration DRC (2007) database.

Migrants from low-HDI countries had the most to gain—and indeed on average saw a 15-fold increase in income (to US$15,000 per annum), a doubling in education enrolment rate (from 47 to 95 percent) and a 16-fold reduction in child mortality (from 112 to 7 deaths per 1,000 live births). Using comparable surveys in a number of developing countries, the study also found that self-selection—the tendency for those who move to be better off and better educated—accounted for only a fraction of these gains. Analysis of bilateral migration flows across countries, prepared as background research for this report, confirmed the positive effect on emigration of all components of human development at destination, while finding that income differences had the most explanatory power.[8] These patterns are discussed in detail in the next chapter.

Paradoxically, despite the fact that people moving out of poor countries have the most to gain from moving, they are the least mobile. For example, despite the high levels of attention given to emigration from Africa to Europe, only 3 percent of Africans live in a country different from where they were born and fewer than 1 percent of Africans live in Europe. Several scholars have observed that if we correlate emigration rates with levels of development, the relationship resembles a 'hump', whereby emigration rates are lower in poor and rich countries than among countries with moderate levels of development.[9] This is illustrated in figure 2.3, which shows that the median emigration rate in countries with low levels of human development is only about one third the rate out of countries with high levels of human development.[10] When we restrict the comparison to out-migration to developed countries, the relationship is even stronger: the median emigration rate among countries with low human development is less than 1 percent, compared to almost 5 percent out of countries with high levels of human development. Analysis of bilateral migration flows prepared as background research for this report confirmed that this pattern holds, even when controlling for characteristics of origin and destination countries such as life expectancy, years of schooling and demographic structure.[11]

Evidence that poverty is a constraint to emigration has also been found in household-level analysis: a study of Mexican households, for example, found that the probability of migration increased with higher income levels for household incomes lower than US$15,000 per annum (figure 2.3, panel B). A commissioned study found that during the *Monga* or growing season in Bangladesh, when people's cash resources are lowest, a randomized monetary incentive significantly increased the likelihood of migrating.[12] The magnitude of the effect was large: giving emigrants an amount equivalent to a week's wages at destination increased the propensity to migrate from 14 to 40 percent. These results shed strong doubts on the idea, often promoted in policy circles, that development in countries of origin will reduce migratory flows.

While many migrant families do improve their standard of living by moving, this is not always the case. As discussed in chapter 3, movement often coincides with adverse outcomes when it occurs under conditions of restricted choice. Conflict-induced migration and trafficking are not a large proportion of overall human movement, but they affect many of the world's poorest people and are thus a special source of concern (box 2.2).

Another key fact about out-migration patterns is their inverse relation to the size of a country's population. For the 48 states with populations below 1.5 million—which include 1 low-, 21 medium-, 12 high- and 11 very high-HDI countries—the average emigration rate is 18.4 percent, considerably higher than the world average of 3 percent. Indeed, the top 13 emigration countries in the world are all small states, with Antigua and Barbuda, Grenada, and Saint Kitts and Nevis having emigration rates above 40 percent. The simple correlation between size and emigration rates is −0.61. In many cases, it is remoteness that leads people born in small states to move in order to take advantage of opportunities elsewhere—the same factor that drives much of the rural to urban migration seen within countries. Cross-country regression analysis confirms that the effect of population size on emigration is higher for countries that are far from world markets—the more remote a small country is, the more people decide to leave.[13] The implications of these patterns are discussed in box 4.4.

The aggregate facts just surveyed tell us where migrants come from and go to, but they do not tell us who moves. While severe data limitations impede presentation of a full global profile of migrants, the existing data nonetheless reveal some interesting patterns.

Approximately half (48 percent) of all international migrants are women. This share has been quite stable during the past five decades: it stood at 47 percent in 1960. This pattern contrasts with that of the 19th century, when the majority of migrants were men.[14] Yet despite recent references to the 'feminization' of migration, it appears that numerical gender balance was largely reached some time ago. However, the aggregate stability hides trends at the regional level. While the share of women going to the European Union has increased slightly from 48

Figure **2.3**	**... but they also move less**

Emigration rates by HDI and income

Panel A: Median emigration rates by origin country HDI group

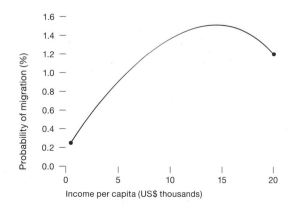

Source: HDR team estimates based on Migration DRC (2007) and UN (2009e).

Panel B: Probability of emigration by income level in Mexican households

Source: Meza and Pederzini (2006).

to 52 percent, that same share has dropped from 47 to 45 percent in Asia.

Of course, the relatively equal gender shares of the migrant population may hide significant differences in the circumstances of movement and the opportunities available.[15] At the same time, a growing literature has challenged conventional views about the subordinate role of women in migration decisions.[16] For example, a qualitative study of decisions taken by Peruvian couples moving to Argentina found that many of the women moved first by themselves, because they were able to secure jobs more rapidly than their partners, who would later follow with the children.[17]

The data also show very large temporary flows of people. In the countries of the Organisation for Economic Co-operation and Development (OECD), temporary migrants typically represent more than a third of arrivals in a given year. However, since most leave after a short period while others transit towards more permanent arrangements, the number of people on temporary visas at any given moment is much smaller than the aggregate flows suggest. Indeed, 83 percent of the foreign-born population in OECD countries has lived there for at least five years.[18] Almost all temporary migrants come for work-related reasons. Some enter into 'circular' arrangements, whereby they repeatedly enter and leave the destination country to carry out seasonal or temporary work, effectively maintaining two places of residence.[19]

It is important not to overemphasize the distinction between categories of migrants, as many migrants shift between categories. Indeed, the migration regime in many countries can perhaps best be understood through the analogy of the multiple doors of a house. Migrants can enter the house through the front door (permanent settlers), the side door (temporary visitors and workers) or the back door (irregular migrants). However, once inside a country, these channels often merge, as when temporary visitors become immigrants or slip into unauthorized status, those with irregular status gain authorization to remain, and people with permanent status decide to return.

This analogy is particularly useful for understanding irregular migration. Overstaying is an important channel through which migrants become irregular, particularly in developed countries. In fact, the distinction between regular and irregular is much less clear-cut than is often assumed. For example, it is common for people to enter a country legally, then work despite lacking a permit to do so.[20] In some island states, such as Australia and Japan, overstaying is practically the only channel to irregular entry; even in many European countries, overstay appears to account for about two thirds of unauthorized migration. In OECD countries, people with irregular residence or work status tend to be workers with low levels of formal education.[21] The best estimates of the number of irregular migrants in the United States amount to about 4 percent of the

---

Box 2.2   Conflict-induced movement and trafficking

People affected by conflict and insecurity can suffer some of the worst human development outcomes of all migrants. The number of people who move as a result of conflict is significant: at the beginning of 2008, there were around 14 million refugees falling under the mandate of either UNHCR or the United Nations Relief and Works Agency for Palestine Refugees in the Near East (UNRWA), accounting for roughly 7 percent of all international migration. The vast majority of refugees originate in and relocate to the poorer countries of the world: in Asia and Africa refugees account respectively for 18 and 13 percent of all international migrants.

Even more individuals displaced by violence and conflict relocate within the borders of their country. It is estimated that, in 2009, internally displaced persons number some 26 million, including 4.9

million in Sudan, 2.8 million in Iraq and 1.4 million in the Democratic Republic of the Congo.

It is much harder to ascertain the magnitude of human trafficking. In fact, there are no accurate estimates of the stocks and flows of people who have been trafficked. Among the reasons for this are the fact that trafficking data are commonly mixed with data on other forms of illegal migration or migrant exploitation, the inherent challenges in distinguishing between what is voluntary and forced, and the very nature of human trafficking as a clandestine and criminal activity. Many of the frequently cited figures are disputed by the countries concerned, and there is a significant gap between estimated numbers and identified cases.

Source: IDMC (2009b), Carling (2006), Kutnick, Belser, and Danailova-Trainor (2007), de Haas (2007) and Lazcko (2009).

population or 30 percent of total migrants.[22] A recent research project funded by the European Commission estimated that in 2005 irregular migrants accounted for 6–15 percent of the total stock of migrants, or about 1 percent of the population of the European Union.[23] Some of these migrants are counted in official estimates of migration, but many are not (box 2.1).

The over-representation of skilled, working-age people in migrant populations is one aspect of migrant selectivity. Not only do migrants tend to have higher income-earning capacity than non-migrants but they often also appear to be healthier and more productive than natives of the destination country with equivalent educational qualifications. Migrant selectivity usually reflects the effect of economic, geographical or policy-imposed barriers that make it harder for low-skilled people to move. This is most evident in terms of formal education. Tertiary graduates, for example, make up 35 percent of working-age immigrants to the OECD but only about 6 percent of the working-age population in non-OECD countries.[24] Immigrants to the OECD from developing countries tend to be of working age: for example, over 80 percent of those from sub-Saharan Africa fall into this group.[25]

What do we know about migrant selectivity in developing countries? When the migration process is more selective, individuals of working age (who have higher earning capacity than those out of the labour force) form a large proportion of movers. Using census data, we compared the age profiles of migrants to people in their countries of origin in 21 developing and 30 developed countries. We found a significant difference between the age profile of immigrants in developed countries and that of their countries of origin: 71 percent of migrants in developed countries are of working age, as opposed to 63 percent of the population in their origin countries; in contrast, the difference is negligible in developing countries (63 versus 62 percent).

New evidence on internal migration paints a more complex picture of migrant selectivity. In Kenya, for example, commissioned research found a positive relationship between measures of human capital and migration,[26] which tends to diminish with successive cohorts of migrants over time,[27] a result that is consistent with the development of social and other networks that facilitate movement. In other words, poorer people may decide to take the risk of migrating as they hear news of others' success and become more confident that they will receive the support they need in order to succeed themselves. Other commissioned research generated education profiles for internal migrants across 34 developing countries. This showed that migrants were more likely than non-migrants to complete secondary school, reflecting both selectivity and better outcomes among migrant children (chapter 3).[28]

What else do we know about the relationship between internal and international migration? Internal migration, particularly from rural to urban areas, can be a first step towards international migration, as found by some studies in Mexico, Thailand and Turkey, but this is far from being a universal pattern.[29] Rather, emigration may foster subsequent internal migration in the home country. In Albania, migration flows to Greece in the early 1990s generated remittances, which helped to finance internal migration to urban centres; in India, international movers from the state of Kerala have freed up positions in their areas of origin and their remittances spurred a construction boom that has attracted low-skilled migrants from surrounding areas.[30]

Comparisons between internal and international migration can yield useful insights into the causes and implications of human movement. For example, background research for this report analysed the relationship between the size of the place of origin (as measured by its population) and skilled labour flows and found that the patterns were broadly similar across countries as well as within them. In particular, emigration rates for skilled workers are higher in small localities than in large ones, just as they are higher in small countries than in large ones.[31] These patterns reflect the importance of human interaction in driving movement. Movement both within and between nations is predominantly driven by the search for better opportunities, and in many cases—in particular those involving skilled labour—opportunities will be greater in places where there are other people with complementary skills. This is one of the reasons why people gravitate to urban centres, and why high-skilled professionals often move to cities and places where their profession is already well established.[32]

> Movement both within and between nations is predominantly driven by the search for better opportunities

Unfortunately, migration data remain weak. It is much easier for policy makers to count the international movements of shoes and cell-phones than of nurses and construction workers

Despite our ability to establish these broad contours of movement, what we know is dwarfed by what we don't know. Unfortunately, migration data remain weak. It is much easier for policy makers to count the international movements of shoes and cell-phones than of nurses and construction workers. Most of our information is based on censuses, but these do not provide time series of migration flows that would enable trends to be recognized nor key data for assessing the impact of migration, such as the income and other characteristics of migrants at the time of admission. Population registers can produce such time series, but very few countries have registers with that capacity. Policy makers typically require information about migrant admissions by type (e.g. contract workers, trainees, family members, skilled professionals, etc.), so administrative data reflecting the number of visas and permits granted to different types of migrants are important. Yet none of these data sources can answer questions about the social or economic impact of international migration.

Advances have been made in recent years. The OECD, the UN, the World Bank and other agencies have compiled and published census and administrative databases that shed new light on some aspects of global flows of people. But public data still cannot answer basic questions, such as: how many Moroccans left France last year? What are the occupations of Latin Americans who took up United States residency in 2004? How has the number of Zimbabweans going to South Africa changed in recent years? How much return or circular migration occurs globally, and what are the characteristics of those migrants? For the most part, migration data remain patchy, non-comparable and difficult to access. Data on trade and investment are vastly more detailed. Many aspects of human movement simply remain a blind spot for policy makers.

While some data limitations are difficult to overcome—including the problem of accurately estimating the number of irregular migrants—others should be surmountable. A logical first step is to ensure that national statistics offices follow international guidelines, such that every census contains core migration questions.[33] Existing surveys could be slightly expanded, or existing administrative data compiled and disseminated, to increase public information on migration

processes. Adding questions on country of birth or country of previous residence to the national census would be a low-cost way forward for many countries. Another would be the public release of existing labour force data, including country of birth, as Brazil, South Africa, the United States and some other countries already do. Yet another would be the inclusion of standard migration questions in household surveys in countries where migration has grown in importance. These improvements are worthy of government attention and increased development assistance.

2.2 Looking back

We now consider how human movement has shaped world history. Doing so sheds light on the extent to which earlier movements differed from or were similar to those of today. It will also reveal the role of migration in the structural transformation of societies, the forces that drive migration and the constraints that frustrate it. We then present a more detailed discussion of the evolution of internal and international movements during the 20th century, with a focus on the post-World War II era. The analysis of trends during the past 50 years is key to understanding the factors causing recent changes in migration patterns and how we can expect these to continue evolving in the future.

2.2.1 The long-term view

Despite the widespread perception that international migration is associated with the rise of globalization and trade in the late 20th century, large-scale long-distance movements were prevalent in the past. At the peak of Iberian rule in the Americas, more than half a million Spaniards and Portuguese and about 700,000 British subjects went to the colonies in the Americas.[34] Through the brutal use of force, 11–12 million Africans were sent as slaves across the Atlantic between the 15th and late 19th centuries. Between 1842 and 1900, some 2.3 million Chinese and 1.3 million Indians travelled as contract labourers to South-East Asia, Africa and North America.[35] At the close of the 19th century the fraction of foreign-born residents in many countries was higher than today.[36]

Going back further in time, we find human movement has been a pervasive phenomenon throughout history, present in nearly every community for which historical or archaeological evidence is available. Recent DNA tests support previous fossil evidence that all human beings evolved from a common ancestor from equatorial Africa, who crossed the Red Sea into Southern Arabia approximately 50,000 years ago.[37] While encounters among different societies often led to conflict, the peaceful coexistence of immigrants in foreign lands is also recorded. An ancient Babylonian tablet from the 18th century BCE, for example, talks about a community of migrants from Uruk who fled their homes when their city was raided and, in their new home, met little resistance to their cultural practices, with their priests being allowed to inhabit the same quarters as those venerating local gods.[38] The idea that migrants should be treated according to basic norms of respect is found in many ancient religious texts. The Old Testament, for example, states that "the alien living with you must be treated as one of your native-born," whereas the Koran requires the faithful to move when their beliefs are in danger and to give *aman* (refuge) to non-Muslims, even if they are in conflict with Muslims.[39]

Population movements have played a vital role in the structural transformation of economies throughout history, thereby contributing greatly to development. Genetic and archaeological evidence from the Neolithic period (9500–3500 BCE) suggests that farming practices spread with the dispersal of communities after they had mastered the techniques of cultivation.[40] The British Industrial Revolution both generated and was fuelled by rapid urban growth, driven mainly by movement from the countryside.[41] The share of rural population has declined markedly in all economies that have become developed, falling in the United States from 79 percent in 1820 to below 4 percent by 1980, and even more rapidly in the Republic of Korea, from 63 percent in 1963 to 7 percent in 2008.[42]

An interesting episode from the standpoint of our analysis was that of the large flows from Europe to the New World during the second half of the 19th century. By 1900, more than a million people were moving out of Europe each year, spurred by the search for better conditions in the face of hunger and poverty at home. The size of these flows is staggering by contemporary standards. At its peak in the 19th century, total

emigrants over a decade accounted for 14 percent of the Irish population, 1 in 10 Norwegians, and 7 percent of the populations of both Sweden and the United Kingdom. In contrast, the number of *lifetime* emigrants from developing countries today is less than 3 percent of the total population of these countries. This historical episode was partly driven by falling travel costs: between the early 1840s and the late 1850s, passenger fares from Britain to New York fell by 77 percent in real terms.[43] There were other determining factors in particular cases, such as the potato famine in Ireland. These population movements had sizeable effects on both source and destination countries. Workers moved from low-wage labour-abundant regions to high-wage labour-scarce regions. This contributed to significant economic convergence: between the 1850s and World War I, real wages in Sweden rose from 24 to 58 percent of those of the United States, while, over the same period, Irish wages rose from 61 to 92 percent of those in Great Britain. According to economic historians, more than two thirds of the wage convergence across countries that occurred in the late 19th century can be traced to the equalizing effect of migration.[44]

Remittances and return migration were also very important in the past. Remittances were sent by courier and through transfers and notes via immigrant banks, mercantile houses, postal services and, after 1900, by telegraph wire. It is estimated that the average British remitter in the United States in 1910 sent up to a fifth of his income back home, and that about a quarter of European migration to the United States around that time was financed through remittances from those already there.[45] Return migration was often the norm, with estimated rates of return from the United States ranging as high as 69 percent for Bulgaria, Serbia and Montenegro and 58 percent for Italy.[46] In Argentina, Italian immigrants were often referred to as *golondrinas* (swallows) because of their tendency to return, and a contemporary observer wrote that "the Italian in Argentina is no colonist; he has no house, he will not make a sustenance... his only hope is a modest saving."[47]

These population movements were enabled by a policy stance that was not only receptive to migration but in many cases actively encouraged it. This is as true of origin countries, which often

Population movements have played a vital role in the structural transformation of economies throughout history

subsidized passage in order to reduce pressures at home, as it was of destination governments, which invited people to come in order to consolidate settlements and take advantage of natural resources. For example, by the 1880s about half of migrants to Argentina received a travel subsidy, while a law passed in Brazil in 1850 allotted land to migrants free of charge.[48] More generally, the late 19th century was marked by the absence of the plethora of mechanisms to control international flows of people that subsequently emerged. Until the passage of restrictive legislation in 1924, for example, there was not even a visa requirement to settle permanently in the United States, and in 1905, only 1 percent of the one million people who made the transatlantic journey to Ellis Island were denied entry into the country.[49]

One key distinction between the pre-World War I period and today lies in the attitudes of destination governments. While anti-immigrant sentiment could run high and often drove the erection of barriers to specific kinds of movement, the prevailing view among governments was that movement was to be expected and was ultimately beneficial to both origin and destination societies.[50] This is all the more remarkable in societies where intolerance of minorities was prevalent and socially accepted to a far larger extent than today.[51] It is also a useful reminder that the barriers to migration that characterize many developed and developing countries today are much less an immutable reality than might at first be supposed.

2.2.2 The 20th century

The pro-migration consensus was not to last. Towards the end of the 19th century, many countries introduced entry restrictions. The causes were varied, from the depletion of unsettled land to labour market pressures and popular sentiment. In countries such as Argentina and Brazil the policy shift occurred through the phasing out of subsidies; in Australia and the United States it came through the imposition of entry barriers.[52] Despite the introduction of these restrictions, estimates from the early 20th century indicate that the share of international migrants in the world's population was similar if not larger than it is today. This is especially striking given the relatively high transport costs at that time.[53]

There was nothing in the area of migration policy even remotely resembling the rapid multilateral liberalization of trade in goods and movements of capital that characterized the post-World War II period.[54] Some countries entered bilateral or regional agreements to respond to specific labour shortages, such as the United States' 1942 Mexican Farm Labour (*Bracero*) Program, which sponsored 4.6 million contracts for work in the United States over a 22-year period,[55] the 1947 United Kingdom–Australia Assisted Passage Agreement, or the flurry of European labour movement agreements and guest-worker programmes.[56] But early enthusiasm for guest-worker programmes had fizzled out by the 1970s. The United States phased out its *Bracero* Program in 1964, and most Western European countries that had heavily relied on guest-worker programmes ceased recruitment during the 1970s oil shock.[57]

This lack of liberalization is consistent with the observed stability in the global share of migrants. As shown in table 2.1, this share (which excludes Czechoslovakia and the former Soviet Union for comparability reasons—see below) has inched up from 2.7 to 2.8 percent between 1960 and 2010. The data nonetheless reveal a

Table **2.1**	**Five decades of aggregate stability, with regional shifts**

Regional distribution of international migrants, 1960–2010

	1960			2010		
	Total migrants (millions)	Share of world migrants	Share of population	Total migrants (millions)	Share of world migrants	Share of population
World (excluding the former Soviet Union and former Czechoslovakia)	**74.1**		**2.7%**	**188.0**		**2.8%**
BY REGION						
Africa	9.2	12.4%	3.2%	19.3	10.2%	1.9%
Northern America	13.6	18.4%	6.7%	50.0	26.6%	14.2%
Latin America and the Caribbean	6.2	8.3%	2.8%	7.5	4.0%	1.3%
Asia	28.5	38.4%	1.7%	55.6	29.6%	1.4%
GCC states	0.2	0.3%	4.6%	15.1	8.0%	38.6%
Europe	14.5	19.6%	3.5%	49.6	26.4%	9.7%
Oceania	2.1	2.9%	13.5%	6.0	3.2%	16.8%
BY HUMAN DEVELOPMENT CATEGORY						
Very high HDI	31.1	41.9%	4.6%	119.9	63.8%	12.1%
OECD	27.4	37.0%	4.2%	104.6	55.6%	10.9%
High HDI	10.6	14.2%	3.2%	23.2	12.3%	3.0%
Medium HDI	28.2	38.1%	1.7%	35.9	19.1%	0.8%
Low HDI	4.3	5.8%	3.8%	8.8	4.7%	2.1%

Source: HDR team estimates based on UN (2009d).
Note: Estimates exclude the former Soviet Union and former Czechoslovakia.

remarkable shift in destination places. The share in developed countries more than doubled, from 5 percent to more than 12 percent.[58] An even larger increase—from 5 to 39 percent of the population—occurred in the GCC countries, which have experienced rapid oil-driven growth. In the rest of the world, however, the fraction of foreign-born people has been stable or declining. The declines are most marked in Latin America and the Caribbean, where international migration has more than halved, but are also evident in Africa and the rest of Asia.

An important caveat is that these trends exclude two sets of countries for which it is difficult to construct comparable time series on international migrants, namely the states of the former Soviet Union, and the two components of former Czechoslovakia. The independence of these new nations generated an artificial increase in the number of migrants, which should not be interpreted as a real increase in the prevalence of international movement (box 2.3).[59]

Where are recent migrants to developed countries coming from? We do not have a full picture of bilateral flows over time, but figure 2.4 displays the evolution of the share of people from developing countries in eight developed economies that have comparable information. In all but one case (the United Kingdom), there were double-digit increases in the share of migrants from developing countries.[60] In many European countries, this shift is driven by the increase in migrants from Eastern European countries classed as developing according to their HDI. For example, during the 1960s only 18 percent of developing country immigrants into Germany came from Eastern Europe; 40 years later that ratio was 53 percent.

In developing countries, the picture is more mixed, although data are limited. We can compare the source of migrants today and several decades ago for a few countries, revealing some interesting contrasts (figure 2.5). In Argentina and Brazil, the decline in the share of foreign-born people was driven by a fall in those coming from the poorer countries of Europe, as those countries experienced dramatic postwar growth while much of Latin America

---

| Box **2.3** | **Migration trends in the former Soviet Union** |

When the Soviet Union broke up in 1991, 28 million people became international migrants overnight—even if they hadn't moved an inch. This is because statistics define an international migrant as a person who is living outside their country of birth. These people had moved within the Soviet Union before 1991 and were now classified as foreign-born. Without their knowing it, they were now 'statistical migrants'.

At one level, the reclassification makes sense. A Russian in Minsk was living in the country of her birth in 1990; by the end of 1991, she was technically a foreigner. But interpreting the resulting increase in the number of migrants as an increase in international movement, as some authors have done, is mistaken. Hence we have excluded them, together with migrants in the former Czechoslovakia, from the calculation of trends in table 2.1.

Has human movement increased in the former Soviet Union since 1991? On the one hand, the relaxation of *propiska* controls increased human mobility. On the other, the erection of national boundaries may have reduced the scope for movement. The picture is further complicated by the fact that many movements after 1991 were returns to the region of origin: for example, people of Russian origin returning from central Asia.

Any attempt to understand trends in the former Soviet Union should use comparable territorial entities. One way to do this is to consider inter-republic migration before and after the break-up. In this approach, anyone who moved between two republics that would later become independent nations would be considered an international migrant. Thus, a Latvian in St. Petersburg would be classified as an international migrant both before and after 1991.

In background research for this report, Soviet census data were used to construct such a series. Thus defined, the share of foreign-born people in the republics of the USSR rose slightly from 10 percent in 1959 to 10.6 percent in 1989. After 1990, there were divergent trends across the different states. In the Russian Federation, which became something of a magnet in the region, the migrant stock increased from 7.8 to 9.3 percent of the population. For Ukraine and the three Baltic states, migrant shares declined, as large numbers of foreign-born people left. In all the other states of the former Soviet Union, the absolute number of migrants declined until 2000 and in most cases the migrant share of the population also declined. Thus, while 30.3 million foreign-born people lived in the territory of the Soviet Union at the time of its dissolution, the aggregate number fell to 27.4 million in 2000 and to 26.5 million in 2005, as many in the post-Soviet space chose to return home.

Source: Heleniak (2009), UN (2002), Zlotnik (1998), and Ivakhnyuk (2009).

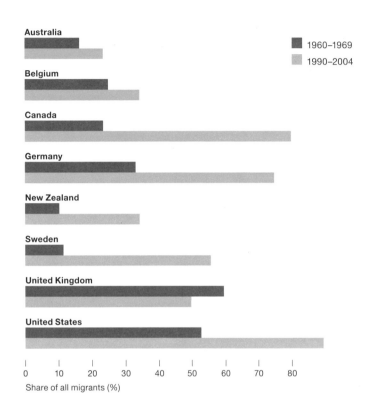

Figure **2.4** **An increasing share of migrants come from developing countries**
Share of migrants from developing countries in selected developed countries

Source: HDR team estimates based on UN (2006a).

A levelling off or even a decline in internal migration flows is to be expected in developed and high-HDI countries, where past flows were associated with rapid urbanization that has now abated. But in many developing countries urbanization has not slowed and is expected to continue. In fact, estimates from UNDESA suggest that the urban share of the world's population will nearly double by 2050 and will increase from 40 percent to over 60 percent in Africa. Urbanization is spurred in part by natural population growth in urban areas, alongside migration from rural areas and from abroad. Although it is difficult to determine the precise contributions of these different sources, it is clear that migration is an important factor in many countries.[61]

Urbanization can be associated with major challenges to city dwellers and the government authorities responsible for urban planning and service provision. The most visible of these challenges is the 2 billion people—40 percent of urban residents—who are expected to be living in slums by 2030.[62] As is well known, living conditions are often very poor in the slums, with inadequate access to safe water and sanitation and insecure land tenure. As we discuss in chapters 4 and 5, it is important that urban local authorities be accountable to residents and adequately financed to tackle these challenges, since local planning and programmes can play a critical role in improving matters.

In sum, the period since 1960 has been marked by a growing concentration of migrants in developed countries against a background of aggregate stability in overall migration. How do we explain these patterns? Our research shows that three key factors—trends in income, population and transport costs—tended to increase movement, which simultaneously faced an increasingly significant constraint: growing legal and administrative barriers.

Divergence in incomes across regions, combined with a general increase in incomes around most of the world, is a major part of the explanation of movement patterns. The evolution of income inequalities shows remarkable divergence between most developing and developed regions, even if the East Asia–Pacific and South Asia regions have seen a mild convergence (figure 2.7, panel A).[63] China presents an exception to the broad pattern of lack of convergence, with

stagnated. In contrast, the rise in the immigration rate in Costa Rica was driven by large flows of Nicaraguan migrants, while the reduction in Mali reflects significant declines in immigration from Burkina Faso, Guinea and Mauritania.

Many countries have experienced increases in internal migration, as shown in figure 2.6. However, this trend is far from uniform. For the 18 countries for which we have comparable information over time, there is an increasing trend in 11 countries, no clear trend in four, and a decline in two developed countries. The average rate of increase for this set of countries is around 7 percent over a decade. However, our research has also found that the share of recent migrants (defined as those who have moved between regions in the past five years) has not increased in most countries in our sample, indicating a possible stabilization of internal migration patterns.

national per capita income rising from 3 to 14 percent of the developed country average between 1960 and 2007.[64] Overall, the data indicate that income incentives to move from poor to rich countries have strongly increased.[65]

Attempts to account for this divergence have generated a vast literature, in which differences in labour and capital accumulation, technological change, policies and institutions have all been investigated.[66] Whatever the ultimate driving forces, one of the key contributing factors has been differing population growth rates. As is well known, between 1960 and 2010 the spatial demographic composition of the world population shifted: of the additional 2.8 billion working-aged people in the world, 9 out of 10 were in developing countries. Because labour became much more abundant in developing countries, wage differentials widened. This meant that moving to developed countries became more attractive and patterns of movement shifted as a result, despite—as we shall see—the raising of high barriers to admission. At the same time, average income levels in the world as a whole were increasing, as shown in panel B of figure 2.7 (even if some developing regions also saw periods of decline). Since poverty is an important constraint on movement, higher average incomes made long-distance movement more feasible. In other words, as incomes rose, poorer countries moved up the 'migration hump', broadening the pool of potential migrants to developed countries.

Recent declines in transport and communication costs have also increased movement. The real price of air travel fell by three fifths between 1970 and 2000, while the cost of communications fell massively.[67] The real cost of a 3-minute telephone call from Australia to the United Kingdom fell from about US$350 in 1926 to US$0.65 in 2000—and, with the advent of internet telephony, has now effectively fallen to zero.[68] Such trends have made it easier than ever before for people to reach and establish themselves in more distant destinations.

Given these drivers, we would expect to see significant growth in international migration in recent decades. However, this potential has been constrained by increased policy barriers to movement, especially against the entry of low-skilled applicants. We turn now to a more in-depth

examination of the role that these barriers play in shaping and constraining movement today.

2.3 Policies and movement

Since the emergence of modern states in the 17th century, the international legal system has been built on the bedrock of two principles: sovereignty and territorial integrity. Within this system, which includes a series of norms and constraints imposed by international law, governments police their country's borders and enforce their right to restrict entry. This section discusses the different ways in which government policy determines how many people to admit, where these people come from, and what status is accorded to them.

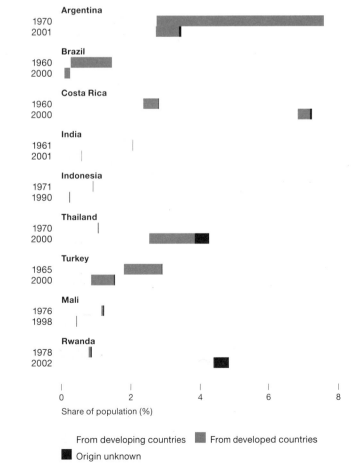

Figure **2.5** **Sources and trends of migration into developing countries**
Migrants as a share of total population in selected countries, 1960–2000s

Source: HDR team estimates based on Minnesota Population Center (2008) and national census data for indicated years.

Figure 2.6 **Internal migration rates have increased only slightly**

Trends in lifetime internal migration intensity in selected countries, 1960–2000s

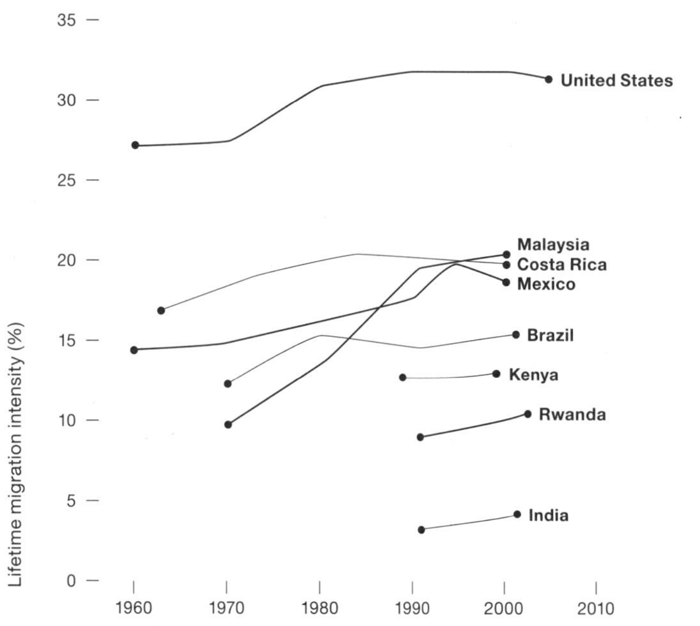

Source: Bell and Muhidin (2009).

Table 2.2 **Policy makers say they are trying to maintain existing immigration levels**

Views and policies towards immigration by HDI category, 2007

HDI categories	Government's view on immigration: Too high	Satis-factory	Too low	Total	Policy on immigration: Lower levels	Maintain levels	Raise levels	No inter-vention	Total
VERY HIGH HDI									
No. of Countries	7	26	6	39	7	24	7	1	39
Percent (%)	18	67	15	100	18	62	18	3	100
HIGH HDI									
No. of Countries	6	40	1	47	9	37	1	0	47
Percent (%)	13	85	2	100	19	79	2	0	100
MEDIUM HDI									
No. of Countries	17	62	4	83	18	47	3	15	83
Percent (%)	20	75	5	100	22	57	4	18	100
LOW HDI									
No. of Countries	4	22	0	26	4	6	0	16	26
Percent (%)	15	85	0	100	15	23	0	62	100
TOTAL									
No. of Countries	34	150	11	195	38	114	11	32	195
Percent (%)	17	77	6	100	19	58	6	16	100

Source: UN (2008b).

While there is a wealth of qualitative country-level analysis of policies—especially for developed countries—severe data limitations impede comparisons of policy across countries. Measurement is intrinsically difficult because the rules take many forms and are enforced in different ways and to varying degrees, with results that are generally not amenable to quantification. In contrast to most aspects of economic policy, for example, national statistical bureaux do not measure the effects of migration policy in ways that are consistent across countries. Most of the measures used in this report have been developed by international research and non-governmental organizations (NGOs), not by national public-sector agencies.

The measure that covers the largest number of countries and the longest time span comes from a periodic survey of policy makers conducted by UNDESA, in which governments report their views and responses to migration. The survey covers 195 countries and reflects the views of policy makers regarding the level of immigration and whether their policy is to lower, maintain or raise future levels. While it is a self-assessment, and official intentions rather than practice are indicated, some interesting patterns emerge (table 2.2). In 2007, some 78 percent of respondent governments viewed current immigration levels as satisfactory, while 17 percent felt them to be too high and 5 percent too low. A similar picture emerges when governments are asked to describe their policies. On both questions, developed country governments appear to be more restrictive than those of developing countries.

These patterns indicate a significant gap between the policies that the public appears to favour in most countries—namely greater restrictions on immigration—and actual policies, which in fact allow for significant amounts of immigration.[69] While explanations for this gap are complex, several factors likely come into play.

The first is that opposition to immigration is not as monolithic as first appears, and voters often have mixed views. As we show below, in many countries, concerns about adverse employment or fiscal effects are mixed with the recognition that tolerance of others and ethnic diversity are positive values. Second, organized groups such as labour unions, employer organizations and NGOs can have a significant effect on the formulation of public policies; in many cases these groups do not advocate for tight restrictions to immigration. Third, many governments implicitly tolerate irregular migration, suggesting that policy makers are aware of the high economic and social costs of a crackdown. For example, in the United States employers are not required to verify the authenticity of immigration documents, but must deduct federal payroll taxes from migrants' pay: through this mechanism, illegal immigrant workers provide around US$7 billion annually to the US Treasury.[70]

For the purposes of this report, we sought to address existing gaps in knowledge by working with national migration experts and the IOM to conduct an assessment of migration policies in 28 countries.[71] The key value added of this exercise lies in the coverage of developing countries (half the sample), which have typically been excluded from such assessments in the past, and the rich information we collected on aspects such as admissions regimes, treatment and entitlements, and enforcement.

Comparing the migration policy regimes of developed and developing countries reveals striking differences as well as similarities. Some of the restrictions commonly noted (and criticized) in developed countries are also present in many developing countries (figure 2.8). The regimes in both groups of countries are biased in favour of high-skilled workers: 92 percent of developing and all of developed countries in our sample were open to temporary skilled migrants; for permanent skilled migration, the corresponding figures were 62 and 93 percent. In our country sample, 38 percent of developing and half of developed countries were closed to permanent migration of unskilled workers.[72]

Temporary regimes have long been used and most countries provide such permits. These programmes stipulate rules for the time-bound admission, stay and employment of foreign workers. The H1B visas of the United States, for instance, grant temporary admission to high-skilled workers for up to six years, while H2B visas are available for low-skilled seasonal workers for up to three. Similarly, Singapore's immigration policy has Employment Passes—for skilled professionals—and a Work Permit or R-Pass for unskilled or semi-skilled workers.[73] Among the countries in our policy assessment,

developing countries were much more likely to have temporary regimes for low-skilled workers.

Rules concerning changes in visa status and family reunion differ widely across countries.[74] Some temporary schemes offer a path to

Figure **2.7**   **Global income gaps have widened**
Trends in real per capita GDP, 1960–2007

Panel A: Ratio of income of developing countries to income of developed countries

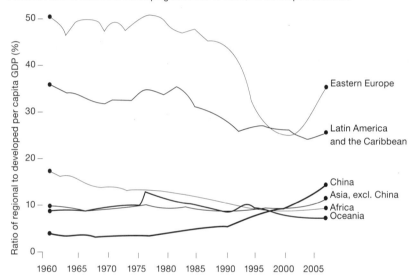

Panel B: Real per capita income of developing countries by region

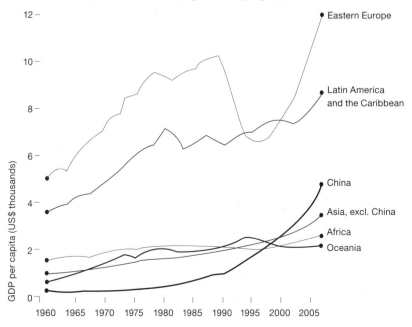

Source: HDR team estimates based on World Bank (2009b) and Heston, Summers, and Aten (2006).

Figure **2.8**

Welcome the high-skilled, rotate the low-skilled

Openness to legal immigration in developed versus developing countries, 2009

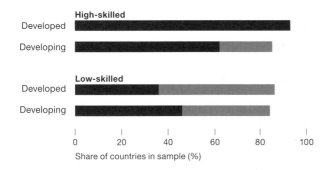

Panel A: Permanent immigration

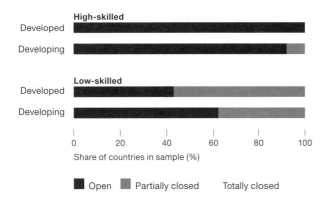

Panel B: Temporary immigration

Source: Klugman and Pereira (2009).

long-term or even permanent residence and allow foreign workers to bring in their dependents. An example is the US's H2B visas, although their annual number is capped at a low level and the dependents are not entitled to work. Other governments explicitly prohibit status change and family reunion, or severely restrict them.

The temporary worker or *kafala* (literally meaning 'guaranteeing and taking care of' in Arabic) programmes of the GCC countries are a special case.[75] Under these programmes, foreign migrant workers receive an entry visa and residence permit only if a citizen of the host country sponsors them. The *khafeel*, or sponsor-employer, is responsible financially and legally for the worker, signing a document from the Labour Ministry to that effect.[76] If the worker is found to have breached the contract, they have to leave the country immediately at their own expense.

Kafala programmes are restrictive on several counts, including family reunification. Human rights abuses—including non-payment of wages and sexual exploitation of domestic workers—are well documented, especially among the increasing share of migrants originating in the Indian subcontinent.[77]

In recent years, some countries in the region have taken moderate steps in the direction of reforming their immigration regimes. Saudi Arabia recently passed a series of regulations facilitating the transfer of workers employed by companies providing services (e.g. maintenance) to government departments.[78] Other initiatives have also been implemented to monitor the living and working conditions of foreign migrants. In the United Arab Emirates, the Ministry of Labour has introduced a hotline to receive complaints from the general public. In 2007, the authorities inspected 122,000 establishments, resulting in penalties for almost 9,000 violations of workers' rights and of legislation on working conditions. However, more ambitious proposals for reform, such as Bahrain's proposal in early 2009 to abolish the *kafala* system, have floundered, reportedly in the face of intense political opposition by business interests.[79]

In some developed countries—including Australia, Canada and New Zealand—the preference for high-skilled workers is implemented through a points system. The formulae take into account such characteristics as education, occupation, language proficiency and age. This confers some objectivity to what otherwise might seem an arbitrary selection process, although other countries attract large numbers of graduates without a point-based system.[80]

Points systems are uncommon in developing countries. Formal restrictions on entry include requirements such as a previous job offer and, in some cases, quotas. One aspect on which developing countries appear to be relatively restrictive is family reunification. About half the developing countries in our sample did not allow the family members of temporary immigrants to come and work—as opposed to one third of developed countries.

Family reunification and marriage migration represent a significant share of inflows into virtually all OECD countries. Indeed, some countries are dominated by flows linked to family ties, as in

France and the United States, where these account for 60 and 70 percent of annual flows respectively. While it is common to distinguish between family reunification and labour migration, it is important to note that family migrants often either have or can acquire authorization to work.

Of course the stated policy may differ from what happens in practice. Significant variations exist in migration law enforcement across countries (figure 2.9). In the United States, research has found that border enforcement varies over the economic cycle, increasing during recessions and easing during expansions.[81] In South Africa, deportations more than doubled between 2002 and 2006 without a change in legislation, as the police force became more actively involved in enforcement.[82] Our policy assessment suggested that while developing countries were somewhat less likely to enforce border controls and less likely to detain violators of immigration laws, other aspects of enforcement including raids by law enforcement agencies and random checks, as well as fines, were at least as frequent as in developed countries. Lower institutional capacity may explain part of this variation. Even after detection, developing countries are reportedly more likely to do nothing or simply to impose fines on irregular migrants. In some countries, courts weigh family unity concerns and the strength of an immigrant's ties to a country in deportation procedures.[83] Further discussion of the role of enforcement in immigration policies is provided in chapter 5.

One question that emerges from these rules on entry and treatment, which can be investigated using cross-country data, is whether there is a 'numbers versus rights' trade-off. It is possible that countries will open their borders to a larger number of immigrants only if access to some basic rights is limited. This could arise if, for example, immigration is seen to become too costly, so that neither voters nor policy makers will support it.[84] Data on the treatment of immigrants allow us to empirically examine this question. The Economist Intelligence Unit (EIU) has created an accessibility index for 61 countries (34 developed, 27 developing) that summarizes official policy in terms of ease of hiring, licensing requirements, ease of family reunification and official integration programmes for migrants. The Migrant Integration

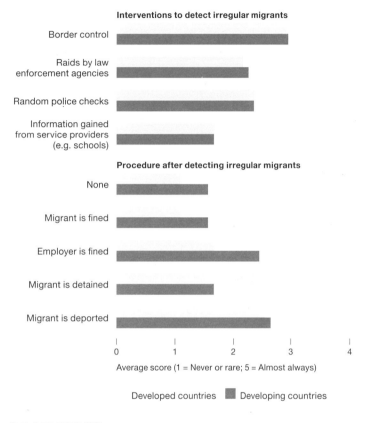

Figure **2.9**   **Enforcement practices vary**

Interventions and procedures regarding irregular migrants, 2009

Average score (1 = Never or rare; 5 = Almost always)

Developed countries   Developing countries

Source: Klugman and Pereira (2009).

Policy Index (MIPEX) measures policies to integrate migrants in six policy areas (long-term residence, family reunion, citizenship, political participation, anti-discrimination measures and labour market access).

Our analysis suggests that there is no systematic relation between various measures of rights and migrant numbers (figure 2.10). Comparison with the EIU index (panel A), which has a broader sample of developed and developing countries, reflects essentially no correlation between the number of migrants and their access to basic rights, suggesting that the various regimes governing such access are compatible with both high and low numbers of migrants. Restricting the analysis to the smaller sample of countries covered by the MIPEX allows us to take advantage of OECD data, which distinguish the share of immigrants with low levels of formal education from developing countries. Again, we find essentially no correlation (panel B). For example,

Figure **2.10** **Cross-country evidence shows little support for the 'numbers versus rights' hypothesis**
Correlations between access and treatment

Panel A: Foreign-born migrants and EIU accessibility score, 2008

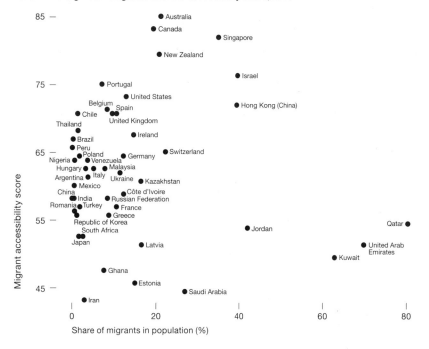

Panel B: Low-skilled foreign-born migrants in OECD and MIPEX aggregate score

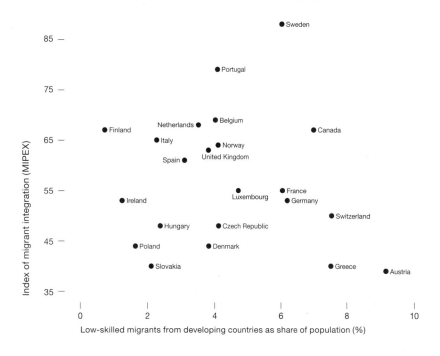

Source: UN (2009d), The Economist Intelligence Unit (2008), OECD (2009a) and Migration Policy Group and British Council (2007).

countries like Poland and Ireland have very low shares of low-skilled workers from developing countries, yet score poorly in the MIPEX. We have also found that countries that have seen increases in their migrant shares over time did not curtail the rights and entitlements provided to immigrants.[85] For example, between 1980 and 2005 the share of immigrants in Spain increased from 2 to 11 percent; during the same period the Spanish government extended the provision of emergency and non-emergency health care to irregular migrants.[86]

Similar results were found in our policy assessment, which allowed us to distinguish between different components of migration policy. In fact, if there was any indication of a correlation, it was often the opposite of that proposed by the numbers versus rights hypothesis. What the data reveal is that, in general, across many measures, developing countries have lower median shares of foreign-born workers and lower protection of migrant rights. Developed countries, which have more migrants, also tend to have rules that provide for better treatment of migrants. For example, India has the lowest score on provision of entitlements and services to international migrants in our assessment, but has an immigrant share of less than 1 percent of the population; Portugal has the highest score while having an immigrant share of 7 percent.

Policies towards migration are not determined solely at the national level. Supra-national agreements, which can be bilateral or regional in nature, can have significant effects on migration flows. Regional agreements have been established under various political unions, such as the Economic Community of West African States (ECOWAS), the European Union and the Mercado Común del Sur (MERCOSUR), while a good example of a bilateral agreement is that of the Trans-Tasman Travel Arrangement between Australia and New Zealand. These agreements have had significant effects on migration flows between signatory countries. They are most likely to allow freedom of movement when participating member states have similar economic conditions and when there are strong political or other motivations for socio-economic integration. For the countries in our policy assessment, about half of the special mobility agreements of developed countries were with other developed

Box **2.4**   ### Global governance of mobility

Beyond a well-established convention on refugees, international mobility lacks a binding multilateral regime. The ILO has long had conventions on the rights of migrant workers, but they are heavily undersubscribed (chapter 5). The IOM has expanded beyond its historic role in the post-war repatriation of refugees towards a more general mission to improve migration management and has increased its membership, but it is outside the UN system and remains largely oriented towards service provision to member states on a project basis. Under the General Agreement on Trade in Services (GATS) of the World Trade Organization (WTO), some 100 member states have made commitments to the temporary admission of foreign nationals who provide services, but these mostly involve business visitor visas for up to 90 days and fixed-term intra-company transfers involving high-skilled professionals.

The lack of multilateral cooperation on migration has been attributed to several related factors. In contrast to trade negotiations, where countries negotiate over the reciprocal reduction of barriers to each other's exports, developing countries are in a weaker bargaining position on the migration front. Most migrants from developed countries go to other developed countries, so there is little pressure from developed country governments to open channels for entering developing countries. This asymmetry, as well as the political sensitivity of the migration issue in most developed destination countries, has led to a lack of leadership from these states in international

negotiations. International discussions have also been characterized by lack of cooperation among sending countries. These obstacles have so far defied the best efforts of international organizations and a handful of governments to promote cooperation and binding international commitments.

Further liberalization is currently being canvassed in the Doha Round of trade negotiations, which began in 2000 but have long since stalled. Existing commitments under GATS are limited, referring mainly to high-skilled workers. GATS also excludes "measures affecting natural persons seeking access to the employment market of another country [or] measures regarding citizenship, residence, or employment on a permanent basis". Nor does GATS apply to permanent migration: most WTO members limit service providers to less than five years in their country.

During the Doha Round it became clear that developing countries want to liberalize the movement of natural persons, whereas industrial countries prefer trade in services. It could be argued that the importance of GATS to labour migration does not lie in the relatively small amount of additional mobility facilitated thus far, but rather in the creation of an institutional framework for future negotiations. However, better progress might be made if the WTO took a more inclusive and people-centred approach, which allowed greater participation by other stakeholders and linked more closely with existing legal regimes for the protection of human rights.

Source: Castles and Miller (1993), Neumayer (2006), Leal-Arcas (2007), Charnovitz (2003), p.243, Mattoo and Olarreaga (2004), Matsushita, Schoenbaum, and Mavroidis (2006), Solomon (2009), and Opeskin (2009).

countries, while more than two thirds of those of developing countries were with other developing countries. There are examples where mobility is granted only to some workers, such as the higher skilled. For example, the migration system of the North American Free Trade Agreement (NAFTA) covers only nationals of Canada, Mexico and the United States who have a B.A. degree and a job offer in another member country. Box 2.4 briefly overviews the multilateral arrangements related to human movement.

However, there can be large differences between the letter of these agreements and actual practice, particularly in countries where the rule of law is weak. For example, despite the provisions for comprehensive rights of entry, residence and establishment provided for in the ECOWAS agreement signed in 1975 (which were to be implemented in three phases over a 15-year period), only the first phase of the protocol—elimination of the need for visas for stays up to 90 days—has been achieved. The reasons

for slow implementation range from inconsistency between the protocol and national laws, regulations and practices to border disputes and full-scale wars which have often led to the expulsion of foreign citizens.[87]

We also find restrictions on human movement within nations as well as on exit. One source of data on these restrictions is the NGO Freedom House, which has collected information on formal and informal restrictions on foreign and internal travel as a component of its assessment of the state of freedom in the world.[88] The results are striking, particularly given that the Universal Declaration of Human Rights guarantees the right to move freely within one's country and to exit and return to one's own country: over a third of countries in the world impose significant restrictions on these freedoms (table 2.3).

Formal restrictions on internal movement are present in many countries with a legacy of central planning, including Belarus, China, Mongolia,

Table **2.3** **Over a third of countries significantly restrict the right to move**
Restrictions on internal movement and emigration by HDI category

HDI categories	Restrictions on mobility, 2008					
	Most restrictive	1	2	3	Least restrictive	Total
VERY HIGH HDI						
No. of Countries	0	3	1	3	31	38
Percent (%)	0	8	3	8	81	100
HIGH HDI						
No. of Countries	2	4	4	10	27	47
Percent (%)	4	9	9	21	57	100
MEDIUM HDI						
No. of Countries	2	13	24	27	16	82
Percent (%)	2	16	29	33	20	100
LOW HDI						
No. of Countries	2	5	13	5	0	25
Percent (%)	8	20	52	20	0	100
TOTAL						
No. of Countries	6	25	42	45	74	192
Percent (%)	3	13	22	23	39	100

Source: Freedom House (2009).

the Russian Federation and Viet Nam.[89] These restrictions are costly, time-consuming and cumbersome to maintain, as are informal barriers, albeit to a lesser extent. Although many people in these countries are able to travel without the proper documentation, they later find that they cannot access services and jobs without them. In several countries, corruption is a key impediment to internal movement. Checkpoints on local roads, where bribes are levied, are commonplace in parts of sub-Saharan Africa. For instance, in Côte d'Ivoire, people living in northern areas controlled by rebel groups were routinely harassed and forced to pay US$40–60 when attempting to travel south to government-controlled areas.[90] Examples of corruption were also reported from Myanmar, the Russian Federation and Viet Nam, where bribes were required to process applications for changes in place of residence. In several South Asian countries, migrants living in urban slums face constant threats of clearance, eviction and rent-seeking from government officials.[91] Internal movement is also impeded by regulations and administrative procedures that

exclude migrants from access to the public services and legal rights accorded to local people (chapter 3).

Countries can limit exit by nationals from their territory by several means, ranging from formal prohibitions to practical barriers created by fees and administrative requirements. Exorbitant passport fees can make it all but impossible for a poor person to leave the country through regular channels: a recent study found that 14 countries had passport fees that exceeded 10 percent of annual per capita income.[92] In many countries, a labyrinth of procedures and regulations, often exacerbated by corruption, causes excessive delays and compounds the costs of leaving. For example, Indonesian emigrants have to visit numerous government offices in order to acquire the necessary paperwork to leave. Not surprisingly, these exit restrictions are negatively correlated with emigration rates.[93]

A handful of countries have formal restrictions on exit. These are strictly enforced in Cuba and the Democratic People's Republic of Korea, and are in place in China, Eritrea, Iran, Myanmar, and Uzbekistan.[94] Eritrea, for example, requires exit visas for citizens and foreign nationals and has reportedly denied the exit visas of children whose parents (living abroad) had not paid the 2 percent tax on foreign income.[95] Twenty countries restrict the exit of women—including Myanmar, Saudi Arabia and Swaziland—while eight impose age-specific restrictions related to the travel of citizens of military service age.[96]

2.4 Looking ahead: the crisis and beyond

The future of the global economy is a central concern for policy makers. Like everyone else, we hold no crystal ball, but we can examine the impacts and implications of the current crisis as the basis for identifying probable trends for the coming decades. Demographic trends, in particular, can be expected to continue to play a significant role in shaping the pressures for movement between regions, as we have seen over the past half-century. But new phenomena such as climate change are also likely to come into play, with effects that are much more difficult to predict.

2.4.1 The economic crisis and the prospects for recovery

Many people are now suffering the consequences of the worst economic recession in post-war history. At the time of writing, world GDP was expected to fall by approximately 1 percent in 2009, marking the first contraction of global output in 60 years.[97] This year's contraction in developed countries is much larger, approaching 4 percent. However, initial optimism that emerging economies might be able to 'decouple' from the financial crisis has been dampened by mounting evidence that they too are, or will be, hard hit. Asian countries have suffered from collapsing export demand, while increases in the cost of external credit have adversely affected Central and Eastern Europe. African countries are battling with collapsing commodity prices, the drying up of capital liquidity, a sharp decline in remittances and uncertainty concerning future flows of development aid. Some of the largest emerging economies, such as Brazil and the Russian Federation, will dip into negative growth, while others, notably China and India, will see severe slowdowns.[98]

Typical recessions do not have a large impact on long-run economic trends.[99] However, it is now clear that this is anything but a typical recession. As such it is likely to have long-lasting and maybe even permanent effects on incomes and employment opportunities, which are likely to be experienced unequally by developing and developed countries.[100] For example, the recession set off by the Federal Reserve's increase of interest rates in 1980 lasted just 3 years in the United States, but the ensuing debt crisis led to a period of stagnation that became known as the 'lost decade' in Africa and Latin America, as the terms of trade of countries in these regions deteriorated by 25 and 37 percent respectively. As commodity prices have fallen significantly from the peak levels of 2008, a similar scenario is probable this time round.

The financial crisis has quickly turned into a jobs crisis (figure 2.11). The OECD unemployment rate is expected to hit 8.4 percent in 2009.[101] That rate has already been exceeded in the United States, which by May 2009 had lost nearly six million jobs since December 2007, with the total number of jobless rising to 14.5 million.[102] In Spain, the unemployment rate climbed as high as 15 percent by April 2009 and

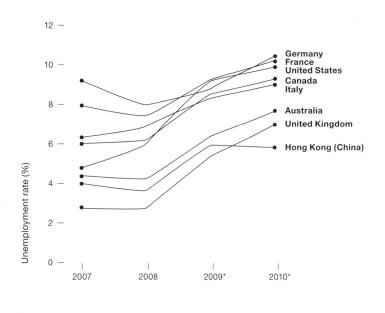

Figure **2.11** **Unemployment is increasing in key migrant destinations**
Unemployment rates in selected destinations, 2007–2010

Unemployment rate (%)

Germany
France
United States
Canada
Italy

Australia

United Kingdom

Hong Kong (China)

2007 2008 2009* 2010*

* Forecasts
Source: Consensus Economics (2009a,b).

topped 28 percent among migrants.[103] The places hit hardest by the crisis thus far are those where most migrants live—the more developed economies. The negative correlation between numbers of immigrants and economic growth suggests that migrants are likely to be badly affected not only in OECD countries but also in the Gulf, East Asia and South Africa (figure 2.12).[104]

A jobs crisis is generally bad news for migrants. Just as economies tend to call on people from abroad when they face labour shortages, so they tend to lay off migrants first during times of recession. This is partly because, on average, migrants have a profile typical of workers who are most vulnerable to recessions—that is, they are younger, have less formal education and less work experience, tend to work as temporary labourers and are concentrated in cyclical sectors.[105] Even controlling for education and gender, labour force analysis in Germany and the United Kingdom found that migrants are much more likely to lose their job during a downturn than non-migrants.[106] Using quarterly GDP and unemployment data from 14 European countries between 1998 and 2008, we also found that, in countries that experienced recessions,

2

HUMAN DEVELOPMENT REPORT 2009
Overcoming barriers: Human mobility and development

Figure **2.12**   **Migrants are in places hardest hit by the recession**
Immigrants' location and projected GDP growth rates, 2009

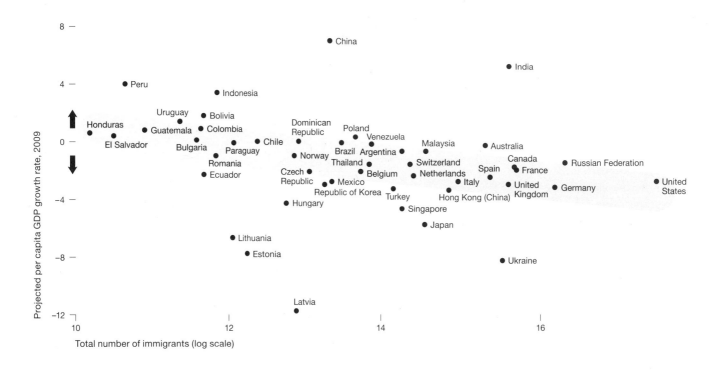

Source: HDR team estimates based on Consensus Economics (2009a,b,c,d) and UN (2009d)

the unemployment rate of migrants tended to increase faster than that of other groups. Within the OECD, migrants were concentrated in highly cyclical sectors that have suffered the largest job losses—including manufacturing, construction, finance, real estate, hotels and restaurants—sectors that employ more than 40 percent of immigrants in almost every high-income OECD country.[107] The decline in remittances from migrants is likely to have adverse effects on family members in countries of origin, as we discuss in greater detail in chapter 4.

Several factors come into play in determining how the crisis affects—and will affect—the movement of people. They include immediate prospects at home and abroad, the perceived risks of migrating, staying or returning, and the increased barriers that are likely to come into place. Several major destination countries have introduced incentives to return (bonuses, tickets, lump sum social security benefits) and increased restrictions on entry and stay. Some governments are discouraging foreign recruitment and

reducing the number of visa slots, especially for low-skilled workers but also for skilled workers. In some cases these measures are seen as a short-term response to circumstances and have involved marginal adjustments rather than outright bans (e.g. Australia plans to reduce its annual intake of skilled migrants by 14 percent).[108] But there is also a populist tone to many of the announcements and provisions. For example, the United States economic stimulus package restricts H1B hires among companies that receive funds from the Troubled Asset Relief Program;[109] the Republic of Korea has stopped issuing new visas through its Employment Permit System; and Malaysia has revoked more than 55,000 visas for Bangladeshis in order to boost job prospects for locals.[110]

There is some evidence of a decline of flows into developed countries during 2008, as the crisis was building. In the United Kingdom, applications for National Insurance cards from foreign-born people fell by 25 percent.[111] Data from surveys carried out by the US Census

Bureau show a 25 percent decline in the flow of Mexican migrants to the United States in the year ending in August 2008.[112] These trends can be expected to continue in 2009 and 2010, as the full effect of the crisis plays out in rising domestic unemployment. There are reasons to be sceptical, however, that major return flows will emerge. As the experience of European guest-worker programmes in the 1970s demonstrates, the size of return flows are affected by the prospects of re-entry to the host country, the generosity of the host country's welfare system, the needs of family members and conditions back home—all of which tend to encourage migrants to stay put and ride out the recession.

Whether this crisis will have major structural effects on migration patterns is not yet clear. Evidence from previous recessions shows that the outcomes have varied. A historical review of several countries—Argentina, Australia, Brazil, Canada, the United States and the United Kingdom—showed that, between 1850 and 1920, declines in domestic wages led to tighter restrictions on immigration.[113] Several scholars have argued that the 1973 oil crisis, which heralded a prolonged period of economic stagnation, structural unemployment and lower demand for unskilled workers in Europe, affected migration patterns as a wealthier Middle East emerged as the new destination hub.[114] During the 1980s, the collapse of Mexican import substitution set in motion an era of mass migration to the United States that was unintentionally accelerated by the 1986 United States immigration reform.[115] In contrast, there is little evidence that the East Asian financial crisis of the late 1990s had a lasting impact on international migration flows.[116]

At this stage it is impossible to predict the type and magnitude of the structural changes that will emerge from the current crisis with any confidence. Some commentators have argued that the origin of the crisis and its fierce concentration in certain sectors in developed countries may strengthen the position of developing countries, particularly in Asia, even leading to a radically different configuration of the global economy.[117] However, there are also reasons for expecting a revival of pre-crisis economic and structural trends once growth resumes. It is certainly true that deeper long-term processes, such

as the demographic trends, will persist regardless of the direction taken by the recession.

2.4.2 Demographic trends

Current forecasts are that the world's population will grow by a third over the next four decades. Virtually all of this growth will be in developing countries. In one in five countries—including Germany, Japan, the Republic of Korea and the Russian Federation—populations are expected to shrink; whereas one in six countries—all of them developing and all but three of them in Africa—will more than double their populations within the next 40 years. Were it not for migration, the population of developed countries would peak in 2020 and fall by 7 percent in the following three decades. The trend evident over the past half century—the fall in the share of people living in Europe and the increase in Africa—is likely to continue.[118]

Aging of populations is a widespread phenomenon. By 2050, the world as a whole and every continent except Africa are projected to have more elderly people (at least 60 years of age) than children (below 15). This is a natural consequence of the decline in death rates and the somewhat slower decline in birth rates that has occurred in most developing countries, a well-known phenomenon known as the 'demographic transition'. By 2050, the average age in developing countries will be 38 years, compared to 45 years in developed countries. Even this seven-year difference will have marked effects. The global working-age population is expected to increase by 1.1 billion by 2050, whereas the working-age population in developed countries, even assuming a continuation of current migration flows, will decline slightly. Over the next 15 years, new entrants to the labour force in developing countries will exceed the total number of working-age people currently living in developed countries (figure 2.13). As in the past, these trends will put pressure on wages and increase the incentives for moving among potential employees in poor countries—and for seeking out workers from abroad among employers in rich countries.

This process affects the dependency ratio—that is, the ratio of elderly and young to the working-age population (table 2.4). For every 100 working-age people in developed countries, there are currently 49 who are not of working

Current forecasts are that the world's population will grow by a third over the next four decades

age, roughly half of whom are children or elderly. In contrast, in developing countries, the ratio is higher, at 53, but three quarters of the dependents are children. Over the next 40 years, as the effect of lower birth rates is felt and the proportion of children falls as they reach working age, the dependency ratio will remain roughly stable in developing countries, reaching just 55 by 2050. However, the proportion of elderly will rise markedly in developed countries, so that there will then be 71 non-working-age people for every 100 of working age, a significantly higher fraction than today. These dependency ratios would increase even more rapidly without the moderate levels of immigration included in these scenarios: if developed countries were to become completely closed to new immigration, the ratio would rise to 78 by 2050.

As is well known, this scenario makes it much more difficult for developed countries to pay for the care of their children and old people. Publicly funded education and health systems are paid with taxes levied on the working population, so that as the share of potential taxpayers

shrinks it becomes more difficult to maintain expenditure levels.

These demographic trends argue in favour of relaxing the barriers to the entry of migrants. However, we do not suggest that migration is the only possible solution to these challenges. Greater labour scarcity can lead to a shift in specialization towards high-technology and capital-intensive industries, and technological innovations are possible for services that were traditionally labour-intensive, such as care of the old. The sustainability of pensions and health care systems can also be addressed, at least in part, by increases in the retirement age and in social security contributions.[119] Growing dependency ratios will occur sooner or later in all countries undergoing demographic transitions—and migrants themselves grow old. Nevertheless, the growing labour abundance of developing countries suggests that we are entering a period when increased migration to developed countries will benefit not only migrants and their families but will also be increasingly advantageous for the populations of destination countries.

Figure **2.13** **Working-age population will increase in developing regions**
Projections of working-age population by region, 2010–2050

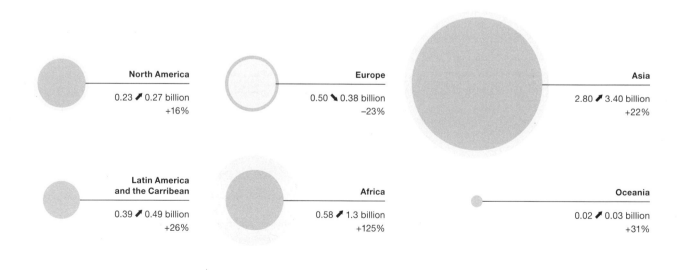

North America
0.23 ✎ 0.27 billion
+16%

Europe
0.50 ↘ 0.38 billion
−23%

Asia
2.80 ✎ 3.40 billion
+22%

Latin America
and the Carribean
0.39 ✎ 0.49 billion
+26%

Africa
0.58 ✎ 1.3 billion
+125%

Oceania
0.02 ✎ 0.03 billion
+31%

2010   2050

Source: HDR team calculations based on UN(2009e).

2.4.3 Environmental factors

The environment can be a key driver of human movement. From nomadic pastoralists, who follow the favourable grazing conditions that arise after rain, to the people displaced by natural disasters such as the Indian Ocean tsunami and Hurricane Katrina, environmental conditions have been intimately linked to movements of people and communities throughout human history. Some are now expecting that the continuing warming of the earth will generate massive population shifts.

Climate change is projected to increase environmental stress in already marginal lands and to raise the frequency of natural hazards. Continued greenhouse gas emissions are likely to be associated with changes in rainfall patterns, desertification, more frequent storms and rises in sea level, all of which have implications for human movement.[120] Changing rainfall patterns, for example, will affect the availability of water and hence the production of food, possibly increasing food prices and the risk of famine.

Existing estimates indicate that several developing areas will be strongly affected by climate change, although the range of estimates is still very wide and predictions are subject to considerable uncertainty. At one extreme, by 2020 it is expected that the yields from rainfed agriculture in Southern Africa could be halved by drought.[121] Over the medium term, as glacial water banks run down, river flows are expected to diminish, severely affecting irrigated agriculture, especially around major massifs such as the Himalayas.

Rises in sea level most directly affect people in coastal areas. One scenario suggests that 145 million people are presently at risk from a rise of one meter, three quarters of whom live in East and South Asia.[122] In some cases, rises will imply the relocation of entire communities. The government of the Maldives, for example, is considering buying land in other countries as a safe haven, given the probability that their archipelago will become submerged.[123]

Some estimates of the numbers of people who will be forced to move as a result of climate change have been presented, ranging from 200 million to 1 billion.[124] Regrettably, there is little hard science backing these numbers. For the most part, they represent the number of people

Table **2.4**	Dependency ratios to rise in developed countries and remain steady in developing countries

Dependency ratio forecasts of developed versus developing countries, 2010–2050

Year	Developed countries		Developing countries	
	Baseline scenario	No Migration scenario	Baseline scenario	No Migration scenario
2010	49	50	53	53
2020	55	56	52	52
2030	62	65	52	52
2040	68	74	53	53
2050	71	78	55	54

Source: UN (2009e).

exposed to the risk of major climatic events and do not take into account the adaptation measures that individuals, communities and governments may undertake.[125] It is thus difficult to know whether such inevitably crude estimates facilitate or obstruct reasoned public debate.

The effect of climate change on human settlement depends partly on how change comes about—as discrete events or a continuous process. Discrete events often come suddenly and dramatically, forcing people to move quickly to more secure places. Continuous processes, on the other hand, are associated with slow-onset changes like sea level rise, salinization or erosion of agricultural lands and growing water scarcity. In many cases, continuous change leads communities to develop their own adaptation strategies, of which migration—whether seasonal or permanent—may be only one component. Under these conditions movement typically takes the form of income diversification by the household, with some household members leaving and others staying behind.[126] This pattern has been observed, for example, among Ethiopian households hit by severe and recurrent droughts.[127]

Given the uncertainty as to whether climate change will occur through a continuous process or discrete events, the extent and type of resulting adaptation and movement are difficult to predict. Moreover, environmental factors are not the sole determinants of movement but interact with livelihood opportunities and public policy responses. It is often the case that natural disasters do not lead to out-migration of the most vulnerable groups, because the poorest usually do

Movement largely reflects people's need to improve their livelihoods… this movement is constrained by policy and economic barriers

not have the means to move and natural disasters further impair their ability to do so. Empirical studies in Mexico have found that the effects of changes in rainfall on migration patterns are determined by socio-economic conditions and the ability to finance the cost of moving.[128] Background research on migration patterns in Nicaragua during Hurricane Mitch, carried out for this report, found that rural families in the bottom two wealth quintiles were less likely to migrate than other families in the aftermath of Hurricane Mitch.[129]

More fundamentally, what happens in the future is affected by the way we consume and use our natural resources today. This was the key message of the 2007/2008 HDR (*Fighting climate change: Human solidarity in a divided world*): catastrophic risks for future generations can be avoided only if the international community acts now. The demand for increased energy in developing countries, where many people still lack access to electricity, can be met while reducing total carbon emissions. The use of more energy-efficient technologies that already exist in developed countries needs to be expanded in developing countries, while creating the next generation of still more efficient technologies and enabling developing countries to leapfrog through to these better solutions. At the same time, energy consumption in developed countries needs to be rationalized. The policy options for encouraging a transition to a low-carbon energy mix include market-based incentives, new standards for emissions, research to develop new technologies and improved international cooperation.[130]

2.5 Conclusions

Three key findings have emerged from this chapter's analysis of global trends in human movement. First, movement largely reflects people's need to improve their livelihoods. Second, this movement is constrained by policy and economic barriers, which are much more difficult for poor people to surmount than for the relatively wealthy. Third, the pressure for increased flows will grow in the coming decades in the face of divergent economic and demographic trends.

Ultimately, how these structural factors will affect the flow of people in the future depends critically on the stance taken by policy makers,

especially those in host countries. At present, policy makers in countries with large migrant populations face conflicting pressures: significant levels of resistance to increased immigration in public opinion on the one hand, and sound economic and social rationales for the relaxation of entry barriers on the other.

How can we expect policies to evolve in the next few decades? Will they evolve in ways that enable us to realize the potential gains from mobility, or will popular pressures gain the upper hand? Will the economic crisis raise protectionist barriers against immigration, or will it serve as an opportunity to rethink the role of movement in fostering social and economic progress? History and contemporary experience provide contrasting examples. Acute labour scarcity made the Americas very open to migration during the 19th century and allowed rapid rates of economic development despite widespread intolerance and xenophobia. This is analogous in some ways to the situation in the GCC states today. However, the tendency to blame outsiders for society's ills is accentuated during economic downturns. Recent incidents across a range of countries—from the Russian Federation to South Africa to the United Kingdom—could presage a growing radicalization and closing off to people from abroad.[131]

Yet none of these outcomes is predetermined. Leadership and action to change the nature of public debate can make a crucial difference. Shifting attitudes towards internal migrants in the United States during the Great Depression provide us with a compelling example. As a result of severe drought in the nation's southern Midwest region, an estimated 2.5 million people migrated to new agricultural areas during the 1930s. There they met fierce resistance from some residents, who saw these migrants as threats to their jobs and livelihoods. It was in this context that John Steinbeck wrote *The Grapes of Wrath*, one of the most powerful indictments of the mistreatment and intolerance of internal migrants ever written. Steinbeck's novel sparked a national debate, leading to a congressional investigation into the plight of migrant workers and ultimately to a landmark 1941 decision by the Supreme Court establishing that states had no right to interfere with the free movement of people within the United States.[132]

How
movers
fare

3

Movers can reap large gains from the opportunities available in better-off places. These opportunities are shaped by their underlying resources—skills, money and networks—and are constrained by barriers. The policies and laws that affect decisions to move also affect the process of moving and the outcomes. In general, and especially for low-skilled people, the barriers restrict people's choices and reduce the gains from moving.

How movers fare

People are motivated to move by the prospects of improved access to work, education, civil and political rights, security and health care. The majority of movers end up better off—sometimes much better off—than before they moved. The gains are potentially highest for people who move from poor to the wealthiest countries, but this type of movement is only a small share of total flows. Available evidence suggests that people who move to emerging and developing countries, as well as within countries, also tend to gain.

However, movement does not necessarily yield a direct positive impact on the well-being of everyone. Moving is risky, with uncertain outcomes and with the specific impacts determined by a host of contextual factors. For both internal and international mobility, different aspects of the process—including the proximate causes of moving and the resources and capabilities that people start out with—profoundly affect outcomes. Those who are forced to flee and leave behind their homes and belongings often go into the process with limited freedom and very few resources. Likewise, those who are moving in the face of local economic crisis, drought or other causes of desperate poverty, may not know what capabilities they will have; they only know that they cannot remain. Even migrants who end up well off after a move often start out with very restricted capabilities and high uncertainty.

The human development outcomes of moving are thus profoundly affected by the conditions under which people move. These conditions determine what resources and capabilities survive the move. Those who go to an embassy to collect a visa, buy a plane ticket and take up a position as a student in, say, the United Kingdom, arrive at their destination in much better shape than someone who is trafficked—arriving with no papers, no money and in bondage. The distance travelled (geographical, cultural and social) is also important. Travelling to a country where one does not speak the language immediately devalues one's knowledge and skills.

This chapter examines how movement affects those who move, why gains are unevenly distributed and why some people win while others lose out. There may well be trade-offs, such as loss of civic rights, even where earnings are higher. The costs of moving also need to be taken into account. We review evidence about these impacts in turn, to highlight the main findings from a vast literature and experience.

The key related question of how moving affects those who don't move, in source and destination places, is addressed in chapter 4. These distinct areas of focus are of course inextricably linked—successful migrants tend to share their success with those who stay at home, while the policy responses of destination places affect how non-movers, as well as movers, fare. Home and host-country impacts are interconnected. Socioeconomic mobility in a host country and the ability to move up the ladder in the homeland are often two sides of the same coin.

3.1 Incomes and livelihoods

It is important to recall at the outset that estimating the impacts of migration is fraught with difficulties, as we saw in box 1.1. The main problem is that movers may differ from non-movers in their basic characteristics, so straight comparisons can be misleading and the identification of causal relationships is problematic.

That said, the most easily quantifiable impacts of moving can be seen in incomes and consumption. We begin with these, then turn to review the costs of moving, which must be subtracted from the gross benefits.

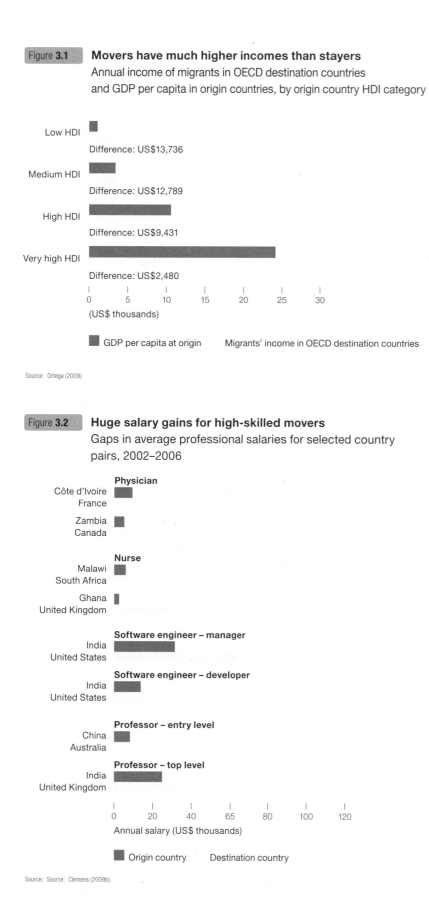

Figure **3.1**

Movers have much higher incomes than stayers

Annual income of migrants in OECD destination countries and GDP per capita in origin countries, by origin country HDI category

Low HDI

Difference: US$13,736

Medium HDI

Difference: US$12,789

High HDI

Difference: US$9,431

Very high HDI

Difference: US$2,480

0   5   10   15   20   25   30

(US$ thousands)

▮ GDP per capita at origin   Migrants' income in OECD destination countries

Source: Ortega (2009)

Figure **3.2**

Huge salary gains for high-skilled movers

Gaps in average professional salaries for selected country pairs, 2002–2006

Physician
Côte d'Ivoire
France

Zambia
Canada

Nurse
Malawi
South Africa

Ghana
United Kingdom

Software engineer – manager
India
United States

Software engineer – developer
India
United States

Professor – entry level
China
Australia

Professor – top level
India
United Kingdom

0   20   40   65   80   100   120

Annual salary (US$ thousands)

▮ Origin country   Destination country

Source: Source: Clemens (2009b).

3.1.1 Impacts on gross income

The evidence consistently reflects very large average income gains for movers. Commissioned research found large differences in income between stayers and movers to OECD countries, with the biggest differences for those moving from low-HDI countries (figure 3.1). Migrant workers in the United States earn about four times as much as they would in their developing countries of origin,[1] while Pacific Islanders in New Zealand increased their net real wages by a factor of three.[2] Evidence from a range of countries suggests that income gains increase over time, as the acquisition of language skills leads to better integration in the labour market.[3]

Gains arise not only when people move to OECD countries. Thai migrants in Hong Kong (China) and Taiwan (Province of China), for example, are paid at least four times as much as they would earn as low-skilled workers at home.[4] In Tajikistan, when the average monthly wage was only US$9, seasonal earnings of US$500–700 in the Russian Federation could cover a family's annual household expenses in the capital city, Dushanbe.[5] However, these average gains are unevenly distributed, and the costs of moving also detract from the gross gains.

Gains can be large for the high-skilled as well as the low-skilled. The wages of Indian software engineers in the late 1990s, for example, were less than 30 percent of their United States counterparts, so those who were able to relocate to this country reaped large gains.[6] Figure 3.2 illustrates the wage gaps, adjusted for purchasing power parity, between high-skilled professionals in selected pairs of countries. A doctor from Côte d'Ivoire can raise her real earnings by a factor of six by working in France. Beyond salaries, many are also often motivated by factors such as better prospects for their children, improved security and a more pleasant working environment.[7]

Internal migrants also tend to access better income-earning opportunities and are able to diversify their sources of livelihood. Commissioned research found that internal migrants in Bolivia experienced significant real income gains, with more than fourfold increases accruing to workers with low education levels moving from the countryside to the cities (figure 3.3). We also found that in 13 out of 16 countries internal migrants had higher incomes than non-migrants.[8] In Brazil and Panama, a series of studies controlling for education found income gains for indigenous groups who move.[9] Studies across a range of countries suggest that internal migration has enabled many households to lift themselves out of poverty, as discussed further in the next chapter.

The segmentation of labour markets in developing countries affects how movers fare. Sometimes this can be traced to administrative restrictions, as in the *hukou* system in China (box 3.1) and the *ho khau* system in Viet Nam. However, segmentation is also widespread in other regions, including South Asia, Africa and Latin America, through barriers that, while not imposed by law, are nonetheless deeply entrenched through social and cultural norms.[10] For example, rural–urban migrants in India are predominantly employed in industries such as construction, brick kilns, textiles and mining, which entail hard physical labour and harsh working and living environments; in Mongolia, rural–urban migrants typically work in informal activities which are temporary, strenuous and without legal protection.[11] In Asia, recent low-skilled migrants from rural areas tend to occupy the lowest social and occupational rungs of urban society and are treated as outsiders.

As we saw in chapter 2, most movers from low-HDI countries are living and working in other low- or medium-HDI countries, in part because barriers to admission are often lower and the costs of moving are less. At the same time, the conditions may well be more difficult than in rich countries and there are risks of both exploitation and expulsion.

Labour market opportunities for migrant women from developing countries tend to be highly concentrated in care activities, paid domestic work and the informal sector.[12] Such women may become trapped in enclaves. For example, in New York City, Hispanic-owned firms were found to provide low wages, few benefits and limited career opportunities to Dominican and Colombian women, reinforcing their social disadvantages.[13] Similar results were found among Chinese migrant women workers.[14] Most Peruvian and Paraguayan women in Argentina (69 and 58 percent respectively) work for low pay on an informal basis

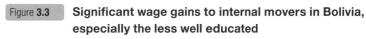

Figure **3.3** **Significant wage gains to internal movers in Bolivia, especially the less well educated**

Ratio of destination to origin wages for internal migrants in Bolivia, 2000

Source: Molina and Yañez (2009).

in the personal service sector.[15] Difficulties are compounded where migrant women are excluded from normal worker protections, as is the case for domestic workers in the GCC states.[16] Although practices are changing in some countries (e.g. Saudi Arabia and the United Arab Emirates), migrants are legally prohibited from joining local unions, and even when this is allowed, they may face resistance and hostility from other workers.[17] NGOs may provide services and protection to migrants, but their coverage tends to be limited.

Labour market discrimination can be a major obstacle to migrants. This is reflected in low call-back rates to job applications where the applicant has a foreign-sounding surname.[18] Yet the picture is often complex, and ethnicity, gender and legal status may all come into play. In the United Kingdom, some studies have found discrimination in hiring migrants in terms of lower employment rates and payments, whereas other studies found that people with Chinese, Indian and Irish backgrounds tended to have employment situations at least as good as white British workers.[19] Our analysis of the 2006 European Social Survey reveals that the vast majority of migrants (more than 75 percent) in this region did not report feeling discriminated against. However, in the much larger country sample provided by the World Values Survey, there was widespread support among locally born people for the proposition, "Employers should give priority to natives when jobs are scarce", albeit with considerable differences across countries (see section 4.2.5).

Box **3.1**   **China: Policies and outcomes associated with internal migration**

Modelled after the Soviet *propiska* system, albeit with roots dating back to ancient times, China's Residence Registration System operates through a permit (*hukou*), needed to gain access to farmland in agricultural areas and to social benefits and public services in urban areas. Until the mid-1980s, the system was administered strictly and movement without a *hukou* was forbidden. Since then, China has liberalized movement but formally maintained the *hukou* system.

As in other areas of reform, China chose a gradual and partial approach. Beginning in the mid-1880s, it allowed people to work outside their place of residence without a *hukou*, but did not allow them access to social benefits, public services or formal-sector jobs. A two-tier migration system analogous to the points system in some developed countries was designed: changes in permanent residency are permitted for the well educated, but only temporary residence is granted for less-educated rural migrants. Many city governments have offered 'blue-stamp' *hukou* to well-off migrants who were able to make sizeable investments.

The evidence suggests that the human development gains for internal migrants and their families have been limited by the persistence of the *hukou* system, along the dimensions illustrated below:

Income gains. In 2004, on average, rural–urban migrants earned RMB780 (US$94) per month, triple the average rural farm income. However, due to the segmentation created by the *hukou* system, temporary migrants typically move to relatively low-paid jobs, and their poverty incidence is double that of urban residents with *hukou*.

Working conditions. Low-skilled migrants tend to work in informal jobs that have inadequate protection and benefits. According to one survey in three provinces, migrants' work hours are 50 percent longer than locals, they are often hired without a written contract and fewer than 1 in 10 have old-age social security and health insurance, compared to average coverage of over 70 percent in China as a whole.

Occupational hazards are high—migrants accounted for about 75 percent of the 11,000 fatalities in 2005 in the notoriously dangerous mining and construction industries.

Access to services. Children who move with temporary status pay additional fees and are denied access to elite schools. An estimated 14–20 million migrant children lack access to schooling altogether. Their drop-out rates at primary and secondary schools exceed 9 percent, compared to close to zero for locals. Access to basic health services is limited. Even in Shanghai, one of the better cities in terms of providing social services to migrants, only two thirds of migrant children were vaccinated in 2004, compared to universal rates for local children. When migrants fall ill, they often move back to rural areas for treatment, due to the costs of urban health care.

Participation. Many migrants remain marginalized in destination places due to institutional barriers. They have few channels for expressing their interests and protecting their rights in the work place. Almost 8 out of 10 have no trade union, workers' representative conference, labour supervisory committees or other labour organization, compared to one fifth of locally born people. Long distances also hinder participation: in a survey of migrants in Wuhan City, only 20 percent had voted in the last village election, mainly because they lived too far away from polling stations.

Discussions about *hukou* reform are reportedly ongoing, while some regional governments have further liberalized their systems. Legislative reforms in 1997 significantly improved the rights of all workers—including migrants, and measures to provide portable pensions for migrant workers were announced in 2008. Other signs of change come from Dongguan, Guangdong, for example, where migrants are now referred to as 'new residents' and the Migrants and Rental Accommodation Administration Office was relabelled the 'Residents Service Bureau'.

Source: Avenarius (2007), Gaige (2006), Chan, Liu, and Yang (1999), Fan (2002), Meng and Zhang (2001), Cai, Du, and Wang (2009), Huang (2006), Ha, Yi, and Zhang (2009b), Fang and Wang (2008), and Mitchell (2009).

One problem facing many migrants on arrival is that their skills and credentials go unrecognized.[20] Coupled with language and other social barriers, this means that they tend to earn much less than similarly qualified local residents.[21] The extent of this problem seems to vary across sectors. Information technology firms tend to be more flexible on credentials, for example, whereas public-sector organizations are often more closed. The failure to fully deploy their skills can cause new immigrants to incur significant costs. The Migration Policy Institute recently estimated that up to 20 percent of college-educated migrants in the United States were unemployed or working in low-skilled jobs, and in Canada, despite the points system, this problem is estimated to drain US$1.7 billion a year from the economy.[22] In response, the Canadian government has launched programmes to speed up the recognition of credentials earned abroad.

Incomes do not depend solely on labour market earnings. In countries with established welfare systems, social transfers reduce poverty rates among disadvantaged groups through unemployment benefits, social assistance and pensions. Whether or not a programme benefits migrant families depends on the design and rules of the system. There are obvious differences across countries in the generosity of these programmes, as their scale tends to be more limited in developing countries due to budgetary constraints. Since most developing countries do not have extensive systems in place, the question of equality of access does not arise. The focus here is therefore on developed countries.

Our policy assessment found that nearly all developed countries in the sample granted permanent migrants access to unemployment benefits and family allowances. However, people with temporary status are less likely to be able to access assistance. Some countries, including Australia and New Zealand, have imposed waiting periods before various benefits can be accessed. And in efforts to avoid welfare dependency, countries such as France and Germany require that applications for family reunification demonstrate that the applicant has stable and sufficient income to support all family members without relying on state benefits.

The Luxembourg Income Study and the European Survey of Income and Living Conditions allow estimates of the effects of social transfers on poverty among families with children.[23] For all 18 countries in the sample, migrant families are more likely to be poor than locally born families. Based on market incomes before social transfers, poverty rates among children exceed 50 and 40 percent among migrant families

in France and the United Kingdom respectively. The redistributive effect of social welfare in these countries is significant, since transfers more than halve these rates for both migrant and locally born children (figure 3.4).[24] In contrast, in the United States the poverty-reducing effect of social transfers for both local and migrant families is negligible, because transfers overall are relatively small. At the same time it is notable that in Australia, Germany and the United States rates of market–income poverty are much lower than in France and the United Kingdom, suggesting that migrant families are doing better in the labour market in those countries.

3.1.2 Financial costs of moving

The gross income gains reported in the literature typically do not account for the monetary costs of moving. These costs arise from various sources, including official fees for documents and clearances, payments to intermediaries, travel expenses and, in some cases, payments of bribes. The costs appear regressive, in that fees for unskilled workers are often high relative to expected wages abroad, especially for those on temporary contracts.[25]

Substantial costs may arise for those without basic documents. Around the world, an

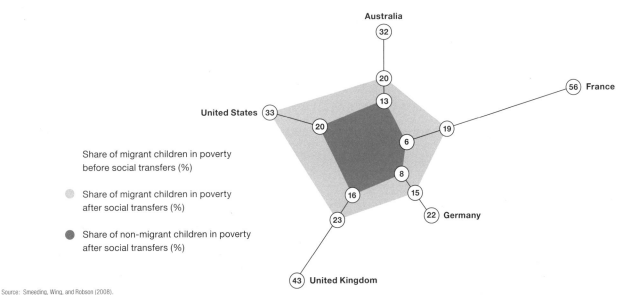

Figure **3.4** **Poverty is higher among migrant children, but social transfers can help**
Effects of transfers on child poverty in selected countries, 1999–2001

Share of migrant children in poverty before social transfers (%)

Share of migrant children in poverty after social transfers (%)

Share of non-migrant children in poverty after social transfers (%)

Source: Smeeding, Wing, and Robson (2008).

Figure **3.5**

Costs of moving are often high

Costs of intermediaries in selected corridors against income per capita, 2006–2008

Viet Nam to Japan (6 years, 5 months and 4 days)

Bangladesh to Saudi Arabia (5 years, 2 months and 3 days)

China to Australia (3 years, 10 months and 16 days)

Colombia to Spain (1 year, 8 months and 3 days)

India to United Kingdom (1 year, 3 months)

Philippines to Singapore (8 months and 26 days)

● = Origin country annual GNI per capita

Source: Bangladesh to Saudi Arabia: Malek (2008); China to Australia: Zhiwu (2009); Colombia to Spain: Grupo de Investigación en Movilidad Humana (2009); Philippines to Singapore: TWC (2006); Viet Nam to Japan: van Thanh (2008).

Figure **3.6**

Moving costs can be many times expected monthly earnings

Costs of movement against expected salary of low-skilled Indonesian workers in selected destinations, 2008

Hong Kong (China)

Taiwan (Province of China)

Malaysia

Singapore

12 months

● = Monthly expected salary

Source: The Institute for ECOSOC Rights (2008).

estimated 48 million children, often from very poor families, lack a birth certificate. The main reason is the fee for obtaining such documents and related factors such as distance to the registration centre.[26]

Lengthy application processes and, in some countries, payments of bribes for routine services can make applying for vital records and basic travel documents very expensive.[27] In the Democratic Republic of the Congo passport applicants can expect to pay up to US$500 (70 percent of average annual income) in bribes.[28] Other countries with limited bureaucratic capacity and corruption in the issuance of travel documents reportedly include Azerbaijan, India and Uzbekistan.[29]

Intermediaries, also known as 'middlemen', perform a specific function in the global labour market. They help to overcome information gaps and meet administrative requirements (such as having a job offer prior to visa application) and sometimes lend money to cover the upfront costs of the move. There are a large number of agencies: in the Philippines alone there are nearly 1,500 licensed recruitment agencies, while India has close to 2,000.[30] The cost of intermediary services appears to vary enormously, but often exceeds per capita income at home (figure 3.5).

The example of Indonesia illustrates how the costs can vary by destination, with moves to Malaysia and Singapore costing about six months' expected salary and to Taiwan a full year (figure 3.6). Legal caps on fees charged by recruiters are generally ignored, as migrants routinely pay much more.[31] The difference between wages at home and expected wages abroad is perhaps the most important determinant of the price of intermediary services. Where relatively few jobs are available, intermediaries who are in a position to allocate these slots are able to charge additional rents. There are cases of abuse and fraud, where prospective movers pay high recruitment fees only to find later on (at the destination) that the work contract does not exist, there have been unilateral changes to the contract, or there are serious violations related to personal safety and working conditions.[32] Some migrants report that employers confiscate their passports, mistreat their employees and deny access to medical care.[33]

Extensive regulations and official fees can encourage irregularity. For Russian employers,

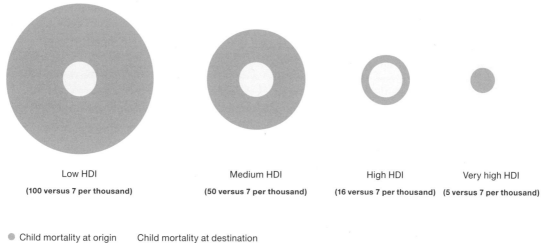

Figure **3.7** The children of movers have a much greater chance of surviving
Child mortality at origin versus destination by origin country HDI category, 2000 census or latest round

Low HDI
(100 versus 7 per thousand)

Medium HDI
(50 versus 7 per thousand)

High HDI
(16 versus 7 per thousand)

Very high HDI
(5 versus 7 per thousand)

● Child mortality at origin   Child mortality at destination

Source: Ortega (2009).

the administrative procedure to apply for a license to hire a foreign worker is reportedly so time-consuming and corrupt that it frequently leads to evasion and perpetuates irregular employment practices.[34] In Singapore, employers of low-skilled migrants must pay a levy, which they in turn deduct from workers' wages.[35] Under agreements between Thailand, Cambodia and the Lao People's Democratic Republic, recruitment fees are equivalent to 4–5 months' salary, processing time averages about four months and 15 percent of wages are withheld pending the migrant's return home. In contrast, smugglers in these corridors reportedly charge the equivalent of one month's salary. Given these cost differences, it is not surprising that only 26 percent of migrant workers in Thailand were registered in 2006.[36]

3.2 Health

This section reviews the impacts of movement on the health of those who move. Gaining better access to services, including health care, may be among the key motivations for moving. Among top high-school graduates from Tonga and Papua New Guinea, 'health care' and 'children's education' were mentioned more often than 'salary' as reasons for migrating, and answers such as 'safety and security' were almost

as frequent.[37] However, the links between migration and health are complex. Migrants' health depends on their personal history before moving, the process of moving itself, and the circumstances of resettlement. Destination governments often rigorously screen applicants for work visas, so successful applicants tend to be healthy.[38] Nevertheless, irregular migrants may have specific health needs that remain unaddressed.

Moving to more developed countries can improve access to health facilities and professionals as well as to health-enhancing factors such as potable water, sanitation, refrigeration, better health information and, last but not least, higher incomes. Evidence suggests that migrant families have fewer and healthier children than they would have had if they had not moved.[39] Recent research conducted in the United States using panel data, which tracks the same individuals over time, found that health outcomes improve markedly during the first year after immigration.[40]

Our commissioned study found a 16-fold reduction in child mortality (from 112 to 7 deaths per 1,000 live births) for movers from low-HDI countries (figure 3.7). Of course these gains are partly explained by self-selection.[41] Nonetheless, the sheer size of these differences suggests that

Barriers to health
services arise due to
financial constraints
as well as status,
cultural and language
differences

similar outcomes would have been very difficult to realize at home. For comparison, as reported in the 2006 HDR, families in the richest quintile in Burkina Faso had a child mortality rate of about 150 deaths per 1,000 live births.

Not surprisingly, given the poor health services, water quality and sanitation in rural areas, studies suggest that migrants to urban centres significantly improve their chances of survival relative to rural residents.[42] The size of this effect has been correlated with duration of stay, which was itself associated with higher incomes and improved knowledge and practices. Sometimes migrants use health care services more than urban locals, suggesting that the availability of these may have motivated their move in the first place. However, the health outcomes associated with urbanization are variable: a broader study found that internal migrants' outcomes were worse than those of urban natives, due to their socio-economic disadvantage, and our commissioned research found that internal migrants had higher life expectancy than non-migrants in only half of the countries studied.[43]

Detailed studies in a number of OECD countries have found that migrants' initial health advantage tends to dissipate over time.[44] This is believed to reflect the adoption of poorer health behaviour and lifestyles as well as, for some, exposure to the adverse working, housing and environmental conditions that often characterize low-income groups in industrial countries. Separation from family and social networks and uncertainty regarding job security and living conditions can affect health. In several studies, migrants have reported higher incidence of stress, anxiety and depression than residents,[45] outcomes that were correlated with worse economic conditions, language barriers, irregular status and recent arrival. Conversely, other studies have found positive effects of migration on mental health, associated with better economic opportunities.[46]

Poor housing conditions and risky occupations can increase accidents and compromise health, which may be worse for irregular migrants.[47] There are well-documented inequalities in health care and status between vulnerable migrant groups and host populations in developed countries.[48] The health of child migrants can also be affected by their type of work, which

may be abusive and/or hazardous.[49] In India, for example, many internal migrants work in dangerous construction jobs, while working conditions in the leather industry expose the mainly migrant workers to respiratory problems and skin infections.[50] Yet these jobs are well paid compared to what was available at home, and interviews in rural Bihar indicate that such jobs are highly sought after.[51]

Not all types of migrants have the same access to health care.[52] Permanent migrants often have greater access than temporary migrants, and the access of irregular migrants tends to be much more restricted (figure 3.8). Movement sometimes deprives internal migrants of access to health services if eligibility is linked to authorized residence, as in China. In contrast, permanent migrants, especially the high-skilled, tend to enjoy relatively good access, while in some countries health care is open to all migrants, regardless of their legal status, as is the case in Portugal and Spain. In the United Arab Emirates coverage varies by emirate, but both Abu Dhabi and Dubai have compulsory insurance schemes to which employers must contribute on behalf of their workers. In Canada all residents are entitled to national health insurance, and the provincial authorities determine who qualifies as a resident.

In practice, barriers to health services arise due to financial constraints as well as status, cultural and language differences,[53] especially for irregular migrants. In France, Germany and Sweden there is a 'responsibility to report' the treatment of an irregular migrant, which can lead to a lack of trust between providers and patients and deter migrants from seeking care.[54] If single female migrants in the GCC states are found to be pregnant, they are deported.[55]

In less-wealthy destination countries there is a tension between the ideal of granting health care access to irregular migrants and the reality of resource constraints. In South Africa many non-nationals report not being able to access antiretroviral drugs against AIDS because facilities deny treatment on the basis of 'being foreign' or not having a national identity booklet.[56] Given that South Africa has one of the highest HIV prevalence rates in the world, combined with improved but still limited access to antiretrovirals, it is not surprising that irregular migrants represent a low priority. But more positive examples are found in other parts of the world. Thailand, for example, provides antiretroviral treatment to migrants from Cambodia and Myanmar, with support from the Global Fund on AIDS, Tuberculosis and Malaria. Thailand also provides migrants with access to health insurance, and efforts are under way to reach irregular migrants.

3.3 Education

Education has both intrinsic value and brings instrumental gains in income-earning potential and social participation. It can provide the language, technical and social skills that facilitate economic and social integration and intergenerational income gains. Movement is likely to enhance educational attainment, especially among children. Many families move with the specific objective of having their children attend better and/or more advanced schools. In many rural areas in developing countries education is available only at primary level and at a lower quality than in urban areas, providing an additional motive for rural–urban migration.[57] Similarly, international migration for educational purposes—school migration—is rising.[58]

In this section we review the evidence concerning school completion levels at places of origin and at destinations, whether migrant children can access state schools and how well they perform relative to children born locally.

School enrolments can change for a number of reasons when a family relocates. Higher incomes are part of the story, but other factors, such as the availability of teachers and schools, the quality of infrastructure and the cost of transport, may be important as well. A natural starting point when measuring education gains is a comparison of enrolment rates. These present a striking picture of the advantages of moving (figure 3.9), with the crude differences being largest for children from low-HDI countries. Two familiar notes of caution should be sounded, however: these results may be overestimated due to positive selection; and mere enrolment guarantees neither a high-quality education nor a favourable outcome from schooling.[59]

The importance of early stimulation to the physical, cognitive and emotional development

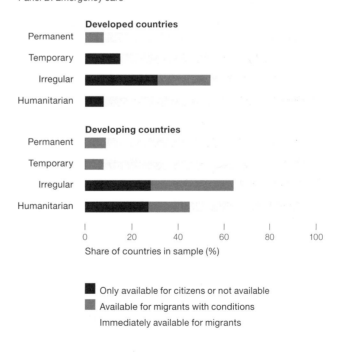

Figure **3.8**

Temporary and irregular migrants often lack access to health care services
Access to health care by migrant status in developed versus developing countries, 2009

Panel A: Preventive care

Developed countries

Permanent
Temporary
Irregular
Humanitarian

Developing countries

Permanent
Temporary
Irregular
Humanitarian

0   20   40   60   80   100

Share of countries in sample (%)

Panel B: Emergency care

Developed countries

Permanent
Temporary
Irregular
Humanitarian

Developing countries

Permanent
Temporary
Irregular
Humanitarian

0   20   40   60   80   100

Share of countries in sample (%)

■ Only available for citizens or not available
■ Available for migrants with conditions
  Immediately available for migrants

Source: Klugman and Pereira (2009)

Figure **3.9** | **Gains in schooling are greatest for migrants from low-HDI countries**

Gross total enrolment ratio at origin versus destination by origin country HDI category, 2000 census or latest round

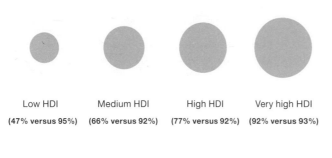

Low HDI	Medium HDI	High HDI	Very high HDI
(47% versus 95%)	**(66% versus 92%)**	**(77% versus 92%)**	**(92% versus 93%)**

⬤ Enrolment ratio at origin   Enrolment ratio at destination

Source: Ortega (2009).

Note: Gross total enrolment includes primary, secondary and tertiary education.

Figure **3.10** | **Migrants have better access to education in developed countries**

Access to public schooling by migrant status in developed versus developing countries, 2009

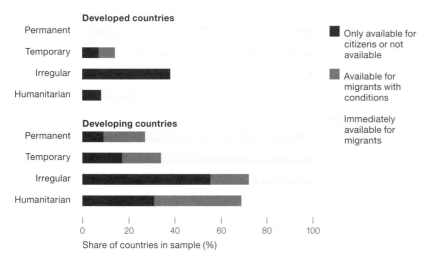

■ Only available for citizens or not available

■ Available for migrants with conditions

Immediately available for migrants

Source: Klugman and Pereira (2009).

However, due to traditional norms, language and cultural barriers and sometimes uncertain legal status, these children are generally less likely to enrol in formal ECD programmes, despite the fact that authorities in Europe and the United States often actively reach out to migrant children.[62] Thailand is among those developing countries that seek to extend informal ECD to migrants, in border areas in the north. Similar arrangements can be found in some other countries; programmes in the Dominican Republic serve Haitian children, for example.

In some countries migrant children may not have access to state schools or their parents may be asked to pay higher fees. Our policy assessment found that developed countries are more likely to allow immediate access to schooling for all types of migrant—permanent, temporary, humanitarian and irregular (figure 3.10). Yet a third of developed countries in our sample, including Singapore and Sweden,[63] did not allow access to children with irregular status, while the same was true for over half the developing countries in the sample, including Egypt and India. Some specific cases: in the United Arab Emirates children with irregular migrant status do not have access to education services; in Belgium education is free and a right for every person, but not compulsory for irregular children; in Poland education for children between 6 and 18 years is a right and is compulsory, but children with irregular status cannot be counted for funding purposes, which may lead the school to decline to enrol such children.[64]

Poverty and discrimination (formal and informal) can inhibit access to basic services. Even if children with irregular status have the right to attend a state school, there may be barriers to their enrolment. In several countries (e.g. France, Italy, the United States), fears that their irregular situation will be reported have been found to deter enrolment.[65] In South Africa close to a third of school-age non-national children are not enrolled, for a combination of reasons including inability to pay for fees, transport, uniforms and books, and exclusion by school administrators, while those in school regularly report being subjected to xenophobic comments by teachers or other students.[66]

The steepest challenges appear to be faced by two groups: children who migrate alone,

of children, and the associated importance of early childhood development (ECD) programmes, is well established.[60] Research from Germany indicates that ECD can bring the children of migrants to par with native children with the same socio-economic background.[61]

who tend to have irregular status (box 3.2), and children who migrate within and between developing countries with their parents, on a temporary basis. The first group is unlikely to be able to access education at all, due to social and cultural isolation, strenuous and hazardous work, extreme poverty, poor health conditions and language barriers.[67] As regards the second group, qualitative studies in Viet Nam and Pakistan have found that seasonal migration disrupts their education.[68] For instance, the Rac Lai minority in Viet Nam migrate with their children to isolated mountainous areas during the harvest season and their children do not attend school during this period.[69]

Even if migrant children gain access to better schools than would have been available to them at origin, they do not all perform well in examinations in comparison with their locally born peers. In the 21 OECD and 12 non-OECD countries covered by the Programme for International Student Assessment,[70] which tested performance in science, pupils who were migrants tended to perform worse in this subject than locally born children. However, foreign-born pupils perform as well as their native peers in Australia, Ireland and New Zealand, as well as in Israel, Macao (China) the Russian Federation and Serbia. Likewise, pupils from the same country of origin performed differently across even neighbouring countries: for example, migrant pupils from Turkey perform better in mathematics in Switzerland than in Germany.[71] The next generation—children of migrants who are born in the destination place—generally do better, but with exceptions, including Denmark, Germany and the Netherlands.

Part of the educational disadvantage of children in migrant families can be traced to low parental education and low income. Children whose parents have less than full secondary completion—which tends to be the case in migrant households in France, Germany, Switzerland and the United States—typically complete fewer years of school. However, while many migrant families live away from relatives and social networks, a study of migrant children in eight developed countries found that they are generally more likely than local children to grow up with both parents.[72] This counters a belief sometimes found in the literature that migrant

Box **3.2** **Independent child migrants**

Trafficking and asylum-seeking are often depicted as accounting for most of the independent movement of children. However, evidence with a long historic record confirms that children also move in search of opportunities for work and education. The Convention on the Rights of the Child goes some way to recognizing children as agents, decision makers, initiators and social actors in their own right. However, the literature and policy responses to children's mobility have largely focused on welfare and protection from harm, and tended to neglect policies of inclusion, facilitation and non-discrimination.

As for other types of movement, the effect of independent child migration is context-specific. Some studies have found a significant link between non-attendance at school and the propensity to migrate to work among rural children, while others find that migration is positively associated with education. A recent study using census data in Argentina, Chile and South Africa shows that independent child migrants had worse shelter at destination, whereas dependent child migrants were similar to non-migrants in their type of shelter. Over a fifth of international independent child migrants aged 15–17 years in these countries were employed, compared to fewer than 4 percent of non-migrant dependent children. Many live with relatives or employers, but shelter and security can be important concerns. Children may be less able than adults to change jobs, find it harder to obtain documents even when eligible, may be more likely to suffer employer violence or encounters with the police, and may be more easily cheated by employers and others.

Source: Bhabha (2008) and Yaqub (2009).

children are often disadvantaged by the absence of a parent.

In OECD countries migrant pupils generally attend schools with teachers and educational resources of similar quality to those attended by locally-born pupils, although there are some exceptions, including Denmark, Greece, the Netherlands and Portugal. In some cases, the quality of schools that migrant children attend is below national standards, but this is more often related to local income levels generally than to migrant status in particular. Studies on school segregation in the United States suggest that children from migrant families have worse test scores if they attend minority, inner-city schools.[73] Studies from the Netherlands and Sweden find that clustering migrant children and separating them from other children is detrimental to school performance.[74] Even if they are not at a disadvantage with regard to instructional materials and equipment, migrant pupils may need special services, such as local language instruction.

Our interest in schooling is partly due to its value in improving the prospects of future

Box **3.3**   **The next generation**

People who move are often motivated by the prospect of better lives for their children. And indeed the children of migrants can represent a key population group requiring the attention of policy makers. In Brussels, for example, they represent over 40 percent of the school-age population, while in New York they are half and in Los Angeles County almost two thirds.

Obtaining a good education is critical to future prospects. Evidence suggests that the children of migrants typically perform better than their parents, but do not fully catch up with children without a migrant background, even after controlling for socio-economic characteristics. There are exceptions, however, including Australia and Canada, where school performance is close to or exceeds that of native peers. Countries with education systems that involve early streaming, such as Germany and the Netherlands, appear to have the biggest gaps in school performance.

How the children of migrants fare in the labour market also tends to differ across countries and groups. Recent findings suggest that

they have higher employment rates compared to migrants in the same age group, but they are at a disadvantage compared to those without a migrant background. In some European countries youth unemployment rates are worse among the children of migrants. Limited access to informal networks and discrimination (whether origin- or class-based) can contribute to these disparities.

Some children of migrants encounter racism, often linked to limited job opportunities. Studies in the United States, for example, have suggested that there is a risk of 'segmented assimilation', meaning that the contacts, networks and aspirations of children of immigrants are limited to their own ethnic group, but also that this risk varies across groups. Teenage children of Mexican migrants have been found to be at higher risk of dropping out of school, going to prison or becoming pregnant. The same studies suggest that economic and social resources at the family and community levels can help to overcome these risks and avert the rise of an underclass of disaffected youth.

Source: Crul (2007), OECD (2007), Castles and Miller (1993), and Portes and Zhou (2009).

generations. Some evidence on the extent to which this happens is presented in box 3.3.

3.4 Empowerment, civic rights and participation

Moving has the potential to affect not only material well-being but also such things as bargaining power, self-respect and dignity. Empowerment, defined as the freedom to act in pursuit of personal goals and well-being,[75] can be enhanced through movement. However, the reception in the host country obviously matters, especially when migrants face local hostility, which can even lead to outbreaks of violence.

Human development is concerned with the full range of capabilities, including social freedoms that cannot be exercised without political and civic guarantees. These form part of the dimension of freedom that some philosophers have labelled "the social bases of self-respect".[76] They can be just as important as gains in income and may be associated with these gains, but are often held in check by deep-seated social, class and racial barriers. In many countries the attitude towards migration is negative, which can diminish migrants' sense of dignity and self-respect. This is not a new phenomenon: in the 19th century, the Irish faced the same prejudices in the United Kingdom, as did the Chinese in Australia.

Movement can allow rural women to gain autonomy. Empowerment tends to occur when migration draws women from rural to urban areas, separating them from other family members and friends and leading them to take paid work outside the home.[77] Qualitative studies in Ecuador, Mexico and Thailand have demonstrated such effects. For the women in these studies, returning to the old rural way of life was an unthinkable proposition.[78] Higher labour force participation and greater autonomy have also been found among Turkish women who emigrated.[79] It is not only women who seek to challenge traditional roles when they move: young migrant men can be similarly empowered to challenge patriarchal structures within the family.[80]

But such positive outcomes are not inevitable. Some migrant communities become caught in a time warp, clinging to the cultural and social practices that prevailed in the home country at the time of migration, even if the country has since moved on.[81] Or the migrant communities may develop radically conservative ideas and practices, as a way to isolate them from the host culture. This can lead to alienation and, occasionally, to extremism. There is a complex dynamic between cultural and community traditions, socio-economic circumstances and public policies. Recent micro-analysis for 10 Latin American countries found that internal migrants of indigenous origin still faced discrimination in urban areas, even while they gained greater access to services than they had in their rural area.[82] Another study found that Bolivian women in Argentina were discriminated against, had only limited employment opportunities and continued to occupy subordinate social positions.[83]

Participation and civic engagement are important aspects of empowerment. Our analysis using the World Values Survey suggests that people with a migrant background are more likely to participate in a range of civic associations. Compared to people who do not have a migrant parent, they are more likely to be a member of, and also tend to have more confidence in, a range of organizations, such as sport, recreational, art and professional organizations. Research also suggests that political participation increases with the ability to speak the host country's language, with duration of stay, education in the destination country, connections to social networks and labour markets, and when institutional barriers to registering and voting are lower.[84]

Institutional factors matter, especially civic and electoral rights. Our policy assessment found that voting in national elections was largely restricted to citizens, although several developed countries allow foreigners to vote in local elections (figure 3.11). The Migrant Integration Policy Index (MIPEX), which assesses the opportunities for migrants to participate in public life in terms of collective associations, voting in, and standing for local elections and support provided to migrant associations, found policies in Western Europe to be favourable to participation, but those in Central, Eastern and South-Eastern Europe were less so. In Sweden any legal resident who has lived in the country for three years can vote in regional and local elections and stand for local elections, while in Spain foreigners can vote in local elections as long as they are registered as residents with their local authority.

Many people move at least partly to enjoy greater physical and personal security, and to places where the rule of law and government accountability are better. This is obviously the case

for many refugees fleeing from conflict, even if their legal situation remains tenuous while they are seeking asylum. Our analysis of determinants of flows between pairs of countries shows that the level of democracy in a country has a positive, significant effect on migrant inflows.[85]

Yet even countries with strong legal traditions are tested when routine police work involves the enforcement of migration law. As we saw in chapter 2, countries vary in their enforcement practices. In some countries, irregular migrants may be seen as easy targets by corrupt officials. In South Africa police hoping to extort bribes often destroy or refuse to recognize documents in order to justify arrest.[86] Mongolian migrants in the Czech Republic also report paying fines during police raids, regardless of whether they are authorized or not.[87] In Malaysia migrants have sometimes been subject to informal enforcement mechanisms, which have led to complaints of abuse (box 3.4).

As we shall see in chapter 4, people in destination places often have concerns about the economic, security and cultural impacts of immigration. In some cases, xenophobia arises. This appears to be most likely where extremists foment fears and insecurities. Outbreaks of violence towards migrants can erupt—such

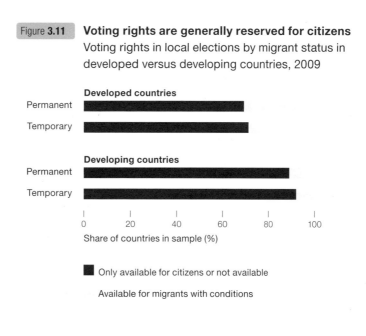

Figure **3.11** **Voting rights are generally reserved for citizens**
Voting rights in local elections by migrant status in developed versus developing countries, 2009

Source: Klugman and Pereira (2009).

Box **3.4** **Enforcement mechanisms in Malaysia**

As one of the most robust economies in South-East Asia, Malaysia has attracted many migrant workers (officially measured at around 7 percent of the population in 2005). The Malaysian labour force at the end of 2008 was almost 12 million, about 44 percent of the 27 million residents, and included about 2.1 million legal migrants from Bangladesh, Indonesia and other Asian countries. The Malaysian government has tended to tolerate unauthorized migration, while regularizations have sometimes been coupled with a ban on new entries and stepped up enforcement.

Since 1972, Malaysia's People's Volunteer Corps (Ikatan Relawan Rakyat or RELA) has helped to enforce laws, including immigration laws. RELA volunteers, who number about 500,000, are allowed to enter workplaces and homes without warrants, to carry firearms and to make arrests after receiving permission from RELA leaders. Migrant activists say that RELA volunteers have become vigilantes, planting evidence to justify arrests of migrants and using excessive force in their policing. The government has recently announced its intention to curb abuses and is currently looking into ways of improving RELA by providing training to its members.

Source: Crush and Ramachandran (2009), Vijayani (2008) and Migration DRC (2007).

as those in Malaysia and South Africa in 2008 and Northern Ireland in 2009, for example—with serious repercussions for both the individuals involved and the societies as a whole.[88] Experience suggests that such outbreaks typically occur where political vacuums allow unscrupulous local actors to manipulate underlying social tensions.[89]

Ironically, although intolerance often results in resistance to social contact, evidence suggests that increased social contact between migrants and non-migrants can improve levels of tolerance for migrant groups and counter existing biases.[90] Clearly, moderate politicians, government authorities and NGOs all have a critical part to play in designing and delivering policies and services that facilitate integration and avert escalated tensions. Having legislation on the books is not enough: it must be accompanied by leadership, accountability and informed public debate (chapter 5).

3.5 Understanding outcomes from negative drivers

Some people move because their luck improves—they win the green card lottery, or a friend or relative offers a helping hand to take up a new opportunity in the city. But many others move in response to difficult circumstances—economic collapse and political unrest in Zimbabwe, war in Sudan, natural disasters such as the Asian tsunami. Moving under these circumstances can expose people to risk, increase their vulnerability and erode their capabilities. But of course in these cases it is not the migration per se but the underlying drivers that cause such deterioration in outcomes. This section reviews the outcomes associated with three broad drivers: conflict, development-induced displacement and trafficking.

3.5.1 When insecurity drives movement

People who flee insecurity and violence typically see an absolute collapse in their human development outcomes. But migration nonetheless protects them from the greater harm they would doubtless come to if they were to stay put. Several forms of protection are available for refugees, especially for those covered by the 1951 Refugee Convention—which defines the criteria under which individuals may be granted asylum by its signatory countries and sets out their associated rights—and thus under the UNHCR mandate. This protection has allowed millions of people to move to new safe and secure environments.

Contemporary conflicts are increasingly associated with large population movements, including deliberate displacement of civilians as a weapon of war.[91] While some are able to flee to more distant places in North America, Western Europe and Australasia, most displaced people relocate within or near their country of origin. Even if camps host only about a third of those displaced by conflicts,[92] these settlements have come to symbolize the plight of people in poor, conflict-affected regions. A contemporary example is the people of Darfur, Sudan, who fled their villages in the wake of attacks that destroyed their cattle and crops, wells and homes, to join what was already the largest displaced population in the world in the wake of the long-running war in southern Sudan.

When the poor and destitute flee combat zones, they run severe risks. Conflict weakens or destroys all forms of capital and people are cut off from their existing sources of income, services and social networks, heightening their vulnerability. After flight, those displaced may have escaped the most direct physical threats, but still face a range of daunting challenges. Security concerns and local hostility rank high among their problems, especially in and around camps.[93] In civil wars, the internally displaced may face harassment from government and animosity from local people.

Nevertheless, it is important to bear in mind that conflict and insecurity drive only a small share of all movement—about one tenth of international movement and around one twentieth of internal movement. There are regional differences: Africa has been more extensively affected, conflict being associated with about 13 percent of international movement on the continent. Map 3.1 shows the location of conflicts and major flows of people displaced within and across borders in Africa. While the map paints a sombre picture, we underline that the vast majority of migration in Africa is not conflict-induced and that most Africans move for the same reasons as everyone else.[94]

Beyond continuing insecurity, trying to earn a decent income is the single greatest challenge that displaced people encounter, especially where they lack identity papers.[95] In commissioned case studies,[96] Uganda was the only one of six countries where refugees were legally allowed to move around freely, to accept work and to access land. About 44 percent of Uganda's working-age camp population was employed, whereas in all five other countries the figure was below 15 percent. Even if the displaced are permitted to work, opportunities are often scarce.

The human development outcomes of those driven to move by insecurity vary considerably. While the UN Guiding Principles on Internal Displacement have raised awareness, internally displaced people—80 percent of whom are women and children—do not benefit from the same legal rights as refugees.[97] Roughly half the world's estimated 26 million internally displaced people receive some support from UNHCR, IOM and others, but sovereignty is often invoked as a justification for restricting international aid efforts. In 2007, Sudan, Myanmar and Zimbabwe each had more than 500,000 crisis-affected people who were beyond the reach of any humanitarian assistance.[98] Even in less extreme cases, malnutrition, poor access to clean water and health care, and lack of documentation and property rights are typical among the internally displaced. However, some governments have made concerted efforts

Map **3.1** **Conflict as a driver of movement in Africa**
Conflict, instability and population movement in Africa

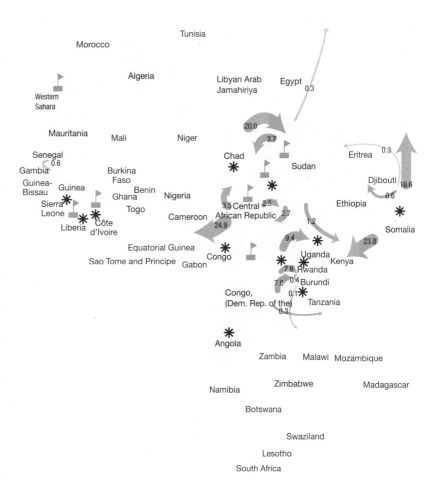

| Recent conflict zones |
| Ongoing UN peacekeeping missions (2009) |
| Refugee flows in 2007 (in thousands) |

Number of refugees (end of 2008)
0–1,000
1,000–10,000
10,000–100,000
100,000–523,032

Internally displaced persons (end of 2008)

Burundi	100,000
Central African Republic	108,000
Chad	180,000
Congo	Up to 7,800
Congo, DRC	1,400,000
Côte d'Ivoire	At least 621,000
Ethiopia	200,000–300,000
Kenya	300,000–600,000
Liberia	Undetermined
Rwanda	Undetermined
Senegal	10,000–70,000
Somalia	1,300,000
Sudan	4,900,000
Uganda	869,000
Zimbabwe	570,000–1,000,000

Source: UNHCR (2008) and IDMC (2008).

Note: This map illustrates refugee flows based on official UNHCR data and misses important flows associated with instability, as in the case of Zimbabweans fleeing to South Africa for example.

to improve the rights and living conditions of their internally displaced populations.[99]

The situation of international refugees also varies, but can be bleak, especially in cases of protracted conflict, such as Palestine. Such cases account for roughly half of all refugees. Our commissioned analysis confirmed overall weak human development outcomes, alongside some heterogeneity across groups and countries. The incidence of sexual and gender-based violence is high. Paradoxically, however, women in Burundi and Sri Lanka were reportedly empowered as they adopted new social roles as protectors and providers for their families.[100]

Education and health indicators in refugee camps are sometimes superior to those of surrounding local populations. Our study found that the share of births attended by skilled medical personnel in camps surveyed in Nepal, Tanzania and Uganda was significantly higher than among these countries' population as a whole. Similarly, education indicators—such as gross primary enrolment ratios and pupil-to-teacher ratios—were better among camp-based

refugees than for the general population (figure 3.12). These patterns reflect both the effects of humanitarian assistance in camps and the generally poor human development conditions and indicators prevailing in countries that host the bulk of refugees.

As noted above, most refugees and internally displaced people do not end up in camps at all, or at least not for long. For example, less than a third of Palestinian refugees live in UNRWA-administered camps.[101] On average, those who relocate to urban centres seem to be younger and better educated, and may enjoy better human development outcomes than those living in camps. Others, usually the better off, may be able to flee to more distant and wealthier countries, sometimes under special government programmes.

Only a minority of asylum seekers succeed in obtaining either refugee status or residency, and those whose request is denied can face precarious situations.[102] Their experience depends on the policies of the destination country. Developed countries in our policy assessment allowed humanitarian migrants access to emergency services, but more restricted access to preventive services, whereas in the developing countries in our sample, access to public health services was even more restricted (figure 3.8).

Finding durable long-term solutions to the problem in the form of sustainable return or successful local integration has proved a major challenge. In 2007, an estimated 2.7 million internally displaced people and 700,000 refugees, representing about 10 and 5 percent of stocks respectively, returned to their areas of origin.[103] Perhaps the Palestinian case, more than any other, illustrates the hardships faced by refugees when conflict is protracted, insecurity is rampant and local economic opportunities are almost non-existent.[104]

In other cases, gradual integration into local communities, sometimes through naturalization, has taken place in a number of developing and developed countries, although refugees tend to be relatively disadvantaged, especially as regards labour market integration.[105]

3.5.2 Development-induced displacement

Outcomes may also be negative when people are displaced by development projects. The classic

Figure **3.12** **School enrolment among refugees often exceeds that of host communities in developing countries**

Gross primary enrolment ratios: refugees, host populations and main countries of origin, 2007

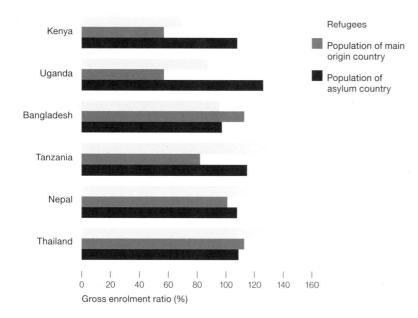

Source: de Bruijn (2009), UNHCR (2008) and UNESCO Institute for Statistics (2008b).

case of this occurs when large dams are built to provide urban water supplies, generate electricity or open up downstream areas for irrigation. Agricultural expansion is another major cause, as when pastoralists lose traditional riverine grazing lands when these are developed for irrigated cash crops. Infrastructure projects such as roads, railways or airports may also displace people, while the energy sector—mining, power plants, oil exploration and extraction, pipelines—may be another culprit. Parks and forest reserves may displace people when managed in a top-down style rather than by local communities.

These types of investment generally expand most people's opportunities—in terms of providing yield-increasing technology, links to markets and access to energy and water, among other things.[106] But how the investments are designed and delivered is critical. By the 1990s it was recognized that such interventions could have negative repercussions for the minority of people directly affected, and were criticized on social justice and human rights grounds.[107] One vocal critic has been the World Commission on Dams, which has stated that, "impoverishment and disempowerment have been the rule rather than the exception with respect to resettled people around the world,"[108] and that these outcomes have been worst for indigenous and tribal peoples displaced by big projects.

Among the impacts observed in indigenous communities are loss of assets, unemployment, debt bondage, hunger and cultural disintegration. There are many such examples, which have been well documented elsewhere.[109] The India Social Institute estimates that there are about 21 million development-induced displaced persons in India, many of whom belong to scheduled castes and tribal groups. In Brazil the construction of the Tucuruí Dam displaced an estimated 25,000 to 30,000 people and significantly altered the lifestyle and livelihood means of the *Parakanã, Asurini* and *Parkatêjê* indigenous groups. Poor resettlement planning split up communities and forced them to relocate several times, often in areas that lacked the necessary infrastructure to serve both the needs of a growing migrant population (pulled in by construction jobs) and those displaced by the project.[110]

This issue was addressed in the Guiding Principles on Internal Displacement mentioned above. The principles provide that, during the planning stage, the authorities should explore all viable options for avoiding displacement. Where it cannot be avoided, it is up to the authorities to make a strong case for it, stating why it is in the best interests of the public. The support and participation of all stakeholders should be sought and, where applicable, agreements should stipulate the conditions for compensation and include a mechanism for resolving disputes. In all instances, displacement should not threaten life, dignity, liberty or security, and should include long-term provisions for adequate shelter, safety, nutrition and health for those displaced. Particular attention should be given to the protection of indigenous peoples, minorities, smallholders and pastoralists.

These principles can help inform development planners as to the social, economic, cultural and environmental problems that large- and even small-scale development projects can create. Incorporating such analysis in planning processes, as has been done for some major sources of development finance—including the World Bank, which has an Involuntary Resettlement Policy—has been an important step forward.[111] Such policies allow for rights of appeal by aggrieved parties through inspection panels and other mechanisms. Approaches of this kind can enable favourable human development outcomes for the majority while helping to mitigate the risks borne by the displaced minority, though the challenges remain large.

3.5.3 Human trafficking

The images associated with trafficking are often horrendous, and attention tends to focus on its association with sexual exploitation, organized crime, violent abuse and economic exploitation. Human trafficking not only adversely affects individuals but can also undermine respect for whole groups. However, the increasing focus on this phenomenon has not yet provided a reliable sense of either its scale or its relative importance in movements within and across borders (chapter 2).

Above all, trafficking is associated with restrictions on human freedom and violations of basic human rights. Once caught in a trafficking

> Above all, trafficking is associated with restrictions on human freedom and violations of basic human rights

Trafficking can be most effectively combated through better opportunities and awareness at home—the ability to say 'no' to traffickers is the best defence

network, people may be stripped of their travel documents and isolated, so as to make escape difficult if not impossible. Many end up in debt bondage in places where language, social and physical barriers frustrate their efforts to seek help. In addition, they may be reluctant to identify themselves, since they risk legal sanctions or criminal prosecution. People trafficked into sex work are also at high risk of infection from HIV and other sexually transmitted diseases.[112]

One basic constraint in assessing the impacts of trafficking relates to data. The IOM's Counter Trafficking Module database contains data on fewer than 14,000 cases that are not a representative sample, and the same applies to the database of the United Nations Office on Drugs and Crime (UNODC).[113] The picture that emerges from these data, alongside existing studies and reports, suggests that most people who are trafficked are young women from minority ethnic groups. This is confirmed by other sources—for example a study in South-eastern Europe, which found that young people and ethnic minorities in the rural areas of post-conflict countries were vulnerable to trafficking, as they tended to experience acute labour market exclusion and disempowerment.[114] However, this picture may be biased, since it is possible that males are less willing to self-report for fear they will be refused victim status. In addition to social and economic exclusion, violence and exploitation at home or in the home community increase vulnerability to trafficking. So too does naïve belief in promises of well-paid jobs abroad.

Sexual exploitation is the most commonly identified form of human trafficking (about 80 percent of cases in the UNODC database), with economic exploitation comprising most of the balance. For women, men and children trafficked for these and other exploitative purposes, bonded labour, domestic servitude, forced marriage, organ removal, begging, illicit adoption and conscription have all been reported.

Alongside the lack of power and assets of the individuals involved, the negative human development outcomes of trafficking can be partly associated with the legal framework of destination countries. Restrictive immigration controls mean that marginalized groups tend to have irregular status and so lack access to the formal labour market and the protections offered by the

state to its citizens and to authorized migrant workers.[115] More generally, of course, trafficking can be most effectively combated through better opportunities and awareness at home—the ability to say 'no' to traffickers is the best defence.

Difficulties in distinguishing trafficking from other types of exploitation, as well as challenges involved in defining exploitative practices, further complicate the rights of trafficked people. Problems can arise over enforcement. It appears that trafficking is sometimes very broadly interpreted to apply to all migrant women who engage in sex work. This can be used to justify their harassment and deportation, making them even more vulnerable to exploitation. And once identified, they are virtually always deported or referred to assistance programmes conditional on cooperation with law enforcement.

Anti-trafficking initiatives have burgeoned in recent years. Interventions to reduce vulnerability in potential source communities, such as awareness campaigns and livelihood projects, have been undertaken. Assistance programmes have also provided counselling, legal aid and support for return and reintegration. Some of these programmes are proving successful, such as the use of entertainment and personal stories as community awareness tools in Ethiopia and Mali, or door-to-door mass communication campaigns as in the Democratic Republic of the Congo.[116] Other initiatives, however, have led to counterproductive and sometimes even disastrous outcomes, including prejudicial limitations on women's rights. In Nepal, for example, prevention messages discouraged girls and women from leaving their villages, while HIV awareness campaigns stigmatized returnees.[117] Anti-trafficking initiatives clearly raise very complex and difficult challenges, which need to be carefully handled.

The lines between traffickers on the one hand and recruiters and smugglers on the other can be blurred. For example, the business of recruitment expands to include numerous layers of informal sub-agents. These sub-agents, working under the umbrella of legitimate recruiters can reduce accountability and increase costs. The risks of detention and deportation are high. Smuggling costs in some cases include bribing corrupt border officials and manufacturing false documents.[118]

3.6 Overall impacts

We have studied the discrete impacts of migration on incomes, health, education and aspects of empowerment and agency—and looked at the negative outcomes that can occur when people move under duress. Differences in the HDI are a simple way to capture overall changes.

Our background research found very large average differences between the HDI of migrants and that of non-migrants, moving internally and across borders. We found that, on average, migrants to OECD countries had an HDI about 24 percent higher than that of people who stayed in their respective countries of origin.[119] But the gains are large not only for those who move to developed countries: we also found substantial differences between internal migrants and non-migrants.[120] Figure 3.13 shows that, in 14 of the 16 developing countries covered by this analysis, the HDI for internal migrants is higher than that of non-migrants.

In some cases the differences are substantial. For internal movers in Guinea, for example, the HDI for migrants is 23 percent higher than for non-migrants—only one percentage point lower than for migrants to OECD countries. If these migrants were thought of as a separate country, they would be ranked about 25 places higher than non-migrants in the global HDI.

There are two major exceptions to the overall pattern of improved well-being from internal movement: in Guatemala and Zambia internal migrants appear to do worse than non-migrants. Both these cases underline the risks that accompany migration. In Guatemala most movers were displaced by violence and civil war in the 1980s and early 1990s, while in Zambia migrants faced extreme urban poverty following the successive economic shocks that have hit this country over the past 20 years. In a few other cases—Bolivia and Peru, for example—the overall human development outcome appears marginal despite sizeable income gains, suggesting poor access to services as a factor inhibiting well-being. However, these exceptional cases serve to emphasize the norm, which is that most movers are winners.

These findings for international movers are borne out by evidence on migrants' own sense of well-being (figure 3.14). We analysed data for 52 countries in 2005 and found that self-reported

| Figure **3.13** | **Significant human development gains to internal movers** |

Ratio of migrants' to non-migrants' estimated HDI in selected developing countries, 1995–2005

Guinea
Madagascar
Uganda
Indonesia
Viet Nam
Côte d'Ivoire
Ghana
Kyrgyzstan
Paraguay
Cameroon
Bolivia
Nicaragua
Colombia
Peru
Zambia
Guatemala

0.6 0.8 1.0 1.2 1.4 1.6

HDI ratio

Source: Harttgen and Klasen (2009).

levels of happiness and health were very similar among migrants and non-migrants: 84 percent of migrants felt happy (compared to 83 percent of non-migrants), while 72 percent felt that their health was good or very good (compared to 70 percent of non-migrants); only 9 percent were 'not satisfied' with life (compared to 11 percent of non-migrants). The share of migrants reporting that they felt quite or very happy was highest in developed countries. Similar shares of foreign and locally born respondents—more than 70 percent—felt that they have 'freedom and choice over their lives'.[121]

Figure **3.14**   **Migrants are generally as happy as locally-born people**
Self-reported happiness among migrants and locally-born people around the world, 2005/2006

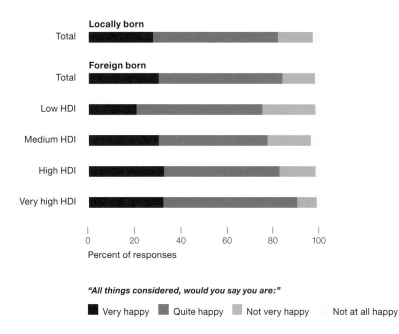

Locally born

Total

Foreign born

Total

Low HDI

Medium HDI

High HDI

Very high HDI

| | | | | | |
| 0 | 20 | 40 | 60 | 80 | 100 |

Percent of responses

"All things considered, would you say you are:"

■ Very happy   ■ Quite happy   ■ Not very happy   □ Not at all happy

Source: HDR team estimates based on WVS (2006).

3.7 Conclusions

The complex effects associated with movement are difficult to summarize simply. The broad findings presented in this chapter underline the role of movement in expanding human freedoms that was outlined in chapter 1. We saw that people who move generally do enhance their opportunities in at least some dimensions, with gains that can be very large. However, we also saw that the gains are reduced by policies at home and destination places as well as by the constraints facing individuals and their families. Since different people face different opportunities and constraints, we observed significant inequalities in the returns to movement. The cases in which people experience deteriorations in their well-being during or following the process of movement—conflict, trafficking, natural disasters, and so on—were associated with constraints that prevent them from choosing their place in life freely.

A key point that emerged is that human movement can also be associated with trade-offs—people may gain in some and lose in other dimensions of freedom. However, the losses can be alleviated and even offset by better policies, as we will show in the final chapter.

Impacts
at origin
and
destination

4

Movement has multiple impacts on other people besides those who move—impacts that critically shape its overall effects. This chapter explores impacts in the country of origin and in the host country while underlining their interconnectedness. Families with members who have moved elsewhere in the country or abroad tend to experience direct gains, but there can also be broader benefits, alongside concerns that people's departure is a loss to origin communities. As regards impacts on places of destination, people often believe that these are negative—because they fear that newcomers take jobs, burden public services, create social tensions and even increase criminality. The evidence suggests that these popular concerns are exaggerated and often unfounded. Still, perceptions matter—and these warrant careful investigation to help frame the discussion of policy.

Impacts at origin and destination

Among people who do not move but can be affected by movement are the families of movers and communities at places of origin and destination. The multiple impacts of movement in these different places are critical in shaping the overall human development effects of movement; this chapter addresses each in turn.

At places of origin, impacts can be seen on income and consumption, education and health, and broader cultural and social processes. These impacts are mostly favourable, but the concern that communities lose out when people move needs to be explored. Our review of the evidence shows that impacts are complex, context-specific and subject to change over time. The nature and extent of impacts depend on who moves, how they fare abroad and their proclivity to stay connected, which may find expression in flows of money, knowledge and ideas, and in the stated intention to return at some date in the future. Because migrants tend to come in large numbers from specific places—e.g. Kerala in India and Fujian Province in China—impacts on local communities may be more pronounced than national impacts. Yet the flow of ideas can also have far-reaching effects on social norms and class structures, rippling out to the broader community over the longer term. Some of these impacts have traditionally been seen as negative, but a broader perspective suggests that a more nuanced view is appropriate. In this light we also examine the extent to which national development plans, such as poverty reduction strategies (PRSs), reflect and frame efforts of developing countries to promote gains from mobility.

Much academic and media attention has been directed to the impacts of migrants on places of destination. One widespread belief is that these impacts are negative—newcomers are seen as 'taking our jobs' if they are employed, living off the taxpayer by claiming welfare benefits if they are not employed, adding an unwanted extra burden to public services in areas such as health and education, creating social tensions with local people or other immigrant groups and even increasing criminal behaviour. We

investigate the vast empirical literature on these issues, which reveals that these fears are exaggerated and often unfounded. Nevertheless, these perceptions matter because they affect the political climate in which policy decisions about the admission and treatment of migrants are made—fears may stoke the flames of a broader hostility to migrants and allow political extremists to gain power. Indeed, historical and contemporary evidence suggests that recessions are times when such hostility can come to the fore. We end this chapter by tackling the thorny issue of public opinion, which imposes constraints on the policy options explored in the final chapter.

4.1 Impacts at places of origin

Typically, only a small share of the total population of an origin country will move. The exceptions—countries with significant shares abroad—are often small states, including Caribbean nations such as Antigua and Barbuda, Grenada, and Saint Kitts and Nevis. In these cases the share can exceed 40 percent. The higher the share, the more likely it is that impacts on people who stay will be more pervasive and more profound. While the discussion below focuses on developing countries, it is important to bear in mind that, as shown in chapter 2, emigration rates for low-HDI countries are the lowest across all country groupings.

In general, the largest impacts at places of origin are felt by the households with an absent migrant. However, the community, the region and even the nation as a whole may be affected. We now look at each of these in turn.

4.1.1 Household level effects

In many developing countries, movement is a household strategy aimed at improving not only the mover's prospects but those of the extended

> Despite these financial rewards, separation is typically a painful decision incurring high emotional costs for both the mover and those left behind

family as well. In return for supporting the move, the family can expect financial remittances when the migrant is established—transfers that typically far outweigh the initial outlay or what the mover might have hoped to earn in the place of origin. These transfers can in turn be used to finance major investments, as well as immediate consumption needs.

Despite these financial rewards, separation is typically a painful decision incurring high emotional costs for both the mover and those left behind. In the words of Filipina poet Nadine Sarreal:

Your loved ones across that ocean
Will sit at breakfast and try not to gaze
Where you would sit at the table
Meals now divided by five
Instead of six, don't feed an emptiness.[1]

The fact that so many parents, spouses and partners are willing to incur these costs gives an idea of just how large they must perceive the rewards to be.

Financial remittances are vital in improving the livelihoods of millions of people in developing countries. Many empirical studies have confirmed the positive contribution of international remittances to household welfare, nutrition, food, health and living conditions in places of origin.[2] This contribution is now well recognized in the literature on migration and reflected in the increasingly accurate data on international remittances published by the World Bank and others, illustrated in map 4.1. Even those whose movement was driven by conflict can be net remitters, as illustrated at various points in history in Bosnia and Herzegovina, Guinea-Bissau, Nicaragua, Tajikistan and Uganda, where remittances helped entire war-affected communities to survive.[3]

In some international migration corridors, money transfer costs have tended to fall over time, with obvious benefits for those sending and receiving remittances.[4] Recent innovations have also seen significant falls in costs at the national level, as in the case of Kenya described in box 4.1. With the reduction in money transfer costs, families who once relied on relatives and close family friends or who used informal avenues such as the local bus driver to remit are now opting to send money through banks, money transfer companies and even via cell-phones.

An important function of remittances is to diversify sources of income and to cushion families against setbacks such as illness or larger shocks caused by economic downturns, political conflicts or climatic vagaries.[5] Studies in countries as diverse as Botswana, El Salvador, Jamaica and the Philippines have found that migrants respond to weather shocks by increasing their remittances, although it is difficult to establish whether these effectively serve as insurance. Recent examples include the 2004 Hurricane Jeanne in Haiti, the 2004 tsunami in Indonesia and Sri Lanka and the 2005 earthquake in Pakistan.[6] In a sample of poor countries, increased remittances were found to offset some 20 percent of the hurricane damage experienced,[7] while in the Philippines about 60 percent of declines in income due to rainfall shocks were offset.[8] In El Salvador crop failure caused by weather shocks increased the probability of households sending a migrant to the United States by 24 percent.[9]

Migrants can provide this kind of protection if their incomes are large enough and do not vary in tandem with their families'. This depends on the nature and breadth of the shock, as well as the location of the migrant. For example, remittances may not provide much insurance against the effects of the current global economic recession, as migrant workers almost everywhere suffer retrenchment just when their families most need support (box 4.2). Remittances to developing countries are expected to fall from US$308 billion in 2008 to US$293 billion in 2009.[10]

Even when the total volume of remittances is large, their direct poverty-reducing impact depends on the socio-economic background of those who moved. Within the Latin America region, for example, a recent study found that in Mexico and Paraguay remittance-receiving households were primarily from the bottom of the income and education distribution, whereas the opposite pattern was found in Peru and Nicaragua.[11] More generally, however, restrictions imposed by the limited opportunities of the low-skilled to move across borders mean that remittances do not tend to flow directly to the poorest families,[12] nor to the poorest countries.[13] Take China, for example: because migrants generally do not come from the poorest households, the aggregate poverty impact of internal migration is limited (an estimated 1 percent

Map **4.1**   **Remittances flow primarily from developed to developing regions**
Flows of international remittances, 2006–2007

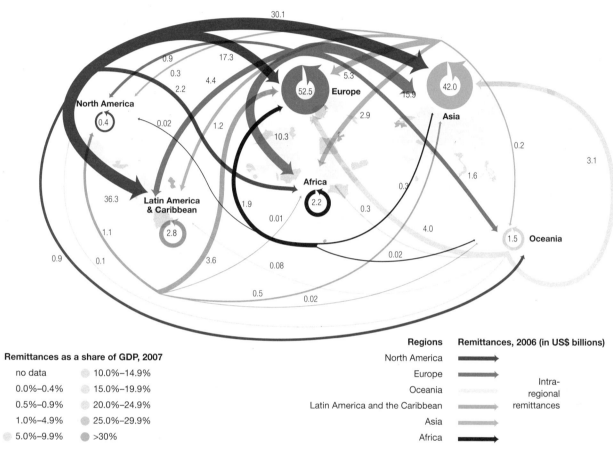

Remittances as a share of GDP, 2007

no data	10.0%–14.9%
0.0%–0.4%	15.0%–19.9%
0.5%–0.9%	20.0%–24.9%
1.0%–4.9%	25.0%–29.9%
5.0%–9.9%	>30%

Regions   **Remittances, 2006 (in US$ billions)**

North America

Europe

Oceania   Intra-
                                       regional
Latin America and the Caribbean   remittances

Asia

Africa

Source: HDR team data based on Ratha and Shaw (2006) and World Bank (2009b).

reduction), although this still translates into al-most 12 million fewer poor.[14] At the same time, some migrants do come from poor households and significant remittances sometimes flow to non-family members, which allows for broader benefits—as has been found for Fiji and Jamaica, for example.[15]

The poverty-reducing effects of internal migration, which have been demonstrated by studies in a diverse range of national situations, may be even more significant. In Andhra Pradesh and Madhya Pradesh in India poverty rates in households with a migrant fell by about half between 2001/02 and 2006/07,[16] and similar results were found for Bangladesh.[17] Large gains have also been reported from panel data, tracking individuals over time, in the Kagera region of Tanzania between 1991 and 2004.[18] Research conducted

for this report, using panel data and controlling for selection bias, examined the cases of Indonesia between 1994 and 2000 and Mexico between 2003 and 2005. In Indonesia, where almost half of all households had an internal migrant, poverty rates for non-migrants were essentially stable for the period (which included the East Asian financial crisis), falling slightly from 40 to 39 percent, but declined rapidly for migrants, from 34 to 19 percent. In Mexico, where about 9 percent of households had an internal migrant, poverty rates rose sharply from 25 to 31 percent for non-migrants for the period (which included the 2001/02 recession), but only slightly, from 29 to 30 percent, for migrants. In both countries, at the outset households with a migrant made up less than half of the top two wealth quintiles, but over time this share rose to nearly two thirds.[19]

Box **4.1**   **How cell-phones can reduce money transfer costs: the case of Kenya**

For many people in remote rural areas of developing countries, the costs of receiving money remain high: recipients typically have to travel long distances to a regional or national capital to collect cash, or the cash has to be hand-delivered by an intermediary, who may take a sizeable margin.

The rapid diffusion of cell-phone technology over the past decade has led to the development of innovative money transfer systems in several countries. For example, in Kenya, a leading cell-phone company, Safaricom, teamed up with donors to pilot a system that subsequently led to the launch in 2007 of M-PESA (meaning 'Mobile-Cash'). Anyone with a cell-phone can deposit money in an account and send it to another cell-phone user, using M-PESA agents distributed across the country.

A recent survey of users across Kenya found that, in just two years, M-PESA has expanded rapidly. It is now used by some 6 million people or 17 percent of the population—out of 26 percent who are cell-phone owners—and is supported by a network of more than 7,500 agents. Transfers can be made from the port city of Mombasa to Kisumu on the shores of Lake Victoria, or from Nairobi in the south to Marsabit in the north—both two-day bus trips—with the push of a few buttons and at a cost of less than a dollar. By mid-2008, the volume of money sent had reached some 8 percent of GDP, mostly in the form of a large number of relatively small transactions.

Source: Jack and Suri (2009).

One dimension of movement that appears to affect remittance flows is gender. Evidence suggests that women tend to send a larger proportion of their incomes home, on a more regular basis, though their lower wages often mean that the absolute amounts are smaller.[20]

There is also a temporal dimension to these flows. Over time, the knock-on effects of remittances may substantially broaden the impacts on poverty and inequality.[21] The poor may gain when remittances are spent in ways that generate local employment, such as building houses, or when businesses are established or expanded.[22] Some studies have found that remittance recipients exhibit greater entrepreneurship and a higher marginal propensity to invest than households without a migrant.[23] Positive investment effects can take decades to materialize in full, however, and are complex and far from automatic. The lag may reflect delays in the sending of remittances as migrants adapt to their new homes, or political and economic conditions in places of origin—such as a poor climate for investment—which can inhibit or deter transfers.[24] Lastly, remittances can also create a store of capital to fund further migration, years after the first family member has left.

Some commentators discount the importance of remittances because they are partly spent on consumption. This critique is mistaken, for two broad reasons. First, consumption can be inherently valuable and often has long-term, investment-like effects, especially in poor communities. Improvements in nutrition and other basic consumption items greatly enhance human capital and hence future incomes.[25] Similarly, spending on schooling is often a priority for families receiving remittances, because it increases the earning power of the next generation. Second, most types of spending, especially on labour-intensive goods and services such as housing and other construction, will benefit the local economy and may have multiplier effects.[26] All of these effects are positive.

Families with migrants appear more likely to send their children to school, using cash from remittances to pay fees and other costs. This reduces child labour. And, once there, the children of migrants are more likely to finish school, as the better prospects associated with migration affect social norms and incentives.[27] In Guatemala internal and international migration is associated with increased educational expenditures (45 and 48 percent respectively), especially on higher levels of schooling.[28] In rural Pakistan temporary migration can be linked with increased enrolment rates and declines in school dropout rates that exceed 40 percent, with larger effects for girls than for boys.[29] In our own commissioned research, similar results were found in Mexico, where children in households with an internal migrant had a 30–45 percent higher probability of being in an appropriate grade for their age.[30]

The prospect of moving can strengthen incentives to invest in education.[31] This has been predicted in theory and shown in practice in some countries. Emigration of Fijians to high-skilled jobs in Australia, for example, has encouraged the pursuit of higher education in Fiji. This effect is so large that, while roughly a third of the Indo-Fijian population has emigrated in the past three decades and skilled workers are over-represented among emigrants, the absolute number of skilled Indo-Fijian workers in Fiji has greatly increased.[32] A number of governments, including the Philippines, have deliberately sought to promote work abroad in part by facilitating the generation of skills at home.[33]

The impacts of migration prospects on schooling incentives are shaped by the context and the prospects themselves. In Mexico, for instance, where low-skilled, often irregular migration predominates, boys were more likely to drop out of school to take up this option.[34] In our commissioned study of Chinese census data at the provincial level, investments in schooling in rural source communities responded to the skills needed for job opportunities outside the province. Thus, where internal migrants had secondary education, this generally encouraged the completion of higher levels by children remaining in the community, whereas in provinces where migrants tended to have completed only middle school, this was associated with lower high school completion rates.[35]

The health outcomes of people who do not move may be affected by migration, through effects on nutrition, living conditions, higher incomes and the transmission of knowledge and practices. There is evidence that the higher incomes and better health knowledge associated with migration have a positive influence on infant and child mortality rates.[36] However, in Mexico at least, it was found that longer term health outcomes may be adversely affected, because levels of preventive health care (e.g. breast feeding and vaccinations) were lower when at least one parent had migrated.[37] This may be associated with the higher work burden and/or reduced levels of knowledge associated with single parenting or families with fewer adults. Moreover, when infectious diseases can be contracted in destination places, return travel can bring significant health risks to families at home. The risks of HIV and other sexually transmitted diseases can be especially high.[38]

Box **4.2**   **The 2009 crisis and remittances**

The 2009 economic crisis, which began in major destination countries and has now gone global, has shrunk flows of remittances to developing countries. There is already evidence of significant declines in flows to countries that depend heavily on remittances, including Bangladesh, Egypt, El Salvador and the Philippines.

Countries and regions vary in their exposure to the crisis via remittance effects. Remittances to Eastern European and Central Asian countries are forecast to suffer the biggest drop in both relative and absolute terms, partly reflecting the reversal of the rapid expansion that had followed European Union accession and the economic boom in the Russian Federation. In Moldova and Tajikistan, where remittance shares of GDP are the highest in the world (45 and 38 percent respectively), flows are projected to shrink by 10 percent in 2009. El Salvador is facing a significant decline in remittances, which account for over 18 percent of its GDP.

About three quarters of remittances to sub-Saharan Africa come from the United States and Europe, which have been badly affected by the downturn (chapter 2). It remains to be seen whether these sources will prove more or less resilient than official development aid and private investment flows.

Source: Ratha and Mohapatra (2009a,b).

Figure **4.1**   **The global recession is expected to impact remittance flows**
Projected trends in remittance flows to developing regions, 2006–2011

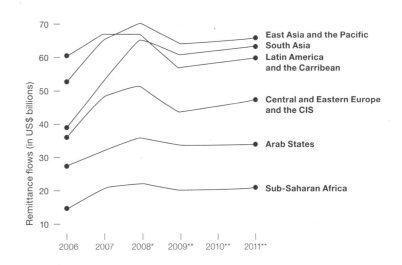

* Estimate ** Forecasts

Source: Ratha and Mohapatra (2009b) and The Economist Intelligence Unit (2009).

Note: These regional groupings include all developing countries as per UNDP Regional Bureaux' classification. For the complete list of countries in each region see 'Classification of Countries' in the Statistical Annex.

Offsetting the potential gains in consumption, schooling and health, children at home can be adversely affected emotionally by the process of migration. One in five Paraguayan mothers residing in Argentina, for example, has

The effects of
skills flows are less
detrimental for origin
communities than is
often assumed

young children in Paraguay.[39] Studies investigating the possible impacts have found that these depend on the age of the child when the separation occurs (in the first years of life the impact may be greater), on the familiarity and attitude of the adult in whose care the child is left, and on whether the separation is permanent or temporary.[40] The advent of cheap and easy communication, for example by cell-phone and Skype, has eased the separation of family members and has greatly helped the maintenance of ties and relationships in recent years.

Movement can affect gender relations at home.[41] When women move, this can change traditional roles, especially those surrounding the care of children and the elderly.[42] When men migrate, rural women can be empowered by their absence: field studies conducted in Ecuador, Ghana, India, Madagascar and Moldova all found that, with male migration, rural women increased their participation in community decision-making.[43] Norms adopted in a migrant's new home—such as a higher age of marriage and lower fertility, greater educational expectations of girls, and labour force participation—can filter back to the place of origin. This diffusion process may be accelerated in cases where the social and cultural gap between sending and receiving countries is large.[44] This has been confirmed by recent findings regarding the transfer of fertility norms from migrants to the extended family and friends at places of origin: lower numbers of children at the national level become the norm in both places.[45]

Overall, however, the evidence about impacts on traditional gender roles is mixed. For example, where the lives of migrants' wives at home remain largely confined to housekeeping, child-rearing and agricultural work, little may change—except that their workloads increase. Gains in authority may be temporary if male migrants resume their position as head of the household on return, as has been reported from Albania and Burkina Faso, for example.[46]

The transmission of norms may extend to participation in civic affairs. Recent studies in six Latin American countries have found that individuals with greater connections to international migrant networks participate more in local community affairs, are more supportive of democratic principles and are also more critical of their own country's democratic performance.[47]

4.1.2 Community and national level economic effects

Beyond its direct impacts on families with migrants, movement may have broader effects. Migration-driven processes of social and cultural change can have significant impacts on entrepreneurship, community norms and political transformations—impacts that are often felt down the generations. For example, Kenya, and indeed most of Africa, may be affected today and in the future by Barack Obama Senior's decision, taken five decades ago, to study in the United States. Most of these effects are highly positive. However, one concern that needs to be addressed is the outflow of skills from source communities.

Fears that the mobility of the skilled harms the economy of origin countries have long been voiced, though the debate has become more nuanced in recent years.[48] The concerns surface regularly in a range of small states and poorer countries, but also extend to such countries as Australia, which sees many of its graduates go abroad. This issue has, over the past few decades, spawned a range of proposals, which are reviewed in chapter 5. But an important underlying point is that mobility is normal and prevalent, even in prosperous societies (chapter 2). Skilled people, like everyone else, move in response to a perceived lack of opportunities at home and/or better opportunities elsewhere, for both themselves and their children. Attempts to curtail these movements without addressing underlying structural causes are unlikely to be effective. There are also reasons to believe that the effects of skills flows are less detrimental for origin communities than is often assumed, as argued in box 4.3.

One traditional concern has been that the departure of able-bodied youth leads to labour shortages and declines in output, particularly in agriculture.[49] In Indonesia, for example, communities faced shortages of labour for cooperative farm work.[50] However, in many developing countries, movements of labour from agriculture to urban areas can be an important part of structural transformation. And to the extent that a shortage of capital, not labour, constrains growth in most developing countries, remittances can be an important source of rural investment finance.

Migration can be a strong force for convergence in wages and incomes between source and destination areas. This is because, as mobility

Box **4.3**   Impacts of skills flows on human development

The emigration of people with university degrees has attracted much popular and academic attention, especially because the shortage of skills is acute in many poor countries. The evidence suggests that improving local working conditions in order to make staying at home more attractive is a more effective strategy than imposing restrictions on exit.

It is important to recognize that the dreadful quality of key service provision in some poor countries cannot be causally traced to the emigration of professional staff. Systematic analysis of a new database on health worker emigration from Africa confirms that low health staffing levels and poor public health conditions are major problems, but tend to reflect factors unrelated to the international movement of health professionals—namely weak incentives, inadequate resources, and limited administrative capacity. Migration is more accurately portrayed as a symptom, not a cause, of failing health systems.

The social cost associated with skilled emigration should not be overestimated. Where graduate unemployment is high, as it often is in poor countries, the opportunity cost of departure may not be large. If a highly productive but modestly paid worker leaves a community, it suffers a significant loss; but if an equally skilled but *un*productive

worker leaves, the community is hardly affected. If, for example, teachers often do not show up to work, the direct impacts of their departure are unlikely to be large. While this should not weaken the drive to address these underlying sources of inefficiency and waste, the fact that staff may not currently be serving their communities is not a point that can simply be wished away in the debate about skills flows.

Like other migrants, skilled people abroad often bring benefits to their countries of origin, through remittances and the development of networks. As shown in figure 3.2, the absolute gain in income from migration can be huge, so that if only a fraction of the difference is remitted, the benefits to the home country can be considerable. Some research has suggested that the share of foreign direct investment in a developing country is positively correlated with the number of that country's graduates present in the investing country. Other studies have found that the more high-skilled emigrants from one country live in another, the more trade occurs between those countries.

Last but not least, significant numbers of skilled emigrants do return—a recent estimate suggested that about half do so, usually after about five years. Recent literature has also emphasized the increasing importance of circular movement as transnational networks grow.

Source: Clemens (2009b), Banerjee and Duflo (2006), Javorcik, Ozden, Spatareanu, and Neagu (2006), Rauch (1999), Felbermayr and Toubal (2008), Findlay and Lowell (2001) and Skeldon (2005).

increases between two regions, their labour markets become more integrated and large differences in wages become more difficult to sustain. There is considerable historical evidence, reviewed in chapter 2, that enhanced mobility is associated with the reduction of wage disparities between countries. Inequalities within countries can follow a bell-shaped pattern over time: progress in some areas creates wealth and thus increases inequality, which encourages migration, which over time in turn tends to reduce inequality. Studies have associated greater internal labour mobility with a reduction in inter-regional income disparities in Brazil, India, Indonesia and Mexico.[51]

Interestingly, emigration rates for skilled workers are substantially higher among women than men in most developing countries.[52] Women with tertiary degrees are at least 40 percent more likely than male graduates to emigrate to OECD countries from a wide range of countries, including Afghanistan, Croatia, Ghana, Guatemala, Malawi, Papua New Guinea, Togo, Uganda and Zambia. While this could reflect various factors, structural and/or cultural barriers to professional achievement at home seem the most likely explanation.[53]

The movement of skilled people happens not only across but also within borders, as people move towards better opportunities. This is illustrated in figure 4.2, which compares movement within Brazil, Kenya, Philippines and United States to international rates. The striking result is that we find very similar patterns of migration of skilled workers within and across nations. In particular, the tendency for a higher proportion of skilled workers to emigrate from small states is echoed in a similar tendency to migrate more from small localities. This suggests that the policy options explored in discussions of local development—such as increased incentives and improved working conditions—may also be relevant to policy-making related to the emigration of skilled professionals abroad.

More broadly, the economic effects of migration at the national level in countries of origin are complex and, for the most part, difficult to measure. Networks may arise that facilitate the diffusion of knowledge, innovation and attitudes and so promote development in the medium to longer term. There is a host of anecdotal evidence indicating that migrants support productive activities in their countries of origin, through technology transfer, the repatriation of enhanced skills and exposure to better working and management practices.[54] The Chinese government has pursued links with Chinese studying abroad to help promote academic excellence in its universities. Similarly, India's 'argonauts'—young graduates who helped fuel the country's high-tech boom in the early 2000s—brought to their jobs the ideas, experience and money they had accumulated in the United States and elsewhere.[55] The entire software industry model changed as firms increasingly outsourced production to India or based themselves there. In this case, skilled migration brought significant external and dynamic effects, which benefit both workers and the industry in the place of origin.

The spread of new industries via international networks of skilled professionals can be rapid and unpredictable, can find niches even amidst otherwise low levels of overall development, and depends crucially on the openness of the business and political environment at home. It appears that countries such as the Islamic Republic of Iran, Viet Nam and the Russian Federation, which have more closed systems, have benefited less in high-tech business formation via their skilled workers abroad than have India and Israel, for example.[56]

Almost all the quantitative macro studies on effects at the national level have focused more narrowly on the scale and contribution of remittances. In 2007 the volume of officially recorded remittances to developing countries was about four times the size of total official development aid.[57] At this scale, remittances are likely to be making a strong contribution to foreign exchange earnings relative to other sources in individual countries. In Senegal, for instance, remittances in 2007 were 12 times larger than foreign direct investment. Remittances represent a significant share of GDP in a range of small and poor states, with Tajikistan topping the list at 45 percent; for all the countries in the top 20 remittance receiving countries, the share exceeded 9 percent in 2007; and in more than 20 developing countries, remittances exceed the earnings from the main commodity export.

However, two major qualifications should be attached to these findings. First, the vast bulk of these flows do not go to the poorest countries. Of the estimated inflows of remittances in 2007, less than 1 percent went to

---

Figure **4.2**   **Skilled workers move similarly across and within nations**

Population and share of skilled workers who migrate internally and internationally

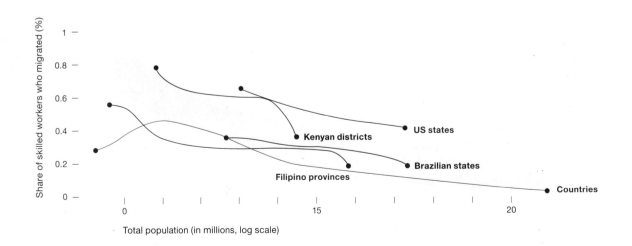

Source: Clemens (2009b).

Note: Shares represented using Kernel density regressions.

countries in the low-HDI category. So, for this group, remittances are only about 15 percent of their official development aid. By contrast, in Latin America and the Caribbean remittances in 2007 amounted to about 60 percent of the combined volume of all foreign direct investment and aid. Second, studies that have sought to trace the impacts of remittances on the long-term growth of the recipient country suggest that these impacts are generally small, although the findings are mixed.[58] This stems in part from the fact that the development impact of remittances is ultimately contingent on local institutional structures.[59]

Concerns have been expressed that remittances create a form of 'resource curse', contributing to undesirable currency appreciation and thereby hampering competitiveness. Here again, however, the evidence is mixed.[60] Moreover, remittances go to individuals and families and are thus distributed more widely than rents from natural resources, which flow only to governments and a handful of companies and thus can tend to exacerbate corruption. One positive macroeconomic feature of remittances is that they tend to be less volatile than either official development aid or foreign direct investment, although still subject to cyclical fluctuations, as seen in 2009 (box 4.2).[61]

In general, 'remittance-led development' would not appear to be a robust growth strategy. Like flows of foreign aid, remittances alone cannot remove the structural constraints to economic growth, social change and better governance that characterize many countries with low levels of human development. That said, for some small states, particularly those facing additional challenges related to remoteness, mobility may be integral to an effective overall strategy for human development (box 4.4).

4.1.3 Social and cultural effects

Mobility can have profound consequences for social, class and ethnic hierarchies in origin communities if lower status groups gain access to substantially higher income streams. This is illustrated by the cases of the *Maya* in Guatemala[62] and the *Haratin*, a group of mainly black sharecroppers, in Morocco.[63] These are welcome changes, which can disrupt traditional, caste-like forms of hereditary inequality based on such things as kinship, skin colour, ethnic group or religion, which are associated with unequal access to land and other resources.

The ideas, practices, identities and social capital that flow back to families and communities at origin are known as *social remittances*.[64] These remittances can arise through visits and through rapidly improving communications. The case of the Dominican village of Miraflores, where two thirds of families sent members to Boston in the 1990s, shows the impacts on gender dynamics. Women's roles changed, not only in Boston, where they went out to work, but also in the Dominican Republic, where they enjoyed a more equal distribution of household tasks and greater empowerment generally. Another example comes from Pakistanis at the Islamic Center of New England in the United States, where women pray and run the mosque alongside men. News of these changes has travelled back to Karachi in Pakistan, where some women still prefer traditional approaches but others are trying to create new spaces where women can pray and study together. Health is another area where social remittances have an impact. As a result of exposure abroad, visiting or returning migrants may bring back practices such as drinking safe water, keeping animals out of living spaces, or going for annual medical check-ups.

The social and cultural effects of migration are not always positive, however. A counterexample is the deportation of youth from the United States back to Central America, which has been likened to the export of gangs and gang cultures.[65] Although detailed data and analysis are not available, a recent regional report found that the distinction between home-grown gangs (*pandillas*) and those exported from the United States (*maras*) is not always clear.[66] In either case, programmes that target at-risk individuals and communities with a view to preventing youth and gang violence are needed, alongside intergovernmental cooperation and greater support and funding for reintegration programmes.[67]

For many young people all over the world, spending time abroad is considered a normal part of life experience and migration marks the transition to adulthood. Field studies in Jordan, Pakistan, Thailand and Viet Nam have found that migration was a means of enhancing a family's social status in the local community. It is

> The ideas, practices, identities and social capital that flow back to families and communities at origin are known as *social remittances*

Box **4.4**   **Mobility and the development prospects of small states**

As noted in chapter 2, it is striking that the countries with the highest rates of emigration are small states. These rates often coincide with underdevelopment. For poorer small states, the disadvantages of being small include over-dependence on a single commodity or sector and vulnerability to exogenous shocks. Small countries cannot easily take advantage of economies of scale in economic activity and in the provision of public goods, and often face high production costs and consumer prices. In the case of small island states, remoteness is an additional factor, raising transport costs and times and making it difficult to compete in external markets. All these factors encourage out-migration.

The financial benefits associated with migration are relatively large for small states. In 2007, remittances averaged US$233 per capita, compared to a developing country average of US$52. The annual highest flows relative to GDP are found in the Caribbean, with remittances accounting for 8 percent of GDP. However, most small states are not among the countries with the highest GDP shares of remittances, so they are not especially exposed to shocks from this source. At the same time, the benefits of migration for small states go well beyond the monetary value of remittances. Moving opens up opportunities for labour linkages, which can enhance integration with economic hubs. Temporary labour migration can be a way of balancing the economic needs of both the origin and destination sides, of providing opportunities for low-skilled workers and of enabling broader benefits at home through the repatriation of skills and business ideas. To the extent that smallness overlaps with fragility and, in some countries, instability, migration can be a safety valve to mitigate the risk of conflict, as well as a diversification strategy over the longer term.

Some small states have integrated emigration into their development strategies, mainly to meet the challenge of job creation. Our commissioned review of PRSs showed that many small states (Bhutan, Cape Verde, Dominica, Guinea-Bissau, Sao Tome and Principe, and Timor-Leste) mention positive elements of international migration in terms of impact on development and/or poverty reduction. Among the goals in Timor-Leste's Poverty Reduction Strategy Paper (PRSP) (2003) was that of developing a plan for 1,000 workers to go abroad annually. However, others (Djibouti, Gambia, Guyana and Maldives) refer to emigration only as a problem. Some see negative aspects, such as exposure to downturns in remittances (Cape Verde) and increased inequality (Bhutan). Dominica's PRS saw emigration both as a cause of poverty and as contributing to poverty reduction.

Small states can make migration a strategic element of development efforts in several ways, some of which involve regional agreements. Some countries focus on temporary employment abroad. Others emphasize the creation of skills, sometimes in concert with neighbours. Mauritius has actively encouraged temporary employment abroad as a way of acquiring skills and capital that migrants can use to set up their own business on return. Supported by donors, the government has established a programme that provides technical and financial support to returning migrants. The Lesotho Development Vision 2020 focuses on generating jobs at home by attracting foreign direct investments, while recognizing the role of work abroad, especially in neighbouring South Africa. Its PRS sets out reform measures that include automation and decentralization of immigration services, establishment of a one-stop shop for efficient processing of immigration and work permits, and anti-corruption measures in the Department of Immigration. Development strategies can take broader measures to deal with the challenges of remoteness. For example, in the South Pacific, regional universities and vocational training have facilitated mobility, and several states have entered into migration agreements with their neighbours.

Emigrants from small states have similar profiles to migrants generally, in that they tend to have more skills and resources than people who stay. In Mauritius, for example, the total emigration rate is 12.5 percent, but about 49 percent for graduates. Overall, however, there is no significant difference in the net supply of skills, measured by the number of doctors per 10,000 population, between small and large states. In terms of simple averages, the number of doctors is actually higher for small states, at 23 per 10,000 compared to 20 per 10,000 on average for all countries.

Source: Luthria (2009), Winters and Martin (2004), Black and Sward (2009), Seewooruthun (2008), Government of Lesotho (2004), Winters, Walmsley, Wang, and Grynberg (2003), Amin and Mattoo (2005), Koettl (2006) and Pritchett (2006).

thus not surprising that the probability of migration increases for those with links to people already abroad.

Sometimes a 'culture of migration' emerges, in which international migration is associated with personal, social and material success while staying home smacks of failure.[68] As the social network grows, the culture is further engrained and migration becomes the norm, particularly among the young and able. This has been observed in cases where there has been large-scale out-migration, such as the Philippines, as well as in West and Southern Africa. A study in Nigeria found that two out five undergraduate students were more interested in leaving Nigeria as a way of gaining social status than in seeking gainful employment at home.[69] This can also be seen with respect to internal migration: a recent study from Ethiopia suggests that shifting preferences and aspirations as a result of education could lead people to migrate out of rural areas, irrespective of the earning potential that migration may provide.[70] The culture can acquire its own self-perpetuating momentum, as illustrated by the Irish, who continued to emigrate at the height of the Celtic Tiger boom.

In West Africa, migration is often not merely a vehicle for economic mobility but is also considered a process through which a boy attains maturity.[71] For some groups in Mali, Mauritania and Senegal, migration is a rite of passage: it is through the knowledge and experience acquired from travel that young adolescent males become men.[72] In the Soninke village of Kounda in Mali mobility distinguishes males and females.[73] Masculinity involves the freedom to move, whereas women in the village are to a large extent fixed inside the household. Men who do not migrate and remain economically dependent on their kin are considered to be immature youngsters and women refer to them with a derogatory term, *tenes*, which means 'being stuck like glue'. In Mali, the colloquial French term used to describe migration is *aller en aventure*, literally, to go on adventure. For the Soninke, being 'on adventure' implies being 'on the path to adulthood'.

The effect of migration on income distribution and social inequality is primarily a function of selection—that is, who moves (see chapter 2).[74] In general, money flows associated with international migration tend to go to the better off, whereas, at least in the longer term, remittances from internal migrants tend to be more equalizing.[75] This type of pattern has been found for Mexico and Thailand, for example.[76] Our commissioned research on China also found that inequality initially rose with internal remittances, then fell.[77]

If it is the better off who tend to migrate, then an appropriate response is to ensure access to basic services and opportunities at home as well as to facilitate the mobility of the poor. As we argue in chapter 5, poor people should not have to move in order to be able to send their children to decent schools: they should have options at home, alongside the possibility of moving.

Collective remittances sent through hometown associations and other community groups have arisen in recent decades.[78] These usually take the form of basic infrastructure projects, such as the construction of roads and bridges, the installation of drinking water and drainage systems, the sinking of wells, the bringing of electricity and telephone lines, and other public goods such as local church or soccer field restorations. Sometimes these are co-financed—the most famous example being Mexico's *Tres Por Uno* programme, which aims to increase collective remittances by assuring migrant associations that, for every peso they invest in local development projects, the federal, municipal and local government will put in three. The amount transferred as collective remittances remains only a fraction of that sent back individually to families, so the potential development impact of such programmes should not be overstated.[79] For example, it has been estimated that, since 1990, Filipinos in the United States have donated US$44 million in financial and material assistance to charitable organizations in the Philippines, an amount equivalent to only 0.04 percent of GDP in 2007.[80]

Mobility can affect social and political life in countries of origin in a broader sense. Migrants and their descendants may return and become directly involved in civic and political activities. Alternatively, business investments, frequent return visits and/or collective initiatives can affect patterns of participation by others at home. For example, in Lebanon, new political forces were formed, particularly after the 1989 Ta'ef Accord, as returning migrants used the wealth earned abroad to engage in politics.[81]

Evidence that emigrants have spurred the improvement of political institutions in their home countries is accumulating. Democratic reform has been found to progress more rapidly in developing countries that have sent more students to universities in democratic countries.[82] Knowledge and expectations brought home by a group of Moroccans returning from France have been found to shape basic infrastructure investments by the government in their home region.[83] However, if emigration serves simply as a safety valve, releasing political pressure, the incentives of the established political elite to reform are diminished.[84]

Just as migrants enrich the social fabric of their adopted homes, so too they can act as agents of political and social change if they return with new values, expectations and ideas shaped by their experiences abroad. Sometimes this has taken the form of supporting civil wars, as in the case of Sri Lanka's diaspora, but in most cases engagement is more constructive.[85] Contemporary high-profile examples include

Evidence that emigrants have spurred the improvement of political institutions in their home countries is accumulating

Box **4.5**   **Mobility and human development: some developing country perspectives**

Several recent National Human Development Reports (NHDRs), including those of Albania, El Salvador and Mexico, have focused on the development implications of mobility. In other countries NHDRs have considered how mobility influences selected aspects of development, such as the role of civil society (Egypt), rural development (Uganda), economic growth (Moldova), social cohesion (Côte d'Ivoire) and inequality (China).

Mexico's NHDR identifies inequality as the most robust determinant of migratory flows, and movement as a factor that modifies the availability of opportunities to others, including stayers. Drawing on the National Employment Survey, the average Mexican migrant is found to have slightly above-average schooling and intermediate income levels but comes from a marginalized municipality, suggesting an initial set of capabilities coupled with lack of opportunities as major driving factors. The report finds that the overall human development impacts of migration in Mexico are complex and conditional on the profile and resources of different groups. For example, while migration tends to reduce education inequality, especially for girls, it can also discourage investment in higher education in communities where most migrants traditionally go abroad for low-skilled jobs.

Different insights come from El Salvador, where emigrants represent 14 percent of the population and the impact of migration is more visible at the macro level. The recent acceleration of migration is seen to have contributed to the country's transition to a service economy, which has relied heavily on remittances and a mosaic of small businesses specialized in delivering goods and services to migrants and their families, including nostalgia products and communications. The report suggests that migration allows some relatively poor people a degree of upward mobility through their links to the global economy.

Source: UNDP (2000; 2004a; 2005a,b; 2006a; 2007c,e; 2008c).

Ellen Johnson-Sirleaf, President of Liberia and Africa's first female head of state, and Joaquim Chissano, former President of Mozambique and now a respected elder statesman. Recognizing the potential benefits of diaspora engagement, some governments have begun to actively reach out.[86] For example, Morocco and Turkey have extended political and economic rights to emigrants and allowed dual citizenship.[87] However, whether these policies of engagement benefit non-migrants or simply subsidize an elite group outside the country remains an open question. By improving its investment climate (presently ranked first in Africa by the World Bank's Doing Business Index), Mauritius has also attracted migrants back; similar patterns have been seen in India and Turkey, among other countries.

4.1.4 Mobility and national development strategies

To date, national development and poverty reduction strategies in developing countries have tended not to recognize the potential of mobility, nor integrated its dynamics into planning and monitoring. This is in part due to the range of other pressing priorities facing these countries, from improving systems of service delivery, through building basic infrastructure, to promoting broad-based growth.

Country-level perspectives on the links between mobility and development can be gleaned from recent National Human Development Reports. The highlights are summarized in box 4.5.

To gain insights into the link between national development strategies and migration in a larger sample of countries, we commissioned a study to review the role of migration in Poverty Reduction Strategies (PRSs). These strategies are statements of development objectives and policy, prepared by poorer countries whose views are often neglected in migration debates. PRSs are of interest since they also involve contributions from, or partnerships with, civil society actors, are intended to be based on quantitative and participatory assessments of poverty, and provide a sense of government priorities.[88] They are also important important because international partners have committed to aligning their assistance to these national strategies, given the importance of country ownership in development.

To date, Bangladesh's PRS has perhaps the most comprehensive treatment of migration and development linkages. The most recent PRSs for Albania, the Kyrgyzstan and Sri Lanka also reflect a major focus on migration-related issues. Many African countries acknowledge the role of remittances, the advantages of return and circular migration of skilled expatriates and the value of knowledge transfer from such people. Several strategies intend to attract development investments from wealthy members of the diaspora.

Earlier analysis of the treatment of international migration in PRSs was based in part on the number of mentions of the word 'migration'.[89] While simple, this indicator is not very meaningful. It is nonetheless striking that there is no significant correlation in PRSs between the number of references to migration and various measures of its possible importance for national development, such as share of the population living abroad, level of remittances and rate of urbanization.[90]

PRSs have laid out a wide range of migration-related policy initiatives, although these are often not explicitly based on prior analysis. In many cases the state of knowledge about the relationship between the proposed initiative and its expected development impact is weak, underlining the importance of better data and analysis.

In general, PRSs appear to recognize the complexity of international migration, acknowledging both its advantages—opportunities for development and poverty reduction—and its possible negative effects. Some tend to stress the positive—for example the most recent PRSs of Ethiopia, Nepal, Senegal and Uzbekistan frame emigration as an opportunity, without mentioning possible downsides. Most recent strategies emphasize the role of remittances, including those of Bangladesh, Democratic Republic of the Congo, Ghana, the Lao People's Democratic Republic, Liberia, Pakistan, Timor-Leste and Uzbekistan.

Several strategies articulate policies towards migration. We can distinguish between policies that are broadly 'proactive/facilitative' and those focused on 'regulation/control' (table 4.1). Combating trafficking, preventing irregular migration and modernizing and strengthening immigration and customs services feature frequently. It is striking how some of these policies echo those promoted by rich country governments.

To sum up, while the PRS framework generally has not been geared towards addressing migration policy per se, it could provide a useful tool for integrating migration and development issues. Fitting this dimension into an overall national strategy for development will require investments in data and analysis and in broad stakeholder consultation. These challenges are discussed further in chapter 5.

4.2 Destination place effects

Debates about migration often dwell on the economic and social impacts on rich destination countries. This report has deliberately sought to redress this imbalance, by beginning with the migrants and their families, then focusing on the places they came from. However, that is not to say that the impacts on people in destination communities are unimportant.

In many developed countries, the percentage of migrants in the total population has risen rapidly over the past 50 years. It is now estimated to be in double figures in more than a dozen OECD countries.[91] As noted in chapter 2 and shown in detail in Statistical Table A, the highest shares are found in Oceania (16 percent)—which includes Australia and New Zealand, North America (13 percent) and Europe (8 percent). The shares range between only 1 and 2 percent in the three major developing regions of Africa, Asia, and Latin America and the Caribbean. The highest country shares are recorded in the GCC states and in South-East Asia, including 63 percent in Qatar, 56 percent in the United Arab Emirates, 47 percent in Kuwait and 40 percent in Hong Kong (China). The real and perceived impacts of immigration are critical, not least because these perceptions shape the political climate in which policy reforms are debated and determined.

We begin this section by reviewing the economic impacts of immigration as a whole, then focus more narrowly on the labour market and

Table **4.1** **PRSs recognize the multiple impacts of migration**
Policy measures aimed at international migration in PRSs, 2000–2008

Proactive/facilitative	No. of countries	Proactive/facilitative	No. of countries	Regulation/control	No. of countries
Export labour	10	Facilitate remittances	9	Combat trafficking	19
Encourage female migration	1	Encourage legal remittance channels	3	Modernise customs	18
Promote student mobility	3	Engage diasporas	17	Strengthen border control	17
Sign bilateral agreements	9	Promote investment by diasporas	8	Combat illegal migration	12
Improve labour conditions abroad	6	Import skills	4	Promote refugee return	10
Pre-departure training	6	Participate in regional cooperation programmes	8	Tackle the 'brain drain'	9
Develop consular services	3	Promote more research/monitoring	8	Support return	7
Regulate recruitment industry	2	Build institutional capacity	5	Sign readmission agreements	2
Facilitate portability of pensions	2	Combat HIV/AIDS amongst migrants	7		
Promote refugee integration	7	Re-integrate trafficking victims	5		

Source: Adapted from Black and Sward (2009)
Note: 84 PRSs reviewed.

Migrants can bring broader economic benefits, including higher rates of innovation

fiscal impacts. For each of these types of impact there are important distributional issues—while there are overall gains, these are not evenly distributed.

4.2.1 Aggregate economic impacts

The impact of migration on aggregate growth rates of destination countries has been much discussed, but robust measurement is difficult. The data requirements and methodological complexities, including the need to disentangle direct and indirect effects and work out their timing, all present challenges (see box 1.1).

Economic theory predicts that there should be significant aggregate gains from movement, both to movers and to destination countries. This is because migration, like international trade, allows people to specialize and take advantage of their relative strengths. The bulk of the gains accrue to the individuals who move, but some part goes to residents in the place of destination as well as to those in the place of origin via financial and other flows. In background research commissioned for this report, estimates using a general equilibrium model of the world economy suggested that destination countries would capture about one-fifth of the gains from a 5 percent increase in the number of migrants in developed countries, amounting to US$190 billion dollars.[92]

To complement our review of the country-level studies, we commissioned research to construct a new dataset on migration flows and stocks, including consistent annual data on nature of employment, hours worked, capital accumulation and changes in immigration laws for 14 OECD destination countries and 74 origin countries for each year over the period 1980–2005.[93] Our research showed that immigration increases employment, with no evidence of crowding out of locals, and that investment also responds vigorously. These results imply that population growth due to migration increases real GDP per capita in the short run, one-for-one (meaning that a 1 percent increase in population due to migration increases GDP by 1 percent). This finding is reasonable, since in most instances annual migration flows are only a fraction of a percentage point of the labour force of the receiving country. Moreover, these flows are largely predictable, implying that the full adjustment of per capita investment levels is plausible even in the short run.

At the individual country level, at least in the OECD countries, similar results have been found—that is, increased migration has neutral or marginally positive effects on per capita income. For example, simulations following the European Union accessions of 2004 suggest that output levels in the United Kingdom and Ireland, which allowed large-scale inflows from the new member states of Eastern Europe, would be 0.5–1.5 percent higher after about a decade.[94] In countries where migrants account for a much higher share of the population and labour force—for example in the GCC states—the aggregate and sectoral contributions to the economy can be expected to be larger. However, detailed empirical analysis is unfortunately not available.

Migrants can bring broader economic benefits, including higher rates of innovation. Productivity gains in a number of destination places have been traced to the contributions of foreign students and scientists to the knowledge base. Data from the United States show that between 1950 and 2000, skilled migrants boosted innovation: a 1.3 percent increase in the share of migrant university graduates increased the number of patents issued per capita by a massive 15 percent, with marked contributions from science and engineering graduates and without any adverse effects on the innovative activity of local people.[95]

Countries explicitly compete for talent at the global level and the share of graduates among migrants varies accordingly.[96] The United States, in particular, has been able to attract migrant talent through the quality of its universities and research infrastructure and its favourable patenting rules.[97] In Ireland and the United Kingdom the share of migrants with tertiary education exceeds 30 percent, while in Austria, Italy and Poland it is below 15 percent.[98] Countries offering more flexible entry regimes and more promising long-term opportunities have done better in attracting skilled people, whereas restrictions on duration of stay, visa conditions and career development, as in Germany for example, limit uptake. This has led to discussions about a blue card or European Union-wide employment permit—an idea that has received preliminary backing from the European Parliament and approval by the European Council.[99] Singapore and Hong Kong (China), have explicit policies to welcome foreign high-skilled professionals. These policies range from allowing immigrants to bring their families, through facilitating permanent residence after defined waiting periods (two years for Singapore, seven for Hong Kong (China)), to the option of naturalization.[100]

Programmes to attract skilled labour can be developed using a general points-based approach, linked to labour market tests and/or employer requirements (chapter 2). A centralized 'manpower' planning approach can be difficult to implement, especially in the face of structural change and economic shocks. Points-based schemes, which have the virtue of simplicity, have been used by destination governments to favour high-skilled migrants or to attract workers for occupations in short supply on the national labour market, as in Australia's General Skilled Migration programme.

Migration can stimulate local employment and businesses, but such effects are likely to be context-specific. Migrants also affect the level and composition of consumer demand, for example in favour of nostalgia goods, as well as locally available goods and services that are close to homes and work-places. Our commissioned study of such effects in California found evidence suggesting that an influx of immigrants over the decade to 2000 into specific areas (selected to capture the potential pool of customers for different firms) was positively correlated with higher employment growth in some sectors, especially in education services. The impact on the composition of demand was mixed: a higher share of migrants was associated with fewer small firms and stand-alone retail stores, but more large-scale discount retailers. At the same time, consistent with expectations, the study found that increased immigration was associated with increased ethnic diversity of restaurants.[101]

4.2.2 Labour market impacts

There is controversy around the effects of migration on employment and wages in the destination country, especially for those with low levels of formal education. Public opinion polls show that there is significant concern that immigration lowers wages.[102] There have also been lively academic debates on the subject, notably in the United States. Yet it is striking that most empirical studies in the OECD draw similar conclusions, namely that the *aggregate* effect of immigration on the wages of local workers may be positive or negative but is fairly small in the short and long run.[103] In Europe, both multi- and single-country studies find little or no impact of migration on the average wages of local people.[104]

At the same time it must be recognized that wage responses to immigration are unlikely to be distributed evenly across all workers and will be most pronounced where locally born workers compete with immigrants. The debates have clarified that it is not just the total number of migrants that matter but their skill mix as well. The kinds of skill that migrants bring affect the wages and employment opportunities of different segments of the local population, sometimes in subtle ways. If the skills of migrant workers complement those of locally born workers, then both groups will benefit.[105] If the skills match exactly, then competition will be heightened, creating the possibility that locally born workers will lose out. However, this is not a foregone conclusion: often the results are mixed, with some individuals in both groups gaining while others lose. Assessing these effects is problematic, because measuring the degree to which different groups' skills complement or substitute for one another is difficult, particularly across international borders.[106]

One striking example of complementarity is how migrants can facilitate higher labour force participation among locally born females.[107] The availability of low-cost child care can free up young mothers, enabling them to go out and find a job. There is consensus in the literature that low-skilled migrant labour generally complements local labour in Europe.[108] This may arise in part because migrants are more mobile than locally born workers—as in Italy, for example.[109] More importantly, migrants are often willing to accept work that locals are no longer prepared to undertake, such as child care, care of the elderly (much in demand in aging societies), domestic work, and restaurant, hotel and other hospitality industry work.

As noted, the small *average* effect on pay may mask considerable variation across types of local workers. There is a vast empirical literature on

Migrants can facilitate higher labour force participation among locally born females

Legal and institutional factors—both their design and their enforcement—matter

the effect of immigration on the distribution of wages in developed countries. In the United States, estimates of the effect on the wages of unskilled workers range from –9 to +0.6 percent.[110] Locals with low levels of formal schooling may still have advantages over migrants due not only to language but also to knowledge of local institutions, networks and technology, which enables them to specialize in complementary and better-paid tasks.[111]

The imperfect substitutability of migrant and local labour is consistent with recent evidence suggesting that the workers affected most by the entry of new migrants are earlier migrants. They feel the brunt of any labour market adjustment, since newcomers primarily compete with them. In the United Kingdom, for example, heightened competition among migrants in the early 2000s may have increased the difference between the wages of locals and migrants by up to 6 percent.[112]

While the evidence about employment impacts is less extensive, the pattern is similar. Detailed investigations have not established a systematic relationship between immigration and unemployment. This is in part because of labour market segmentation, as low-skilled migrants accept jobs that are less attractive to locals, enabling the latter to move to other sectors and jobs. The massive inflows associated with European Union accession led neither to the displacement of local workers nor to increased unemployment in Ireland and the United Kingdom. Recent experience in Europe thus supports the idea that migrant labour does not have a large effect on the employment of locals. One European study found that a 10 percent increase in the share of migrants in total employment would lower the employment of residents by between 0.2 and 0.7 percent.[113]

These econometric results should also be interpreted in the light of the evidence concerning the labour market disadvantage of migrants that was reviewed in chapter 3. Legal and institutional factors—both their design and their enforcement—matter. If migrant workers fall through the net of the formal arrangements that protect wages and working conditions, unfair competition with locally born workers could well follow. A similar outcome can be expected where people are excluded from unions or where

the enforcement of regulations is weak. Even in countries with well-regulated labour markets, workers with irregular status often tend to fall 'under the radar'—the drowning of Chinese cockle gatherers in Morecambe Bay in the United Kingdom was a notorious case of lack of enforcement of health and safety standards. Recent British research found that more general structural trends, particularly the increasing use of agency (temporary) labour contracts, which are associated with fewer rights for workers, are significant factors shaping the pay and working conditions of migrant workers. There is widespread evidence of payment below the legal minimum wage, especially for younger migrants.[114]

Among emerging and developing economies, empirical evidence on the labour market impacts of immigration is sparse. A recent study of Thailand, which investigated whether places with higher concentrations of migrants had lower wages, found that a 10 percent increase in migrants reduced the wages of Thai locals by about 0.2 percent but did not lower employment or reduce internal migration.[115] Simulations conducted for Hong Kong (China), found that even large increases in new immigrants (a 40 percent increase) would lower wages by no more than 1 percent.[116] To the extent that migrants can find employment only in the informal labour market, their arrival will have a larger effect on locals who themselves operate informally. In many developing countries, informality is ubiquitous, so migrants are likely to join an already large segment of the market.

4.2.3 Rapid urbanization

Rapid urban growth, which can be partly attributed to internal migration, can pose major challenges. While people may be attracted by the better opportunities available in cities, it is nonetheless true that local services and amenities may come under severe strain. This can be seen in large cities, such as Calcutta and Lagos, as well as the myriad medium-sized cities, from Colombo to Guayaquil to Nairobi. Many newcomers and their families in developing countries end up in shanty towns and slums, typically on the outskirts of large cities. Residents in these areas often face high service costs. They may also be at risk from flooding and landslides, not to mention harassment from the authorities and violence, theft or extortion at the hands of criminals.

When movement is driven by falling living standards and weak support services in places of origin, the rate of migration to urban centres can exceed the demand for labour and the provision of services there.[117] Under these conditions the outcome is high structural unemployment and underemployment. Moreover, where local authorities are ill prepared for population growth and face severe institutional and financial constraints, the result is likely to be rapidly increasing disparities in incomes and well-being and segmentation of the city into areas that are relatively prosperous and safe, with good services, and 'no-go' areas where living conditions are falling apart. In contrast, when people are attracted to cities because of employment opportunities, net benefits are likely to accrue as the concentration of ideas, talent and capital lead to positive spillovers. This has been found in the Republic of Korea, for example.[118]

These contrasting scenarios underline the importance of good urban governance, which can be defined as the sum of the many ways individuals and institutions—public and private—plan and manage city life. Among the most important aspects of urban governance for migrants are: adequate financial resources, which must often be generated through local taxation; equitable pricing policies for basic social services and utilities; the extension of services to areas where migrants live; even-handed regulation of the informal sector; outreach and support services (such as language classes) targeted to migrant groups; and accountability, through such mechanisms as representation on local authorities, the publication of performance standards for key services, and the regular independent audit and publication of municipal accounts.

Field research provides useful insights into how city authorities are handling flows of people and the more general challenges of urban poverty. The findings suggest that decentralization and democratization can allow the poor more opportunities to lobby and to make incremental gains, at least in terms of infrastructure provision.[119] Having a voice—and having that voice heard—seems to work in terms of protecting the poor from the worst excesses of bad governance, particularly from harassment and removal of informal traders.[120] There are clearly echoes of

Amartya Sen's argument about the positive effects of democratic processes and a free press.[121]

Clearly, however, some municipal governments have wielded levers with negative repercussions for migrants. For instance, a review of urbanization experiences in Asia, commissioned for this report, finds that a number of governments continue to pursue policies aimed at decelerating in-migration. Several countries were found to have forcibly cleared slums, pushing the poor into periphery areas void of services.[122] In Dhaka, Bangladesh, some 29 slum areas, home to 60,000 people, were cleared by the authorities in early 2007. In Jakarta, Indonesia, the 'closed city' policy requires migrants to present proof of employment and housing, making it difficult for them to stay legally, while a law passed in September 2007 makes squatter settlements on river banks and highways illegal. Sometimes this kind of intervention can lead to unrest, as in Bangladesh, for example, following evictions in Agargoan and other settlements.[123] It appears that mass evictions are more likely when democracy and accountability are weak, as the shantytown clearances around Harare in Zimbabwe during 2005 demonstrate.

One final point: popular perceptions among local people in Europe and the United States as well as South Africa, for example, associate migrants with price increases in certain private markets, such as the rental market for housing. To the best of our knowledge, no studies establish the existence of such an effect.

4.2.4 Fiscal impacts

A popular measure of the impact of migration, though not one that necessarily reflects its true economic and social effects, is the perception of the changes it brings to the government's fiscal position.[124] People across the political spectrum often share concerns about the implications of migration for the welfare state. Our analysis of the European Social Survey of 2002 suggested that up to 50 percent of the region's population worry about migrants being a net fiscal burden, with those most concerned tending to be less well educated, older and/or unemployed. The concerns are most acute in the Czech Republic, Greece, Hungary and Ireland, much less so in Italy, Luxembourg, Portugal and Sweden. Some people are worried about increased costs, others

People across the political spectrum often share concerns about the implications of migration for the welfare state

A migrant whose child attends state school may also provide childcare services that facilitate the entry of a high-skilled woman into the labour force—and both pay taxes

about sustainability in the face of reduced social cohesion. Some governments have sought to address these concerns by introducing waiting periods for becoming eligible to receive benefits, as in Australia, New Zealand and the United Kingdom, for example.

Do migrants 'take more than they give,' or vice versa? This is a highly contentious issue, and one that we believe has garnered unwarranted attention. Estimating migrants' use of public services is fraught with measurement difficulties, while calculating their offsetting tax contributions adds another layer of complexity. A migrant whose child attends state school may also provide childcare services that facilitate the entry of a high-skilled woman into the labour force—and both pay taxes.

In practice, there is wide variation across countries in both the existence and generosity of welfare benefits and the eligibility of migrants. Studies in the United States, which has low levels of benefits for a rich country, have found a range of estimates, but the general picture is consistent: first-generation migrants tend to generate net fiscal costs whereas later generations tend to produce large fiscal surpluses.[125] At the same time, taxes paid by migrants may not accrue to the levels of government providing services to migrants. Especially where migrants are under-counted and where fiscal transfers are made to local authorities on a per capita or needs basis, it may be that the localities facing the largest burdens in extending basic services to migrants also lack adequate resources to do so.

Local government typically accounts for a significant share of total government spending and often bears the burden of financing basic services, including services for migrants. According to the International Monetary Fund,[126] the share of spending in 2007 by subnational authorities in developed countries ranged from 63 percent for Denmark to 6 percent for Greece. The share is significant in a number of other major destination countries, including the Russian Federation (51 percent) and South Africa (47 percent). But there are exceptions—for example Thailand, where the share is below 15 percent. Thus, depending on the structure of public finances, migrants could impose net fiscal costs on one level of government while being net contributors to total public revenue.

For example, the costs of providing educational and health services, which may include special programmes such as language courses, may be concentrated in local authorities, while income taxes accrue to the central government.

In the United States, fiscal concerns appear to affect the immigration policy preferences of different groups. One study found that locals tend to be in favour of curbing immigration if they live in states that have large migrant populations and provide migrants with generous welfare benefits.[127] This opinion is strongest among locals with high earnings potential, who tend to be in higher tax brackets. Similar results were obtained using a sample of over 20 countries in Europe.[128]

In countries with progressive tax systems and welfare benefits, low-skilled migrants, refugees and those entering under family reunification programmes are associated with higher net fiscal costs. In some European countries migrants, after accounting for their demographic characteristics, appear to be more dependent on welfare programmes than locals, but this is certainly not the case in all countries.[129] The difference can be traced back at least partly to the relative generosity of the welfare systems.

In the 2008/09 recession, rising unemployment and hardship among migrants can be expected to impose additional costs on public finances, although the degree to which this happens in practice remains to be seen. Determining factors in each country will be the share of migrants among the unemployed and the structure of unemployment benefits, particularly the eligibility rules. Even in countries with well-developed welfare systems, the access of migrants to benefits may be limited. A recent study predicted that, among European countries, Estonia, France and Latvia were likely to face a higher public finance burden due to the costs of migrants' welfare benefits during the 2009 downturn, whereas Austria, Finland, Germany, Ireland and Spain would register less-marked increases.[130] In many developing countries, the issue of rising fiscal costs during a time of recession typically does not arise, because welfare benefits are simply unavailable to anyone.

Migration is sometimes touted as a solution to the looming fiscal crisis associated with rapid aging in many developed countries (chapter 2). This would require that migrants be net contributors to the fiscal system in the short to medium term. The longer term costs when migrants themselves retire need also to be taken into account. Both imply the need either to continually expand immigration or, more realistically, to raise social security contributions from the increased numbers of working migrants while introducing structural changes to the design of social security and retirement systems.

Whether positive or negative, the net fiscal impacts of immigration are not large. Putting the various effects together, relative to GDP, most estimates for the United States and Europe place the net fiscal impact of immigration in the range of ± 1 percent of GDP.[131] For example, the figure for the United Kingdom is ± 0.65 percent of GDP.[132] These estimates indicate that the fiscal consequences of migration should not generally be a key factor in designing policy.

Some destination governments impose additional fees on migrants, based on the principle that individuals receiving a benefit over and above the services enjoyed by the local taxpayer should contribute more. In 1995, Canada introduced a Right of Permanent Residence Fee equivalent to US$838, to be paid before a visa can be issued (but refundable if the client is refused or chooses not to proceed). Several amendments over time have sought to mitigate negative impacts with a loan option, flexibility in the timing of payment, elimination of the fee for refugees, protected persons and dependent children—and then halving of the fee in 2006. In addition to the fee, there is a US$430 administrative charge for adults (US$86 for dependents). However, in the Canadian and other similar cases, there is no direct link between the revenues generated from this fee and funding for integration programmes. The United Kingdom recently introduced a landing fee, at a more symbolic level of UK£50 (US$93). Both these examples seem oriented more towards assuaging popular concerns than towards raising revenue to cover fiscal costs.

4.2.5 Perceptions and concerns about migration

Migration is a controversial issue in many countries. The mere presence of newcomers from different backgrounds can pose challenges, especially in societies that were traditionally homogeneous. Broadly speaking, three interlinked types of concern can be distinguished, related to security and crime, socio-economic factors, and cultural factors.[133] We end this chapter by addressing each of these aspects in turn.

Following the attacks on the United States in 2001, security concerns rose to the top of the political agenda. A major issue was the association, real or imagined, of foreigners with a lack of loyalty and the threat of terrorism. Such fears are far from new, having characterized many historical instances of anti-immigration sentiment. Examples include the ethnic Chinese in Indonesia, who were suspected of political subversion on behalf of Communist China during the 1960s, and the ethnic Russian populations in the Baltic states who were suspected of undermining the states' newly won independence after the collapse of the Soviet Union in the early 1990s. These concerns normally abate somewhat over time, only to resurface in new forms at times of political instability and change.

Security concerns also derive from the perceived links between immigration and crime, which are often cited in popular debates about migration. We found that more than 70 percent of respondents to the European Social Survey of 2002 believed that immigrants worsen a country's crime problems, with the figure rising to more than 85 percent in Germany, the Czech Republic and Norway. As exemplified by the film *The Godfather*, stereotype images associating immigrants with crime have long been propagated through the popular media, which often feature violence perpetrated by a range of immigrant groups including the Italian *mafia*, Chinese triads and Central American gangs such as the Salvadoran *Mara Salvatrucha*.

The data do not confirm these stereotypes. However, they do reveal significant variation in immigrant crime rates across countries. Data from the 2000 US census show that, for every ethnic group, incarceration rates among young men are lowest for immigrants, even those who are the least educated. On average, among men aged 18 to 39 (who comprise the vast majority of the prison population), the incarceration rate of the locally born in 2000 was 3.5 percent, five times higher than the 0.7 percent rate of the

Whether positive or negative, the net fiscal impacts of immigration are not large

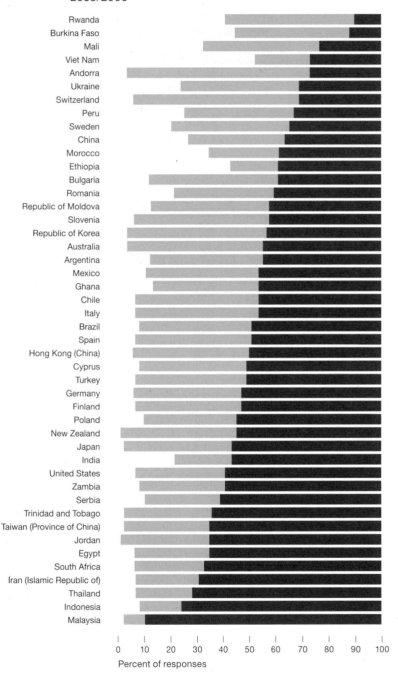

Figure **4.3** **Support for immigration is contingent on job availability**
Attitudes towards immigration and availability of jobs,
2005/2006

Percent of responses

*"How about people from other countries coming here to work.
Which one of the following do you think the government should do?"*

Let anyone come who wants to
Let people come as long as there are jobs available
Limit/prohibit immigration

Source: Kleemans and Klugman (2009).

foreign-born.[134] Earlier studies for the United States yielded similar findings.[135] However, the picture in Europe is more varied. Data from the Council of Europe on 25 countries show that on average there are more than twice as many foreign-born people in prison than locally born. A study on six European countries found that, in Austria, Germany, Luxembourg, Norway and Spain, offense rates are higher for foreigners, while this was not the case in Greece, for example.[136]

Fears that migrants will undermine the socio-economic status of local people have been tested empirically. As already indicated, the effects can be positive for some individuals and groups and negative for others, but are seldom very large. However, the 2008/09 economic recession represents a severe shock to many workers in destination (and other) countries, possibly the worst since the Great Depression of the 1930s. While there is no serious suggestion that this shock has been caused by migrant labour, it has nevertheless stoked the flames of anti-immigrant rhetoric, as local workers search for ways of saving their own jobs. Governments are under enormous pressure—and often fail to withstand it. Opinions are shifting, even in cases where migration has been broadly welcomed by the public thus far—for example, in the United Kingdom against Eastern Europeans, despite the successful experience of large-scale inflows during the long boom.[137]

People's views about migration are conditioned by the availability of jobs. In the majority of the 52 countries covered in the latest World Values Survey, most respondents endorsed restrictions on immigration, but many emphasized that these restrictions should be clearly linked to the availability of jobs (figure 4.3).[138] The demographic and economic projections presented in chapter 2 suggest that, beyond the current recession, structural features will lead to the re-emergence of job vacancies and hence new opportunities for migrants.

Even in normal times, many feel that preference should be given to locally born people (figure 4.4). Our regression analysis found that this view prevailed more among people who were older, had lower incomes, lived in small towns and did not have a migrant background. Interestingly, however, people were more likely to favour equal treatment of migrants in countries where the stock of migrants was relatively high.

Economic and security concerns can sometimes reinforce each other, in what becomes a vicious circle. Migrants who are marginalized—due, for example, to temporary or irregular status or high levels of unemployment—may resort to anti-social or criminal behaviour, confirming the security fears of locals. If this leads to further discrimination in the labour market and in policy formation, such migrants may turn away from the new society back to the old, possibly forming gangs or other anti-social organizations that threaten local populations. This type of pathology has been observed among some young Maghrebians in France and some Central American groups in the United States.

Where labour market disadvantage leads to social exclusion, repercussions for social cohesion can quickly follow. Recent research in seven developed countries has highlighted barriers to socialization encountered by children in immigrant families.[139] These families are often concentrated in certain locations, such as particular low-income urban localities. This fosters educational and socio-economic segregation: residence in segregated neighbourhoods limits contacts with locally born people, a separation reinforced by attendance at schools that are *de facto* segregated. A study we commissioned on Latino immigrant identity in the United States suggested that restrictive migration policies and increasingly adverse public opinion over time, alongside mixed human development outcomes, have affected people's sense of self. The study, based on interviews with immigrants and their children from several Latin American countries, suggests that immigrants have formative experiences that engender group solidarity but promote a rejection of American identity, related to the realities of the labour market during a period of rising inequality.[140]

Concerns are also expressed about the possible impacts of immigration on the political climate.[141] However, in most countries, the relative size of the migrant population is too small to have a direct effect on national electoral politics, particularly since migrants come from a diversity of backgrounds and will have a diversity of political views. In any case migrants

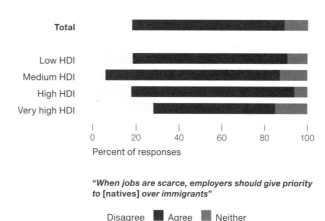

Figure **4.4** **When jobs are limited, people favour the locally born**
Public opinion about job preferences by destination country HDI category, 2005/2006

"*When jobs are scarce, employers should give priority to* [natives] *over immigrants*"

Disagree ■ Agree ■ Neither

Source: Kleemans and Klugman (2009).

are generally not permitted to vote in national elections. Their preferences may be more significant in local elections, where granting of voting rights to first-generation immigrants is more common.[142] Over time, as economic, social and cultural assimilation deepens, the effects of migrants on voting patterns become even less predictable.[143]

Last but not least, in sufficient numbers, migrants can affect the ethnic and cultural diversity of a society, literally changing the face of a nation. Several countries that today are highly prosperous were historically founded by migrants. Australia, Canada, New Zealand and United States have continued to welcome large inflows over time, in successive waves from different countries of origin, and generally have been highly successful in absorbing migrants and giving them a common sense of belonging to the new nation despite their cultural differences.[144] In countries with a long and proud history of independence and a strong sense of national identity, the arrival of newcomers may pose more challenges.

Of course, some cultural attributes are more easily adopted by locals than others. For example, many societies welcome new cuisines (probably the most resistant are the French and Italians, who think they have figured it out already). This confirms Paul Krugman's thesis that a taste for variety, combined with economies of scale, does more to explain international trade patterns than any other factor. But some find it harder to open the door to new religious and social customs such as the wearing of headscarves by women and the payment of dowries.

While specific issues can arise, the evidence suggests that people are generally tolerant of minorities and have a positive view of ethnic diversity (figure 4.5). People who are less well-educated, older, unemployed and without a migrant background are less likely to value ethnic diversity.[145] At the same time, more than 75 percent of respondents in the 2005/2006 World Values Survey did not object to having a migrant as their neighbour. These attitudes point to clear opportunities for building a broad consensus around better treatment of migrants, a policy option that we explore in the next chapter.

Insecurity and adverse reactions may arise when migrant communities are seen to represent alternative and competing social norms and structures, implicitly threatening the local culture. This is associated with the view that ethnic identities compete with each other and vary considerably in their commitment to the nation state, implying that there is a zero sum game between recognizing diversity and unifying the state. Yet individuals can and do have multiple identities that are complementary—in terms of ethnicity, language, religion, race and even citizenship (chapter 1). Thus when migrants integrate more fully and more diffusely with their adopted homeland, which in turn becomes even more diverse, they have a better chance of being valued as enriching society and introducing complementary cultural traits.

4.3 Conclusions

This chapter has explored the impacts of mobility on those who do not move. We began with places of origin and focused on developing countries (although by far the highest regional rates of out-migration are observed for Europe and the lowest for Africa). The greatest impacts are at the household level, for those who have family members who have moved, and these are largely positive for income, consumption, education and health. However, the poverty impacts are limited because those who move are mainly not the poorest. Broader community and national effects can also be observed, although these patterns are often complex, context-specific and subject to change over time.

Given the global recession of 2008/09, it is especially important to assess the impact of migration on host communities and countries. There is no evidence of significant adverse economic, labour market or fiscal impacts, and there is evidence of gains in such areas as social diversity and capacity for innovation. Fears about migrants are generally exaggerated.

These findings, alongside those in the preceding chapter, suggest the possibility of creating virtuous circles through policy measures that enhance and broaden the benefits of mobility. This would increase migrants' economic and social contributions to both destination and origin communities and countries.

The public policies that people encounter when they move play a large part in shaping their futures. Designing these policies well is in the interests of migrants themselves, the communities they leave behind and the other residents in their adopted homes. It is to this topic that we turn in the final chapter of this report.

Figure **4.5**   **Many people value ethnic diversity**

Popular views about the value of ethnic diversity by destination country HDI category, 2005/2006

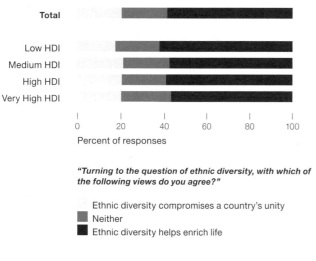

"Turning to the question of ethnic diversity, with which of the following views do you agree?"

Ethnic diversity compromises a country's unity
Neither
Ethnic diversity helps enrich life

Source: Kleemans and Klugman (2009).

Policies
to enhance
human
development
outcomes

5

This final chapter proposes reforms that will allow mobility to contribute to a fuller enhancement of people's freedoms. At present, many people who move have at best only precarious rights and face uncertain futures. The policy mismatch between restrictive entry and high labour demand for low-skilled workers needs to be addressed. We propose a core package of reforms that will improve outcomes for individual movers and their families, their origin communities and host places. The design, timing and acceptability of reforms depend on a realistic appraisal of economic and social conditions and a recognition of public opinion and political constraints.

Policies to enhance human development outcomes

The foregoing analysis has shown that large gains to human development would flow from improved policies towards movers. These would benefit all groups affected by migration. A bold vision is needed to realize these gains—a vision that embraces reform because of its potential pay-offs, while recognizing the underlying challenges and constraints.

We have also shown that the entry policies that have prevailed in many destination countries over recent decades can be largely characterized by denial and delay on the one hand, and heightened border controls and illegal stays on the other. This has worsened the situation of people lacking legal status and, especially during the recession, has created uncertainty and frustration among the wider population.

The factors driving migration—including disparate opportunities and rapid demographic transitions—are expected to persist in the coming decades. Lopsided demographic patterns mean that nine tenths of the growth in the world's labour force since 1950 has been in developing countries, while developed countries are aging. These trends create pressures for people to move, but the regular channels allowing movement for low-skilled people are very restricted. Demographic projections to the year 2050 predict that these trends will continue, even if the demand for labour has been temporarily attenuated by the current economic crisis. This implies a need to rethink the policy of restricting the entry of low-skilled workers, which ill accords with the underlying demand for such workers. This chapter tackles the major challenge of how governments can prepare for the resumption of growth, with its underlying structural trends.

Our proposal consists of a core package of reforms with medium- to long-term pay-offs. The package consists of six 'pillars'. Each pillar is beneficial on its own, but together they offer the best chance of maximizing the human development impacts of migration:

1. Liberalizing and simplifying regular channels that allow people to seek work abroad;
2. Ensuring basic rights for migrants;
3. Reducing transaction costs associated with migration;
4. Improving outcomes for migrants and destination communities;
5. Enabling benefits from internal mobility; and
6. Making mobility an integral part of national development strategies.

Our proposal involves new processes and norms to govern migration, but does not prescribe any particular levels of increased admissions, since these need to be determined at the country level.

Our agenda is largely oriented towards the longer-term reforms needed to enhance the gains from movement, while recognizing the major challenges in the short term. In the midst of what is shaping up to be the worst economic crisis since the Great Depression, unemployment is rising to record highs in many countries. As a result, many migrants find themselves doubly at risk: suffering unemployment, insecurity and social marginalization, yet at the same time often portrayed as the source of these problems. It is important that the current recession must not become an occasion for scapegoating, but rather be seized as an opportunity to institute a new deal for migrants—one that will benefit workers at home and abroad while guarding against a protectionist backlash. Forging that new deal and selling it to the public will require political vision and committed leadership.[1]

Open dialogue is critical if progress is to be made in the public debate about migration. In

Open dialogue is critical if progress is to be made in the public debate about migration

this debate, the benefits should not be overplayed and the concerns about distributional effects—especially among low-skilled workers—need to be recognized and taken into account. The political economy of reform is directly addressed below.

Because this is a global report with diverse stakeholders—governments in origin, destination and transit countries; donors and international organizations; the private sector; and civil society, including migrant groups and diaspora associations, academia and the media—the policy directions we outline are inevitably pitched at a general level. Our intention is to stimulate debate and follow-up in discussing, adapting and implementing these recommendations. At the country level, much more detailed analysis will be needed to ensure relevance to local circumstances and allow for political realities and practical constraints.

5.1 The core package

We will now explore the policy entry points outlined above. Our focus is limited to selected aspects out of the much broader menu of options that have been discussed and implemented around the world.[2] In defining a priority agenda we have been motivated by a focus on the disadvantaged, a realistic consideration of the political constraints and an awareness that trade-offs are inevitable. Whenever possible, we illustrate with examples of good practice.

5.1.1 Liberalizing and simplifying regular channels

Overly restrictive barriers to entry prevent many people from moving and mean that millions who do move have irregular status—an estimated one quarter of the total. This has created uncertainty and frustration, both in the migrant community and among the wider population, especially during the current recession.

When growth resumes, the demand for migrant labour will likewise rebound, since the demographic and economic conditions that created that demand in the first place will still be in place. The need for working-age people in developed countries has been largely structural, and is long-term—not temporary—in nature. This is true even for high-turnover jobs in such sectors as care, construction, tourism and food processing.

If the demand for labour is long-term, then, from the perspective of both migrants and their destination communities and societies, it is better to allow people to come legally. And provided migrants can find and keep jobs, it is better to offer them the option of extending their stay than to limit them to temporary permits. The longer people stay abroad, the greater the social and economic mobility they and their children are likely to enjoy. When the presence of migrants is denied or ignored by host governments, the risk of segmentation is greatly increased, not only in the labour market and economy but also in society more generally. This is one lesson that emerged clearly from the German guest-worker experience. We see it again today, in destinations as diverse as the GCC states, the Russian Federation, Singapore, South Africa and Thailand.

So what would a liberalization and simplification of migration channels look like? There are two broad avenues where reform appears both desirable and feasible: seasonal or circular programmes, and entry for unskilled people, with conditional paths to extension. The difficult issue of what to do about people with irregular status is a third area in which various options for change are possible and should be considered. In each case, the specific design of new measures will need to be discussed and debated at the national level through political processes that permit the balancing of different interests (section 5.2). As high-skilled people are already welcomed in most countries, reforms need to focus on the movement of people without tertiary degrees.

The first avenue, already explored by a number of countries, is to expand schemes for truly seasonal work in sectors such as agriculture and tourism. Key elements when planning and implementing reforms include consultation with source country governments, union and employer involvement, basic wage guarantees, health and safety protection, and provision for repeat visits. These elements are the basis for schemes that have been successfully operating for decades in Canada, for example, and have more recently been introduced in New Zealand (box 5.1). Workers in formal schemes of this kind are typically accorded better protection than those with irregular status. From a human development point of view, that is one of their major advantages.

Box **5.1**   Opening up regular channels—Sweden and New Zealand

Two countries have recently introduced reforms in line with the directions suggested by this report, although both are too new to evaluate in terms of impact.

In late 2008, Sweden introduced a major labour migration reform. The initiative came from the Swedish parliament and began with the appointment of a parliamentary committee with a mandate to propose changes. This was during a period of rapid economic growth and widespread labour shortages. Parliamentary and media debates focused on the risk of displacement of local workers and on whether unsuccessful asylum seekers could apply. A scheme was thus designed that met union concerns about undercutting of wages and labour standards.

Among the scheme's key elements is the provision that employers are the primary judges of needs (self-assessment), with a role for the Swedish Migration Board to ensure consistency with collective agreements and allow for union comment. Portability across employers is allowed after two years, and if individuals change jobs during this initial period they must apply for a new work permit. The duration is initially for two years, extendable to four, after which permanent residence can be granted. During the first quarter of operation, there were 24,000 applications, representing about 15 percent of total applications to come to Sweden.

New Zealand's Recognised Seasonal Employer Scheme (RSE) was launched in April 2007 as part of the government's growth and innovation agenda, to address the acute problems experienced by the horticulture and viticulture industries in finding workers during seasonal labour peaks. It provides a number of seasonal jobs, set annually.

RSE was designed to avoid some of the downsides of the low-wage temporary work cycle, which was seen as unsustainable for both employers and workers, many of whom were irregular migrants. Transiting to RSE shook out existing irregular workers from the system and brought new employers into contact with the government. During the transition period employers were allowed to retain workers already in New Zealand for a limited period and under certain conditions.

Central to the objectives of both the New Zealand government and the union movement, and critical to public acceptance, was to ensure that employers recruit and train New Zealand workers first, before they recruit offshore. However, the scheme allows Pacific Island countries to find a continuing market for their low-skilled labour, provided that they put in place appropriate selection and facilitation processes and help to ensure return. Their workers have the opportunity to be trained and properly remunerated, and to broaden their experience and contacts. So far, no serious problems have been reported.

RSE is not a low-cost scheme. It will not be economically sustainable unless the industries involved can realize productivity and quality gains in partnership with a known group of workers, who can be relied on to return to specific orchards and vineyards each year.

Sources: Government of Sweden (2008) and World Bank (2006a).

The second avenue, which involves more fundamental reforms, is to expand the number of visas for low-skilled people—conditional on employer demand. As is currently the case, the visas can initially be temporary. Issuance can be made conditional on a job offer, or at least experience of, or willingness to work in, a sector that is known to face labour shortages.

Expanding regular entry channels involves taking decisions on the following key issues:

Setting annual inflow numbers. These must be responsive to local conditions and there are several ways of ensuring this. Numbers can be based on employer demand—such that an individual is required to have a job offer prior to arrival—or on the recommendations of a technical committee or similar body that considers projections of demand and submissions from unions, employers and community groups. The United Kingdom's Migration Advisory Committee, set up in late 2007 to provide advice on the designation of so-called

'shortage occupations', is a good example. The disadvantages of requiring a job offer are that the decision is effectively delegated to individual employers, transaction costs for individual migrants may be higher, and portability can become an issue. Caution should be exercised in relation to employers' stated 'needs' for migrants. These could arise because migrants are willing to work longer hours and/or because they are more skilled. Employers should not use migrant labour as a stratagem for evading their legal obligations to provide basic health and safety protection and to guarantee minimum standards in working conditions, which should be accorded to all workers, regardless of origin.

Employer portability. Tying people to specific employers prevents them from finding better opportunities and is therefore both economically inefficient and socially undesirable. Our policy assessment found that governments typically allow employment portability for permanent high-skilled migrants, but not for temporary low-skilled workers. However, there are signs of change. The United Arab Emirates has begun to offer transferable employment sponsorships in response to complaints of abuse from migrants.[3] Sweden's recent labour immigration reform, described in box 5.1, is perhaps the most comprehensive example of employment and benefits portability to date, as work permits are transferable and migrants who lose their jobs—for whatever reason—have three months to find work before the visa is revoked.[4] An employer who has gone abroad to recruit will typically seek some period of non-portability—but even in these cases there are ways of building in a degree of flexibility: for example, allowing the migrant or another employer who wants to employ her to pay a fee reimbursing the original employer for recruitment costs.

Box **5.2**   **Experience with regularization**

Most European countries have operated some form of regularization programme, albeit for a range of motives and, in some cases, despite denying that regularization takes place (Austria and Germany). A recent study estimated that in Europe over 6 million people have applied to transit from irregular to legal status over the decade to 2007, with an approval rate of 80 percent. The numbers in each country vary hugely—Italy having the highest (1.5 million), followed by Spain and Greece.

Regularization programmes are not limited to the OECD. A regional agreement in Latin America, MERCOSUR, means that Argentina, for example, has legislated that any citizen of a MERCOSUR country without a criminal background can obtain legal residence. In South Africa efforts are underway to regularize irregular Zimbabweans, beginning with a temporary residence permit that grants them access to health care and education and the right to stay and work for at least six months. In Thailand 135,000 migrants were regularized in early 2008, although in the past periods of regularization were followed by stepped-up rates of deportation.

The pros and cons of regularization have been hotly debated. The benefits for the destination country relate to security and the rule of law, while the individuals and families who are regularized may be better placed to overcome social and economic exclusion. Among the disadvantages are concerns about encouraging future flows, the undermining of formal admissions programmes and fraudulent applications. At the same time, the benefits of regularization are highly dependent on context. For example, in the United States many irregular immigrants already pay taxes, so the revenue benefits are much lower than in countries with large informal economies, where taxes are avoided on a much larger scale. Surveys of country experiences have tended to conclude that the socio-economic impacts of regularization have been mixed, with the expected positive impacts on wages, mobility and integration not always materializing.

Source: ICMPD (2009), Cerrutti (2009) and Martin (2009b).

Right to apply for extension and pathways to permanence. This will be at the discretion of the host government and, as at present, is usually subject to a set of specific conditions. Nevertheless, extension of temporary permits is possible in many developed countries (e.g. Canada, Portugal, Sweden, United Kingdom and United States), and some developing countries (e.g. Ecuador and Malaysia). Whether the permit is renewed indefinitely may depend on bilateral agreements. Some countries grant the opportunity for migrants to convert temporary into permanent status after several years of regular residence (e.g. in Italy after six years, and in Portugal and the United Kingdom after five). This may be conditional on, for example, the migrant's labour market record and lack of criminal convictions.[5]

Provisions to facilitate circularity. The freedom to move back and forth between host and source country can enhance benefits for migrants and their origin countries. Again, this can be subject to discretion or to certain conditions. Portability of accumulated social security benefits is a further advantage that can encourage circularity.

The issue of irregular status inevitably crops up in almost any discussion of immigration. Various approaches have been used by governments to address the issue. Amnesty schemes are announced and remain open for a finite period—these have been used in various European countries as well as in Latin America. Ongoing administrative mechanisms may grant some type of legal status on a discretionary basis—for example, on the basis of family ties, as is possible in the United States. Forced returns to the country of origin have also been pursued. None of these measures is uncontroversial. Box 5.2 summarizes recent regularization experiences.[6]

So-called 'earned regularizations', as tried in a number of countries, may be the most viable way forward.[7] These provide irregular migrants with a provisional permit to live and work in the host country, initially for a finite period, which can be extended or made permanent through the fulfilment of various criteria, such as language acquisition, maintaining stable employment and paying taxes. There is no initial amnesty but rather a conditional permission to transit to full residence status. This approach has the attraction of potentially garnering broad public acceptance.

The varied European experience suggests that among the key ingredients of successful regularizations are the involvement of civil society organizations, migrant associations and employers in planning and implementation; guarantee against expulsion during the process; and clear qualifying criteria (for example, length of residence, employment record and family ties).[8] Among the challenges faced in practice are long delays. With locally administered schemes, as in France, variable treatment across locations may be an issue.

Forced returns are especially controversial. Their number has been rising sharply in some countries, surpassing 350,000 in the United States and 300,000 in South Africa in 2008 alone. Pushed enthusiastically by rich country governments, forced returns also feature in the European Union's mobility partnerships.[9] Many origin states cooperate with destination countries by signing readmission agreements, although some, for example South Africa, have so far declined to sign.

What should humane enforcement policies look like? Most people argue that there need to be some sanctions for breaches of border control and work rules and that, alongside discretionary regularization, forced returns have a place in the policy armoury. But implementing this sanction raises major challenges, especially in cases where the individuals concerned have lived and worked in the country for many years and may have family members who are legally resident. For example, a recent survey of Salvadorian deportees found that one quarter had resided in the United States for more than 20 years, and that about four fifths were working at the time of their deportation, many with children born in the United States.[10] In various countries, including the United Kingdom, the media have occasionally taken up cases of threatened deportation that have seemed particularly inhumane.

It is clearly important that, where individuals with irregular status are identified, enforcement procedures should follow the rule of law and basic rights should be respected. There is a need to establish the accountability of employers who engage workers with irregular status. This has been a topic of debate in the United

States, for example. Formal processes to determine whether or not individuals have the legal right to stay in the country are clearly better than summary or mass expulsions, which have been observed in the past (e.g. Malaysia's expulsion of irregular Indonesian workers in early 2005)[11], although some procedural aspects, such as the right to counsel, may represent an unwelcome burden on the public purse in developing countries. The United Kingdom Prison Inspectorate has published Immigration Detention Expectations based on international human rights standards. But mere publication does not, of course, ensure that the standards are met. In some countries, NGOs work to improve living conditions in detention camps—the Ukrainian Red Cross is an example. The recent European Union directive on the procedures for return appears to be a step towards transparency and harmonization of regulations, with an emphasis on standard procedures either to expel people with irregular status or to grant them definite legal status. The directive has, however, been criticized as inadequate in guaranteeing respect for human rights.[12]

5.1.2 Ensuring basic rights for migrants

This report has focused on mobility through the lens of expanding freedoms. But not all migrants achieve all the freedoms that migration promises. Depending on where they come from and go to, people frequently find themselves having to trade off one kind of freedom against another, most often in order to access higher earnings by working in a country where one or more fundamental human rights are not respected. Migrants who lack resources, networks, information and avenues of recourse are more likely to lose out in some dimensions, as too are those who face racial or other forms of discrimination. Major problems can arise for those without legal status and for those in countries where governance and accountability structures are weak.

Refugees are a distinct legal category of migrants by virtue of their need for international protection. They have specific rights, set out in the 1951 Refugee Convention and 1967 Protocols, which have been ratified by 144 states (figure 5.1).[13] These agreements provide critical protection to those fleeing across international borders to escape persecution.

Where individuals with irregular status are identified, enforcement procedures should follow the rule of law and basic rights should be respected

More generally, the six core international human rights treaties, which have been ratified by 131 countries around the globe, all contain strong non-discrimination clauses ensuring the applicability of many provisions to migrants.[14] These instruments are universal and apply to both citizens and non-citizens, including those who have moved or presently stay, whether their status is regular or irregular. Of particular relevance are the rights to equality under the law and to be free from discrimination on grounds of race, national origin or other status. These are important legal constraints on state action.[15]

Recently, protocols against the trafficking and smuggling of people have rapidly garnered broad support, building on existing instruments with 129 ratifications.[16] These protocols, which seek to criminalize trafficking, focus more on suppressing organized crime and facilitating orderly migration than on advancing the human rights of the individuals (mainly women) involved.[17] Many states have enacted these principles into national legislation: of the 155 states surveyed in 2008, some 80 percent had introduced a specific offence of trafficking in persons and more than half had created a special anti-trafficking police unit.[18] Progress on this front is

clearly welcome, although some observers have noted that increasingly harsh immigration policies have also tended to promote trafficking and smuggling.[19]

By way of contrast, the series of ILO conventions adopted throughout the 20th century, which seek to promote minimum standards for migrant workers, have not attracted wide endorsement. The causes are several, including the scope and comprehensiveness of the conventions versus the desire for unfettered state discretion in such matters. In 1990, the UN International Convention on the Protection of the Rights of All Migrant Workers and Members of their Families (CMW) reiterated the core principles of the human rights treaties, but also went further, for example in defining discrimination more broadly, in providing stronger safeguards against collective and arbitrary expulsion and in ensuring the right of regular migrants to vote and be elected. However, there are only 41 signatories to date, of which only five are net immigration countries and none belong to the very high-HDI category (figure 5.1).

Looking behind figure 5.1 to examine the migration profiles of ratifying countries, we found that most have immigration and emigration rates below 10 percent. Among the countries where the share of the population who are either migrants or emigrants exceeds 25 percent, the rates of signing are still low—only 3 out of 64 have signed up to the CMW, for example, although 22 have signed the six core human rights treaties. Even among countries with net outmigration rates exceeding 10 percent of their population—which have strong incentives to sign in order to protect their workers abroad—ratification rates of the CMW are low. Only 20 percent of high-emigration country governments have signed the CMW over the almost two decades of its existence, whereas half have ratified the six core human rights treaties and 59 percent are signatories to the more recent trafficking protocol.

Countries that have not ratified the CMW are still obliged to protect migrant workers, through other core human rights treaties. Treaty Monitoring Bodies (TMBs) under existing conventions are now supplemented by periodic review by UNHCR. Recent analysis of a decade of deliberations by TMBs reveals that the relevant

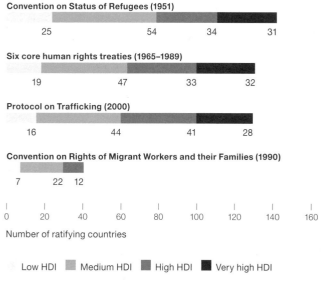

Figure **5.1**

Ratification of migrants' rights convention has been limited
Ratification of selected agreements by HDI category, as of 2009

Convention on Status of Refugees (1951)
25   54   34   31

Six core human rights treaties (1965–1989)
19   47   33   32

Protocol on Trafficking (2000)
16   44   41   28

Convention on Rights of Migrant Workers and their Families (1990)
7   22   12

0   20   40   60   80   100   120   140   160
Number of ratifying countries

Low HDI   Medium HDI   High HDI   Very high HDI

Source: UNODC (2004) and UN (2009b).

provisions of other core human rights treaties can highlight problems and protect the rights of migrants, and have increasingly done so over time.[20] Even if each country naturally seeks to portray its human rights record in the best light, TMBs can, despite the lack of enforcement mechanisms, influence through 'naming and shaming', highlighting egregious cases and seeking moral or political suasion.

Ensuring the rights of migrants has been a recurrent cry in all global forums, as exemplified by the statements made by civil society organizations at the 2008 Global Forum on Migration and Development in Manila. Yet it is also clear that the main challenge is not the lack of a legal framework for the protection of rights—as a series of conventions, treaties and customary law provisions already exist—but rather their effective implementation. In this spirit, in 2005 the ILO developed a Multilateral Framework on Labour Migration, which provides guidelines and good practices within a non-binding framework that recognizes the sovereign right of all states to determine their own migration policies. This 'soft law' type of approach accommodates the inherent differences between states and allows for gradual implementation.[21]

Even if there is no appetite to sign up to formal conventions, there is no sound reason for any government to deny such basic migrant rights as the right to:
- Equal remuneration for equal work, decent working conditions and protection of health and safety;
- Organize and bargain collectively;
- Not be subject to arbitrary detention, and be subject to due process in the event of deportation;
- Not be subject to cruel, inhumane or degrading treatment; and
- Return to countries of origin.

These should exist alongside basic human rights of liberty, security of person, freedom of belief and protection against forced labour and trafficking.

One argument against ensuring basic rights has been that this would necessarily reduce the numbers of people allowed to enter. However as we showed in chapter 2, this trade-off does not generally hold such and an argument is in any case not justifiable on moral grounds.

The prime responsibility for ensuring basic rights while abroad lies with host governments. Attempts by source country governments, such as India and the Philippines, to mandate minimum wages paid to emigrants have typically failed due to the lack of jurisdiction over this matter. Source country governments can nonetheless provide support in terms of advising about migrants' rights and responsibilities through migrant resource centres and pre-departure orientation about what to expect while abroad.

Consular services can play an important part in providing a channel for complaints and possible recourse, while bilateral agreements can establish key principles. However, a collective and coordinated effort by countries of origin to raise standards is more likely to be effective than isolated national efforts.

Employers, unions, NGOs and migrant associations also have a role. Employers are the main source of breaches of basic rights—hence their behaviour is paramount. Some employers have sought to set a good example by developing codes of conduct and partnering with the Business for Social Responsibility programme for migrant workers' rights, which focuses on situations where there are no effective mechanisms for enforcing existing labour laws.[22] Among the measures available to unions and NGOs are: informing migrants about their rights, working more closely with employers and government officials to ensure that these rights are respected, unionizing migrant workers and advocating for regularization. One active NGO, is the Collectif de défense des travailleurs étrangers dans l'agriculture (CODESTRAS), which seeks to improve the situation of seasonal workers in the South of France through awareness-raising, information, dissemination and legal support.[23]

The role of trade unions is particularly important. Over time, unions have accorded greater attention to migrants' rights. The World Values Survey of 2005/2006, covering 52 countries, suggests that rates of union membership are higher among people with a migrant background: 22 percent of those who have a migrant parent are members of a labour union, compared to 17 percent of those who do not. This difference is especially large in low-HDI countries.[24]

The prime responsibility for ensuring basic rights while abroad lies with host governments... Employers, unions, NGOs and migrant associations also have a role

Rationalizing 'paper walls' in countries of origin is an important part of reducing the barriers to legal migration

Last but not least, migrants themselves can affect the way destination communities and societies perceive immigration. Sometimes, negative public opinion partly reflects past incidents of unlawful behaviour associated with migrants. By supporting more inclusive societies and communities, where everyone—including migrants—understands and respects the law and pursues peaceful forms of participation and, if necessary, protest, migrants can alleviate the risk of such negative reactions. Civil society and local authorities can help by supporting migrant networks and communities.[25]

5.1.3 Reducing transaction costs associated with movement

Moving across borders inevitably involves transaction costs. Distance complicates job matching, both within countries and, more acutely, across national borders, because of information gaps, language barriers and varying regulatory frameworks. This creates a need for intermediation and facilitation services. Given the magnitude of income differences between low- and very high-HDI countries, it is not surprising that there is a market for agents who can match individuals with jobs abroad and help navigate the administrative restrictions associated with international movement.

Under current migration regimes, the major cost is typically the administrative requirement that a job offer be obtained from a foreign employer before departure. Especially in Asia, many migrant workers rely on commercial agents to organize the offer and make all the practical arrangements. Most agents are honest brokers and act through legal channels, but some lack adequate information on the employers and/or the workers or smuggle people through borders illegally.

This market for intermediation services can be problematic, however. In the worst cases it can result in trafficking and years of bondage, violent abuse and sometimes even death. A much more common problem is high fees, especially for low-skilled workers. Intermediation often generates surplus profits for recruiters, due to the combination of restrictive entry and high labour demand for low-skilled workers, who frequently lack adequate information and have unequal bargaining power. The costs also appear to be regressive, rising as the level of skills falls,

meaning that, for example, few migrant nurses pay recruitment fees but most domestic helpers do. Asian migrants moving to the Gulf states often pay 25–35 percent of what they expect to earn over two or three years in recruitment and other fees.[26] In some cases, corruption imposes additional costs. Extensive administrative regulation can be counterproductive in that it is more likely to expose migrants to corruption and creates rents for middlemen, officials and others who grease the wheels of the system.

Governments can help to reduce transaction costs for migrant workers in several ways. Six areas deserve priority consideration:

Opening corridors and introducing regimes that allow free movement. Because of MERCOSUR, for example, Bolivian workers can travel relatively freely to Argentina, as well as learn about jobs and opportunities from friends and relatives through deepening social networks. The same dynamic was observed on an accelerated basis following European Union enlargement in 2004. Another example is facilitated access for seasonal workers across the Guatemala–Mexico border.

Reducing the cost of and easing access to official documents, such as birth certificates and passports. Rationalizing 'paper walls' in countries of origin is an important part of reducing the barriers to legal migration.[27] Analysis at the level of the country and migration corridor is needed to identify the types and amounts of upfront costs, which can range from travelling multiple times from the village to the capital to apply for a passport, to the fees for other pre-departure requirements such as health checks, police clearances, insurance fees and bank guarantees. Prospective migrants in the Mexico–Canada programme go to the capital city six times on average—a requirement that prompted the government to offer a stipend to cover travel costs (although rationalizing the administrative requirements would have been more efficient).[28] Some costs arise from destination country requirements. For example, the Republic of Korea requires that migrants learn the language before arrival: while language training increases earnings and promotes integration, it also increases pre-arrival debt.[29] A number of countries have attempted to speed up paperwork for migrants, with varying degrees of success (box 5.3).

Empowerment of migrants, through access to information, rights of recourse abroad and stronger social networks. The latter, in particular, can do much to plug the information gap between migrant workers and employers, limiting the need for costly recruitment agencies and enabling migrants to pick and choose among a wider variety of employment opportunities.[30] In Malaysia migrant networks allow Indonesians to learn about new job openings before the news even reaches local residents.[31] Similarly, improved telecommunication has helped prospective migrants in Jamaica become better informed.[32] Information centres, such as the pilot launched by the European Union in Bamako, Mali in 2008, can provide potential migrants with accurate (if disappointing!) information about opportunities for work and study abroad.

Regulation of private recruiters to prevent abuses and fraud. Prohibitions do not tend to work, in part because bans in destination places do not apply to recruiters in source areas.[33] Yet some regulations can be effective, for example joint liability between employers and recruiters, which can help to avert fraud and deceit. In the Philippines recruitment agencies are treated as 'co-employers', liable jointly and separately for failure to comply with a given contract. An agency found to be at fault risks having its license revoked, although suspension is often avoided by payment of a fine. Self-regulation through industry associations and codes of conduct is another means of promoting ethical standards. Industry associations can collect and disseminate information on high-risk agencies and best practices. Many such associations exist in South and East Asia, although none has emerged as a self-regulatory body similar to those found in developed countries, since most have focused on ensuring that government policy on migration is friendly to the recruitment industry—as, for example, in Bangladesh, the Philippines and Sri Lanka.[34] Such associations could develop over time to play a more effective role in assuring the quality of services and, where necessary, censuring members for lax standards.

Direct administration of recruitment by public agencies. In Guatemala, for example, the IOM administers a programme that sends seasonal farm workers to Canada at no charge to the worker. However there is debate about the

Box **5.3** **Reducing paperwork: a challenge for governments and partners**

A prime example of streamlined deployment despite extensive administrative requirements is the Philippine Overseas Employment Administration, which regulates all aspects of recruitment and works closely with other agencies to ensure the protection of its workers abroad. Indonesia has attempted to follow suit, establishing the National Agency for the Placement and Protection of Indonesian Migrant Workers (BNP2TKI) in 2006, although low bureaucratic capacity and weak intergovernmental coordination have reportedly compromised BNP2TKI's effectiveness. Other countries have attempted to address issues related to delays and costs, but few have succeeded. In Gabon the government instituted a 3-day limit on the waiting time for passports, but the delays remain long and the process arduous. Similarly, the Myanmar government recently instituted a policy for passports to be issued within one week, but continuing complaints suggest that delays and demands for bribes remain common.

Development assistance programmes could support and finance administrative improvements for vital records registration with shorter processing times and lower costs. This would allow governments to offer their citizens proper travel documents at affordable prices. Bangladesh, which has a birth registration rate of below 10 percent, has partnered with the United Nations Children's Fund (UNICEF) on this front.

Source: Agunias (2008), Tirtosudarmo (2009), United States Department of State (2009e), Koslowski (2009), and UNICEF (2007).

appropriate role for government agencies. In most poor countries, the capacity of national employment agencies to match workers with suitable jobs at home, let alone abroad, is very weak.[35] Some bilateral agreements, such as those signed by the Republic of Korea, require migrants to use government agencies, prompting complaints from recruiters and workers about high costs and lack of transparency. The fees charged by public recruiters are sometimes lower, but the costs in terms of time can be significant and can discourage prospective migrants from using regular channels.[36]

Intergovernmental cooperation. This can play an important role. The Colombo Process and the Abu Dhabi Dialogue are two recent intergovernmental initiatives designed to cooperatively address transactions costs and other issues. This process, which took place for the first time in January 2008, involved almost a dozen source and several destination countries in the GCC states and South East Asia, with the United Arab Emirates and IOM serving as the co-hosts. It focuses on developing key partnerships between countries of origin and destination around the subject of temporary contractual labour to, among other things, develop and share

Inclusion and integration are critical from a human development perspective

knowledge on labour market trends, prevent illegal recruitment, and promote welfare and protection measures for contractual workers. The ministerial consultation is intended to take place every two years. A pilot project followed where under the initiative of the governments of India, the Philippines and the United Arab Emirates there will be a test and identification of best practices in different aspects of temporary and circular migration, beginning with a group of Filipino and Indian workers in the sectors of construction, health and hospitality.[37]

5.1.4 Improving outcomes for migrants and destination communities

While the weight of evidence shows that the aggregate economic impact of migration in the long run is likely to be positive, local people with specific skills or in certain locations may experience adverse effects. To a large extent these can be minimized and offset by policies and programmes that recognize and plan for the presence of migrants, promoting inclusion and ensuring that receiving communities are not unduly burdened. It is important to recognize the actual and perceived costs of immigration at the community level, and consider how these might be shared.

Inclusion and integration are critical from a human development perspective, since they have positive effects not only for individual movers and their families but also for receiving communities. The ways in which the status and rights of immigrants are recognized and enforced will determine the extent of such integration. In some developing countries, support for integration could be an appropriate candidate for development assistance.

Yet institutional and policy arrangements may often be more important than targeted migrant integration policies. For example, the quality of state schooling in poor neighbourhoods is likely to be critical—and not only for migrants. Within this broader context, the policy priorities for improving outcomes for migrants and destination communities are as follows:

Provide access to basic services—particularly schooling and health care. These services are not only critical to migrants and their families, but also have broader positive externalities. Here the key is equity of access and treatment. Our review

suggests that access is typically most restricted for temporary workers and people with irregular status. Access to schooling should be provided on the same basis and terms as for locally born residents. The same applies for health care—both emergency care in the case of accidents or severe illness and preventive services such as vaccinations, which are typically also in the best interests of the whole community and highly effective in the long term. Some developing countries, for example Costa Rica, grant migrants access to public health facilities regardless of status.[38]

Help newcomers acquire language proficiency. Services in this area can contribute greatly to labour market gains and inclusion more generally. They need to be designed with the living and working constraints faced by migrants in mind. The needs of adults vary, depending on whether or not they are working outside the home, while children can access school-based programmes. Among good practice examples are Australia, which provides advanced language training to migrants and indigenous populations.[39] Examples of targeted language learning for children include the Success for All programme in the United States, which combines group instruction and individual tutoring at the pre-school and primary school levels.[40] Several European countries provide language courses for newcomers through programmes offered by central government, state schools, municipalities and NGOs, such as the Swedish for Immigrants programme that dates back to 1965, the Portugal Acolhe programme offered since 2001, and the Danish Labour Market programme introduced in 2007.

Allow people to work. This is the single most important reform for improving human development outcomes for migrants, especially poorer and more vulnerable migrants. Access to the labour market is vital not just because of the associated economic gains but also because employment greatly increases the prospects for social inclusion. Restrictions on seeking paid work, as have traditionally been applied to asylum seekers and refugees in many developed countries, are damaging both to short- and medium-term outcomes, since they encourage dependency and destroy self-respect. They should be abolished. Allowing people to move among employers is a further basic principle of well-designed programmes, which are concerned with the interests of migrants and not solely with those of employers. In many countries, high-skilled newcomers also face problems in accreditation of the qualifications they bring from abroad (box 5.4).

Support local government roles. Strong local government, accountable to local users, is essential for the delivery of services such as primary health and education. However, in some countries, government officials implicitly deny the existence of migrants by excluding them from development plans and allowing systematic discrimination to thrive. Improving individual and community outcomes associated with migration requires local governments that aim to[41]:

- Promote inclusive local governance structures to enable participation and accountability;
- Avoid institutional practices that contribute to discrimination;
- Ensure that law and order plays a facilitating role, including an effective and responsive police service;
- Provide relevant information for the public and for civil society organizations, including migrants' associations;[42] and
- Ensure equitable land use planning, consistent with the needs of the poor—for example, options to alleviate tenure insecurity and related constraints.

Address local budget issues, including fiscal transfers to finance additional local needs. Often, responsibility for the provision of basic services such as schools and clinics lies with local authorities, whose budgets may be strained by growing populations and who may lack the tax base to address their responsibilities for service delivery. Where subnational governments have an important role in financing basic services, redistributive fiscal mechanisms can help offset imbalances between revenue and expenditure allocations. Intergovernmental transfers are typically made across states and localities on the basis of at least two criteria: need (such as population, poverty rates, and so on) and revenue-generating capacity (so as not to discourage local taxation efforts). Since circumstances and objectives differ from country to country, no single pattern of transfers is universally appropriate. Per capita grants require that all people present, including irregular migrants and their families, should be counted. Transfers may also be used to reimburse specific

---

| Box **5.4** | **Recognition of credentials** |

Many migrants, especially from poorer countries, are well qualified yet unable to use their skills abroad. Accreditation of skills is rarely practised in Europe, for example, even where there are institutional arrangements in place that are supposed to facilitate recognition.

There are reasons why immediate accreditation is not allowed. For example, it may be difficult to judge the quality of overseas qualifications, and there may be a premium on local knowledge (e.g. lawyers, with respect to applicable legislation).

Among the strategies available to promote the use of skills and qualifications held by foreigners are the following:

- *Mutual recognition agreements.* These are most common between countries with similar systems of education and levels of economic development, as in the European Union.
- *Prior vetting.* Both source and destination governments can vet the credentials of potential migrants before they leave. Australia has pioneered this approach. However, if an individual's goal is to enhance her human development via migration, the wait for credential recognition may be more costly than trying her luck in some other country, especially if she is unable to practise her profession at home or works there for a low wage.
- *Fast-track consideration.* Governments can facilitate fast-track consideration of credentials and establish national offices to expedite recognition. Mentors and short courses abroad can help migrants fill any gaps. Some states in the United States have established 'New Americans' offices to help newcomers navigate what can be a maze, even for internal migrants.
- *Recognition of on-the-job skills.* Many skills are learned on the job and mechanisms for recognizing such informally learned skills may be lacking. Developing the capacity to recognize and certify on-the-job skills could make it easier for workers to have their skills recognized abroad.

Source: Iredale (2001).

---

costs, especially in social services, where there is a strong argument for equalization of access. Well-designed transfer systems do not rely heavily on earmarking, and the grants should be made in as simple, reliable and transparent a way as possible.[43]

Address discrimination and xenophobia. Appropriate interventions by governments and civil society can foster tolerance at the community level. This is especially important where there is a risk of violence, although in practice policy responses tend to emerge *ex post*. In response to violence in Côte d'Ivoire, for example, an Anti-Xenophobia Law was passed in August 2008 to impose sanctions on conduct that incites such violence.[44] Civil society can also work to engender tolerance and protect diversity, as demonstrated recently in South Africa, where the 'No to Xenophobia' emergency mobile phone

It is critical to ensure fair treatment of migrants during recessions

SMS network was initiated after the violence of May 2008.[45] Another example is the Campaign for Diversity, Human Rights and Participation, organized by the Council of Europe in partnership with the European Commission and the European Youth Forum. This emphasized the role of the media in combating prejudice against Muslim and Roma peoples, and offered awards for municipalities that actively advance protection and inclusion.[46] Of course, where discrimination and tensions are deep-seated and have erupted in violence, and especially where the rule of law is weak, it will take time as well as much effort and goodwill for such efforts to bear fruit.

Ensure fair treatment during recession. This has assumed some urgency in 2009, which has brought reports of backlashes and deportations around the world. Among the provisions that can protect migrant workers against undue hardship are to[47]:

• Allow those laid off to look for a new job, at least until their existing work and residence permits expire;

• Ensure that those who are laid off before the end of their contracts can claim severance payments and/or unemployment benefits when entitled to do so;

• Step up labour law enforcement so as to minimize abuses (e.g. wage arrears) where workers are fearful of layoffs;

• Ensure continued access to basic services (health and education) and to job search services;

• Support institutions in origin countries that help laid-off workers to return and provide training grants and support; and

• Improve disaggregated data—including data on layoffs and wages, by sector and gender—so that origin governments and communities can become aware of changes in employment prospects.

If governments take these types of measures, the economic crisis could become an opportunity to promote better treatment and avoid conflict.

It is important to give credit where it is due. There are examples where state and local governments have embraced migration and its broader social and cultural implications. The recent West Australian Charter on Multiculturalism is an interesting example of a state-level commitment to the elimination of discrimination and the promotion of cohesion and inclusion among individuals and groups.[48] Many of the foregoing recommendations are already standard policy in some OECD countries, although there tends to be plenty of variability in practice. The boldest reforms are needed in a number of major destination countries, including, for example, South Africa and the United Arab Emirates, where current efforts to enable favourable human development outcomes for individuals and communities fall far short of what is needed.

5.1.5 Enabling benefits from internal mobility

In terms of the number of people involved, internal migration far exceeds external migration. An estimated 136 million people have moved in China alone, and 42 million in India, so the totals for just these two countries approach the global stock of people who have crossed frontiers. This reflects the fact that mobility is not only a natural part of human history but a continuing dimension of development and of modern societies, in which people seek to connect to emerging opportunities and change their circumstances accordingly.

Given these realities, government policies should seek to facilitate, not hinder, the process of internal migration. The policies and programmes in place should not adversely affect those who move. By the same token, they should not require people to move in order to access basic services and livelihood opportunities. These two principles lead to a series of recommendations that are entirely within the jurisdiction of all national governments to implement:

Remove the barriers to internal mobility. To ensure full and equal civic, economic and social rights for all, it is vital to lift legal and administrative constraints to mobility and to combat discrimination against movers. As reviewed in chapter 2, administrative barriers are less common since the demise of central planning in large parts of the world—but some are remarkably persistent, despite typically failing to curb mobility to any marked degree. Such barriers are contrary to international law. They are also costly and time-consuming to maintain for government and to negotiate for movers. Many opt to travel without the proper documentation, only to find later that they cannot access key services. Internal migrants should have equal access to the full range of public services and benefits, especially education and health, but also pensions and social assistance where these are provided.

Freedom of movement is especially important for seasonal and temporary workers, who are typically among the poorest migrants and have often been neglected or actively discriminated against. These types of migration flows can present acute challenges for local authorities responsible for the provision of services, which need to learn to cater to more fluid populations. Partial reforms that allow migrants to work but not to access services on an equal basis (as is the case in China) are not enough. Reforms have been introduced in some states in India—for example, allowing seasonal migrants to obtain temporary ration cards—but implementation has been slow.[49]

Provide appropriate support to movers at destination. Just as they should do for people coming from abroad, governments should provide appropriate support to people who move internally. This may be done in partnership with local communities and NGOs. Some people who move are disadvantaged—due to lack of education, prejudice against ethnic minorities and linguistic differences—and therefore need targeted support programmes. Support could be provided in areas ranging from job search to language training. Access to social assistance and other entitlements should be ensured. Above all, it is vital to ensure that basic health care and education needs are met. India has examples of NGO-run children's hostels to help children of migrants access accommodation, schooling and extra classes to catch up.

Redistribute tax revenues. Intergovernmental fiscal arrangements should ensure the redistribution of revenues so that poorer localities, where internal migrants often live, do not bear a disproportionate burden in providing adequate local public services. The same principles as apply to fiscal redistribution to account for the location of international migrants also apply here.

Enhance responsiveness. This may sound obvious and should by now go without saying, but it is vital to build the capacity of local government

and programmes to respond to people's needs. Inclusive and accountable local government can play a central role not only in service provision but also in averting and alleviating social tensions. Proactive urban planning, rather than denial, is needed to avoid the social and economic marginalization of migrants.

The Millennium Development Goals (MDGs) call for action plans to create 'Cities without Slums' to, inter alia, improve sanitation and secure land tenure. However, progress has been slow: according to the most recent global MDG report, more than a third of the world's urban population lives in slum conditions, rising to over 60 percent in sub-Saharan Africa.[50]

Governments sometimes respond to concerns about slums by seeking to curb inflows of migrants to cities, as revealed by the review of PRSs presented in chapter 4. However, a more constructive policy approach would be to meet the needs of a growing and shifting population by addressing the serious water and sanitation challenges that tend to prevail in slum areas. With proactive planning and sufficient resources, it is possible to ensure that growing cities can provide decent living conditions. Some cities, recognizing the importance of sustainable urban development, have come up with innovative solutions for improving the lives of city dwellers. Singapore's experience with urban renewal is widely cited as a best practice example: virtually all of its squatter settlements were replaced with high-rise public housing, complemented by expanded public transport and improved environmental management. A more recent example comes from Alexandria, Egypt, where participatory approaches have been used to develop medium- and long-term plans for economic development, urban upgrading of slum areas and environmental regeneration.[51]

Last but not least, many rural migrants describe being pushed rather than pulled to urban areas because of inadequate public facilities in their place of origin. The universal provision of services and infrastructure should extend to places experiencing net out-migration. This will provide opportunities for people to develop the skills to be productive and to compete for jobs in their place of origin, while also preparing them for jobs elsewhere if they so choose.

Inclusive and accountable local government can play a central role not only in service provision but also in averting and alleviating social tensions

Migration can be a vital strategy for households and families seeking to diversify and improve their livelihoods

5.1.6 Making mobility an integral part of national development strategies

A central theme of the 2009 Global Forum on Migration and Development, hosted by Greece, is the integration of migration into national development strategies. This raises the broader question of the role of mobility in strategies for improving human development. Our analysis of PRSs since 2000 helped to identify current policy attitudes and constraints, while recognizing that migration has played a major role in national visions of development at different moments and periods in history.

The links between mobility and development are complex, in large part because mobility is best seen as a component of human development rather than an isolated cause or effect of it. The relationship is further complicated by the fact that, in general, the largest developmental gains from mobility accrue to those who go abroad—and are thus beyond the realm of the territorial and place-focused approaches that tend to dominate policy thinking.

Migration can be a vital strategy for households and families seeking to diversify and improve their livelihoods, especially in developing countries. Flows of money have the potential to improve well-being, stimulate economic growth and reduce poverty, directly and indirectly. However, migration, and remittances in particular, cannot compensate for an institutional environment that hinders economic and social development more generally. A critical point that emerges from experience is the importance of national economic conditions and strong public-sector institutions in enabling the broader benefits of mobility to be reaped.

We have seen that the mobility choices of the poor are often constrained. This can arise from underlying inequalities in their skills, but also from policy and institutional barriers. Needed now is country-specific identification of the constraints surrounding people's choices, using quantitative and qualitative data and analysis. Improvements in data, alongside such recent initiatives as the development of migration profiles (supported by the European Commission and other partners), will be crucial to this effort. This would highlight barriers and inform attempts to improve national strategies.

Some development strategies—8 of the 84 PRSs prepared between 2000 and 2008[52]—raise concerns about the exit of graduates. There is broad agreement that coercive policies to limit exit, as well as being contrary to international law, are not the right way to proceed, for both ethical and economic reasons.[53] However, there is less agreement as to what alternative policies should look like. Box 5.5 looks at the merits of different options.

Finally, while this topic is beyond the focus of this report, we underline the importance of sustained efforts to promote human development at home.[54] A comprehensive investigation of the sources of human development success and failure and its implications for national development strategies will be a major theme of the next HDR, which marks the 20th anniversary of the global report.

5.2 The political feasibility of reform

Against a background of popular scepticism about migration, a critical issue is the political feasibility of our proposals. This section argues that reform is possible, but only if steps are taken to address the concerns of local people, so that they no longer view immigration as a threat, either to themselves individually or to their society.

While the evidence on mobility points to significant gains for movers and, in many cases, benefits also for destination and origin countries, any discussion of policy must recognize that in many destination countries, both developed and developing, attitudes among the local population towards migration are at best mildly permissive and often quite negative. An array of opinion polls and other surveys suggest that residents see controls on immigration as essential and most would prefer to see existing rules on entry tightened rather than relaxed. Interestingly, however, attitudes to migration appear to be more positive in countries where the migrant population share in 1995 was large and where rates of increase over the past decade have been high.[55] In terms of the treatment of migrants, the picture is more positive, as people tend to support equitable treatment of migrants already within their borders.

We begin with the vexed issue of liberalizing entry. The evidence suggests that opposition to liberalization is widespread, but the picture is

Box **5.5**   **When skilled people emigrate: some policy options**

Taxing citizens abroad—sometimes termed a Bhagwati tax—has been a longstanding proposal and is an established feature of the United States tax system. It can be justified by the notion that citizenship implies responsibilities, including the payment of tax, especially by the better off. If entry barriers create a shortage of skilled labour in destination countries and hence higher incomes for those who do manage to move, taxing these rents is non-distortionary and would not affect the global allocation of labour.

However, there are several arguments against imposing a surcharge on nationals abroad, who may already be paying tax to their new host countries. First, implementation would either be on a voluntary basis or through bilateral tax agreements. But people do not like paying taxes—and there is no consensus among governments as to the desirability of migrant taxation, largely because it is administratively costly. Second, while some emigrants will have benefited from attending a public university at home, others will have been educated abroad or privately. Third, through remittances, investment and other mechanisms, migrants often generate substantial benefits back home. Taxation could discourage these flows and persuade emigrants to relinquish their citizenship in favour of their new homeland.

Hence implementation of such taxes has been very limited. The Philippines tried, but experience was very mixed and the approach was shelved nearly a decade ago. Today most governments, including the Philippines, grant tax holidays to emigrants.

An alternative way to compensate for skill losses could be direct transfers between governments. Whether self-standing or part of an official development aid package, these have the advantage of simplicity and relatively low transaction costs. However, skill loss is hard to measure. And such transfers would not address the underlying issues that stimulated exit in the first place, such as low-quality educational and health services and/or thin markets for skilled individuals.

Aid is largely fungible, as many studies have shown, so even aid that is earmarked to support the higher education system mostly supports whatever the government is spending money on.

There may still be a case for policy to address skilled emigration in those sectors, such as health and education, where there are potentially large divergences between private and public benefits and costs. Which policy approach has merit depends on local circumstances. For example:

- Targeted incentives in the form of wage supplements for public-sector workers. Such an approach would have to be carefully calibrated, given its possible effects on labour supply. A major constraint here is that the wage differentials are often too great to lie within the fiscal capacity of poor governments.
- Training tailored to skills that are useful in origin countries but less tradable across borders. For example, while an international market for doctors exists, training in paramedic skills may promote better retention of skilled people as well as being more relevant to local health care needs.
- Reform of education financing. This would allow private-sector provision so that people seeking training as a way of moving abroad do not rely on public funding. The Philippines has been taking this route for training its nurses.
- Investment in alternative technologies. Distance services, dispensed by cell-phone, internet telephony or websites, can allow skills that are in short supply to benefit larger numbers of people.
- Targeted development assistance. Where loss of talent is associated with lack of innovation and investment—for example, in agriculture—development assistance could prioritize regional and national research institutions.

Providing incentives for skilled migrants to return has also been tried, but experience has been mixed and it is not clear that this is the best use of scarce public funds. Effectiveness depends partly on the strength of the home institution to which the migrant would return but also, and perhaps more importantly, on the performance and prospects of the whole country. Evidence suggests that returns occur anyway when countries offer sufficiently attractive opportunities. China, India and Mauritius are recent cases in point.

Sources: Clemens (2009b), Bhagwati (1979), Clemens (2009a), Pomp (1989) and World Bank (1998).

not as monochrome as it initially appears. There are four main reasons why this is so.

First, as mentioned in chapter 4, many people are willing to accept immigration if jobs are available. Our proposal links future liberalization to the demand for labour, such that inflows of migrants will respond to vacancy levels. This alleviates the risk that migrants will substitute for or undercut local workers. Indeed, conditions of this kind are already widely applied by governments, particularly in the developed economies,

to the entry of skilled migrants. Our proposal is that this approach be extended to low-skilled workers, with an explicit link to the state of the national labour market, and sectoral needs.

Second, our focus on improving the transparency and efficiency of the pathways to permanence for migrants can help address the persistent impression, shared by many local people, that a significant part of cross-border migration is irregular or illegal. Certainly, in the United States the size of the irregular migrant

Figure **5.2**   **Support for opportunity to stay permanently**

Preferences for temporary versus permanent migration, 2008

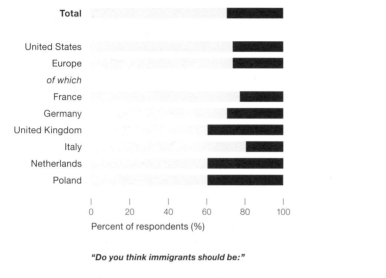

"*Do you think immigrants should be:*"

Allowed the opportunity to stay permanently

■ Only admitted temporarily, then required to return to their country of origin

Source: Transatlantic Trends (2008)

labour force is a major political issue, on which a policy consensus has yet to be reached. Irregular migration is also prominent in other destination countries, both developed and developing. Interestingly, recent data suggest that there is considerable support in developed countries for permanent migration, with over 60 percent of respondents feeling that legal migrants should be given an opportunity to stay permanently (figure 5.2).

To translate this support into action will require the design of policies for legal migration that are explicitly linked to job availability—and the marketing of this concept to the public so as to build on existing levels of support. Parallel measures to address the problem of irregular migration will also need to be designed and implemented, so that the policy vacuum in this area is no longer a source of concern to the public. Large-scale irregular migration, although often convenient for employers and skirted around by policy makers, tends not only to have adverse consequences for migrants themselves (as documented in chapter 3) but also to weaken the acceptability of—and hence the overall case for—further liberalization of entry rules.

Sustainable solutions would have to include incentives for employers to hire regular migrants, as well as incentives for migrants to prefer regular status.

Third, some of the resistance to migration is shaped by popular misperceptions of its consequences. Many believe, for example, that immigrants have a negative impact on the earnings of existing residents or that they are responsible for higher crime levels. These concerns again tend to be more pronounced in relation to irregular migrants, not least because their status is associated with an erosion of the rule of law. There are several broad approaches to these issues that have promise. Public information campaigns and awareness-raising activities are vital. Because migration is a contentious issue, information is often used selectively at present, to support the arguments of specific interest groups. While this is a natural and usually desirable feature of democratic discussion, it can come at the cost of objectivity and factual understanding. For example, a recent review of 20 European countries found that, in every case, the perceived number of immigrants greatly exceeded the actual number, often by a factor of two or more.[56]

To address such vast gaps between perceptions and reality, there is a need to provide the public with more impartial sources of information and analysis on the scale, scope and consequences of migration. A recurring feature of the migration debate is the pervasive mistrust of official statistics and interpretation. Because migration is so vexed a policy issue, more attention needs to be paid to informing public debate on it in ways that are recognized and respected for their objectivity and reliability. Governments can benefit significantly from technical advice given by expert bodies, such as the United Kingdom's Migration Advisory Committee. These should be deliberately kept at arm's length from the administration, so that they are seen as impartial.

Fourth, migration policy is normally formed through the complex interaction of a multitude of players, who form different interest groups and belong to different political parties. Organized groups can and do mobilize to bring about reform, often forming coalitions to pursue change in areas where their interests coincide.[57] For example, employer groups have often been in the vanguard of calls for changes in entry rules in response to labour and/or skill shortages. Destination countries should decide on the design of migration policies and target numbers of migrants through political processes that permit public debate and the balancing of different interests. Further, what may be feasible at the national level needs to be discussed and debated locally, and the design further adapted to meet local constraints. Partly out of fear that debate over migration will take on racist overtones, discussion of migration among mainstream political parties and organizations has often been more muted than might have been expected. While the reasons for caution are laudable, there is a danger that self-censorship will be counter-productive.

How migrants are treated is a further area of policy in which reform may turn out to be easier than at first expected. Equitable treatment of migrants not only accords with basic notions of fairness but can also bring instrumental benefits for destination communities, associated with cultural diversity, higher rates of innovation and other aspects explored in chapter 4. Indeed, the available evidence suggests that people are generally quite tolerant of minorities and have a positive view of ethnic diversity. These attitudes suggest that there are opportunities for building a broad consensus around the better treatment of migrants.

The protection of migrants' rights is increasingly in the interest of the major destination countries that have large numbers of their own nationals working abroad.[58] By 2005, more than 80 countries had significant shares of their populations—in excess of 10 percent—as either immigrants or emigrants. For these countries, observance of the rights of migrants is obviously an important policy objective. This suggests that bilateral or regional arrangements that enable reciprocity could have an important role to play in enacting reforms in a coordinated manner.

While there is clear scope for improving the quality of public debates and of resulting policies, our proposals also recognize that there are very real and important choices and trade-offs to be made. In particular, our proposals have been designed in such a way as to ensure that the gains from further liberalization can be used in part to offset the losses suffered by particular groups

and individuals. Further, while the fiscal costs of migration are not generally significant (as shown in chapter 3), there may be a political case for measures that help improve the perception of burden sharing. For example, Canada has had administrative fees in place for over a decade; other countries, such as the United Kingdom, have followed this approach.

Moreover, the design of policy has to address the potential costs associated with migration. The suggested design of the reform package already ensures that the number of entrants is responsive to labour demand, and helps assure that migrants have regular status. Further measures could include compensation for communities and localities that bear a disproportionate share of the costs of migration in terms of providing access to public services and welfare benefits. This will help to dispel resentments against migrants among specific groups and reduce the support for extremist political parties in areas where immigration is a political issue. An example of this can be found in the case of financial transfers to schools with high migrant pupil numbers, a measure taken in a number of developed countries.

Another important measure to minimize disadvantages to local residents lies in the observance of national and local labour standards. This is a core concern of unions and also of the public, whose distress at the exploitation and abuse of migrants is commendable and a clear sign that progressive reform will prove acceptable. Contemporary examples of union involvement in scheme design and implementation include Barbados, New Zealand and Sweden, which have thereby improved the design and acceptability of their programmes.

Lastly, it should go without saying (but often does not) that participation in decision-making increases the acceptance of reform. This is perhaps the most important measure that governments can take to ensure that changes to migration policy are negotiated with and agreed by different stakeholder groups. The Netherlands is an example where the government has undertaken regular consultations with migrant organizations. Similarly, in New Zealand, 'Kick-Start Forums' have successfully been used to bring together stakeholders to resolve problems in the Recognised Seasonal Employment Scheme.[59]

Equitable treatment of migrants not only accords with basic notions of fairness but can also bring instrumental benefits for destination communities

Mobility has
the potential to
enhance human
development—among
movers, stayers
and the majority of
those in destination
societies

5.3 Conclusions

We began this report by pointing to the extraordinarily unequal global distribution of opportunities and how this is a major driver of the movement of people. Our main message is that mobility has the potential to enhance human development—among movers, stayers and the majority of those in destination societies. However, processes and outcomes can be adverse, sometimes highly so, and there is therefore scope for significant improvements in policies and institutions at the national, regional and international levels. Our core package calls for a bold vision and identifies an ambitious long-term agenda for capturing the large unrealized gains to human development from current and future mobility.

Existing international forums—most notably the Global Forum on Migration and Development—provide valuable opportunities to review challenges and share experiences. Consultations at this level need to be matched by action at other levels. Even on a unilateral basis, governments can take measures to improve outcomes for both international and internal movers. Most of the recommendations

we have made are not conditional on new international agreements. The key reforms with respect to the treatment of migrants and the improvement of destination community outcomes are entirely within the jurisdiction of national governments. In some cases actions are needed at subnational levels—for example to ensure access to basic services. Unilateral action needs to be accompanied by progress in bilateral and regional arrangements. Many governments, both at origin and destination, as well as countries of transit, have signed bilateral agreements. These are typically used to set quotas, establish procedures and define minimum standards. Regional agreements can play an especially important role, especially in establishing free movement corridors.

Our suggested reforms to government policies and institutions could bring about sizeable human development gains from mobility at home and abroad. Advancing this agenda will require committed leadership, extensive consultation with stakeholders and bold campaigning for changes in public opinion to move the debates and policy discussions forward.

Notes

Chapter 1

1 OECD (2009a).

2 Few developing countries have data on flows of migrants. However, the sum of the stock of internal migrants and international migrants in developing countries is considerably larger than the stock of migrants in developed countries (see section 2.1).

3 See the Statistical Tables for life expectancy and income, and Barro and Lee (2001) for years of education.

4 For a discussion of the reasons behind the poor living conditions in the Lower Rio Grande Valley, see Betts and Slottje (1994). Anderson and Gerber (2007b) provide an overview of living conditions along both sides of the border and their evolution over time. Comprehensive data and analysis on human development within the United States can be found in Burd-Sharps, Lewis, and Martins (2008).

5 The number of Chinese who changed their district of residence over the period 1979–2003 is estimated to exceed 250 million (Lu and Wang, 2006). Inter-provincial flows (corresponding to the definition of internal migration we use in the report—see box 1.3) accounted for about a quarter of these movements.

6 Clemens, Montenegro, and Pritchett (2008).

7 Clemens, Montenegro, and Pritchett (2008), Ortega (2009).

8 UNDP (2008d).

9 The practice of compulsory testing of immigrants is not unique to the Arab states. For example, the United States severely restricts the entry of HIV-positive travellers and bars HIV-positive non-citizens from obtaining permanent residence. See U.S.Citizenship and Immigration Services (2008).

10 A search for scholarly articles on international migration using the Social Sciences Citation Index yielded only 1,441 articles—less than a fifth of those dealing with international trade (7,467) and less than one twentieth of those dealing with inflation (30,227).

11 Koslowski (2008).

12 IOM (2008b), World Bank (2006b), ILO (2004), and GFMD (2008).

13 Aliran (2007).

14 Branca (2005).

15 In particular, questioning of the distinction between voluntary and involuntary migration led to terms like 'mixed migration' and the 'migration–asylum nexus'. The use of some of these terms is not uncontroversial, as recognition of economic motives among asylum seekers can have implications for admissions and treatment. See Richmond (1994), van Hear (2003), van Hear, Brubaker, and Bessa (2009), and UNHCR (2001).

16 Bakewell (2008) shows that the return to Angola of many of these migrants since the end of the civil war in 2002 coincided with the attempt by many Zambians to move to Angola in order to participate in expected improvements in social and economic conditions. This suggests that economic motives were at least as important among expatriate Angolans as the desire to return to their country of origin.

17 Van Hear, Brubaker, and Bessa (2009) and Van Engeland and Monsutti (2005).

18 An interesting example of migration flows being disconnected from economic growth differentials was the 1985/86 recession, when Malaysian per capita GDP shrank by 5.4 percent while the Indonesian economy was unaffected, yet migration flows between the two countries continued unabated. See Hugo (1993).

19 This does not mean that migrants in Malaysia are free from discrimination. See Hugo (1993).

20 Attempts to develop a conceptual framework for understanding migration go back at least to Ravenstein (1885), who proposed a set of 'laws of migration' and emphasized the development of cities as 'poles of attraction'. Within neoclassical economic theory, initial expositions include Lewis (1954), and Harris and Todaro (1970), while the tradition of Marxist studies was initiated by discussion of the 'agrarian question' by Kautsky (1899).

21 Stark and Bloom (1985), Stark (1991).

22 Mesnard (2004), Yang (2006).

23 Massey (1988).

24 Gidwani and Sivaramakrishnan (2003).

25 See Nussbaum (1993) on the origins of this idea.

26 Huan-Chang (1911).

27 Plato (2009).

28 Nussbaum (2000).

29 This definition is consistent with more conventional usage. For example, the Oxford English Dictionary defines mobility as "the ability to move or to be moved; capacity for movement or change of place; ... " (Oxford University Press, 2009). The idea of labour mobility as indicating the absence of restrictions on movement, as distinguished from the action of movement itself, also has a long tradition in international economics; see Mundell (1968).

30 Sainath (2004).

31 Sen (2006), p.4.

32 UNDP (1990), p.89.

33 UNDP (1997).

34 UNDP (2004b).

35 See, for example, the idea of using international transfers to reduce emigration pressures in poor countries, which was featured in the 1994 Human Development Report, UNDP (1994).

Chapter 2

1. Bell and Muhidin (2009).

2. Less conservative definitions raise the estimates significantly. For example, while our estimate of 42 million internal migrants (4 percent of the population) in India includes all those who have moved between states, there are 307 million people (28 percent of the population) who live in a different city from where they were born (Deshingkar and Akter, 2009). Montenegro and Hirn (2008) use an intermediate zonal denomination and calculate an average internal migration rate of 19.4 percent for 34 developing countries. Seasonal migration is excluded from both of these estimates. To the best of our knowledge, no comparable cross-country estimates of seasonal migration exist, although country-specific research suggests that it is often high.

3. Immigrants, for example, are defined on the basis of place of birth in 177 countries but on the basis of citizenship in 42 countries. A few countries (including China) do not have information on either their foreign-born or foreign citizens, which means that these countries must be dropped from the sample or that their immigrant share must be estimated. The UN (2009e) estimates used throughout this report do the latter.

4. Migration DRC (2007).

5. HDR team calculations based on Migration DRC (2007) and CEPII (2006).

6. The destination country HDI is calculated as the weighted average of the HDI of all destination countries, where the weights are the shares in the population of migrants. The magnitude presented in figure 2.2 is only a rough approximation of the human development gains from international migration, because the human development of migrants may be different from the average of populations at both home and destination countries, and because the HDI itself is only a partial measure of human development. Box 1.1 and chapter 3 provide a more detailed discussion of the methodological problems inherent in estimating individual gains from migration.

7. Ortega (2009).

8. Cummins, Letouze, Purser, and Rodríguez (2009). These authors use the Migration DRC (2007) database on bilateral stocks of migrants to develop the first gravity (bilateral flows) model covering both OECD and non-OECD countries. Other findings include large and statistically significant effects of characteristics such as land area, population structures, a common border and geographic distance, as well as former colonial ties and having a common language.

9. Martin (1993) observed that development in poor countries typically went hand in hand with increasing rather than decreasing rates of emigration and hypothesized that there may be a non-linear inverted-U relationship between migration and development. The theory has since been discussed by several authors including Martin and Taylor (1996), Massey (various) and Hatton and Williamson (various). The first cross-country test of the theory using data on bilateral flows was carried out by de Haas (2009).

10. A similar figure was first presented by de Haas (2009).

11. Cummins, Letouze, Purser, and Rodríguez (2009).

12. Mobarak, Shyamal, and Gharad (2009).

Notes

HUMAN DEVELOPMENT REPORT **2009**
Overcoming barriers: Human mobility and development

13. HDR team analysis based on UN (2009e), Migration DRC (2007) and CEPII (2006). These regressions control for a linear and quadratic term in HDI as well as for linear terms and a multiplicative interaction of size and remoteness. Remoteness is measured by the average distance to OECD countries, as calculated by the CEPII (2006). Size is measured by the log of population.

14. For example, female migrants accounted for less than a third of immigrants into the United States 200 years ago (Hatton and Williamson (2005), p.33).

15. See Ramírez, Domínguez, and Morais (2005) for a comprehensive discussion of the key issues.

16. Nava (2006).

17. Rosas (2007).

18. OECD (2008b).

19. Newland (2009) provides a comprehensive survey of the key issues involved in circular migration.

20. Sabates-Wheeler (2009).

21. OECD (2008b).

22. Passel and Cohn (2008).

23. Vogel and Kovacheva (2009).

24. Docquier and Marfouk (2004). If we use a broader definition of the labour force and count as economically active all individuals over the age of 15, we find that 24 percent of immigrants to the OECD have a tertiary degree, as opposed to 5 percent of the population of non-OECD countries.

25. OECD (2009a).

26. Miguel and Hamory (2009).

27. Sun and Fan (2009).

28. Background research carried out by the HDR team in collaboration with the World Bank. This profile of internal migrants also found that those with lower levels of formal education were more likely to migrate in the upper middle-income countries of Latin America. This result suggests that when the average level of income of a country is sufficiently high, even relatively poor people are able to move.

29. King, Skeldon, and Vullnetari (2008).

30. Skeldon (2006) on India and Pakistan, and King, Skeldon, and Vullnetari (2008) on Italy, Korea and Japan.

31. Clemens (2009b).

32. See Jacobs (1970) and Glaeser, Kallal, Scheinkman, and Shleifer (1992). For a comprehensive discussion of the relationship between agglomeration economies, economic development and flows of international and internal migration; see World Bank (2009e).

33. These guidelines are outlined in OECD (2008b).

34. Altman and Horn (1991).

35. Sanjek (2003).

36. In 1907 alone, almost 1.3 million people or 1.5 percent of the population were granted permanent resident status in the United States; a century later, in 2007, both the absolute number and fraction were lower: 1.05 million and only 0.3 percent of the population (DHS, 2007). Hatton and Williamson (2005) estimated for a sample of countries—Denmark, France, Germany, Norway, Sweden, United Kingdom and six 'New World' countries (Argentina, Australia, Brazil, Canada,

New Zealand and United States)—that the stock of foreign-born migrants in 1910–1911 was around 23 million, or about 8 percent of their population.

37. Linz et al. (2007).

38. van Lerberghe and Schoors (1995).

39. Rahaei (2009).

40. Bellwood (2005).

41. Williamson (1990).

42. Lucas (2004); 2008 figure from OECD (2008a).

43. By the late 19th century, the cost of steerage passage from the United Kingdom to the United States had fallen to one tenth of average annual income, making the trip feasible for many more people. However, the costs from elsewhere were much higher: for example, from China to California in 1880, it cost approximately six times Chinese per capita income. See Hatton and Williamson (2005) and Galenson (1984).

44. Taylor and Williamson (1997) and Hatton and Williamson (2005). For the Ireland–Great Britain comparison the period is 1852–1913, while for Sweden–United States it is 1856–1913.

45. Magee and Thompson (2006) and Baines (1985).

46. Gould (1980).

47. Cinel (1991), p.98.

48. Nugent and Saddi (2002).

49. Foner (2002).

50. For example, Canada's open policy towards immigration following confederation was seen as a pillar of the national policy to generate economic prosperity through population growth. See Kelley and Trebilcock (1998).

51. See, e.g. Ignatiev (1995).

52. See Timmer and Williamson (1998), who find evidence of tightening between 1860 and 1930 in Argentina, Australia, Brazil, Canada and the United States.

53. A report by the ILO counted 33 million foreign nationals in 1910, equivalent to 2.5 percent of the population covered by the study (which was 76 percent of the world population at the time). In contrast to modern statistics, it counted those with a different nationality than their country of residence as foreigners, thereby probably underestimating the share of foreign-born people (International Labour Office (1936), p. 37). It is also important to note that, since the number of nations has increased significantly during the past century, the rate of international migration could be expected to have increased even if no genuine increases in movement has taken place.

54. Since 1960, world trade as a share of global GDP has more than doubled, increasing at an average rate of 2.2 percent a year.

55. García y Griego (1983).

56. Appleyard (2001).

57. The German restrictions appear to have started before the oil shock but gained intensity after it. See Martin (1994).

58. These percentages refer to the migrants in countries that are developed according to the most recent HDI (See box 1.3). We might expect these patterns to be different if we instead calculated the share of migrants in the countries that were developed in 1960, but in fact the

share of migrants in the 17 most developed countries in 1960 (covering 15 percent of the world population, the same share covered by developed countries today) was 6.2 percent, not very different from our 5 percent figure.

59. Czechoslovakia and the Soviet Union were not the only cases where new nations emerged during this period. However, in background analysis carried out for this report, we studied the patterns of changes in the share of migrants that occurred after reunifications or break-ups since 1960 and in other cases (e.g. Germany, former Yugoslavia), the changes in the migrant share were not large enough to have a significant impact on aggregate trends.

60. The exception is the United Kingdom, where large shares of immigrants from developing Commonwealth countries took place during the 1960s.

61. UN-HABITAT (2003).

62. UN (2008c) and UN-HABITAT (2003).

63. This divergence has not occurred for other dimensions of human development, such as health and education (school enrolment rates). These dimensions are critical, although income appears to have a larger impact on the propensity to move (see Cummins, Letouze, Purser, and Rodríguez, 2009).

64. Moreover, China was different from other developing regions during the 1960s because of the restrictions on exit, which also affect comparisons of migration flows over time.

65. Since our exercise compares countries classified according to their current HDI levels, it does not take into account the convergence of some fast-growing developing countries, which moved into the top HDI category. Our method seems better suited to understanding the growing concentration of migrants in the subset of countries that are developed today. Furthermore, if we do the comparison for the group of countries classed as developing in 1960, we get very similar patterns (see endnote 58).

66. For a comprehensive survey of this literature see UN (2006b). The debate on divergence is related to the discussion on whether world inequality has been increasing, although the latter depends also on the evolution of inequality within countries.

67. Doganis (2002).

68. Department of Treasury and Finance (2002).

69. Facchini and Mayda (2009) find that, while greater public opposition towards immigration is associated with higher policy restrictions, there is still a significant gap between the policies desired by most voters and those that are adopted by policy makers. See also Cornelius, Tsuda, Martin, and Hollifield (2004).

70. Hanson (2007).

71. The assessment evaluated several dimensions of migration policy, including admissions criteria, integration policies, the treatment of authorized migrants and the situation of irregular migrants. The openness of each regime was assessed through subjective evaluation by respondents as well as according to a set of objective criteria, such as the existence of numerical limits, entry requirements and international agreements

on free movement. The developing countries covered were Chile, China (internal mobility only), Costa Rica, Côte d'Ivoire, Ecuador, Egypt, India, Kazakhstan, Malaysia, Mexico, Morocco, Russian Federation, Thailand and Turkey. The developed countries were Australia, Canada, France, Germany, Italy, Japan, Portugal, Republic of Korea, Singapore, Spain, Sweden, United Arab Emirates, United Kingdom and United States. Further details of the assessment are provided in Klugman and Pereira (2009).

72. Governments often differ in the criteria they use to classify workers as skilled. In order to achieve some degree of homogeneity across countries, we classified as skilled all workers coming under regimes requiring a university degree. When the classification was based on occupation, we tried to match the type of occupation with the education level typically required to perform the job. When there was no explicit distinction in visa regimes based on education level or occupation, we either made a distinction based on information on the most common workers in each visa class, or, in the case of clearly mixed flows, we treated the regulation as applying to both high-skilled and low-skilled workers.

73. Ruhs (2005) and Singapore Government Ministry of Manpower (2009).

74. Ruhs (2002) and OECD (2008b).

75. This concept originated as a mechanism in Arab countries' legislation—which typically does not recognize adoption—whereby adults pledged to take care of orphaned or abandoned children. See Global Legal Information Network (2009).

76. Longva (1997), pp. 20–21.

77. See, for example, Bahrain Center for Human Rights (2008) and UNDP (2008d).

78. Under the new regulation, the Labor Ministry will transfer the sponsorship of the workers from previous government contractors to new ones and the state will bear their iqama (residence permit) and sponsorship transfer fees. See Thaindian News (2009) and Arab News (2009).

79. Khaleej Times (2009).

80. Jasso and Rosenzweig (2009).

81. Hanson and Spilimbergo (2001).

82. Lawyers for Human Rights (2008).

83. Human Rights Watch (2007a).

84. Ruhs and Martin (2008) and Ruhs (2009).

85. See Cummins and Rodríguez (2009). These authors also address potential issues of reverse causation by using the predicted immigration shares from a bilateral gravity model as an exogenous source of cross-national variation. Their results still point to a statistically insignificant correlation between numbers and rights; indeed, in most of their instrumental variable estimates the correlation turns positive, shedding further doubts on the numbers versus rights hypothesis.

86. Muñoz de Bustillo and Antón (2009).

87. Adepoju (2005).

88. Freedom House (2009).

89. United States Department of State (2009b), Wang (2005), National Statistics Office (2006), Ivakhnyuk (2009), and Anh (2005).

90. United States Department of State (2009d).

91. Kundu (2009).

92. McKenzie (2007).

93. Tirtosudarmo (2009).

94. On Cuba, see Human Rights Watch (2005a) and Amnesty International (2009). On the Democratic People's Republic of Korea, see Freedom House (2005). For other countries, see United States Department of State (2009a), Immigration and Refugee Board of Canada (2008) and IATA (2006).

95. Human Rights Watch (2007b).

96. United States Department of State (2009a) and McKenzie (2007).

97. IMF (2009a).

98. See IMF (2009c), Consensus Economics (2009a), Consensus Economics (2009c), Consensus Economics (2009d).

99. Recessions in developed countries tend to last two years, after which trend economic growth is re-established: Chauvet and Yu (2006). However, the mean duration and intensity of recessions is much longer in developing countries. See Hausmann, Rodríguez, and Wagner (2008).

100. See Perron (1989) and Perron and Wada (2005), who find evidence of persistent effects of the oil shock and the Great Depression on incomes.

101. OECD (2009b).

102. United States Bureau of Labor Statistics (2009).

103. INE (2009).

104. The correlation is statistically significant at 5 percent. The Asian Development Bank has projected contractions in the key migrant destinations of the region, ranging up to 5 percent in Singapore. In South Africa, home to 1.2 million migrants, the EIU expects the economy to contract by 0.8 percent in 2009, and the economy of the United Arab Emirates is projected to contract by 1.7 percent in 2009. Business Monitor International (2009).

105. Betcherman and Islam (2001).

106. Dustmann, Glitz, and Vogel (2006).

107. OECD (2008a).

108. Taylor (2009).

109. Kalita (2009).

110. The Straits Times (2009) and Son (2009).

111. Local Government Association (2009).

112. Preston (2009).

113. Timmer and Williamson (1998).

114. de Haas (2009).

115. See Martin (2003) and Martin (2009a).

116. Skeldon (1999) and Castles and Vezzoli (2009). There were deportations in order to demonstrate support for local workers, but once governments realized that locals were not interested in migrants' jobs, these restrictions were reversed.

117. See for example Rodrik (2009) and Castles and Vezzoli (2009).

118. While all forecasts are inherently uncertain, population projections tend to be quite accurate. The UN has produced 12 different estimates of the 2000 world population since 1950, and all but one of these estimates were within 4 percentage points of the actual number (Population Reference Bureau, 2001). One recent study found average prediction errors of the order of 2 percent even for age sub-groups of the population.

119. However, these alternative solutions are in themselves costly: technological innovation to substitute for a globally abundant factor uses up resources, and raising retirement ages or contributions reduces leisure or consumption.

120. Barnett and Webber (2009).

121. IPCC (2007), chapter 9.

122. Anthoff, Nicholls, Richard, and Vafeidis (2009).

123. Revkin (2008).

124. Myers (2005) and Christian Aid (2007).

125. Barnett and Webber (2009).

126. Stark (1991).

127. Ezra and Kiros (2001).

128. Black et al. (2008).

129. Carvajal and Pereira (2009).

130. UNDP (2007a) and UNDP (2008e).

131. See Friedman (2005).

132. Steinbeck (1939). On the Great Dust Bowl Migration see Worster (1979) and Gregory (1989). For the landmark 1941 US Supreme Court decision in the case of *California vs. Edwards* see ACLU (2003).

Chapter 3

1. Clemens, Montenegro, and Pritchett (2008).

2. McKenzie, Gibson, and Stillman (2006).

3. Chiswick and Miller (1995).

4. Sciortino and Punpuing (2009).

5. Maksakova (2002).

6. Commander, Chanda, Kangasniemi, and Winters (2008).

7. Clemens (2009b).

8. Harttgen and Klasen (2009). Migrants had lower income in two countries (Guatemala and Zambia) and there was no statistically significant difference in one (Viet Nam). See section 3.6.

9. Del Popolo, Oyarce, Ribotta, and Rodríguez (2008).

10. Srivastava and Sasikumar (2003), Ellis and Harris (2004) and ECLAC (2007).

11. See Deshingkar and Akter (2009) on India and MOSWL, PTRC, and UNDP (2004) on Mongolia.

12. Ghosh (2009).

13. Gilbertson (1995).

14. Zhou and Logan (1989).

15. Cerrutti (2009).

16. UNDP (2008d).

17. Castles and Miller (1993) and ICFTU (2009).

18. Bursell (2007) and Bovenkerk, Gras, Ramsoedh, Dankoor, and Havelaar (1995).

19. Clark and Drinkwater (2008) and Dustmann and Fabbri (2005).

20. Iredale (2001).

21. Chiswick and Miller (1995).

22. Reitz (2005).

23. The social transfer programmes included in this analysis are all forms of universal and social insurance benefits, minus income and payroll taxes and social assistance (including all forms of targeted income-tested benefits). The poverty line is defined as half the median income. See Smeeding, Wing, and Robson (2009).

24. These estimates may over- or underestimate the effect of transfers on poverty because the endogenous response of labour supply decisions to transfers is not factored in.

25. Martin (2005) and Kaur (2007).

26. UNICEF (2005a).
27. Koslowski (2009).
28. McKenzie (2007) and United States Department of State (2006).
29. United States Department of State (2009a).
30. Agunias (2009) and Martin (2005).
31. Martin (2005).
32. Agunias (2009) and Martin (2005).
33. UNFPA (2006).
34. Ivakhnyuk (2009).
35. Martin (2009b).
36. Martin (2009b).
37. Gibson and McKenzie (2009).
38. The so-called 'healthy migrant effect' has been well documented; see, for example, Fennelly (2005).
39. Rossi (2008).
40. Jasso, Massey, Rosenzweig, and Smith (2004), using the US Citizenship and Immigration Service's New Immigrant Survey.
41. Ortega (2009).
42. Brockerhoff (1990).
43. Brockerhoff (1995) and Harttgen and Klasen (2009).
44. See Chiswick and Lee (2006), and Antecol and Bedard (2005). Another factor clouding these estimates is the possibility that 'regression to the mean' may account for part of the apparent deterioration in health. In particular, if not being ill is an important condition enabling migration, then those who migrate may include people who are not inherently healthier but who nevertheless have had the good luck not to fall ill. These people will also be more likely to fall ill after migrating than those whose lack of illness is due truly to good health.
45. Garcia-Gomez (2007) on Catalonia, Spain; Barros and Pereira (2009) on Portugal.
46. Stillman, McKenzie, and Gibson (2006), Steel, Silove, Chey, Bauman, and Phan T. (2005) and Nazroo (1997).
47. McKay, Macintyre, and Ellaway (2003).
48. Benach, Muntaner, and Santana (2007).
49. Whitehead, Hashim, and Iversen (2007).
50. Tiwari (2005).
51. Deshingkar and Akter (2009).
52. Some migrants gain access to services over time. For example, in many countries, asylum seekers who apply for refugee status often do not have access unless and until their application is successful. In other countries, Australia for example, payment of limited income support is available to some asylum seekers living in the community who have reached a certain stage in visa processing and meet other criteria (such as passing a means test).
53. Carballo (2007) and Goncalves, Dias, Luck, Fernandes, and Cabral (2003).
54. PICUM (2009).
55. Kaur (2007).
56. Landau and Wa Kabwe-Segatti (2009).
57. Hashim (2006) and Pilon (2003)
58. OECD (2008b).
59. Our commissioned research of HDI differences between internal migrants and non-migrants in 16 countries found that the educational level of migrants was higher in 10 countries,

not significantly different in 4 and lower in 2 countries.
60. UNICEF (2008). Other studies find similar returns. For a comprehensive review of the evidence on early childhood interventions, see Heckman (2006).
61. Clauss and Nauck (2009).
62. For example, Norwegian authorities are obliged to inform refugee families about the importance and availability of ECD within three months of arrival.
63. For further information on undocumented migrants in Sweden, see PICUM (2009).
64. PICUM (2008a).
65. PICUM (2008a).
66. Landau and Wa Kabwe-Segatti (2009).
67. Rossi (2008).
68. Government of Azad Jammu and Kashmir (2003) and Poverty Task Force (2003).
69. Poverty Task Force (2003).
70. The Programme for International Student Assessment is a triennial survey of pupils aged 15 years.
71. OECD (2007). The Programme for International Student Assessment study focuses on science but also assesses reading and mathematics, which yielded similar comparisons.
72. Australia, France, Germany, Italy, Netherlands, Switzerland, United Kingdom and United States. See Hernandez (2009).
73. Portes and Rumbaut (2001).
74. Karsten et al. (2006), Nordin (2006) and Szulkin and Jonsson (2007).
75. Sen (1992).
76. Rawls (1971).
77. Hugo (2000).
78. Petros (2006), Zambrano and Kattya (2005) and Mills (1997).
79. Içduygu (2009).
80. Piper (2005).
81. Ghosh (2009) and Kabeer (2000).
82. Del Popolo, Oyarce, Ribotta, and Rodriguez (2008).
83. Cerrutti (2009).
84. Uhlaner, Cain, and Kiewiet (1989), Cho (1999), Rosenstone and Hansen (1993), Wolfinger and Rosenstone (1980) and Ramakrishnan and Espenshade (2001).
85. A standard deviation increase of 1 in destination country democracy, as measured by the Polity IV index, leads to an 11 log point increase in immigration, significant at 1 percent. See Cummins, Letouze, Purser, and Rodríguez (2009).
86. Landau (2005).
87. Ministry of Social Welfare and Labour, United Nations Population Fund, and Mongolian Population and Development Association (2005).
88. Crush and Ramachandran (2009).
89. Misago, Landau, and Monson (2009).
90. Pettigrew and Tropp (2005) and Pettigrew (1998).
91. Human Security Centre (2005) and Newman and van Selm (2003).
92. UNHCR (2008). There is no reliable estimate of the share of internally displaced people living in camps, but 70 percent are estimated to live with host-country relatives, families and communities.

93. IDMC (2008).
94. Bakewell and de Haas (2007).
95. van Hear, Brubaker, and Bessa (2009) and Crisp (2006).
96. Camps located in Bangladesh, Kenya, Nepal, Tanzania, Thailand and Uganda: de Bruijn (2009).
97. ECOSOC (1998). Presented to the UN Commission on Human Rights by the Representative of the Secretary General in 1998, the Guiding Principles on Internal Displacement set the basic standards and norms to guide governments, international organizations and all other relevant actors in providing assistance and protection to internally displaced persons in internal conflict situations, natural disasters and other situations of forced displacement worldwide.
98. Estimates in this paragraph come from IDMC (2008).
99. IDMC (2008) lists Azerbaijan, Bosnia and Herzegovina, Côte d'Ivoire, Croatia, Georgia, Lebanon, Liberia, Turkey and Uganda in this category. Noteworthy efforts include financial compensation as part of Turkey's return programme and specific efforts towards property restitution across the Balkans, which had largely been completed by 2007.
100. Ghosh (2009).
101. UNRWA (2008).
102. Gibney (2009) and Hatton and Williamson (2005). In the United Kingdom, for example, only 19 out of every 100 people who applied for asylum in 2007 were recognized as refugees and had their applications granted, while another nine who applied for asylum but did not qualify were given permission to stay for humanitarian or other reasons.
103. UNHCR (2008).
104. UNRWA-ECOSOC (2008).
105. UNHCR (2002).
106. See, for example, UNECA (2005).
107. Robinson (2003).
108. Bartolome, de Wet, Mander, and Nagraj (2000), p. 7.
109. See IIED and WBCSD (2003), Global IDP Project and Norwegian Refugee Council (2005) and Survival International (2007).
110. La Rovere and Mendes (1999).
111. For World Bank, CIEL (2009); there are other examples: for ADB, see Asian Development Bank (2009); for IDB, see IDB (2009).
112. UNDP (2007b).
113. UNODC (2009).
114. Clert, Gomart, Aleksic, and Otel (2005).
115. See, for example, Carling (2006).
116. USAID (2007).
117. Laczko and Danailova-Trainor (2009) .
118. Koser (2008).
119. Ortega (2009).
120. Harttgen and Klasen (2009).
121. These numbers are taken from the 2005/2006 World Values Survey. The survey records whether at least one parent is a migrant, which we use as a proxy for migrant status. These particular results are consistent with data from the 1995 World Values Survey, which show whether or not the respondent is foreign-born.

Chapter 4

1. Sarreal (2002).
2. Yang (2009).
3. UNDP (2008b).
4. For a list of least and most costly international corridors, see World Bank (2009c).
5. Stark (1991).
6. Savage and Harvey (2007).
7. Yang (2008a).
8. Yang and Choi (2007).
9. Halliday (2006).
10. Ratha and Mohapatra (2009a). This is the 'base case' scenario, which assumes that new migration flows to major destination countries will be zero, implying that the stock of existing migrants will remain unchanged.
11. Fajnzylber and Lopez (2007).
12. Schiff (1994).
13. Kapur (2004).
14. Zhu and Luo (2008).
15. Lucas and Chappell (2009).
16. Deshingkar and Akter (2009).
17. Rayhan and Grote (2007).
18. Beegle, De Weerdt, and Dercon (2008).
19. Deb and Seck (2009).
20. Murison (2005). For example, Bangladeshi women working in the Middle East remit up to 72 percent of their earnings on average, and Colombian women working in Spain remit more than men (68 versus 54 percent).
21. Docquier, Rapoport, and Shen (2003) and Stark, Taylor, and Yitzhaki (1986).
22. Adelman and Taylor (1988) and Durand, Kandel, Emilio, and Massey (1996).
23. Yang (2009).
24. Massey et al. (1998), Taylor et al. (1996) and Berriane (1997).
25. Behrman et al. (2008).
26. Adelman and Taylor (1988), Durand, Kandel, Emilio, and Massey (1996) and Stark (1980) (1980).
27. Adams Jr. (2005), Cox Edwards and Ureta (2003) and Yang (2008b).
28. Adams Jr. (2005).
29. Mansuri (2006).
30. Deb and Seck (2009).
31. Fan and Stark (2007) and Stark, Helmenstein, and Prskawetz (1997).
32. Chand and Clemens (2008).
33. Castles and Delgado Wise (2008).
34. McKenzie and Rapoport (2006).
35. Ha, Yi, and Zhang (2009a).
36. Frank and Hummer (2002).
37. Hildebrandt, McKenzie, Esquivel, and Schargrodsky (2005).
38. Wilson (2003).
39. Cerrutti (2009).
40. Bowlby (1982), Cortes (2008), Smith, Lalaonde, and Johnson (2004) and Suarez-Orozco, Todorova, and Louie (2002).
41. For a review of gender empowerment and migration see Ghosh (2009).
42. King and Vullnetari (2006).
43. See Deshingkar and Grimm (2005).
44. Fargues (2006).
45. Beine, Docquier, and Schiff (2008).
46. Hampshire (2006) and King, Skeldon, and Vullnetari (2008).
47. Cordova and Hiskey (2009). The countries covered were Dominican Republic, El Salvador, Guatemala, Honduras, Mexico and Nicaragua.
48. See the review of this literature in Clemens (2009b).
49. Lipton (1980) and Rubenstein (1992).
50. Tirtosudarmo (2009).
51. World Bank (2009e), p. 165.
52. Docquier and Rapoport (2004) and Dumont, Martin, and Spielvogel (2007).
53. An analogy can be drawn with the sharp decline in the skills and qualifications of schoolteachers in the United States over the past half century, which is attributed to the fact that skilled women now have a much broader range of career choices available to them than teaching (Corcoran, William, and Schwab, 2004).
54. Saxenian (2002).
55. Commander, Chanda, Kangasniemi, and Winters (2008).
56. Saxenian (2006).
57. The World Bank, which has been closely tracking flows, estimates that unrecorded flows would add at least 50 percent to the total remittance figure.
58. Chami, Fullenkamp, and Jahjah (2005) and Leon-Ledesma and Piracha (2004).
59. Eckstein (2004) and Ahoure (2008).
60. World Bank (2006b) and Kireyev (2006).
61. Buch, Kuckulenz, and Le Manchec (2002) and de Haas and Plug (2006).
62. Taylor, Moran-Taylor and Ruiz (2006).
63. de Haas (2006).
64. Levitt (1998) and Levitt (2006).
65. Quirk (2008).
66. World Bank (2009a).
67. World Bank (2009a).
68. Massey, Arango, Hugo, Kouaouci, Pellegrino and Taylor (1993) and Thomas-Hope (2009).
69. Adesina (2007).
70. Ali (2009).
71. Bakewell (2009).
72. Ba, Awumbila, Ndiaye, Kassibo, and Ba (2008).
73. Jonsson (2007).
74. Black, Natali and Skinner (2005).
75. If the incomes and consumption of those abroad were included in these measures of inequality the distribution would widen considerably, since incomes abroad are so much higher.
76. Taylor, Mora, Adams, and Lopez-Feldman (2005) for Mexico; Yang (2009) for Thailand.
77. Ha, Yi, and Zhang (2009b).
78. Goldring (2004) and Lacroix (2005).
79. Orozco and Rouse (2007) and Zamora (2007).
80. HDR team estimates based on figures cited in Anonuevo and Anonuevo (2008).
81. Tabar (2009).
82. Spilimbergo (2009).
83. Iskander (2009).
84. Castles and Delgado Wise (2008).
85. Massey et al. (1998).
86. Eckstein (2004), Massey et al. (1998), Newland and Patrick (2004) and van Hear, Pieke, and Vertovec (2004).
87. Gamlen (2006) and Newland and Patrick (2004).
88. IMF and World Bank (1999).
89. Jobbins (2008) and Martin (2008).
90. Black and Sward (2009).
91. These countries are Australia, Austria, Belgium, Canada, France, Germany, Ireland, Luxembourg, Netherlands, New Zealand, Spain, Sweden, Switzerland and United States; see Statistical Table A. The share of foreign-born migrants in the United Kingdom was estimated at about 9 percent at that time.
92. Van der Mensbrugghe and Roland-Holst (2009). These simulations extend and update those presented in World Bank (2006b).
93. Ortega and Peri (2009).
94. See Barrell, Fitzgerald, and Railey (2007). In the United States, Borjas (1999) estimated the aggregate effect to be positive but small, at 0.1 percent of GDP.
95. Hunt and Gauthier-Loiselle (2008).
96. See, for example, the Council of the European Union (2009).
97. See, *inter alia*, Baumol, Litan, and Schramm (2007) and Zucker and Darby (2008).
98. OECD (2008b).
99. EurActiv.com News (2008).
100. Martin (2009b).
101. This finding must be qualified because of the inability to distinguish the labour supply (immigrants tend to work in these restaurants) from labour demand effects (if they consume there); see Mazzolari and Neumark (2009).
102. For example, 38 percent of Britons believe this is the case: Dustmann, Frattini, and Preston (2008a).
103. For instance, see Longhi, Nijkamp, and Poot (2005), Ottaviano and Peri (2008), and Münz, Straubhaar, Vadean, and Vadean (2006).
104. For Spain, see Carrasco, Jimeno, and Ortega (2008), for France, Constant (2005), for the United Kingdom, Dustmann, Frattini, and Preston (2008).
105. See, for example, Borjas (1995). A substitute is when an increased supply of one input lowers the price of the other input, while a complement is when an increased supply raises the price of the other input.
106. For example, in the United States, workers with less than high-school education may in most respects be perfect substitutes for high-school graduates, throwing doubt on the assumption that completion per se matters; see Card (2009).
107. Kremer and Watt (2006) and Castles and Miller (1993).
108. For a survey, see Münz, Straubhaar, Vadean, and Vadean (2006).
109. Reyneri (1998).
110. The first estimate comes from Borjas (2003), for the period 1980–2000, while the second comes from Ottaviano and Peri (2008) and refers to the 1990–2006 period. Using Borjas's methodology for the 1990–2006 period gives an estimate of -7.8 percent (Ottaviano and Peri (2008), p. 59). The approaches differ in their assumptions regarding the substitutability between high-school dropouts and high-school graduates. See also Card (1990) and Borjas, Grogger, and Hanson (2008).
111. Peri, Sparber, and Drive (2008); Amuedo-Dorantes and de la Rica (2008) for Spain.

112. Manacorda, Manning, and Wadsworth (2006).
113. Angrist and Kugler (2003).
114. Jayaweera and Anderson (2009).
115. Bryant and Rukumnuaykit (2007).
116. Suen (2002).
117. A comprehensive discussion of this issue can be found in World Bank (2009e).
118. Henderson, Shalizi, and Venables (2001).
119. Amis (2002).
120. The Cities Alliance (2007).
121. Dreze and Sen (1999).
122. Kundu (2009).
123. See Hossain, Khan, and Seeley (2003) and Afsar (2003).
124. Hanson (2009).
125. For example, Borjas (1995) and Lee and Miller (2000).
126. IMF (2009b).
127. Hanson, Scheve, and Slaughter (2007).
128. Facchini and Mayda (2008).
129. Brucker et al. (2002). Countries with greater migrant dependence on welfare included Austria, Belgium, Denmark, Finland, France and Netherlands, while those with less dependence included Germany, Greece, Spain, Portugal and United Kingdom.
130. Vasquez, Alloza, Vegas, and Bertozzi (2009).
131. Rowthorn (2008).
132. Alternative estimates could be derived by considering the entire future stream of taxes and spending associated with immigrants and their dependents, plus future generations. However, estimating the net present value would be very difficult given all the assumptions needed about people's future behaviour (fertility, schooling, employment prospects, and so on), so in practice a static approach is used: see Rowthorn (2008). Some authors have estimated the net present fiscal value of an immigrant in the United States and have found largely positive estimates; see Lee and Miller (2000).
133. Lucassen (2005).
134. IPC (2007).
135. Butcher and Piehl (1998).
136. Australian Institute of Criminology (1999).
137. Savona, Di Nicola, and Da Col (1996).
138. However, particularly in medium-HDI countries (such as Egypt, Indonesia, Islamic Republic of Iran, Jordan, South Africa and Thailand), a significant proportion did favour more restrictions on access. Similarly, in countries with higher income inequality, people were more likely to favour limiting migration and said that employers should give priority to local people when jobs are scarce. See Kleemans and Klugman (2009).
139. Zimmermann (2009).
140. Massey and Sánchez R. (2009).
141. O'Rourke and Sinnott (2003).
142. Earnest (2008).
143. Several studies have investigated the long-run effects of immigration on political values, with differing results. Bueker (2005) finds significant differences in turnout and participation among US voters of different immigrant backgrounds, while

Rodríguez and Wagner (2009) find that the well-documented patterns of civic engagement and attitudes towards redistribution across different regions of Italy are not reflected in the political behaviour of Italians from these regions who are living in Venezuela.
144. Castles and Miller (1993).
145. Kleemans and Klugman (2009).

Chapter 5

1. Scheve and Slaughter (2007).
2. This chapter does not provide a comprehensive review of policies that are relevant to migration, since these have been well documented elsewhere: see OECD (2008b), IOM (2008a), Migration Policy Group and British Council (2007) and ILO (2004).
3. Agunias (2009) and Klugman and Pereira (2009).
4. Government of Sweden (2008).
5. Khoo, Hugo, and McDonald (2008) and Klugman and Pereira (2009).
6. See ICMPD (2009) for an excellent review.
7. Papademetriou (2005).
8. ICMPD (2009), p. 47.
9. For example, in the United Kingdom the Foreign and Commonwealth Office team working on promoting the return of irregular migrants and failed asylum seekers is currently five times larger than the team focused on migration and development in the Department for International Development. See Black and Sward (2009).
10. Hagan, Eschbach, and Rodriguez (2008).
11. Migrant Forum in Asia (2006) and Human Rights Watch (2005b).
12. See European Parliament (2008); on criticisms, see, for example, Amnesty International (2008).
13. UNHCR (2007).
14. See international conventions on Economic, Social and Cultural Rights (ICESCR 1966), on Civil and Political Rights (ICCPR 1966), on the Elimination of All Forms of Racial Discrimination (ICERD 1966), on the Elimination of All Forms of Discrimination against Women (CEDAW 1979), Against Torture, and Other Cruel, Inhuman or Degrading Treatment or Punishment (CAT 1984), and on the Rights of the Child (CRC 1989). The ratification rates are lowest among Asian and Middle Eastern states (47 percent) and stand at 58 and 70 percent for Latin America and Africa respectively. While 131 countries have ratified all six core human rights treaties, some of these treaties have more than 131 signatories. The total number of parties for individual treaties can be found in the Statistical Annex.
15. ICCPR Art 2, 26; ICESCR Art 2; see Opeskin (2009).
16. The European Community, which is listed as a separate signatory, is not included here.
17. IOM (2008b), p. 62.
18. UNODC (2009).
19. See for example Carling (2006) (on trafficking from Nigeria) and de Haas (2008).
20. December 18 vzw (2008).
21. Alvarez (2005) and Betts (2008).

22. Martin and Abimourchad (2008).
23. PICUM (2008b).
24. Kleemans and Klugman (2009).
25. For examples of such activities, see the Joint Initiative of the European Commission and the United Nations (EC-UN Joint Migration and Development Initiative, 2008). The joint initiative has at its heart a knowledge management platform of activities related to remittances, communities, capacities and rights led by civil society and local authorities. See GFMD (2008).
26. Martin (2009b) and Agunias (2009).
27. McKenzie (2007).
28. Martin (2005), p. 20.
29. Martin (2009a), p. 47.
30. Hamel (2009).
31. Martin (2009a).
32. Horst (2006).
33. The 1997 ILO Convention on Private Employment Agencies prohibits the charging of fees to workers, but this has been ratified by only 21 countries.
34. Agunias (2008), Ruhunage (2006) and Siddiqui (2006).
35. Betcherman, Olivas, and Dar (2004) review the effectiveness of active labour market programmes, drawing on 159 evaluations in developing and developed countries.
36. Martin (2009b) and Sciortino and Punpuing (2009).
37. See Colombo Process (2008).
38. Marquette (2006).
39. Christensen and Stanat (2007).
40. Success for All Foundation (2008).
41. Misago, Landau, and Monson (2009).
42. This might include, for example, leaflets explaining who does what and where to go to complain.
43. World Bank (2002).
44. Zamble (2008).
45. One World Net (2008).
46. Council of Europe (2006).
47. Martin (2009a).
48. Government of Western Australia (2004).
49. Deshingkar and Akter (2009), pp. 38-40.
50. UN (2008a).
51. The Cities Alliance (2007).
52. Black and Sward (2009).
53. For example, in Myanmar, college graduates must reimburse the government for the cost of their education before they can receive a passport; United States Department of State (2009c).
54. As Ranis and Stewart (2000) note, while there are many paths to good human development performance, in general successes have been characterized by initiatives that give priority to girls and women (education, incomes), effective expenditure policies (e.g. Chile) and good economic performance (e.g. Viet Nam).
55. Kleemans and Klugman (2009).
56. Sides and Citrin (2007).
57. Facchini and Mayda (2009).
58. Ghosh (2007).
59. Bedford (2008).

Bibliography

ACLU (American Civil Liberties Union). 2003. "Edwards v. California." www.aclu.org. Accessed July 2009.

ActionAid International. 2004. "Participatory Poverty Assessment (PPA) Lower Songkhram River Basin, Thailand". Bangkok: ActionAid International and Mekong Wetlands Biodiversity Programme.

Adams Jr., R. H. 2005. "Remittances, Household Expenditure and Investment in Guatemala". *Policå Research Working Paper No. 3532.* Washington DC: World Bank.

Adelman, I. and J. E. Taylor. 1988. "Life in a Mexican Village: A SAM Perspective." *Journal of Development Studies* 25 (1): 5-24.

Adepoju, A. 2005. *Migration in West Africa.* Geneva: Global Commission on International Migration.

Adesina, O. A. 2007. "'Checking out': Migration, Popular Culture, and the Articulation and Formation of Class Identity". Paper presented at African Migrations Workshop on Understanding Migration Dynamics in the Continent, 18-21 September 2007, Accra, Ghana.

Afsar, R. 2003. "Internal Migration and the Development Nexus: The Case of Bangladesh". Paper presented at Regional Conference on Migration and Pro-Poor Policy Changes in Asia, 22-24 June 2003, Dhaka, Bangladesh.

Agunias, D. R. 2008. *Managing Temporary Migration: Lessons from the Philippine Model.* Washington DC: Migration Policy Institute.

Agunias, D. R. 2009. "Migration Intermediaries: Agents of Human Development?" *Human Development Research Paper No. 22.* New York: United Nations Development Programme, Human Development Report Office.

Ahoure, A. A. E. 2008. "Transferts, Gouvernance et Développement Economique dans les Pays de l'Afrique Sub-saharienne: Une Analyse à Partir de Données de Panel". Paper presented at African Migration Workshop, 26-29 November 2008, Rabat, Morocco.

Ali, S. N. 2009. "Education as a Means of Rural Transformation through Smooth Rural-Urban Migration: Some Evidence from Ethiopia". Paper presented at the 7th International Conference on the Ethiopian Economy, 25-27 June 2009, Addis Ababa, Ethiopia.

Aliran. 2007. "Chin Asylum Seekers Detained in Rela Raid." http://www.aliran.com/index.php?option=com_content&view=article&id=184:chin-asylum-seekers-detained-in-rela-raid&catid=32:2006-9&Itemid=10. Accessed May 2009.

Altman, I. and J. Horn (Eds.). 1991. *To Make America: European Emigration in the Early Modern Period.* Berkeley: University of California Press.

Alvarez, J. E. 2005. *International Organizations as Law-Makers.* New York: Oxford University Press.

Amin, M. and A. Mattoo. 2005. "Does Temporary Migration have to be Permanent?" *Policy Research Working Paper Series No. 3582.* Washington DC: World Bank.

Amis, P. 2002. "African Urban Poverty and What is the Role of Local Government in its Alleviation?". Unpublished report. Washington DC: World Bank.

Amnesty International. 2008. "Amnesty International EU Office reaction to Return Directive Vote." http://www.amnesty-eu.org/static/html/pressrelease.asp?cfid=7&id=366&cat=4&l=1. Accessed June 2009.

——. **2009.** "Urgent Action: Cuba UA 115/09." http://www.amnestyusa.org/actioncenter/actions/uaa11509.pdf. Accessed June 2009.

Amuedo-Dorantes, C. and S. de la Rica. 2008. "Complements or Substitutes? Immigrant and Native Task Specialization in Spain". *Discussion Paper Series No. 16/08.* London: Centre for Research and Analysis of Migration.

Anderson, J. B. and J. Gerber. 2007a. "Data Appendix to Fifty Years of Change on the U.S.-Mexico Border: Growth, Development, and Quality of Life." http://latinamericanstudies.sdsu.edu/BorderData.html. Accessed June 2009a.

——. **2007b.** *Fifty Years of Change on the U.S.-Mexico Border: Growth, Development, and Quality of Life.* Austin: University of Texas Press.

Andrienko, Y. and S. Guriev. 2005. "Understanding Migration in Russia". *Policy paper series No. 23.* Moscow: Center for Economic and Financial Research.

Angrist, J. D. and A. D. Kugler. 2003. "Protective or Counter-Productive? Labour Market Institutions and The Effect of Immigration on EU Natives." *The Economic Journal* 113 (488): 302-331.

Anh, D. N. 2005. "Enhancing the Development Impact of Migrant Remittances and Diasporas: The Case of Viet Nam." *Asia Pacific Population Journal* 20 (3): 111-122.

Anonuevo, E. and A. T. Anonuevo. 2008. "Diaspora Giving: An Agent of Change in Asia Pacific Communities". Paper presented at Diaspora Giving: An Agent of Change in Asia Pacific Communities?, 21-23 May 2008, Ha Noi, Viet Nam.

Antecol, H. and K. Bedard. 2005. "Unhealthy Assimilation: Why do Immigrants Converge to American Health Status Levels". *Discussion Paper Series No. 1654.* Bonn: Institut zur Zukunft der Arbeit.

Anthoff, D., R. J. Nicholls, S. J. T. Richard and A. T. Vafeidis. 2009. "Global and Regional Exposure to Large

Rises in Sea-Level: A Sensitivity Analysis". *Working Paper No. 96*. Norwich: Tyndall Centre for Climate Change Research.

Appleyard, R. 2001. "International Migration Policies: 1950-2000." *International Migration* 39 (6): 7-20.

Arab News. 2009. "Cabinet Passes Regulations Simplifying Iqama Transfer." *Arab News,* 21 April.

Asian Development Bank. 2009. "About the Safeguard Policy Update." http://www.adb.org/Safeguards/about.asp. Accessed June 2009.

Australian Institute of Criminology. 1999. *Ethnicity and Crime: An Australian Research Study.* Canberra: Department of Immigration and Multicultural Affairs.

Avenarius, C. 2007. "Cooperation, Conflict and Integration among Sub-ethnic Immigrant Groups from Taiwan." *Population, Space and Place* 13 (2): 95-112.

Azcona, G. 2009. "Migration in Participatory Poverty Assessments: A Review." *Human Development Research Paper No. 56.* New York: United Nations Development Programme, Human Development Report Office.

Ba, C. O., M. Awumbila, A. I. Ndiaye, B. Kassibo and D. Ba. 2008. *Irregular Migration in West Africa.* Dakar: Open Society Initiative for West Africa.

Bahrain Center for Human Rights. 2008. "The Situation of Women Migrant Domestic Workers in Bahrain". *Report submitted to the 42nd session of the CEDAW Committee.* Manama: Bahrain Center for Human Rights.

Baines, D. 1985. *Migration in a Mature Economy: Emigration and Internal Migration in England and Wales, 1861-1900.* Cambridge: Cambridge University Press.

Bakewell, O. 2008. "Research Beyond the Categories: The Importance of Policy Irrelevant Research into Forced Migration." *Journal of Refugee Studies* 21: 432-453.

———. **2009.** "South-South Migration and Human Development: Reflections on African Experiences." *Human Development Research Paper No. 7.* New York: United Nations Development Programme, Human Development Report Office.

Bakewell, O. and H. de Haas. 2007. "African Migrations: Continuities, Discontinuities and Recent Transformations." In L. de Haan, U. Engel, and P. Chabal (Eds.), *African Alternatives*: 95-117. Leiden: Brill.

Banerjee, A. and E. Duflo. 2006. "Addressing Absence." *Journal of Economic Perspectives* 20 (1): 117-132.

Barnett, J. and M. Webber. 2009. "Accommodating Migration to Promote Adaptation to Climate Change". Melbourne: Commission on Climate Change and Development, University of Melbourne.

Barrell, R., J. Fitzgerald and R. Railey. 2007. "EU Enlargement and Migration: Assessing the Macroeconomic Consequences". *Discussion Paper No. 292.* London: National Institute of Economic and Social Research.

Barro, R. J. and J.-W. Lee. 2001. "International Data on Educational Attainment: Updates and Implications." *Oxford Economic Papers* 53 (3): 541-563.

Barros, P. P. and I. M. Pereira. 2009. "Access to Health Care and Migration: Evidence from Portugal." *Human Development Research Paper No. 28.* New York: United Nations Development Programme, Human Development Report Office.

Bartolome, L. J., C. de Wet, H. Mander and V. K. Nagraj. 2000. "Displacement, Resettlement, Rehabilitation, Reparation, and Development". *Working paper.* Cape Town: Secretariat of the World Commission on Dams.

Baumol, W. J., R. Litan and C. Schramm. 2007. *Good Capitalism, Bad Capitalism.* New Haven: Yale University Press.

Bedford, R. 2008. "Migration Policies, Practices and Cooperation Mechanisms in the Pacific". Paper presented at United Nations Expert Group Meeting on International Migration and Development in Asia and the Pacific, 20-21 September 2008, Bangkok, Thailand: Department of Social and Economic Affairs.

Beegle, K., J. De Weerdt and S. Dercon. 2008. "Migration and Economic Mobility in Tanzania: Evidence from a Tracking Survey". *Policy Research Working Paper No. 4798.* Washington DC: World Bank.

Behrman, J. R., J. Hoddinott, J. A. Maluccio, E. Soler-Hampejsek, E. L. Behrman, R. Martorell, Ramírez M. and A. D. Stein. 2008. *What Determines Adult Skills? Impacts of Preschool, School-Years, and Post-School Experiences in Guatemala.* Philadelphia: University of Pennsylvania.

Beine, M., F. Docquier and M. Schiff. 2008. "International Migration, Transfers of Norms and Home Country Fertility". *Discussion Paper No. 3912.* Bonn: Institut zur Zukunft der Arbeit.

Bell, M. and S. Muhidin. 2009. "Cross-National Comparisons of Internal Migration." *Human Development Research Paper No. 30.* New York: United Nations Development Programme, Human Development Report Office.

Bellwood, P. 2005. *First Farmers: The Origins of Agricultural Societies.* Oxford: Blackwell Publishing.

Benach, J., C. Muntaner and V. Santana. 2007. "Employment Conditions and Health Inequalities". *Final Report to the WHO Commission on Social Determinants of Health.* Geneva: Employment Conditions Knowledge Network.

Berriane, M. 1997. "Emigration Internationale du Travail et Micro-Urbanisation dans le Rif Oriental: Cas du Centre de Toauima". *Migration Internationale et Changements Sociaux dans le Maghreb*: 75-97. Tunis: Université de Tunis.

Betcherman, G. and R. Islam (Eds.). 2001. *East Asian Labor Markets and the Economic Crisis: Impacts Responses and Lessons.* Washington DC: World Bank.

Bibliography

Betcherman, G., K. Olivas and A. Dar. 2004. "Impacts of Active Labour Market Programmes: New Evidence from Evaluations with Particular Attention to Developing and Transition Countries". *Social Protection Discussion Paper Series No. 0402*. Washington DC: World Bank.

Betts, A. 2008. *Towards a 'Soft Law' Framework for the Protection of Vulnerable Migrants.* Geneva: UNHCR.

Betts, D. C. and D. J. Slottje. 1994. *Crisis on the Rio-Grande: Poverty, Unemployment, and Economic Development on the Texas-Mexico Border.* Boulder: Westview Press.

Bhabha, J. 2008. "Independent Children, Inconsistent Adults: International Child Migration and the Legal Framework". *Discussion Paper No. 2008-02.* Florence: Innocenti Research Centre, UNICEF.

Bhagwati, J. N. 1979. "International Migration of the Highly Skilled: Economics, Ethics and Taxes." *Third World Quarterly* 1 (3): 17-30.

Black, R., D. Coppard, D. Kniveton, A. Murata, K. Schmidt-Verkerk and R. Skeldon. 2008. "Demographics and Climate Change: Future Trends and their Policy Implications for Migration". *Globalisation and Poverty Working Paper No. T27.* Brighton: Development Research Centre on Migration.

Black, R. and J. Sward. 2009. "Migration, Poverty Reduction Strategies and Human Development." *Human Development Research Paper No. 38.* New York: United Nations Development Programme, Human Development Report Office.

Borjas, G. J. 1995. "The Economic Benefits from Immigration." *The Journal of Economic Perspectives* 9 (2): 3-22.

———. **1999.** "Immigration and Welfare Magnets." *Journal of Labor Economics* 17 (4): 607-637.

———. **2003.** "The Labor Demand Curve is Downward Sloping: Reexamining the Impact of Immigration on the Labor Market." *The Quarterly Journal of Economics* 118 (4): 1335-1374.

Borjas, G. J., J. T. Grogger and G. H. Hanson. 2008. "Imperfect Substitution Between Immigrants and Natives: A Reappraisal". *Working Paper No. W13887.* Cambridge: National Bureau of Economic Research.

Bovenkerk, F., M. J. I. Gras, D. Ramsoedh, M. Dankoor and A. Havelaar. 1995. "Discrimination Against Migrant Workers and Ethnic Minorities in Access to Employment in the Netherlands". *Labor Market Papers No. 4.* Geneva: International Labour Organization.

Bowlby, J. 1982. *Attachment.* New York: Basic Books.

Branca, M. 2005. *Border Deaths and Arbitrary Detention of Migrant Workers.* Berkeley: Human Rights Advocates.

Brockerhoff, M. 1990. "Rural to Urban Migration and Child Survival in Senegal." *Demography* 27 (4): 601-616.

———. **1995.** "Child Survival in Big Cities: The Disadvantages of Migrants." *Social Science and Medicine* 40 (10): 1371-1383.

Brucker, H., G. S. Epstein, B. McCormick, G. Saint-Paul,

A. Venturini and K. Zimmermann. 2002. "Managing Migration in the European Welfare State." In T. Boeri, G. Hanson, and B. McCormick (Eds.), *Immigration Policy and the Welfare System*: 1-168. New York: Oxford University Press.

Bryant, J. and P. Rukumnuaykit. 2007. "Labor Migration in the Greater Mekong Sub-region: Does Migration to Thailand Reduce the Wages of Thai Workers?" *Working Paper No. 40889.* Washington DC: World Bank.

Buch, C. M., A. Kuckulenz and M.-H. Le Manchec. 2002. "Worker Remittances and Capital Flows". *Working Paper No. 1130.* Kiel: Kiel Institute for World Economics.

Bueker, C. S. 2005. "Political Incorporation among Immigrants from Ten Areas of Origin: The Persistence of Source Country Effects." *International Migration Review* 39 (1): 103-140.

Burd-Sharps, S., K. Lewis and E. Martins. 2008. *The Measure of America: American Human Development Report, 2008-2009.* New York: Columbia University Press.

Bursell, M. 2007. "What's in a Name? A Field Experiment Test for the Existence of Ethnic Discrimination in the Hiring Process". *Working Paper No. 2007-7.* The Stockholm University Linnaeus Center for Integration Studies.

Business Monitor International. 2009. "Downturn Raises Employment Questions." *Business Monitor International Forecasts.* March.

Butcher, K. F. and A. M. Piehl. 1998. "Recent Immigrants: Unexpected Implications for Crime and Incarceration." *Industrial and Labor Relations Review* 51 (4): 654-679.

Cai, F., Y. Du and M. Wang. 2009. «Migration and Labor Mobility in China.» *Human Development Research Paper No. 9.* New York: United Nations Development Programme, Human Development Report Office.

Carballo, M. 2007. "The Challenge of Migration and Health." *World Hospitals and Health Services: The Official Journal of the International Hospital Federation* 42 (4): 9-18.

Card, D. 1990. "The Impact of the Mariel Boat Lift on the Miami Labor Market." *Industrial and Labor Relation Review* 43 (2): 245-257.

———. **2009.** "Immigration and Inequality". *Working Paper No. 14683.* Cambridge: National Bureau of Economic Research, Inc.

Carling, J. 2006. "Migration, Human Smuggling and Trafficking from Nigeria to Europe". Geneva: International Organization for Migration.

Carrasco, R., J. F. Jimeno and A. C. Ortega. 2008. "The Impact of Immigration on the Wage Structure: Spain 1995-2002". *Economics Working Papers No. 080603.* Universidad Carlos III, Departamento de Economía.

Carvajal, L. and I. M. Pereira. 2009. "Evidence on the Link between Migration, Climate Disasters and Adaptive Capacity". *Human Development Report Office Working Paper.* New York: United Nations Development Programme.

Castles, S. and R. Delgado Wise (Eds.). 2008. *Migration*

Bibliography

and Development: Perspectives from the South. Geneva: International Organization for Migration.

Castles, S. and M. Miller. 1993. The Age of Migration. New York: The Guilford Press.

Castles, S. and S. Vezzoli. 2009. "The Global Economic Crisis and Migration: Temporary Interruption or Structural Change?". Unpublished Manuscript for Paradigmes (Spain).

CEPII (Research Center in International Economics). 2006. "Distance Database." http://www.cepii.fr/anglaisgraph/bdd/distances.htm. Accessed July 2009.

Cerrutti, M. 2009. "Gender and Intra-regional Migration in South America." Human Development Research Paper No. 12. New York: United Nations Development Programme, Human Development Report Office.

Chami, R., C. Fullenkamp and S. Jahjah. 2005. "Are Immigrant Remittance Flows a Source of Capital for Development?" IMF Staff Papers 52 (1): 55-81.

Chan, Liu and Yang. 1999. "Hukou and Non-Hukou Migration in China: Comparisons and Contrasts." International Journal of Population Geography 5: 425-448.

Chand, S. and M. A. Clemens. 2008. "Skilled Emigration and Skill Creation: A Quasi-experiment". International and Development Economics Working Paper No. 08-05. Canberra: Crawford School of Economics and Government.

Charnovitz, S. 2003. "Trade Law Norms on International Migration." In T. Aleinikoff and V. Chetail (Eds.), Migration and International Legal Norms: 241-253. The Hague: TMC Asser Press.

Chauvet, M. and C. Yu. 2006. "International Business Cycles: G7 and OECD Countries". Economic Review, First Quarter 2006. Atlanta: Federal Reserve Bank of Atlanta.

Chiswick, B. and Y. L. Lee. 2006. "Immigrant Selection Systems and Immigrant Health". Discussion Paper No. 2345. Bonn: Institut zur Zukunft der Arbeit.

Chiswick, B. and P. Miller. 1995. "The Endogenity Between Language and Earnings: An International Analysis." Journal of Labour Economics 13: 201-246.

Cho, W. K. T. 1999. "Naturalization, Socialization, Participation: Immigrants and Non-Voting." The Journal of Politics 61 (4): 1140-1155.

Christensen, G. and P. Stanat. 2007. "Language Policies and Practices for Helping Immigrants and Second-Generation Students Succeed". Unpublished Report of The Transatlantic Task Force on Immigration and Integration. Migration Policy Institute and Bertelsmann Stiftung.

Christian Aid. 2007. "Human Tide: The Real Migration Crisis". A Christian Aid Report.

CIEL (Center for International and Environmental Law). 2009. "The World Bank's Involuntary Resettlement Policy." http://www.ciel.org/Ifi/wbinvolresettle.html. Accessed June 2009.

Cinel, D. 1991. The National Integration of the Italian Return Migration, 1870-1929. Cambridge: Cambridge University Press.

Clark, K. and S. Drinkwater. 2008. "The Labour-Market Performance of Recent Migrants." Oxford Review of Economic Policy 24 (3): 495-516.

Clauss, S. and B. Nauck. 2009. "The Situation Among Children of Migrant Origin in Germany". Working Paper. Forthcoming. Florence: Innocenti Research Centre, UNICEF.

Clemens, M. 2009a. "Should Skilled Emigrants be Taxed? New Data on African Physicians Abroad". Working Paper. Forthcoming. Washington DC: Center for Global Development.

——. **2009b.** "Skill Flow: A Fundamental Reconsideration of Skilled-Worker Mobility and Development." Human Development Research Paper No. 8. New York: United Nations Development Programme, Human Development Report Office.

Clemens, M., C. Montenegro and L. Pritchett. 2008. "The Place Premium: Wage Differences for Identical Workers Across the U.S. Border". Policy Research Working Paper No. 4671. Washington DC: World Bank and Center For Global Development.

Clemens, M. and L. Pritchett. 2008. "Income Per Natural: Measuring Development as if People Mattered More than Places". Working Paper No. 143. Washington DC: Center for Global Development.

Clert, C., E. Gomart, I. Aleksic and N. Otel. 2005. "Human Trafficking in South Eastern Europe: Beyond Crime Control, an Agenda for Social Inclusion and Development". Processed Paper. Washington DC: World Bank.

Colombo Process. 2008. "Ministerial Consultation on Overseas Employment and Contractual Labour for Countries of Origin and Destination in Asia (Abu Dhabi Dialogue)". Ministerial Consultation on Overseas Employment and Contractual Labour for Countries of Origin and Destination in Asia (Abu Dhabi Dialogue), 21-22 January 2008, Abu Dhabi, UAE.

Comelatto, P. A., A. E. Lattes and C. M. Levit. 2003. "Migración Internacional y Dinámica Demográfica en la Argentina Durante la Segunda Mitad del Siglo XX." Estudios Migratorios Latinoamericanos 17 (50): 69-110.

Commander, S., R. Chanda, M. Kangasniemi and L. A. Winters. 2008. "The Consequences of Globalisation: India's Software Industry and Cross-border Labour Mobility." The World Economy 31 (2): 187-211.

Consensus Economics. 2009a. "Asia Pacific Consensus Forecasts." Consensus Economics: 1-36.

——. **2009b.** "Consensus Forecasts." Consensus Economics: 1-32.

——. **2009c.** "Eastern Europe Consensus Forecasts." Consensus Economics: 1-24.

——. **2009d.** "Latin American Consensus Forecasts." *Consensus Economics*: 1-31.

Constant, A. 2005. "Immigrant Adjustment in France and Impacts on the Natives." In K. F. Zimmermann (Ed.), *European Migration: What Do We Know?*: 263-302. New York: Oxford University Press.

Corcoran, S. P., E. N. William and R. M. Schwab. 2004. "Changing Labor-Market Opportunities for Women and the Quality of Teachers, 1957-2000." *American Economic Review* 94 (2): 230-235.

Cordova, A. and J. Hiskey. 2009. "Migrant Networks and Democracy in Latin America". Unpublished Working Paper. Nashville: Vanderbilt University.

Cornelius, W. A., T. Tsuda, P. L. Martin and J. Hollifield (Eds.). 2004. *Controlling immigration: A Global Perspective (Second Edition)*. Stanford: Stanford University Press.

Cortes, R. 2008. "Children and Women Left Behind in Labour Sending Countries: An Appraisal of Social Risks". Unpublished Working Paper. New York: UNICEF, Division of Policy and Practice.

Council of Europe. 2006. "Roma Campaign Dosta." http://www.coe.int/t/dg3/romatravellers/documentation/youth/Romaphobia_en.asp. Accessed May 2009.

Council of the European Union. 2009. *Council Directive on the Conditions of Entry and Residence of Third-country Nationals for the Purpose of Highly Qualified Employment 17426/08.* Brussels: Council of the European Union.

Cox Edwards, A. and M. Ureta. 2003. "International Migration Remittances, and Schooling: Evidence from El Salvador." *Journal of Development Economics* 72 (2): 429-461.

Crisp, J. 2006. "Forced Displacement in Africa: Dimensions, Difficulties and Policy Directions". *Research Paper No. 126.* Geneva, Switzerland: United Nations High Commissioner for Refugees.

Crul, M. 2007. "Pathways to Success for the Children of Immigrants". Unpublished Report of The Transatlantic Task Force on Immigration and Integration. Migration Policy Institute and Bertelsmann Stiftung.

Crush, J. and S. Ramachandran. 2009. "Xenophobia, International Migration, and Human Development." *Human Development Research Paper No. 47.* New York: United Nations Development Programme, Human Development Report Office.

Cummins, M., E. Letouzé, M. Purser and F. Rodríguez. 2009. "Revisiting the Migration-Development Nexus: A Gravity Model Approach." *Human Development Research Paper No. 44.* New York: United Nations Development Programme, Human Development Report Office.

Cummins, M. and F. Rodríguez. 2009. "Is There a Numbers Versus Rights Trade-Off in Immigration Policy? What the Data Say." *Human Development Research Paper No. 21.* New York: United Nations Development Programme, Human Development Report Office.

de Bruijn, B. J. 2009. "The Living Conditions and Well-Being of Refugees." *Human Development Research Paper No. 25.* New York: United Nations Development Programme, Human Development Report Office.

de Haas, H. 2007. *The Myth of Invasion: Irregular Migration from West Africa to the Maghreb and the European Union.* Oxford: International Migration Institute (IMI), James Martin 21st Century School, University of Oxford.

——. **2008.** "The Myth of Invasion: The Inconvenient Realities of African Migration to Europe." *Third World Quarterly* 29 (7): 1305-1322.

——. **2009.** "Mobility and Human Development." *Human Development Research Paper No. 1.* New York: United Nations Development Programme, Human Development Report Office.

de Haas, H. and R. Plug. 2006. "Cherishing the Goose with the Golden Eggs: Trends in Migrant Remittances from Europe to Morocco 1970-2004." *International Migration Review* 40 (3): 603-634.

Deb, P. and P. Seck. 2009. "Internal Migration, Selection Bias and Human Development: Evidence from Indonesia and Mexico." *Human Development Research Paper No. 31.* New York: United Nations Development Programme, Human Development Report Office.

December 18 vzw. 2008. *The UN Treaty Monitoring Bodies and Migrant Workers: A Samzidat.* Geneva: December 18 vzw.

Del Popolo, F., A. M. Oyarce, B. Ribotta and J. Rodríguez. 2008. *Indigenous Peoples and Urban Settlements: Spatial Distribution, Internal Migration and Living Conditions.* Santiago: United Nations Economic Commission for Latin America and the Caribbean.

Department of Treasury and Finance. 2002. "Globalisation and the Western Australian Economy". *Economic Research Paper.* Perth: Government of Western Australia.

Deshingkar, P. and S. Akter. 2009. "Migration and Human Development in India." *Human Development Research Paper No. 13.* New York: United Nations Development Programme, Human Development Report Office.

Deshingkar, P. and S. Grimm. 2005. "Internal Migration and Development: A Global Perspective". *Migration Research Series No. 19.* Geneva: International Organization for Migration.

DHS (Department of Homeland Security). 2007. "Yearbook of Immigration Statistics: 2007, Table 1." http://www.dhs.gov/ximgtn/statistics/publications/LPR07.shtm. Accessed June 2009.

Docquier, F. and A. Marfouk. 2004. "International Migration by Educational Attainment (1990-2000) - Release 1.1". Unpublished Working Paper.

Docquier, F., H. Rapoport and I. L. Shen. 2003. "Remittances and Inequality: A Dynamic Migration Model". *Discussion Paper No. 808.* Bonn: Institut zur Zukunft der Arbeit.

Doganis, R. 2002. *Flying Off Course.* London: Routledge.

Drèze, J. and A. Sen. 1999. *The Political Economy of Hunger Volume 1: Entitlement and Well-Being.* Oxford: Clarendon Press.

Dumont, J.-C., J. P. Martin and G. Spielvogel. 2007. "Women on the Move: The Neglected Gender Dimension of the Brain Drain". *Discussion Paper No. 2920.* Bonn: Institut zur Zukunft der Arbeit.

Durand, J., W. Kandel, A. P. Emilio and D. S. Massey. 1996. "International Migration and Development in Mexican Communities." *Demography* 33 (2): 249-264.

Dustmann, C. and F. Fabbri. 2005. "Immigrants in the British Labour Market." *Fiscal Studies* 26 (4): 423-470.

Dustmann, C., T. Frattini and I. Preston. 2008. "The Effect of Immigration Along the Distribution of Wages". *Discussion Paper No. 0803.* London: Centre for Research and Analysis of Migration.

Dustmann, C., A. Glitz and T. Vogel. 2006. "Employment, Wage Structure, and the Economic Cycle: Difference Between Immigrants and Natives in Germany and the UK". *Discussion Paper No. 0906.* London: Centre for Research and Analysis of Migration.

Earnest, D. C. 2008. *Old Nations, New Voters: Nationalism, Transnationalism and Democracy in the Era of Global Migration.* Albany: State University of New York Press.

EC-UN Joint Migration and Development Initiative. 2008. "Migrant Communities." In *Migration for Development: Knowledge Fair Handbook*: 39-53. Brussels: EC-UN Joint Migration and Development Initiative.

Eckstein, S. 2004. "Dollarization and its Discontents: Remittances and the Remaking of Cuba in the Post-Soviet Era." *Comparative Politics* 36 (3): 313-330.

ECLAC (Economic Commission for Latin America and the Caribbean). 2007. "Internal Migration and Development in Latin America and the Caribbean: Continuity, Changes and Policy Challenges." In *Social Panorama of Latin America*: 195-232. Santiago: United Nations.

ECOSOC (Economic and Social Council of the United Nations, Commission on Human Rights). 1998. "Further Promotion and Encouragement of Human Rights and Fundamental Freedoms Including the Question of the Programme and Methods of Work of the Commission: Human Rights, Mass Exoduses, and Displaced Persons". Commission on Human Rights, Fifth-fourth session. UN Doc. No. E/CN.4/1998/53/Add.2.

Ellis, F. and N. Harris. 2004. "Development Patterns, Mobility and Livelihood Diversification". Paper presented at Department for International Development Sustainable Development Retreat, 13 July 2004, Guildford, UK.

EurActiv.com News. 2008. "Divided Parliament Approves EU Blue Card System." http://www.euractiv.com/en/socialeurope/divided-parliament-approves-eu-blue-card-system/article-177380.

European Parliament. 2008. "European Parliament Legislative Resolution of 18 June 2008 on the Proposal for a Directive of the European Parliament and of the Council on Common Standards and Procedures in Member States for Returning Illegally Staying Third-Country Nationals P6_TA(2008)0293." http://www.europarl.europa.eu/sides/getDoc.do?pubRef=-//EP//TEXT+TA+P6-TA-2008-0293+0+DOC+XML+V0//EN&language=EN#BKMD-5. Accessed June 2009.

Ezra, M. and G. E. Kiros. 2001. "Rural Out-Migration in the Drought Prone Areas of Ethiopia: A Multilevel Analysis." *International Migration Review* 35 (3): 749-771.

Facchini, G. and A. M. Mayda. 2008. "From Individual Attitudes Towards Migrants to Migration Policy Outcomes: Theory and Evidence." *Economic Policy* 23 (56): 651-713.

———. **2009.** "The Political Economy of Immigration Policy." *Human Development Research Paper No. 3.* New York: United Nations Development Programme, Human Development Report Office.

Fajnzylber, P. and J. H. Lopez. 2007. *Close to Home: The Development Impact of Remittances in Latin America.* Washington DC: World Bank Publications.

Fan, C. C. 2002. "The Elite, the Natives, and the Outsiders: Migration and Labor Market Segmentation in Urban China." *Annals of the Association of American Geographers* 92 (1): 103-124.

Fan, C. S. and O. Stark. 2007. "The Brain Drain, 'Educated Unemployment', Human Capital Formation, and Economic Betterment." *Economics of Transition* 15 (4): 629-660.

Fang, C. and D. Wang. 2008. "Impacts of Internal Migration on Economic Growth and Urban Development in China." In J. DeWind and J. Holdaway (Eds.), *Migration and Development Within and Across Borders: Research and Policy Perspectives on Internal and International Migration*: 245-272. Geneva: International Organization for Migration.

Fang, Z. Z. 2009. "Potential of China in Global Nurse Migration." *Health Services Research* 42 (1): 1419-1428.

Fargues, P. 2006. "The Demographic Benefit of International Migration: Hypothesis and Application to Middle Eastern and North African Contexts". *Policy Research Working Paper No. 4050.* Washington DC: World Bank.

Felbermayr, G. J. and F. Toubal. 2008. "Revisiting the Trade-Migration Nexus: Evidence from New OECD Data". Unpublished Working Paper.

Fennelly, K. 2005. "The 'Healthy Migrant' Effect." *Healthy Generations* 5 (3): 1-4.

Findlay, A. M. and B. L. Lowell. 2001. *Migration of Highly Skilled Persons from Developing Countries: Impact and Policy Responses.* Geneva: International Labour Office.

Foner, N. 2002. *From Ellis Island to JFK.* New Haven: Yale University Press.

Frank, R. and R. A. Hummer. 2002. "The Other Side of the Paradox: The Risk of Low Birth Weight Among Infants of Migrant and Nonmigrant Households within Mexico." *International Migration Review* 36 (3): 746-765.

Freedom House. 2005. *Freedom in the World 2005: The Annual Survey of Political Rights and Civil Liberties.* Boston: Rowman & Littlefield Publishers.

——. 2009. "Freedom in the World Survey". Washington DC: Freedom House.

Friedman, B. M. 2005. *The Moral Consequences of Economic Growth.* New York: Knopf.

Gaige. 2006. *Zhongguo nongmingong wenti yanjiu zongbaogao (Report on the Problems of Chinese Farmer-Turned Workers)* (Rep. No. 5).

Galenson, D. W. 1984. "The Rise and Fall of Indentured Servitude in the Americas: An Economic Analysis." *Journal of Economic History* 44 (1): 1-26.

Gamlen, A. 2006. "Diasporas Engagement Policies: What are They, and What Kinds of States Use Them?". *Working Paper No. 32.* Oxford: Centre on Migration, Policy and Society.

García y Griego, M. 1983. "The Importation of Mexican Contract Laborers to the United States, 1942-1964: Antecedents, Operation and Legacy." In P. Brown and H. Shue (Eds.), *The Border that Joins: Mexican Migrants and US Responsibility*: 49-98. New Jersey: Rowman and Littlefield.

Garcia-Gomez, P. 2007. "Salud y Utilización de Recursos Sanitarios: Un Análisis de las Diferencias y Similitudes Entre Población Inmigrante y Autóctona." *Presupuesto y Gasto Publico* 49: 67-85.

GFMD (Global Forum on Migration and Development). 2008. "Report of the Proceedings". Prepared for the Global Forum on Migration and Development, 29-30 October 2008, Manila, Philippines.

Ghosh, B. 2007. "Restrictions in EU Immigration and Asylum Policies in the Light of International Human Rights Standards." *Essex Human Rights Review* 4 (2).

Ghosh, J. 2009. "Migration and Gender Empowerment: Recent Trends and Emerging Issues." *Human Development Research Paper No. 4.* New York: United Nations Development Programme, Human Development Report Office.

Gibney, M. J. 2009. "Precarious Residents: Migration Control, Membership and the Rights of Non-Citizens." *Human Development Research Paper No. 10.* New York: United Nations Development Programme, Human Development Report Office.

Gibson, J. and S. D. McKenzie. 2009. "The Microeconomic Determinants of Emigration and Return Migration of the Best and Brightest: Evidence from the Pacific". *Discussion Paper Series No. 03/09.* London: Centre for Research and Analysis of Migration.

Gidwani, V. and K. Sivaramakrishnan. 2003. "Circular Migration and the Spaces of Cultural Assertion." *Annals of the Association of American Geographers* 93 (1): 186-213.

Gilbertson, G. A. 1995. "Women's Labor and Enclave Employment: The Case of Dominican and Colombian Women in New York City." *International Migration Review* 29 (3): 657-670.

Glaeser, E. L., H. D. Kallal, J. A. Scheinkman and A. Shleifer. 1992. "Growth in Cities." *Journal of Political Economy* 100 (6): 1126-1152.

Global IDP Project and Norwegian Refugee Council. 2005. *Internal Displacement: Global Overview of Trends and Developments in 2004.* Geneva: Global IDP Project.

Global Legal Information Network. 2009. "Kafala." http://www.glin.gov/subjectTermIndex. action?search=&searchDetails. queryType=BOOLEAN&searchDetails.queryString=mt%3A ^%22Kafala%22%24. Accessed June 2009.

Goldring, L. 2004. "Family and Collective Remittances to Mexico: A Multi-Dimensional Typology." *Development and Change* 35: 799-840.

Goncalves, A., S. Dias, M. Luck, M. J. Fernandes and J. Cabral. 2003. "Acesso aos Cuidados de Saúde de Comunidades Migrantes: Problemas e Perspectivas e Intervenção." *Revista Portuguesa de Saude Publica* 21 (1): 55-64.

Gould, J. D. 1980. "European Inter-Continental Emigration. The Road Home: Return Migration from the USA." *Journal of European Economic History* 9: 41-112.

Government of Azad Jammu and Kashmir. 2003. *Between Hope and Despair: Pakistan Participatory Poverty Assessment Azad Jammu and Kashmir Report.* Islamabad: Planning Commission, Government of Pakistan.

Government of Lesotho. 2004. "Kingdom of Lesotho Poverty Reduction Strategy 2004/2005 - 2006/2007." http://www. lesotho.gov.ls/documents/PRSP_Final.pdf. Accessed June 2009.

Government of Sweden. 2008. "Swedish Code of Statutes." http://www.sweden.gov.se/. Accessed June 2009.

Government of Western Australia. 2004. "WA Charter of Multiculturalism." http://www.omi.wa.gov.au/Publications/ wa_charter_multiculturalism.pdf. Accessed June 2009.

Gregory, J. N. 1989. *American Exodus: The Dust Bowl Migration and Okie Culture in California.* New York: Oxford University Press.

Ha, W., J. Yi and J. Zhang. 2009a. "Brain Drain, Brain Gain, and Economic Growth in China." *Human Development*

Research Paper No. 37. New York: United Nations Development Programme, Human Development Report Office.

——. **2009b.** "Internal Migration and Inequality in China: Evidence from Village Panel Data." *Human Development Research Paper No. 27.* New York: United Nations Development Programme, Human Development Report Office.

Hagan, J., K. Eschbach and N. Rodriguez. 2008. "US Deportation Policy, Family Separation, and Circular Migration." *International Migration Review* 42 (1): 64-88.

Halliday, T. 2006. "Migration, Risk, and Liquidity Constraints in El Salvador." *Economic Development and Cultural Change* 54 (4): 893-925.

Hamel, J. Y. 2009. "Information and Communication Technologies and Migration." *Human Development Research Paper No. 39.* New York: United Nations Development Programme, Human Development Report Office.

Hampshire, K. 2006. "Flexibility in Domestic Organization and Seasonal Migration Among the Fulani of Northern Burkina Faso." *Africa* 76: 402-426.

Hanson, G. 2007. "The Economic Logic of Illegal Immigration". *Working Paper No. 26.* New York: Council on Foreign Relations.

—— **2009.** "The Governance of Migration Policy." *Human Development Research Paper No. 2.* New York: United Nations Development Programme, Human Development Report Office.

Hanson, G., K. F. Scheve and M. J. Slaughter. 2007. "Public Finance and Individual Preferences Over Globalization Strategies." *Economics and Politics* 19 (1): 1-33.

Hanson, G. and A. Spilimbergo. 2001. "Political Economy, Terms of Trade, and Border Enforcement." *Canadian Journal of Economics* 34 (3): 612-638.

Harris, J. R. and M. P. Todaro. 1970. "Migration, Unemployment, and Development: A Two-Sector Analysis." *The American Economic Review* 60 (1): 126-142.

Harttgen, K. and S. Klasen. 2009. "A Human Development Index by Internal Migration Status." *Human Development Research Paper No. 54.* New York: United Nations Development Programme, Human Development Report Office.

Hashim, I. M. 2006. "The Positives and Negatives of Children's Independent Migration: Assessing the Evidence and the Debates". *Working Paper No. T16.* Brighton: Development Research Centre on Migration.

Hatton, T. J. and J. G. Williamson. 1998. *The Age of Mass Migration: Causes and Economic Impact.* New York: Oxford University Press.

——. **2005.** *Global Migration and the World Economy: Two Centuries of Policy Performance.* Cambridge: MIT Press.

Hausmann, R., F. Rodríguez and R. Wagner. 2008. "Growth Collapses." In C. M. Reinhart, C. A. Végh, and A. Velasco (Eds.), *Money, Crises, and Transition: Essays in Honor of Guillermo A. Calvo*: 377-428. Cambridge: MIT Press.

He, Y. 2004. "Hukou and Non-Hukou Migrations in China: 1995-2000". *Working Paper Series No. C2004016.* China Center for Economic Research.

Heckman, J. J. 2006. "Skill Formation and the Economics of Investing in Disadvantaged Children." *Science* 312 (5782): 1900-1902.

Heleniak, T. 2009. "Migration Trends and Patterns in the Former Soviet Union and Czechoslovakia 1960-1990". *Commissioned by the Human Development Report Office.* New York: United Nations Development Programme.

Henderson, J. V., Z. Shalizi and A. J. Venables. 2001. "Geography and Development." *Journal of Economic Geography* (1): 81-105.

Hernandez, D. 2009. "Children in Immigrant Families in Eight Affluent Societies". Florence: Innocenti Research Centre, UNICEF.

Heston, A., R. Summers and B. Aten. 2006. "Penn World Table Version 6.2". Philadelphia: Center for International Comparisons of Production, Income and Prices at the University of Pennsylvania.

Hildebrandt, N., D. J. McKenzie, G. Esquivel and E. Schargrodsky. 2005. "The Effects of Migration on Child Health in Mexico." *Economia* 6 (1): 257-289.

Horst, H. 2006. "The Blessings and Burdens of Communication: Cell Phones in Jamaican Transnational Social Fields." *Global Networks* 6 (2): 143-159.

Hossain, M. I., I. A. Khan and J. Seeley. 2003. "Surviving on their Feet: Charting the Mobile Livelihoods of the Poor in Rural Bangladesh". Paper presented at Staying Poor: Chronic Poverty and Development Policy, 7-9 April 2003, Manchester, UK.

Huan-Chang, C. 1911. *The Economic Principles of Confucius and his School.* Whitefish: Kessinger Publishing.

Huang, Q. 2006. "Three Government Agencies Emphasize the Need to Pay Close Attention to the Safety and Health of Migrant Workers (Sanbumen Kaizhan Guanai Nongmingong Shenming Anquan Yu Jiankang Tebie Xingdong)." *Xinhua News Agency.*

Hugo, G. 2000. "Migration and Women's Empowerment." In H. B. Presser and G. Sen (Eds.), *Women's Empowerment and Demographic Processes.* Oxford, U.K.: Oxford University Press.

Hugo, G. 1993. "Indonesian Labour Migration to Malaysia: Trends and Policy Implications." *Southeast Asian Journal of Social Science* 21 (1): 36-70.

Human Rights Watch. 2005a. *Families Torn Apart: The High Cost of U.S. and Cuban Travel Restrictions.* New York: Human Rights Watch.

——. **2005b.** "Malaysia: Migrant Workers Fall Prey to Abuse." *Human Rights Watch News Release,* 16 May.

——. **2007a.** "Forced Apart." http://www.hrw.org/en/reports/2007/07/16/forced-apart. Accessed June 2009.

——. **2007b.** "World Report 2007". New York: Human Rights Watch.

Human Security Centre. 2005. *Human Security Report 2005: War and Peace in the 21st Century.* New York: Oxford University Press.

Hunt, J. and M. Gauthier-Loiselle. 2008. "How Much Does Immigration Boost Innovation?" *Working Paper No. 14312.* Cambridge: National Bureau of Economic Research.

IATA (International Air Transport Association). 2006. *Travel Information Manual.* Badhoevedorp: IATA.

Içduygu, A. 2009. "International Migration and Human Development in Turkey." *Human Development Research Paper No. 52.* New York: United Nations Development Programme, Human Development Report Office.

ICFTU (International Confederation of Free Trade Unions). 2009. "International Confederation of Free Trade Unions." http://www.icftu.org/default.asp?Language=EN. Accessed July 2009.

ICMPD (International Centre for Migration Policy Development). 2009. "Regularisations in Europe: Study on Practices in the Area of Regularisation of Illegally Staying Third-Country Nationals in the Member States of the EU". Vienna: ICMPD.

IDB (Inter-American Development Bank). 2009. "Sectoral Operational Policies: Involuntary Resettlement." http://www.iadb.org/aboutus/pi/OP_710.cfm. Accessed June 2009.

IDMC (Internal Displacement Monitoring Centre). 2008. *Internal Displacement: Global Overview of Trends and Developments in 2007.* Geneva: IDMC.

——. **2009a.** "Global Statistics on IDPs." http://www.internal-displacement.org. Accessed February 2009.

——. **2009b.** *Internal Displacement: Global Overview of Trends and Developments in 2008.* Geneva: IDMC.

Ignatiev, N. 1995. *How the Irish Became White.* New York: Routledge.

IIED and WBCSD (International Institute for Environment and Development and World Business Council for Sustainable Development). 2003. *Breaking New Ground: Mining, Minerals and Sustainable Development.* Virginia: Earthscan.

ILO (International Labour Organization). 2004. "Towards a Fair Deal for Migrant Workers in the Global Economy." International Labour Conference, 92nd Session, 1-12 June 2004, Geneva, Switzerland.

——. **2009a.** "Economically Active Population Estimates and Projections." http://laborsta.ilo.org/applv8/data/EAPEP/eapep_E.html. Accessed July 2009.

——. **2009b.** "LABORSTA database." http://laborsta.ilo.org/. Accessed July 2009.

IMF (International Monetary Fund). 2009a. "Global Economic Policies and Prospects". Executive Summary of the Meeting of the Ministers and Central Bank Governors of the Group of Twenty, 13-14 March, London.

——. **2009b.** "Government Finance Statistics Online." http://www.imfstatistics.org/gfs/. Accessed July 2009.

——. **2009c.** *World Economic Outlook Update: Global Economic Slump Challenges Policies.* Washington DC: International Monetary Fund.

IMF (International Monetary Fund) and World Bank. 1999. "Poverty Reduction Strategy Papers--Operational Issues." http://www.imf.org/external/np/pdr/prsp/poverty1.htm.

Immigration and Refugee Board of Canada. 2008. "Responses to Information Requests (CHN102869.E)." http://www2.irb-cisr.gc.ca/en/research/rir/?action=record.viewrec&gotorec=451972. Accessed July 2009.

INE (Instituto Nacional de Estadística). 2009. "Encuesta de Población Activa: Primer Trimestre". Madrid: Government of Spain.

International Labour Office. 1936. *World Statistics of Aliens: A Comparative Study of Census Returns, 1910-1920-1930.* Westminster: P.S. King & Son Ltd.

IOM (International Organization for Migration). 2008a. "The Diversity Initiative: Fostering Cultural Understanding in Ukraine." http://www.iom.int/jahia/Jahia/facilitating-migration/migrant-integration/pid/2026. Accessed June 2009.

——. **2008b.** *World Migration 2008: Managing Labour Mobility in the Evolving Global Economy.* Geneva: International Organization for Migration.

IPC (Immigration Policy Center). 2007. *The Myth of Immigrant Criminality and the Paradox of Assimilation: Incarceration Rates Among Native and Foreign-Born Men.* Washington DC: IPC.

IPCC (Intergovernmental Panel on Climate Change). 2007. "Climate Change 2007: The Physical Science Basis. Contribution of Working Group I to the Fourth Assessment Report of the Intergovernmental Panel on Climate Change." In S. Solomon, D. Qin, M. Manning, Z. Chen, M. Marquis, K. B. Averyt, M. Tignor, and H. L. Miller (Eds.). New York: Cambridge University Press.

IPU (Inter-Parliamentary Union). 2009. Correspondence on year women received the right to vote and to stand for election and year first woman was elected or appointed to parliament. June. Geneva.

Iredale, R. 2001. "The Migration of Professionals: Theories and Typologies." *International Migration* 39 (5, Special Issue 1): 7-26.

Iskander, N. 2009. "The Creative State: Migration, Development and the State in Morocco and Mexico, 1963-2005". New York: New York University. Forthcoming.

Ivakhnyuk, I. 2009. "The Russian Migration Policy and its Impact on Human Development: The Historical Perspective." *Human Development Research Paper No. 14.* New York: United Nations Development Programme, Human Development Report Office.

Jack, B. and T. Suri. 2009. "Mobile Money: The Economics of Kenya's M-PESA". Cambridge: MIT Sloan School of Business, Forthcoming.

Jacobs, J. 1970. *The Economy of Cities.* New York: Vintage Books.

Jasso, G., D. Massey, M. Rosenzweig and J. Smith. 2004. "Immigrant Health - Selectivity and Acculturation." In N. B. Anderson, R. A. Bulatao, and B. Cohen (Eds.), *Critical Perspectives on Racial and Ethnic Differences in Health in Late Life*: 227-266. Washington, D.C.: National Academies Press.

Jasso, G. and M. Rosenzweig. 2009. "Selection Criteria and the Skill Composition of Immigrants: A Comparative Analysis of Australian and US Employment Immigration." In J. N. Bhagwati and G. Hanson (Eds.), *Skilled Immigration Today: Prospects, Problems and Policies*: 153-183. New York: Oxford University Press.

Javorcik, B. S., C. Ozden, M. Spatareanu and C. Neagu. 2006. "Migrant Networks and Foreign Direct Investment". *Working Paper No. 3.* Newark: Rutgers University.

Jayaweera, H. and B. Anderson. 2009. "Migrant Workers and Vulnerable Employment: A Review of Existing Data". *Project Undertaken by Compas for the TUC Comission on Vulnerable Employment.* Oxford: Centre on Migration, Policy, and Society.

Jobbins, M. 2008. "Migration and Development: Poverty Reduction Strategies." Prepared for the Global Forum on Migration and Development, 29-30 October 2008, Manila, Philippines.

Kabeer, N. 2000. *The Power to Choose: Bangladeshi Women and Labour Market Decisions in London and Dhaka.* London: Verso.

Kalita, M. 2009. "U.S. Deters Hiring of Foreigners as Joblessness Grows." *The Wall Street Journal,* 27 March.

Kapur, D. 2004. "Remittances: The New Development Matra?" *G-24 Discussion Paper Series No. 29.* Geneva: United Nations Conference on Trade and Development.

Karsten, S., C. Felix, G. Ledoux, W. Meijnen, J. Roeleveld and E. Van Schooten. 2006. "Choosing Segregation or Integration?: The Extent and Effects of Ethnic Segregation in Dutch Cities." *Education and Urban Society* 38 (2): 228-247.

Kaur, A. 2007. "International Labour Migration in Southeast Asia: Governance of Migration and Women Domestic Workers." *Intersections: Gender, History and Culture in the Asian Context* (15).

Kautsky, K. 1899. *The Agrarian Question.* London: Zwan Publications.

Kelley, N. and M. Trebilcock. 1998. *The Making of the Mosaic: A History of Canadian Immigration Policy.* Toronto: University of Toronto Press.

Khaleej Times. 2009. "Bahrain Commerce Body Denies Abolition of Sponsorship." *Khaleej Times Online,* 15 June.

Khoo, S. E., G. Hugo and P. McDonald. 2008. "Which Skilled Temporary Migrants Become Permanent Residents and Why?" *International Migration Review* 42 (1): 193-226.

King, R., R. Skeldon and J. Vullnetari. 2008. "Internal and International Migration: Bridging the Theoretical Divide". Paper presented at Theories of Migration and Social Change Conference, 1-3 July 2008, Oxford University, Oxford, UK.

King, R. and J. Vullnetari. 2006. "Orphan Pensioners and Migrating Grandparents: The Impact of Mass Migration on Older People in Rural Albania." *Ageing and Society* 26 (5): 783-816.

Kireyev, A. 2006. "The Macroeconomics of Remittances: The Case of Tajikistan". *IMF Working Paper No. 06/2.* Washington D.C.: International Monetary Fund.

Kleemans, M. and J. Klugman. 2009. "Public Opinions towards Migration." *Human Development Research Paper No. 53.* New York: United Nations Development Programme, Human Development Report Office.

Klugman, J. and I. M. Pereira. 2009. "Assessment of National Migration Policies." *Human Development Research Paper No. 48.* New York: United Nations Development Programme, Human Development Report Office.

Koettl, J. 2006. "The Relative Merits of Skilled and Unskilled Migration, Temporary, and Permanent Labor Migration, and Portability of Social Security Benefits". *Working Paper Series No. 38007.* Washington DC: World Bank.

Koser, K. 2008. "Why Migrant Smuggling Pays." *International Migration* 46 (2): 3-26.

Koslowski, R. 2008. "Global Mobility and the Quest for an International Migration Regime." In J. Chamie and L. Dall'Oglio (Eds.), *International migration and development: Continuing the dialogue: Legal and policy perspectives*: 103-144. Geneva: International Organization for Migration.

——. **2009.** "Global Mobility Regimes: A Conceptual Reframing". Paper presented at International Studies Association Meeting, 15 February 2009, New York, US.

Kremer, M. and S. Watt. 2006. "The Globalisation of Household Production". *Working Paper No. 2008-0086.* Cambridge: Weatherhead Center for International Affairs, Harvard University.

Kundu, A. 2009. "Urbanisation and Migration: An Analysis of Trends, Patterns and Policies in Asia." *Human Development Research Paper No. 16.* New York: United Nations Development Programme, Human Development Report

Office.

Kutnick, B., P. Belser and G. Danailova-Trainor. 2007. "Methodologies for Global and National Estimation of Human Trafficking Victims: Current and Future Approaches". *Working Paper No. 29.* Geneva: International Labour Organization.

La Rovere, E. L. and F. E. Mendes. 1999. "Tucuruí Hydropower Complex Brazil". *Working Paper.* Cape Town: World Commission on Dams.

Lacroix, T. 2005. "Les Réseaux Marocains du Développement: Géographie du Transnational et Politiques du Territorial". Paris: Presses de Sciences Po.

Laczko, F. and G. Danailova-Trainor. 2009. "Trafficking in Persons and Human Development: Towards a More Integrated Policy Response." *Human Development Research Paper No. 51.* New York: United Nations Development Programme, Human Development Report Office.

Landau, L. B. 2005. "Urbanization, Nativism and the Rule of Law in South Africa's 'Forbidden Cities'." *Third World Quarterly* 26 (7): 1115-1134.

Landau, L. B. and A. Wa Kabwe-Segatti. 2009. "Human Development Impacts of Migration: South Africa Case Study." *Human Development Research Paper No. 5.* New York: United Nations Development Programme, Human Development Report Office.

Lawyers for Human Rights. 2008. "Monitoring Immigration Detention in South Africa". Pretoria: Lawyers for Human Rights.

Leal-Arcas, R. 2007. "Bridging the Gap in the Doha Talks: A Look at Services Trade." *Journal of International Commercial Law and Technology* 2 (4): 241-249.

Lee, R. and T. Miller. 2000. "Immigration, Social Security, and Broader Fiscal Impacts." *American Economic Review: Papers and Proceedings* 90 (2): 350-354.

Leon-Ledesma, M. and M. Piracha. 2004. "International Migration and the Role of Remittances in Eastern Europe." *International Migration* 42 (4): 65-83.

Levitt, P. 1998. "Social Remittances: Migration Driven Local-Level Forms of Cultural Diffusion." *International Migration Review* 32 (4): 926-948.

——. **2006.** "Social Remittances - Culture as a Development Tool". Unpublished Working Paper. Santo Domingo: United Nations International Research and Training Institute for the Advancement of Women.

Lewis, W. A. 1954. "Economic Development with Unlimited Supplies of Labor." *Manchester School of Economic and Social Studies* 22 (2): 139-191.

Linz, B., F. Balloux, Y. Moodley, A. Manica, H. Liu, P. Roumagnac, D. Falush, C. Stamer, F. Prugnolle, S. W. van der Merwe, Y. Yamaoka, D. Y. Graham, E. Perez-Trallero, T. Wadstrom, S. Suerbaum and M. Achtman.

2007. "An African Origin for the Intimate Association Between Humans and Helicobacter Pylori." *Nature* 445: 915-918.

Lipton, M. 1980. "Migration from Rural Areas of Poor Countries: The Impact on Rural Productivity and Income Distribution." *World Development* 8 (1): 1-24.

LIS (Luxembourg Income Study). 2009. "Key Figures." http://www.lisproject.org/key-figures/key-figures.htm. Accessed June 2009.

Local Government Association. 2009. "The Impact of the Recession on Migrant Labour". London: Local Government Association.

Longhi, S., P. Nijkamp and J. Poot. 2005. "A Meta-Analytic Assessment of the Effect of Immigration on Wages." *Journal of Economic Surveys* 19 (3): 451-477.

Longva, A. N. 1997. *Walls Built on Sand: Migration, Exclusion and Society in Kuwait.* Boulder: Westview Press.

Lu, X. and Y. Wang. 2006. "'Xiang-Cheng' Renkou Qianyi Guimo De Cesuan Yu Fenxi (1979-2003) (Estimation and Analysis on Chinese Rural-Urban Migration Size)." *Xibei Renkou (Northwest Population)* 1: 14-16.

Lucas, R. E. B. 2004. "Life Earnings and Rural-Urban Migration." *The Journal of Political Economy* 112 (1): S29-S59.

Lucas, R. E. B. and L. Chappell. 2009. "Measuring Migration's Development Impacts: Preliminary Evidence from Jamaica". *Working Paper.* Global Development Network and Institute for Public Policy Research.

Lucassen, L. 2005. *The Immigrant Threat: The Integration of Old and New Migrants in Western Europe since 1890.* Champaign: University of Illinois Press.

Luthria, M. 2009. "The Importance of Migration to Small Fragile Economies." *Human Development Research Paper No. 55.* New York: United Nations Development Programme, Human Development Report Office.

Magee, G. B. and A. S. Thompson. 2006. "Lines of Credit, Debts of Obligation: Migrant Remittances to Britain, C.1875-1913." *Economic History Review* 59 (3): 539-577.

Maksakova, L. P. 2002. "Migratsia I Rinok Truda V Stranakh Srednei Azii [Migration and Labor Market in the Middle Asian Countries]". Proceedings of the Regional Seminar, 11-12 October 2001, Tashkent, Uzbekistan.

Malek, A. 2008. "Training for Overseas Employment". Paper presented at International Labour Organization Symposium on Deployment of Workers Overseas: A Shared Responsibility, 15-16 July 2008, Dhaka, Bangladesh.

Manacorda, M., A. Manning and J. Wadsworth. 2006. "The Impact of Immigration on the Structure of Male Wages: Theory and Evidence from Britain". *Discussion Paper Series No. 0608.* London: Centre for Research and Analysis of Migration.

Mansuri, G. 2006. "Migration, Sex Bias, and Child Growth in Rural Pakistan". *Policy Research Working Paper No. 3946.* Washington, D.C.: World Bank.

Marcelli, E. A. and P. M. Ong. 2002. "2000 Census Coverage of Foreign Born Mexicans in Los Angeles Country: Implications for Demographic Analysis". Paper presented at the 2002 Annual Meeting of the Population Association of America, 9-11 May 2002, Atlanta, US.

Marquette, C. M. 2006. "Nicaraguan Migrants in Costa Rica." *Poblacion y Salud en Mesoamerica 4* (1).

Martin, P. 1993. *Trade and Migration: NAFTA and Agriculture.* Washington DC: Institute for International Economics.

——. **1994.** "Germany: Reluctant Land of Immigration." In W. Cornelius, P. Martin, and J. Hollifield (Eds.), *Controlling Immigration: A Global Perspective*: 189-225. Stanford: Stanford University Press.

——. **2003.** *Promise Unfulfilled: Unions, Immigration, and Farm Workers.* Ithaca: Cornell University Press.

——. **2005.** "Merchant of Labor: Agents of the Evolving Migration Infrastructure". *Discussion Paper No. 158.* Geneva: International Institute for Labour Studies.

——. **2009a.** "Demographic and Economic Trends: Implications for International Mobility." *Human Development Research Paper No. 17.* New York: United Nations Development Programme, Human Development Report Office.

——. **2009b.** "Migration in the Asia-Pacific Region: Trends, Factors, Impacts." *Human Development Research Paper No. 32.* New York: United Nations Development Programme, Human Development Report Office.

Martin, P. and J. E. Taylor. 1996. "The Anatomy of a Migration Hump." In J. E. Taylor (Ed.), *Development Strategy, Employment, and Migration: Insights from Models*: 43-62. Paris: Organisation for Economic Co-operation and Development (OECD).

Martin, S. F. 2008. "Policy and Institutional Coherence at the Civil Society Days of the GFMD". Prepared for the Global Forum on Migration and Development, 29-30 October 2008, Manila, Philippines.

Martin, S. F. and R. Abimourchad. 2008. "Promoting the Rights of Migrants". Prepared for the Civil Society Days of the Global Forum on Migration and Development, 27-30 October 2008, Manila, Philippines.

Massey, D. S. 1988. "International Migration and Economic Development in Comparative Perspective." *Population and Development Review* 14: 383-414.

——. **2003.** "Patterns and Processes of International Migration in the 21st Century". Paper prepared for Conference on African Migration in Comparative Perspective, 4-7 June 2003, Johannesburg, South Africa.

Massey, D. S., J. Arango, G. Hugo, A. Kouaouci, A. Pellegrino and J. E. Taylor. 1998. *Worlds in Motion: Understanding International Mgiration at the End of the Milliennium.* New York: Oxford University Press.

Massey, D. S. and M. Sánchez R. 2009. "Restrictive Immigration Policies and Latino Immigrant Identity in the United States." *Human Development Research Paper No. 43.* New York: United Nations Development Programme, Human Development Report Office.

Matsushita, M., T. J. Schoenbaum and P. C. Mavroidis (Eds.). 2006. *The World Trade Organization: Law, Practice, and Policy.* New York: Oxford University Press.

Mattoo, A. and M. Olarreaga. 2004. "Reciprocity across Modes of Supply in the WTO: A Negotiating Formula." *International Trade Journal* 18: 1-24.

Mazzolari, F. and D. Neumark. 2009. "The Effects of Immigration on the Scale and Composition of Demand: A Study of California Establishments." *Human Development Research Paper No. 33.* New York: United Nations Development Programme, Human Development Report Office.

McKay, L., S. Macintyre and A. Ellaway. 2003. "Migration and Health: A Review of the International Literature". *Occasional Paper No. 12.* Glasgow: Medical Research Council Social and Public Health Sciences Unit.

McKenzie, D. 2007. "Paper Walls are Easier to Tear Down: Passport Costs and Legal Barriers to Emigration." *World Development* 35 (11): 2026-2039.

McKenzie, D., J. Gibson and S. Stillman. 2006. "How Important is Selection? Experimental versus Non-Experimental Measures of the Income Gains from Migration". *Policy Research Working Paper Series No. 3906.* Washington DC: World Bank.

Meng, X. and J. Zhang. 2001. "The Two-Tier Labor Market in Urban China: Occupational Segregation and Wage Differentials Between Urban Residents and Rural Migrants in Shanghai." *Journal of Comparative Economics* 29 (3): 485-504.

Mesnard, A. 2004. "Temporary Migration and Capital Market Imperfections." *Oxford Economic Paper* 56: 242-262.

Meza, L. and C. Pederzini. 2006. "Condiciones Laborales Familiares y la Decision de Migracion: El Caso de México". *Documento de apoyo del Informe sobre Desarrollo Humano México 2006-2007.* Mexico City: Programa de las Naciones Unidas para el Desarrollo.

Migrant Forum in Asia. 2006. "Asylum Seekers and Migrants at Risk of Violent Arrest, Overcrowded Detention Centers and Inhumane Deportation." *Migrant Forum in Asia, Urgent Appeal,* 2 November.

Migration DRC (Development Research Centre). 2007. "Global Migrant Origin Database (Version 4)." Development Research Centre on Migration, Globalisation and Poverty, University of Sussex.

Migration Policy Group and British Council. 2007. "Migrant Integration Policy Index." http://www.integrationindex.eu/. Accessed June 2009.

Miguel, E. and J. Hamory. 2009. "Individual Ability and Selection into Migration in Kenya." *Human Development Research Paper No. 45.* New York: United Nations Development Programme, Human Development Report Office.

Mills, M. B. 1997. "Contesting the Margins of Modernity: Women, Migration, and Consumption in Thailand." *American Ethnologist* 24 (1): 37-61.

Ministry of Social Welfare and Labour, United Nations Population Fund and Mongolian Population and Development Association. 2005. *Status and Consequences of Mongolian Citizens Working Abroad.* Ulaanbaatar: Mongolian Population and Development Association.

Minnesota Population Center. 2008. "Integrated Public Use Microdata Series - International: Version 4.0." University of Minnesota. http://www.ipums.umn.edu/. Accessed July 2009.

Misago, J. P., L. B. Landau and T. Monson. 2009. *Towards Tolerance, Law and Dignity: Addressing Violence Against Foreign Nationals in South Africa.* Arcadia: International Organization for Migration, Regional Office for Southern Africa.

Mitchell, T. 2009. "An Army Marching to Escape Medieval China." *Financial Times,* 15 April.

Mobarak, A. M., C. Shyamal and B. Gharad. 2009. "Migrating away from a Seasonal Famine: A Randomized Intervention in Bangladesh." *Human Development Research Paper No. 41.* New York: United Nations Development Programme, Human Development Report Office.

Molina, G. G. and E. Yañez. 2009. "The Moving Middle: Migration, Place Premiums and Human Development in Bolivia." *Human Development Research Paper No. 46.* New York: United Nations Development Programme, Human Development Report Office.

Montenegro, C. E. and M. L. Hirn. 2008. "A New Set of Disaggregated Labor Market Indicators Using Standardized Household Surveys from Around the World". *World Development Report Background Paper.* Washington DC: World Bank.

MOSWL, PTRC and UNDP (Ministry of Labour and Social Welfare, Population Teaching and Research Center, National University of Mongolia and United Nations Development Programme). 2004. *Urban Poverty and In-Migration Survey Report on Mongolia.* Ulaanbaatar: MOSWL, PRTC and UNDP.

Mundell, R. A. 1968. *International Economics.* New York: Macmillan.

Muñoz de Bustillo, R. and J.-I. Antón. 2009. "Health Care Utilization and Immigration in Spain". *Munich Personal RePEc Archive Paper No. 12382.* Munich: University Library of Munich.

Münz, R., T. Straubhaar, F. Vadean and N. Vadean. 2006. "The Costs and Benefits of European Immigration". *Hamburg Institute of International Economics (HWWI) Policy Report No. 3.* Hamburg: HWWI Research Program.

Murillo C., A. M. and J. Mena. 2009. "Informe de las Migraciones Colombianas". *Special Tabulation for the Human Development Report 2009.* New York: Grupo de Investigación en Movilidad Humana, Red Alma Mater.

Murison, S. 2005. "Evaluation of DFID Development Assistance: Gender Equality and Women's Empowerment: Phase II Thematic Evaluation: Migration and Development". *Working Paper No. 13.* London: British Government's Department for International Development.

Myers, N. 2005. "Environmental Refugees: An Emergent Security Issue". Paper presented at 13th Economic Forum, 23-27 May 2005, Prague, Czech Republic.

Narayan, D., L. Pritchett and S. Kapoor. 2009. *Moving Out of Poverty: Success from the Bottom Up (Volume 2).* New York: Palgrave Macmillan.

National Statistics Office. 2006. *Participatory Poverty Assessment in Mongolia.* Ulaanbaatar: National Statistics Office.

Nava, A. 2006. "Spousal Control and Intra-Household Decision Making: An Experimental Study in the Philippines". *American Economic Review.* Forthcoming.

Nazroo, J. Y. 1997. *Ethnicity and Mental Health: Findings from a National Community Survey.* London: Policy Studies Institute.

Neumayer, E. 2006. "Unequal Access to Foreign Spaces: How States Use Visa Restrictions to Regulate Mobility in a Globalized World." *Transactions of the Institute of British Geographers* 31 (1): 72-84.

Newland, K. 2009. "Circular Migration and Human Development." *Human Development Research Paper No. 42.* New York: United Nations Development Programme, Human Development Report Office.

Newland, K. and E. Patrick. 2004. *Beyond Remittances: The Role of Diaspora in Poverty Reduction in the their Countries of Origin.* Washington D.C.: Migration Policy Institute.

Newman, E. and J. van Selm. 2003. *Refugees and Forced Displacement: International Security, Human Vulnerability and the State.* Tokyo: United Nations University Press.

Nordin, M. 2006. "Ethnic Segregation and Educational Attainment in Sweden". Unpublished Working Paper. Lund: Department of Economics, Lund University.

Nugent, J. B. and V. Saddi. 2002. "When and How Do Land Rights Become Effective? Historical Evidence from Brazil". Unpublished paper. Los Angeles: Department of Economics,

Bibliography

HUMAN DEVELOPMENT REPORT **2009**
Overcoming barriers: Human mobility and development

University of Southern California.

Nussbaum, M. 1993. "Non-Relative Virtues: An Aristotelian
Approach." In M. Nussbaum and A. Sen (Eds.), *Quality of Life*:
242-269. New York: Oxford University Press.

——. **2000.** *Women and Human Development: The Capabilities
Approach.* Cambridge: Cambridge University Press.

O'Rourke, K. H. and R. Sinnott. 2003. "Migration Flows:
Political Economy of Migration and the Empirical Challenges".
Discussion Paper Series No. 06. Dublin: Institute for
International Integration Studies.

**OECD (Organisation for Economic Co-operation and
Development). 2007.** *PISA 2006: Science Competencies for
Tomorrow's World Executive Summary.* Paris: OECD.

——. **2008a.** *A Profile of Immigrant Populations in the 21st
Century: Data from OECD Countries.* Paris: OECD Publishing.

——. **2008b.** *International Migration Outlook.* Paris: OECD
Publishing.

——. **2009a.** "OECD Database on Immigrants in OECD
Countries." http://stats.oecd.org/index.aspx?lang=en.
Accessed March 2009.

——. **2009b.** "OECD Economic Outlook, Interim Report March
2009". Paris: OECD.

——. **2009c.** "OECD.Stat Extracts database." http://stats.oecd.
org/index.aspx. Accessed July 2009.

**OECD (Organisation for Economic Co-operation and
Development) and Statistics Canada. 2000.** "Literacy
in the Information Age: Final Report of the International Adult
Literacy Survey". Paris: OECD Publishing.

——. **2005.** *Learning a Living: First Results of the Adult Literacy
and Life Skills Survey.* Paris: OECD.

**OECD-DAC (Organisation for Economic Co-operation and
Development, Development Assistance Committee).
2009.** "Creditor Reporting System (CRS) Database." http://
www.oecd.org/dataoecd/50/17/5037721.htm. Accessed
July 2009.

One World Net. 2008. "South Africans Text No To Xenophobia."
http://us.oneworld.net/places/southern-africa/-/article/
south-africans-text-no-xenophobia. Accessed July 2009.

Opeskin, B. 2009. "The Influence of International Law on the
International Movement of Persons." *Human Development
Research Paper No. 18.* New York: United Nations
Development Programme, Human Development Report Office.

Orozco, M. and R. Rouse. 2007. "Migrant Hometown
Associations and Opportunities for Development: A Global
Perspective." *Migration Information Source,* February.

Ortega, D. 2009. "The Human Development of Peoples." *Human
Development Research Paper No. 49.* New York: United
Nations Development Programme, Human Development
Report Office.

Ortega, F. and G. Peri. 2009. "The Causes and Effects of
International Labor Mobility: Evidence from OECD Countries

1980-2005." *Human Development Research Paper No. 6.*
New York: United Nations Development Programme, Human
Development Report Office.

Ottaviano, G. I. P. and G. Peri. 2008. "Immigration and
National Wages: Clarifying the Theory and the Empirics".
Working Paper No. 14188. Cambridge: National Bureau of
Economic Research.

Oxford University Press. 2009. "Oxford English
Dictionary Online." http://dictionary.oed.com/cgi/
entry/00312893?query_type=word&querywor
d=mobility&first=1&max_to_show=10&sort_
type=alpha&result_place=1&search_id=ofqh-nRqx50-
11785&hilite=00312893. Accessed June 2006.

Papademetriou, D. 2005. "The 'Regularization' Option in
Managing Illegal Migration More Effectively: A Comparative
Perspective". *Policy Brief No. 4.* Washington DC: Migration
Policy Institute.

Passel, J. S. and D. Cohn. 2008. "Trends in Unauthorized
Immigration: Undocumented Inflow Now Trails Legal Inflow".
Washington DC: Pew Hispanic Center.

Peri, G., C. Sparber and O. S. Drive. 2008. "Task
Specialisation, Immigration and Wages." *American Economic
Journal: Applied Economics.* Forthcoming.

Perron, P. 1989. "The Great Crash, the Oil Price Shock, and the
Unit Root Hypothesis." *Econometrica* 57 (6): 1361-1401.

Perron, P. and T. Wada. 2005. "Let's Take a Break: Trends and
Cycles in US Real GDP". *Working Paper.* Boston: Department
of Economics, Boston University.

Petros, K. 2006. "Motherhood, Mobility and the Maquiladora
in Mexico: Women's Migration from Veracruz to Reynosa".
Summer Funds Research Report. Austin: Center for Latin
American Social Policy, Lozano Long Institute of Latin
America Studies, The University of Texas at Austin.

Pettigrew, T. 1998. "Intergroup Contact Theory." *Annual Review
of Psychology* 49: 65-85.

Pettigrew, T. and L. Tropp. 2005. "Allport's Intergroup Contact
Hypothesis: Its History and Influence." In J. F. Dovidio, P.
Glick, and L. Rudman (Eds.), *On the Nature of Prejudice:
Fifty Years after Allport*: 262-277. Oxford: Wiley-Blackwell
Publishing.

**PICUM (Platform for International Cooperation on
Undocumented Migrants). 2008a.** "Platform for
International Cooperation on Undocumented Migrants."
http://www.picum.org/. Accessed July 2009.

——. **2008b.** *Undocumented Children in Europe: Invisible Victims
of Immigration Restrictions.* Belgium: PICUM.

——. **2009.** "Human rights of Undocumented Migrants:
Sweden." http://www.picum.org/?pid=51. Accessed July
2009.

Pilon, M. 2003. "Schooling in West Africa". *Background paper
prepared for the UNESCO 2003 Education for All Global*

132

Monitoring Report 2003/2004. Paris: United Nations Educational, Scientific and Cultural Organization.

Piper, N. 2005. "Gender and Migration". *Paper presented for the Policy Analysis and Research Programme of the Global Commission on International Migration*. Switzerland: Global Commission on International Migration.

Plato. 2009. *The Socratic Dialogues*. New York, NY: Kaplan Publishing.

Pomp, R. D. 1989. "The Experience of the Philippines in Taxing its Nonresident Citizens." In J. N. Bahagwati and J. D. Wilson (Eds.), *Income Taxation and International Mobility*: 43-82. Cambridge: MIT Press.

Population Reference Bureau. 2001. "Understanding and Using Population Projections". *Measure Communication Policy Brief*. Washington DC: Population Reference Bureau.

Portes, A. and R. G. Rumbaut. 2001. *Ethnicities: Children of Immigrants in America*. Berkeley: University of California Press and Russell Sage Foundation.

Portes, A. and m. Zhou. 2009. "The New Second Generation: Segmented Assimilation and its Variants." *Annals of the American Academy of Political and Social Science* 530 (1): 74-96.

Poverty Task Force. 2003. "Ninh Thuan Participatory Poverty Assessment". Ha Noi: CRP and World Bank.

Preston, J. 2009. "Mexican Data Say Migration to U.S. has Plummeted." *New York Times,* 15 May.

Pritchett, L. 2006. *Let the People Come: Breaking the Gridlock on International Labor Mobility*. Washington DC: Center for Global Development.

Quirk, M. 2008. "How to Grow a Gang." *The Atlantic Monthly,* May.

Rahaei, S. 2009. "Islam, Human Rights and Displacement." *Forced Migration Review* Supplement: 1-12.

Rajan, S. I. and K. C. Zachariah. 2009. "Annual Migration Survey 2008: Special Tabulation". Trivandrum: Centre for Development Studies.

Ramakrishnan, S. and T. J. Espenshade. 2001. "Immigrant Incorporation and Political Participation in the United States." *International Migration Review* 35 (3): 870-909.

Ramírez, C., M. G. Domínguez and J. M. Morais. 2005. "Crossing Borders: Remittances, Gender and Development". *Working paper*. Santo Domingo: United Nations International Training and Research Institute for the Advancement of Women.

Ranis, G. and F. Stewart. 2000. "Strategies for Success in Human Development." *Journal of Human Development* 1 (1): 49-70.

Ratha, D. and S. Mohapatra. 2009a. "Revised Outlook for Remittance Flows 2009-2011: Remittances Expected to Fall by 5 to 8 Percent in 2009". *Migration and Development Brief 9*. Washington DC: World Bank.

Ratha, D. and S. Mohapatra. 2009b. "Revised Outlook for Remittances Flows 2009-2011."

Ratha, D. and W. Shaw. 2006. "South-South Migration and Remittances (The Bilateral Remittances Matrix Version 4)". Washington DC: World Bank.

Rauch, J. E. 1999. "Networks versus Markets in International Trade." *Journal of International Economics* 48 (1): 7-35.

Ravenstein, E. G. 1885. "The Laws of Migration." *Journal of the Statistical Society of London* 48 (2): 167-235.

Rawls, J. 1971. *A Theory of Justice*. Cambridge: Harvard University Press.

Rayhan, I. and U. Grote. 2007. "1987-94 Dynamics of Rural Poverty in Bangladesh." *Journal of Identity and Migration Studies* 1 (2): 82-98.

Reitz, J. G. 2005. "Tapping Immigrants' Skills: New Directions for Canadian Immigration Policy in the Knowledge Economy." *Law and Business Review of the Americas* 11: 409.

Revkin, A. C. 2008. "Maldives Considers Buying Dry Land if Seas Rise." *New York Times,* 10 November.

Reyneri, E. 1998. "The Role of the Underground Economy in Irregular Migration to Italy: Cause or Effect?" *Journal of Ethnic and Migration Studies* 24 (2): 313-331.

Richmond, A. 1994. *Global Apartheid: Refugees, Racism, and the New World Order*. Toronto: Oxford University Press.

Robinson, C. W. 2003. "Risks and Rights: The Causes, Consequences, and Challenges of Development-Induced Displacement". *Occasional Paper*. Washington DC: The Brookings Institution-SAIS Project on Internal Displacement.

Rodríguez, F. and R. Wagner. 2009. "How Would your Kids Vote if I Open my Doors? Evidence from Venezuela." *Human Development Research Paper No. 40*. New York: United Nations Development Programme, Human Development Report Office.

Rodrik, D. 2009. "Let Developing Nations Rule." http://www.voxeu.org/index.php?q=node/2885. Accessed July 2009.

Rosas, C. 2007. "¿Migras tú, Migro yo o Migramos Juntos? Los Condicionantes de Género en las Decisiones Migratorias de Parejas Peruanas Destinadas en Buenos Aires". Paper presented at IX Jornadas Argentinas de Estudios de Población (AEPA), 31 October-2 November 2007, Córdoba, Spain.

Rosenstone, S. J. and J. M. Hansen. 1993. *Mobilization, Participation, and Democracy in America*. New York: Macmillan.

Rossi, A. 2008. "The Impact of Migration on Children Left Beyond in Developing Countries". Paper presented at Building Migration into Development Strategies Conference, 28-29 April 2008, London, UK.

Rowthorn, R. 2008. "The Fiscal Impact of Immigration on the Advanced Economies." *Oxford Review of Economic Policy* 24 (3): 560-580.

Bibliography

Rubenstein, H. 1992. "Migration, Development and Remittances in Rural Mexico." *International Migration* 30 (2): 127-153.

Ruhs, M. and P. Martin. 2008. "Numbers vs Rights: Trade-offs and Guest Worker Programs." *International Migration Review* 42 (1): 249-265.

Ruhs, M. 2002. "Temporary Foreign Workers Programmes: Policies, Adverse Consequences, and the Need to Make them Work". *Working Paper No. 56*. San Diego: The Center for Comparative Immigration Studies, University of California, San Diego.

——. **2005.** "The Potential of Temporary Migration Programmes in Future International Migration Policy". *Paper prepared for the Policy Analysis and Research Programme*. Geneva: Global Commission on International Migration.

——. **2009.** "Migrant Rights, Immigration Policy and Human Development." *Human Development Research Paper No. 23*. New York: United Nations Development Programme, Human Development Report Office.

Ruhunage, L. K. 2006. "Institutional Monitoring of Migrant Recruitment in Sri Lanka." In C. Kuptsch (Ed.), *Merchants of Labour*: 53-62. Geneva: International Labour Organization.

Sabates-Wheeler, R. 2009. "The Impact of Irregular Status on Human Development Outcomes for Migrants." *Human Development Research Paper No. 26*. New York: United Nations Development Programme, Human Development Report Office.

Sainath, P. 2004. "The Millions who Cannot Vote." *The Hindu*, 15 March.

Sanjek, R. 2003. "Rethinking Migration, Ancient to Future." *Global Networks* 3 (3): 315-336.

Sarreal, N. 2002. "A Few Degrees." In J. Son (Ed.), *Risk and Rewards: Stories from the Philippine Migration Trail*: 153. Bangkok: Inter Press Service Asia-Pacific.

Savage, K. and P. Harvey. 2007. "Remittance during Crises: Implications for Humanitarian Response". *Briefing Paper No. 26*. London: Overseas Development Institute.

Savona, E. U., A. Di Nicola and G. Da Col. 1996. "Dynamics of Migration and Crime in Europe: New Patterns of an Old Nexus". *Working Paper No. 8*. Trento: School of Law, University of Trento.

Saxenian, A. 2002. "The Silicon Valley Connection: Transnational Networks and Regional Development in Taiwan, China and India." *Science Technology and Society* 7 (1): 117-149.

——. **2006.** *International Mobility of Engineers and the Rise of Entrepreneurship in the Periphery*. Helsinki: United Nations University - World Institute for Development Economics Research.

Scheve, K. F. and M. J. Slaughter. 2007. "A New Deal for Globalization." *Foreign Affairs* 86 (4): 34-46.

Schiff, M. 1994. "How Trade, Aid and Remittances Affect International Migration". *Policy Research Working Paper Series No. 1376*. Washington DC: World Bank.

Sciortino, R. and S. Punpuing. 2009. *International Migration in Thailand*. Bangkok: International Organization for Migration.

Seewooruthun, D. C. R. 2008. "Migration and Development: The Mauritian Perspective". Paper presented at the workshop on Enhancing the Role of Return Migration in Fostering Development, 7-8 July 2008, Geneva, International Organization for Migration.

Sen, A. 1992. *Inequality Reexamined*. Oxford: Oxford University Press.

——. **2006.** *Identity and Violence: The Illusion of Destiny*. New York: W.W. Norton and Co.

Siddiqui, T. 2006. "Protection of Bangladeshi Migrants through Good Governance." In C. Kuptsch (Ed.), *Merchants of Labour*: 63-90. Geneva: International Labour Organization.

Sides, J. and J. Citrin. 2007. "European Opinion About Immigration: The Role of Identities, Interests and Information." *B.J.Pol.S.* 37: 477-504.

Singapore Government Ministry of Manpower. 2009. "Work Permit." http://www.mom.gov.sg/publish/momportal/en/communities/work_pass/work_permit.html. Accessed July 2009.

Skeldon, R. 1999. "Migration in Asia after the Economic Crisis: Patterns and Issues." *Asia-Pacific Population Journal* 14 (3): 3-24.

——. **2005.** "Globalization, Skilled Migration and Poverty Alleviation: Brain Drains in Context". *Working Paper No. T15*. Sussex: Development Research Centre on Migration, Globalisation and Poverty.

——. **2006.** "Interlinkages between Internal and International Migration and Development in the Asian Region." *Population Space and Place* 12 (1): 15-30.

Smeeding, T., C. Wing and K. Robson. 2009. "Differences in Social Transfer Support and Poverty for Immigrant Families with Children: Lessons from the LIS". Unpublished tabulation.

Smeeding, T. 1997. "Financial Poverty in Developed Countries: The Evidence from the Luxembourg Income Study". *Background Paper for UNDP, Human Development Report 1997*. United Nations Development Programme.

Smith, A., R. N. Lalaonde and S. Johnson. 2004. "Serial Migration and Its Implications for the Parent-Child Relationship: A Retrospective Analysis of the Experiences of the Children of Caribbean Immigrants." *Cultural Diversity and Ethnic Minority Psychology* 10 (2): 107-122.

Solomon, M. K. 2009. "GATS Mode 4 and the Mobility of Labor." In R. Cholewinski, R. Perruchoud, and E. MacDonald (Eds.), *International migration Law: Developing Paradigms and Key Challenges*: 107-128. The Hague: TMC Asser

Press.

Son, G. Y. 2009. "Where Work is the Only Bonus." *Bangkok Post,* 16 March.

Spilimbergo, A. 2009. "Democracy and Foreign Education." *American Economic Review* 99 (1): 528-543.

Srivastava, R. and S. Sasikumar. 2003. "An Overview of Migration in India, its Impacts and Key Issues". Paper presented at the Regional Conference on Migration Development and Pro-Poor Policy Choices in Asia, 22-24 June 2003, Dhaka, Bangladesh.

Stark, O. 1980. "On the Role of Urban-to-Rural Remittances in Rural Development." *Journal of Development Studies* 16 (3): 369-374.

——. **1991.** *The Migration of Labor.* Cambridge: Basil Blackwell.

Stark, O. and D. Bloom. 1985. "The New Economics of Labour Migration." *American Economic Review* 75 (2): 173-178.

Stark, O., C. Helmenstein and A. Prskawetz. 1997. "A Brain Gain with a Brain Drain." *Economics Letters* 55: 227-234.

Stark, O., J. E. Taylor and S. Yitzhaki. 1986. "Remittances and Inequality." *The Economic Journal* 96 (383): 722-740.

STATEC (Central Service for Statistics and Economic Studies). 2008. Correspondence on gross enrolment ratio for Luxembourg. May. Luxembourg.

Steel, Z., D. Silove, T. Chey, A. Bauman and Phan T. 2005. "Mental Disorders, Disability and Health Service Use Amongst Vietnamese Refugees and the Host Australian Population." *Acta Psychiatrica Scandinavica* 111 (4): 300-309.

Steinbeck, J. 1939. *The Grapes of Wrath.* New York: Viking Press-James Lloyd.

Stillman, S., D. McKenzie and J. Gibson. 2006. "Migration and Mental Health: Evidence from a Natural Experiment". *Department of Economics Working Paper in Economics.* University of Waikato.

Suarez-Orozco, C., I. L. G. Todorova and J. Louie. 2002. "Making Up for Lost Time: The Experience of Separation and Reunification Among Immigrant Families." *Family Process* 41 (4): 625-643.

Success for All Foundation. 2008. "About SFAF: Our Approach to Increasing Student Achievement and History." http://www.successforall.net/. Accessed June 2009.

Suen, W. 2002. *Economics: A Mathematical Analysis.* Boston: McGraw-Hill.

Sun, M. and C. C. Fan. 2009. "China's Permanent and Temporary Migrants: Differentials and Changes, 1990-2000". Forthcoming.

Survival International. 2007. "Progress Can Kill: How Imposed Development Destroys the Health of Tribal Peoples". London: Survival International.

Szulkin, R. and J. O. Jonsson. 2007. "Ethnic Segregation and Educational Outcomes in Swedish Comprehensive Schools".

Working Paper No. 2. Stockholm: The Stockholm University Linnaeus Centre for Integration Studies.

Tabar, P. 2009. "Immigration and Human Development: Evidence from Lebanon." *Human Development Research Paper No. 35.* New York: United Nations Development Programme, Human Development Report Office.

Taylor, A. M. and J. G. Williamson. 1997. "Convergence in the Age of Mass Migration." *European Review of Economic History* 1: 27-63.

Taylor, E. J., J. Arango, G. Hugo, A. Kouaouci, D. S. Massey and A. Pellegrino. 1996. "International Migration and Community Development." *Population Index* 62 (3): 397-418.

Taylor, J. E., J. Mora, R. Adams and A. Lopez-Feldman. 2005. "Remittances, Inequality and Poverty: Evidence from Rural Mexico". *Working paper No. 05-003.* Davis: University of California, Davis.

Taylor, R. 2009. "Australia Slashes Immigration as Recession Looms." *Reuters UK,* 16 March.

Thaindian News. 2009. "New Law in Saudi Arabia to Benefit Two Mn Bangladeshi Workers." *Thaindian News,* 24 April.

The Cities Alliance. 2007. *Liveable Cities: The Benefits of Urban Environmental Planning.* Washington DC: The Cities Alliance.

The Economist Intelligence Unit. 2008. "The Global Migration Barometer." http://www.eiu.com. Accessed July 2009.

——. **2009.** "Economist Intelligence Unit." http://www.eiu.com. Accessed July 2009.

The Institute for ECOSOC Rights. 2008. "Kebijakan Ilegal Migrasi Buruh Migran dan Mitos Pembaharuan Kebijakan: Antara Malaysia-Singapura" (Migrant Worker Illegal Policy and the Myth of Policy Reform: Between Malaysia and Singapore)". *Research Draft Report.* Jakarta: Institute of ECOSOC Rights.

The Straits Times. 2009. "No Visas for 55,000 Workers." *The Straits Times,* 11 March.

Thomas-Hope, E. (Ed.). 2009. *Freedom and Constraint in Caribbean: Migration and Diaspora.* Kingston: Ian Randle Publishers.

Timmer, A. and J. G. Williamson. 1998. "Racism, Xenophobia or Markets? The Political Economy of Immigration Policy Prior to the Thirties." *Population and Development Review* 24 (4): 739-771.

Tirtosudarmo, R. 2009. "Mobility and Human Development in Indonesia." *Human Development Research Paper No. 19.* New York: United Nations Development Programme, Human Development Report Office.

Tiwari, R. 2005. "Child Labour in Footwear Industry: Possible Occupational Health Hazards." *Indian Journal of Occupational and Environmental Medicine* 9 (1): 7-9.

Transatlantic Trends. 2008. *Transatlantic Trends 2008: Immigration.* Brussels: Transatlantic Trends.

TWC2 (Transient Workers Count Too). 2006. "Debt, Delays, Deductions: Wage Issues Faced by Foreign Domestic Workers in Singapore". Singapore: TWC2.

U.S. Citizenship and Immigration Services. 2008. "Issuance of a Visa and Authorization for Temporary Admission into the United States for Certain Nonimmigrant Aliens Infected with HIV [73 FR 58023] [FR 79-08]." http://www.uscis.gov/propub/ProPubVAP.jsp?dockey=c56119ee231ea5ba9dac1a0e9b277bc6. Accessed June 2009.

Uhlaner, C., B. Cain and R. Kiewiet. 1989. "Political Participation of the Ethnic Minorities in the 1980s." *Political Behaviour* 11 (3): 195-231.

UN (United Nations). 1998. "Recommendations on Statistics of International Migration". *Statistical Paper Series M No. 58.* New York: Department of Economic and Social Affairs.

———. **2002.** "Trends in Total Migrant Stock: The 2001 Revision." New York: Department of Social and Economic Affairs.

———. **2006a.** "Trends in the Total Migrant Stock: The 2005 Revision." New York: Department of Economic and Social Affairs.

———. **2006b.** "World Economic and Social Survey 2006: Diverging Growth and Development". New York: Department of Economic and Social Affairs.

———. **2008a.** *The Millennium Development Goals Report 2008.* New York: Department of Economic and Social Affairs.

———. **2008b.** "World Population Policies: 2007". New York: Department of Social and Economic Affairs.

———. **2008c.** "World Urbanization Prospects: The 2007 Revision CD-ROM Edition". New York: UN.

———. **2009a.** "Millennium Development Goals Indicators Database." http://mdgs.un.org. Accessed July 2009.

———. **2009b.** "Multilateral Treaties Deposited with the Secretary-General." http://untreaty.un.org. Accessed July 2009.

———. **2009c.** "National Accounts Main Aggregates Database." http://unstats.un.org/unsd/snaama/SelectionCountry.asp. Accessed July 2009.

———. **2009d.** "Trends in Total Migrant Stock: The 2008 Revision." New York: Department of Economic and Social Affairs.

———. **2009e.** "World Population Prospects: The 2008 Revision". New York: Department of Economic and Social Affairs.

UN-HABITAT (United Nations Human Settlements Programme). 2003. *Global Report on Human Settlements 2003: The Challenge of Slums.* London: Earthscan.

UNDP (United Nations Development Programme).
1990. *Human Development Report 1990: Concept and Measurement of Human Development.* New York: Oxford University Press.

———. **1994.** *Human Development Report 1994: New Dimensions of Human Security.* New York: Oxford University Press.

———. **1997.** *Human Development Report 1997: Human Development to Eradicate Poverty.* New York: Oxford University Press.

———. **2000.** *Albania Human Development Report 2000: Economic and Social Insecurity, Emigration and Migration.* Tirana: UNDP.

———. **2004a.** *Côte d'Ivoire Human Development Report 2004: Social Cohesion and National Reconstruction.* Abidjan: UNDP.

———. **2004b.** *Human Development Report 2004: Cultural Liberty in Today's Diverse World.* New York: UNDP.

———. **2005a.** *China Human Development Report 2005: Towards Human Development with Equity.* Beijing: UNDP.

———. **2005b.** *El Salvador Human Development Report 2005: Una Mirada al Nuevo Nosotros, El Impacto de las Migraciones.* San Salvador: UNDP.

———. **2006a.** *Moldova Human Development Report 2006: Quality of Economic Growth and its Impact on Human Development.* Chisinau: UNDP.

———. **2006b.** *Timor-Leste: Human Development Report 2006: The Path Out of Poverty.* Dili: UNDP.

———. **2007a.** *Human Development Report 2007/2008: Fighting Climate Change: Human Solidarity in a Divided World.* New York: Palgrave Macmillan.

———. **2007b.** *Human Trafficking and HIV: Exploring Vulnerabilities and Responses in South Asia.* Colombo: UNDP Regional HIV and Development Programme for Asia Pacific.

———. **2007c.** *Mexico Human Development Report 2006/2007: Migracion y Desarrollo Humano.* Mexico City: UNDP.

———. **2007d.** *National Human Development Report 2007: Social Inclusion in Bosnia and Herzegovina.* Sarajevo: UNDP.

———. **2007e.** *Uganda Human Development Report 2007: Rediscovering Agriculture for Human Development.* Kampala: UNDP.

———. **2008a.** *China Human Development Report 2007/08: Basic Public Services for 1.3 Billion People.* Beijing: UNDP.

———. **2008b.** *Crisis Prevention and Recovery Report 2008: Post-Conflict Economic Recovery, Enabling Local Ingenuity.* New York: UNDP.

———. **2008c.** *Egypt Human Development Report 2008: Egypt's Social Contract; The Role of Civil Society.* Cairo: UNDP.

———. **2008d.** "HIV Vulnerabilities of Migrant Women: From Asia to the Arab States". Colombo: Regional Centre in Colombo.

———. **2008e.** "The Bali Road Map: Key Issues Under Negotiation". New York: Environment and Energy Group.

UNECA (United Nations Economic Commission for Africa).
2005. *Africa's Sustainable Development Bulletin 2005: Assessing Sustainable Development in Africa.* Addis Ababa: SDD (The Sustainable Development Division), UNECA The United Nations Economic Commission for Africa.

UNESCO Institute for Statistics (United Nations Educational, Scientific and Cultural Organization).

1999. *Statistical Yearbook*. Paris: UNESCO.

——. **2003.** Correspondence on adult and youth literacy rates. March. Montreal.

——. **2007.** Correspondence on gross and net enrolment ratios. April. Montreal.

——. **2008a.** "Data Centre Education Module." UNESCO.

——. **2008b.** "Global Education Digest 2008: Comparing Education Statistics Across the World." UNESCO.

——. **2009a.** Correspondence on adult and youth literacy rates. February. Montreal.

——. **2009b.** Correspondence on education indicators. February. Montreal.

——. **2009c.** "Data Centre Education Module." UNESCO.

UNFPA (United Nations Population Fund). 2006. "State of World Population 2006: A Passage to Hope - Women and International Migration". New York: UNFPA.

UNHCR (United Nations High Commission for Refugees). 2001. "The Asylum-Migration Nexus: Refugee Protection and Migration Perspectives from ILO". Paper presented at Global Consultations on International Protection, 28 June 2001, Geneva, Switzerland.

——. **2002.** "Local Integration EC/GC/02/6". Paper presented at Global Consultations on Internal Protection, 25 April, Geneva, Switzerland.

——. **2007.** "1951 Convention Relating to the Status of Refugees, Text of the 1967 Protocol, Relating to the Status of Refugees, Resolution 2198 (XXI) adopted by the United Nations General Assembly." http://www.unhcr.org/protect/PROTECTION/3b66c2aa10.pdf.

——. **2008.** *Statistical yearbook 2007: Trends in Displacement, Protection and Solutions*. Geneva: UNHCR.

——. **2009a.** Correspondence on asylum seekers. Marcha. Geneva.

——. **2009b.** Correspondence on refugees. March. Geneva.

UNICEF (United Nations Children's Fund). 2004. *The State of the World's Children 2005*. New York: UNICEF.

——. **2005a.** "The 'Rights' Start to Life: A Statistical Analysis of Birth Registration". New York: UNICEF.

——. **2005b.** *The State of the World's Children 2006*. New York: UNICEF.

——. **2007.** "Birth Registration Day Helps Ensure Basic Human Rights in Bangladesh." http://www.unicef.org/infobycountry/bangladesh_40265.html. Accessed June 2009.

——. **2008.** "The Child Care Transition: Innocenti Report Card 8. A League Table of Early Childhood Education and Care in Economically Advanced Countries". Florence: Innocenti Research Centre, UNICEF.

United States Bureau of Labor Statistics. 2009. "The Employment Situation: May 2009." http://www.bls.gov/news.release/empsit.nr0.htm. Accessed June 2009.

United States Department of State. 2006. *2005 Human Rights Report: Democratic Republic of the Congo*. Washington: Bureau of Democracy, Human Rights and Labor, United States Department of State.

——. **2009a.** "2008 Country Reports on Human Rights Practices". Washington DC: Bureau of Democracy, Human Rights and Labor, United States Department of State.

——. **2009b.** "2008 Country Reports on Human Rights Practices: Belarus". Washington DC: Bureau of Democracy, Human Rights and Labor, United States Department of State.

——. **2009c.** "2008 Country Reports on Human Rights Practices: Burma". Washington DC: Bureau of Democracy, Human Rights and Labor, United States Department of State.

——. **2009d.** "2008 Country Reports on Human Rights Practices: Côte d'Ivoire". Washington DC: Bureau of Democracy, Human Rights and Labor, United States Department of State.

——. **2009e.** "2008 Country Reports on Human Rights Practices: Gabon". Washington DC: Bureau of Democracy, Human Rights and Labor, United States Department of State.

UNODC (United Nations Office of Drugs and Crime). 2004. "United Nations Convention against Transnational Organized Crime and the Protocols Thereto." http://www.unodc.org/documents/treaties/UNTOC/Publications/TOC%20Convention/TOCebook-e.pdf. Accessed June 2009.

——. **2009.** *Global Report on Trafficking in Persons*. Vienna: UNODC.

UNRWA (United Nations Relief and Works Agency). 2008. "UNRWA in Figures." http://www.un.org/unrwa/publications/pdf/uif-dec08.pdf. Accessed May 2009.

UNRWA-ECOSOC (United Nations Relief and Works Agency - United Nations Economic and Social Council). 2008. "Assistance to the Palestinian People: Report of the Secretary-General". Economic and Social Council Substantive Session of 2008, 30 June - 25 July 2008, New York City.

USAID (United States Agency for International Development). 2007. "Anti-Trafficking in Persons Programs in Africa: A Review". Washington DC: USAID.

van der Mensbrugghe, D. and D. Roland-Holst. 2009. "Global Economic Prospects for Increasing Developing Country Migration into Developed Countries." *Human Development Research Paper No. 50*. New York: United Nations Development Programme, Human Development Report Office.

van Engeland, A. and A. Monsutti. 2005. *War and Migration: Social Networks and Economic Strategies of the Hazaras of Afghanistan*. London: Routledge.

van Hear, N. 2003. "From Durable Solutions to Transnational Relations: Home and Exile Among Refugee Diasporas". *New Issues in Refugee Research Working Paper No. 83*. Geneva:

United Nations High Commissioner for Refugees.

van Hear, N., R. Brubaker and T. Bessa. 2009. "Managing Mobility for Human Development: The Growing Salience of Mixed Migration." *Human Development Research Paper No. 20.* New York: United Nations Development Programme, Human Development Report Office.

van Hear, N., F. Pieke and S. Vertovec. 2004. "The Contribution of UK-Based Diasporas to Development and Poverty Reduction". Oxford: Centre on Migration, Policy, and Society (COMPAS).

van Lerberghe, K. and A. Schoors (Eds.). 1995. *Immigration and Emigration within the Ancient Near East.* Leuven: Peeters Publishers.

van Thanh, T. 2008. "Exportation of Migrants as a Development Strategy in Viet Nam". Paper presented at Workshop on Migrants, Migration and Development in the Greater Mekong Subregion, 15-16 July 2008, Vientiane, Laos.

Vasquez, P., M. Alloza, R. Vegas and S. Bertozzi. 2009. "Impact of the Rise in Immigrant Unemployment on Public Finances". *Working Paper No. 2009-15.* Madrid: Fundación de Estudios De Economía Aplicada.

Vijayani, M. 2008. "No Plans to Disband Rela, Says Syed Hamid." *The Star,* 8 December.

Vogel, D. and V. Kovacheva. 2009. "Calculation Table 2005: A Dynamic Aggregate Country Estimate of Irregular Foreign Residents in the EU in 2005." http://irregular-migration. hwwi.net/Europe.5248.0.html. Accessed June 2009.

Wang, F.-L. 2005. *Organizing Through Division and Exclusion: China's Hukou System.* Stanford: Stanford University Press.

Whitehead, A., I. Hashim and V. Iversen. 2007. "Child Migration, Child Agency and Inter-Generational Relations in Africa and South Asia". *Working Paper No. T24.* Brighton: Development Research Centre on Migration, Globalisation and Poverty.

WHO (World Health Organization). 2009. "World Health Statistics." http://www.who.int/whosis/whostat/2009/en/ index.html. Accessed July 2009.

Williamson, J. G. 1990. *Coping with City Growth During the British Industrial Revolution.* New York: Cambridge University Press.

Wilson, M. E. 2003. "The Traveller and Emerging Infections: Sentinel, Courier, Transmitter." *Journal of Applied Microbiology* 94 (Suppl 1): S1-S11.

Winters, L. A. and P. Martin. 2004. "When Comparative Advantage is Not Enough: Business Costs in Small Remote Economies." *World Trade Review* 3 (3): 347-384.

Winters, L. A., T. L. Walmsley, Z. K. Wang and R. Grynberg. 2003. "Liberalising the Temporary Movement of Natural Persons: An Agenda for the Development Round." *The World Economy* 26 (8): 1137-1161.

Wolfinger, R. E. and S. J. Rosenstone. 1980. *Who Votes?*

New Haven: Yale University Press.

World Bank. 1998. *Assessing Aid: What Works, What Doesn't, and Why.* New York: Oxford University Press.

——. **2000.** "Voices of the Poor." http://go.worldbank.org/ H1N8746X10. Accessed June 2009.

——. **2002.** "Governance." In J. Klugman (Ed.), *A Sourcebook for Poverty Reduction Strategies. Volume 1: Core Techniques and Cross-Cutting Issues*: 269-300. Washington DC: World Bank.

——. **2003.** "Participatory Poverty Assessment Niger". Washington DC: World Bank.

——. **2006a.** *At Home and Away: Expanding Job Opportunities for Pacific Islanders Through Labor Mobility.* Washington DC: World Bank.

——. **2006b.** *Global Economic Prospects: Economic Implications of Remittances and Migration 2006.* Washington DC: World Bank.

——. **2009a.** "Crime and Violence in Central America". Washington DC: Central America Unit and Poverty Reduction and Economic Management Unit, World Bank.

——. **2009b.** "Migration and Remittances Factbook 2008: March 2009 Update". Washington DC: World Bank.

——. **2009c.** "Remittance Prices Worldwide." http:// remittanceprices.worldbank.org/. Accessed June 2009.

——. **2009d.** "World Development Indicators". Washington DC: World Bank.

——. **2009e.** *World Development Report 2009: Reshaping Economic Geography.* Washington DC: World Bank.

Worster, D. 1979. *Dust Bowl.* New York: Oxford University Press.

WVS (World Values Survey). 2006. "World Values Survey 2005/6."

http://www.worldvaluessurvey.org/.

Yang, D. 2006. "Why Do Migrants Return to Poor Countries? Evidence from Philippine Migrants' Responses to Exchange Rate Shocks." *Review of Economics and Statistics* 88 (4): 715-735.

——. **2008a.** "Coping with Disaster: The Impact of Hurricanes on International Financial Flows, 1970-2002." *The B.E. Journal of Economic Analysis & Policy* 8 (1 (Advances), Article 13): 1903-1935.

——. **2008b.** "International Migration, Remittances, and Household Investment: Evidence from Philippine Migrants' Exchange Rate Shocks." *The Economic Journal* 118 (528): 591-630.

——. **2009.** "International Migration and Human Development." *Human Development Research Paper No. 29.* New York: United Nations Development Programme, Human Development Report Office.

Yang, D. and H. Choi. 2007. "Are Remittances Insurance? Evidence from Rainfall Shocks in the Philippines." *World*

Bank Economic Review 21 (2): 219-248.

Yaqub, S. 2009. "Independent Child Migrants in Developing Countries: Unexplored Links in Migration and Development". *Working Paper 1.* Florence: Innocenti Research Centre, UNICEF.

Zamble, F. 2008. "Politics Côte d'Ivoire: Anti-Xenophobia Law Gets Lukewarm Reception." *Inter Press News Service Agency,* 21 August.

Zambrano, G. C. and H. B. Kattya. 2005. "My Life Changed: Female Migration, Perceptions and Impacts". Quito: Centro de Planificación y Estudios Sociales Ecuador and UNIFEM.

Zamora, R. G. 2007. "El Programa Tres por uno de Remesas Colectivas en México: Lecciones y Desafíos." *Migraciones Internacionales* 4 (001): 165-172.

Zhou, M. and J. R. Logan. 1989. "Returns on Human Capital in Ethnic Enclaves: New York City's Chinatown." *American Sociological Review* 54: 809-820.

Zhu, N. and X. Luo. 2008. "The Impact of Remittances on Rural Poverty and Inequality in China". *Policy Research Working Paper Series No. 4637.* World Bank.

Zimmermann, R. 2009. "Children in Immigrant Families in Seven Affluent Societies: Overview, Definitions and Issues". *Working Paper, Special Series on Children in Immigrant Families in Affluent Societies.* Florence: Innocenti Research Center, UNICEF.

Zlotnik, H. 1998. "International Migration 1965-96: An Overview." *Population and Development Review* 24: 429-468.

Zucker, L. G. and M. R. Darby. 2008. "Defacto and Deeded Intellectual Property Rights". *Working Paper No. 14544.* Cambridge: National Bureau of Economic Research.

Statistical
annex

TABLE A

Human movement: snapshots and trends

	International migration											Internal migration	
	Immigration								Emigration			Lifetime internal migrationᵇ	
	Stock of immigrants (000)				Annual rate of growth (%)	Share of population (%)		Proportion female (%)		Emigration rate (%)	International movement rate (%)	Total migrants (000)	Migration rate (%)
HDI rank	1960	1990	2005	2010ᵃ	1960–2005	1960	2005	1960	2005	2000–2002	2000–2002	1990–2005	1990–2005
VERY HIGH HUMAN DEVELOPMENT													
1 Norway	61.6	195.2	370.6	485.4	4.0	1.7	8.0	54.3	51.1	3.9	11.0	..	..
2 Australia	1,698.1	3,581.4	4,335.8	4,711.5	2.1	16.5	21.3	44.3	50.9	2.2	22.5	..	..
3 Iceland	3.3	9.6	22.6	37.2	4.3	1.9	7.6	52.3	52.0	10.6	16.4	..	..
4 Canada	2,766.3	4,497.5	6,304.0	7,202.3	1.8	15.4	19.5	48.1	52.0	4.0	21.5	..	..
5 Ireland	73.0	228.0	617.6	898.6	4.7	2.6	14.8	51.7	49.9	20.0	28.1	..	..
6 Netherlands	446.6	1,191.6	1,735.4	1,752.9	3.0	3.9	10.6	58.8	51.6	4.7	14.2	..	..
7 Sweden	295.6	777.6	1,112.9	1,306.0	2.9	4.0	12.3	55.1	52.2	3.3	15.0	..	..
8 France	3,507.2	5,897.3	6,478.6	6,684.8	1.4	7.7	10.6	44.5	51.0	2.9	13.1	..	..
9 Switzerland	714.2	1,376.4	1,659.7	1,762.8	1.9	13.4	22.3	53.3	49.7	5.6	26.0	..	..
10 Japan	692.7	1,075.6	1,998.9	2,176.2	2.4	0.7	1.6	46.0	54.0	0.7	1.7	..	..
11 Luxembourg	46.4	113.8	156.2	173.2	2.7	14.8	33.7	53.8	50.3	9.5	38.3	..	..
12 Finland	32.1	63.3	171.4	225.6	3.7	0.7	3.3	56.3	50.6	6.6	9.0	..	..
13 United States	10,825.6	23,251.0	39,266.5	42,813.3	2.9	5.8	13.0	51.1	50.1	0.8	12.4	44,400 ᶜ	17.8 ᶜ
14 Austria	806.6	793.2	1,156.3	1,310.2	0.8	11.5	14.0	56.6	51.2	5.5	17.2	..	..
15 Spain	210.9	829.7	4,607.9	6,377.5	6.9	0.7	10.7	52.2	47.7	3.2	8.3	8,600 ᶜ	22.4 ᶜ
16 Denmark	94.0	235.2	420.8	483.7	3.3	2.1	7.8	64.3	51.9	4.3	10.7	..	..
17 Belgium	441.6	891.5	882.1	974.8	1.5	4.8	8.5	45.1	48.9	4.4	14.6	..	..
18 Italy	459.6	1,428.2	3,067.7	4,463.4	4.2	0.9	5.2	57.3	53.5	5.4	8.1	..	..
19 Liechtenstein	4.1	10.9	11.9	12.5	2.4	24.6	34.2	53.8	48.8	12.6	42.0	..	..
20 New Zealand	333.9	523.2	857.6	962.1	2.1	14.1	20.9	47.1	51.9	11.8	27.3	..	..
21 United Kingdom	1,661.9	3,716.3	5,837.8	6,451.7	2.8	3.2	9.7	48.7	53.2	6.6	14.3	..	..
22 Germany	2,002.9ᵈ	5,936.2	10,597.9	10,758.1	3.7	2.8 ᵈ	12.9	35.1 ᵈ	46.7	4.7	15.3	..	..
23 Singapore	519.2	727.3	1,494.0	1,966.9	2.3	31.8	35.0	44.0	55.8	6.3	19.1	..	..
24 Hong Kong, China (SAR)	1,627.5	2,218.5	2,721.1	2,741.8	1.1	52.9	39.5	48.0	56.5	9.5	45.6	..	..
25 Greece	52.5	412.1	975.0	1,132.8	6.5	0.6	8.8	46.1	45.1	7.8	17.2	..	..
26 Korea (Republic of)	135.6	572.1	551.2	534.8	3.1	0.5	1.2	47.7	51.4	3.1	3.4	..	..
27 Israel	1,185.6	1,632.7	2,661.3	2,940.5	1.8	56.1	39.8	49.5	55.9	13.1	40.3	..	..
28 Andorra	2.5	38.9	50.3	55.8	6.7	18.7	63.1	44.2	47.4	9.7	79.6	..	..
29 Slovenia	..	178.1	167.3	163.9	..	..	8.4	..	46.8	5.2	7.6	..	..
30 Brunei Darussalam	20.6	73.2	124.2	148.1	4.0	25.1	33.6	42.0	44.8	4.9	33.4	..	..
31 Kuwait	90.6	1,585.3	1,869.7	2,097.5	6.7	32.6	69.2	25.6	30.0	16.6	54.5	..	..
32 Cyprus	29.6	43.8	116.2	154.3	3.0	5.2	13.9	50.3	57.1	18.4	23.4	..	..
33 Qatar	14.4	369.8	712.9	1,305.4	8.7	32.0	80.5	25.8	25.8	2.3	60.7	..	..
34 Portugal	38.9	435.8	763.7	918.6	6.6	0.4	7.2	58.4	50.6	16.1	21.4	1,200 ᶜ	12.8 ᶜ
35 United Arab Emirates	2.2	1,330.3	2,863.0	3,293.3	15.9	2.4	70.0	15.0	27.7	3.3	55.1	..	..
36 Czech Republic	60.1ᵉ	424.5	453.3	453.0	4.5	0.4 ᵉ	4.4	59.5 ᵉ	53.8	3.5	7.7	..	..
37 Barbados	9.8	21.4	26.2	28.1	2.2	4.2	10.4	59.8	60.1	29.8	36.6	90 ᶠ	31.1 ᶠ
38 Malta	1.7	5.8	11.7	15.5	4.3	0.5	2.9	59.7	51.6	22.3	24.0	..	..
HIGH HUMAN DEVELOPMENT													
39 Bahrain	26.7	173.2	278.2	315.4	5.2	17.1	38.2	27.9	31.9	15.9	47.3	..	..
40 Estonia	..	382.0	201.7	182.5	..	..	15.0	..	59.6	12.2	28.5	..	..
41 Poland	2,424.9	1,127.8	825.4	827.5	-2.4	8.2	2.2	53.9	59.0	5.1	7.1	..	..
42 Slovakia	..	41.3	124.4	130.7	..	..	2.3	..	56.0	8.2	10.3	..	..
43 Hungary	518.1	347.5	333.0	368.1	-1.0	5.2	3.3	53.1	56.1	3.9	6.6	..	..
44 Chile	104.8	107.5	231.5	320.4	1.8	1.4	1.4	43.7	52.3	3.3	4.5	3,100 ᶜ	21.3 ᶜ
45 Croatia	..	475.4	661.4	699.9	..	..	14.9	..	53.0	12.0	23.8	800 ᵍ	26.6 ᵍ
46 Lithuania	..	349.3	165.3	128.9	..	..	4.8	..	56.6	8.6	13.9	..	..
47 Antigua and Barbuda	4.9	12.0	18.2	20.9	2.9	8.9	21.8	50.2	55.1	45.3	56.1	24,000 ᶠ	28.4 ᶠ
48 Latvia	..	646.0	379.6	335.0	..	..	16.6	..	59.0	9.1	33.0	..	..
49 Argentina	2,601.2	1,649.9	1,494.1	1,449.3	-1.2	12.6	3.9	45.4	53.4	1.6	5.6	6,700 ᶜ	19.9 ᶜ
50 Uruguay	192.2	98.2	84.1	79.9	-1.8	7.6	2.5	47.8	54.0	7.0	9.5	800 ᶠ	24.1 ᶠ
51 Cuba	143.6	34.6	15.3	15.3	-5.0	2.0	0.1	30.6	29.0	8.9	9.6	1,800 ᶠ	15.2 ᶠ
52 Bahamas	11.3	26.9	31.6	33.4	2.3	10.3	9.7	43.7	48.5	10.8	19.3	..	..
53 Mexico	223.2	701.1	604.7	725.7	2.2	0.6	0.6	46.2	49.4	9.0	9.5	17,800 ᶜ	18.5 ᶜ
54 Costa Rica	32.7	417.6	442.6	489.2	5.8	2.5	10.2	44.2	49.8	2.6	9.7	700 ᶜ	20.0 ᶜ
55 Libyan Arab Jamahiriya	48.2	457.5	617.5	682.5	5.7	3.6	10.4	49.0	35.5	1.4	11.5	..	..
56 Oman	43.7	423.6	666.3	826.1	6.1	7.7	25.5	21.2	20.8	0.7	28.0	..	..
57 Seychelles	0.8	3.7	8.4	10.8	5.1	1.9	10.2	35.4	42.5	17.0	21.6	..	..
58 Venezuela (Bolivarian Republic of)	509.5	1,023.8	1,011.4	1,007.4	1.5	6.7	3.8	37.9	49.9	1.4	5.3	5,200 ᶜ	23.8 ᶜ
59 Saudi Arabia	63.4	4,743.0	6,336.7	7,288.9	10.2	1.6	26.8	36.4	30.1	1.1	24.8	..	..

Human movement: snapshots and trends

		International migration											Internal migration	
		Immigration								Emigration			Lifetime internal migration[b]	
		Stock of immigrants (000)				Annual rate of growth (%)	Share of population (%)		Proportion female (%)		Emigration rate (%)	International movement rate (%)	Total migrants (000)	Migration rate (%)
HDI rank		1960	1990	2005	2010[a]	1960–2005	1960	2005	1960	2005	2000–2002	2000–2002	1990–2005	1990–2005
60	Panama	68.3	61.7	102.2	121.0	0.9	6.1	3.2	42.7	50.2	5.7	8.2	600[c]	20.6[c]
61	Bulgaria	20.3	21.5	104.1	107.2	3.6	0.3	1.3	57.9	57.9	10.5	11.6	800[g]	14.3[g]
62	Saint Kitts and Nevis	3.5	3.2	4.5	5.0	0.5	6.9	9.2	48.6	46.3	44.3	49.3	..	..
63	Romania	330.9	142.8	133.5	132.8	-2.0	1.8	0.6	54.8	52.1	4.6	5.0	2,300[g]	15.1[g]
64	Trinidad and Tobago	81.0	50.5	37.8	34.3	-1.7	9.6	2.9	49.8	53.9	20.2	22.8	..	..
65	Montenegro	..	..[h]	54.6	42.5	..	..	8.7	..	60.9	..[h]	..[h]	..	..
66	Malaysia	56.9	1,014.2	2,029.2	2,357.6	7.9	0.7	7.9	42.2	45.0	3.1	10.1	4,200[c]	20.7[c]
67	Serbia	155.4[e]	99.3	674.6	525.4	3.3	0.9[e]	6.8	56.9[e]	56.1	13.6	18.7	..	..
68	Belarus	..	1,249.0	1,106.9	1,090.4	..	..	11.3	..	54.2	15.2	26.1	900[c]	10.8[c]
69	Saint Lucia	2.4	5.3	8.7	10.2	2.8	2.7	5.3	50.1	51.3	24.1	27.9	30[f]	18.5[f]
70	Albania	48.9	66.0	82.7	89.1	1.2	3.0	2.7	53.7	53.1	21.0	21.4	500[g]	24.1[g]
71	Russian Federation	2,941.7[e]	11,524.9	12,079.6	12,270.4	3.1	1.4[e]	8.4	47.9[e]	57.8	7.7	15.3	..	..
72	Macedonia (the Former Yugoslav Rep. of)	..	95.1	120.3	129.7	..	..	5.9	..	58.3	11.3	12.8	..	..
73	Dominica	2.4	2.5	4.5	5.5	1.4	4.0	6.7	50.9	46.2	38.3	41.6	..	..
74	Grenada	4.0	4.3	10.8	12.6	2.2	4.5	10.6	51.2	53.3	40.3	45.0	..	..
75	Brazil	1,397.1	798.5	686.3	688.0	-1.6	1.9	0.4	44.4	46.4	0.5	0.8	17,000[c]	10.1[c]
76	Bosnia and Herzegovina	..	56.0	35.1	27.8	..	..	0.9	..	49.8	25.1	27.0	1,400[g]	52.5[g]
77	Colombia	58.7	104.3	110.0	110.3	1.4	0.4	0.3	43.9	48.3	3.9	4.1	8,100[c]	20.3[c]
78	Peru	66.5	56.0	41.6	37.6	-1.0	0.7	0.1	44.3	52.4	2.7	2.9	6,300[f]	22.4[f]
79	Turkey	947.6	1,150.5	1,333.9	1,410.9	0.8	3.4	1.9	48.1	52.0	4.2	6.0	..	..
80	Ecuador	24.1	78.7	123.6	393.6	3.6	0.5	0.9	45.5	49.1	5.3	5.9	2,400[c]	20.2[c]
81	Mauritius	10.2	8.7	40.8	42.9	3.1	1.6	3.3	39.3	63.3	12.5	13.1	..	..
82	Kazakhstan	..	3,619.2	2,973.6	3,079.5	..	..	19.6	..	54.0	19.4	35.8	1,000[g]	9.3[g]
83	Lebanon	151.4	523.7	721.2	758.2	3.5	8.0	17.7	49.2	49.1	12.9	27.1	..	..
MEDIUM HUMAN DEVELOPMENT														
84	Armenia	..	658.8	492.6	324.2	..	..	16.1	..	58.9	20.3	28.1	500[g]	24.5[g]
85	Ukraine	..	6,892.9	5,390.6	5,257.5	..	..	11.5	..	57.2	10.9	23.8	..	..
86	Azerbaijan	..	360.6	254.5	263.9	..	..	3.0	..	57.0	14.3	15.8	1,900[g]	33.2[g]
87	Thailand	484.8	387.5	982.0	1,157.3	1.6	1.8	1.5	36.5	48.4	1.3	2.0	..	..
88	Iran (Islamic Republic of)	48.4	4,291.6	2,062.2	2,128.7	8.3	0.2	2.9	50.6	39.7	1.3	4.7	..	..
89	Georgia	..	338.3	191.2	167.3	..	..	4.3	..	57.0	18.3	22.1	..	..
90	Dominican Republic	144.6	291.2	393.0	434.3	2.2	4.3	4.1	25.9	40.1	9.1	10.4	1,700[f]	17.7[f]
91	Saint Vincent and the Grenadines	2.5	4.0	7.4	8.6	2.4	3.1	6.8	50.6	51.8	34.4	39.0	..	..
92	China	245.7	376.4	590.3	685.8	1.9	0.0	0.0	47.3	50.0	0.5	0.5	73,100[c]	6.2[c]
93	Belize	7.6	30.4	40.6	46.8	3.7	8.2	14.4	46.1	50.5	16.5	27.4	40[f]	14.2[f]
94	Samoa	3.4	3.2	7.2	9.0	1.6	3.1	4.0	45.9	44.9	37.2	39.4	..	..
95	Maldives	1.7	2.7	3.2	3.3	1.4	1.7	1.1	46.3	44.8	0.4	1.5	..	..
96	Jordan	385.8	1,146.3	2,345.2	2,973.0	4.0	43.1	42.1	49.2	49.1	11.6	45.3	..	..
97	Suriname	22.5	18.0	34.0	39.5	0.9	7.7	6.8	47.4	45.6	36.0	36.9	..	..
98	Tunisia	169.2	38.0	34.9	33.6	-3.5	4.0	0.4	51.0	49.5	5.9	6.3	..	..
99	Tonga	0.1	3.0	1.2	0.8	5.0	0.2	1.1	45.5	48.7	33.7	34.7	..	..
100	Jamaica	21.9	20.8	27.2	30.0	0.5	1.3	1.0	48.4	49.4	26.7	27.0	..	..
101	Paraguay	50.0	183.3	168.2	161.3	2.7	2.6	2.8	47.4	48.1	6.9	9.8	1,600[f]	26.4[f]
102	Sri Lanka	1,005.3	458.8	366.4	339.9	-2.2	10.0	1.9	46.6	49.8	4.7	6.6	..	..
103	Gabon	20.9	127.7	244.6	284.1	5.5	4.3	17.9	42.9	42.9	4.3	22.8	..	..
104	Algeria	430.4	274.0	242.4	242.3	-1.3	4.0	0.7	50.1	45.2	6.2	6.9	..	..
105	Philippines	219.7	159.4	374.8	435.4	1.2	0.8	0.4	43.9	50.1	4.0	5.6	6,900[c]	11.7[c]
106	El Salvador	34.4	47.4	35.9	40.3	0.1	1.2	0.6	72.8	52.8	14.3	14.6	1,200[f]	16.7[f]
107	Syrian Arab Republic	276.1	690.3	1,326.4	2,205.8	3.5	6.0	6.9	48.7	48.9	2.4	7.4	..	..
108	Fiji	20.1	13.7	17.2	18.5	-0.3	5.1	2.1	37.6	47.9	15.0	16.6	..	..
109	Turkmenistan	..	306.5	223.7	207.7	..	..	4.6	..	57.0	5.3	9.8	..	..
110	Occupied Palestinian Territories	490.3	910.6	1,660.6	1,923.8	2.7	44.5	44.1	49.2	49.1	23.9	61.3	..	..
111	Indonesia	1,859.5	465.6	135.6	122.9	-5.8	2.0	0.1	48.0	46.0	0.9	1.0	8,100[c]	4.1[c]
112	Honduras	60.0	270.4	26.3	24.3	-1.8	3.0	0.4	45.4	48.6	5.3	5.9	1,200[f]	17.2[f]
113	Bolivia	42.7	59.6	114.0	145.8	2.2	1.3	1.2	43.4	48.1	4.3	5.3	1,500[f]	15.2[f]
114	Guyana	14.0	4.1	10.0	11.6	-0.8	2.5	1.3	42.2	46.5	33.5	33.6	..	..
115	Mongolia	3.7	6.7	9.1	10.0	2.0	0.4	0.4	47.4	54.0	0.3	0.6	200[g]	9.7[g]
116	Viet Nam	4.0	29.4	54.5	69.3	5.8	0.0	0.1	46.4	36.6	2.4	2.4	12,700[g]	21.9[g]
117	Moldova	..	578.5	440.1	408.3	..	..	11.7	..	56.0	14.3	24.6	..	..
118	Equatorial Guinea	19.4	2.7	5.8	7.4	-2.7	7.7	1.0	30.2	47.0	14.5	14.7	..	..

TABLE

A

	International migration											Internal migration	
	Immigration							Emigration				Lifetime internal migration[b]	
	Stock of immigrants (000)				Annual rate of growth (%)	Share of population (%)		Proportion female (%)		Emigration rate (%)	International movement rate (%)	Total migrants (000)	Migration rate (%)
HDI rank	1960	1990	2005	2010[a]	1960–2005	1960	2005	1960	2005	2000–2002	2000–2002	1990–2005	1990–2005
119 Uzbekistan	..	1,653.0	1,267.8	1,175.9	..	..	4.8	..	57.0	8.5	13.4	..	..
120 Kyrgyzstan	..	623.1	288.1	222.7	..	..	5.5	..	58.2	10.5	20.6	600 [g]	16.2 [g]
121 Cape Verde	6.6	8.9	11.2	12.1	1.2	3.4	2.3	50.4	50.4	30.5	32.1	..	..
122 Guatemala	43.3	264.3	53.4	59.5	0.5	1.0	0.4	48.3	54.4	4.9	5.2	1,500 [f]	11.1 [f]
123 Egypt	212.4	175.6	246.7	244.7	0.3	0.8	0.3	47.8	46.7	2.9	3.1	..	..
124 Nicaragua	12.4	40.8	35.0	40.1	2.3	0.7	0.6	46.6	48.8	9.1	9.6	800 [f]	13.3 [f]
125 Botswana	7.2	27.5	80.1	114.8	5.4	1.4	4.4	43.8	44.3	0.9	3.8	..	..
126 Vanuatu	2.8	2.2	1.0	0.8	-2.2	4.4	0.5	39.0	46.5	2.0	2.7	..	..
127 Tajikistan	..	425.9	306.4	284.3	..	..	4.7	..	57.0	11.4	16.1	400 [g]	9.9 [g]
128 Namibia	27.2	112.1	131.6	138.9	3.5	4.5	6.6	36.9	47.3	1.3	8.7	..	..
129 South Africa	927.7	1,224.4	1,248.7	1,862.9	0.7	5.3	2.6	29.0	41.4	1.7	3.9	6,700 [c]	15.4 [c]
130 Morocco	394.3	57.6	51.0	49.1	-4.5	3.4	0.2	51.5	49.9	8.1	8.5	6,800 [g]	33.4 [g]
131 Sao Tome and Principe	7.4	5.8	5.4	5.3	-0.7	11.6	3.5	46.4	47.9	13.5	17.9	..	..
132 Bhutan	9.7	23.8	37.3	40.2	3.0	4.3	5.7	18.5	18.5	2.2	3.8	..	..
133 Lao People's Democratic Republic	19.6	22.9	20.3	18.9	0.1	0.9	0.3	48.9	48.1	5.9	6.2	..	..
134 India	9,410.5	7,493.2	5,886.9	5,436.0	-1.0	2.1	0.5	46.0	48.6	0.8	1.4	42,300 [c]	4.1 [c]
135 Solomon Islands	3.7	4.7	6.5	7.0	1.2	3.1	1.4	45.6	44.0	1.0	1.7	..	..
136 Congo	26.3	129.6	128.8	143.2	3.5	2.6	3.8	51.6	49.6	14.7	20.0	..	..
137 Cambodia	381.3	38.4	303.9	335.8	-0.5	7.0	2.2	48.3	51.3	2.3	3.9	1,300 [c]	11.7 [c]
138 Myanmar	286.6	133.5	93.2	88.7	-2.5	1.4	0.2	44.9	47.7	0.7	0.9	..	..
139 Comoros	1.5	14.1	13.7	13.5	4.9	0.8	2.2	46.6	53.1	7.7	10.7	..	..
140 Yemen	159.1	343.5	455.2	517.9	2.3	3.0	2.2	38.3	38.3	3.0	4.3	..	..
141 Pakistan	6,350.3	6,555.8	3,554.0	4,233.6	-1.3	13.0	2.1	46.4	44.8	2.2	4.8	..	..
142 Swaziland	16.9	71.4	38.6	40.4	1.8	4.9	3.4	48.5	47.4	1.1	4.8	..	..
143 Angola	122.1	33.5	56.1	65.4	-1.7	2.4	0.3	41.7	51.1	5.5	5.8	..	..
144 Nepal	337.6	430.7	818.7	945.9	2.0	3.5	3.0	64.1	69.1	3.9	6.2	..	..
145 Madagascar	126.3	46.1	39.7	37.8	-2.6	2.5	0.2	49.2	46.1	0.9	1.3	1,000 [g]	9.3 [g]
146 Bangladesh	661.4	881.6	1,031.9	1,085.3	1.0	1.2	0.7	46.4	13.9	4.5	5.1	..	..
147 Kenya	59.3	163.0	790.1	817.7	5.8	0.7	2.2	37.1	50.8	1.4	2.3	3,500 [c]	12.6 [c]
148 Papua New Guinea	20.2	33.1	25.5	24.5	0.5	1.0	0.4	43.3	37.6	0.9	1.3	..	..
149 Haiti	14.5	19.1	30.1	35.0	1.6	0.4	0.3	50.5	43.2	7.7	8.0	1,000 [g]	17.5 [g]
150 Sudan	242.0	1,273.1	639.7	753.4	2.2	2.1	1.7	47.2	48.3	1.7	3.8	..	..
151 Tanzania (United Republic of)	477.0	576.0	797.7	659.2	1.1	4.7	2.0	45.0	50.2	0.8	3.3	..	..
152 Ghana	529.7	716.5	1,669.3	1,851.8	2.6	7.8	7.6	36.4	41.8	4.5	7.3	3,300 [c]	17.8 [c]
153 Cameroon	175.4	265.3	211.9	196.6	0.4	3.2	1.2	44.3	45.6	1.0	1.9	..	..
154 Mauritania	12.1	93.9	66.1	99.2	3.8	1.4	2.2	41.1	42.1	4.1	6.3	400 [g]	24.2 [g]
155 Djibouti	11.8	122.2	110.3	114.1	5.0	13.9	13.7	41.8	46.5	2.2	5.8	..	..
156 Lesotho	3.2	8.2	6.2	6.3	1.5	0.4	0.3	50.5	45.7	2.6	2.8	..	..
157 Uganda	771.7	550.4	652.4	646.5	-0.4	11.4	2.3	41.3	49.9	0.7	2.7	1,300 [c]	5.2 [c]
158 Nigeria	94.1	447.4	972.1	1,127.7	5.2	0.2	0.7	36.2	46.5	0.8	1.4	..	..
LOW HUMAN DEVELOPMENT													
159 Togo	101.3	162.6	182.8	185.4	1.3	6.5	3.1	51.8	50.4	3.7	6.8	..	..
160 Malawi	297.7	1,156.9	278.8	275.9	-0.1	8.4	2.0	51.2	51.6	1.2	3.4	200 [g]	2.7 [g]
161 Benin	34.0	76.2	187.6	232.0	3.8	1.5	2.4	48.5	46.0	7.5	8.8	..	..
162 Timor-Leste	7.1	9.0	11.9	13.8	1.1	1.4	1.2	46.0	52.6	2.6	3.2	..	..
163 Côte d'Ivoire	767.0	1,816.4	2,371.3	2,406.7	2.5	22.3	12.3	40.8	45.1	1.0	13.8	..	..
164 Zambia	360.8	280.0	287.3	233.1	-0.5	11.9	2.4	47.0	49.4	2.2	5.6	..	..
165 Eritrea	7.7	11.8	14.6	16.5	1.4	0.5	0.3	41.9	46.5	12.5	12.8	..	..
166 Senegal	168.0	268.6	220.2	210.1	0.6	5.5	2.0	41.7	51.0	4.4	7.0	..	..
167 Rwanda	28.5	72.9	435.7	465.5	6.1	1.0	4.8	53.9	53.9	2.7	3.7	800 [c]	10.4 [c]
168 Gambia	31.6	118.1	231.7	290.1	4.4	9.9	15.2	42.7	48.7	3.6	16.4	..	..
169 Liberia	28.8	80.8	96.8	96.3	2.7	2.7	2.9	37.8	45.1	2.7	7.8	..	..
170 Guinea	11.3	241.1	401.2	394.6	7.9	0.4	4.4	48.0	52.8	6.3	14.3	..	..
171 Ethiopia	393.3	1,155.4	554.0	548.0	0.8	1.7	0.7	41.9	47.1	0.4	1.4	..	..
172 Mozambique	8.9	121.9	406.1	450.0	8.5	0.1	1.9	43.6	52.1	4.2	6.0	900 [g]	8.1 [g]
173 Guinea-Bissau	11.6	13.9	19.2	19.2	1.1	2.0	1.3	50.0	50.0	8.6	9.9	..	..
174 Burundi	126.3	333.1	81.6	60.8	-1.0	4.3	1.1	46.0	53.7	5.4	6.5	..	..
175 Chad	55.1	74.3	358.4	388.3	4.2	1.9	3.6	44.0	48.0	3.2	3.7	..	..
176 Congo (Democratic Republic of the)	1,006.9	754.2	480.1	444.7	-1.6	6.5	0.8	49.8	52.9	1.5	2.9	8,500 [g]	27.1 [g]
177 Burkina Faso	62.9	344.7	772.8	1,043.0	5.6	1.3	5.6	52.3	51.1	9.8	17.9	..	..

Human movement: snapshots and trends

	International migration											Internal migration	
	Immigration								Emigration			Lifetime internal migration[b]	
	Stock of immigrants (000)				Annual rate of growth (%)	Share of population (%)		Proportion female (%)		Emigration rate (%)	International movement rate (%)	Total migrants (000)	Migration rate (%)
HDI rank	1960	1990	2005	2010[a]	1960–2005	1960	2005	1960	2005	2000–2002	2000–2002	1990–2005	1990–2005
178 Mali	167.6	165.3	165.4	162.7	0.0	3.3	1.4	50.0	47.8	12.5	12.9	..	..
179 Central African Republic	43.1	62.7	75.6	80.5	1.2	2.9	1.8	49.6	46.6	2.7	4.2	..	..
180 Sierra Leone	45.9	154.5	152.1	106.8	2.7	2.0	3.0	35.6	45.7	2.0	3.0	600[g]	19.0[g]
181 Afghanistan	46.5	57.7	86.5	90.9	1.4	0.5	0.4	43.6	43.6	10.6	10.8	..	..
182 Niger	55.0	135.7	183.0	202.2	2.7	1.7	1.4	50.0	53.6	4.0	5.0	..	..
OTHER UN MEMBER STATES													
Iraq	87.8	83.6	128.1	83.4	0.8	1.2	0.5	40.9	31.1	4.1	4.6	..	..
Kiribati	0.6	2.2	2.0	2.0	2.6	1.8	2.2	38.2	48.8	4.0	6.7	..	..
Korea (Democratic People's Rep. of)	25.1	34.1	36.8	37.1	0.9	0.2	0.2	47.3	52.0	2.0	2.2	..	..
Marshall Islands	0.8	1.5	1.7	1.7	1.5	5.8	2.9	41.0	41.0	17.7	20.1	..	..
Micronesia (Federated States of)	5.8	3.7	2.9	2.7	-1.6	13.1	2.6	40.9	46.4	18.6	21.0	1[g]	1.2[g]
Monaco	15.4	20.1	22.6	23.6	0.9	69.5	69.8	57.5	51.3	39.3	82.6	..	..
Nauru	0.4	3.9	4.9	5.3	5.5	9.3	48.7	5.1	45.0	9.3	50.4	..	..
Palau	0.3	2.9	6.0	5.8	6.5	3.3	30.0	34.9	40.2	39.3	58.7	..	..
San Marino	7.5	8.7	11.4	11.7	0.9	48.9	37.7	53.5	53.5	18.1	45.0	..	..
Somalia	11.4	633.1	21.3	22.8	1.4	0.4	0.3	41.9	46.5	6.5	6.7	..	..
Tuvalu	0.4	0.3	0.2	0.2	-1.6	6.1	1.9	42.2	45.4	15.4	18.2	..	..
Zimbabwe	387.2	627.1	391.3	372.3	0.0	10.3	3.1	24.1	37.8	2.3	7.4	..	..
Africa	9,175.9[T]	15,957.6[T]	17,678.6[T]	19,191.4[T]	1.7	3.2	1.9	43.1	47.8	2.9	..	..	..
Asia	28,494.9[T]	50,875.7[T]	55,128.5[T]	61,324.0[T]	0.7	1.7	1.4	46.6	47.1	1.7	..	..	..
Europe	17,511.7[T]	49,360.5[T]	64,330.1[T]	69,744.5[T]	2.9	3.0	8.8	49.0	52.9	7.3	..	..	..
Latin America and the Caribbean	6,151.4[T]	7,130.3[T]	6,869.4[T]	7,480.3[T]	0.2	2.8	1.2	44.6	48.4	5.0	..	..	..
Northern America	13,603.5[T]	27,773.9[T]	45,597.1[T]	50,042.4[T]	2.8	6.7	13.6	50.8	50.3	1.1	..	..	..
Oceania	2,142.6[T]	4,365.0[T]	5,516.3[T]	6,014.7[T]	1.7	13.5	16.4	44.3	48.2	4.9	..	..	..
OECD	31,574.9[T]	61,824.3[T]	97,622.8[T]	108,513.7[T]	2.6	4.1	8.4	48.7	51.1	3.9	..	..	..
European Union (EU27)	13,555.3[T]	26,660.0[T]	41,596.8[T]	46,911.3[T]	2.8	3.5	8.5	49.1	51.4	5.7	..	..	..
GCC	241.0[T]	8,625.2[T]	12,726.6[T]	15,126.6[T]	10.2	4.9	37.1	33.5	29.1	3.2	..	..	..
Very high human development	31,114.9[T]	66,994.9[T]	107,625.9[T]	120,395.2[T]	3.1	4.6	11.1	48.6	50.9	3.4	..	..	..
Very high HD: OECD	27,461.0[T]	58,456.2[T]	94,401.4[T]	105,050.9[T]	3.1	4.1	10.0	48.6	50.9	3.2	..	..	..
Very high HD: non-OECD	3,653.8[T]	8,538.7[T]	13,224.6[T]	15,344.3[T]	4.7	41.5	46.5	47.4	50.3	11.6	..	..	..
High human development	13,495.1[T]	34,670.2[T]	38,078.0[T]	40,383.6[T]	1.1	2.8	3.8	47.2	50.5	6.0	..	..	..
Medium human development	28,204.2[T]	44,870.0[T]	40,948.6[T]	44,206.5[T]	0.6	1.7	0.8	46.1	46.8	1.9	..	..	..
Low human development	4,265.7[T]	8,928.0[T]	8,467.5[T]	8,812.0[T]	1.6	3.9	2.3	45.0	48.9	3.9	..	..	..
World (excluding the former Soviet Union and Czechoslovakia)	74,078.1[T]	125,389.2[T]	168,780.5[T]	187,815.1[T]	1.1	2.7	2.7	46.8	47.8	2.4	..	..	..
World	77,114.7[Ti]	155,518.1[Ti]	195,245.4[Ti]	213,943.8[Ti]	1.1	2.6 i	3.0 i	47.0 i	49.2 i	3.0 i	..	..	..

NOTES

a 2010 projections are based on long-run tendencies and may not accurately predict the effect of unexpected short-term fluctuations such as the 2009 economic crisis. See UN (2009d) for further details.

b Due to differences in definition of the underlying data, cross country comparisons should be made with caution. Data are from different censuses and surveys and refer to different time periods and so are not strictly comparable.

c Data are estimates based on censuses from Bell and Muhidin (2009). Internal migrants are expressed as a percentage of the total population.

d Estimates for 1960 for Germany refer to the former Federal Republic of Germany and the former German Democratic Republic.

e Estimates for 1960 for the Czech Republic, the Russian Federation and Serbia refer to the former states of Czechoslovakia, the Soviet Union and Yugoslavia respectively.

f Data are estimates based on censuses from ECLAC (2007). Internal migrants are expressed as a percentage of the total population.

g Data are estimates based on household surveys from the World Bank (2009e). Internal migrants are expressed as a percentage of the working age population only.

h Data for Montenegro are included with those for Serbia.

i Data are aggregates from original data source.

SOURCES

Columns 1–4 and 6–9: UN (2009d).

Column 5: calculated based on data from UN (2009d).

Column 10: calculated based on data from Migration DRC 2007 and population data from UN (2009e).

Column 11: calculated based on data from Migration DRC (2007).

Column 12–13: various (as indicated).

International emigrants by area of residence

B

HDI rank	Continent of residence 2000–2002 (% of total emigrant stocks)						Human develoment category of countries of residence[a] 2000–2002 (% of total emigrant stocks)				Share of continents' immigrants from country 2000–2002 (% of total immigrant stocks in the continent)					
	Africa	Asia	Europe	Latin America and the Caribbean	Northern America	Oceania	Very high	High	Medium	Low	Africa	Asia	Europe	Latin America and the Caribbean	Northern America	Oceania
VERY HIGH HUMAN DEVELOPMENT																
1 Norway	1.7	9.3	62.1	1.0	23.3	2.6	87.0	5.1	7.1	0.8	0.02	0.03	0.19	0.03	0.11	0.10
2 Australia	2.5	10.9	46.9	0.9	21.9	17.1	83.4	3.6	12.1	0.9	0.07	0.10	0.35	0.06	0.24	1.47
3 Iceland	1.7	4.3	61.4	0.7	30.3	1.6	92.4	2.7	4.1	0.8	0.00	0.00	0.04	0.00	0.03	0.01
4 Canada	1.3	5.8	15.2	2.2	72.7	2.7	91.6	3.0	4.8	0.7	0.11	0.15	0.34	0.48	2.35	0.70
5 Ireland	1.6	3.4	69.2	0.6	19.4	5.8	93.4	2.6	3.3	0.8	0.10	0.07	1.16	0.10	0.47	1.13
6 Netherlands	2.0	7.1	46.5	2.3	28.6	13.5	88.0	7.0	4.2	0.9	0.10	0.11	0.62	0.30	0.56	2.10
7 Sweden	3.3	6.3	65.5	1.7	20.6	2.6	87.2	6.3	4.7	1.9	0.06	0.04	0.34	0.09	0.15	0.16
8 France	16.0	6.5	54.5	4.6	15.9	2.4	70.4	13.0	9.7	6.9	1.79	0.24	1.67	1.37	0.71	0.85
9 Switzerland	2.5	6.9	68.4	2.7	16.4	3.2	86.8	7.1	5.3	0.9	0.07	0.06	0.50	0.19	0.18	0.27
10 Japan	1.3	12.9	13.4	8.6	59.5	4.3	78.8	10.9	9.7	0.6	0.07	0.23	0.20	1.26	1.30	0.76
11 Luxembourg	1.6	3.2	87.2	0.7	6.9	0.4	92.9	3.3	3.1	0.7	0.00	0.00	0.07	0.01	0.01	0.00
12 Finland	1.8	4.4	80.5	0.7	10.2	2.4	91.2	4.1	4.0	0.8	0.04	0.03	0.50	0.04	0.09	0.17
13 United States	2.7	20.1	28.3	32.2	12.6	4.2	45.7	35.7	17.3	1.4	0.38	0.91	1.08	11.97	0.70	1.89
14 Austria	1.9	9.1	63.0	1.8	19.8	4.4	84.7	8.8	5.7	0.8	0.06	0.09	0.50	0.14	0.23	0.41
15 Spain	1.8	3.4	61.2	23.5	9.1	1.0	70.4	24.8	3.9	0.8	0.15	0.09	1.43	5.34	0.31	0.27
16 Denmark	2.1	6.9	63.8	1.1	21.7	4.4	88.3	5.2	5.8	0.8	0.03	0.03	0.26	0.05	0.13	0.21
17 Belgium	2.0	6.3	75.6	1.6	13.3	1.2	88.4	6.1	4.6	0.9	0.06	0.06	0.61	0.12	0.16	0.11
18 Italy	2.0	3.5	51.1	10.7	26.0	6.7	82.9	12.4	3.9	0.8	0.42	0.23	2.86	5.81	2.12	4.38
19 Liechtenstein	1.5	3.1	92.0	0.6	2.5	0.2	93.1	3.2	3.0	0.7	0.00	0.00	0.01	0.00	0.00	0.00
20 New Zealand	1.1	6.6	16.6	0.3	6.9	68.6	92.1	1.6	5.7	0.5	0.03	0.07	0.15	0.03	0.09	7.17
21 United Kingdom	2.2	9.9	22.1	1.2	34.6	30.0	87.2	3.7	8.1	1.0	0.57	0.84	1.58	0.87	3.60	24.92
22 Germany	2.3	17.0	41.0	1.6	35.2	2.9	75.6	17.2	6.4	0.9	0.59	1.40	2.85	1.07	3.55	2.35
23 Singapore	0.9	51.2	21.9	0.2	12.3	13.5	49.1	34.4	16.0	0.5	0.02	0.29	0.10	0.01	0.09	0.74
24 Hong Kong, China (SAR)	1.0	3.9	20.5	0.4	63.2	11.0	94.8	1.5	3.2	0.5	0.04	0.06	0.25	0.05	1.12	1.55
25 Greece	1.9	14.4	42.6	1.0	27.4	12.7	83.4	10.5	5.3	0.8	0.11	0.27	0.68	0.15	0.63	2.33
26 Korea (Republic of)	0.9	35.7	7.4	1.6	50.3	4.2	86.5	2.4	10.6	0.5	0.09	1.08	0.19	0.38	1.86	1.23
27 Israel	1.0	76.1	6.8	0.7	14.6	0.8	24.8	4.3	70.4	0.4	0.06	1.47	0.11	0.12	0.35	0.14
28 Andorra	10.2	3.2	84.4	0.8	1.2	0.2	84.5	3.1	11.3	1.1	0.00	0.00	0.01	0.00	0.00	0.00
29 Slovenia	1.7	3.4	68.6	0.8	19.1	6.3	72.1	23.9	3.2	0.8	0.01	0.01	0.13	0.01	0.05	0.14
30 Brunei Darussalam	1.4	25.3	31.9	0.2	28.3	12.9	73.3	1.5	24.7	0.4	0.00	0.01	0.01	0.00	0.01	0.05
31 Kuwait	5.0	84.1	3.6	0.2	6.5	0.6	13.4	28.1	58.2	0.3	0.15	0.83	0.03	0.01	0.08	0.06
32 Cyprus	1.0	10.8	68.1	0.2	9.0	10.9	87.6	8.2	3.8	0.5	0.01	0.04	0.21	0.01	0.04	0.39
33 Qatar	7.6	59.3	12.6	0.2	18.4	1.9	35.2	7.3	57.2	0.4	0.01	0.02	0.00	0.00	0.01	0.01
34 Portugal	5.6	3.2	59.6	12.1	18.7	0.8	78.3	13.8	3.3	4.5	0.70	0.13	2.01	3.97	0.92	0.32
35 United Arab Emirates	6.6	71.9	8.3	0.2	11.5	1.5	21.6	6.2	71.6	0.5	0.05	0.18	0.02	0.00	0.04	0.04
36 Czech Republic	2.0	7.1	66.9	0.8	21.0	2.1	69.2	26.0	4.0	0.8	0.05	0.05	0.42	0.05	0.19	0.15
37 Barbados	1.1	3.4	25.6	4.7	64.9	0.4	90.7	5.0	3.7	0.5	0.01	0.01	0.05	0.08	0.17	0.01
38 Malta	1.8	3.4	35.9	0.5	16.5	42.0	93.9	1.9	3.4	0.8	0.01	0.01	0.07	0.01	0.05	0.94
HIGH HUMAN DEVELOPMENT																
39 Bahrain	4.7	86.1	5.3	0.2	3.1	0.7	11.4	5.4	82.8	0.4	0.04	0.22	0.01	0.00	0.01	0.02
40 Estonia	1.6	6.7	81.1	0.2	9.1	1.4	47.2	42.0	10.1	0.7	0.02	0.03	0.26	0.01	0.04	0.05
41 Poland	1.7	8.9	53.3	1.4	31.8	2.9	74.8	18.0	6.4	0.8	0.22	0.37	1.88	0.46	1.63	1.20
42 Slovakia	1.7	4.7	83.1	0.6	9.2	0.7	84.9	10.7	3.5	0.8	0.05	0.05	0.68	0.05	0.11	0.07
43 Hungary	1.7	6.7	48.6	1.5	35.6	5.9	86.6	8.8	3.8	0.8	0.04	0.05	0.34	0.10	0.36	0.47
44 Chile	1.1	3.6	20.2	50.1	20.6	4.5	45.3	49.5	4.7	0.5	0.04	0.04	0.19	4.49	0.28	0.48
45 Croatia	1.6	3.2	72.2	0.5	13.4	9.0	87.0	9.1	3.2	0.8	0.06	0.04	0.75	0.05	0.20	1.08
46 Lithuania	1.7	8.7	76.4	0.4	11.6	1.2	28.2	62.0	9.0	0.8	0.03	0.06	0.42	0.02	0.09	0.08
47 Antigua and Barbuda	1.0	46.6	8.4	11.4	32.5	0.0	41.1	11.7	46.7	0.5	0.00	0.06	0.01	0.13	0.05	0.00
48 Latvia	1.6	7.8	71.6	0.3	15.7	3.0	35.3	52.2	11.8	0.8	0.02	0.04	0.29	0.01	0.09	0.14
49 Argentina	1.1	10.6	28.6	34.6	23.3	1.8	59.1	21.2	19.1	0.5	0.04	0.13	0.30	3.58	0.36	0.22
50 Uruguay	1.1	3.5	17.2	61.4	13.0	3.8	34.0	60.4	5.1	0.5	0.02	0.02	0.07	2.55	0.08	0.19
51 Cuba	1.1	3.5	9.0	4.2	82.2	0.0	91.3	3.8	4.3	0.5	0.07	0.08	0.17	0.75	2.21	0.01
52 Bahamas	1.1	3.5	8.2	1.9	84.7	0.6	93.7	2.5	3.2	0.5	0.00	0.00	0.01	0.01	0.08	0.00
53 Mexico	1.1	3.9	1.6	0.8	92.5	0.0	94.8	1.2	3.4	0.5	0.68	0.80	0.28	1.39	23.24	0.07
54 Costa Rica	1.1	3.8	6.2	16.7	71.9	0.3	78.8	10.0	10.8	0.5	0.01	0.01	0.01	0.31	0.20	0.01
55 Libyan Arab Jamahiriya	16.3	39.8	26.7	0.4	14.7	2.0	68.1	7.7	18.9	5.3	0.08	0.06	0.04	0.01	0.03	0.03
56 Oman	8.6	60.4	17.6	0.2	10.7	2.5	33.1	8.6	57.9	0.3	0.01	0.02	0.01	0.00	0.01	0.01
57 Seychelles	39.7	2.7	32.1	0.2	10.4	14.9	57.0	1.6	30.7	10.7	0.04	0.00	0.01	0.00	0.00	0.05
58 Venezuela (Bolivarian Republic of)	1.0	3.4	37.1	22.5	35.6	0.4	72.7	21.6	5.2	0.5	0.02	0.02	0.22	1.32	0.31	0.02
59 Saudi Arabia	8.3	66.5	8.0	0.8	15.5	0.8	26.8	10.4	62.3	0.4	0.13	0.33	0.03	0.03	0.09	0.04

International emigrants by area of residence

		Areas of residence																
		Continent of residence 2000–2002 (% of total emigrant stocks)						Human development category of countries of residence[a] 2000–2002 (% of total emigrant stocks)					Share of continents' immigrants from country 2000–2002 (% of total immigrant stocks in the continent)					
HDI rank		Africa	Asia	Europe	Latin America and the Caribbean	Northern America	Oceania	Very high	High	Medium	Low		Africa	Asia	Europe	Latin America and the Caribbean	Northern America	Oceania
60	Panama	1.1	3.5	4.5	10.2	80.6	0.1	85.5	10.0	4.0	0.5		0.01	0.01	0.01	0.31	0.37	0.00
61	Bulgaria	1.5	68.3	24.3	0.6	4.9	0.4	24.2	57.8	17.2	0.7		0.09	1.28	0.38	0.09	0.11	0.07
62	Saint Kitts and Nevis	1.0	3.1	29.1	29.4	37.3	0.1	66.2	30.0	3.3	0.5		0.00	0.00	0.02	0.18	0.03	0.00
63	Romania	1.7	19.7	57.4	1.0	19.0	1.3	74.9	19.2	5.1	0.8		0.11	0.42	1.03	0.17	0.50	0.28
64	Trinidad and Tobago	1.1	3.4	9.7	4.0	81.4	0.4	91.6	3.9	3.9	0.6		0.02	0.02	0.05	0.22	0.67	0.03
65	Montenegro	1.6[b]	11.3[b]	72.3[b]	0.4[b]	10.8[b]	3.5[b]	76.2[b]	19.0[b]	4.0[b]	0.8[b]		0.17[b]	0.38[b]	2.07[b]	0.12[b]	0.45[b]	1.16
66	Malaysia	1.4	66.8	10.7	0.2	9.4	11.6	78.8	1.0	19.6	0.5		0.07	1.06	0.14	0.03	0.18	1.79
67	Serbia	1.6[b]	11.3[b]	72.3[b]	0.4[b]	10.8[b]	3.5[b]	76.2[b]	19.0[b]	4.0[b]	0.8[b]		0.17[b]	0.38[b]	2.07[b]	0.12[b]	0.45[b]	1.16
68	Belarus	1.8	8.6	86.8	0.2	2.6	0.1	7.7	67.4	24.1	0.8		0.20	0.31	2.64	0.05	0.11	0.04
69	Saint Lucia	1.1	3.3	21.3	40.4	33.8	0.1	55.1	38.5	5.8	0.5		0.00	0.00	0.02	0.34	0.04	0.00
70	Albania	1.6	3.9	88.2	0.5	5.6	0.2	89.6	6.2	3.4	0.7		0.08	0.06	1.23	0.06	0.11	0.04
71	Russian Federation	1.9	35.3	58.9	0.3	3.4	0.2	13.0	31.7	54.5	0.8		1.44	8.63	12.14	0.51	1.03	0.45
72	Macedonia (the Former Yugoslav Rep. of)	1.6	17.9	52.8	0.4	10.2	17.1	75.7	18.8	4.8	0.8		0.03	0.09	0.23	0.02	0.07	0.87
73	Dominica	1.0	3.6	25.9	23.9	45.5	0.0	71.5	24.3	3.7	0.5		0.00	0.00	0.02	0.17	0.05	0.00
74	Grenada	1.1	3.4	18.4	20.1	56.9	0.2	75.4	20.0	4.0	0.5		0.00	0.00	0.02	0.23	0.10	0.00
75	Brazil	1.0	30.4	23.8	18.9	25.3	0.6	69.3	8.8	21.4	0.5		0.06	0.59	0.39	3.00	0.60	0.11
76	Bosnia and Herzegovina	1.7	3.5	82.7	0.3	10.0	2.0	57.1	38.9	3.2	0.8		0.13	0.09	1.78	0.05	0.31	0.49
77	Colombia	1.1	3.5	18.9	43.3	33.0	0.3	52.2	43.8	3.5	0.5		0.11	0.12	0.53	11.80	1.35	0.09
78	Peru	1.0	9.4	20.0	27.4	41.3	0.8	66.6	26.7	6.2	0.5		0.05	0.14	0.25	3.36	0.76	0.12
79	Turkey	0.9	10.2	84.0	0.2	3.7	1.0	85.4	9.8	4.4	0.5		0.17	0.62	4.32	0.11	0.27	0.61
80	Ecuador	1.0	3.3	41.7	8.5	45.3	0.2	86.7	9.6	3.2	0.5		0.04	0.05	0.50	0.99	0.79	0.03
81	Mauritius	32.8	2.6	49.7	0.2	4.9	9.8	63.7	1.7	24.4	10.2		0.36	0.01	0.15	0.01	0.02	0.34
82	Kazakhstan	1.0	13.6	84.8	0.2	0.4	0.0	6.2	73.6	19.7	0.5		0.22	0.99	5.19	0.11	0.04	0.03
83	Lebanon	10.3	18.6	22.7	4.8	31.2	12.5	67.2	16.7	11.6	4.4		0.37	0.22	0.22	0.46	0.45	1.42
MEDIUM HUMAN DEVELOPMENT																		
84	Armenia	1.0	11.3	78.2	0.2	9.2	0.1	17.7	65.4	16.4	0.5		0.05	0.18	1.04	0.03	0.18	0.02
85	Ukraine	1.8	12.1	79.7	0.2	5.9	0.3	14.5	76.6	8.1	0.8		0.65	1.44	7.98	0.21	0.86	0.34
86	Azerbaijan	1.0	23.3	74.3	0.2	1.2	0.0	6.9	67.6	24.9	0.5		0.08	0.65	1.73	0.04	0.04	0.01
87	Thailand	1.0	60.1	13.0	0.2	22.3	3.4	43.7	30.3	25.5	0.5		0.06	1.04	0.19	0.03	0.47	0.57
88	Iran (Islamic Republic of)	5.1	17.9	34.9	0.3	39.6	2.3	82.8	6.6	10.1	0.5		0.30	0.33	0.55	0.04	0.91	0.41
89	Georgia	1.0	15.7	81.8	0.2	1.2	0.1	15.5	63.5	20.5	0.5		0.06	0.33	1.44	0.03	0.03	0.01
90	Dominican Republic	1.1	3.8	10.7	6.4	77.9	0.0	88.8	6.3	4.3	0.5		0.06	0.07	0.17	0.97	1.75	0.00
91	Saint Vincent and the Grenadines	1.1	3.4	16.5	27.1	51.9	0.1	68.5	27.5	3.4	0.5		0.00	0.00	0.02	0.25	0.07	0.00
92	China	1.1	64.0	7.2	0.9	23.3	3.5	79.5	6.5	13.5	0.5		0.41	7.53	0.71	0.89	3.35	3.99
93	Belize	1.1	3.5	4.4	7.6	83.3	0.1	88.1	4.0	7.3	0.5		0.00	0.00	0.00	0.07	0.11	0.00
94	Samoa	0.8	5.4	1.5	0.3	16.6	75.3	76.5	1.1	21.9	0.5		0.01	0.01	0.00	0.00	0.04	1.57
95	Maldives	1.4	38.9	34.5	0.7	4.8	19.8	60.6	3.1	35.8	0.5		0.00	0.00	0.00	0.00	0.00	0.00
96	Jordan	5.9	81.3	3.7	0.3	8.2	0.6	15.8	27.5	56.3	0.5		0.25	1.10	0.04	0.04	0.14	0.07
97	Suriname	1.0	3.1	82.2	11.0	2.7	0.0	83.7	3.9	12.0	0.5		0.02	0.02	0.38	0.49	0.02	0.00
98	Tunisia	9.3	9.9	78.3	0.2	2.3	0.1	81.1	6.8	8.7	3.4		0.35	0.12	0.81	0.02	0.03	0.01
99	Tonga	0.8	5.5	2.2	0.9	35.8	54.8	90.2	1.6	7.7	0.5		0.00	0.01	0.00	0.01	0.04	0.55
100	Jamaica	1.1	3.4	19.8	2.6	73.0	0.1	92.9	3.5	3.1	0.5		0.06	0.07	0.32	0.41	1.72	0.02
101	Paraguay	1.1	3.9	2.9	87.4	4.6	0.1	8.2	87.1	4.2	0.5		0.03	0.03	0.02	5.99	0.05	0.01
102	Sri Lanka	0.9	54.1	25.7	0.2	12.7	6.5	46.4	18.0	35.1	0.5		0.05	1.02	0.41	0.03	0.29	1.18
103	Gabon	69.9	2.1	26.1	0.2	1.7	0.0	27.6	1.2	59.8	11.4		0.25	0.00	0.03	0.00	0.00	0.00
104	Algeria	9.5	6.8	81.6	0.2	1.8	0.1	83.7	5.2	7.6	3.5		1.23	0.28	2.88	0.06	0.09	0.02
105	Philippines	0.9	35.4	8.7	0.2	49.9	4.9	66.5	25.4	7.6	0.5		0.20	2.43	0.50	0.14	4.20	3.30
106	El Salvador	1.1	3.5	2.4	5.1	86.8	1.0	90.5	2.9	6.1	0.5		0.07	0.07	0.04	0.84	2.15	0.19
107	Syrian Arab Republic	7.7	49.5	19.5	4.6	17.0	1.7	40.9	38.3	19.8	1.0		0.20	0.42	0.14	0.32	0.18	0.14
108	Fiji	0.8	5.0	4.4	0.3	38.0	51.6	92.5	1.1	5.9	0.5		0.01	0.01	0.01	0.01	0.13	1.46
109	Turkmenistan	1.0	12.1	86.2	0.2	0.5	0.0	10.2	71.7	17.6	0.5		0.02	0.06	0.38	0.01	0.00	0.00
110	Occupied Palestinian Territories	11.1	85.4	2.3	0.3	0.6	0.3	6.4	14.9	78.3	0.4		0.74	1.84	0.04	0.06	0.02	0.06
111	Indonesia	1.0	77.5	13.7	0.2	4.8	2.9	25.5	60.3	13.7	0.5		0.11	2.87	0.43	0.07	0.22	1.04
112	Honduras	1.1	3.6	3.4	10.8	81.1	0.1	84.9	3.7	10.9	0.5		0.02	0.03	0.02	0.65	0.73	0.00
113	Bolivia	1.1	4.9	8.2	70.5	15.1	0.2	24.4	70.7	4.4	0.5		0.03	0.04	0.05	4.56	0.15	0.02
114	Guyana	1.1	3.4	8.8	8.0	78.6	0.2	87.6	7.7	4.2	0.6		0.03	0.03	0.06	0.51	0.74	0.01
115	Mongolia	0.9	21.0	40.7	0.4	35.1	1.8	75.8	17.4	6.3	0.4		0.00	0.00	0.01	0.00	0.09	0.01
116	Viet Nam	0.9	15.1	18.3	0.2	57.4	8.0	85.0	2.7	11.8	0.5		0.12	0.61	0.63	0.07	2.86	3.16
117	Moldova	1.8	7.7	86.7	0.2	3.5	0.1	12.0	50.1	37.1	0.8		0.07	0.10	0.98	0.02	0.06	0.02
118	Equatorial Guinea	77.9	3.0	18.3	0.2	0.6	0.0	18.7	1.1	72.0	8.2		0.46	0.01	0.03	0.00	0.00	0.00

HDI rank	Africa	Asia	Europe	Latin America and the Caribbean	Northern America	Oceania	Very high	High	Medium	Low	Africa	Asia	Europe	Latin America and the Caribbean	Northern America	Oceania
	Continent of residence 2000–2002 (% of total emigrant stocks)						**Human develoment category of countries of residence[a] 2000–2002 (% of total emigrant stocks)**				**Share of continents' immigrants from country 2000–2002 (% of total immigrant stocks in the continent)**					
119 Uzbekistan	1.0	39.7	57.9	0.2	1.2	0.0	8.5	49.9	41.1	0.5	0.14	1.88	2.31	0.08	0.07	0.02
120 Kyrgyzstan	1.0	10.4	87.8	0.2	0.6	0.0	6.9	80.7	11.9	0.5	0.04	0.13	0.89	0.02	0.01	0.00
121 Cape Verde	33.8	3.0	49.1	0.2	14.0	0.0	62.3	1.7	10.8	25.2	0.42	0.01	0.17	0.01	0.07	0.00
122 Guatemala	1.1	3.7	3.0	9.1	83.0	0.1	86.4	5.6	7.5	0.5	0.04	0.05	0.03	0.91	1.25	0.01
123 Egypt	10.5	70.5	9.7	0.3	7.4	1.6	21.8	54.5	20.3	3.5	1.43	3.10	0.36	0.11	0.40	0.69
124 Nicaragua	1.1	3.5	2.5	48.4	44.4	0.1	47.3	46.0	6.2	0.5	0.04	0.04	0.02	4.23	0.58	0.02
125 Botswana	60.3	2.7	21.3	0.2	10.8	4.7	36.6	1.3	43.2	18.9	0.06	0.00	0.01	0.00	0.00	0.02
126 Vanuatu	0.8	5.3	25.4	0.3	2.8	65.4	57.2	1.6	40.8	0.4	0.00	0.00	0.00	0.00	0.00	0.05
127 Tajikistan	1.0	42.8	55.6	0.2	0.4	0.0	6.3	50.3	42.9	0.5	0.05	0.70	0.77	0.03	0.01	0.00
128 Namibia	77.8	2.5	11.3	0.2	5.4	2.7	19.5	1.1	36.6	42.8	0.12	0.00	0.00	0.00	0.00	0.01
129 South Africa	38.6	3.3	30.5	0.3	13.8	13.5	57.5	1.6	12.5	28.4	1.89	0.05	0.41	0.04	0.27	2.09
130 Morocco	9.1	13.2	74.5	0.2	2.8	0.1	82.8	5.8	7.8	3.5	1.48	0.69	3.29	0.09	0.18	0.03
131 Sao Tome and Principe	27.2	3.0	69.0	0.2	0.6	0.0	68.5	2.0	20.1	9.4	0.04	0.00	0.03	0.00	0.00	0.00
132 Bhutan	0.7	89.3	6.4	0.2	2.8	0.5	10.5	0.9	87.9	0.6	0.00	0.02	0.00	0.00	0.00	0.00
133 Lao People's Democratic Republic	0.9	15.6	17.4	0.2	62.9	3.0	84.2	1.3	14.0	0.5	0.02	0.11	0.10	0.01	0.55	0.21
134 India	1.7	72.0	9.7	0.2	15.0	1.3	47.9	20.4	30.7	1.0	0.97	13.18	1.49	0.35	3.37	2.41
135 Solomon Islands	0.9	5.6	11.4	0.3	4.5	77.3	60.4	1.3	37.9	0.4	0.00	0.00	0.00	0.00	0.00	0.06
136 Congo	80.1	2.1	16.5	0.2	1.1	0.0	17.5	1.1	73.8	7.6	2.74	0.02	0.15	0.02	0.01	0.00
137 Cambodia	0.9	13.1	26.3	0.2	50.5	8.9	86.5	1.5	11.5	0.5	0.02	0.08	0.14	0.01	0.39	0.55
138 Myanmar	0.8	77.6	5.9	0.2	11.8	3.7	23.1	0.9	75.4	0.5	0.02	0.49	0.03	0.01	0.09	0.23
139 Comoros	42.0	4.8	52.4	0.2	0.6	0.0	52.2	4.5	37.8	5.5	0.13	0.00	0.04	0.00	0.00	0.00
140 Yemen	6.1	85.4	4.6	0.2	3.6	0.1	17.5	65.9	16.2	0.4	0.23	1.04	0.05	0.02	0.05	0.01
141 Pakistan	1.4	72.5	16.4	0.2	9.1	0.4	27.7	24.1	47.4	0.9	0.30	5.02	0.96	0.11	0.78	0.28
142 Swaziland	72.5	3.2	14.9	0.2	7.1	2.1	24.0	1.9	25.8	48.4	0.05	0.00	0.00	0.00	0.00	0.00
143 Angola	65.8	3.8	28.6	0.8	1.0	0.0	29.2	2.0	33.7	35.2	3.62	0.07	0.43	0.11	0.02	0.01
144 Nepal	0.7	95.0	2.4	0.2	1.3	0.3	5.6	2.2	91.6	0.6	0.05	1.99	0.04	0.03	0.03	0.07
145 Madagascar	28.2	3.0	65.8	0.5	2.4	0.1	67.2	15.3	8.7	8.9	0.27	0.01	0.17	0.01	0.01	0.00
146 Bangladesh	0.7	92.4	4.7	0.2	1.8	0.2	7.7	8.4	83.2	0.6	0.31	12.76	0.55	0.17	0.30	0.25
147 Kenya	41.5	4.2	37.9	0.2	14.4	1.8	53.6	1.6	39.8	5.0	1.18	0.04	0.29	0.02	0.16	0.16
148 Papua New Guinea	0.8	8.9	4.9	0.3	4.4	80.7	59.1	1.1	39.3	0.5	0.00	0.01	0.00	0.00	0.01	0.81
149 Haiti	1.1	3.4	5.5	25.7	64.3	0.0	70.0	12.1	17.3	0.5	0.05	0.05	0.07	3.19	1.20	0.00
150 Sudan	42.9	45.9	5.7	0.2	4.6	0.8	12.5	38.8	42.0	6.7	1.72	0.60	0.06	0.02	0.07	0.10
151 Tanzania (United Republic of)	67.5	2.8	17.4	0.2	11.4	0.7	29.4	1.3	45.7	23.7	1.21	0.02	0.09	0.01	0.08	0.04
152 Ghana	74.8	3.4	12.2	0.2	9.1	0.2	21.6	1.0	16.5	60.8	4.48	0.07	0.20	0.03	0.22	0.05
153 Cameroon	48.9	3.2	38.8	0.2	8.9	0.1	47.2	1.5	36.7	14.6	0.52	0.01	0.11	0.01	0.04	0.00
154 Mauritania	75.9	4.5	17.1	0.2	2.3	0.0	19.3	3.6	18.9	58.2	0.55	0.01	0.03	0.00	0.01	0.00
155 Djibouti	41.7	5.0	48.0	0.2	4.7	0.5	52.4	4.5	11.5	31.5	0.04	0.00	0.01	0.00	0.00	0.00
156 Lesotho	93.5	2.3	2.8	0.1	1.1	0.2	4.2	0.9	23.6	71.3	0.30	0.00	0.00	0.00	0.00	0.00
157 Uganda	37.5	3.7	43.9	0.2	13.9	0.9	58.1	1.6	31.8	8.5	0.40	0.01	0.13	0.01	0.06	0.03
158 Nigeria	62.3	4.4	18.1	0.2	14.8	0.2	33.0	2.3	44.5	20.2	4.06	0.09	0.32	0.04	0.38	0.04
LOW HUMAN DEVELOPMENT																
159 Togo	83.8	2.7	11.3	0.2	2.0	0.0	13.2	0.9	51.4	34.5	1.12	0.01	0.04	0.01	0.01	0.00
160 Malawi	83.7	2.5	11.6	0.2	1.7	0.4	13.6	1.1	43.4	41.9	0.79	0.01	0.03	0.00	0.01	0.01
161 Benin	91.6	3.1	4.6	0.2	0.5	0.0	5.2	0.8	43.5	50.4	3.30	0.04	0.05	0.02	0.01	0.00
162 Timor-Leste	0.8	39.5	18.2	0.2	0.2	41.0	59.8	1.2	38.5	0.4	0.00	0.02	0.01	0.00	0.00	0.19
163 Côte d'Ivoire	47.7	3.1	43.4	0.2	5.6	0.1	48.4	1.6	10.4	39.6	0.53	0.01	0.13	0.01	0.02	0.00
164 Zambia	78.3	2.9	13.2	0.2	3.8	1.6	18.5	1.1	53.8	26.5	1.21	0.01	0.06	0.01	0.02	0.08
165 Eritrea	78.2	11.5	5.6	0.2	4.3	0.3	10.4	9.4	13.1	67.1	2.78	0.13	0.05	0.02	0.06	0.03
166 Senegal	55.7	3.0	38.1	0.2	2.9	0.0	40.6	1.5	24.7	33.2	1.67	0.03	0.31	0.02	0.03	0.00
167 Rwanda	85.2	3.2	9.1	0.2	2.3	0.0	11.4	1.0	79.7	8.0	1.28	0.02	0.04	0.01	0.01	0.00
168 Gambia	44.7	2.9	39.7	0.2	12.4	0.1	51.6	1.5	16.5	30.4	0.14	0.00	0.03	0.00	0.02	0.00
169 Liberia	34.9	4.4	11.5	0.2	48.8	0.2	60.4	1.1	24.9	13.6	0.19	0.01	0.02	0.00	0.10	0.00
170 Guinea	90.3	3.0	5.1	0.2	1.4	0.0	6.6	0.8	10.2	82.4	3.29	0.04	0.05	0.02	0.02	0.00
171 Ethiopia	8.6	37.5	21.4	0.2	30.7	1.5	75.1	10.0	10.5	4.4	0.15	0.22	0.10	0.01	0.22	0.08
172 Mozambique	83.8	2.5	12.8	0.3	0.6	0.1	13.3	1.2	50.1	35.4	4.44	0.04	0.18	0.04	0.01	0.01
173 Guinea-Bissau	65.0	2.8	31.3	0.2	0.6	0.0	31.5	1.3	13.1	54.1	0.52	0.01	0.07	0.00	0.00	0.00
174 Burundi	90.8	3.2	4.6	0.2	1.1	0.0	5.8	0.9	84.2	9.1	2.21	0.03	0.03	0.01	0.01	0.00
175 Chad	90.7	5.5	3.1	0.2	0.5	0.0	3.8	3.7	74.3	18.1	1.72	0.06	0.02	0.01	0.00	0.00
176 Congo (Dem. Republic of the)	79.7	2.6	15.3	0.2	2.2	0.0	17.4	1.1	48.6	32.8	4.09	0.04	0.21	0.02	0.04	0.01
177 Burkina Faso	94.0	3.0	2.4	0.2	0.3	0.0	2.9	0.8	8.9	87.5	7.93	0.08	0.06	0.04	0.01	0.00

International emigrants by area of residence

	Areas of residence															
	Continent of residence 2000–2002 (% of total emigrant stocks)						Human develoment category of countries of residence[a] 2000–2002 (% of total emigrant stocks)				Share of continents' immigrants from country 2000–2002 (% of total immigrant stocks in the continent)					
HDI rank	Africa	Asia	Europe	Latin America and the Caribbean	Northern America	Oceania	Very high	High	Medium	Low	Africa	Asia	Europe	Latin America and the Caribbean	Northern America	Oceania
178 Mali	91.1	3.1	5.1	0.2	0.5	0.0	5.7	0.9	17.5	76.0	8.99	0.10	0.14	0.05	0.02	0.00
179 Central African Republic	84.1	2.1	13.0	0.2	0.6	0.1	13.5	1.0	70:9	14.6	0.58	0.00	0.02	0.00	0.00	0.00
180 Sierra Leone	40.9	3.0	31.5	0.2	24.0	0.5	55.4	1.4	11.1	32.1	0.24	0.01	0.05	0.00	0.06	0.01
181 Afghanistan	0.8	91.4	4.4	0.2	2.7	0.5	11.0	4.6	84.0	0.4	0.14	4.82	0.20	0.08	0.17	0.25
182 Niger	93.3	3.0	3.0	0.2	0.5	0.0	3.6	0.8	20.6	75.0	2.90	0.03	0.02	0.02	0.01	0.00
OTHER UN MEMBER STATES																
Iraq	5.1	59.2	22.1	0.2	10.7	2.7	44.2	6.6	48.7	0.4	0.35	1.33	0.42	0.03	0.29	0.59
Kiribati	0.8	5.5	7.9	0.3	28.6	57.0	62.6	1.2	35.8	0.4	0.00	0.00	0.00	0.00	0.00	0.04
Korea (Dem. People's Rep. of)	0.9	47.5	2.0	0.9	48.6	0.0	85.9	1.5	12.2	0.5	0.03	0.46	0.02	0.07	0.58	0.00
Marshall Islands	0.8	25.1	3.5	1.0	64.2	5.4	69.1	4.0	26.4	0.5	0.00	0.01	0.00	0.00	0.02	0.01
Micronesia (Federated States of)	0.8	23.1	3.9	1.1	30.4	40.7	35.7	30.2	33.6	0.5	0.00	0.01	0.00	0.00	0.02	0.20
Monaco	2.0	5.9	87.9	0.6	3.4	0.2	90.1	2.9	6.3	0.7	0.00	0.00	0.03	0.00	0.00	0.00
Nauru	0.7	5.6	6.9	4.2	11.1	71.5	86.3	4.7	8.7	0.4	0.00	0.00	0.00	0.00	0.00	0.01
Palau	0.7	55.3	3.3	1.6	17.6	21.6	22.3	12.7	64.5	0.5	0.00	0.01	0.00	0.00	0.01	0.05
San Marino	1.5	3.1	86.2	1.1	8.0	0.1	92.9	3.4	3.0	0.7	0.00	0.00	0.01	0.00	0.00	0.00
Somalia	50.8	9.6	27.5	0.2	10.8	1.0	39.2	8.2	11.7	41.0	1.71	0.10	0.25	0.02	0.14	0.11
Tuvalu	0.7	5.1	17.0	0.3	1.6	75.3	83.0	4.3	12.3	0.3	0.00	0.00	0.00	0.00	0.00	0.03
Zimbabwe	61.8	3.0	24.1	0.2	5.7	5.1	34.7	1.5	28.2	35.7	1.12	0.02	0.12	0.01	0.04	0.29
Africa	52.6	12.5	28.9	0.2	4.9	0.9	35.9	8.3	25.7	30.0	82.39T	6.31T	12.34T	0.97T	3.07T	4.41
Asia	1.7	54.7	24.5	0.5	16.4	2.2	41.7	23.2	34.5	0.6	6.83T	72.37T	27.34T	5.62T	26.57T	28.68
Europe	2.5	16.0	59.0	2.5	15.4	4.6	52.6	28.1	18.1	1.2	8.39T	17.25T	53.66T	21.75T	20.39T	48.18
Latin America and the Caribbean	1.1	5.1	10.3	13.4	69.8	0.3	81.7	12.1	5.6	0.5	1.77T	2.73T	4.69T	59.05T	46.01T	1.70
Northern America	2.2	14.7	23.6	21.0	34.9	3.7	62.8	23.5	12.6	1.1	0.49T	1.07T	1.44T	12.46T	3.09T	2.60
Oceania	1.4	8.7	20.1	0.6	22.5	46.7	84.3	2.8	12.3	0.6	0.13T	0.28T	0.54T	0.16T	0.87T	14.44
OECD	2.4	9.0	36.4	4.8	41.2	6.2	83.1	9.7	6.0	1.2	6.84T	8.22T	28.10T	35.99T	46.29T	55.89
European Union (EU27)	3.1	10.7	49.1	4.4	24.6	8.0	77.4	14.9	6.2	1.5	5.47T	6.04T	23.25T	20.41T	16.91T	43.70
GCC	6.1	77.9	5.9	0.3	9.1	0.8	18.0	17.6	63.9	0.4	0.39T	1.60T	0.10T	0.05T	0.23T	0.17
Very high human development	3.0	14.3	39.2	6.3	28.2	9.0	76.7	11.9	9.9	1.4	6.08T	9.43T	21.71T	34.20T	22.75T	57.60
Very high HD: OECD	3.1	10.7	41.4	7.0	28.5	9.3	79.4	12.1	7.0	1.5	5.68T	6.32T	20.60T	33.87T	20.67T	53.47
Very high HD: non-OECD	1.9	46.4	19.6	0.6	25.3	6.3	53.8	10.4	35.3	0.5	0.39T	3.11T	1.11T	0.33T	2.08T	4.14
High human development	1.7	16.5	43.8	4.4	32.4	1.3	56.4	23.9	18.9	0.7	5.53T	17.75T	39.74T	38.67T	42.85T	13.42
Medium human development	7.4	43.3	27.8	2.1	17.6	1.8	42.6	25.3	28.9	3.2	35.37T	66.96T	36.26T	26.71T	33.33T	27.88
Low human development	64.1	21.9	10.2	0.2	3.2	0.4	15.0	2.6	40.8	41.6	53.02T	5.85T	2.29T	0.42T	1.07T	1.10
World (excluding the former Soviet Union and Czechoslovakia)	10.8	29.2	24.8	4.2	27.4	3.5	59.6	13.3	21.1	6.0	96.81T	84.39T	60.44T	98.72T	97.03T	98.57
World	9.1	28.2	33.4	3.4	23.0	2.9	51.1	20.7	23.3	5.0	100.00T	100.00T	100.00T	100.00T	100.00T	100.00

NOTES

a Percentages may not sum to 100% due to movements to areas not classified by human development categories.

b Data refer to Serbia and Montenegro prior to its separation into two independent states in June 2006.

SOURCES

All columns: calculated based on data from Migration DRC (2007).

Education and employment of international migrants in OECD countries

(aged 15 years and above)

TABLE C

HDI rank	Stock of international migrants in OECD countries (thousands)	Educational attainment levels of international migrants[a] — Low: less than upper secondary	Educational attainment levels of international migrants[a] — Medium: upper secondary or post-secondary non-tertiary	Educational attainment levels of international migrants[a] — High: tertiary (% of all migrants)	Tertiary emigration rate (%)	Labour force participation rate[b] (both sexes) (% of all migrants)	Total unemployment rate[b] (both sexes)	Unemployment rates of international migrants by level of educational attainment[a] — Low: less than upper secondary	Unemployment rates — Medium: upper secondary or post-secondary non-tertiary	Unemployment rates — High: tertiary (% of labour force)
VERY HIGH HUMAN DEVELOPMENT										
1 Norway	123.3	21.7	38.1	31.7	4.5	45.1	5.7	8.5	6.8	3.8
2 Australia	291.9	16.6	36.1	42.3	2.5	73.4	6.1	10.7	7.5	3.7
3 Iceland	22.7	15.3	39.0	33.5	18.0	65.2	4.8	9.0	4.4	3.9
4 Canada	1,064.1	18.3	40.7	39.4	3.0	58.3	4.1	7.9	5.1	2.5
5 Ireland	788.1	37.8	25.3	22.4	22.1	55.2	5.1	7.7	4.8	3.0
6 Netherlands	583.4	25.9	36.6	31.8	6.2	55.7	4.5	6.8	4.5	3.4
7 Sweden	201.5	18.0	37.5	36.8	4.6	62.4	7.2	15.4	8.8	3.9
8 France	1,135.6	32.0	30.7	32.2	4.2	60.2	7.7	13.2	7.6	4.6
9 Switzerland	427.2	34.6	40.0	24.0	9.8	60.3	10.4	14.8	9.9	6.3
10 Japan	565.4	10.4	38.9	49.0	1.1	57.7	4.4	8.5	5.3	3.2
11 Luxembourg	31.3	39.0	32.4	23.7	..	50.4	8.8	13.2	8.9	4.8
12 Finland	257.2	30.4	42.5	23.5	6.1	53.6	4.7	5.8	5.0	3.3
13 United States	840.6	19.6	29.3	46.6	0.4	60.3	5.7	9.6	7.8	3.9
14 Austria	383.1	23.4	45.0	27.3	9.8	55.3	3.2	5.1	3.0	2.3
15 Spain	757.6	51.7	26.8	17.6	2.4	52.7	7.5	9.4	7.6	4.7
16 Denmark	159.5	20.3	38.3	33.3	6.3	54.2	5.0	7.8	5.5	3.7
17 Belgium	350.8	34.5	32.4	30.8	5.8	54.7	8.7	14.4	9.8	4.6
18 Italy	2,357.1	57.5	26.3	11.5	3.8	48.4	8.0	11.0	6.5	3.6
19 Liechtenstein	3.5	27.5	46.9	19.5	..	59.6	3.7	5.1	3.4	2.8
20 New Zealand	413.1	30.6	34.7	26.5	8.2	76.4	6.9	10.4	6.5	3.7
21 United Kingdom	3,241.3	25.7	36.7	33.1	10.3	59.7	5.4	9.5	5.6	3.3
22 Germany	3,122.5	26.6	43.0	27.4	7.1	57.2	7.9	14.2	7.9	4.6
23 Singapore	106.6	19.7	32.2	43.5	12.9	63.9	5.9	7.0	7.4	4.4
24 Hong Kong, China (SAR)	388.4	27.9	31.4	37.9	16.8	61.7	6.8	7.1	9.0	5.4
25 Greece	685.8	55.3	26.0	15.1	7.9	49.6	6.3	8.8	3.9	4.6
26 Korea (Republic of)	975.3	16.4	39.3	43.6	..	58.8	5.5	8.8	6.1	4.3
27 Israel	162.7	18.3	37.0	42.7	5.4	65.6	6.2	11.2	7.4	4.0
28 Andorra	3.4	46.3	27.2	25.6	..	47.7	11.9	12.8	11.9	10.8
29 Slovenia	78.4	47.3	39.1	11.4	..	39.1	6.3	7.4	6.2	4.5
30 Brunei Darussalam	8.9	19.1	41.1	37.7	..	63.3	6.3	5.8	9.2	4.3
31 Kuwait	37.1	16.7	36.9	44.2	6.5	53.8	9.6	18.9	12.3	6.3
32 Cyprus	140.5	41.0	28.4	23.0	24.8	54.4	6.8	8.9	7.0	4.7
33 Qatar	3.3	16.1	37.0	43.9	..	45.7	10.7	14.5	15.8	6.9
34 Portugal	1,260.2	67.2	23.4	6.2	6.3	71.0	7.7	8.5	6.7	5.3
35 United Arab Emirates	14.4	21.0	50.2	24.2	..	40.8	14.9	18.8	17.1	10.6
36 Czech Republic	242.5	22.6	51.6	23.7	..	55.9	11.0	30.5	10.9	3.6
37 Barbados	88.4	30.0	40.2	26.3	47.3	66.0	6.3	9.2	6.5	4.0
38 Malta	98.0	53.2	24.5	13.5	..	54.0	4.9	5.8	4.6	3.2
HIGH HUMAN DEVELOPMENT										
39 Bahrain	7.2	15.8	40.6	40.2	5.3	61.7	7.9	6.1	10.1	6.7
40 Estonia	36.0	26.6	36.6	30.6	..	37.2	11.4	15.4	13.8	7.5
41 Poland	2,112.6	30.6	46.2	21.1	12.3	59.5	10.7	15.8	11.1	6.1
42 Slovakia	361.5	40.7	45.5	12.9	..	48.8	15.7	34.8	10.8	3.9
43 Hungary	331.5	25.6	44.1	27.4	8.4	46.6	6.5	11.1	6.2	5.0
44 Chile	207.9	25.1	41.8	29.9	3.8	65.8	8.8	12.6	9.2	6.1
45 Croatia	488.9	45.7	39.4	12.4	..	56.7	8.4	15.9	3.6	3.6
46 Lithuania	134.4	35.8	39.6	21.8	..	28.9	11.6	19.3	13.6	6.1
47 Antigua and Barbuda	24.3	29.7	41.4	26.6	..	68.0	8.1	12.8	8.9	3.9
48 Latvia	54.8	19.5	36.1	35.8	..	39.7	6.5	11.0	7.3	5.2
49 Argentina	322.3	31.1	34.8	32.6	2.0	62.8	9.9	13.6	9.8	7.6
50 Uruguay	74.4	34.7	37.0	26.3	5.1	67.3	9.5	12.5	9.4	6.6
51 Cuba	924.6	40.8	35.1	23.9	..	52.5	8.0	12.0	7.5	5.2
52 Bahamas	30.1	23.3	46.9	29.4	..	63.8	9.7	16.8	11.2	4.6
53 Mexico	8,327.9	69.6	24.7	5.7	6.5	60.1	9.4	10.6	7.7	5.2
54 Costa Rica	75.7	31.5	43.7	24.4	3.9	64.8	6.6	10.4	6.1	3.8
55 Libyan Arab Jamahiriya	64.8	44.3	30.6	23.6	..	51.2	7.6	8.0	6.9	7.4
56 Oman	2.6	13.6	44.6	37.5	..	34.4	7.7	7.5	10.4	7.4
57 Seychelles	8.1	42.6	31.5	17.3	..	60.3	9.7	12.6	8.4	7.4
58 Venezuela (Bolivarian Republic of)	233.3	27.0	35.8	36.7	3.8	64.3	11.3	15.0	12.7	8.1
59 Saudi Arabia	34.1	22.8	38.8	35.8	..	43.5	11.8	18.4	13.2	8.2

Education and employment of international migrants in OECD countries
(aged 15 years and above)

		Educational attainment levels of international migrants[a]				Economic activity status of international migrants		Unemployment rates of international migrants		
								By level of educational attainment[a]		
		Low	Medium	High				Low	Medium	High
HDI rank	Stock of international migrants in OECD countries	less than upper secondary	upper secondary or post-secondary non-tertiary	tertiary	Tertiary emigration rate	Labour force participation rate[b] (both sexes)	Total unemployment rate[b] (both sexes)	less than upper secondary	upper secondary or post-secondary non-tertiary	tertiary
	(thousands)	(% of all migrants)			(%)	(% of all migrants)		(% of labour force)		
60 Panama	139.8	16.9	50.0	32.9	11.1	65.5	6.1	13.3	6.8	3.3
61 Bulgaria	604.4	51.0	31.3	13.0	..	59.2	9.3	8.9	10.1	8.7
62 Saint Kitts and Nevis	20.0	33.0	35.5	26.6	..	66.8	6.6	10.5	6.1	4.2
63 Romania	1,004.6	32.7	43.9	22.3	..	59.8	8.8	12.1	8.8	5.9
64 Trinidad and Tobago	274.2	23.3	46.2	29.7	66.4	70.2	7.1	11.5	7.6	4.1
65 Montenegro	..[c]	52.1[d]	30.2[d]	10.6[d]	..	55.9[d]	13.6[d]	16.3[d]	12.2[d]	7.8[d]
66 Malaysia	214.3	18.4	28.8	47.6	11.3	65.7	6.2	8.3	9.0	4.3
67 Serbia	1,044.4	52.1[d]	30.2[d]	10.6[d]	..	55.9[d]	13.6[d]	16.3[d]	12.2[d]	7.8[d]
68 Belarus	151.1	37.1	37.3	25.0	..	29.1	10.4	14.7	13.9	6.4
69 Saint Lucia	24.5	37.9	37.0	20.3	..	65.6	9.0	12.6	8.4	5.5
70 Albania	524.1	54.0	34.6	8.7	..	68.8	10.0	10.3	9.3	10.6
71 Russian Federation	1,524.4	33.9	37.9	27.1	..	58.0	15.7	19.6	15.7	13.0
72 Macedonia (the Former Yugoslav Rep. of)	175.7	57.1	24.4	7.4	..	59.6	10.0	11.0	8.1	8.0
73 Dominica	25.7	40.4	34.0	21.7	..	64.3	9.9	13.1	9.9	6.4
74 Grenada	46.4	34.2	39.6	23.3	..	69.0	8.3	12.3	7.9	4.7
75 Brazil	544.1	30.6	38.8	25.9	1.6	70.9	6.8	9.0	6.2	5.7
76 Bosnia and Herzegovina	569.9	44.3	42.0	9.6	..	68.3	11.0	14.2	9.0	7.8
77 Colombia	691.7	33.9	40.5	24.8	5.8	63.9	11.5	16.3	10.2	8.3
78 Peru	415.1	24.7	44.8	28.6	3.0	67.7	8.4	12.0	8.0	6.8
79 Turkey	2,085.5	69.0	21.6	6.7	3.2	58.1	19.6	23.2	15.9	5.2
80 Ecuador	503.7	48.8	35.8	15.0	5.8	69.8	10.9	12.6	9.9	8.1
81 Mauritius	91.4	42.9	27.9	24.4	48.5	69.3	11.7	16.2	12.6	4.8
82 Kazakhstan	415.7	35.1	48.0	16.6	..	60.0	13.0	17.9	12.4	8.9
83 Lebanon	335.5	33.8	31.6	30.9	..	56.9	10.4	15.3	11.0	6.9
MEDIUM HUMAN DEVELOPMENT										
84 Armenia	79.4	27.3	41.5	30.3	..	56.6	14.4	21.4	13.8	11.4
85 Ukraine	773.0	36.8	34.8	27.0	..	36.1	9.8	12.3	10.9	7.9
86 Azerbaijan	30.1	25.2	33.0	39.8	..	57.1	16.9	21.2	16.8	14.8
87 Thailand	269.7	34.8	31.9	27.6	1.5	58.7	9.0	13.5	8.5	5.3
88 Iran (Islamic Republic of)	616.0	17.2	34.4	45.9	8.3	62.5	8.6	19.4	9.5	6.2
89 Georgia	84.7	35.8	35.4	24.8	..	58.6	16.9	19.6	16.1	15.1
90 Dominican Republic	695.3	53.2	34.2	12.3	9.8	56.7	13.3	17.1	11.3	7.2
91 Saint Vincent and the Grenadines	34.8	34.4	38.6	24.5	..	68.1	8.9	11.8	9.5	5.5
92 China	2,068.2	31.0	25.1	39.4	3.0	58.5	6.1	7.8	6.9	4.9
93 Belize	42.6	30.5	48.7	20.4	..	66.0	8.4	11.2	8.5	5.7
94 Samoa	71.5	31.1	44.1	8.7	..	62.0	13.5	15.9	12.6	7.8
95 Maldives	0.4	25.8	40.5	30.0	..	30.0	13.1	18.2	4.7	14.5
96 Jordan	63.9	20.0	37.8	41.0	4.6	61.9	7.9	12.0	8.5	6.2
97 Suriname	7.1	23.9	43.2	30.9	..	61.0	6.9	15.6	6.2	3.5
98 Tunisia	427.5	55.5	27.8	15.9	14.3	57.0	20.6	26.4	18.8	10.3
99 Tonga	40.9	34.6	44.8	9.5	..	62.0	11.3	14.1	9.9	6.5
100 Jamaica	789.7	33.1	39.6	24.2	72.6	68.9	7.9	11.9	7.9	4.3
101 Paraguay	20.1	37.1	37.5	23.9	1.9	69.3	6.9	7.5	6.9	6.3
102 Sri Lanka	316.9	32.7	34.4	26.4	19.4	67.8	10.5	13.5	10.9	7.0
103 Gabon	10.8	29.9	33.1	35.9	..	49.7	23.1	32.6	24.3	17.2
104 Algeria	1,313.3	55.4	27.8	16.4	15.4	53.0	21.9	29.0	20.3	11.7
105 Philippines	1,930.3	17.4	35.1	45.9	7.4	68.7	4.9	8.9	5.6	3.5
106 El Salvador	835.6	62.9	29.2	7.7	14.1	64.7	8.4	9.6	6.9	5.7
107 Syrian Arab Republic	130.2	33.0	30.3	33.3	3.8	55.3	10.5	13.7	10.5	8.6
108 Fiji	119.0	30.8	41.5	21.4	38.3	69.9	7.5	9.6	7.4	5.3
109 Turkmenistan	4.9	25.4	48.4	24.8	..	45.8	16.3	17.3	17.0	14.6
110 Occupied Palestinian Territories	15.5	23.5	28.2	40.5	..	46.7	12.1	13.9	13.6	10.9
111 Indonesia	339.4	24.8	38.3	34.5	1.8	48.8	4.4	3.4	4.4	4.5
112 Honduras	275.6	57.2	32.2	10.6	12.0	63.7	10.0	12.0	8.5	5.5
113 Bolivia	76.8	24.9	44.1	29.4	3.3	66.6	8.5	11.0	8.9	6.3
114 Guyana	303.6	31.0	42.9	25.0	76.9	68.6	6.6	10.2	6.4	4.0
115 Mongolia	4.3	16.5	35.1	45.7	..	58.6	9.7	9.2	7.6	11.3
116 Viet Nam	1,518.1	40.7	34.8	22.9	..	64.6	7.7	10.5	7.2	4.7
117 Moldova	41.4	26.8	37.4	34.6	..	63.7	12.3	16.9	11.4	10.3
118 Equatorial Guinea	12.1	52.0	25.5	22.4	..	63.3	22.3	26.9	20.9	15.0

TABLE C

		Educational attainment levels of international migrants[a]				Economic activity status of international migrants		Unemployment rates of international migrants		
								By level of educational attainment[a]		
		Low	Medium	High				Low	Medium	High
	Stock of international migrants in OECD countries	less than upper secondary	upper secondary or post-secondary non-tertiary	tertiary	Tertiary emigration rate	Labour force participation rate[b] (both sexes)	Total unemployment rate[b] (both sexes)	less than upper secondary	upper secondary or post-secondary non-tertiary	tertiary
HDI rank	(thousands)	(% of all migrants)			(%)	(% of all migrants)		(% of labour force)		
119 Uzbekistan	45.2	25.0	40.0	33.9	..	59.0	12.5	16.0	12.7	10.5
120 Kyrgyzstan	34.1	33.5	47.9	18.4	..	58.8	12.8	17.3	12.3	9.7
121 Cape Verde	87.9	73.7	19.1	5.9	..	70.5	9.4	9.7	9.7	5.1
122 Guatemala	485.3	63.6	27.9	8.4	11.2	63.5	8.2	9.1	7.4	5.4
123 Egypt	308.7	18.8	30.7	47.3	3.7	59.9	8.3	12.9	9.7	6.5
124 Nicaragua	221.0	40.7	41.1	18.1	14.3	61.6	8.7	12.0	8.0	5.2
125 Botswana	4.1	12.3	46.3	37.1	4.2	45.3	14.3	10.6	17.6	10.6
126 Vanuatu	1.7	27.8	39.1	27.2	..	63.4	12.6	16.6	10.1	12.1
127 Tajikistan	8.9	30.4	45.1	24.1	..	57.5	12.4	18.0	12.3	8.5
128 Namibia	3.1	15.3	34.8	45.9	..	70.3	6.0	10.6	6.1	4.8
129 South Africa	351.7	14.6	34.6	44.8	6.8	74.2	5.5	10.1	6.6	3.7
130 Morocco	1,505.0	61.1	23.1	13.9	..	60.9	19.8	22.6	19.0	12.2
131 Sao Tome and Principe	11.6	72.2	16.9	10.7	..	73.7	9.3	9.8	9.9	5.8
132 Bhutan	0.7	39.1	30.6	23.7	..	57.4	14.1	13.4	12.7	14.1
133 Lao People's Democratic Republic	264.2	49.5	35.7	14.2	..	63.0	9.6	12.4	8.4	6.0
134 India	1,952.0	25.5	19.5	51.2	3.5	66.6	5.9	9.8	7.0	4.3
135 Solomon Islands	1.8	25.3	29.5	36.8	..	63.5	10.8	18.3	15.0	5.7
136 Congo	68.7	27.1	34.2	34.9	25.7	72.4	26.4	37.4	28.3	18.5
137 Cambodia	239.1	52.4	30.8	15.2	..	62.2	11.2	14.6	9.5	6.4
138 Myanmar	61.2	25.0	26.2	40.9	2.5	61.7	5.8	8.2	6.5	4.5
139 Comoros	17.6	63.6	25.6	10.7	..	66.8	40.8	45.4	36.1	25.7
140 Yemen	31.9	47.0	30.2	19.3	..	56.3	9.1	8.8	10.6	6.8
141 Pakistan	669.0	43.6	21.4	30.3	9.8	55.2	10.9	15.1	10.6	7.3
142 Swaziland	1.8	19.8	32.9	42.9	3.2	69.6	7.4	12.2	6.6	6.1
143 Angola	196.2	52.9	26.5	19.5	..	77.0	9.7	11.4	10.2	4.9
144 Nepal	23.9	21.3	33.0	39.2	3.0	72.0	6.3	6.2	7.2	5.8
145 Madagascar	76.6	33.3	34.6	31.7	..	67.2	17.7	25.0	18.3	11.9
146 Bangladesh	285.7	46.2	22.3	27.2	3.2	54.8	12.5	17.9	12.0	7.5
147 Kenya	198.1	26.0	32.7	36.9	27.2	73.6	6.1	8.2	7.0	4.1
148 Papua New Guinea	25.9	28.0	33.8	31.2	15.1	70.3	8.7	13.2	9.5	4.9
149 Haiti	462.9	39.3	40.6	20.0	67.5	66.2	11.3	15.2	10.8	6.6
150 Sudan	42.1	23.4	32.9	39.7	4.6	59.4	16.2	25.1	14.8	13.9
151 Tanzania (United Republic of)	70.2	25.1	30.4	40.7	15.6	69.9	5.9	8.1	7.4	4.2
152 Ghana	165.6	26.5	38.4	31.3	33.7	75.7	9.6	14.2	9.7	6.4
153 Cameroon	58.5	23.3	32.3	41.9	12.5	68.9	21.8	32.6	24.5	15.9
154 Mauritania	15.2	63.1	19.1	17.2	..	72.0	22.2	23.1	24.8	15.8
155 Djibouti	5.4	34.1	34.7	29.7	..	56.5	24.9	37.4	23.2	16.8
156 Lesotho	0.9	18.3	31.6	45.8	3.8	62.5	6.0	..	9.9	3.8
157 Uganda	82.1	27.4	29.0	39.0	24.2	72.9	6.9	9.0	8.1	5.0
158 Nigeria	261.0	15.5	28.4	53.1	..	75.4	11.2	20.7	13.9	7.9
LOW HUMAN DEVELOPMENT										
159 Togo	18.4	27.9	34.1	35.8	11.8	71.9	21.3	28.0	22.2	16.2
160 Malawi	14.9	32.5	28.5	34.8	15.5	70.4	7.2	10.2	7.7	4.7
161 Benin	14.4	25.8	30.5	42.2	11.3	70.9	19.7	26.9	22.8	14.3
162 Timor-Leste	11.1	57.1	23.4	12.4	..	62.6	12.1	14.8	11.6	4.5
163 Côte d'Ivoire	62.6	38.1	34.2	26.4	..	70.7	22.7	28.0	22.9	16.1
164 Zambia	34.9	14.2	34.4	47.9	15.5	77.1	6.3	11.9	7.7	4.1
165 Eritrea	48.0	36.0	39.3	20.7	..	65.2	11.3	14.8	10.3	7.8
166 Senegal	133.2	56.6	23.6	19.1	18.6	74.8	18.5	20.4	19.2	12.3
167 Rwanda	14.8	25.4	32.6	34.9	20.8	59.0	26.4	37.4	27.3	21.5
168 Gambia	20.9	47.9	30.9	16.5	44.6	67.9	15.0	20.3	12.1	7.5
169 Liberia	41.0	20.6	44.8	33.5	24.7	73.7	9.3	20.8	9.2	5.0
170 Guinea	21.3	49.6	25.4	22.4	..	68.2	24.6	31.6	20.2	15.7
171 Ethiopia	124.4	24.3	43.6	29.2	..	68.4	9.5	14.9	8.9	7.0
172 Mozambique	85.7	44.2	28.8	26.4	53.6	77.9	6.7	8.9	7.0	3.5
173 Guinea-Bissau	30.0	66.3	20.5	12.8	71.5	76.5	16.7	18.0	16.3	11.2
174 Burundi	10.6	24.3	28.7	38.0	..	60.5	24.5	37.0	26.5	18.1
175 Chad	5.8	22.7	33.1	42.2	..	73.5	20.5	30.6	20.6	16.5
176 Congo (Democratic Republic of the)	100.7	25.0	32.5	35.5	9.6	66.5	21.8	31.9	24.4	15.1
177 Burkina Faso	8.3	46.9	22.6	28.5	..	72.3	15.3	16.8	13.9	13.8

153

C

Education and employment of international migrants in OECD countries
(aged 15 years and above)

	Stock of international migrants in OECD countries	Educational attainment levels of international migrants[a]			Tertiary emigration rate	Economic activity status of international migrants		Unemployment rates of international migrants		
		Low	Medium	High		Labour force participation rate[b] (both sexes)	Total unemployment rate[b] (both sexes)	By level of educational attainment[a]		
		less than upper secondary	upper secondary or post-secondary non-tertiary	tertiary				Low	Medium	High
								less than upper secondary	upper secondary or post-secondary non-tertiary	tertiary
HDI rank	(thousands)	(% of all migrants)			(%)	(% of all migrants)		(% of labour force)		
178 Mali	45.2	68.3	18.7	12.6	14.6	74.9	24.9	27.1	24.4	14.4
179 Central African Republic	9.8	33.4	33.1	32.7	9.1	69.1	24.2	35.6	23.6	17.8
180 Sierra Leone	40.2	23.5	37.4	33.7	34.5	71.8	10.7	19.1	10.5	6.5
181 Afghanistan	141.2	44.7	28.9	19.4	6.4	47.3	13.6	13.9	13.1	12.5
182 Niger	4.8	26.6	34.3	37.5	5.8	68.1	18.5	27.8	17.8	14.1
OTHER UN MEMBER STATES										
Iraq	335.5	38.9	26.9	26.6	8.4	49.5	17.8	27.4	12.5	12.6
Kiribati	1.7	38.3	33.9	20.2	..	57.5	8.4	7.7	11.6	4.8
Korea (Democratic People's Rep. of)	1.2	21.7	32.1	38.6	..	58.3	6.5	8.3	4.7	6.7
Marshall Islands	5.3	34.9	54.1	10.9	..	58.1	19.9	27.9	20.5	4.8
Micronesia (Federated States of)	6.5	26.9	59.7	13.3	..	68.9	11.5	17.9	11.1	4.6
Monaco	12.3	41.4	35.1	23.0	..	50.8	11.1	16.4	12.3	5.7
Nauru	0.5	35.3	34.7	21.6	..	62.4	8.2	22.2	6.0	2.4
Palau	2.1	12.7	58.9	28.3	..	71.5	8.1	12.1	9.2	5.1
San Marino	2.8	61.6	25.7	12.4	..	44.3	4.3	6.2	2.7	3.6
Somalia	125.1	44.0	30.6	12.5	..	42.0	28.2	37.0	24.0	18.9
Tuvalu	0.9	38.9	27.2	6.2	..	57.2	16.1	19.2	13.0	6.8
Zimbabwe	77.4	14.9	39.9	40.6	9.4	73.4	7.0	11.0	8.6	4.4
Africa	6,555.3[T]	44.6	28.6	24.5	9.3	63.4	16.5	22.8	15.7	9.0
Asia	17,522.0[T]	33.0	29.8	34.3	3.6	60.9	9.0	14.6	8.6	5.0
Europe	27,318.1[T]	38.6	35.7	21.6	7.0	56.5	8.8	12.6	8.5	5.3
Latin America and the Caribbean	18,623.0[T]	53.8	31.9	13.8	6.0	61.4	9.4	11.6	8.3	5.7
Northern America	1,923.8[T]	18.8	35.8	42.5	0.7	59.3	4.8	8.6	6.1	3.2
Oceania	1,098.2[T]	26.6	38.7	27.4	4.0	71.4	7.8	11.8	7.9	4.2
OECD	33,500.2[T]	44.5	32.3	20.3	2.9	58.3	8.5	12.2	7.7	4.1
European Union (EU27)	20,514.2[T]	37.1	35.9	23.0	7.0	56.7	7.6	11.5	7.6	4.3
GCC	98.6[T]	19.2	40.0	37.9	6.3	48.1	11.0	17.6	13.4	7.3
Very high human development	21,480.5[T]	33.4	34.5	27.9	2.7	57.9	6.6	10.4	6.7	3.9
Very high HD: OECD	20,281.1[T]	33.5	34.6	27.6	2.6	57.8	6.6	10.5	6.6	3.8
Very high HD: non-OECD	1,199.3[T]	30.6	33.2	32.2	12.2	59.3	6.6	8.2	7.9	4.8
High human development	28,213.0[T]	49.4	33.2	15.7	5.1	59.3	10.9	14.0	9.8	6.6
Medium human development	22,102.2[T]	37.8	30.4	29.2	5.2	61.8	10.3	15.2	9.9	6.0
Low human development	1,244.8[T]	37.7	32.1	25.8	12.8	65.9	16.1	21.5	15.2	10.4
World (excluding the former Soviet Union and Czechoslovakia)	69,018.3[T]	41.4	32.3	23.5	3.7	60.3	9.3	13.3	8.7	5.2
World	75,715.9[Te]	41.0	32.7	23.5	3.7	59.7	9.5	13.6	9.0	5.5

NOTES

a. Percentages may not sum to 100% as those whose educational attainment levels are unknown are excluded.

b. Persons whose economic activity status is unknown are excluded.

c. Data for Montenegro are included with those from Serbia.

d. Data refer to Serbia and Montenegro prior to its separation into two independent states in June 2006.

e. Data are aggregates from original data source.

SOURCES

Columns 1–4 and 8–10: OECD (2009a).

Columns 5: OECD (2008a).

Columns 6 and 7: calculated based on data from OECD (2009a).

Conflict and insecurity-induced movement

	By country of origin — International					Internal	By country of asylum — International				
	Stock of refugees			People in refugee-like situations	Stock of asylum seekers (pending cases)	Internally displaced people[d]	Stock of refugees			People in refugee-like situations	Stock of asylum seekers (pending cases)
HDI rank	Total (thousands) 2007	Share of international emigrant stock (%)	Share of world refugees (%) 2007	Total (thousands) 2007	Total (thousands) 2007	Total (thousands) 2008	Total (thousands) 2007	Share of international immigrant stock (%)	Share of world refugees (%) 2007	Total (thousands) 2007	Total (thousands) 2007
VERY HIGH HUMAN DEVELOPMENT											
1 Norway	0.0	0.0	0.0	0.0	0.0	..	34.5	9.3	0.2	0.0	6.7
2 Australia	0.1	0.0	0.0	0.0	0.0	..	22.2	0.5	0.2	0.0	1.5
3 Iceland	0.0	0.0	0.0	0.0	..	..	0.0	0.2	0.0	0.0	0.0
4 Canada	0.5	0.0	0.0	0.0	0.1	..	175.7	2.8	1.2	0.0	37.5
5 Ireland	0.0	0.0	0.0	0.0	0.0	..	9.3	1.5	0.1	0.0	4.4
6 Netherlands	0.0	0.0	0.0	0.0	0.0	..	86.6	5.0	0.6	0.0	5.8
7 Sweden	0.0	0.0	0.0	0.0	0.0	..	75.1	6.7	0.5	0.0	27.7
8 France	0.1	0.0	0.0	0.0	0.1	..	151.8	2.3	1.1	0.0	31.1
9 Switzerland	0.0	0.0	0.0	0.0	0.0	..	45.7	2.8	0.3	0.0	10.7
10 Japan	0.5	0.1	0.0	0.0	0.0	..	1.8	0.1	0.0	0.0	1.5
11 Luxembourg	0.0	0.0	0.0	0.0	..	..	2.7	1.8	0.0	0.0	0.0
12 Finland	0.0	0.0	0.0	0.0	..	..	6.2	3.6	0.0	0.0	0.7
13 United States	2.2	0.1	0.0	0.0	1.1	..	281.2	0.7	2.0	0.0	83.9
14 Austria	0.0	0.0	0.0	0.0	0.0	..	30.8	2.7	0.2	0.0	38.4
15 Spain	0.0	0.0	0.0	0.0	0.0	..	5.1	0.1	0.0	0.0	0.0
16 Denmark	0.0	0.0	0.0	0.0	0.0	..	26.8	6.4	0.2	0.0	0.6
17 Belgium	0.1	0.0	0.0	0.0	0.0	..	17.6	2.0	0.1	0.0	15.2
18 Italy	0.1	0.0	0.0	0.0	0.0	..	38.1	1.2	0.3	0.0	1.5
19 Liechtenstein	0.0	0.0	0.0	0.0	..	..	0.3	2.4	0.0	0.0	0.0
20 New Zealand	0.0	0.0	0.0	0.0	0.0	..	2.7	0.3	0.0	0.0	0.2
21 United Kingdom	0.2	0.0	0.0	0.0	0.0	..	299.7	5.1	2.1	0.0	10.9
22 Germany	0.1	0.0	0.0	0.0	0.1	..	578.9	5.5	4.0	0.0	34.1
23 Singapore	0.1	0.0	0.0	0.0	0.0	..	0.0	0.0	0.0	0.0	0.0
24 Hong Kong, China (SAR)	0.0	0.0	0.0	0.0	0.0	..	0.1	0.0	0.0	0.0	1.9
25 Greece	0.1	0.0	0.0	0.0	0.0	..	2.2	0.2	0.0	0.0	28.5
26 Korea (Republic of)	1.2	0.1	0.0	0.0	0.4	..	0.1	0.0	0.0	0.0	1.2
27 Israel	1.5	0.2	0.0	0.0	0.9	150–420 [b]	1.2	0.0	0.0	0.0	5.8
28 Andorra	0.0	0.1	0.0	0.0	0.0	..	..	..	..	..	..
29 Slovenia	0.1	0.0	0.0	0.0	0.0	..	0.3	0.2	0.0	0.0	0.1
30 Brunei Darussalam	0.0	0.0	0.0	0.0	..	..	..	..	..	..	..
31 Kuwait	0.7	0.2	0.0	0.0	0.1	..	0.2	0.0	0.0	38.0	0.7
32 Cyprus	0.0	0.0	0.0	0.0	0.0	..	1.2	1.0	0.0	0.0	11.9
33 Qatar	0.1	0.4	0.0	0.0	0.0	..	0.0	0.0	0.0	0.0	0.0
34 Portugal	0.0	0.0	0.0	0.0	0.0	..	0.4	0.0	0.0	0.0	0.0
35 United Arab Emirates	0.3	0.2	0.0	0.0	0.0	..	0.2	0.0	0.0	0.0	0.1
36 Czech Republic	1.4	0.4	0.0	0.0	0.1	..	2.0	0.4	0.0	0.0	2.2
37 Barbados	0.0	0.0	0.0	0.0	0.0	..	..	..	..	..	..
38 Malta	0.0	0.0	0.0	0.0	0.0	..	3.0	25.7	0.0	0.0	0.9
HIGH HUMAN DEVELOPMENT											
39 Bahrain	0.1	0.1	0.0	0.0	0.0	..	0.0	0.0	0.0	0.0	0.0
40 Estonia	0.3	0.1	0.0	0.0	0.1	..	0.0	0.0	0.0	0.0	0.0
41 Poland	2.9	0.1	0.0	0.0	0.2	..	9.8	1.2	0.1	0.0	5.9
42 Slovakia	0.3	0.1	0.0	0.0	0.1	..	0.3	0.2	0.0	0.0	0.6
43 Hungary	3.4	0.8	0.0	0.0	0.1	..	8.1	2.4	0.1	0.0	1.6
44 Chile	1.0	0.2	0.0	0.0	0.1	..	1.4	0.6	0.0	0.0	0.5
45 Croatia	100.4	16.5	0.7	0.0	0.1	3 [c]	1.6	0.2	0.0	0.0	0.1
46 Lithuania	0.5	0.1	0.0	0.0	0.1	..	0.7	0.4	0.0	0.0	0.0
47 Antigua and Barbuda	0.0	0.0	0.0	0.0	..	..	..	..	..	..	..
48 Latvia	0.7	0.3	0.0	0.0	0.0	..	0.0	0.0	0.0	0.0	0.0
49 Argentina	1.2	0.2	0.0	0.0	0.1	..	3.3	0.2	0.0	0.0	1.1
50 Uruguay	0.2	0.1	0.0	0.0	0.0	..	0.1	0.2	0.0	0.0	0.0
51 Cuba	7.1	0.7	0.0	0.4	1.1	..	0.6	4.0	0.0	0.0	0.0
52 Bahamas	0.0	0.0	0.0	0.0	0.0	..	..	..	..	..	..
53 Mexico	5.6	0.1	0.0	0.0	14.8	6	1.6	0.3	0.0	0.0	0.0
54 Costa Rica	0.4	0.4	0.0	0.0	0.1	..	11.6	2.6	0.1	5.6	0.5
55 Libyan Arab Jamahiriya	2.0	2.5	0.0	0.0	0.6	..	4.1	0.7	0.0	0.0	2.8
56 Oman	0.0	0.2	0.0	0.0	0.0	..	0.0	0.0	0.0	0.0	0.0
57 Seychelles	0.1	0.3	0.0	0.0	0.0	..	..	..	..	..	..
58 Venezuela (Bolivarian Republic of)	5.1	1.4	0.0	0.0	1.8	..	0.9	0.1	0.0	200.0	9.6
59 Saudi Arabia	0.8	0.3	0.0	0.0	0.0	..	240.7	3.8	1.7	0.0	0.3

D

Conflict and insecurity-induced movement

	By country of origin					Internal	By country of asylum				
	International						International				
	Stock of refugees			People in refugee-like situations	Stock of asylum seekers (pending cases)	Internally displaced people[d]	Stock of refugees			People in refugee-like situations	Stock of asylum seekers (pending cases)
HDI rank	Total (thousands) 2007	Share of international emigrant stock (%)	Share of world refugees (%) 2007	Total (thousands) 2007	Total (thousands) 2007	Total (thousands) 2008	Total (thousands) 2007	Share of international immigrant stock (%)	Share of world refugees (%) 2007	Total (thousands) 2007	Total (thousands) 2007
60 Panama	0.1	0.1	0.0	0.0	0.0	..	1.9	1.8	0.0	15.0	0.5
61 Bulgaria	3.3	0.4	0.0	0.0	0.4	..	4.8	4.6	0.0	0.0	1.0
62 Saint Kitts and Nevis	0.0	0.0	0.0	0.0	0.0	..	..	..	..	..	..
63 Romania	5.3	0.5	0.0	0.0	0.6	..	1.8	1.3	0.0	0.0	0.2
64 Trinidad and Tobago	0.2	0.1	0.0	0.0	0.2	..	0.0	0.1	0.0	0.0	0.1
65 Montenegro	0.6	..	0.0	0.0	0.3	..	8.5	15.6	0.1	0.0	0.0
66 Malaysia	0.6	0.1	0.0	0.0	0.1	..	32.2	1.6	0.2	0.4	6.9
67 Serbia	165.6	9.8	1.2	0.1	14.2	248 [d]	98.0	14.5	0.7	0.0	0.0
68 Belarus	5.0	0.3	0.0	0.0	1.2	..	0.6	0.1	0.0	0.0	0.0
69 Saint Lucia	0.2	0.4	0.0	0.0	0.2	..	0.0	0.0	0.0	0.0	0.0
70 Albania	15.3	1.9	0.1	0.0	1.6	..	0.1	0.1	0.0	0.0	0.0
71 Russian Federation	92.9	0.8	0.6	0.0	17.6	18–137 [e]	1.7	0.0	0.0	0.0	3.1
72 Macedonia (the Former Yugoslav Rep. of)	8.1	3.1	0.1	0.0	1.1	1	1.2	1.0	0.0	0.1	0.2
73 Dominica	0.1	0.1	0.0	0.0	0.0	..	..	..	..	..	..
74 Grenada	0.3	0.4	0.0	0.0	0.1	..	..	..	..	..	..
75 Brazil	1.6	0.2	0.0	0.0	0.3	..	3.8	0.6	0.0	17.0	0.4
76 Bosnia and Herzegovina	78.3	6.2	0.5	0.0	1.1	125	7.4	21.0	0.1	0.0	0.6
77 Colombia	70.1	4.3	0.5	481.6	43.1	2,650–4,360 [c]	0.2	0.2	0.0	0.0	0.1
78 Peru	7.7	1.0	0.1	0.0	3.1	150 [c]	1.0	2.4	0.0	0.0	0.5
79 Turkey	221.9	7.4	1.6	0.0	9.2	954–1,200	7.0	0.5	0.0	0.0	5.2
80 Ecuador	1.3	0.2	0.0	0.0	0.3	..	14.9	12.1	0.1	250.0	27.4
81 Mauritius	0.1	0.0	0.0	0.0	0.0	..	0.0	0.0	0.0	0.0	0.0
82 Kazakhstan	5.2	0.1	0.0	0.0	0.5	..	4.3	0.1	0.0	0.0	0.1
83 Lebanon	13.1	2.3	0.1	0.0	2.6	90–390 [f]	466.9 [g]	64.7 [g]	3.3 [g]	0.1	0.6
MEDIUM HUMAN DEVELOPMENT											
84 Armenia	15.4	2.0	0.1	0.0	4.0	8 [c]	4.6	0.9	0.0	0.0	0.1
85 Ukraine	26.0	0.4	0.2	0.0	2.4	..	2.3	0.0	0.0	5.0	1.3
86 Azerbaijan	15.9	1.2	0.1	0.0	1.9	573 [h]	2.4	0.9	0.0	0.0	0.1
87 Thailand	2.3	0.3	0.0	0.0	0.4	..	125.6	12.8	0.9	0.0	13.5
88 Iran (Islamic Republic of)	68.4	7.4	0.5	0.0	10.4	..	963.5	46.7	6.7	0.0	1.2
89 Georgia	6.8	0.7	0.0	5.0	4.1	0 [i]	1.0	0.5	0.0	0.0	0.0
90 Dominican Republic	0.4	0.0	0.0	0.0	0.1	..	..	..	..	..	..
91 Saint Vincent and the Grenadines	0.6	1.1	0.0	0.0	0.5	..	..	..	..	..	..
92 China	149.1	2.6	1.0	0.0	15.5	..	301.1	51.0	2.1	0.0	0.1
93 Belize	0.0	0.0	0.0	0.0	0.0	..	0.4	0.9	0.0	0.0	0.0
94 Samoa	0.0	0.0	0.0	0.0	0.0	..	..	..	..	..	..
95 Maldives	0.0	1.6	0.0	0.0	0.0	..	..	..	..	..	..
96 Jordan	1.8	0.3	0.0	0.0	0.7	..	2,431.0 [g]	..	17.0 [g]	0.0	0.4
97 Suriname	0.1	0.0	0.0	0.0	0.0	..	0.0	0.0	0.0	0.0	0.0
98 Tunisia	2.5	0.4	0.0	0.0	0.3	..	0.1	0.3	0.0	0.0	0.1
99 Tonga	0.0	0.0	0.0	0.0	0.0	..	..	..	..	..	..
100 Jamaica	0.8	0.1	0.0	0.0	0.2	..	..	..	..	..	..
101 Paraguay	0.1	0.0	0.0	0.0	0.0	..	0.1	0.0	0.0	0.0	0.0
102 Sri Lanka	134.9	14.5	0.9	0.0	6.0	500	0.2	0.0	0.0	0.0	0.2
103 Gabon	0.1	0.2	0.0	0.0	0.0	..	8.8	3.6	0.1	0.0	4.3
104 Algeria	10.6	0.5	0.1	0.0	1.4	.. [j]	94.1	38.8	0.7	0.0	1.6
105 Philippines	1.5	0.0	0.0	0.0	0.8	314 [k]	0.1	0.1	0.0	0.0	0.0
106 El Salvador	6.0	0.6	0.0	0.0	18.6	..	0.0	0.1	0.0	0.0	0.0
107 Syrian Arab Republic	13.7	3.2	0.1	0.0	6.9	433	1,960.8 [g]	..	13.7 [g]	0.0	5.9
108 Fiji	1.8	1.3	0.0	0.0	0.2	..	0.0	0.0	0.0	0.0	0.0
109 Turkmenistan	0.7	0.3	0.0	0.0	0.1	..	0.1	0.1	0.0	0.0	0.0
110 Occupied Palestinian Territories	4,953.4 [g]	..	34.6 [g]	6.0	2.4	25–115 [c,l]	1,813.8 [g]	..	12.7 [g]	0.0	0.0
111 Indonesia	20.2	1.1	0.1	0.3	2.4	150–250 [c]	0.3	0.2	0.0	0.0	0.2
112 Honduras	1.2	0.3	0.0	0.0	0.7	..	0.0	0.1	0.0	0.0	0.0
113 Bolivia	0.4	0.1	0.0	0.0	0.4	..	0.6	0.6	0.0	0.0	0.2
114 Guyana	0.7	0.2	0.0	0.0	0.2	..	..	..	..	..	..
115 Mongolia	1.1	14.5	0.0	0.0	2.0	..	0.0	0.1	0.0	0.0	0.0
116 Viet Nam	327.8	16.3	2.3	0.0	1.8	..	2.4	4.3	0.0	0.0	0.0
117 Moldova	4.9	0.7	0.0	0.0	0.9	..	0.2	0.0	0.0	0.0	0.1
118 Equatorial Guinea	0.4	0.4	0.0	0.0	0.0	..	0.0	0.0	0.0	0.0	0.0

	By country of origin					Internal	By country of asylum				
	International						International				
	Stock of refugees			People in refugee-like situations	Stock of asylum seekers (pending cases)	Internally displaced people[d]	Stock of refugees			People in refugee-like situations	Stock of asylum seekers (pending cases)
HDI rank	Total (thousands) 2007	Share of international emigrant stock (%) 2007	Share of world refugees (%) 2007	Total (thousands) 2007	Total (thousands) 2007	Total (thousands) 2008	Total (thousands) 2007	Share of international immigrant stock (%) 2007	Share of world refugees (%) 2007	Total (thousands) 2007	Total (thousands) 2007
119 Uzbekistan	5.7	0.2	0.0	0.0	1.8	3	1.1	0.1	0.0	0.0	0.0
120 Kyrgyzstan	2.3	0.4	0.0	0.0	0.4	..	0.4	0.1	0.0	0.4	0.7
121 Cape Verde	0.0	0.0	0.0	0.0	0.0	..	..	..	..	..	..
122 Guatemala	6.2	1.0	0.0	0.0	15.0	..	0.4	0.7	0.0	0.0	0.0
123 Egypt	6.8	0.3	0.0	0.0	1.6	..	97.6	39.5	0.7	0.0	14.9
124 Nicaragua	1.9	0.4	0.0	0.0	0.8	..	0.2	0.5	0.0	0.0	0.0
125 Botswana	0.0	0.1	0.0	0.0	0.1	..	2.5	3.1	0.0	0.0	0.0
126 Vanuatu	0.0	0.0	0.0	0.0	..	..	0.0	0.1	0.0	0.0	0.0
127 Tajikistan	0.5	0.1	0.0	0.4	0.1	..	1.1	0.4	0.0	0.0	0.1
128 Namibia	1.1	4.6	0.0	0.0	0.0	..	6.5	5.0	0.0	0.0	1.2
129 South Africa	0.5	0.1	0.0	0.0	0.1	..	36.7	2.9	0.3	0.0	170.9
130 Morocco	4.0	0.2	0.0	0.0	0.5	..	0.8	1.5	0.0	0.0	0.7
131 Sao Tome and Principe	0.0	0.1	0.0	0.0	..	..	0.0	0.0	0.0	0.0	0.0
132 Bhutan	108.1	..	0.8	2.5	1.6	..	..	..	..	..	..
133 Lao People's Democratic Republic	10.0	2.8	0.1	0.0	0.2	..	0.0	0.0	0.0	0.0	0.0
134 India	20.5	0.2	0.1	0.0	7.1	500 [k]	161.5	2.7	1.1	0.0	2.4
135 Solomon Islands	0.0	1.1	0.0	0.0	0.0	..	..	..	..	..	..
136 Congo	19.7	3.6	0.1	0.0	6.1	8 [c]	38.5	29.9	0.3	0.0	4.8
137 Cambodia	17.7	5.7	0.1	0.0	0.4	..	0.2	0.1	0.0	0.0	0.2
138 Myanmar	191.3	60.8	1.3	0.1	19.0	503 [m]	0.0	0.0	0.0	0.0	0.0
139 Comoros	0.1	0.2	0.0	0.0	..	..	0.0	0.0	0.0	0.0	0.0
140 Yemen	1.6	0.3	0.0	0.0	0.3	25–35	117.4	25.8	0.8	0.0	0.7
141 Pakistan	31.9	0.9	0.2	0.0	8.6	.. [n]	887.3	25.0	6.2	1,147.8	3.1
142 Swaziland	0.0	0.2	0.0	0.0	0.1	..	0.8	2.0	0.0	0.0	0.3
143 Angola	186.2	21.2	1.3	0.0	0.8	20 [c,o]	12.1	21.5	0.1	0.0	2.9
144 Nepal	3.4	0.3	0.0	0.0	2.1	50–70	128.2	15.7	0.9	2.5	1.6
145 Madagascar	0.3	0.2	0.0	0.0	0.0	..	0.0	0.0	0.0	0.0	0.0
146 Bangladesh	10.2	0.1	0.1	0.0	7.3	500 [c]	27.6	2.7	0.2	0.0	0.1
147 Kenya	7.5	1.7	0.1	0.0	1.7	400 [p]	265.7	33.6	1.9	0.0	5.8
148 Papua New Guinea	0.0	0.1	0.0	0.0	0.0	..	10.0	39.2	0.1	0.0	0.0
149 Haiti	22.3	3.0	0.2	0.0	10.3	..	0.0	0.0	0.0	0.0	0.0
150 Sudan	523.0	81.4	3.7	0.0	19.4	6,000 [q]	222.7	34.8	1.6	0.0	7.3
151 Tanzania (United Republic of)	1.3	0.4	0.0	0.0	2.9	..	435.6	54.6	3.0	0.0	0.3
152 Ghana	5.1	0.5	0.0	0.0	1.7	..	35.0	2.1	0.2	0.0	0.4
153 Cameroon	11.5	6.8	0.1	0.0	3.0	..	60.1	28.4	0.4	0.0	2.2
154 Mauritania	33.1	28.3	0.2	0.0	1.0	..	1.0	1.5	0.0	29.5	0.0
155 Djibouti	0.6	3.8	0.0	0.0	0.0	..	6.7	6.0	0.0	0.0	0.5
156 Lesotho	0.0	0.0	0.0	0.0	0.0	..	0.0	0.0	0.0	0.0	0.0
157 Uganda	21.3	12.5	0.1	0.0	3.2	869 [r]	229.0	35.1	1.6	0.0	5.8
158 Nigeria	13.9	1.3	0.1	0.0	9.7	..	8.5	0.9	0.1	0.0	0.7
LOW HUMAN DEVELOPMENT											
159 Togo	22.5	10.5	0.2	0.0	1.3	2 [c]	1.3	0.7	0.0	0.0	0.1
160 Malawi	0.1	0.1	0.0	0.0	8.2	..	2.9	1.1	0.0	0.0	6.8
161 Benin	0.3	0.0	0.0	0.0	0.2	..	7.6	4.1	0.1	0.0	0.5
162 Timor-Leste	0.0	0.0	0.0	0.0	0.0	30	0.0	0.0	0.0	0.0	0.0
163 Côte d'Ivoire	22.2	12.6	0.2	0.0	7.4	621	24.6	1.0	0.2	0.0	1.8
164 Zambia	0.2	0.1	0.0	0.0	0.5	..	112.9	39.3	0.8	0.0	0.0
165 Eritrea	208.7	36.7	1.5	0.0	12.2	32 [c]	5.0	34.4	0.0	0.0	2.0
166 Senegal	15.9	3.3	0.1	0.0	0.9	10–70	20.4	9.3	0.1	0.0	2.5
167 Rwanda	81.0	33.7	0.6	0.0	8.2	..	53.6	12.3	0.4	0.0	0.7
168 Gambia	1.3	2.5	0.0	0.0	1.0	..	14.9	6.4	0.1	0.0	0.0
169 Liberia	91.5	..	0.6	0.0	3.5	..	10.5	10.8	0.1	0.0	0.1
170 Guinea	8.3	1.4	0.1	0.0	1.9	..	25.2	6.3	0.2	0.0	4.0
171 Ethiopia	59.8	21.0	0.4	0.0	29.5	200 [c]	85.2	15.4	0.6	0.0	0.2
172 Mozambique	0.2	0.0	0.0	0.0	0.7	..	2.8	0.7	0.0	0.0	4.2
173 Guinea-Bissau	1.0	0.8	0.0	0.0	0.3	..	7.9	40.9	0.1	0.0	0.3
174 Burundi	375.7	96.7	2.6	0.0	7.1	100	24.5	30.0	0.2	0.0	7.5
175 Chad	55.7	18.4	0.4	0.0	2.7	186	294.0	82.0	2.1	0.0	0.0
176 Congo (Democratic Republic of the)	370.4	45.1	2.6	0.0	36.3	1,400 [s]	177.4	36.9	1.2	0.0	0.1
177 Burkina Faso	0.6	0.0	0.0	0.0	0.3	..	0.5	0.1	0.0	0.0	0.6

D

Conflict and insecurity-induced movement

	By country of origin					By country of asylum				
	International					Internal	International				
	Stock of refugees			People in refugee-like situations	Stock of asylum seekers (pending cases)	Internally displaced people[d]	Stock of refugees			People in refugee-like situations	Stock of asylum seekers (pending cases)
HDI rank	Total (thousands) 2007	Share of international emigrant stock (%) 2007	Share of world refugees (%) 2007	Total (thousands) 2007	Total (thousands) 2007	Total (thousands) 2008	Total (thousands) 2007	Share of international immigrant stock (%)	Share of world refugees (%) 2007	Total (thousands) 2007	Total (thousands) 2007
178 Mali	1.0	0.1	0.0	3.5	0.6	..	9.2	5.6	0.1	0.0	1.9
179 Central African Republic	98.1	89.5	0.7	0.0	1.3	108	7.5	10.0	0.1	0.0	2.0
180 Sierra Leone	32.1	34.0	0.2	0.0	4.7	..	8.8	5.8	0.1	0.0	0.2
181 Afghanistan	1,909.9	73.2	13.4	1,147.8	16.1	200 [t]	0.0	0.0	0.0	0.0	0.0
182 Niger	0.8	0.2	0.0	0.0	0.3	..	0.3	0.2	0.0	0.0	0.0
OTHER UN MEMBER STATES											
Iraq	2,279.2	..	15.9	30.0	27.7	2,842 [v]	42.4	33.1	0.3	0.0	2.4
Kiribati	0.0	1.0	0.0	0.0	..	..	..	..	..	..	..
Korea (Democratic People's Rep. of)	0.6	0.1	0.0	0.0	0.2	..	..	..	..	..	..
Marshall Islands	0.0	0.0	0.0	0.0	..	..	..	..	..	..	..
Micronesia (Federated States of)	0.0	0.0	0.0	0.0	..	..	0.0	0.1	0.0	0.0	0.0
Monaco	0.0	0.0	0.0	0.0	..	..	..	..	..	..	..
Nauru	0.0	0.3	0.0	0.0	0.0	..	..	..	..	..	..
Palau	0.0	0.0	0.0	0.0	0.0	..	..	..	..	..	..
San Marino	0.0	0.0	0.0	0.0	0.0	..	..	..	..	..	..
Somalia	455.4	84.5	3.2	2.0	16.4	1,100	0.9	4.2	0.0	0.0	8.7
Tuvalu	0.0	0.1	0.0	0.0	..	..	..	..	..	..	..
Zimbabwe	14.4	5.0	0.1	0.0	34.3	880–960	4.0	1.0	0.0	0.0	0.5
Africa	2,859.7[T]	11.4	20.0[T]	31.6[T]	234.2[T]	..	2,468.8[T]	14.0	17.3[T]	29.5[T]	272.3[T]
Asia	10,552.2[T]	16.1	73.8[T]	1,192.1[T]	166.4[T]	..	9,729.8[T]	17.6	68.1[T]	1,189.1[T]	69.3[T]
Europe	516.0[T]	0.9	3.6[T]	0.1[T]	42.7[T]	..	1,564.1[T]	2.4	10.9[T]	5.1[T]	234.2[T]
Latin America and the Caribbean	142.9[T]	0.5	1.0[T]	482.0[T]	112.2[T]	..	43.0[T]	0.6	0.3[T]	487.6[T]	41.2[T]
Northern America	2.7[T]	0.1	0.0[T]	0.0[T]	1.2[T]	..	457.0[T]	1.0	3.2[T]	0.0[T]	121.4[T]
Oceania	2.0[T]	0.1	0.0[T]	0.0[T]	0.3[T]	..	34.9[T]	0.6	0.2[T]	0.0[T]	1.7[T]
OECD	240.9[T]	0.5	1.7[T]	0.0[T]	26.4[T]	..	1,924.1[T]	2.0	13.5[T]	0.0[T]	357.7[T]
European Union (EU27)	19.0[T]	0.1	0.1[T]	0.0[T]	2.0[T]	..	1,363.3[T]	3.3	9.5[T]	0.0[T]	223.3[T]
GCC	2.0[T]	0.2	0.0[T]	0.0[T]	0.2[T]	..	241.1[T]	1.9	1.7[T]	38.0[T]	1.2[T]
Very high human development	9.7[T]	0.0	0.1[T]	0.0[T]	3.2[T]	..	1,903.7[T]	1.8	13.3[T]	38.0[T]	365.7[T]
Very high HD: OECD	6.8[T]	0.0	0.0[T]	0.0[T]	2.0[T]	..	1,897.3[T]	2.0	13.3[T]	0.0[T]	344.4[T]
Very high HD: non-OECD	2.9[T]	0.1	0.0[T]	0.0[T]	1.2[T]	..	6.4[T]	0.0	0.0[T]	38.0[T]	21.3[T]
High human development	828.8[T]	1.5	5.8[T]	482.1[T]	117.2[T]	..	941.1[T]	2.5	6.6[T]	488.1[T]	70.1[T]
Medium human development	9,410.0[T]	12.3	65.8[T]	70.3[T]	240.6[T]	..	10,550.7[T]	25.8	73.8[T]	1,185.1[T]	259.2[T]
Low human development	3,827.1[T]	28.9	26.8[T]	1,153.3[T]	195.9[T]	..	902.1[T]	10.7	6.3[T]	0.0[T]	45.0[T]
World (excluding the former Soviet Union and Czechoslovakia)	13,891.2[T]	9.6	97.2[T]	1,700.3[T]	521.4[T]	..	14,274.8[T]	8.5	99.8[T]	1,705.9[T]	731.6[T]
World	14,297.5[T]	7.3	100.0[T]	1,711.3[Tu]	740.0[Tu]	26,000 [Tu]	14,297.5[T]	7.3	100.0[T]	1,711.3[Tu]	740.0[Tu]

NOTES

a Estimates maintained by the IDMC are based on various sources and are associated with high levels of uncertainty.

b Higher figure includes an estimate of internally displaced Bedouin.

c Data refer to a year or period other than that specified.

d Figure includes 206,000 registered IDPs in Serbia plus an estimated 20,000 unregistered Roma displaced in Serbia and 21,000 IDPs in Kosovo.

e Figure includes forced migrants registered in Ingushetia and Chechnya.

f Figure includes 32,000 Palestinian refugees displaced as a result of fighting between Lebanese forces and Fatah al Islam in May–August 2007.

g Including Palestinian refugees under the responsibility of UNRWA (2008).

h Figure refers to those displaced from Nagorno Karabakh and seven occupied territories.

i Some 59,000 people displaced since the August 2008 crisis have not been able to return. There are some 221,597 IDPs based on the result of a survey conducted by UNHCR and the government but these are yet to be endorsed.

j There are no reliable estimates but in 2002, the EU estimated the number to be 100,000.

k Figures are suspected to be underestimate.

l Lower figure relates to IDPs evicted by home demolitions in Gaza between 2000 and 2004 whilst higher figure is cumulative since 1967.

m Figure relates to the eastern border areas only.

n Exact IDP numbers are unknown but conflict induced displacement has taken place in the North-West Frontier province, Baluchistan and Waziristan.

o Figure refers to IDPs in Cabinda region only.

p Figure takes into account the government's return programme which claims that some 172,000 displaced due to the post-election violence returned in May 2008.

q Figures are based on separate estimates for Darfur, Khartoum and Southern Sudan.

r Excludes IDPs in urban areas.

s Figure includes an estimated 250,000 civilians who fled their homes in North Kiva due to fighting between the national army and CNDP rebels.

t It is believed that there are more than 200,000 IDPs.

u Data are aggregates from the original data source.

v Figure is cumulative since 2001 and includes 1.5 million people displaced due to a rise in inter-communal violence since February 2006.

SOURCES

Columns 1, 3, 4, 7, 9 and 10: UNHCR (2009b).

Column 2: calculated based on data from UNHCR (2009b) and Migration DRC (2007).

Columns 5 and 11: UNHCR (2009a).

Column 6: IDMC (2009a).

Column 8: calculated based on UNHCR (2009b) and UN (2009d).

International financial flows: remittances, official development assistance and foreign direct investment

HDI rank	Remittances			ODA received (net disbursements) per capita (US$)	Relative size of remittance inflows				Remittance inflows by continent of origin					
	Inflows total (US$ millions)	Outflows total (US$ millions)	Outflows per migrant (US$)		per capita (US$)	as % of net ODA receipts	as % of GDP	ratio of remittances to FDI	Africa	Asia	Europe	Latin American and the Caribbean	Northern America	Oceania
	2007								(% of total remittance inflows)					
VERY HIGH HUMAN DEVELOPMENT														
1 Norway	613	3,642	10,588	..	130	..	0.2	0.2	0.0	4.2	66.2	0.7	26.3	2.7
2 Australia	3,862	3,559	869	..	186	..	0.4	0.1	0.7	6.7	49.3	0.8	25.7	16.8
3 Iceland	41	100	4,333	..	137	..	0.2	0.0	0.0	0.5	63.4	0.3	34.1	1.6
4 Canada	..	..	..	..	..	..	..	..	..	..	..	..	..	..
5 Ireland	580	2,554	4,363	..	135	..	0.2	0.0	0.0	0.2	70.6	0.1	22.9	6.1
6 Netherlands	2,548	7,830	4,780	..	155	..	0.3	0.0	0.0	3.4	51.5	1.8	30.4	12.9
7 Sweden	775	1,142	1,022	..	85	..	0.2	0.1	0.6	3.2	69.4	1.4	22.9	2.6
8 France	13,746	4,380	677	..	223	..	0.5	0.1	13.5	3.8	58.8	4.7	16.8	2.3
9 Switzerland	2,035	16,273	9,805	..	272	..	0.4	0.0	0.1	3.2	75.4	2.3	16.2	2.8
10 Japan	1,577	4,037	1,971	..	12	..	0.0	0.1	0.1	8.8	15.8	9.0	62.3	4.0
11 Luxembourg	1,565	9,281	53,446	..	3,355	..	3.3	0.0	0.0	0.2	90.7	0.2	8.5	0.4
12 Finland	772	391	2,506	..	146	..	0.3	0.1	0.2	1.0	83.7	0.2	12.3	2.6
13 United States	2,972	45,643	1,190	..	10	..	0.0	0.0	0.7	12.0	31.2	38.2	13.4	4.5
14 Austria	2,945	2,985	2,420	..	352	..	0.8	0.1	0.0	3.7	73.6	1.2	17.9	3.5
15 Spain	10,687	14,728	3,075	..	241	..	0.7	0.2	0.1	0.3	63.8	24.2	10.8	1.0
16 Denmark	989	2,958	7,612	..	182	..	0.3	0.1	0.3	2.6	67.4	0.7	24.6	4.5
17 Belgium	8,562	3,192	4,438	..	819	..	1.9	0.1	0.2	2.4	79.7	1.3	15.3	1.2
18 Italy	3,165	11,287	4,481	..	54	..	0.2	0.1	0.1	0.2	56.2	9.8	27.4	6.3
19 Liechtenstein	..	..	..	..	..	..	..	..	..	..	..	..	..	..
20 New Zealand	650	1,207	1,880	..	155	..	0.5	0.2	0.1	2.1	16.5	0.1	8.2	73.0
21 United Kingdom	8,234	5,048	933	..	135	..	0.3	0.0	0.3	4.4	26.2	0.7	38.4	29.9
22 Germany	8,570	13,860	1,366	..	104	..	0.3	0.2	0.2	12.1	44.3	1.5	39.1	2.8
23 Singapore	..	..	..	..	..	..	..	..	..	..	..	..	..	..
24 Hong Kong, China (SAR)	348	380	127	..	48	..	0.2	0.0	0.0	2.5	17.7	0.2	68.9	10.8
25 Greece	2,484	1,460	1,499	..	223	..	0.7	1.3	0.0	8.2	58.1	0.4	23.6	9.7
26 Korea (Republic of)	1,128	4,070	7,384	..	23	..	0.1	0.7	0.0	36.1	6.9	1.3	52.0	3.7
27 Israel	1,041	2,770	1,041	..	150	..	0.6	0.1	0.0	70.0	7.8	0.8	20.5	0.9
28 Andorra	..	..	..	..	..	..	..	..	..	..	..	..	..	..
29 Slovenia	284	207	1,236	..	142	..	0.7	0.2	0.0	0.1	77.0	0.5	17.1	5.2
30 Brunei Darussalam	..	405	3,263	..	..	..	..	..	..	..	..	..	..	..
31 Kuwait	..	3,824	2,291	..	..	..	..	..	..	..	..	..	..	..
32 Cyprus	172	371	3,195	..	201	..	..	0.1	0.0	6.3	69.8	0.0	11.5	12.4
33 Qatar	..	..	..	..	..	..	..	..	..	..	..	..	..	..
34 Portugal	3,945	1,311	1,717	..	371	..	1.8	0.7	3.1	0.3	62.4	12.1	21.2	0.8
35 United Arab Emirates	..	..	..	..	..	..	..	..	..	..	..	..	..	..
36 Czech Republic	1,332	2,625	5,790	..	131	..	0.8	0.1	0.0	4.1	70.2	0.4	23.3	2.0
37 Barbados	140	40	1,534	46	476	1,025.6	..	..	..	..	..	..	..	..
38 Malta	40	54	5,011	..	99	..	..	0.0	0.0	0.1	36.1	0.0	19.3	44.5
HIGH HUMAN DEVELOPMENT														
39 Bahrain	..	1,483	5,018	..	..	..	..	..	..	..	..	..	..	..
40 Estonia	426	96	474	..	319	..	2.3	0.2	0.0	4.5	81.5	0.1	12.3	1.6
41 Poland	10,496	1,278	1,818	..	276	..	2.6	0.5	0.0	5.5	54.2	1.0	36.4	2.9
42 Slovakia	1,483	73	588	..	275	..	2.0	0.4	0.0	1.8	85.4	0.1	12.0	0.7
43 Hungary	413	235	742	..	41	..	0.3	0.0	0.0	3.4	52.4	0.9	37.8	5.5
44 Chile	3	6	25	7	0	2.1	0.0	0.0	0.0	0.0	25.7	42.0	27.2	5.1
45 Croatia	1,394	86	129	36	306	850.8	2.9	0.3	0.0	0.0	77.8	0.3	13.7	8.1
46 Lithuania	1,427	566	3,424	..	421	..	3.8	0.7	0.0	6.8	74.2	0.3	17.2	1.5
47 Antigua and Barbuda	24	2	113	49	276	560.9	2.0	0.1	0.0	14.2	11.7	10.6	63.3	0.1
48 Latvia	552	45	100	..	242	..	2.1	0.2	0.0	5.9	67.4	0.2	22.7	3.7
49 Argentina	604	472	315	2	15	737.0	0.2	0.1	0.0	6.5	41.1	24.5	26.2	1.7
50 Uruguay	97	4	42	10	29	285.6	0.4	0.1	0.0	0.1	29.2	48.4	17.9	4.5
51 Cuba	..	..	..	8	..	..	..	..	..	..	..	..	..	..
52 Bahamas	..	171	5,397	..	..	..	..	..	..	..	..	..	..	..
53 Mexico	27,144	..	..	1	255	22,416.0	3.0	1.1	0.0	0.0	0.8	0.3	98.9	0.0
54 Costa Rica	635	271	616	12	142	1,205.1	2.3	0.3	0.0	0.2	6.5	11.8	81.2	0.3
55 Libyan Arab Jamahiriya	16	762	1,234	3	3	84.1	..	0.0	14.3	34.0	32.1	0.1	17.4	2.0
56 Oman	39	3,670	5,847	..	15	..	0.1	0.0	..	..	..	..	..	..
57 Seychelles	11	21	4,309	32	129	402.5	1.9	0.0	7.6	0.2	51.2	0.0	17.7	23.3
58 Venezuela (Bolivarian Republic of)	136	598	592	3	5	191.0	0.1	0.2	0.0	0.1	47.1	14.7	37.8	0.3
59 Saudi Arabia	..	16,068	2,526	..	..	..	..	..	..	..	..	..	..	..

E

International financial flows: remittances, official development assistance and foreign direct investment

	Remittances			ODA received (net disbursements) per capita (US$)	Relative size of remittance inflows				Remittance inflows by continent of origin					
HDI rank	Inflows total (US$ millions)	Outflows total (US$ millions)	Outflows per migrant (US$)		per capita (US$)	as % of net ODA receipts	as % of GDP	ratio of remittances to FDI	Africa	Asia	Europe	Latin American and the Caribbean	Northern America	Oceania
				2007					(% of total remittance inflows)					
60 Panama	180	151	1,476	..	54	..	0.8	0.1	0.0	0.1	3.9	8.1	87.8	0.1
61 Bulgaria	2,086	86	822	..	273	..	5.7	0.2	0.0	53.8	37.2	0.1	8.5	0.5
62 Saint Kitts and Nevis	37	6	1,352	57	739	1,289.0	..	..	..	..	..	..	..	..
63 Romania	8,533	351	2,630	..	398	..	5.6	0.9	0.0	15.0	61.3	0.4	22.0	1.3
64 Trinidad and Tobago	92	..	..	14	69	503.0	0.4	..	0.0	0.0	8.0	2.0	89.6	0.4
65 Montenegro	..	..	..	177	..	..	..	..	..	..	..	..	..	..
66 Malaysia	1,700	6,385	3,895	8	64	851.4	1.0	0.2	0.0	80.3	6.0	0.0	6.7	7.0
67 Serbia	..	..	..	85	..	..	..	..	..	..	..	..	..	..
68 Belarus	354	109	92	9	37	425.4	0.8	0.2	0.0	6.1	88.4	0.0	5.4	0.1
69 Saint Lucia	31	4	488	143	188	131.5	3.5	0.1	..	..	..	..	..	..
70 Albania	1,071	7	85	96	336	350.9	10.1	2.2	0.0	0.4	91.2	0.0	8.2	0.2
71 Russian Federation	4,100	17,716	1,467	..	29	..	0.3	0.1	0.0	31.3	61.8	0.1	6.5	0.2
72 Macedonia (the Former Yugoslav Rep. of)	267	18	147	105	131	124.9	3.6	0.8	0.0	6.1	71.0	0.1	9.5	13.3
73 Dominica	26	0	37	288	385	133.8	8.0	0.6	0.0	0.3	27.5	13.3	58.9	0.0
74 Grenada	55	4	329	215	524	244.3	..	0.4	0.0	0.0	17.6	12.6	69.6	0.2
75 Brazil	4,382	896	1,396	2	23	1,475.0	0.3	0.1	0.0	31.9	27.3	11.2	29.1	0.5
76 Bosnia and Herzegovina	2,520	65	1,601	113	640	568.6	..	1.2	0.0	0.1	85.1	0.1	12.7	2.0
77 Colombia	4,523	95	775	16	98	618.9	3.0	0.5	0.0	0.2	29.1	26.7	43.7	0.3
78 Peru	2,131	137	3,294	9	76	810.2	1.9	0.4	0.0	7.5	26.7	16.4	48.7	0.8
79 Turkey	1,209	106	80	11	16	151.7	0.2	0.1	0.0	3.7	92.4	0.0	3.2	0.7
80 Ecuador	3,094	83	726	16	232	1,436.6	6.9	16.9	0.0	0.0	52.7	3.9	43.3	0.2
81 Mauritius	215	12	557	59	170	288.3	2.9	0.6	1.0	0.2	75.1	0.0	8.2	15.5
82 Kazakhstan	223	4,303	1,720	13	14	110.1	0.2	0.0	0.0	9.6	89.6	0.0	0.8	0.0
83 Lebanon	5,769	2,845	4,332	229	1,407	614.1	24.4	2.0	2.1	11.0	33.1	4.0	36.9	12.9
MEDIUM HUMAN DEVELOPMENT														
84 Armenia	846	176	749	117	282	240.6	9.0	1.2	0.0	6.2	72.7	0.0	20.9	0.2
85 Ukraine	4,503	42	6	9	97	1,111.1	3.9	0.5	0.0	9.1	77.0	0.1	13.4	0.5
86 Azerbaijan	1,287	435	2,395	27	152	571.4	4.4	..	0.0	16.3	80.1	0.0	3.5	0.0
87 Thailand	1,635	..	..	..	26	..	0.7	0.2	0.0	32.4	25.3	0.0	37.8	4.5
88 Iran (Islamic Republic of)	1,115	..	..	1	16	1,094.5	0.5	1.5	0.0	9.5	40.1	0.1	48.1	2.2
89 Georgia	696	28	148	87	158	182.0	6.8	0.4	0.0	10.4	86.3	0.0	3.2	0.1
90 Dominican Republic	3,414	28	180	13	350	2,674.2	9.3	2.0	0.0	0.1	12.7	2.9	84.4	0.0
91 Saint Vincent and the Grenadines	31	7	702	545	254	46.6	6.7	0.3	..	..	..	..	..	..
92 China	32,833	4,372	7,340	1	25	2,282.3	1.1	0.2	0.1	61.9	7.4	0.4	27.3	3.0
93 Belize	75	22	555	81	260	319.4	5.3	0.7	0.0	0.0	2.8	4.9	92.2	0.1
94 Samoa	120	13	1,422	197	640	324.3	..	48.1	0.0	0.0	0.0	0.0	26.9	73.1
95 Maldives	3	103	30,601	122	10	8.0	..	0.2	0.0	37.5	38.5	0.4	5.3	18.4
96 Jordan	3,434	479	215	85	580	680.8	22.7	1.9	0.0	74.2	7.6	0.1	17.1	0.9
97 Suriname	140	65	12,233	329	305	92.7	..	1.1	0.0	0.0	89.0	7.3	3.8	0.1
98 Tunisia	1,716	15	402	30	166	553.2	5.0	1.1	8.9	4.3	84.0	0.0	2.6	0.1
99 Tonga	100	12	10,525	304	992	326.8	..	3.6	0.0	0.2	1.3	0.5	48.0	50.0
100 Jamaica	2,144	454	25,724	10	790	8,231.9	19.4	2.5	0.0	0.0	17.3	1.3	81.3	0.1
101 Paraguay	469	..	..	18	77	434.1	3.2	2.4	0.0	1.1	4.6	82.9	11.3	0.2
102 Sri Lanka	2,527	314	853	31	131	429.1	8.1	4.2	0.0	26.2	45.7	0.0	19.4	8.6
103 Gabon	11	110	451	36	8	22.8	0.1	0.0	33.5	0.0	61.5	0.0	4.8	0.2
104 Algeria	2,120	..	..	12	63	543.9	1.6	1.3	0.7	2.3	94.7	0.0	2.2	0.1
105 Philippines	16,291	35	93	7	185	2,567.7	11.6	5.6	0.0	20.1	9.6	0.0	66.2	4.1
106 El Salvador	3,711	29	1,213	13	541	4,211.6	18.4	2.4	0.0	0.0	1.1	2.7	95.3	0.9
107 Syrian Arab Republic	824	235	239	4	41	1,099.7	2.2	..	4.7	33.0	31.9	2.7	25.7	2.0
108 Fiji	165	32	1,836	69	197	287.9	5.0	0.6	0.0	0.3	3.5	0.0	46.2	50.0
109 Turkmenistan	..	..	..	6	..	..	..	..	..	..	..	..	..	..
110 Occupied Palestinian Territories	598	16	9	465	149	32.0	..	..	..	..	..	..	..	..
111 Indonesia	6,174	1,654	10,356	3	27	776.1	1.5	0.9	0.0	65.1	20.3	0.0	9.9	4.6
112 Honduras	2,625	2	94	65	369	565.4	24.5	3.2	0.0	0.1	2.6	4.3	93.0	0.0
113 Bolivia	927	72	621	50	97	194.4	6.6	4.5	0.0	2.0	16.7	49.3	31.7	0.3
114 Guyana	278	61	54,887	168	377	224.6	23.5	1.8	0.0	0.0	7.0	2.9	90.0	0.1
115 Mongolia	194	77	8,443	87	74	85.1	..	0.6	0.0	11.0	63.2	0.1	24.8	1.0
116 Viet Nam	5,500	..	..	29	63	220.3	7.9	0.8	0.0	4.1	17.9	0.0	70.6	7.5
117 Moldova	1,498	87	197	71	395	556.6	38.3	3.0	0.0	6.4	83.2	0.0	10.2	0.2
118 Equatorial Guinea	..	..	..	62	..	..	..	..	..	..	..	..	..	..

		Remittances				Relative size of remittance inflows			Remittance inflows by continent of origin					
		Inflows total (US$ millions)	Outflows total (US$ millions)	Outflows per migrant (US$)	ODA received (net disbursements) per capita (US$)	per capita (US$)	as % of net ODA receipts	as % of GDP	ratio of remittances to FDI	Africa	Asia	Europe	Latin American and the Caribbean	Northern America	Oceania
HDI rank		2007								(% of total remittance inflows)					
119	Uzbekistan	..	..	..	6	..	..	..	..	..	..	..	..	..	..
120	Kyrgyzstan	715	220	763	51	134	261.1	19.0	3.4	0.0	8.6	89.2	0.0	2.0	0.1
121	Cape Verde	139	6	537	308	262	85.0	9.2	1.1	12.7	0.0	62.0	0.0	25.2	0.0
122	Guatemala	4,254	18	347	34	319	945.6	10.6	5.9	0.0	0.0	1.9	5.1	92.9	0.0
123	Egypt	7,656	180	1,082	14	101	706.6	6.0	0.7	12.5	58.6	13.3	0.1	13.1	2.3
124	Nicaragua	740	..	..	149	132	88.7	12.1	1.9	0.0	0.0	1.7	32.5	65.6	0.2
125	Botswana	141	120	1,495	56	75	135.2	1.2	..	76.2	0.1	12.9	0.0	7.8	2.9
126	Vanuatu	5	18	17,274	251	22	8.8	1.2	0.1	0.0	0.2	39.6	0.0	5.6	54.6
127	Tajikistan	1,691	184	600	33	251	764.0	45.5	4.7	0.0	28.6	69.2	0.0	2.1	0.0
128	Namibia	17	16	112	99	8	8.2	0.2	0.1	48.9	0.0	29.9	0.1	14.9	6.2
129	South Africa	834	1,186	1,072	16	17	105.0	0.3	0.1	23.6	0.6	38.3	0.1	20.4	17.0
130	Morocco	6,730	52	394	35	216	617.8	9.0	2.4	0.2	8.0	88.4	0.0	3.3	0.1
131	Sao Tome and Principe	2	1	92	228	13	5.6	..	0.1	8.4	0.0	90.5	0.0	1.1	0.0
132	Bhutan	..	..	..	135	..	..	..	..	..	..	..	..	..	..
133	Lao People's Democratic Republic	1	1	20	68	0	0.3	0.0	0.0	0.0	6.3	12.5	0.0	79.2	2.1
134	India	35,262	1,580	277	1	30	2,716.2	3.1	1.5	0.3	58.2	12.8	0.1	26.9	1.8
135	Solomon Islands	20	3	854	500	41	8.2	..	0.5	0.0	0.5	16.2	0.0	8.9	74.3
136	Congo	15	102	355	34	4	11.7	0.2	0.0	25.8	0.4	67.7	0.0	6.1	0.1
137	Cambodia	353	157	517	46	24	52.5	4.2	0.4	0.0	4.6	22.7	0.0	64.4	8.3
138	Myanmar	125	32	270	4	3	65.9	..	0.3	..	..	..	..	..	..
139	Comoros	12	..	..	53	14	27.0	2.6	15.0	10.8	0.1	88.1	0.0	0.9	0.1
140	Yemen	1,283	120	455	10	57	569.1	6.1	1.4	0.2	84.7	6.5	0.0	8.5	0.1
141	Pakistan	5,998	3	1	13	37	271.1	4.2	1.1	0.2	45.2	32.2	0.0	21.6	0.7
142	Swaziland	99	8	180	55	86	156.9	3.5	2.6	94.3	0.1	3.2	0.0	1.9	0.5
143	Angola	..	603	10,695	14	..	..	..	..	..	..	..	..	..	..
144	Nepal	1,734	4	5	21	61	289.8	15.5	302.1	0.0	75.3	10.2	0.0	12.4	2.1
145	Madagascar	11	21	338	45	1	1.2	0.1	0.0	5.8	0.1	90.3	0.1	3.7	0.1
146	Bangladesh	6,562	3	3	9	41	436.9	9.5	10.1	0.0	69.7	18.4	0.0	11.2	0.7
147	Kenya	1,588	16	47	34	42	124.5	5.4	2.2	8.8	0.4	61.0	0.0	27.2	2.6
148	Papua New Guinea	13	135	5,301	50	2	4.2	0.2	0.1	0.0	0.7	6.1	0.0	8.5	84.7
149	Haiti	1,222	96	3,208	73	127	174.3	20.0	16.4	0.0	0.0	4.1	6.1	89.7	0.0
150	Sudan	1,769	2	3	55	46	84.1	3.7	0.7	16.7	55.5	12.5	0.0	13.3	2.0
151	Tanzania (United Republic of)	14	46	59	69	0	0.5	0.1	0.0	11.0	0.5	49.3	0.0	37.3	1.9
152	Ghana	117	6	4	49	5	10.2	0.8	0.1	29.7	0.7	38.8	0.0	30.2	0.6
153	Cameroon	167	103	750	104	9	8.7	0.8	0.4	30.0	0.1	56.1	0.0	13.8	0.0
154	Mauritania	2	..	..	116	1	0.5	0.1	0.0	37.1	0.5	54.3	0.0	8.1	0.0
155	Djibouti	28	5	233	135	34	25.3	..	0.1	..	..	..	..	..	..
156	Lesotho	443	21	3,567	65	221	342.3	28.7	3.4	98.3	0.0	1.0	0.0	0.6	0.1
157	Uganda	849	364	702	56	27	49.1	7.2	1.8	4.3	0.5	69.0	0.0	25.0	1.3
158	Nigeria	9,221	103	106	14	62	451.5	6.7	1.5	15.2	2.0	42.9	0.0	39.5	0.4
LOW HUMAN DEVELOPMENT															
159	Togo	229	35	193	18	35	189.4	8.4	3.3	38.1	0.0	54.8	0.0	7.0	0.0
160	Malawi	1	1	4	53	0	0.1	0.0	0.0	28.0	0.0	59.1	0.0	10.8	2.2
161	Benin	224	67	383	52	25	47.7	4.1	4.7	81.2	0.0	17.0	0.0	1.8	0.0
162	Timor-Leste	..	..	..	241	..	..	..	..	..	..	..	..	..	..
163	Côte d'Ivoire	179	19	8	9	9	108.7	0.9	0.4	13.9	0.1	74.1	0.0	11.7	0.1
164	Zambia	59	124	451	88	5	5.7	0.5	0.1	..	..	..	..	..	..
165	Eritrea	..	..	..	32	..	..	..	..	..	..	..	..	..	..
166	Senegal	925	96	296	68	75	109.8	8.5	11.9	20.0	0.1	73.5	0.0	6.2	0.1
167	Rwanda	51	68	562	73	5	7.2	1.9	0.8	40.6	0.1	43.8	0.0	15.2	0.2
168	Gambia	47	12	52	42	28	65.4	6.9	0.7	5.4	0.0	73.1	0.0	21.4	0.1
169	Liberia	65	0	5	186	17	9.3	..	0.5	..	..	..	..	..	..
170	Guinea	151	119	294	24	16	67.2	3.0	1.4	65.8	0.2	25.8	0.0	8.2	0.0
171	Ethiopia	359	15	26	29	4	14.8	2.0	1.6	4.7	24.1	28.7	0.0	41.0	1.5
172	Mozambique	99	45	111	83	5	5.6	1.3	0.2	63.7	0.0	34.0	0.2	1.8	0.3
173	Guinea-Bissau	29	5	280	73	17	23.5	8.3	4.1	17.7	0.0	80.5	0.0	1.8	0.0
174	Burundi	0	0	2	55	0	0.0	0.0	0.0	100.0	0.0	0.0	0.0	0.0	0.0
175	Chad	..	..	..	33	..	..	..	..	..	..	..	..	..	..
176	Congo (Democratic Republic of the)	..	..	..	19	..	..	..	..	..	..	..	..	..	..
177	Burkina Faso	50	44	57	63	3	5.4	0.7	0.1	91.6	0.0	7.8	0.0	0.7	0.0

International financial flows: remittances, official development assistance and foreign direct investment

		Remittances				Relative size of remittance inflows			Remittance inflows by continent of origin					
HDI rank	Inflows total (US$ millions)	Outflows total (US$ millions)	Outflows per migrant (US$)	ODA received (net disbursements) per capita (US$)	per capita (US$)	as % of net ODA receipts	as % of GDP	ratio of remittances to FDI	Africa	Asia	Europe	Latin American and the Caribbean	Northern America	Oceania
				2007							(% of total remittance inflows)			
178 Mali	212	57	1,234	82	17	20.8	3.3	0.6	74.1	0.0	23.8	0.0	2.0	0.0
179 Central African Republic	..	..	..	41	..	..	..	..	..	..	..	..	..	..
180 Sierra Leone	148	136	1,140	91	25	27.7	9.4	1.6	1.5	0.0	55.1	0.0	42.9	0.5
181 Afghanistan	..	..	..	146	..	..	..	..	..	..	..	..	..	..
182 Niger	78	29	237	38	5	14.4	1.9	2.9	82.7	0.0	14.3	0.0	3.0	0.0
OTHER UN MEMBER STATES														
Iraq	..	781	27,538	314	..	..	..	..	..	..	..	..	..	..
Kiribati	7	..	..	285	74	25.9	..	..	0.0	0.3	34.0	0.0	34.0	31.6
Korea (Democratic People's Rep. of)	..	..	..	4	..	..	..	..	..	..	..	..	..	..
Marshall Islands	..	..	..	879	..	..	..	..	..	..	..	..	..	..
Micronesia (Federated States of)	..	..	..	1,034	..	..	..	..	..	..	..	..	..	..
Monaco	..	..	..	..	..	..	..	..	..	..	..	..	..	..
Nauru	..	..	..	2,518	..	..	..	..	..	..	..	..	..	..
Palau	..	..	..	1,100	..	..	..	..	..	..	..	..	..	..
San Marino	..	..	..	..	..	..	..	..	..	..	..	..	..	..
Somalia	..	..	..	44	..	..	..	..	..	..	..	..	..	..
Tuvalu	..	..	..	1,115	..	..	..	..	..	..	..	..	..	..
Zimbabwe	..	..	..	35	..	..	..	..	..	..	..	..	..	..
Africa	36,850 T	4,754 T	324	36	44	..	..	..	12.2	16.4	57.4	0.0	12.5	1.5
Asia	141,398 T	62,220 T	1,448	9	36	..	..	..	0.3	45.8	17.3	0.5	32.8	3.4
Europe	119,945 T	126,169 T	1,990	..	160	..	..	..	2.2	6.3	62.0	4.2	20.4	4.8
Latin America and the Caribbean	63,408 T	3,947 T	798	10	114	..	..	..	0.0	2.7	9.7	6.2	81.2	0.2
Northern America	2,972 T	45,643 T	..	..	..	..	..	..	..	..	..	..	..	..
Oceania	6,193 T	5,090 T	..	..	..	..	..	..	..	..	..	..	..	..
OECD	124,520 T	165,254 T	1,884	..	108	..	..	..	2.0	3.6	44.1	5.2	39.5	5.6
European Union (EU27)	96,811 T	88,391 T	2,208	..	196	..	..	..	2.7	5.9	58.5	5.1	22.5	5.4
GCC	39 T	25,044 T	2,797	..	..	..	..	..	..	..	..	..	..	..
Very high human development	86,313 T	172,112 T	1,845	..	92	..	..	..	2.7	5.0	55.3	6.8	22.8	7.5
Very high HD: OECD	83,776 T	163,562 T	1,919	..	91	..	..	..	2.8	4.6	55.5	6.9	22.7	7.5
Very high HD: non-OECD	2,537 T	8,550 T	..	..	..	..	..	..	..	..	..	..	..	..
High human development	92,453 T	59,434 T	1,705	9	101	..	..	..	0.2	9.1	35.8	3.4	49.4	2.2
Medium human development	189,093 T	15,403 T	446	12	44	..	..	..	1.6	37.8	21.3	1.0	35.9	2.3
Low human development	2,907 T	874 T	133	51	11	..	..	..	34.7	2.5	53.0	0.0	9.6	0.2
World (excluding the former Soviet Union and Czechoslovakia)	349,632 T	221,119 T	1,540	14	57	..	..	..	1.8	21.4	33.2	3.4	36.4	3.8
World	370,765 Ta	248,283 Ta	1,464	14	58	..	..	..	1.8	21.1	34.7	3.2	35.4	3.7

NOTES

a Data are aggregates from original data source.

SOURCES

Columns 1, 2 and 7: World Bank (2009b).

Column 3: calculated based on data on remittances and stocks of migrants from World Bank (2009b).

Column 4: calculated based on data on ODA from OECD-DAC (2009) and population data from UN (2009e).

Column 5: calculated based on data on remittances from World Bank (2009b) and population data from UN (2009e).

Column 6: calculated based on data on remittances from World Bank (2009b) and on ODA from OECD-DAC (2009).

Column 8: calculated based on data on remittances and FDI from World Bank (2009b).

Columns 9–14: calculated based on data from Ratha and Shaw (2006).

TABLE

Selected conventions related to human rights and migration

(by year of ratification)

F

HDI rank	International Convention on the Protection of the Rights of All Migrant Workers and Members of their Families 1990	Protocol to Prevent, Suppress and Punish Trafficking in Persons, Especially Women and Children, supplementing the UN Convention against Transnational Organized Crime 2000	Convention relating to the Status of Refugees 1951	International Convention on the Elimination of All Forms of Racial Discrimination 1966	International Covenant on Civil and Political Rights 1966	International Covenant on Economic, Social and Cultural Rights 1966	Convention on the Elimination of All Forms of Discrimination against Women 1979	Convention against Torture and Other Cruel, Inhuman or Degrading Treatment or Punishment 1984	Convention on the Rights of the Child 1989
VERY HIGH HUMAN DEVELOPMENT									
1 Norway	..	2003	1953	1970	1972	1972	1981	1986	1991
2 Australia	..	2005	1954	1975	1980	1975	1983	1989	1990
3 Iceland	..	**2000**	1955	1967	1979	1979	1985	1996	1992
4 Canada	..	2002	1969	1970	1976	1976	1981	1987	1991
5 Ireland	..	**2000**	1956	2000	1989	1989	1985	2002	1992
6 Netherlands	..	2005	1956	1971	1978	1978	1991	1988	1995
7 Sweden	..	2004	1954	1971	1971	1971	1980	1986	1990
8 France	..	2002	1954	1971	1980	1980	1983	1986	1990
9 Switzerland	..	2006	1955	1994	1992	1992	1997	1986	1997
10 Japan	..	**2002**	1981	1995	1979	1979	1985	1999	1994
11 Luxembourg	..	2009	1953	1978	1983	1983	1989	1987	1994
12 Finland	..	2006	1968	1970	1975	1975	1986	1989	1991
13 United States	..	2005	..	1994	1992	**1977**	**1980**	1994	**1995**
14 Austria	..	2005	1954	1972	1978	1978	1982	1987	1992
15 Spain	..	2002	1978	1968	1977	1977	1984	1987	1990
16 Denmark	..	2003	1952	1971	1972	1972	1983	1987	1991
17 Belgium	..	2004	1953	1975	1983	1983	1985	1999	1991
18 Italy	..	2006	1954	1976	1978	1978	1985	1989	1991
19 Liechtenstein	..	2008	1957	2000	1998	1998	1995	1990	1995
20 New Zealand	..	2002	1960	1972	1978	1978	1985	1989	1993
21 United Kingdom	..	2006	1954	1969	1976	1976	1986	1988	1991
22 Germany	..	2006	1953	1969	1973	1973	1985	1990	1992
23 Singapore	..	..	..	..	..	..	1995	..	1995
24 Hong Kong, China (SAR)	..	..	..	..	..	..	..	..	..
25 Greece	..	**2000**	1960	1970	1997	1985	1983	1988	1993
26 Korea (Republic of)	..	**2000**	1992	1978	1990	1990	1984	1995	1991
27 Israel	..	2008	1954	1979	1991	1991	1991	1991	1991
28 Andorra	..	..	..	2006	2006	..	1997	2006	1996
29 Slovenia	..	2004	1992	1992	1992	1992	1992	1993	1992
30 Brunei Darussalam	..	..	..	..	..	..	2006	..	1995
31 Kuwait	..	2006	..	1968	1996	1996	1994	1996	1991
32 Cyprus	..	2003	1963	1967	1969	1969	1985	1991	1991
33 Qatar	..	2009	..	1976	..	..	2009	2000	1995
34 Portugal	..	2004	1960	1982	1978	1978	1980	1989	1990
35 United Arab Emirates	..	2009	..	1974	..	..	2004	..	1997
36 Czech Republic	..	**2002**	1993	1993	1993	1993	1993	1993	1993
37 Barbados	..	**2001**	..	1972	1973	1973	1980	..	1990
38 Malta	..	2003	1971	1971	1990	1990	1991	1990	1990
HIGH HUMAN DEVELOPMENT									
39 Bahrain	..	2004	..	1990	2006	2007	2002	1998	1992
40 Estonia	..	2004	1997	1991	1991	1991	1991	1991	1991
41 Poland	..	2003	1991	1968	1977	1977	1980	1989	1991
42 Slovakia	..	2004	1993	1993	1993	1993	1993	1993	1993
43 Hungary	..	2006	1989	1967	1974	1974	1980	1987	1991
44 Chile	2005	2004	1972	1971	1972	1972	1989	1988	1990
45 Croatia	..	2003	1992	1992	1992	1992	1992	1992	1992
46 Lithuania	..	2003	1997	1998	1991	1991	1994	1996	1992
47 Antigua and Barbuda	..	..	1995	1988	..	..	1989	1993	1993
48 Latvia	..	2004	1997	1992	1992	1992	1992	1992	1992
49 Argentina	2007	2002	1961	1968	1986	1986	1985	1986	1990
50 Uruguay	2001	2005	1970	1968	1970	1970	1981	1986	1990
51 Cuba	..	..	..	1972	**2008**	**2008**	1980	1995	1991
52 Bahamas	..	2008	1993	1975	2008	2008	1993	**2008**	1991
53 Mexico	1999	2003	2000	1975	1981	1981	1981	1986	1990
54 Costa Rica	..	2003	1978	1967	1968	1968	1986	1993	1990
55 Libyan Arab Jamahiriya	2004	2004	..	1968	1970	1970	1989	1989	1993
56 Oman	..	2005	..	2003	..	..	2006	..	1996
57 Seychelles	1994	2004	1980	1978	1992	1992	1992	1992	1990
58 Venezuela (Bolivarian Republic of)	..	2002	..	1967	1978	1978	1983	1991	1990
59 Saudi Arabia	..	2007	..	1997	..	..	2000	1997	1996

F

Selected conventions related to human rights and migration
(by year of ratification)

HDI rank	International Convention on the Protection of the Rights of All Migrant Workers and Members of their Families 1990	Protocol to Prevent, Suppress and Punish Trafficking in Persons, Especially Women and Children, supplementing the UN Convention against Transnational Organized Crime 2000	Convention relating to the Status of Refugees 1951	International Convention on the Elimination of All Forms of Racial Discrimination 1966	International Covenant on Civil and Political Rights 1966	International Covenant on Economic, Social and Cultural Rights 1966	Convention on the Elimination of All Forms of Discrimination against Women 1979	Convention against Torture and Other Cruel, Inhuman or Degrading Treatment or Punishment 1984	Convention on the Rights of the Child 1989
60 Panama	..	2004	1978	1967	1977	1977	1981	1987	1990
61 Bulgaria	..	2001	1993	1966	1970	1970	1982	1986	1991
62 Saint Kitts and Nevis	..	2004	2002	2006	..	..	1985	..	1990
63 Romania	..	2002	1991	1970	1974	1974	1982	1990	1990
64 Trinidad and Tobago	..	2007	2000	1973	1978	1978	1990	..	1991
65 Montenegro	**2006**	2006	2006	2006	2006	2006	2006	2006	2006
66 Malaysia	..	2009		..	..	..	1995	..	1995
67 Serbia	**2004**	2001	2001	..	..	..	2001	..	2001
68 Belarus	..	2003	2001	1969	1973	1973	1981	1987	1990
69 Saint Lucia	..	..	..	1990	..	..	1982	..	1993
70 Albania	2007	2002	1992	1994	1991	1991	1994	1994	1992
71 Russian Federation	..	2004	1993	1969	1973	1973	1981	1987	1990
72 Macedonia (the Former Yugoslav Rep. of)	..	2005	1994	1994	1994	1994	1994	1994	1993
73 Dominica	..	..	1994	..	1993	1993	1980	..	1991
74 Grenada	..	2004	..	**1981**	1991	1991	1990	..	1990
75 Brazil	..	2004	1960	1968	1992	1992	1984	1989	1990
76 Bosnia and Herzegovina	1996	2002	1993	1993	1993	1993	1993	1993	1993
77 Colombia	1995	2004	1961	1981	1969	1969	1982	1987	1991
78 Peru	2005	2002	1964	1971	1978	1978	1982	1988	1990
79 Turkey	2004	2003	1962	2002	2003	2003	1985	1988	1995
80 Ecuador	2002	2002	1955	1966	1969	1969	1981	1988	1990
81 Mauritius	..	2003	..	1972	1973	1973	1984	1992	1990
82 Kazakhstan	..	2008	1999	1998	2006	2006	1998	1998	1994
83 Lebanon	..	2005	..	1971	1972	1972	1997	2000	1991
MEDIUM HUMAN DEVELOPMENT									
84 Armenia	..	2003	1993	1993	1993	1993	1993	1993	1993
85 Ukraine	..	2004	2002	1969	1973	1973	1981	1987	1991
86 Azerbaijan	1999	2003	1993	1996	1992	1992	1995	1996	1992
87 Thailand	..	**2001**	..	2003	1996	1999	1985	2007	1992
88 Iran (Islamic Republic of)	..	..	1976	1968	1975	1975	..	..	1994
89 Georgia	..	2006	1999	1999	1994	1994	1994	1994	1994
90 Dominican Republic	..	2008	1978	1983	1978	1978	1982	**1985**	1991
91 Saint Vincent and the Grenadines	..	**2002**	1993	1981	1981	1981	1981	2001	1993
92 China	..	..	1982	1981	**1998**	2001	1980	1988	1992
93 Belize	2001	2003	1990	2001	1996	**2000**	1990	1986	1990
94 Samoa	..	..	1988	..	2008	..	1992	..	1994
95 Maldives	..	..	..	1984	2006	2006	1993	2004	1991
96 Jordan	..	..	..	1974	1975	1975	1992	1991	1991
97 Suriname	..	2007	1978	1984	1976	1976	1993	..	1993
98 Tunisia	..	2003	1957	1967	1969	1969	1985	1988	1992
99 Tonga	..	..	..	1972	..	..	..	..	1995
100 Jamaica	2008	2003	1964	1971	1975	1975	1984	..	1991
101 Paraguay	2008	2004	1970	2003	1992	1992	1987	1990	1990
102 Sri Lanka	1996	**2000**	..	1982	1980	1980	1981	1994	1991
103 Gabon	**2004**	..	1964	1980	1983	1983	1983	2000	1994
104 Algeria	2005	2004	1963	1972	1989	1989	1996	1989	1993
105 Philippines	1995	2002	1981	1967	1986	1974	1981	1986	1990
106 El Salvador	2003	2004	1983	1979	1979	1979	1981	1996	1990
107 Syrian Arab Republic	2005	**2000**	..	1969	1969	1969	2003	2004	1993
108 Fiji	..	..	1972	1973	..	..	1995	..	1993
109 Turkmenistan	..	2005	1998	1994	1997	1997	1997	1999	1993
110 Occupied Palestinian Territories	..	..	..	..	..	..	..	..	..
111 Indonesia	**2004**	**2000**	..	1999	2006	2006	1984	1998	1990
112 Honduras	2005	2008	1992	2002	1997	1981	1983	1996	1990
113 Bolivia	2000	2006	1982	1970	1982	1982	1990	1999	1990
114 Guyana	**2005**	2004	..	1977	1977	1977	1980	1988	1991
115 Mongolia	..	2008	..	1969	1974	1974	1981	2002	1990
116 Viet Nam	..	..	..	1982	1982	1982	1982	..	1990
117 Moldova	..	2005	2002	1993	1993	1993	1994	1995	1993
118 Equatorial Guinea	..	2003	1986	2002	1987	1987	1984	2002	1992

TABLE

F

HDI rank	International Convention on the Protection of the Rights of All Migrant Workers and Members of their Families 1990	Protocol to Prevent, Suppress and Punish Trafficking in Persons, Especially Women and Children, supplementing the UN Convention against Transnational Organized Crime 2000	Convention relating to the Status of Refugees 1951	International Convention on the Elimination of All Forms of Racial Discrimination 1966	International Covenant on Civil and Political Rights 1966	International Covenant on Economic, Social and Cultural Rights 1966	Convention on the Elimination of All Forms of Discrimination against Women 1979	Convention against Torture and Other Cruel, Inhuman or Degrading Treatment or Punishment 1984	Convention on the Rights of the Child 1989
119 Uzbekistan	..	2008	..	1995	1995	1995	1995	1995	1994
120 Kyrgyzstan	2003	2003	1996	1997	1994	1994	1997	1997	1994
121 Cape Verde	1997	2004	..	1979	1993	1993	1980	1992	1992
122 Guatemala	2003	2004	1983	1983	1992	1988	1982	1990	1990
123 Egypt	1993	2004	1981	1967	1982	1982	1981	1986	1990
124 Nicaragua	2005	2004	1980	1978	1980	1980	1981	2005	1990
125 Botswana	..	2002	1969	1974	2000	..	1996	2000	1995
126 Vanuatu	..	..	..	..	2008	..	1995	..	1993
127 Tajikistan	2002	2002	1993	1995	1999	1999	1993	1995	1993
128 Namibia	..	2002	1995	1982	1994	1994	1992	1994	1990
129 South Africa	..	2004	1996	1998	1998	**1994**	1995	1998	1995
130 Morocco	1993	..	1956	1970	1979	1979	1993	1993	1993
131 Sao Tome and Principe	**2000**	2006	1978	**2000**	**1995**	**1995**	2003	**2000**	1991
132 Bhutan	..	..	..	**1973**	..	..	1981	..	1990
133 Lao People's Democratic Republic	..	2003	..	1974	**2000**	2007	1981	..	1991
134 India	..	**2002**	..	1968	1979	1979	1993	**1997**	1992
135 Solomon Islands	..	..	1995	1982	..	1982	2002	..	1995
136 Congo	**2008**	**2000**	1962	1988	1983	1983	1982	2003	1993
137 Cambodia	**2004**	2007	1992	1983	1992	1992	1992	1992	1992
138 Myanmar	..	2004	..	..	..	..	1997	..	1991
139 Comoros	**2000**	..	..	2004	**2008**	**2008**	1994	**2000**	1993
140 Yemen	..	..	1980	1972	1987	1987	1984	1991	1991
141 Pakistan	..	..	..	1966	**2008**	2008	1996	**2008**	1990
142 Swaziland	..	**2001**	2000	1969	2004	2004	2004	2004	1995
143 Angola	..	..	1981	..	1992	1992	1986	..	1990
144 Nepal	..	..	..	1971	1991	1991	1991	1991	1990
145 Madagascar	..	2005	1967	1969	1971	1971	1989	2005	1991
146 Bangladesh	**1998**	..	..	1979	2000	1998	1984	1998	1990
147 Kenya	..	2005	1966	2001	1972	1972	1984	1997	1990
148 Papua New Guinea	..	..	1986	1982	2008	2008	1995	..	1993
149 Haiti	..	**2000**	1984	1972	1991	..	1981	..	1995
150 Sudan	..	..	1974	1977	1986	1986	..	**1986**	1990
151 Tanzania (United Republic of)	..	2006	1964	1972	1976	1976	1985	..	1991
152 Ghana	2000	..	1963	1966	2000	2000	1986	2000	1990
153 Cameroon	..	2006	1961	1971	1984	1984	1994	1986	1993
154 Mauritania	2007	2005	1987	1988	2004	2004	2001	2004	1991
155 Djibouti	..	2005	1977	**2006**	2002	2002	1998	2002	1990
156 Lesotho	2005	2003	1981	1971	1992	1992	1995	2001	1992
157 Uganda	1995	**2000**	1976	1980	1995	1987	1985	1986	1990
158 Nigeria	..	2001	1967	1967	1993	1993	1985	2001	1991
LOW HUMAN DEVELOPMENT									
159 Togo	**2001**	2009	1962	1972	1984	1984	1983	1987	1990
160 Malawi	..	2005	1987	1996	1993	1993	1987	1996	1991
161 Benin	**2005**	2004	1962	2001	1992	1992	1992	1992	1990
162 Timor-Leste	2004	..	2003	2003	2003	2003	2003	2003	2003
163 Côte d'Ivoire	..	..	1961	1973	1992	1992	1995	1995	1991
164 Zambia	..	2005	1969	1972	1984	1984	1985	1998	1991
165 Eritrea	..	..	..	2001	2002	2001	1995	..	1994
166 Senegal	1999	2003	1963	1972	1978	1978	1985	1986	1990
167 Rwanda	2008	2003	1980	1975	1975	1975	1981	2008	1991
168 Gambia	..	2003	1966	1978	1979	1978	1993	**1985**	1990
169 Liberia	**2004**	2004	1964	1976	2004	2004	1984	2004	1993
170 Guinea	2000	2004	1965	1977	1978	1978	1982	1989	1990
171 Ethiopia	..	..	1969	1976	1993	1993	1981	1994	1991
172 Mozambique	..	2006	1983	1983	1993	..	1997	1999	1994
173 Guinea-Bissau	**2000**	2007	1976	**2000**	**2000**	1992	1985	**2000**	1990
174 Burundi	..	**2000**	1963	1977	1990	1990	1992	1993	1990
175 Chad	..	..	1981	1977	1995	1995	1995	1995	1990
176 Congo (Democratic Republic of the)	..	2005	1965	1976	1976	1976	1986	1996	1990
177 Burkina Faso	2003	2002	1980	1974	1999	1999	1987	1999	1990

F

Selected conventions related to human rights and migration
(by year of ratification)

HDI rank	International Convention on the Protection of the Rights of All Migrant Workers and Members of their Families 1990	Protocol to Prevent, Suppress and Punish Trafficking in Persons, Especially Women and Children, supplementing the UN Convention against Transnational Organized Crime 2000	Convention relating to the Status of Refugees 1951	International Convention on the Elimination of All Forms of Racial Discrimination 1966	International Covenant on Civil and Political Rights 1966	International Covenant on Economic, Social and Cultural Rights 1966	Convention on the Elimination of All Forms of Discrimination against Women 1979	Convention against Torture and Other Cruel, Inhuman or Degrading Treatment or Punishment 1984	Convention on the Rights of the Child 1989
178 Mali	2003	2002	1973	1974	1974	1974	1985	1999	1990
179 Central African Republic	..	2006	1962	1971	1981	1981	1991	..	1992
180 Sierra Leone	**2000**	**2001**	1981	1967	1996	1996	1988	2001	1990
181 Afghanistan	..	..	2005	1983	1983	1983	2003	1987	1994
182 Niger	2009	2004	1961	1967	1986	1986	1999	1998	1990
OTHER UN MEMBER STATES									
Iraq	..	2009	..	1970	1971	1971	1986	..	1994
Kiribati	..	2005	..	..	..	..	2004	..	1995
Korea (Democratic People's Rep. of)	..	..	..	..	1981	1981	2001	..	1990
Marshall Islands	..	..	..	..	..	..	2006	..	1993
Micronesia (Federated States of)	..	..	..	..	..	..	2004	..	1993
Monaco	..	2001	1954	1995	1997	1997	2005	1991	1993
Nauru	..	**2001**	..	**2001**	**2001**	..	..	**2001**	1994
Palau	..	..	..	..	..	..	..	..	1995
San Marino	..	**2000**	..	2002	1985	1985	2003	2006	1991
Somalia	..	..	1978	1975	1990	1990	..	1990	**2002**
Tuvalu	..	..	1986	..	..	..	1999	..	1995
Zimbabwe	..	..	1981	1991	1991	1991	1991	..	1990
Total state parties ●	**41**	**129**	**144**	**173**	**164**	**160**	**186**	**146**	**193**
Treaties signed, not yet ratified ○	**15**	**21**	**0**	**6**	**8**	**6**	**1**	**10**	**2**
Africa ●	16	36	48	49	50	48	51	43	52
○	9	5	0	3	3	3	0	5	1
Asia ●	8	25	19	41	35	38	45	33	47
○	3	6	0	1	3	0	0	2	0
Europe ●	2	37	42	44	43	42	43	44	44
○	2	5	0	0	0	0	0	0	0
Latin America and the Caribbean ●	15	26	27	31	29	27	33	22	33
○	1	3	0	1	1	2	0	2	0
Northern America ●	0	2	1	2	2	1	1	2	1
○	0	0	0	0	0	1	1	0	1
Oceania ●	0	3	7	6	5	4	12	2	16
○	0	1	0	1	1	0	0	1	0
Very high human development ●	0	26	31	37	34	32	36	36	38
○	0	8	0	0	0	1	1	0	1
High human development ●	12	41	34	43	39	39	47	37	47
○	2	1	0	1	1	1	0	1	0
Medium human development ●	22	44	54	68	66	64	77	52	83
○	8	11	0	4	6	4	0	7	0
Low human development ●	7	15	25	25	25	25	25	21	25
○	5	3	0	1	1	0	0	2	1

NOTES

Data refer to the year of ratification, accession or succession unless otherwise specified. All these stages have the same legal effect. **Bold** signifies signature not yet followed by ratification. Data are as of June 2009.

● Total state parties
○ Treaties signed, but not yet ratified.

SOURCES

All columns: UN (2009b).

TABLE G

Human development index trends

G

HDI rank	1980	1985	1990	1995	2000	2005	2006	2007	Rank 2006	Change in rank 2006–2007	Long term 1980–2007	Medium term 1990–2007	Short term 2000–2007
VERY HIGH HUMAN DEVELOPMENT													
1 Norway	0.900	0.912	0.924	0.948	0.961	0.968	0.970	0.971	1	0	0.28	0.29	0.16
2 Australia	0.871	0.883	0.902	0.938	0.954	0.967	0.968	0.970	2	0	0.40	0.43	0.24
3 Iceland	0.886	0.894	0.913	0.918	0.943	0.965	0.967	0.969	3	0	0.33	0.35	0.39
4 Canada	0.890	0.913	0.933	0.938	0.948	0.963	0.965	0.966	4	0	0.31	0.21	0.27
5 Ireland	0.840	0.855	0.879	0.903	0.936	0.961	0.964	0.965	5	0	0.52	0.55	0.44
6 Netherlands	0.889	0.903	0.917	0.938	0.950	0.958	0.961	0.964	7	1	0.30	0.30	0.21
7 Sweden	0.885	0.895	0.906	0.937	0.954	0.960	0.961	0.963	6	-1	0.32	0.36	0.14
8 France	0.876	0.888	0.909	0.927	0.941	0.956	0.958	0.961	11	3	0.34	0.32	0.30
9 Switzerland	0.899	0.906	0.920	0.931	0.948	0.957	0.959	0.960	9	0	0.25	0.25	0.19
10 Japan	0.887	0.902	0.918	0.931	0.943	0.956	0.958	0.960	10	0	0.29	0.26	0.25
11 Luxembourg	..	..	..	..	..	0.956	0.959	0.960	8	-3	..	..	..
12 Finland	0.865	0.882	0.904	0.916	0.938	0.952	0.955	0.959	13	1	0.38	0.35	0.32
13 United States	0.894	0.909	0.923	0.939	0.949	0.955	0.955	0.956	12	-1	0.25	0.21	0.11
14 Austria	0.865	0.878	0.899	0.920	0.940	0.949	0.952	0.955	16	2	0.37	0.35	0.23
15 Spain	0.855	0.869	0.896	0.914	0.931	0.949	0.952	0.955	15	0	0.41	0.37	0.36
16 Denmark	0.882	0.891	0.899	0.917	0.936	0.950	0.953	0.955	14	-2	0.29	0.36	0.28
17 Belgium	0.871	0.885	0.904	0.933	0.945	0.947	0.951	0.953	17	0	0.34	0.31	0.13
18 Italy	0.857	0.866	0.889	0.906	0.927	0.947	0.950	0.951	19	1	0.39	0.40	0.36
19 Liechtenstein	..	..	..	..	..	..	0.950	0.951	18	-1	..	..	..
20 New Zealand	0.863	0.874	0.884	0.911	0.930	0.946	0.948	0.950	20	0	0.36	0.42	0.30
21 United Kingdom	0.861	0.870	0.891	0.929	0.932	0.947	0.945	0.947	21	0	0.35	0.36	0.24
22 Germany	0.869	0.877	0.896	0.919	..	0.942	0.945	0.947	22	0	0.32	0.33	..
23 Singapore	0.785	0.805	0.851	0.884	..	..	0.942	0.944	24	1	0.68	0.61	..
24 Hong Kong, China (SAR)	..	..	..	..	..	0.939	0.943	0.944	23	-1	..	..	..
25 Greece	0.844	0.857	0.872	0.874	0.895	0.935	0.938	0.942	25	0	0.41	0.45	0.73
26 Korea (Republic of)	0.722	0.760	0.802	0.837	0.869	0.927	0.933	0.937	26	0	0.97	0.92	1.08
27 Israel	0.829	0.853	0.868	0.883	0.908	0.929	0.932	0.935	28	1	0.44	0.44	0.42
28 Andorra	..	..	..	..	..	..	0.933	0.934	27	-1	..	..	..
29 Slovenia	..	..	0.853	0.861	0.892	0.918	0.924	0.929	29	0	..	0.51	0.58
30 Brunei Darussalam	0.827	0.843	0.876	0.889	0.905	0.917	0.919	0.920	30	0	0.39	0.29	0.22
31 Kuwait	0.812	0.826	..	0.851	0.874	0.915	0.912	0.916	31	0	0.44	..	0.67
32 Cyprus	..	..	0.849	0.866	0.897	0.908	0.911	0.914	32	0	..	0.43	0.26
33 Qatar	..	..	..	..	0.870	0.903	0.905	0.910	34	1	..	..	0.64
34 Portugal	0.768	0.789	0.833	0.870	0.895	0.904	0.907	0.909	33	-1	0.63	0.52	0.23
35 United Arab Emirates	0.743	0.806	0.834	0.845	0.848	0.896	0.896	0.903	37	2	0.72	0.47	0.91
36 Czech Republic	..	..	0.847	0.857	0.868	0.894	0.899	0.903	36	0	..	0.38	0.56
37 Barbados	..	..	..	..	..	0.890	0.891	0.903	39	2	..	..	..
38 Malta	..	0.809	0.836	0.856	0.874	0.897	0.899	0.902	35	-3	0.50[a]	0.45	0.45
HIGH HUMAN DEVELOPMENT													
39 Bahrain	0.761	0.784	0.829	0.850	0.864	0.888	0.894	0.895	38	-1	0.60	0.45	0.50
40 Estonia	..	..	0.817	0.796	0.835	0.872	0.878	0.883	40	0	..	0.46	0.80
41 Poland	..	..	0.806	0.823	0.853	0.871	0.876	0.880	42	1	..	0.52	0.45
42 Slovakia	..	..	..	0.827	0.840	0.867	0.873	0.880	44	2	..	..	0.66
43 Hungary	0.802	0.813	0.812	0.816	0.844	0.874	0.878	0.879	41	-2	0.34	0.47	0.58
44 Chile	0.748	0.762	0.795	0.822	0.849	0.872	0.874	0.878	43	-1	0.59	0.58	0.48
45 Croatia	..	..	0.817	0.811	0.837	0.862	0.867	0.871	45	0	..	0.38	0.58
46 Lithuania	..	..	0.828	0.791	0.830	0.862	0.865	0.870	46	0	..	0.29	0.68
47 Antigua and Barbuda	..	..	..	..	..	0.860	0.860	0.868	48	1	..	..	..
48 Latvia	..	..	0.803	0.765	0.810	0.852	0.859	0.866	50	2	..	0.44	0.96
49 Argentina	0.793	0.797	0.804	0.824	..	0.855	0.861	0.866	47	-2	0.33	0.44	..
50 Uruguay	0.776	0.783	0.802	0.817	0.837	0.855	0.860	0.865	49	-1	0.40	0.45	0.47
51 Cuba	..	..	..	..	..	0.839	0.856	0.863	51	0	..	..	..
52 Bahamas	..	..	..	..	..	0.852	0.854	0.856	52	0	..	..	..
53 Mexico	0.756	0.768	0.782	0.794	0.825	0.844	0.849	0.854	54	1	0.45	0.52	0.50
54 Costa Rica	0.763	0.770	0.791	0.807	0.825	0.844	0.849	0.854	53	-1	0.42	0.45	0.48
55 Libyan Arab Jamahiriya	..	..	..	..	0.821	0.837	0.842	0.847	56	1	..	..	0.44
56 Oman	..	..	..	..	..	0.836	0.843	0.846	55	-1	..	..	..
57 Seychelles	..	..	..	..	0.841	0.838	0.841	0.845	57	0	..	..	0.06
58 Venezuela (Bolivarian Republic of)	0.765	0.765	0.790	0.793	0.802	0.822	0.833	0.844	62	4	0.37	0.39	0.74
59 Saudi Arabia	..	..	0.744	0.765	..	0.837	0.840	0.843	58	-1	..	0.74	..

G

Human development index trends

HDI rank	1980	1985	1990	1995	2000	2005	2006	2007	Rank 2006	Change in rank 2006–2007	Average annual growth rates (%) Long term 1980–2007	Medium term 1990–2007	Short term 2000–2007
60 Panama	0.759	0.769	0.765	0.784	0.811	0.829	0.834	0.840	61	1	0.38	0.55	0.50
61 Bulgaria	..	..	..	..	0.803	0.829	0.835	0.840	59	-2	..	..	0.65
62 Saint Kitts and Nevis	..	..	..	..	..	0.831	0.835	0.838	60	-2	..	..	..
63 Romania	..	..	0.786	0.780	0.788	0.824	0.832	0.837	64	1	..	0.37	0.87
64 Trinidad and Tobago	0.794	0.791	0.796	0.797	0.806	0.825	0.832	0.837	63	-1	0.19	0.30	0.53
65 Montenegro	..	..	..	..	0.815	0.823	0.828	0.834	65	0	..	..	0.34
66 Malaysia	0.666	0.689	0.737	0.767	0.797	0.821	0.825	0.829	66	0	0.81	0.69	0.56
67 Serbia	..	..	..	..	0.797	0.817	0.821	0.826	67	0	..	..	0.51
68 Belarus	..	..	0.795	0.760	0.786	0.812	0.819	0.826	69	1	..	0.22	0.70
69 Saint Lucia	..	..	..	..	..	0.817	0.821	0.821	68	-1	..	..	..
70 Albania	..	..	..	..	0.784	0.811	0.814	0.818	70	0	..	..	0.61
71 Russian Federation	..	..	0.821	0.777	..	0.804	0.811	0.817	73	2	..	-0.03	..
72 Macedonia (the Former Yugoslav Rep. of)	..	..	..	0.782	0.800	0.810	0.813	0.817	72	0	..	..	0.30
73 Dominica	..	..	..	..	..	0.814	0.814	0.814	71	-2	..	..	..
74 Grenada	..	..	..	..	..	0.812	0.810	0.813	74	0	..	..	..
75 Brazil	0.685	0.694	0.710	0.734	0.790	0.805	0.808	0.813	75	0	0.63	0.79	0.41
76 Bosnia and Herzegovina	..	..	..	..	..	0.803	0.807	0.812	76	0	..	..	..
77 Colombia	0.688	0.698	0.715	0.757	0.772	0.795	0.800	0.807	82	5	0.59	0.71	0.63
78 Peru	0.687	0.703	0.708	0.744	0.771	0.791	0.799	0.806	83	5	0.59	0.76	0.63
79 Turkey	0.628	0.674	0.705	0.730	0.758	0.796	0.802	0.806	78	-1	0.93	0.79	0.87
80 Ecuador	0.709	0.723	0.744	0.758	..	..	0.805	0.806	77	-3	0.48	0.47	..
81 Mauritius	..	..	0.718	0.735	0.770	0.797	0.801	0.804	79	-2	..	0.67	0.63
82 Kazakhstan	..	..	0.778	0.730	0.747	0.794	0.800	0.804	81	-1	..	0.20	1.05
83 Lebanon	..	..	..	..	..	0.800	0.800	0.803	80	-3	..	..	..
MEDIUM HUMAN DEVELOPMENT													
84 Armenia	..	..	0.731	0.693	0.738	0.777	0.787	0.798	85	1	..	0.51	1.12
85 Ukraine	..	..	..	..	0.754	0.783	0.789	0.796	84	-1	..	..	0.76
86 Azerbaijan	..	..	..	..	..	0.755	0.773	0.787	88	2	..	..	..
87 Thailand	0.658	0.684	0.706	0.727	0.753	0.777	0.780	0.783	86	-1	0.64	0.61	0.57
88 Iran (Islamic Republic of)	0.561	0.620	0.672	0.712	0.738	0.773	0.777	0.782	87	-1	1.23	0.89	0.83
89 Georgia	..	..	..	..	0.739	0.765	0.768	0.778	91	2	..	..	0.73
90 Dominican Republic	0.640	0.659	0.667	0.686	0.748	0.765	0.771	0.777	89	-1	0.72	0.90	0.54
91 Saint Vincent and the Grenadines	..	..	..	..	..	0.763	0.767	0.772	93	2	..	..	..
92 China	0.533	0.556	0.608	0.657	0.719	0.756	0.763	0.772	99	7	1.37	1.40	1.00
93 Belize	..	..	0.705	0.723	0.735	0.770	0.770	0.772	90	-3	..	0.54	0.70
94 Samoa	..	0.686	0.697	0.716	0.742	0.764	0.766	0.771	96	2	0.53[a]	0.59	0.55
95 Maldives	..	..	..	0.683	0.730	0.755	0.765	0.771	97	2	..	..	0.78
96 Jordan	0.631	0.638	0.666	0.656	0.691	0.764	0.767	0.770	95	-1	0.73	0.85	1.55
97 Suriname	..	..	..	..	..	0.759	0.765	0.769	98	1	..	..	..
98 Tunisia	..	0.605	0.627	0.654	0.678	0.758	0.763	0.769	100	2	1.09[a]	1.20	1.79
99 Tonga	..	..	..	..	0.759	0.765	0.767	0.768	94	-5	..	..	0.16
100 Jamaica	..	..	..	..	0.750	0.765	0.768	0.766	92	-8	..	..	0.29
101 Paraguay	0.677	0.677	0.711	0.726	0.737	0.754	0.757	0.761	101	0	0.43	0.40	0.45
102 Sri Lanka	0.649	0.670	0.683	0.696	0.729	0.752	0.755	0.759	102	0	0.58	0.62	0.57
103 Gabon	..	..	..	0.748	0.735	0.747	0.750	0.755	103	0	..	..	0.39
104 Algeria	..	0.628	0.647	0.653	0.713	0.746	0.749	0.754	104	0	0.83[a]	0.90	0.79
105 Philippines	0.652	0.651	0.697	0.713	0.726	0.744	0.747	0.751	105	0	0.53	0.44	0.49
106 El Salvador	0.573	0.585	0.660	0.691	0.704	0.743	0.746	0.747	106	0	0.99	0.73	0.85
107 Syrian Arab Republic	0.603	0.625	0.626	0.649	0.715	0.733	0.738	0.742	109	2	0.77	1.00	0.53
108 Fiji	..	..	..	..	..	0.744	0.744	0.741	107	-1	..	..	..
109 Turkmenistan	..	..	..	..	..	..	0.739	0.739	108	-1	..	..	..
110 Occupied Palestinian Territories	..	..	..	..	..	0.736	0.737	0.737	110	0	..	..	..
111 Indonesia	0.522	0.562	0.624	0.658	0.673	0.723	0.729	0.734	111	0	1.26	0.95	1.25
112 Honduras	0.567	0.593	0.608	0.623	0.690	0.725	0.729	0.732	112	0	0.94	1.09	0.84
113 Bolivia	0.560	0.577	0.629	0.653	0.699	0.723	0.726	0.729	113	0	0.98	0.87	0.62
114 Guyana	..	..	..	..	..	0.722	0.721	0.729	114	0	..	..	..
115 Mongolia	..	..	..	..	0.676	0.713	0.720	0.727	116	1	..	..	1.02
116 Viet Nam	..	0.561	0.599	0.647	0.690	0.715	0.720	0.725	115	-1	1.16[a]	1.13	0.71
117 Moldova	..	..	0.735	0.682	0.683	0.712	0.718	0.720	117	0	..	-0.12	0.77
118 Equatorial Guinea	..	..	..	..	0.655	0.715	0.712	0.719	118	0	..	..	1.33

HDI rank	1980	1985	1990	1995	2000	2005	2006	2007	Rank 2006	Change in rank 2006–2007	Long term 1980–2007	Medium term 1990–2007	Short term 2000–2007
												Average annual growth rates (%)	
119 Uzbekistan	..	..	..	..	0.687	0.703	0.706	0.710	119	0	..	..	0.48
120 Kyrgyzstan	..	..	..	..	0.687	0.702	0.705	0.710	120	0	..	..	0.46
121 Cape Verde	..	..	0.589	0.641	0.674	0.692	0.704	0.708	121	0	..	1.08	0.71
122 Guatemala	0.531	0.538	0.555	0.621	0.664	0.691	0.696	0.704	123	1	1.05	1.40	0.85
123 Egypt	0.496	0.552	0.580	0.631	0.665	0.696	0.700	0.703	122	-1	1.30	1.13	0.81
124 Nicaragua	0.565	0.569	0.573	0.597	0.667	0.691	0.696	0.699	124	0	0.79	1.17	0.67
125 Botswana	0.539	0.579	0.682	0.665	0.632	0.673	0.683	0.694	126	1	0.94	0.10	1.34
126 Vanuatu	..	..	..	..	0.663	0.681	0.688	0.693	125	-1	..	..	0.62
127 Tajikistan	..	..	0.707	0.636	0.641	0.677	0.683	0.688	127	0	..	-0.16	1.03
128 Namibia	..	..	0.657	0.675	0.661	0.672	0.678	0.686	129	1	..	0.26	0.53
129 South Africa	0.658	0.680	0.698	..	0.688	0.678	0.680	0.683	128	-1	0.14	-0.13	-0.10
130 Morocco	0.473	0.499	0.518	0.562	0.583	0.640	0.648	0.654	130	0	1.20	1.37	1.63
131 Sao Tome and Principe	..	..	..	..	..	0.639	0.645	0.651	131	0	..	..	..
132 Bhutan	..	..	..	..	..	0.602	0.608	0.619	133	1	..	..	..
133 Lao People's Democratic Republic	..	..	..	0.518	0.566	0.607	0.613	0.619	132	-1	..	..	1.26
134 India	0.427	0.453	0.489	0.511	0.556	0.596	0.604	0.612	134	0	1.33	1.32	1.36
135 Solomon Islands	..	..	..	..	..	0.599	0.604	0.610	135	0	..	..	..
136 Congo	..	..	0.597	0.575	0.536	0.600	0.603	0.601	136	0	..	0.04	1.65
137 Cambodia	..	..	..	..	0.515	0.575	0.584	0.593	137	0	..	..	2.01
138 Myanmar	..	0.492	0.487	0.506	..	0.583	0.584	0.586	138	0	0.79[a]	1.08	..
139 Comoros	0.447	0.461	0.489	0.513	0.540	0.570	0.573	0.576	139	0	0.94	0.96	0.92
140 Yemen	..	..	..	0.486	0.522	0.562	0.568	0.575	141	1	..	..	1.36
141 Pakistan	0.402	0.423	0.449	0.469	..	0.555	0.568	0.572	142	1	1.30	1.42	..
142 Swaziland	0.535	0.587	0.619	0.626	0.598	0.567	0.569	0.572	140	-2	0.24	-0.47	-0.63
143 Angola	..	..	..	..	..	0.541	0.552	0.564	143	0	..	..	..
144 Nepal	0.309	0.342	0.407	0.436	0.500	0.537	0.547	0.553	144	0	2.16	1.81	1.46
145 Madagascar	..	..	..	..	0.501	0.532	0.537	0.543	145	0	..	..	1.14
146 Bangladesh	0.328	0.351	0.389	0.415	0.493	0.527	0.535	0.543	148	2	1.86	1.96	1.39
147 Kenya	..	..	..	..	0.522	0.530	0.535	0.541	147	0	..	..	0.51
148 Papua New Guinea	0.418	0.427	0.432	0.461	..	0.532	0.536	0.541	146	-2	0.95	1.32	..
149 Haiti	0.433	0.442	0.462	0.483	..	..	0.526	0.532	149	0	0.77	0.83	..
150 Sudan	..	..	..	..	0.491	0.515	0.526	0.531	150	0	..	..	1.12
151 Tanzania (United Republic of)	..	..	0.436	0.425	0.458	0.510	0.519	0.530	151	0	..	1.15	2.09
152 Ghana	..	..	..	..	0.495	0.512	0.518	0.526	154	2	..	..	0.88
153 Cameroon	0.460	0.498	0.485	0.457	0.513	0.520	0.519	0.523	152	-1	0.48	0.44	0.26
154 Mauritania	..	..	..	..	0.495	0.511	0.519	0.520	153	-1	..	..	0.71
155 Djibouti	..	..	..	..	..	0.513	0.517	0.520	155	0	..	..	..
156 Lesotho	..	..	..	..	0.533	0.508	0.511	0.514	156	0	..	..	-0.52
157 Uganda	..	..	0.392	0.389	0.460	0.494	0.505	0.514	158	1	..	1.59	1.57
158 Nigeria	..	..	0.438	0.450	0.466	0.499	0.506	0.511	157	-1	..	0.91	1.31
LOW HUMAN DEVELOPMENT													
159 Togo	0.404	0.387	0.391	0.404	..	0.495	0.498	0.499	159	0	0.78	1.44	..
160 Malawi	..	0.379	0.390	0.453	0.478	0.476	0.484	0.493	161	1	1.20[a]	1.38	0.44
161 Benin	0.351	0.364	0.384	0.411	0.447	0.481	0.487	0.492	160	-1	1.25	1.46	1.37
162 Timor-Leste	..	..	..	..	..	0.488	0.484	0.489	162	0	..	..	..
163 Côte d'Ivoire	..	..	0.463	0.456	0.481	0.480	0.482	0.484	163	0	..	0.26	0.08
164 Zambia	..	..	0.495	0.454	0.431	0.466	0.473	0.481	164	0	..	-0.17	1.57
165 Eritrea	..	..	..	..	0.431	0.466	0.467	0.472	165	0	..	..	1.29
166 Senegal	..	..	0.390	0.399	0.436	0.460	0.462	0.464	166	0	..	1.02	0.88
167 Rwanda	0.357	0.361	0.325	0.306	0.402	0.449	0.455	0.460	167	0	0.94	2.04	1.90
168 Gambia	..	..	..	..	..	0.450	0.453	0.456	168	0	..	..	..
169 Liberia	0.365	0.370	0.325	0.280	0.419	0.427	0.434	0.442	169	0	0.71	1.81	0.77
170 Guinea	..	..	..	..	..	0.426	0.433	0.435	170	0	..	..	..
171 Ethiopia	..	..	..	0.308	0.332	0.391	0.402	0.414	171	0	..	..	3.13
172 Mozambique	0.280	0.258	0.273	0.310	0.350	0.390	0.397	0.402	172	0	1.34	2.28	1.97
173 Guinea-Bissau	0.256	0.278	0.320	0.349	0.370	0.386	0.391	0.396	174	1	1.62	1.25	0.99
174 Burundi	0.268	0.292	0.327	0.299	0.358	0.375	0.387	0.394	175	1	1.43	1.10	1.38
175 Chad	..	..	..	0.324	..	0.350	0.394	0.393	0.392	173	-2	..	..	1.61
176 Congo (Democratic Republic of the)	..	..	..	..	0.353	0.370	0.371	0.389	177	1	..	..	1.41
177 Burkina Faso	0.248	0.264	0.285	0.297	0.319	0.367	0.384	0.389	176	-1	1.67	1.82	2.85

Human development index trends

HDI rank	1980	1985	1990	1995	2000	2005	2006	2007	Rank 2006	Change in rank 2006–2007	Average annual growth rates (%) Long term 1980–2007	Medium term 1990–2007	Short term 2000–2007
178 Mali	0.245	0.239	0.254	0.267	0.316	0.361	0.366	0.371	179	1	1.53	2.23	2.30
179 Central African Republic	0.335	0.344	0.362	0.347	0.378	0.364	0.367	0.369	178	-1	0.36	0.12	-0.33
180 Sierra Leone	..	..	..	..	..	0.350	0.357	0.365	180	0	..	..	..
181 Afghanistan	..	..	..	..	..	0.347	0.350	0.352	181	0	..	..	..
182 Niger	..	..	..	..	0.258	0.330	0.335	0.340	182	0	..	..	3.92

NOTES

The human development index values in this table were calculated using a consistent methodology and data series. They are not strictly comparable with those published in earlier Human Development Reports. See the Reader's guide for more details.

a Average annual growth rate between 1985 and 2007.

SOURCES

Columns 1–8: calculated based on data on life expectancy from UN (2009e); data on adult literacy rates from UNESCO Institute for Statistics (2003) and (2009a); data on combined gross enrolment ratios from UNESCO Institute for Statistics (1999) and (2009b); and data on GDP per capita (2007 PPP US$) from World Bank (2009d).

Column 9: calculated based on revised HDI values for 2006 in column 7.

Column 10: calculated based on revised HDI ranks for 2006 and new HDI ranks for 2007.

Column 11: calculated based on the HDI values for 1980 and 2007.

Column 12: calculated based on the HDI values for 1990 and 2007.

Column 13: calculated based on the HDI values for 2000 and 2007.

TABLE

Human development index 2007 and its components

HDI rank	Human development index value	Life expectancy at birth (years)	Adult literacy rate (% aged 15 and above)	Combined gross enrolment ratio in education (%)	GDP per capita (PPP US$)	Life expectancy index	Education index	GDP index	GDP per capita rank minus HDI rank[b]
	2007	2007	1999–2007[a]	2007	2007	2007	2007	2007	2007
VERY HIGH HUMAN DEVELOPMENT									
1 Norway	0.971	80.5	.. [c]	98.6 [d]	53,433 [e]	0.925	0.989	1.000	4
2 Australia	0.970	81.4	.. [c]	114.2 [d,f]	34,923	0.940	0.993	0.977	20
3 Iceland	0.969	81.7	.. [c]	96.0 [d]	35,742	0.946	0.980	0.981	16
4 Canada	0.966	80.6	.. [c]	99.3 [d,g]	35,812	0.927	0.991	0.982	14
5 Ireland	0.965	79.7	.. [c]	97.6 [d]	44,613 [e]	0.911	0.985	1.000	5
6 Netherlands	0.964	79.8	.. [c]	97.5 [d]	38,694	0.914	0.985	0.994	8
7 Sweden	0.963	80.8	.. [c]	94.3 [d]	36,712	0.930	0.974	0.986	9
8 France	0.961	81.0	.. [c]	95.4 [d]	33,674	0.933	0.978	0.971	17
9 Switzerland	0.960	81.7	.. [c]	82.7 [d]	40,658	0.945	0.936	1.000	4
10 Japan	0.960	82.7	.. [c]	86.6 [d]	33,632	0.961	0.949	0.971	16
11 Luxembourg	0.960	79.4	.. [c]	94.4 [h]	79,485 [e]	0.906	0.975	1.000	-9
12 Finland	0.959	79.5	.. [c]	101.4 [d,f]	34,526	0.908	0.993	0.975	11
13 United States	0.956	79.1	.. [c]	92.4 [d]	45,592 [e]	0.902	0.968	1.000	-4
14 Austria	0.955	79.9	.. [c]	90.5 [d]	37,370	0.915	0.962	0.989	1
15 Spain	0.955	80.7	97.9 [i]	96.5 [d]	31,560	0.929	0.975	0.960	12
16 Denmark	0.955	78.2	.. [c]	101.3 [d,f]	36,130	0.887	0.993	0.983	1
17 Belgium	0.953	79.5	.. [c]	94.3 [d]	34,935	0.908	0.974	0.977	4
18 Italy	0.951	81.1	98.9 [i]	91.8 [d]	30,353	0.935	0.965	0.954	11
19 Liechtenstein	0.951	.. [k]	.. [c]	86.8 [d,l]	85,382 [e,m]	0.903	0.949	1.000	-18
20 New Zealand	0.950	80.1	.. [c]	107.5 [d,f]	27,336	0.919	0.993	0.936	12
21 United Kingdom	0.947	79.3	.. [c]	89.2 [d,g]	35,130	0.906	0.957	0.978	-1
22 Germany	0.947	79.8	.. [c]	88.1 [d,g]	34,401	0.913	0.954	0.975	2
23 Singapore	0.944	80.2	94.4 [j]	.. [n]	49,704 [e]	0.920	0.913	1.000	-16
24 Hong Kong, China (SAR)	0.944	82.2	.. [o]	74.4 [d]	42,306	0.953	0.879	1.000	-13
25 Greece	0.942	79.1	97.1 [j]	101.6 [d,f]	28,517	0.902	0.981	0.944	6
26 Korea (Republic of)	0.937	79.2	.. [c]	98.5 [d]	24,801	0.904	0.988	0.920	9
27 Israel	0.935	80.7	97.1 [i]	89.9 [d]	26,315	0.928	0.947	0.930	7
28 Andorra	0.934	.. [k]	.. [c]	65.1 [d,l]	41,235 [e,p]	0.925	0.877	1.000	-16
29 Slovenia	0.929	78.2	99.7 [c,j]	92.8 [d]	26,753	0.886	0.969	0.933	4
30 Brunei Darussalam	0.920	77.0	94.9 [j]	77.7	50,200 [e]	0.867	0.891	1.000	-24
31 Kuwait	0.916	77.5	94.5 [j]	72.6 [d]	47,812 [d,e]	0.875	0.872	1.000	-23
32 Cyprus	0.914	79.6	97.7 [j]	77.6 [d,l]	24,789	0.910	0.910	0.920	4
33 Qatar	0.910	75.5	93.1 [j]	80.4	74,882 [d,e]	0.841	0.888	1.000	-30
34 Portugal	0.909	78.6	94.9 [j]	88.8 [d]	22,765	0.893	0.929	0.906	8
35 United Arab Emirates	0.903	77.3	90.0 [l]	71.4	54,626 [d,e,q]	0.872	0.838	1.000	-31
36 Czech Republic	0.903	76.4	.. [c]	83.4 [d]	24,144	0.856	0.938	0.916	1
37 Barbados	0.903	77.0	.. [c,o]	92.9	17,956 [d,q]	0.867	0.975	0.866	11
38 Malta	0.902	79.6	92.4 [r]	81.3 [d]	23,080	0.910	0.887	0.908	1
HIGH HUMAN DEVELOPMENT									
39 Bahrain	0.895	75.6	88.8 [j]	90.4 [d,g]	29,723 [d]	0.843	0.893	0.950	-9
40 Estonia	0.883	72.9	99.8 [c,j]	91.2 [d]	20,361	0.799	0.964	0.887	3
41 Poland	0.880	75.5	99.3 [c,j]	87.7 [d]	15,987	0.842	0.952	0.847	12
42 Slovakia	0.880	74.6	.. [c]	80.5 [d]	20,076	0.827	0.928	0.885	3
43 Hungary	0.879	73.3	98.9 [j]	90.2 [d]	18,755	0.805	0.960	0.874	3
44 Chile	0.878	78.5	96.5 [j]	82.5 [d]	13,880	0.891	0.919	0.823	15
45 Croatia	0.871	76.0	98.7 [j]	77.2 [d]	16,027	0.850	0.916	0.847	7
46 Lithuania	0.870	71.8	99.7 [c,j]	92.3 [d]	17,575	0.780	0.968	0.863	3
47 Antigua and Barbuda	0.868	.. [k]	99.0 [r]	.. [n]	18,691 [q]	0.786	0.945	0.873	0
48 Latvia	0.866	72.3	99.8 [c,j]	90.2 [d]	16,377	0.788	0.961	0.851	3
49 Argentina	0.866	75.2	97.6 [j]	88.6 [d]	13,238	0.836	0.946	0.815	13
50 Uruguay	0.865	76.1	97.9 [i]	90.9 [d]	11,216	0.852	0.955	0.788	20
51 Cuba	0.863	78.5	99.8 [c,j]	100.8	6,876 [d,s]	0.891	0.993	0.706	44
52 Bahamas	0.856	73.2	.. [o]	71.8 [d,g]	20,253 [d,s]	0.804	0.878	0.886	-8
53 Mexico	0.854	76.0	92.8 [j]	80.2 [d]	14,104	0.850	0.886	0.826	5
54 Costa Rica	0.854	78.7	95.9 [j]	73.0 [d,g]	10,842 [q]	0.896	0.883	0.782	19
55 Libyan Arab Jamahiriya	0.847	73.8	86.8 [j]	95.8 [d,g]	14,364 [q]	0.814	0.898	0.829	2
56 Oman	0.846	75.5	84.4 [j]	68.2	22,816 [d,l]	0.841	0.790	0.906	-15
57 Seychelles	0.845	.. [k]	91.8 [r]	82.2 [d,l]	16,394 [q]	0.797	0.886	0.851	-7
58 Venezuela (Bolivarian Republic of)	0.844	73.6	95.2 [i]	85.9 [l]	12,156	0.811	0.921	0.801	7
59 Saudi Arabia	0.843	72.7	85.0 [j]	78.5 [d,l]	22,935	0.794	0.828	0.907	-19

Human development index 2007 and its components

HDI rank	Human development index value	Life expectancy at birth (years)	Adult literacy rate (% aged 15 and above)	Combined gross enrolment ratio in education (%)	GDP per capita (PPP US$)	Life expectancy index	Education index	GDP index	GDP per capita rank minus HDI rank[b]
	2007	2007	1999–2007[a]	2007	2007	2007	2007	2007	2007
60 Panama	0.840	75.5	93.4 [j]	79.7 [d]	11,391 [q]	0.842	0.888	0.790	7
61 Bulgaria	0.840	73.1	98.3 [j]	82.4 [d]	11,222	0.802	0.930	0.788	8
62 Saint Kitts and Nevis	0.838	.. [k]	97.8 [t]	73.1 [d,g]	14,481 [q]	0.787	0.896	0.830	-6
63 Romania	0.837	72.5	97.6 [j]	79.2 [d]	12,369	0.792	0.915	0.804	1
64 Trinidad and Tobago	0.837	69.2	98.7 [j]	61.1 [d,g]	23,507 [q]	0.737	0.861	0.911	-26
65 Montenegro	0.834	74.0	96.4 [r,u]	74.5 [d,u,v]	11,699	0.817	0.891	0.795	1
66 Malaysia	0.829	74.1	91.9 [j]	71.5 [d]	13,518	0.819	0.851	0.819	-5
67 Serbia	0.826	73.9	96.4 [r,u]	74.5 [d,u,v]	10,248 [w]	0.816	0.891	0.773	8
68 Belarus	0.826	69.0	99.7 [c,j]	90.4	10,841	0.733	0.961	0.782	6
69 Saint Lucia	0.821	73.6	94.8 [x]	77.2	9,786 [q]	0.810	0.889	0.765	8
70 Albania	0.818	76.5	99.0 [c,j]	67.8 [d]	7,041	0.858	0.886	0.710	23
71 Russian Federation	0.817	66.2	99.5 [c,j]	81.9 [d]	14,690	0.686	0.933	0.833	-16
72 Macedonia (the Former Yugoslav Rep. of)	0.817	74.1	97.0 [j]	70.1 [d]	9,096	0.819	0.880	0.753	8
73 Dominica	0.814	.. [k]	88.0 [x]	78.5 [d,g]	7,893 [q]	0.865	0.848	0.729	10
74 Grenada	0.813	75.3	96.0 [x]	73.1 [d,g]	7,344 [q]	0.838	0.884	0.717	18
75 Brazil	0.813	72.2	90.0 [i]	87.2 [d]	9,567	0.787	0.891	0.761	4
76 Bosnia and Herzegovina	0.812	75.1	96.7 [y]	69.0 [d,z]	7,764	0.834	0.874	0.726	11
77 Colombia	0.807	72.7	92.7 [i]	79.0	8,587	0.795	0.881	0.743	4
78 Peru	0.806	73.0	89.6 [i]	88.1 [d,g]	7,836	0.800	0.891	0.728	7
79 Turkey	0.806	71.7	88.7 [i]	71.1 [d,g]	12,955	0.779	0.828	0.812	-16
80 Ecuador	0.806	75.0	91.0 [r]	.. [n]	7,449	0.833	0.866	0.719	11
81 Mauritius	0.804	72.1	87.4 [i]	76.9 [d,g]	11,296	0.785	0.839	0.789	-13
82 Kazakhstan	0.804	64.9	99.6 [c,j]	91.4	10,863	0.666	0.965	0.782	-10
83 Lebanon	0.803	71.9	89.6 [i]	78.0	10,109	0.781	0.857	0.770	-7
MEDIUM HUMAN DEVELOPMENT									
84 Armenia	0.798	73.6	99.5 [c,j]	74.6	5,693	0.810	0.909	0.675	16
85 Ukraine	0.796	68.2	99.7 [c,j]	90.0	6,914	0.720	0.960	0.707	9
86 Azerbaijan	0.787	70.0	99.5 [c,i]	66.2 [d,aa]	7,851	0.751	0.881	0.728	-2
87 Thailand	0.783	68.7	94.1 [j]	78.0 [d,g]	8,135	0.728	0.888	0.734	-5
88 Iran (Islamic Republic of)	0.782	71.2	82.3 [i]	73.2 [d,g]	10,955	0.769	0.793	0.784	-17
89 Georgia	0.778	71.6	100.0 [c,ab]	76.7	4,662	0.777	0.916	0.641	21
90 Dominican Republic	0.777	72.4	89.1 [i]	73.5 [d,g]	6,706 [q]	0.790	0.839	0.702	7
91 Saint Vincent and the Grenadines	0.772	71.4	88.1 [x]	68.9 [d]	7,691 [q]	0.774	0.817	0.725	-2
92 China	0.772	72.9	93.3 [j]	68.7 [d]	5,383	0.799	0.851	0.665	10
93 Belize	0.772	76.0	75.1 [x]	78.3 [d,g]	6,734 [q]	0.851	0.762	0.703	3
94 Samoa	0.771	71.4	98.7 [i]	74.1 [d,g]	4,467 [q]	0.773	0.905	0.634	19
95 Maldives	0.771	71.1	97.0 [i]	71.3 [d,g]	5,196	0.768	0.885	0.659	9
96 Jordan	0.770	72.4	91.1 [i]	78.7 [d]	4,901	0.790	0.870	0.650	11
97 Suriname	0.769	68.8	90.4 [i]	74.3 [d,g]	7,813 [q]	0.729	0.850	0.727	-11
98 Tunisia	0.769	73.8	77.7 [i]	76.2 [d]	7,520	0.813	0.772	0.721	-8
99 Tonga	0.768	71.7	99.2 [c,j]	78.0 [d,g]	3,748 [q]	0.778	0.920	0.605	21
100 Jamaica	0.766	71.7	86.0 [i]	78.1 [d,g]	6,079 [q]	0.778	0.834	0.686	-2
101 Paraguay	0.761	71.7	94.6 [i]	72.1 [d,g]	4,433	0.778	0.871	0.633	13
102 Sri Lanka	0.759	74.0	90.8 [i]	68.7 [d,g]	4,243	0.816	0.834	0.626	14
103 Gabon	0.755	60.1	86.2 [i]	80.7 [d,g]	15,167	0.584	0.843	0.838	-49
104 Algeria	0.754	72.2	75.4 [i]	73.6 [d,g]	7,740 [q]	0.787	0.748	0.726	-16
105 Philippines	0.751	71.6	93.4 [i]	79.6 [d]	3,406	0.777	0.888	0.589	19
106 El Salvador	0.747	71.3	82.0 [r]	74.0	5,804 [q]	0.771	0.794	0.678	-7
107 Syrian Arab Republic	0.742	74.1	83.1 [i]	65.7 [d,g]	4,511	0.818	0.773	0.636	5
108 Fiji	0.741	68.7	.. [o]	71.5 [d,g]	4,304	0.728	0.868	0.628	7
109 Turkmenistan	0.739	64.6	99.5 [c,j]	.. [n]	4,953 [d,q]	0.661	0.906	0.651	-3
110 Occupied Palestinian Territories	0.737	73.3	93.8 [i]	78.3	.. [d,ac]	0.806	0.886	0.519	
111 Indonesia	0.734	70.5	92.0 [i]	68.2 [d]	3,712	0.758	0.840	0.603	10
112 Honduras	0.732	72.0	83.6 [i]	74.8 [d,g]	3,796 [q]	0.783	0.806	0.607	7
113 Bolivia	0.729	65.4	90.7 [i]	86.0 [d,g]	4,206	0.673	0.892	0.624	4
114 Guyana	0.729	66.5	.. [o]	83.9	2,782 [q]	0.691	0.939	0.555	13
115 Mongolia	0.727	66.2	97.3 [i]	79.2	3,236	0.687	0.913	0.580	10
116 Viet Nam	0.725	74.3	90.3 [r]	62.3 [d,g]	2,600	0.821	0.810	0.544	13
117 Moldova	0.720	68.3	99.2 [c,j]	71.6	2,551	0.722	0.899	0.541	14
118 Equatorial Guinea	0.719	49.9	87.0 [y]	62.0 [d,g]	30,627	0.415	0.787	0.955	-90

HDI rank	Human development index value 2007	Life expectancy at birth (years) 2007	Adult literacy rate (% aged 15 and above) 1999–2007[a]	Combined gross enrolment ratio in education (%) 2007	GDP per capita (PPP US$) 2007	Life expectancy index 2007	Education index 2007	GDP index 2007	GDP per capita rank minus HDI rank[b] 2007
119 Uzbekistan	0.710	67.6	96.9 [y]	72.7	2,425 [q]	0.711	0.888	0.532	14
120 Kyrgyzstan	0.710	67.6	99.3 [c,j]	77.3	2,006	0.710	0.918	0.500	20
121 Cape Verde	0.708	71.1	83.8 [j]	68.1	3,041	0.769	0.786	0.570	5
122 Guatemala	0.704	70.1	73.2 [j]	70.5	4,562	0.752	0.723	0.638	-11
123 Egypt	0.703	69.9	66.4 [r]	76.4 [d,g]	5,349	0.749	0.697	0.664	-20
124 Nicaragua	0.699	72.7	78.0 [r]	72.1 [d,g]	2,570 [q]	0.795	0.760	0.542	6
125 Botswana	0.694	53.4	82.9 [j]	70.6 [d,g]	13,604	0.473	0.788	0.820	-65
126 Vanuatu	0.693	69.9	78.1 [j]	62.3 [d,g]	3,666 [q]	0.748	0.728	0.601	-4
127 Tajikistan	0.688	66.4	99.6 [c,j]	70.9	1,753	0.691	0.896	0.478	17
128 Namibia	0.686	60.4	88.0 [j]	67.2 [d]	5,155	0.590	0.811	0.658	-23
129 South Africa	0.683	51.5	88.0 [j]	76.8 [d]	9,757	0.442	0.843	0.765	-51
130 Morocco	0.654	71.0	55.6 [j]	61.0	4,108	0.767	0.574	0.620	-12
131 Sao Tome and Principe	0.651	65.4	87.9 [j]	68.1	1,638	0.673	0.813	0.467	17
132 Bhutan	0.619	65.7	52.8 [r]	54.1 [d,g]	4,837	0.678	0.533	0.647	-24
133 Lao People's Democratic Republic	0.619	64.6	72.7 [r]	59.6 [d]	2,165	0.659	0.683	0.513	2
134 India	0.612	63.4	66.0 [j]	61.0 [d]	2,753	0.639	0.643	0.553	-6
135 Solomon Islands	0.610	65.8	76.6 [j]	49.7 [d]	1,725 [q]	0.680	0.676	0.475	10
136 Congo	0.601	53.5	81.1 [j]	58.6 [d,g]	3,511	0.474	0.736	0.594	-13
137 Cambodia	0.593	60.6	76.3 [j]	58.5	1,802	0.593	0.704	0.483	6
138 Myanmar	0.586	61.2	89.9 [y]	56.3 [d,g,aa]	904 [d,q]	0.603	0.787	0.368	29
139 Comoros	0.576	64.9	75.1 [j]	46.4 [d,g]	1,143	0.666	0.655	0.407	20
140 Yemen	0.575	62.5	58.9 [j]	54.4 [d]	2,335	0.624	0.574	0.526	-6
141 Pakistan	0.572	66.2	54.2 [j]	39.3 [d]	2,496	0.687	0.492	0.537	-9
142 Swaziland	0.572	45.3	79.6 [y]	60.1 [d]	4,789	0.339	0.731	0.646	-33
143 Angola	0.564	46.5	67.4 [y]	65.3 [d]	5,385	0.359	0.667	0.665	-42
144 Nepal	0.553	66.3	56.5 [j]	60.8 [d,g]	1,049	0.688	0.579	0.392	21
145 Madagascar	0.543	59.9	70.7 [y]	61.3	932	0.582	0.676	0.373	21
146 Bangladesh	0.543	65.7	53.5 [j]	52.1 [d]	1,241	0.678	0.530	0.420	9
147 Kenya	0.541	53.6	73.6 [y]	59.6 [d,g]	1,542	0.477	0.690	0.457	2
148 Papua New Guinea	0.541	60.7	57.8 [j]	40.7 [d,v]	2,084 [q]	0.594	0.521	0.507	-10
149 Haiti	0.532	61.0	62.1 [j]	.. [n]	1,155 [q]	0.600	0.588	0.408	9
150 Sudan	0.531	57.9	60.9 [y,ad]	39.9 [d,g]	2,086	0.548	0.539	0.507	-13
151 Tanzania (United Republic of)	0.530	55.0	72.3 [j]	57.3	1,208	0.500	0.673	0.416	6
152 Ghana	0.526	56.5	65.0 [j]	56.5	1,334	0.525	0.622	0.432	1
153 Cameroon	0.523	50.9	67.9 [j]	52.3	2,128	0.431	0.627	0.510	-17
154 Mauritania	0.520	56.6	55.8 [j]	50.6 [d,l]	1,927	0.526	0.541	0.494	-12
155 Djibouti	0.520	55.1	.. [o]	25.5 [d]	2,061	0.501	0.554	0.505	-16
156 Lesotho	0.514	44.9	82.2 [j]	61.5 [d,g]	1,541	0.332	0.753	0.457	-6
157 Uganda	0.514	51.9	73.6 [j]	62.3 [d,g]	1,059	0.449	0.698	0.394	6
158 Nigeria	0.511	47.7	72.0 [j]	53.0 [d,g]	1,969	0.378	0.657	0.497	-17
LOW HUMAN DEVELOPMENT									
159 Togo	0.499	62.2	53.2 [y]	53.9	788	0.620	0.534	0.345	11
160 Malawi	0.493	52.4	71.8 [j]	61.9 [d,g]	761	0.456	0.685	0.339	12
161 Benin	0.492	61.0	40.5 [j]	52.4 [d,g]	1,312	0.601	0.445	0.430	-7
162 Timor-Leste	0.489	60.7	50.1 [ae]	63.2 [d,g]	717 [q]	0.595	0.545	0.329	11
163 Côte d'Ivoire	0.484	56.8	48.7 [y]	37.5 [d,g]	1,690	0.531	0.450	0.472	-17
164 Zambia	0.481	44.5	70.6 [j]	63.3 [d,g]	1,358	0.326	0.682	0.435	-12
165 Eritrea	0.472	59.2	64.2 [j]	33.3 [d,g]	626 [q]	0.570	0.539	0.306	12
166 Senegal	0.464	55.4	41.9 [j]	41.2 [d,g]	1,666	0.506	0.417	0.469	-19
167 Rwanda	0.460	49.7	64.9 [y]	52.2 [d,g]	866	0.412	0.607	0.360	1
168 Gambia	0.456	55.7	.. [o]	46.8 [d,g]	1,225	0.511	0.439	0.418	-12
169 Liberia	0.442	57.9	55.5 [j]	57.6 [d]	362	0.548	0.562	0.215	10
170 Guinea	0.435	57.3	29.5 [y]	49.3 [d]	1,140	0.538	0.361	0.406	-10
171 Ethiopia	0.414	54.7	35.9 [j]	49.0	779	0.496	0.403	0.343	0
172 Mozambique	0.402	47.8	44.4 [j]	54.8 [d,g]	802	0.380	0.478	0.348	-3
173 Guinea-Bissau	0.396	47.5	64.6 [j]	36.6 [d,g]	477	0.375	0.552	0.261	5
174 Burundi	0.394	50.1	59.3 [y]	49.0	341	0.418	0.559	0.205	6
175 Chad	0.392	48.6	31.8 [j]	36.5 [d,g]	1,477	0.393	0.334	0.449	-24
176 Congo (Democratic Republic of the)	0.389	47.6	67.2 [y]	48.2	298	0.377	0.608	0.182	5
177 Burkina Faso	0.389	52.7	28.7 [j]	32.8	1,124	0.462	0.301	0.404	-16

H Human development index 2007 and its components

HDI rank	Human development index value 2007	Life expectancy at birth (years) 2007	Adult literacy rate (% aged 15 and above) 1999–2007[a]	Combined gross enrolment ratio in education (%) 2007	GDP per capita (PPP US$) 2007	Life expectancy index 2007	Education index 2007	GDP index 2007	GDP per capita rank minus HDI rank[b] 2007
178 Mali	0.371	48.1	26.2 [i]	46.9	1,083	0.385	0.331	0.398	-16
179 Central African Republic	0.369	46.7	48.6 [y]	28.6 [d,g]	713	0.361	0.419	0.328	-5
180 Sierra Leone	0.365	47.3	38.1 [i]	44.6 [d]	679	0.371	0.403	0.320	-5
181 Afghanistan	0.352	43.6	28.0 [y]	50.1 [d,g]	1,054 [d,ag]	0.310	0.354	0.393	-17
182 Niger	0.340	50.8	28.7 [i]	27.2	627	0.431	0.282	0.307	-6
OTHER UN MEMBER STATES									
Iraq	..	67.8	74.1 [y]	60.5 [d,g,i]	..	0.714	0.695	..	..
Kiribati	..	.. [k]	..	75.8 [d,g]	1,295 [q]	0.699	..	0.427	..
Korea (Democratic People's Rep. of)	..	67.1	..	..	..	0.702	..	..	..
Marshall Islands	..	.. [k]	..	71.1 [d,g]	..	0.758	..	..	..
Micronesia (Federated States of)	..	68.4	..	..	2,802 [q]	0.724	..	0.556	..
Monaco	..	.. [k]	.. [c]	..	..	0.948	..	..	..
Nauru	..	.. [k]	..	55.0 [d,g]	..	0.906	..	..	..
Palau	..	.. [k]	91.9 [d,r]	96.9 [d,g]	..	0.758	0.936	..	..
San Marino	..	.. [k]	.. [c]	..	..	0.940	..	..	..
Somalia	..	49.7	..	..	..	0.412	..	..	..
Tuvalu	..	.. [k]	..	69.2 [d,g]	..	0.683	..	..	..
Zimbabwe	..	43.4	91.2 [i]	54.4 [d,g]	..	0.306	0.789	..	..
Arab States	0.719	68.5	71.2	66.2	8,202	0.726	0.695	0.736	..
Central and Eastern Europe and the CIS	0.821	69.7	97.6	79.5	12,185	0.745	0.916	0.802	..
East Asia and the Pacific	0.770	72.2	92.7	69.3	5,733	0.786	0.849	0.676	..
Latin America and the Caribbean	0.821	73.4	91.2	83.4	10,077	0.806	0.886	0.770	..
South Asia	0.612	64.1	64.2	58.0	2,905	0.651	0.621	0.562	..
Sub-Saharan Africa	0.514	51.5	62.9	53.5	2,031	0.441	0.597	0.503	..
OECD	0.932	79.0	..	89.1	32,647	0.900	..	0.966	..
European Union (EU27)	0.937	79.0	..	91.0	29,956	0.899	..	0.952	..
GCC	0.868	74.0	86.8	77.0	30,415	0.816	0.835	0.954	..
Very high human development	0.955	80.1	..	92.5	37,272	0.918	..	0.988	..
Very high HD: OECD	..	80.1	..	92.9	37,122	0.919	..	0.988	..
Very high HD: non-OECD	..	79.7	..	..	41,887	0.912	..	1.000	..
High human development	0.833	72.4	94.1	82.4	12,569	0.790	0.902	0.807	..
Medium human development	0.686	66.9	80.0	63.3	3,963	0.698	0.744	0.614	..
Low human development	0.423	51.0	47.7	47.6	862	0.434	0.477	0.359	..
World	0.753	67.5 [af]	83.9 [af]	67.5	9,972	0.708	0.784	0.768	..

NOTES

a Data refer to national literacy estimates from censuses or surveys conducted between 1999 and 2007, unless otherwise specified. Due to differences in methodology and timeliness of underlying data, comparisons across countries and over time should be made with caution. For more details, see http://www.uis.unesco.org/.

b A positive figure indicates that the HDI rank is higher than the GDP per capita (PPP US$) rank; a negative figure, the opposite.

c For the purposes of calculating the HDI, a value of 99.0% was applied.

d Data refer to a year other than that specified.

e For the purposes of calculating the HDI, a value of 40,000 (PPP US$) was applied.

f For the purposes of calculating the HDI, a value of 100% was applied.

g UNESCO Institute for Statistics estimate.

h Statec (2008). Data refer to nationals enrolled both in the country and abroad and thus differ from the standard definition.

i Data are from a national household survey.

j UNESCO Institute for Statistics estimates based on its Global Age-specific Literacy Projections model, April 2009.

k For the purposes of calculating the HDI unpublished estimates from UN (2009e) were used: Andorra 80.5, Antigua and Barbuda 72.2, Dominica 76.9, Liechtenstein 79.2, Saint Kitts and Nevis 72.2 and the Seychelles 72.8.

l National estimate.

m HDRO estimate based on GDP from UN (2009c) and the PPP exchange rate for Switzerland from World Bank (2009d).

n Because the combined gross enrolment ratio was unavailable, the following HDRO estimates were used: Antigua and Barbuda 85.6, Ecuador 77.8, Haiti 52.1, Singapore 85.0 and Turkmenistan 73.9.

o In the absence of recent data, estimates for 2005 from UNESCO Institute for Statistics (2003), based on outdated census or survey information, were used and should be interpreted with caution: the Bahamas 95.8, Barbados 99.7, Djibouti 70.3, Fiji 94.4, the Gambia 42.5, Guyana 99.0 and Hong Kong, China (SAR) 94.6.

p HDRO estimate based on GDP from UN (2009c).

q World Bank estimate based on regression.

r Data are from a national census of population.

s Heston, Summers and Aten (2006). Data differ from the standard definition.

t Data are from the Secretariat of the Organization of Eastern Caribbean States, based on national sources.

u Data refer to Serbia and Montenegro prior to its separation into two independent states in June 2006. Data exclude Kosovo.

v UNESCO Institute for Statistics (2007).

w Data exclude Kosovo.

x Data are from the Secretariat of the Caribbean Community, based on national sources.

y Data are from UNICEF's Multiple Indicator Cluster Survey.

z UNDP (2007d).

aa UNESCO Institute for Statistics (2008a).

ab UNICEF (2004).

ac In the absence of an estimate of GDP per capita (PPP US$), an HDRO estimate of 2,243 (PPP US$) was used, derived from the value of GDP for 2005 in US$ and the weighted average ratio of PPP US$ to US$ in the Arab States. The value is expressed in 2007 prices.

ad Data refer to North Sudan only.

ae UNDP (2006b).

af Data are aggregates provided by original data source.

ag Calculated on the basis of GDP in PPP US$ for 2006 from World Bank (2009d) and total population for the same year from UN (2009e).

SOURCES

Column 1: calculated based on data in columns 6–8.
Column 2: UN (2009e).
Column 3: UNESCO Institute for Statistics (2009a).
Column 4: UNESCO Institute for Statistics (2009b).
Column 5: World Bank (2009d).
Column 6: calculated based on data in column 2.
Column 7: calculated based on data in columns 3 and 4.
Column 8: calculated based on data in column 5.
Column 9: calculated based on data in columns 1 and 5.

TABLE

Human and income poverty

1

HDI rank	Human poverty index (HPI-1) Rank	Value (%)	Probability of not surviving to age 40[a,†] (% of cohort) 2005–2010	Adult illiteracy rate[b,†] (% aged 15 and above) 1999–2007	Population not using an improved water source[†] (%) 2006	Children under weight for age (% aged under 5) 2000–2006[c]	Population below income poverty line (%) $1.25 a day 2000–2007[c]	$2 a day 2000–2007[c]	National poverty line 2000–2006[c]	HPI-1 rank minus income poverty rank[d]
VERY HIGH HUMAN DEVELOPMENT										
23 Singapore	14	3.9	1.6	5.6[i]	0[f]	3	..	..	..	..
24 Hong Kong, China (SAR)	..	..	1.4	..[k]	..	..	..	..	..	..
26 Korea (Republic of)	..	..	1.9	..[e]	8[j]	..	<2[f,g]	<2[f,g]	..	..
27 Israel	..	..	1.9	2.9[i]	0	..	..	..	..	..
29 Slovenia	..	..	1.9	0.3[e,i]	..	..	<2	<2	..	..
30 Brunei Darussalam	..	..	2.6	5.1[i]	..	..	..	..	..	..
31 Kuwait	..	..	2.5	5.5[h]	..	10[g]	..	..	..	..
32 Cyprus	..	..	2.1	2.3[i]	0	..	..	..	..	..
33 Qatar	19	5.0	3.0	6.9[h]	0	6[g]	..	..	..	..
35 United Arab Emirates	35	7.7	2.3	10.0[h]	0	14[g]	..	..	..	..
36 Czech Republic	1	1.5	2.0	..[e]	0	1[g]	<2[g]	<2[g]	..	0
37 Barbados	4	2.6	3.0	..[e,k]	0	6[g,m]	..	..	..	..
38 Malta	..	..	1.9	7.6[n]	0	..	..	..	..	..
HIGH HUMAN DEVELOPMENT										
39 Bahrain	39	8.0	2.9	11.2[i]	0[f]	9[g]	..	..	..	..
40 Estonia	..	..	5.2	0.2[e,i]	0	..	<2	<2	8.9[g]	..
41 Poland	..	..	2.9	0.7[e,i]	0[f]	..	<2	<2	14.8	..
42 Slovakia	..	..	2.7	..[e]	0	..	<2[g]	<2[g]	..	..
43 Hungary	3	2.2	3.1	1.1[i]	0	2[g,m]	<2	<2	17.3[g]	2
44 Chile	10	3.2	3.1	3.5[i]	5	1	<2	2.4	17.0[g]	6
45 Croatia	2	1.9	2.6	1.3[i]	1	1[g]	<2	<2	..	1
46 Lithuania	..	..	5.7	0.3[e,i]	..	..	<2	<2	..	..
47 Antigua and Barbuda	..	..	..	1.1[n]	9[j]	10[g,m]	..	..	..	..
48 Latvia	..	..	4.8	0.2[e,i]	1	..	<2	<2	5.9	..
49 Argentina	13	3.7	4.4	2.4[i]	4	4	4.5[f]	11.3[f]	..	-18
50 Uruguay	6	3.0	3.8	2.1[h]	0	5	<2[f]	4.2[f]	..	4
51 Cuba	17	4.6	2.6	0.2[e,i]	9	4	..	..	..	..
52 Bahamas	..	..	7.3	..[k]	3[j]	..	..	..	..	..
53 Mexico	23	5.9	5.0	7.2[h]	5	5	<2	4.8	17.6	16
54 Costa Rica	11	3.7	3.3	4.1[i]	2	5[g]	2.4	8.6	23.9	-13
55 Libyan Arab Jamahiriya	60	13.4	4.0	13.2[i]	29[j]	5[g]	..	..	..	..
56 Oman	64	14.7	3.0	15.6[i]	18[j]	18[g]	..	..	..	..
57 Seychelles	..	..	..	8.2[n]	13[j]	6[g,m]	..	..	..	..
58 Venezuela (Bolivarian Republic of)	28	6.6	6.7	4.8[h]	10[j]	5	3.5	10.2	..	-5
59 Saudi Arabia	53	12.1	4.7	15.0[i]	10[j]	14[g]	..	..	..	..
60 Panama	30	6.7	5.9	6.6[i]	8	7[g]	9.5	17.8	37.3[g]	-15
61 Bulgaria	..	..	3.8	1.7[i]	1	..	<2	2.4	12.8	..
62 Saint Kitts and Nevis	..	..	..	2.2[o]	1	..	..	..	..	..
63 Romania	20	5.6	4.3	2.4[i]	12	3	<2	3.4	28.9	13
64 Trinidad and Tobago	27	6.4	8.4	1.3[i]	6	6	4.2[g]	13.5[g]	21.0[g]	-7
65 Montenegro	8	3.1	3.0	3.6[n,p]	2	3	..	..	..	..
66 Malaysia	25	6.1	3.7	8.1[i]	1	8	<2	7.8	..	17
67 Serbia	7	3.1	3.3	3.6[n,p]	1	2	..	..	..	..
68 Belarus	16	4.3	6.2	0.3[e,i]	0	1	<2	<2	18.5	11
69 Saint Lucia	26	6.3	4.6	5.2[q]	2	14[g,m]	20.9[g]	40.6[g]	..	-35
70 Albania	15	4.0	3.6	1.0[e,i]	3	8	<2	7.8	25.4	10
71 Russian Federation	32	7.4	10.6	0.5[e,i]	3	3[g]	<2	<2	19.6	24
72 Macedonia (the Former Yugoslav Rep. of)	9	3.2	3.4	3.0[i]	0	6[g]	<2	3.2	21.7	5
73 Dominica	..	..	..	12.0[q]	3[j]	5[g,m]	..	..	..	..
74 Grenada	..	..	3.2	4.0[q]	6[j]	..	..	..	..	..
75 Brazil	43	8.6	8.2	10.0[h]	9	6[g]	5.2	12.7	21.5	1
76 Bosnia and Herzegovina	5	2.8	3.0	3.3[r]	1	2	<2	<2	19.5	3
77 Colombia	34	7.6	8.3	7.3[h]	7	7	16.0	27.9	64.0[g]	-21
78 Peru	47	10.2	7.4	10.4[h]	16	8	7.9	18.5	53.1	0
79 Turkey	40	8.3	5.7	11.3[h]	3	4	2.7	9.0	27.0	6
80 Ecuador	38	7.9	7.3	9.0[h]	5	9	4.7	12.8	46.0[g]	0
81 Mauritius	45	9.5	5.8	12.6[i]	0	15[g]	..	..	..	..
82 Kazakhstan	37	7.9	11.2	0.4[e,i]	4	4	3.1	17.2	15.4	3
83 Lebanon	33	7.6	5.5	10.4[h]	0	4	..	..	..	..

HDI rank	Human poverty index (HPI-1) Rank	Human poverty index (HPI-1) Value (%)	Probability of not surviving to age 40[a],† (% of cohort) 2005–2010	Adult illiteracy rate[b],† (% aged 15 and above) 1999–2007	Population not using an improved water source† (%) 2006	Children under weight for age (% aged under 5) 2000–2006[c]	Population below income poverty line (%) $1.25 a day 2000–2007[c]	Population below income poverty line (%) $2 a day 2000–2007[c]	Population below income poverty line (%) National poverty line 2000–2006[c]	HPI-1 rank minus income poverty rank[d]
MEDIUM HUMAN DEVELOPMENT										
84 Armenia	12	3.7	5.0	0.5 [e,i]	2	4	10.6	43.4	50.9	-30
85 Ukraine	21	5.8	8.4	0.3 [e,i]	3	1	<2	<2	19.5	14
86 Azerbaijan	50	10.7	8.6	0.5 [e,h]	22	7	<2	<2	49.6	38
87 Thailand	41	8.5	11.3	5.9 [i]	2	9	<2	11.5	13.6 [g]	30
88 Iran (Islamic Republic of)	59	12.8	6.1	17.7 [h]	6 [j]	11 [g]	<2	8.0	..	44
89 Georgia	18	4.7	6.7	0.0 [e,s]	1	3 [g]	13.4	30.4	54.5	-29
90 Dominican Republic	44	9.1	9.4	10.9 [i]	5	5	5.0	15.1	42.2	3
91 Saint Vincent and the Grenadines	..	..	5.8	11.9 [q]	..	..	..	..	..	..
92 China	36	7.7	6.2	6.7 [i]	12	7	15.9 [t]	36.3 [t]	2.8	-19
93 Belize	73	17.5	5.6	24.9 [q]	9 [j]	7	..	..	..	..
94 Samoa	..	..	5.6	1.3 [i]	12	..	..	..	..	..
95 Maldives	66	16.5	6.0	3.0 [i]	17	30	..	..	..	..
96 Jordan	29	6.6	5.3	8.9 [h]	2	4	<2	3.5	14.2	21
97 Suriname	46	10.1	10.0	9.6 [i]	8	13	15.5 [g]	27.2 [g]	..	-9
98 Tunisia	65	15.6	4.1	22.3 [i]	6	4	2.6	12.8	7.6 [g]	26
99 Tonga	..	..	5.4	0.8 [e,i]	0	..	..	..	..	..
100 Jamaica	51	10.9	9.9	14.0 [i]	7	4	<2	5.8	18.7	39
101 Paraguay	49	10.5	8.9	5.4 [h]	23	5	6.5	14.2	..	5
102 Sri Lanka	67	16.8	5.5	9.2 [h]	18	29	14.0	39.7	22.7	7
103 Gabon	72	17.5	22.6	13.8 [i]	13	12	4.8	19.6	..	24
104 Algeria	71	17.5	6.4	24.6 [i]	15	4	6.8 [g]	23.6 [g]	22.6 [g]	19
105 Philippines	54	12.4	5.7	6.6 [i]	7	28	22.6	45.0	25.1 [g]	-19
106 El Salvador	63	14.6	10.7	18.0 [n]	16	10	11.0	20.5	37.2	8
107 Syrian Arab Republic	56	12.6	3.9	16.9 [i]	11	10	..	..	..	..
108 Fiji	79	21.2	6.2	.. [k]	53	8 [g]	..	..	..	..
109 Turkmenistan	..	..	13.0	0.5 [e,i]	..	11	24.8 [g]	49.6 [g]	..	..
110 Occupied Palestinian Territories	24	6.0	4.3	6.2 [h]	11	3	..	..	..	..
111 Indonesia	69	17.0	6.7	8.0 [h]	20	28	..	..	16.7	..
112 Honduras	61	13.7	9.3	16.4 [h]	16	11	18.2	29.7	50.7	-3
113 Bolivia	52	11.6	13.9	9.3 [h]	14	8	19.6	30.3	65.2	-10
114 Guyana	48	10.2	12.8	.. [k]	7	14	7.7 [g]	16.8 [g]	35.0 [g]	2
115 Mongolia	58	12.7	10.3	2.7 [i]	28	6	22.4	49.0	36.1	-15
116 Viet Nam	55	12.4	5.8	9.7 [n]	8	25	21.5	48.4	28.9	-13
117 Moldova	22	5.9	6.2	0.8 [e,i]	10	4	8.1	28.9	48.5	-21
118 Equatorial Guinea	98	31.9	34.5	13.0 [r]	57	19	..	..	..	..
119 Uzbekistan	42	8.5	10.7	3.1 [r]	12	5	46.3	76.7	27.5	-46
120 Kyrgyzstan	31	7.3	9.2	0.7 [e,i]	11	3	21.8	51.9	43.1	-34
121 Cape Verde	62	14.5	6.4	16.2 [i]	20 [j]	14 [g]	20.6	40.2	..	-6
122 Guatemala	76	19.7	11.2	26.8 [i]	4	23	11.7	24.3	56.2	15
123 Egypt	82	23.4	7.2	33.6 [n]	2	6	<2	18.4	16.7	58
124 Nicaragua	68	17.0	7.9	22.0 [n]	21	10	15.8	31.8	47.9 [g]	6
125 Botswana	81	22.9	31.2	17.1 [i]	4	13	31.2 [g]	49.4 [g]	..	-8
126 Vanuatu	83	23.6	7.1	21.9 [i]	41 [j]	20 [g,m]	..	..	..	..
127 Tajikistan	74	18.2	12.5	0.4 [e,i]	33	17	21.5	50.8	44.4	-2
128 Namibia	70	17.1	21.2	12.0 [i]	7	24	49.1 [g]	62.2 [g]	..	-29
129 South Africa	85	25.4	36.1	12.0 [i]	7	12 [g]	26.2	42.9	..	-2
130 Morocco	96	31.1	6.6	44.4 [i]	17	10	2.5	14.0	..	50
131 Sao Tome and Principe	57	12.6	13.9	12.1 [i]	14	9	..	..	..	..
132 Bhutan	102	33.7	14.2	47.2 [n]	19	19 [g]	26.2	49.5	..	13
133 Lao People's Democratic Republic	94	30.7	13.1	27.3 [n]	40	40	44.0	76.8	33.0	-6
134 India	88	28.0	15.5	34.0 [i]	11	46	41.6 [t]	75.6 [t]	28.6	-10
135 Solomon Islands	80	21.8	11.6	23.4 [i]	30	21 [g,m]	..	..	..	..
136 Congo	84	24.3	29.7	18.9 [i]	29	14	54.1	74.4	..	-27
137 Cambodia	87	27.7	18.5	23.7 [i]	35	36	40.2	68.2	35.0	-10
138 Myanmar	77	20.4	19.1	10.1 [r]	20	32	..	..	..	..
139 Comoros	78	20.4	12.6	24.9 [i]	15	25	46.1	65.0	..	-20
140 Yemen	111	35.7	15.6	41.1 [i]	34	46	17.5	46.6	41.8 [g]	35
141 Pakistan	101	33.4	12.6	45.8 [h]	10	38	22.6	60.3	32.6 [g]	16
142 Swaziland	108	35.1	47.2	20.4 [r]	40	10	62.9	81.0	69.2	-15
143 Angola	118	37.2	38.5	32.6 [r]	49	31	54.3	70.2	..	2

I1 TABLE

Human and income poverty

HDI rank	Human poverty index (HPI-1) Rank	Human poverty index (HPI-1) Value (%)	Probability of not surviving to age 40[a,†] (% of cohort) 2005–2010	Adult illiteracy rate[b,†] (% aged 15 and above) 1999–2007	Population not using an improved water source[†] (%) 2006	Children under weight for age (% aged under 5) 2000–2006[c]	Population below income poverty line (%) $1.25 a day 2000–2007[c]	$2 a day 2000–2007[c]	National poverty line 2000–2006[c]	HPI-1 rank minus income poverty rank[d]
144 Nepal	99	32.1	11.0	43.5[i]	11	39	55.1[t]	77.6[t]	30.9	-16
145 Madagascar	113	36.1	20.8	29.3[r]	53	42	67.8	89.6	71.3[g]	-14
146 Bangladesh	112	36.1	11.6	46.5[i]	20[u]	48	49.6[v]	81.3[v]	40.0	2
147 Kenya	92	29.5	30.3	26.4[r]	43	20	19.7	39.9	52.0[g]	16
148 Papua New Guinea	121	39.6	15.9	42.2[i]	60	35[g,m]	35.8[g]	57.4[g]	37.5[g]	23
149 Haiti	97	31.5	18.5	37.9[j,n]	42	22	54.9	72.1	..	-16
150 Sudan	104	34.0	23.9	39.1[r,w]	30	41	..	..	..	..
151 Tanzania (United Republic of)	93	30.0	28.2	27.7[i]	45	22	88.5	96.6	35.7	-37
152 Ghana	89	28.1	25.8	35.0[i]	20	18	30.0	53.6	28.5	0
153 Cameroon	95	30.8	34.2	32.1[h]	30	19	32.8	57.7	40.2	4
154 Mauritania	115	36.2	21.6	44.2[i]	40	32	21.2	44.1	46.3	32
155 Djibouti	86	25.6	26.2	..[k]	8	29	18.8	41.2	..	12
156 Lesotho	106	34.3	47.4	17.8[h]	22	20	43.4	62.2	68.0[g]	3
157 Uganda	91	28.8	31.4	26.4[i]	36	20	51.5	75.6	37.7	-17
158 Nigeria	114	36.2	37.4	28.0[i]	53	29	64.4	83.9	34.1[g]	-11
LOW HUMAN DEVELOPMENT										
159 Togo	117	36.6	18.6	46.8[r]	41	26	38.7	69.3	..	18
160 Malawi	90	28.2	32.6	28.2[i]	24	19	73.9	90.4	65.3[g]	-35
161 Benin	126	43.2	19.2	59.5[i]	35	23	47.3	75.3	29.0[g]	19
162 Timor-Leste	122	40.8	18.0	49.9[x]	38	46	52.9	77.5	..	9
163 Côte d'Ivoire	119	37.4	24.6	51.3[r]	19	20	23.3	46.8	..	29
164 Zambia	110	35.5	42.9	29.4[i]	42	20	64.3	81.5	68.0	-14
165 Eritrea	103	33.7	18.2	35.8[i]	40	40	..	..	53.0[g]	..
166 Senegal	124	41.6	22.4	58.1[h]	23	17	33.5	60.3	33.4[g]	28
167 Rwanda	100	32.9	34.2	35.1[r]	35	23	76.6	90.3	60.3	-28
168 Gambia	123	40.9	21.8	..[k]	14	20	34.3	56.7	61.3	26
169 Liberia	109	35.2	23.2	44.5[i]	36	26[g]	83.7	94.8	..	-24
170 Guinea	129	50.5	23.7	70.5[r]	30	26	70.1	87.2	40.0[g]	1
171 Ethiopia	130	50.9	27.7	64.1[h]	58	38	39.0	77.5	44.2	30
172 Mozambique	127	46.8	40.6	55.6[i]	58	24	74.7	90.0	54.1	-3
173 Guinea-Bissau	107	34.9	37.4	35.4[i]	43	19	48.8	77.9	65.7	-1
174 Burundi	116	36.4	33.7	40.7[r]	29	39	81.3	93.4	68.0[g]	-16
175 Chad	132	53.1	35.7	68.2[i]	52	37	61.9	83.3	64.0[g]	11
176 Congo (Democratic Republic of the)	120	38.0	37.3	32.8[r]	54	31	59.2	79.5	..	0
177 Burkina Faso	131	51.8	26.9	71.3[h]	28	37	56.5	81.2	46.4	12
178 Mali	133	54.5	32.5	73.8[h]	40	33	51.4	77.1	63.8[g]	22
179 Central African Republic	125	42.4	39.6	51.4[r]	34	29	62.4	81.9	..	3
180 Sierra Leone	128	47.7	31.0	61.9[i]	47	30	53.4	76.1	70.2	14
181 Afghanistan	135	59.8	40.7	72.0[r]	78	39	..	..	..	..
182 Niger	134	55.8	29.0	71.3[h]	58	44	65.9	85.6	63.0[g]	8
OTHER UN MEMBER STATES										
Iraq	75	19.4	10.0	25.9[r]	23	8	..	..	..	..
Kiribati	..	..	..	..	35	13[g]	..	..	..	..
Korea (Democratic People's Rep. of)	..	..	10.0	..	0	23	..	..	..	..
Marshall Islands	..	..	..	..	12[j]	..	..	..	..	..
Micronesia (Federated States of)	..	..	8.8	..	6	15[g]	..	..	..	..
Nauru	..	..	..	..	..	..	..	..	..	..
Palau	..	..	..	8.1[j,n]	11	..	..	..	..	..
Somalia	..	..	34.1	..	71	36	..	..	..	..
Tuvalu	..	..	..	..	7	..	..	..	..	..
Zimbabwe	105	34.0	48.1	8.8i	19	17	..	..	34.9[g]	..

NOTES

† Denotes indicators used to calcualte the human poverty index (HPI-1). For further details, see Technical note 1: www.hdr.undp.org/en/statistics/tn1

a Data refer to the probability at birth of not surviving to age 40, multiplied by 100.

b Data refer to national illiteracy estimates from censuses or surveys conducted between 1999 and 2007, unless otherwise specified. Due to differences in methodology and timeliness of underlying data, comparisons across countries and over time should be made with caution. For more details, see http://www.uis.unesco.org/.

c Data refer to the most recent year available during the period specified.

d Income poverty refers to the share of the population living on less than $1.25 a day. All countries with an income poverty rate of less than 2% were given equal rank. The rankings are based on countries for which data are available for both indicators. A positive figure indicates that the country performs better in income poverty than in human poverty, a negative the opposite.

e For the purposes of calculating the HPI-1 a value of 1% was assumed.

f Estimates cover urban areas only.

g Data refer to an earlier year outside the range of years specified.

h Data are from a national household survey.

i UNESCO Institute for Statistics estimates based on its Global Age-specific Literacy Projections model, April 2009.

j Data refer to an earlier year than that specified.

k In the absence of recent data, estimates for 2005 from UNESCO Institute for Statistics (2003), based on outdated census or survey information, were used and should be interpreted with caution: Bahamas 4.2, Barbados 0.3, Djibouti 29.7, Fiji 5.6, Gambia 57.5, Guyana 1.0 and Hong Kong, China (SAR) 5.4.

l National estimate.

m UNICEF (2005b).

n Data are from a national census of population.

o Data are from the Secretariat of the Organization of Eastern Caribbean States, based on national sources.

p Data refer to Serbia and Montenegro prior to its separation into two independent states in June 2006. Data exclude Kosovo.

q Data are from the Secretariat of the Caribbean Community, based on national sources.

r Data are from UNICEF's Multiple Indicator Cluster Survey.

s UNICEF (2004).

t Estimates are weighted averages of urban and rural values.

u Estimates have been adjusted for arsenic contamination levels based on national surveys conducted and approved by the government.

v Estimates are adjusted by spatial consumer price index information.

w Data refer to North Sudan only.

x UNDP (2006b).

SOURCES

Column 1: determined on the basis of HPI-1 values.
Column 2: calculated on the basis of data in columns 3–6.
Column 3: UN (2009e).
Column 4: UNESCO Institute for Statistics (2009a).
Columns 5 and 6: UN (2009a) based on a joint effort by UNICEF and WHO.
Columns 7–9: World Bank (2009d).
Column 10: calculated based on HPI-1 values and the income poverty measures.

HPI-1 RANKS FOR 135 COUNTRIES AND AREAS

1 Czech Republic	36 China	71 Algeria	106 Lesotho
2 Croatia	37 Kazakhstan	72 Gabon	107 Guinea-Bissau
3 Hungary	38 Ecuador	73 Belize	108 Swaziland
4 Barbados	39 Bahrain	74 Tajikistan	109 Liberia
5 Bosnia and Herzegovina	40 Turkey	75 Iraq	110 Zambia
6 Uruguay	41 Thailand	76 Guatemala	111 Yemen
7 Serbia	42 Uzbekistan	77 Myanmar	112 Bangladesh
8 Montenegro	43 Brazil	78 Comoros	113 Madagascar
9 Macedonia (the Former Yugoslav Rep. of)	44 Dominican Republic	79 Fiji	114 Nigeria
10 Chile	45 Mauritius	80 Solomon Islands	115 Mauritania
11 Costa Rica	46 Suriname	81 Botswana	116 Burundi
12 Armenia	47 Peru	82 Egypt	117 Togo
13 Argentina	48 Guyana	83 Vanuatu	118 Angola
14 Singapore	49 Paraguay	84 Congo	119 Côte d'Ivoire
15 Albania	50 Azerbaijan	85 South Africa	120 Congo (Democratic Republic of the)
16 Belarus	51 Jamaica	86 Djibouti	121 Papua New Guinea
17 Cuba	52 Bolivia	87 Cambodia	122 Timor-Leste
18 Georgia	53 Saudi Arabia	88 India	123 Gambia
19 Qatar	54 Philippines	89 Ghana	124 Senegal
20 Romania	55 Viet Nam	90 Malawi	125 Central African Republic
21 Ukraine	56 Syrian Arab Republic	91 Uganda	126 Benin
22 Moldova	57 Sao Tome and Principe	92 Kenya	127 Mozambique
23 Mexico	58 Mongolia	93 Tanzania (United Republic of)	128 Sierra Leone
24 Occupied Palestinian Territories	59 Iran (Islamic Republic of)	94 Lao People's Democratic Republic	129 Guinea
25 Malaysia	60 Libyan Arab Jamahiriya	95 Cameroon	130 Ethiopia
26 Saint Lucia	61 Honduras	96 Morocco	131 Burkina Faso
27 Trinidad and Tobago	62 Cape Verde	97 Haiti	132 Chad
28 Venezuela (Bolivarian Republic of)	63 El Salvador	98 Equatorial Guinea	133 Mali
29 Jordan	64 Oman	99 Nepal	134 Niger
30 Panama	65 Tunisia	100 Rwanda	135 Afghanistan
31 Kyrgyzstan	66 Maldives	101 Pakistan	
32 Russian Federation	67 Sri Lanka	102 Bhutan	
33 Lebanon	68 Nicaragua	103 Eritrea	
34 Colombia	69 Indonesia	104 Sudan	
35 United Arab Emirates	70 Namibia	105 Zimbabwe	

TABLE

Human and income poverty: OECD countries

2

HDI rank	Human poverty index (HPI-2) Rank	Human poverty index (HPI-2) Value (%)	Probability at birth of not surviving to age 60[a†] (% of cohort) 2005–2010	People lacking functional literacy skills[b†] (% aged 16–65) 1994–2003	Long-term unemployment[†] (% of labour force) 2007	Population living below 50% of median income[†] 2000–2005[c]	HPI-2 rank minus income poverty rank[d]
VERY HIGH HUMAN DEVELOPMENT							
1 Norway	2	6.6	6.6	7.9	0.2	7.1	-6
2 Australia	14	12.0	6.4	17.0 [e]	0.7	12.2	-4
3 Iceland	..	..	5.4	..	0.1	..	..
4 Canada	12	11.2	7.3	14.6	0.4	13.0	-8
5 Ireland	23	15.9	6.9	22.6 [e]	1.4	16.2	0
6 Netherlands	3	7.4	7.1	10.5 [e]	1.3	4.9 [f]	1
7 Sweden	1	6.0	6.3	7.5 [e]	0.7	5.6	-3
8 France	8	11.0	7.7	.. [g]	3.1	7.3	-1
9 Switzerland	7	10.6	6.4	15.9	1.5	7.6	-3
10 Japan	13	11.6	6.2	.. [g]	1.2	11.8 [f,h]	-4
11 Luxembourg	10	11.2	7.8	.. [g]	1.3	8.8	-4
12 Finland	5	7.9	8.2	10.4 [e]	1.5	6.5	-1
13 United States	22	15.2	9.7	20.0	0.5	17.3	-2
14 Austria	9	11.0	7.6	.. [g]	1.2	7.7	-2
15 Spain	17	12.4	7.1	.. [g]	2.0	14.2	-4
16 Denmark	4	7.7	9.2	9.6 [e]	0.7	5.6	1
17 Belgium	15	12.2	8.0	18.4 [e,i]	3.8	8.1	3
18 Italy	25	29.8	6.8	47.0	2.8	12.8	6
20 New Zealand	..	..	7.6	18.4 [e]	0.2	..	..
21 United Kingdom	21	14.6	7.8	21.8 [e]	1.3	11.6	5
22 Germany	6	10.1	7.6	14.4 [e]	4.8	8.4	-7
25 Greece	18	12.5	7.0	.. [g]	4.1	14.3	-4
26 Korea (Republic of)	..	..	8.1	..	0.0	..	..
34 Portugal	..	..	8.7	..	3.7	..	..
36 Czech Republic	11	11.2	10.2	.. [g]	2.8	4.9 [f]	10
HIGH HUMAN DEVELOPMENT							
41 Poland	19	12.8	13.2	.. [g]	4.4	11.5	4
42 Slovakia	16	12.4	13.3	.. [g]	7.8	7.0 [f]	9
43 Hungary	20	13.2	16.4	.. [g]	3.5	6.4 [f]	15
53 Mexico	24	28.1	13.0	43.2 [j]	0.1	18.4	-1
79 Turkey	..	..	14.9	..	3.1	..	..

NOTES

† Denotes indicators used to calculate the HPI-2. For further details see Technical note 1.

a Data refer to the probability at birth of not surviving to age 60, multiplied by 100.

b Based on scoring at level 1 on the prose literacy scale of the IALS. Data refer to the most recent year available during the period specified.

c Data refer to the most recent year available during the period specified.

d Income poverty refers to the share of the population living on less than 50% of the median adjusted disposable household income. A positive figure indicates that the country performs better in income poverty than in human poverty, a negative the opposite.

e OECD and Statistics Canada (2000).

f Data refer to an earlier year than the period specified.

g For calculating HPI-2 an estimate of 16.4%, the unweighted average of countries with available data, was applied.

h Smeeding (1997).

i Data refer to Flanders only.

j Data refer to the state of Nuevo Leon only.

SOURCES

Column 1: Determined on the basis of HPI-2 values in column 2.

Column 2: calculated based on data in columns 3–6.

Column 3: UN (2009e).

Column 4: OECD and Statistics Canada (2005), unless otherwise specified.

Column 5: calculated on the basis of data on long-term unemployment and labour force from OECD (2009c).

Column 6: LIS (2009).

Column 7: calculated based on data in columns 1 and 6.

TABLE

Gender-related development index and its components

J

HDI rank	Gender-related development index (GDI) 2007			Life expectancy at birth (years) 2007		Adult literacy rate[a] (% aged 15 and above) 1999–2007		Combined gross enrolment ratio in education[b] (%) 2007		Estimated earned income[c] (PPP US$) 2007		HDI rank minus GDI rank[d]
	Rank	Value	as a % of HDI value	Female	Male	Female	Male	Female	Male	Female	Male	
VERY HIGH HUMAN DEVELOPMENT												
1 Norway	2	0.961	98.9	82.7	78.2	..[e]	..[e]	102.7[f,g]	94.7[f,g]	46,576[g]	60,394[g]	-1
2 Australia	1	0.966	99.6	83.7	79.1	..[e]	..[e]	115.7[f,g]	112.8[f,g]	28,759[g]	41,153[g]	1
3 Iceland	3	0.959	99.0	83.3	80.2	..[e]	..[e]	102.1[f,g]	90.1[f,g]	27,460[g]	43,959[g]	0
4 Canada	4	0.959	99.2	82.9	78.2	..[e]	..[e]	101.0[f,g,h]	97.6[f,g,h]	28,315[g,i]	43,456[g,i]	0
5 Ireland	10	0.948	98.2	82.0	77.3	..[e]	..[e]	99.1[f]	96.2[f]	31,978[g,i]	57,320[g,i]	-5
6 Netherlands	7	0.954	98.9	81.9	77.6	..[e]	..[e]	97.1[f]	97.9[f]	31,048	46,509	-1
7 Sweden	5	0.956	99.3	83.0	78.6	..[e]	..[e]	99.0[f]	89.8[f]	29,476[g,i]	44,071[g,i]	2
8 France	6	0.956	99.4	84.5	77.4	..[e]	..[e]	97.4[f]	93.5[f]	25,677[g]	42,091[g]	2
9 Switzerland	13	0.946	98.5	84.1	79.2	..[e]	..[e]	81.4[f]	84.0[f]	31,442[g]	50,346[g]	-4
10 Japan	14	0.945	98.4	86.2	79.0	..[e]	..[e]	85.4[f]	87.7[f]	21,143[g]	46,706[g]	-4
11 Luxembourg	16	0.943	98.2	82.0	76.5	..[e]	..[e]	94.7[j]	94.0[j]	57,676[g,i]	101,855[g,i]	-5
12 Finland	8	0.954	99.5	82.8	76.0	..[e]	..[e]	105.1[f,g]	97.9[f,g]	29,160[g]	40,126[g]	4
13 United States	19	0.942	98.5	81.3	76.7	..[e]	..[e]	96.9[f]	88.1[f]	34,996[g,i]	56,536[g,i]	-6
14 Austria	23	0.930	97.4	82.5	77.0	..[e]	..[e]	92.1[f]	89.0[f]	21,380[g]	54,037[g]	-9
15 Spain	9	0.949	99.4	84.0	77.5	97.3	98.6	99.9[f]	93.3[f]	21,817[g,i]	41,597[g,i]	6
16 Denmark	12	0.947	99.2	80.5	75.9	..[e]	..[e]	105.3[f,g]	97.6[f,g]	30,745[g]	41,630[g]	4
17 Belgium	11	0.948	99.4	82.4	76.5	..[e]	..[e]	95.9[f]	92.8[f]	27,333[g]	42,866[g]	6
18 Italy	15	0.945	99.3	84.0	78.1	98.6	99.1	94.7[f]	89.1[f]	20,152[g,i]	41,158[g,i]	3
19 Liechtenstein	..	..	..	..[k]	..[k]	..[e]	..[e]	79.6[f,l]	94.0[f,l]	..	..	..
20 New Zealand	18	0.943	99.3	82.1	78.1	..[e]	..[e]	113.4[f,g]	102.0[f,g]	22,456	32,375	1
21 United Kingdom	17	0.943	99.5	81.5	77.1	..[e]	..[e]	92.8[f,h]	85.9[f,h]	28,421[g]	42,133[g]	3
22 Germany	20	0.939	99.2	82.3	77.0	..[e]	..[e]	87.5	88.6	25,691[g,i]	43,515[g,i]	1
23 Singapore	..	..	..	82.6	77.8	91.6	97.3	..	..	34,554[g,i]	64,656[g,i]	..
24 Hong Kong, China (SAR)	22	0.934	98.9	85.1	79.3	..[m]	..[m]	73.4[f]	75.4[f]	35,827[g]	49,324[g]	0
25 Greece	21	0.936	99.4	81.3	76.9	96.0	98.2	103.2[f,g]	100.1[f,g]	19,218[i]	38,002[i]	2
26 Korea (Republic of)	25	0.926	98.8	82.4	75.8	..[e]	..[e]	90.6[f,g]	105.8[f,g]	16,931[i]	32,668[i]	-1
27 Israel	26	0.921	98.5	82.7	78.5	88.7[f]	95.0[f]	92.1[f]	87.8[f]	20,599[i]	32,148[i]	-1
28 Andorra	..	..	..	..[k]	..[k]	..[e]	..[e]	66.3[f,h]	64.0[f,g]	..	..	..
29 Slovenia	24	0.927	99.7	81.7	74.4	99.6	99.7	98.1[f]	87.7[f]	20,427[i]	33,398[i]	2
30 Brunei Darussalam	29	0.906	98.5	79.6	74.9	93.1	96.5	79.1	76.5	36,838[g,i]	62,631[g,i]	-2
31 Kuwait	34	0.892	97.4	79.8	76.0	93.1	95.2	77.8[f]	67.8[f]	24,722[f,g,i]	68,673[f,g,i]	-6
32 Cyprus	27	0.911	99.7	81.9	77.3	96.6	99.0	77.8[f,l]	77.3[f,l]	18,307	31,625	2
33 Qatar	35	0.891	97.9	76.8	74.8	90.4	93.8	87.7	74.2	24,584[g,i]	88,264[g,i]	-5
34 Portugal	28	0.907	99.7	81.8	75.3	93.3	96.6	91.6[f]	86.2[f]	17,154	28,762	3
35 United Arab Emirates	38	0.878	97.2	78.7	76.6	91.5	89.5	78.7[h]	65.4[h]	18,361[g,i]	67,556[g,i]	-6
36 Czech Republic	31	0.900	99.7	79.4	73.2	..[e]	..[e]	85.1[f]	81.9[f]	17,706[i]	30,909[i]	2
37 Barbados	30	0.900	99.7	79.7	74.0	..[g,m]	..[g,m]	100.2[g]	85.8[g]	14,735[f,i]	22,830[f,i]	4
38 Malta	32	0.895	99.3	81.3	77.7	93.5[f]	91.2[f]	81.7[f]	81.0[f]	14,458	31,812	3
HIGH HUMAN DEVELOPMENT												
39 Bahrain	33	0.895	99.9	77.4	74.2	86.4	90.4	95.3[f,h]	85.8[f,h]	19,873[f]	39,060[f]	3
40 Estonia	36	0.882	99.8	78.3	67.3	99.8[g]	99.8[g]	98.2[f]	84.6[f]	16,256[i]	25,169[i]	1
41 Poland	39	0.877	99.6	79.7	71.3	99.0	99.6	91.4[f]	84.2[f]	11,957[i]	20,292[i]	-1
42 Slovakia	40	0.877	99.7	78.5	70.7	..[e]	..[e]	83.1[f]	77.9[f]	14,790[i]	25,684[i]	-1
43 Hungary	37	0.879	99.9	77.3	69.2	98.8	99.0	94.0[f]	86.6[f]	16,143	21,625	3
44 Chile	41	0.871	99.2	81.6	75.5	96.5	96.6	82.0[f,h]	83.0[f,h]	8,188[i]	19,694[i]	0
45 Croatia	43	0.869	99.7	79.4	72.6	98.0	99.5	79.4[f]	75.2[f]	12,934	19,360	-1
46 Lithuania	42	0.869	99.9	77.7	65.9	99.7	99.7	97.6[f]	87.2[f]	14,633	20,944	1
47 Antigua and Barbuda	..	..	..	..[k]	..[k]	99.4	98.4	..	..	..	..	..
48 Latvia	44	0.865	99.8	77.1	67.1	99.8[g]	99.8[g]	97.5[f]	83.2[f]	13,403	19,860	0
49 Argentina	46	0.862	99.5	79.0	71.5	97.7	97.6	93.3[f]	84.0[f]	8,958[i]	17,710[i]	-1
50 Uruguay	45	0.862	99.7	79.8	72.6	98.2	97.4	96.3[f]	85.6[f]	7,994[i]	14,668[i]	1
51 Cuba	49	0.844	97.7	80.6	76.5	99.8	99.8	110.7[g]	91.5[g]	4,132[f,i,n]	8,442[f,i,n]	-2
52 Bahamas	..	..	..	76.0	70.4	..[m]	..[m]	72.2[f,h]	71.4[f,h]	..	..	..
53 Mexico	48	0.847	99.2	78.5	73.6	91.4	94.4	79.0[f]	81.5[f]	8,375[i]	20,107[i]	0
54 Costa Rica	47	0.848	99.4	81.3	76.4	96.2	95.7	74.4[f,h]	71.6[f,h]	6,788	14,763	2
55 Libyan Arab Jamahiriya	54	0.830	98.0	76.8	71.6	78.4	94.5	98.5[f,h]	93.1[f,h]	5,590[i]	22,505[i]	-4
56 Oman	56	0.826	97.7	77.3	74.1	77.5	89.4	68.3	68.1	7,697[i]	32,797[i]	-5
57 Seychelles	..	..	..	..[k]	..[k]	92.3	91.4	83.6[f,l]	80.9[f,l]	..	..	..
58 Venezuela (Bolivarian Republic of)	55	0.827	97.9	76.7	70.7	94.9	95.4	75.7[f]	72.7[f]	7,924[i]	16,344[i]	-3
59 Saudi Arabia	60	0.816	96.7	75.1	70.8	79.4	89.1	78.0[f]	79.1[f]	5,987[i]	36,662[i]	-7

J

Gender-related development index and its components

HDI rank	Gender-related development index (GDI) 2007			Life expectancy at birth (years) 2007		Adult literacy rate[a] (% aged 15 and above) 1999–2007		Combined gross enrolment ratio in education[b] (%) 2007		Estimated earned income[c] (PPP US$) 2007		HDI rank minus GDI rank[d]
	Rank	Value	as a % of HDI value	Female	Male	Female	Male	Female	Male	Female	Male	
60 Panama	51	0.838	99.7	78.2	73.0	92.8	94.0	83.5[f]	76.1[f]	8,331	14,397	3
61 Bulgaria	50	0.839	99.9	76.7	69.6	97.9	98.6	82.9[f]	81.8[f]	9,132	13,439	5
62 Saint Kitts and Nevis	..	..	..	..[k]	..[k]	..	..	74.1[f]	72.1[f]	..	..	..
63 Romania	52	0.836	99.9	76.1	69.0	96.9	98.3	81.7f	76.7[f]	10,053	14,808	4
64 Trinidad and Tobago	53	0.833	99.5	72.8	65.6	98.3	99.1	62.2[f,h]	59.9[f,h]	16,686[i]	30,554[i]	4
65 Montenegro	..	..	..	76.5	71.6	94.1[f,o]	98.9[f,o]	..	..	8,611[i,p]	14,951[i,p]	..
66 Malaysia	58	0.823	99.2	76.6	71.9	89.6	94.2	73.1[f]	69.8[f]	7,972[i]	18,886[i]	0
67 Serbia	..	..	..	76.3	71.6	94.1[f,o]	98.9[f,o]	..	..	7,654[i,p]	12,900[i,p]	..
68 Belarus	57	0.824	99.8	75.2	63.1	99.7[g]	99.8[g]	93.8	87.1	8,482	13,543	2
69 Saint Lucia	..	..	..	75.5	71.7	..	..	80.6	73.8	6,599[i]	13,084[i]	..
70 Albania	61	0.814	99.5	79.8	73.4	98.8[g]	99.3[g]	67.6[f]	68.0[f]	4,954[i]	9,143[i]	-1
71 Russian Federation	59	0.816	99.9	72.9	59.9	99.4	99.7	86.1[f]	78.0[f]	11,675[i]	18,171[i]	2
72 Macedonia (the Former Yugoslav Rep. of)	62	0.812	99.4	76.5	71.7	95.4	98.6	71.1[f]	69.1[f]	5,956[i]	12,247[i]	0
73 Dominica	..	..	..	..[k]	..[k]	..	..	82.7[f,h]	74.5[f,h]	..	..	..
74 Grenada	..	..	..	76.7	73.7	..	..	73.8[f,h]	72.4[f,h]	..	..	..
75 Brazil	63	0.810	99.7	75.9	68.6	90.2	89.8	89.4[f]	85.1[f]	7,190	12,006	0
76 Bosnia and Herzegovina	..	..	..	77.7	72.4	94.4	99.0	..	..	5,910[i]	9,721[i]	..
77 Colombia	64	0.806	99.9	76.5	69.1	92.8	92.4	80.9	77.2	7,138	10,080	0
78 Peru	65	0.804	99.7	75.8	70.4	84.6	94.9	89.9[f,h]	86.4[f,h]	5,828[i]	9,835[i]	0
79 Turkey	70	0.788	97.7	74.2	69.4	81.3	96.2	66.3[f,h]	75.7[f,h]	5,352[i]	20,441[i]	-4
80 Ecuador	..	..	..	78.0	72.1	89.7	92.3	..	..	4,996[i]	9,888[i]	..
81 Mauritius	67	0.797	99.1	75.7	68.5	84.7	90.2	75.7[f,h]	78.0[f,h]	6,686[i]	15,972[i]	0
82 Kazakhstan	66	0.803	99.8	71.2	59.1	99.5	99.8	95.1	87.8	8,831[i]	13,080[i]	2
83 Lebanon	71	0.784	97.7	74.1	69.8	86.0	93.4	80.3	75.7	4,062[i]	16,404[i]	-2
MEDIUM HUMAN DEVELOPMENT												
84 Armenia	68	0.794	99.5	76.7	70.1	99.3	99.7	77.8	71.6	4,215	7,386	2
85 Ukraine	69	0.793	99.7	73.8	62.7	99.6	99.8	93.2[i]	87.0[i]	5,249	8,854	2
86 Azerbaijan	73	0.779	99.0	72.3	67.6	99.2[g]	99.8[g]	..	..	4,836	11,037	-1
87 Thailand	72	0.782	99.8	72.1	65.4	92.6	95.9	79.6[f,h]	76.6[f,h]	6,341[i]	10,018[i]	1
88 Iran (Islamic Republic of)	76	0.770	98.4	72.5	69.9	77.2	87.3	73.0[f,h]	73.4[f,h]	5,304[i]	16,449[i]	-2
89 Georgia	..	..	..	75.0	68.1	..	..	77.7[h]	75.8[h]	2,639	6,921	..
90 Dominican Republic	74	0.775	99.7	75.2	69.8	89.5	88.8	76.7[f]	70.4[f]	4,985[i]	8,416[i]	1
91 Saint Vincent and the Grenadines	..	..	..	73.6	69.4	..	..	70.3[f]	67.6[f]	5,180[i]	10,219[i]	..
92 China	75	0.770	99.8	74.7	71.3	90.0	96.5	68.5[f]	68.9[f]	4,323[i]	6,375[i]	1
93 Belize	..	..	..	78.0	74.2	..	..	79.2[f,h]	77.4[f,h]	4,021	9,398	..
94 Samoa	80	0.763	99.0	74.7	68.4	98.4	98.9	76.3[f,h]	72.0[f,h]	2,525[i]	6,258[i]	-3
95 Maldives	77	0.767	99.5	72.7	69.7	97.1	97.0	71.4[f,h]	71.3[f,h]	3,597[i]	6,714[i]	1
96 Jordan	87	0.743	96.5	74.3	70.7	87.0	95.2	79.9[f]	77.5[f]	1,543	8,065	-8
97 Suriname	79	0.763	99.3	72.5	65.3	88.1	92.7	79.3[f,h]	69.4[f,h]	4,794[i]	10,825[i]	1
98 Tunisia	84	0.752	97.8	76.0	71.8	69.0	86.4	78.9[f,h]	73.6[f,h]	3,249[i]	11,731[i]	-3
99 Tonga	78	0.765	99.6	74.6	69.0	99.3	99.2	78.8[f,h]	77.2[f,h]	2,705[i]	4,752[i]	4
100 Jamaica	81	0.762	99.5	75.1	68.3	91.1	80.5	82.0[f,h]	74.3[f,h]	4,469[i]	7,734[i]	2
101 Paraguay	82	0.759	99.8	73.8	69.6	93.5	95.7	72.2[f,h]	72.1[f,h]	3,439[i]	5,405[i]	2
102 Sri Lanka	83	0.756	99.6	77.9	70.3	89.1	92.7	69.9[f,h]	67.5[f,h]	3,064	5,450	2
103 Gabon	85	0.748	99.1	61.5	58.7	82.2	90.2	75.0[f]	79.8[f]	11,221[i]	19,124[i]	1
104 Algeria	88	0.742	98.4	73.6	70.8	66.4	84.3	74.5[f,h]	72.8[f,h]	4,081[i]	11,331[i]	-1
105 Philippines	86	0.748	99.6	73.9	69.4	93.7	93.1	81.6[f]	77.8[f]	2,506[i]	4,293[i]	2
106 El Salvador	89	0.740	99.0	75.9	66.4	79.7	84.9	74.8	73.3	3,675[i]	8,016[i]	0
107 Syrian Arab Republic	98	0.715	96.4	76.0	72.2	76.5	89.7	63.9[f,h]	67.5[f,h]	1,512[i]	7,452[i]	-8
108 Fiji	90	0.732	98.7	71.0	66.5	..[m]	..[m]	73.2[f,h]	70.0[f,h]	2,349[i]	6,200[i]	1
109 Turkmenistan	..	..	..	68.8	60.6	99.3	99.7	..	..	3,594[i]	5,545[i]	..
110 Occupied Palestinian Territories	..	..	..	74.9	71.7	90.3	97.2	80.8	75.9	..	..	..
111 Indonesia	93	0.726	99.0	72.5	68.5	88.8	95.2	66.8[f,h]	69.5[f,h]	2,263[i]	5,163[i]	-1
112 Honduras	95	0.721	98.4	74.4	69.6	83.5	83.7	78.3[f,h]	71.3[f,h]	1,951[i]	5,668[i]	-2
113 Bolivia	91	0.728	99.8	67.5	63.3	86.0	96.0	83.6[f]	89.7[f]	3,198[i]	5,222[i]	3
114 Guyana	96	0.721	98.9	69.6	63.7	..[g,m]	..[g,m]	83.0	84.7	1,607[i]	3,919[i]	-1
115 Mongolia	92	0.727	100.0	69.6	63.0	97.7	96.8	84.9	73.7	3,019	3,454	4
116 Viet Nam	94	0.723	99.7	76.1	72.3	86.9	93.9	60.7[f,h]	63.9[f,h]	2,131[i]	3,069[i]	3
117 Moldova	97	0.719	99.8	72.1	64.5	98.9	99.6	74.6[i]	68.6[i]	2,173[i]	2,964[i]	1
118 Equatorial Guinea	102	0.700	97.3	51.1	48.7	80.5	93.4	55.8[f]	68.2[f]	16,161[i]	45,418[i]	-3

HDI rank	Gender-related development index (GDI) 2007			Life expectancy at birth (years) 2007		Adult literacy rate[a] (% aged 15 and above) 1999–2007		Combined gross enrolment ratio in education[b] (%) 2007		Estimated earned income[c] (PPP US$) 2007		HDI rank minus GDI rank[d]
	Rank	Value	as a % of HDI value	Female	Male	Female	Male	Female	Male	Female	Male	
119 Uzbekistan	99	0.708	99.7	70.9	64.5	95.8	98.0	71.4	74.0	1,891[i]	2,964[i]	1
120 Kyrgyzstan	100	0.705	99.4	71.4	63.9	99.1	99.5	79.7	74.9	1,428[i]	2,600[i]	1
121 Cape Verde	101	0.701	98.9	73.5	68.2	78.8	89.4	69.7	66.6	2,015[i]	4,152[i]	1
122 Guatemala	103	0.696	98.9	73.7	66.7	68.0	79.0	67.8	73.2	2,735[i]	6,479[i]	0
123 Egypt	..	..	..	71.7	68.2	57.8	74.6	..	..	2,286	8,401	..
124 Nicaragua	106	0.686	98.2	75.9	69.8	77.9	78.1	72.7[f,h]	71.5[f,h]	1,293[i]	3,854[i]	-2
125 Botswana	105	0.689	99.3	53.3	53.2	82.9	82.8	71.3[f,h]	70.0[f,h]	9,961[i]	17,307[i]	0
126 Vanuatu	104	0.692	99.9	72.0	68.1	76.1	80.0	60.3[f,h]	64.2[f,h]	2,970[i]	4,332[i]	2
127 Tajikistan	107	0.686	99.6	69.3	63.7	99.5	99.8	64.6	77.2	1,385[i]	2,126[i]	0
128 Namibia	108	0.683	99.5	61.2	59.3	87.4	88.6	68.2[f]	66.3[f]	4,006[i]	6,339[i]	0
129 South Africa	109	0.680	99.6	53.2	49.8	87.2	88.9	77.3[f]	76.3[f]	7,328[i]	12,273[i]	0
130 Morocco	111	0.625	95.7	73.3	68.8	43.2	68.7	55.1[f,h]	64.0[f,h]	1,603[i]	6,694[i]	-1
131 Sao Tome and Principe	110	0.643	98.8	67.3	63.5	82.7	93.4	68.6	67.7	1,044[i]	2,243[i]	1
132 Bhutan	113	0.605	97.7	67.6	64.0	38.7	65.0	53.7[f,h]	54.6[f,h]	2,636[i]	6,817[i]	-1
133 Lao People's Democratic Republic	112	0.614	99.3	65.9	63.2	63.2	82.5	54.3[f]	64.8[f]	1,877[i]	2,455[i]	1
134 India	114	0.594	97.1	64.9	62.0	54.5	76.9	57.4[f]	64.3 f	1,304[i]	4,102[i]	0
135 Solomon Islands	..	..	..	66.7	64.9	..	..	47.8[f]	51.4[f]	1,146[i]	2,264[i]	..
136 Congo	115	0.594	98.8	54.4	52.5	71.8[f]	90.6[f]	55.2[f,h]	62.0[f,h]	2,385[i]	4,658[i]	0
137 Cambodia	116	0.588	99.2	62.3	58.6	67.7	85.8	54.8[h]	62.1[h]	1,465[i]	2,158[i]	0
138 Myanmar	..	..	..	63.4	59.0	86.4	93.9	..	..	640[i]	1,043[i]	..
139 Comoros	117	0.571	99.2	67.2	62.8	69.8	80.3	42.3[f,h]	50.4[f,h]	839[i]	1,446[i]	0
140 Yemen	122	0.538	93.6	64.1	60.9	40.5	77.0	42.3[f]	65.9[f]	921[i]	3,715[i]	-4
141 Pakistan	124	0.532	93.0	66.5	65.9	39.6	67.7	34.4[f]	43.9[f]	760[i]	4,135[i]	-5
142 Swaziland	118	0.568	99.3	44.8	45.7	78.3	80.9	58.4[f]	61.8[f]	3,994[i]	5,642[i]	2
143 Angola	..	..	..	48.5	44.6	54.2	82.9	..	..	4,212[i]	6,592[i]	..
144 Nepal	119	0.545	98.4	66.9	65.6	43.6	70.3	58.1[f,h]	63.4[f,h]	794[i]	1,309[i]	2
145 Madagascar	120	0.541	99.6	61.5	58.3	65.3	76.5	60.2	62.5	774	1,093	2
146 Bangladesh	123	0.536	98.7	66.7	64.7	48.0	58.7	52.5[f]	51.8[f]	830[i]	1,633[i]	0
147 Kenya	121	0.538	99.4	54.0	53.2	70.2	77.7	58.2[f,h]	61.0[f,h]	1,213[i]	1,874[i]	3
148 Papua New Guinea	..	..	..	63.0	58.7	53.4	62.1	..	..	1,775[i]	2,383[i]	..
149 Haiti	..	..	..	62.9	59.1	64.0 f	60.1 f	..	..	626[i]	1,695[i]	..
150 Sudan	127	0.516	97.0	59.4	56.3	51.8	71.1	37.6[f,h]	42.2[f,h]	1,039[i]	3,119[i]	-2
151 Tanzania (United Republic of)	125	0.527	99.4	55.8	54.2	65.9	79.0	56.2[h]	58.4[h]	1,025[i]	1,394[i]	1
152 Ghana	126	0.524	99.5	57.4	55.6	58.3	71.7	54.5[h]	58.3[h]	1,133[i]	1,531[i]	1
153 Cameroon	129	0.515	98.6	51.4	50.3	59.8	77.0	47.7[f]	56.7[f]	1,467[i]	2,791[i]	-1
154 Mauritania	128	0.516	99.1	58.5	54.7	48.3	63.3	50.5[f,j]	50.7[f,j]	1,405[i]	2,439[i]	1
155 Djibouti	130	0.514	98.8	56.5	53.7	..[m]	..[m]	21.9[f]	29.0[f]	1,496[i]	2,627[i]	0
156 Lesotho	132	0.509	99.1	45.5	43.9	90.3	73.7	62.3[f,h]	60.6[f,h]	1,315[i]	1,797[i]	-1
157 Uganda	131	0.509	99.2	52.4	51.4	65.5	81.8	61.6[f,h]	62.9[f,h]	861[i]	1,256[i]	1
158 Nigeria	133	0.499	97.7	48.2	47.2	64.1	80.1	48.1[f,h]	57.9[f,h]	1,163[i]	2,777[i]	0
LOW HUMAN DEVELOPMENT												
159 Togo	..	..	..	63.9	60.4	38.5	68.7	..	..	494[i]	1,088[i]	..
160 Malawi	134	0.490	99.4	53.4	51.3	64.6	79.2	61.7[f,h]	62.1[f,h]	646[i]	877[i]	0
161 Benin	135	0.477	97.0	62.1	59.8	27.9	53.1	44.5[f,h]	60.1[f,h]	892	1,726	0
162 Timor-Leste	..	..	..	61.5	59.8	..	..	62.1[f,h]	64.2[f,h]	493[i]	934[i]	..
163 Côte d'Ivoire	137	0.468	96.6	58.3	55.7	38.6	60.8	31.3[f,h]	43.7[f,h]	852[i]	2,500[i]	-1
164 Zambia	136	0.473	98.3	45.0	44.0	60.7	80.8	60.7[f,h]	66.0[f,h]	980[i]	1,740[i]	1
165 Eritrea	138	0.459	97.3	61.4	56.8	53.0	76.2	27.6[f,h]	39.1[f,h]	422[i]	839[i]	0
166 Senegal	140	0.457	98.5	56.9	53.9	33.0	52.3	39.0[f,h]	43.3[f,h]	1,178[i]	2,157[i]	-1
167 Rwanda	139	0.459	99.8	51.4	47.9	59.8	71.4	52.4[f]	52.0[f]	770[i]	970[i]	1
168 Gambia	141	0.452	99.1	57.3	54.1	..[m]	..[m]	47.2[f,h]	46.4[f,h]	951[i]	1,499[i]	0
169 Liberia	142	0.430	97.3	59.3	56.5	50.9	60.2	48.6[f]	66.5[f]	240[i]	484[i]	0
170 Guinea	143	0.425	97.7	59.3	55.3	18.1	42.6	41.5[f]	56.9[f]	919[i]	1,356[i]	0
171 Ethiopia	144	0.403	97.3	56.2	53.3	22.8	50.0	44.0[h]	54.0[h]	624[i]	936[i]	0
172 Mozambique	145	0.395	98.3	48.7	46.9	33.0	57.2	50.2[f,h]	59.4[f,h]	759[i]	848[i]	0
173 Guinea-Bissau	148	0.381	96.2	49.1	46.0	54.4	75.1	28.8[f,h]	44.5[f,h]	301[i]	658[i]	-2
174 Burundi	146	0.390	99.1	51.4	48.6	52.2	67.3	46.2[h]	51.8[h]	296[i]	387[i]	1
175 Chad	149	0.380	96.8	49.9	47.3	20.8	43.0	27.5[f,h]	45.5[f,h]	1,219[i]	1,739[i]	-1
176 Congo (Democratic Republic of the)	150	0.370	95.1	49.2	46.1	54.1	80.9	40.5[f]	55.9[f]	189[i]	410[i]	-1
177 Burkina Faso	147	0.383	98.4	54.0	51.4	21.6	36.7	29.2	36.3	895[i]	1,354[i]	3

Gender-related development index and its components

J

HDI rank	Gender-related development index (GDI) 2007			Life expectancy at birth (years) 2007		Adult literacy rate[a] (% aged 15 and above) 1999–2007		Combined gross enrolment ratio in education[b] (%) 2007		Estimated earned income[c] (PPP US$) 2007		HDI rank minus GDI rank[d]
	Rank	Value	as a % of HDI value	Female	Male	Female	Male	Female	Male	Female	Male	
178 Mali	153	0.353	95.2	48.8	47.4	18.2	34.9	37.5 [f,h]	51.0 [f,h]	672 [i]	1,517 [i]	-2
179 Central African Republic	151	0.354	95.8	48.2	45.1	33.5	64.8	22.9 [f,h]	34.4 [f,h]	535 [i]	900 [i]	1
180 Sierra Leone	152	0.354	97.1	48.5	46.0	26.8	50.0	37.6 [f,h]	51.7 [f,h]	577 [i]	783 [i]	1
181 Afghanistan	154	0.310	88.0	43.5	43.6	12.6	43.1	35.4 [f,h]	63.6 [f,h]	442 [f,i,q]	1,845 [f,i,q]	0
182 Niger	155	0.308	90.8	51.7	50.0	15.1	42.9	22.1	32.3	318 [i]	929 [i]	0
OTHER UN MEMBER STATES												
Iraq	..	..	..	71.8	64.2	64.2	84.1	52.1 [f,h]	68.5 [f,h]	..	..	..
Kiribati	..	..	..	.. [k]	.. [k]	..	..	77.9 [f,h]	73.8 [f,h]	..	..	..
Korea (Democratic People's Rep. of)	..	..	..	69.1	64.9	..	..	..	..	..	..	..
Marshall Islands	..	..	..	.. [k]	.. [k]	..	..	71.2 [f,h]	71.1 [f,h]	..	..	..
Micronesia (Federated States of)	..	..	..	69.2	67.6	..	..	..	..	..	..	..
Monaco	..	..	..	.. [k]	.. [k]	..	..	..	..	..	..	..
Nauru	..	..	..	.. [k]	.. [k]	..	..	56.1 [f,h]	54.0 [f,h]	..	..	..
Palau	..	..	..	.. [k]	.. [k]	90.5 [f]	93.3 [f]	91.2 [f,h]	82.4 [f,h]	..	..	..
San Marino	..	..	..	.. [k]	.. [k]	.. [e]	.. [e]	..	..	..	..	..
Somalia	..	..	..	51.2	48.3	..	..	..	..	..	..	..
Tuvalu	..	..	..	.. [k]	.. [k]	..	..	70.8 [f,h]	67.8 [f,h]	..	..	..
Zimbabwe	..	..	..	43.6	42.6	88.3	94.1	53.4 [f,h]	55.5 [f,h]	..	..	..

NOTES

a Data refer to national literacy estimates from censuses or surveys conducted between 1999 and 2007, unless otherwise specified. Due to differences in methodology and timeliness of underlying data, comparisons across countries and over time should be made with caution. For more details, see http://www.uis.unesco.org/.

b Data for some countries may refer to national or UNESCO Institute for Statistics estimates. For details, see http://www.uis.unesco.org/.

c Because of the lack of gender-disaggregated income data, female and male earned income are crudely estimated on the basis of data on the ratio of the female nonagricultural wage to the male nonagricultural wage, the female and male shares of the economically active population, the total female and male population and GDP per capita in PPP US$ (see http://hdr.undp.org/en/statistics/tn1). The wage ratios used in this calculation are based on data for the most recent year available between 1999 and 2007.

d The HDI ranks used in this calculation are recalculated for the countries with a GDI value. A positive figure indicates that the GDI rank is higher than the HDI rank; a negative figure, the opposite.

e For the purposes of calculating the HDI, a value of 99.0% was applied.

f Data refer to an earlier year than that specified.

g For the purpose of calculating the GDI, the female and male values appearing in this table were scaled downward to reflect the maximum values for adult literacy (99%), gross enrolment ratios (100%), and GDP per capita (40,000 (PPP US$)). For more details, see http://hdr.undp.org/en/statistics/tn1.

h UNESCO Institute for Statistics estimate.

i No wage data are available. For the purposes of calculating the estimated female and male earned income, a value of 0.75 was used for the ratio of the female nonagricultural wage to the male nonagricultural wage.

j Statec (2008). Data refer to nationals enrolled both in the country and abroad and thus differ from the standard definition.

k For the purposes of calculating the HDI unpublished estimates from UN (2009e) were used: Andorra 84.3 (for females) and 77.5 (for males), Antigua and Barbuda 74.6 and 69.7, Dominica 80.3 and 73.7, Liechtenstein 82.4 and 76.0, Saint Kitts and Nevis 74.6 and 69.8 and the Seychelles 77.7 and 68.4.

l National estimate from the UNESCO Institute for Statistics.

m In the absence of recent data, estimates for 2005 from UNESCO Institute for Statistics (2003), based on outdated census or survey information, were used and should be interpreted with caution: the Bahamas 96.7 (for females) and 95.0 (for males), Barbados 99.8 and 99.7, Djibouti 61.4 and 79.9, Fiji 92.9 and 95.9, the Gambia 35.4 and 49.9, Guyana 98.7 and 99.2 and Hong Kong, China (SAR) 91.4 and 97.3.

n Heston, Summers and Aten (2006). Data differ from the standard definition.

o Data refer to Serbia and Montenegro prior to its separation into two independent states in June 2006. Data exclude Kosovo.

p Earned income is estimated using data on the economic activity rate for Serbia and Montenegro prior to its separation into two independent states in June 2006.

q Calculated on the basis of GDP in PPP US$ for 2006 from World Bank (2009d) and total population for the same year from UN (2009e).

SOURCES

Column 1: determined on the basis of the GDI values.

Column 2: calculated based on data in columns 4–11.

Column 3: calculated based on GDI and HDI values.

Columns 4 and 5: UN (2009e).

Columns 6 and 7: UNESCO Institute for Statistics (2009a.)

Columns 8 and 9: UNESCO Institute for Statistics (2009b).

Columns 10 and 11: calculated based on data on GDP (in PPP US$) and population from the World Bank (2009d), data on wages and economically active population from ILO (2009b).

Column 12: calculated based on recalculated HDI ranks and GDI ranks in column 1.

GDI RANKS FOR 155 COUNTRIES AND AREAS

1 Australia	41 Chile	81 Jamaica	121 Kenya
2 Norway	42 Lithuania	82 Paraguay	122 Yemen
3 Iceland	43 Croatia	83 Sri Lanka	123 Bangladesh
4 Canada	44 Latvia	84 Tunisia	124 Pakistan
5 Sweden	45 Uruguay	85 Gabon	125 Tanzania (United Republic of)
6 France	46 Argentina	86 Philippines	126 Ghana
7 Netherlands	47 Costa Rica	87 Jordan	127 Sudan
8 Finland	48 Mexico	88 Algeria	128 Mauritania
9 Spain	49 Cuba	89 El Salvador	129 Cameroon
10 Ireland	50 Bulgaria	90 Fiji	130 Djibouti
11 Belgium	51 Panama	91 Bolivia	131 Uganda
12 Denmark	52 Romania	92 Mongolia	132 Lesotho
13 Switzerland	53 Trinidad and Tobago	93 Indonesia	133 Nigeria
14 Japan	54 Libyan Arab Jamahiriya	94 Viet Nam	134 Malawi
15 Italy	55 Venezuela (Bolivarian Republic of)	95 Honduras	135 Benin
16 Luxembourg	56 Oman	96 Guyana	136 Zambia
17 United Kingdom	57 Belarus	97 Moldova	137 Côte d'Ivoire
18 New Zealand	58 Malaysia	98 Syrian Arab Republic	138 Eritrea
19 United States	59 Russian Federation	99 Uzbekistan	139 Rwanda
20 Germany	60 Saudi Arabia	100 Kyrgyzstan	140 Senegal
21 Greece	61 Albania	101 Cape Verde	141 Gambia
22 Hong Kong, China (SAR)	62 Macedonia (the Former Yugoslav Rep. of)	102 Equatorial Guinea	142 Liberia
23 Austria	63 Brazil	103 Guatemala	143 Guinea
24 Slovenia	64 Colombia	104 Vanuatu	144 Ethiopia
25 Korea (Republic of)	65 Peru	105 Botswana	145 Mozambique
26 Israel	66 Kazakhstan	106 Nicaragua	146 Burundi
27 Cyprus	67 Mauritius	107 Tajikistan	147 Burkina Faso
28 Portugal	68 Armenia	108 Namibia	148 Guinea-Bissau
29 Brunei Darussalam	69 Ukraine	109 South Africa	149 Chad
30 Barbados	70 Turkey	110 Sao Tome and Principe	150 Congo (Democratic Republic of the)
31 Czech Republic	71 Lebanon	111 Morocco	151 Central African Republic
32 Malta	72 Thailand	112 Lao People's Democratic Republic	152 Sierra Leone
33 Bahrain	73 Azerbaijan	113 Bhutan	153 Mali
34 Kuwait	74 Dominican Republic	114 India	154 Afghanistan
35 Qatar	75 China	115 Congo	155 Niger
36 Estonia	76 Iran (Islamic Republic of)	116 Cambodia	
37 Hungary	77 Maldives	117 Comoros	
38 United Arab Emirates	78 Tonga	118 Swaziland	
39 Poland	79 Suriname	119 Nepal	
40 Slovakia	80 Samoa	120 Madagascar	

TABLE

Gender empowerment measure and its components

K

HDI rank	Gender empowerment measure (GEM) Rank	Value	Seats in parliament held by women[a] (% of total)	Female legislators, senior officials and managers[b] (% of total)	Female professional and technical workers[b] (% of total)	Ratio of estimated female to male earned income[c]	Year women received right to[d] vote	stand for election	Year a woman became Presiding Officer of parliament or of one of its houses for the first time[e]	Women in ministerial positions[f] (% of total)
VERY HIGH HUMAN DEVELOPMENT										
1 Norway	2	0.906	36[g]	31	51	0.77	1913	1907, 1913	1993	56
2 Australia	7	0.870	30[g]	37	57	0.70	1902, 1962	1902, 1962	1987	24
3 Iceland	8	0.859	33[g]	30	56	0.62	1915, 1920	1915, 1920	1974	36
4 Canada	12	0.830	25[g]	37	56	0.65	1917, 1960	1920, 1960	1972	16
5 Ireland	22	0.722	15[g]	31	53	0.56	1918, 1928	1918, 1928	1982	21
6 Netherlands	5	0.882	39[g]	28	50	0.67	1919	1917	1998	33
7 Sweden	1	0.909	47[g]	32	51	0.67	1919, 1921	1919, 1921	1991	48
8 France	17	0.779	20[g]	38	48	0.61	1944	1944	..	47
9 Switzerland	13	0.822	27[g]	30	46	0.62	1971	1971	1977	43
10 Japan	57	0.567	12	9[h]	46[h]	0.45	1945, 1947	1945, 1947	1993	12
11 Luxembourg	..	..	23[g]	..	..	0.57	1919	1919	1989	14
12 Finland	3	0.902	42	29	55	0.73	1906	1906	1991	58
13 United States	18	0.767	17[g]	43	56	0.62	1920, 1965	1788[j]	2007	24
14 Austria	20	0.744	27[g]	27	48	0.40	1918	1918	1927	38
15 Spain	11	0.835	34[g]	32	49	0.52	1931	1931	1999	44
16 Denmark	4	0.896	38[g]	28	52	0.74	1915	1915	1950	37
17 Belgium	6	0.874	36[g]	32	49	0.64	1919, 1948	1921	2004	23
18 Italy	21	0.741	20[g]	34	47	0.49	1945	1945	1979	24
19 Liechtenstein	..	..	24	..	..	..	1984	1984	..	20
20 New Zealand	10	0.841	34	40	54	0.69	1893	1919	2005	32
21 United Kingdom	15	0.790	20[g]	34	47	0.67	1918, 1928	1918, 1928	1992	23
22 Germany	9	0.852	31[g]	38	50	0.59	1918	1918	1972	33
23 Singapore	16	0.786	24	31	45	0.53	1947	1947	..	0
24 Hong Kong, China (SAR)	..	..	..	30	42	0.73	..	..	..	..
25 Greece	28	0.677	15[g]	28	49	0.51	1952	1952	2004	12
26 Korea (Republic of)	61	0.554	14[g]	9	40	0.52	1948	1948	..	5
27 Israel	23	0.705	18[g]	30	52	0.64	1948	1948	2006	12
28 Andorra	..	..	25	..	..	..	1970	1973	..	38
29 Slovenia	34	0.641	10[g]	34	56	0.61	1946	1946	..	18
30 Brunei Darussalam	..	..	..	35[h]	37[h]	0.59	—	—	..	7
31 Kuwait	..	..	3	..	..	0.36	2005	2005	..	7
32 Cyprus	48	0.603	14[g]	15	48	0.58	1960	1960	..	18
33 Qatar	88	0.445	0	7	25	0.28	2003[k]	2003	..	8
34 Portugal	19	0.753	28[g]	32	51	0.60	1931, 1976	1931, 1976	..	13
35 United Arab Emirates	25	0.691	23	10	21	0.27	2006[l]	2006[l]	..	8
36 Czech Republic	31	0.664	16[g]	29	53	0.57	1920	1920	1998	13
37 Barbados	37	0.632	14	43	52	0.65	1950	1950	..	28
38 Malta	74	0.531	9[g]	19	41	0.45	1947	1947	1996	15
HIGH HUMAN DEVELOPMENT										
39 Bahrain	46	0.605	14	13[h]	19[h]	0.51	1973, 2002	1973, 2002	..	4
40 Estonia	30	0.665	21	34	69	0.65	1918	1918	2003	23
41 Poland	38	0.631	18[g]	36	60	0.59	1918	1918	1997	26
42 Slovakia	32	0.663	19[g]	31	58	0.58	1920	1920	..	13
43 Hungary	52	0.590	11[g]	35	60	0.75	1918, 1945	1918, 1945	1963	21
44 Chile	75	0.526	13[g]	23[h]	50[h]	0.42	1949	1949	2002	41
45 Croatia	44	0.618	21[g]	21	51	0.67	1945	1945	1993	24
46 Lithuania	40	0.628	18[g]	38	70	0.70	1919	1919	..	23
47 Antigua and Barbuda	..	..	17	45	55	..	1951	1951	1994	9
48 Latvia	33	0.648	20	41	66	0.67	1918	1918	1995	22
49 Argentina	24	0.699	40[g]	23	54	0.51	1947	1947	1973	23
50 Uruguay	63	0.551	12[g]	40	53	0.55	1932	1932	1963	29
51 Cuba	29	0.676	43	31[h]	60[h]	0.49	1934	1934	..	19
52 Bahamas	..	..	25	43	63	..	1961, 1964	1961, 1964	1997	8
53 Mexico	39	0.629	22[g]	31	42	0.42	1947	1953	1994	16
54 Costa Rica	27	0.685	37[g]	27	43	0.46	1949	1949	1986	29
55 Libyan Arab Jamahiriya	..	..	8	..	..	0.25	1964	1964	..	0
56 Oman	87	0.453	9	9	33	0.23	1994, 2003	1994, 2003	..	9
57 Seychelles	..	..	24	..	..	..	1948	1948	..	20
58 Venezuela (Bolivarian Republic of)	55	0.581	19[g]	27[h]	61[h]	0.48	1946	1946	1998	21
59 Saudi Arabia	106	0.299	0	10	29	0.16	—	—	..	0

HDI rank	Gender empowerment measure (GEM)		Seats in parliament held by women[a] (% of total)	Female legislators, senior officials and managers[b] (% of total)	Female professional and technical workers[b] (% of total)	Ratio of estimated female to male earned income[c]	Year women received right to[d]		Year a woman became Presiding Officer of parliament or of one of its houses for the first time[e]	Women in ministerial positions[f] (% of total)
	Rank	Value					vote	stand for election		
60 Panama	47	0.604	17[g]	44	52	0.58	1941, 1946	1941, 1946	1994	23
61 Bulgaria	45	0.613	22	31	61	0.68	1937, 1945	1945	..	24
62 Saint Kitts and Nevis	..	..	7	..	..	..	1951	1951	2004	..
63 Romania	77	0.512	10g	28	56	0.68	1929, 1946	1929, 1946	2008	0
64 Trinidad and Tobago	14	0.801	33[g]	43	53	0.55	1946	1946	1991	36
65 Montenegro	84	0.485	11	20	60	0.58	1946[m]	1946[m]	..	6
66 Malaysia	68	0.542	15	23	41	0.42	1957	1957	..	9
67 Serbia	42	0.621	22[g]	35	55	0.59	1946[m]	1946[m]	2008	17
68 Belarus	..	..	33	..	..	0.63	1918	1918	..	6
69 Saint Lucia	51	0.591	17	52	56	0.50	1951	1951	2007	..
70 Albania	..	..	7[g]	..	..	0.54	1920	1920	2005	7
71 Russian Federation	60	0.556	11	39	64	0.64	1918	1918	..	10
72 Macedonia (the Former Yugoslav Rep. of)	35	0.641	28[g]	29	53	0.49	1946	1946	..	14
73 Dominica	..	..	19	48	55	..	1951	1951	1980	21
74 Grenada	..	..	21	49	53	..	1951	1951	1990	50
75 Brazil	82	0.504	9[g]	35	53	0.60	1932	1932	..	11
76 Bosnia and Herzegovina	..	..	12[g]	..	..	0.61	1946	1946	2009	0
77 Colombia	80	0.508	10[g]	38[h]	50[h]	0.71	1954	1954	..	23
78 Peru	36	0.640	29[g]	29	47	0.59	1955	1955	1995	29
79 Turkey	101	0.379	9	8	33	0.26	1930	1930	..	4
80 Ecuador	41	0.622	28[g,n]	28	49	0.51	1929	1929	..	35
81 Mauritius	71	0.538	17	20	45	0.42	1956	1956	..	10
82 Kazakhstan	73	0.532	12[g]	38	67	0.68	1924, 1993	1924, 1993	..	6
83 Lebanon	..	..	5[g]	..	..	0.25	1952	1952	..	5
MEDIUM HUMAN DEVELOPMENT										
84 Armenia	93	0.412	8[g]	24	65	0.57	1918	1918	..	6
85 Ukraine	86	0.461	8	39	64	0.59	1919	1919	..	4
86 Azerbaijan	100	0.385	11	5	53	0.44	1918	1918	..	7
87 Thailand	76	0.514	13[g]	30	53	0.63	1932	1932	..	10
88 Iran (Islamic Republic of)	103	0.331	3	13	34	0.32	1963	1963	..	3
89 Georgia	95	0.408	6	34	62	0.38	1918, 1921	1918, 1921	2001	18
90 Dominican Republic	64	0.550	17[g]	31	51	0.59	1942	1942	1999	14
91 Saint Vincent and the Grenadines	..	..	18	..	..	0.51	1951	1951	..	21
92 China	72	0.533	21[g]	17	52	0.68	1949	1949	..	9
93 Belize	81	0.507	11	41	50	0.43	1954	1954	1984	18
94 Samoa	89	0.431	8	29	39	0.40	1948, 1990	1948, 1990	..	23
95 Maldives	90	0.429	12	14	49	0.54	1932	1932	..	14
96 Jordan	..	..	8[g]	..	..	0.19	1974	1974	..	15
97 Suriname	58	0.560	25	28[h]	23	0.44	1948	1948	1997	17
98 Tunisia	..	..	20[g]	..	..	0.28	1959	1959	..	7
99 Tonga	102	0.363	3[o]	27	43	0.57	1960	1960	..	..
100 Jamaica	..	..	14	..	..	0.58	1944	1944	1984	11
101 Paraguay	79	0.510	14[g]	35	50	0.64	1961	1961	..	19
102 Sri Lanka	98	0.389	6[g]	24	46	0.56	1931	1931	..	6
103 Gabon	..	..	17	..	..	0.59	1956	1956	2009	17
104 Algeria	105	0.315	6[g]	5	35	0.36	1962	1962	..	11
105 Philippines	59	0.560	20[g]	57	63	0.58	1937	1937	..	9
106 El Salvador	70	0.539	19[g]	29	48	0.46	1939	1961	1994	39
107 Syrian Arab Republic	..	..	12	..	40[h]	0.20	1949, 1953	1953	..	6
108 Fiji	..	..	..[p]	51[h]	9	0.38	1963	1963	..	8
109 Turkmenistan	..	..	..	..	..	0.65	1927	1927	2006	7
110 Occupied Palestinian Territories	..	..	..[g]	10	34	..	..	..	..	..
111 Indonesia	96	0.408	12[g]	14[h]	48[h]	0.44	1945, 2003	1945	..	11
112 Honduras	54	0.589	23[g]	41[h]	52[h]	0.34	1955	1955	..	..
113 Bolivia	78	0.511	15[g]	36	40	0.61	1938, 1952	1938, 1952	1979	24
114 Guyana	53	0.590	30[g]	25	59	0.41	1953	1945	..	26
115 Mongolia	94	0.410	4	48	54	0.87	1924	1924	..	20
116 Viet Nam	62	0.554	26	22	51	0.69	1946	1946	..	4
117 Moldova	66	0.547	22[g]	40	68	0.73	1924, 1993	1924, 1993	2001	11
118 Equatorial Guinea	..	..	6[g]	..	..	0.36	1963	1963	..	14

Gender empowerment measure and its components

HDI rank	Gender empowerment measure (GEM) Rank	Value	Seats in parliament held by women[a] (% of total)	Female legislators, senior officials and managers[b] (% of total)	Female professional and technical workers[b] (% of total)	Ratio of estimated female to male earned income[c]	Year women received right to[d] vote	stand for election	Year a woman became Presiding Officer of parliament or of one of its houses for the first time[e]	Women in ministerial positions[f] (% of total)
119 Uzbekistan	..	..	16[g]	..	..	0.64	1938	1938	2008	5
120 Kyrgyzstan	56	0.575	26[g]	35	62	0.55	1918	1918	..	19
121 Cape Verde	..	..	18	..	..	0.49	1975	1975	..	36
122 Guatemala	..	..	12[g]	..	..	0.42	1946	1946, 1965	1991	7
123 Egypt	107	0.287	4[g]	11	32	0.27	1956	1956	..	6
124 Nicaragua	67	0.542	18[g]	41	51	0.34	1950	1955	1990	33
125 Botswana	65	0.550	11[g]	33	51	0.58	1965	1965	..	28
126 Vanuatu	..	..	4	..	..	0.69	1975, 1980	1975, 1980	..	8
127 Tajikistan	..	..	20	..	..	0.65	1924	1924	..	6
128 Namibia	43	0.620	27[g]	36	52	0.63	1989	1989	..	25
129 South Africa	26	0.687	34[g,q]	34	55	0.60	1930, 1994	1930, 1994	1994	45
130 Morocco	104	0.318	6[g]	12	35	0.24	1959	1963	..	19
131 Sao Tome and Principe	..	..	7	..	..	0.47	1975	1975	1980	25
132 Bhutan	..	..	14	..	..	0.39	1953	1953	..	0
133 Lao People's Democratic Republic	..	..	25	..	..	0.76	1958	1958	..	11
134 India	..	..	9[g]	..	..	0.32	1935, 1950	1935, 1950	2009	10
135 Solomon Islands	..	..	0	..	..	0.51	1974	1974	..	0
136 Congo	..	..	9	..	..	0.51	1947, 1961	1963	..	13
137 Cambodia	91	0.427	16	14	41	0.68	1955	1955	..	7
138 Myanmar	..	..	..[r]	..	..	0.61	1935	1946	..	0
139 Comoros	..	..	3	..	..	0.58	1956	1956	..	..
140 Yemen	109	0.135	1	4	15	0.25	1967, 1970	1967, 1970	..	6
141 Pakistan	99	0.386	21[g]	3	25	0.18	1956	1956	2008	4
142 Swaziland	..	..	22	..	..	0.71	1968	1968	2006	19
143 Angola	..	..	37[g]	..	..	0.64	1975	1975	..	6
144 Nepal	83	0.486	33[g]	14	20	0.61	1951	1951	..	20
145 Madagascar	97	0.398	9	22	43	0.71	1959	1959	..	13
146 Bangladesh	108	0.264	6[g,s]	10[h]	22[h]	0.51	1935, 1972	1935, 1972	..	8
147 Kenya	..	..	10[g]	..	..	0.65	1919, 1963	1919, 1963	..	..
148 Papua New Guinea	..	..	1	..	..	0.74	1964	1963	..	4
149 Haiti	..	..	5[g]	..	..	0.37	1957	1957	..	11
150 Sudan	..	..	17[g]	..	..	0.33	1964	1964	..	6
151 Tanzania (United Republic of)	69	0.539	30[g]	16	38	0.74	1959	1959	..	21
152 Ghana	..	..[e]	8[g]	..	..	0.74	1954	1954	2009	16
153 Cameroon	..	..	14[g]	..	..	0.53	1946	1946	..	12
154 Mauritania	..	..	20[g]	..	..	0.58	1961	1961	..	12
155 Djibouti	..	..	14[g]	..	..	0.57	1946	1986	..	9
156 Lesotho	50	0.591	26[g]	52	58	0.73	1965	1965	2000	32
157 Uganda	49	0.591	31[g]	33	35	0.69	1962	1962	..	28
158 Nigeria	..	..	7	..	..	0.42	1958	1958	2007	23
LOW HUMAN DEVELOPMENT										
159 Togo	..	..	11	..	..	0.45	1945	1945	..	10
160 Malawi	..	..	13[g]	..	..	0.74	1961	1961	..	24
161 Benin	..	..	11	..	..	0.52	1956	1956	..	22
162 Timor-Leste	..	..	29[g]	..	..	0.53	..	..	..	25
163 Côte d'Ivoire	..	..	9[g]	..	..	0.34	1952	1952	..	13
164 Zambia	92	0.426	15	19[h]	31[h]	0.56	1962	1962	..	17
165 Eritrea	..	..	22[g]	..	..	0.50	1955[t]	1955[t]	..	18
166 Senegal	..	..	29[g]	..	..	0.55	1945	1945	..	18
167 Rwanda	..	..	51[g]	..	..	0.79	1961	1961	2008	17
168 Gambia	..	..	9	..	..	0.63	1960	1960	2006	28
169 Liberia	..	..	14[g]	..	..	0.50	1946	1946	2003	20
170 Guinea	..	..	..[u]	..	..	0.68	1958	1958	..	16
171 Ethiopia	85	0.464	21[g]	16	33	0.67	1955	1955	1995	10
172 Mozambique	..	..	35[g]	..	..	0.90	1975	1975	..	26
173 Guinea-Bissau	..	..	10	..	..	0.46	1977	1977	..	25
174 Burundi	..	..	32[g]	..	..	0.77	1961	1961	2005	30
175 Chad	..	..	5	..	..	0.70	1958	1958	..	17
176 Congo (Democratic Republic of the)	..	..	8	..	..	0.46	1967	1970	..	12
177 Burkina Faso	..	..	15[g]	..	..	0.66	1958	1958	..	14

HDI rank	Gender empowerment measure (GEM) Rank	Gender empowerment measure (GEM) Value	Seats in parliament held by women[a] (% of total)	Female legislators, senior officials and managers[b] (% of total)	Female professional and technical workers[b] (% of total)	Ratio of estimated female to male earned income[c]	Year women received right to[d] vote	Year women received right to[d] stand for election	Year a woman became Presiding Officer of parliament or of one of its houses for the first time[e]	Women in ministerial positions[f] (% of total)
178 Mali	..	..	10 [g]	..	..	0.44	1956	1956	..	23
179 Central African Republic	..	..	10	..	..	0.59	1986	1986	..	13
180 Sierra Leone	..	..	13 [g]	..	..	0.74	1961	1961	..	14
181 Afghanistan	..	..	26 [g]	..	..	0.24	1963	1963	..	4
182 Niger	..	..	12 [g]	..	..	0.34	1948	1948	..	26
OTHER UN MEMBER STATES										
Iraq	..	..	25 [g]	..	..	..	1980	1980	..	10
Kiribati	..	..	4	27 [h]	44 [h]	..	1967	1967	..	8
Korea (Democratic People's Rep. of)	..	..	20 [g]	..	..	..	1946	1946	..	0
Marshall Islands	..	..	3	19 [h]	36 [h]	..	1979	1979	..	10
Micronesia (Federated States of)	..	..	0	..	..	..	1979	1979	..	14
Monaco	..	..	25	..	..	..	1962	1962	..	0
Nauru	..	..	0	..	..	..	1968	1968	..	0
Palau	..	..	7	36 [h]	44 [h]	..	1979	1979	..	0
San Marino	..	..	15	19	52	..	1959	1973	1981	20
Somalia	..	..	.. [g]	..	..	..	1956	1956	..	..
Tuvalu	..	..	0	25	50	..	1967	1967	..	0
Zimbabwe	..	..	18 [g]	..	..	..	1919, 1957	1919, 1978	2005	16

NOTES

a Data are as of 28 February 2009, unless otherwise specified. Where there are lower and upper houses, data refer to the weighted average of women's shares of seats in both houses.

b Data refer to the most recent year available between 1999 and 2007. Estimates for countries that have implemented the International Standard Classification of Occupations (ISCO-88) are not strictly comparable with those for countries using the previous classification (ISCO-68).

c Calculated on the basis of data in columns 10 and 11 in Table J. Estimates are based on data for the most recent year available between 1996 and 2007. Following the methodology implemented in the calculation of the GDI, the income component of the GEM has been scaled downward for countries whose income exceeds the maximum goalpost GDP per capita value of 40,000 (PPP US$). For more details, For more details see http://hdr.undp.org/en/statistics/tn1

d Data refer to the year in which the right to vote or stand for national election on a universal and equal basis was recognized. Where two years are shown, the first refers to the first partial recognition of the right to vote or stand for election. In some countries, women were granted the right to vote or stand at local elections before obtaining these rights for national elections; however, data on local election rights are not included in this table.

e Date at which, for the first time in the country's parliamentary history, a woman became speaker/presiding officer of parliament or of one of its houses. As of May 2009, women occupy only 12.6% of the total number of 269 posts of Presiding Officers of parliament or of one of its houses.

f Data are as of January 2008. The total includes deputy prime ministers and ministers. Prime ministers were also included when they held ministerial portfolios. Vice-presidents and heads of governmental or public agencies are not included.

g Countries with established quota systems for women. Quota systems aim at ensuring that women constitute at least a 'critical minority' of 30 or 40 percent. Today women constitute 16 percent of the members of parliaments around the world.

h Data follow the ISCO-68 classification.

i The total refers to all voting members of the House.

j No information is available on the year all women received the right to stand for election. As the country's constitution does not mention gender with regard to this right.

k According to the new constitution approved in 2003, women are granted suffrage. To date, no legislative elections have been held.

l In December 2006, the Federal National Council was renewed. Men and women were entitled to vote, under similar conditions. One woman was elected to the Council and 7 subsequently appointed.

m Serbia and Montenegro separated into two independent states in June 2006. Women received the right to vote and to stand for elections in 1946, when Serbia and Montenegro were part of the former Yugoslavia.

n The 2008 Constitution provides that the National Congress shall be replaced by a 124-member National Assembly. Elections to that body are due to take place on 26 April 2009. During the transitional period, a Legislative and Oversight Commission, comprising the members of the Constituent Assembly, assumes the legislative and oversight functions. The date refers to the date when the Commission held its first session.

o No woman candidate was elected in the 2008 elections. One woman was appointed to the cabinet. As cabinet ministers also sit in parliament, there was one woman out of a total of 32 members in October 2008.

p The parliament was dissolved following a coup d'état in December 2006.

q The figures on the distribution of seats do not include the 36 special rotating delegates appointed on an ad hoc basis, and all percentages given are therefore calculated on the basis of the 54 permanent seats.

r The parliament elected in 1990 has never been convened nor authorized to sit, and many of its members were detained or forced into exile.

s Forty five seats reserved for women are yet to be filled.

t In November 1955, Eritrea was part of Ethiopia. The Constitution of sovereign Eritrea adopted on 23 May 1997 stipulates that "All Eritrean citizens, of eighteen years of age or more, shall have the right to vote".

u The parliament was dissolved following a coup d'état in December 2008.

SOURCES

Column 1: detemined on the basis of GEM values in column 2.

Column 2: calculated on the basis of data in columns 3–6; see Technical note 1 for details (http://hdr.undp.org/en/statistics/tn1).

Column 3: calculated on the basis of data on parliamentary seats from IPU (2009).

Column 4: calculated on the basis of occupational data from ILO (2009b).

Column 5: calculated on the basis of occupational data from ILO (2009b).

Column 6: calculated on the basis of data in columns 10 and 11 of table J.

Columns 7 and 8: IPU (2009).

Columns 9 and 10: IPU (2009).

K

Gender empowerment measure and its components

GEM RANKS FOR 109 COUNTRIES OR AREAS

1 Sweden	29 Cuba	57 Japan	85 Ethiopia
2 Norway	30 Estonia	58 Suriname	86 Ukraine
3 Finland	31 Czech Republic	59 Philippines	87 Oman
4 Denmark	32 Slovakia	60 Russian Federation	88 Qatar
5 Netherlands	33 Latvia	61 Korea (Republic of)	89 Samoa
6 Belgium	34 Slovenia	62 Viet Nam	90 Maldives
7 Australia	35 Macedonia (the Former Yugoslav Rep. of)	63 Uruguay	91 Cambodia
8 Iceland	36 Peru	64 Dominican Republic	92 Zambia
9 Germany	37 Barbados	65 Botswana	93 Armenia
10 New Zealand	38 Poland	66 Moldova	94 Mongolia
11 Spain	39 Mexico	67 Nicaragua	95 Georgia
12 Canada	40 Lithuania	68 Malaysia	96 Indonesia
13 Switzerland	41 Ecuador	69 Tanzania (United Republic of)	97 Madagascar
14 Trinidad and Tobago	42 Serbia	70 El Salvador	98 Sri Lanka
15 United Kingdom	43 Namibia	71 Mauritius	99 Pakistan
16 Singapore	44 Croatia	72 China	100 Azerbaijan
17 France	45 Bulgaria	73 Kazakhstan	101 Turkey
18 United States	46 Bahrain	74 Malta	102 Tonga
19 Portugal	47 Panama	75 Chile	103 Iran (Islamic Republic of)
20 Austria	48 Cyprus	76 Thailand	104 Morocco
21 Italy	49 Uganda	77 Romania	105 Algeria
22 Ireland	50 Lesotho	78 Bolivia	106 Saudi Arabia
23 Israel	51 Saint Lucia	79 Paraguay	107 Egypt
24 Argentina	52 Hungary	80 Colombia	108 Bangladesh
25 United Arab Emirates	53 Guyana	81 Belize	109 Yemen
26 South Africa	54 Honduras	82 Brazil	
27 Costa Rica	55 Venezuela (Bolivarian Republic of)	83 Nepal	
28 Greece	56 Kyrgyzstan	84 Montenegro	

Demographic trends

TABLE

L

L

	Total population (millions)			Rate of natural increase (%)		Net international migration rate (%)		Urban population[a] (% of total)		Child dependency ratio		Old age dependency ratio		Total fertility rate (births per woman)	
HDI rank	1990	2007	2020[b]	1990 to 1995	2005 to 2010	1990 to 1995	2005 to 2010	1990	2010	1990	2010	1990	2010	1990 to 1995	2005 to 2010
VERY HIGH HUMAN DEVELOPMENT															
1 Norway	4.2	4.7	5.2	0.4	0.4	0.2	0.6	72.0	77.6	29.3	28.4	25.2	22.7	1.9	1.9
2 Australia	17.1	20.9	23.7	0.7	0.6	0.4	0.5	85.4	89.1	32.9	28.1	16.8	20.7	1.9	1.8
3 Iceland	0.3	0.3	0.4	1.1	0.9	-0.1	1.3	90.8	92.3	38.7	29.8	16.5	17.4	2.2	2.1
4 Canada	27.7	32.9	37.1	0.7	0.3	0.5	0.6	76.6	80.6	30.4	23.5	16.6	20.3	1.7	1.6
5 Ireland	3.5	4.4	5.1	0.5	0.9	0.0	0.9	56.9	61.9	44.6	30.6	18.5	16.7	2.0	2.0
6 Netherlands	15.0	16.5	17.1	0.4	0.3	0.3	0.1	68.7	82.9	26.5	26.3	18.6	22.9	1.6	1.7
7 Sweden	8.6	9.2	9.7	0.3	0.2	0.3	0.3	83.1	84.7	27.9	25.3	27.7	28.1	2.0	1.9
8 France	56.8	61.7	64.9	0.3	0.4	0.1	0.2	74.1	77.8	30.5	28.4	21.6	26.2	1.7	1.9
9 Switzerland	6.7	7.5	7.9	0.3	0.1	0.7	0.3	73.2	73.6	24.9	22.4	21.3	25.5	1.5	1.5
10 Japan	123.2	127.4	123.7	0.3	-0.1	0.1	0.0	63.1	66.8	26.3	20.5	17.2	35.1	1.5	1.3
11 Luxembourg	0.4	0.5	0.5	0.3	0.3	1.1	0.8	80.9	82.2	25.1	25.7	19.4	20.5	1.7	1.7
12 Finland	5.0	5.3	5.5	0.3	0.2	0.2	0.2	61.4	63.9	28.7	25.0	19.9	25.9	1.8	1.8
13 United States	254.9	308.7	346.2	0.7	0.6	0.5	0.3	75.3	82.3	33.0	30.3	18.7	19.4	2.0	2.1
14 Austria	7.7	8.3	8.5	0.1	0.0	0.6	0.4	65.8	67.6	25.8	21.8	22.1	25.9	1.5	1.4
15 Spain	38.8	44.1	48.6	0.1	0.2	0.2	0.8	75.4	77.4	29.8	22.0	20.5	25.3	1.3	1.4
16 Denmark	5.1	5.4	5.6	0.1	0.1	0.2	0.1	84.8	87.2	25.3	27.6	23.2	25.6	1.7	1.8
17 Belgium	9.9	10.5	11.0	0.1	0.2	0.2	0.4	96.4	97.4	27.0	25.4	22.3	26.4	1.6	1.8
18 Italy	57.0	59.3	60.4	0.0	-0.1	0.1	0.6	66.7	68.4	24.0	21.7	22.2	31.3	1.3	1.4
19 Liechtenstein	0.0	0.0	0.0	..	..	..	..	16.9	14.2	..	..	..	..	..	..
20 New Zealand	3.4	4.2	4.7	0.9	0.7	0.8	0.2	84.7	86.8	35.1	30.3	16.9	19.4	2.1	2.0
21 United Kingdom	57.2	60.9	65.1	0.2	0.2	0.1	0.3	88.7	90.1	29.1	26.3	24.1	25.1	1.8	1.8
22 Germany	79.4	82.3	80.4	-0.1	-0.2	0.7	0.1	73.1	73.8	23.3	20.2	21.7	30.9	1.3	1.3
23 Singapore	3.0	4.5	5.2	1.3	0.3	1.5	2.2	100.0	100.0	29.4	21.0	7.7	13.8	1.8	1.3
24 Hong Kong, China (SAR)	5.7	6.9	7.7	0.7	0.2	1.0	0.3	99.5	100.0	30.7	15.3	12.1	17.0	1.3	1.0
25 Greece	10.2	11.1	11.3	0.1	-0.1	0.9	0.3	58.8	61.4	28.7	21.1	20.4	27.2	1.4	1.4
26 Korea (Republic of)	43.0	48.0	49.5	1.0	0.4	-0.3	0.0	73.8	81.9	36.9	22.3	7.2	15.2	1.7	1.2
27 Israel	4.5	6.9	8.3	1.5	1.5	2.0	0.2	90.4	91.7	52.5	44.4	15.2	16.4	2.9	2.8
28 Andorra	0.1	0.1	0.1	..	..	..	..	94.7	88.0	..	..	..	..	..	..
29 Slovenia	1.9	2.0	2.1	0.0	0.0	0.4	0.2	50.4	48.0	30.9	19.8	16.3	23.5	1.4	1.4
30 Brunei Darussalam	0.3	0.4	0.5	2.5	1.7	0.3	0.2	65.8	75.7	54.9	37.5	4.3	4.9	3.1	2.1
31 Kuwait	2.1	2.9	3.7	1.9	1.6	-6.2	0.8	98.0	98.4	58.9	31.3	1.9	3.2	3.2	2.2
32 Cyprus	0.7	0.9	1.0	1.0	0.4	0.4	0.6	66.8	70.3	40.8	25.2	17.3	19.0	2.4	1.5
33 Qatar	0.5	1.1	1.7	1.8	1.0	0.6	9.4	92.2	95.8	38.9	19.2	1.6	1.3	4.1	2.4
34 Portugal	10.0	10.6	10.8	0.1	0.0	0.0	0.4	47.9	60.7	30.8	22.7	20.3	26.7	1.5	1.4
35 United Arab Emirates	1.9	4.4	5.7	2.1	1.3	3.2	1.6	79.1	78.0	43.4	24.0	1.8	1.3	3.9	1.9
36 Czech Republic	10.3	10.3	10.6	0.0	0.0	0.0	0.4	75.2	73.5	32.4	19.9	19.0	21.6	1.7	1.4
37 Barbados	0.3	0.3	0.3	0.6	0.4	-0.8	-0.1	32.7	40.8	36.4	23.5	15.1	14.4	1.6	1.5
38 Malta	0.4	0.4	0.4	0.7	0.1	0.3	0.2	90.4	94.7	35.5	21.7	15.8	21.2	2.0	1.3
HIGH HUMAN DEVELOPMENT															
39 Bahrain	0.5	0.8	1.0	2.3	1.6	0.9	0.5	88.1	88.6	47.5	36.2	3.4	3.1	3.4	2.3
40 Estonia	1.6	1.3	1.3	-0.3	-0.1	-1.4	0.0	71.1	69.5	33.5	22.7	17.5	25.2	1.6	1.6
41 Poland	38.1	38.1	37.5	0.3	0.0	0.0	-0.1	61.3	61.2	38.8	20.6	15.5	18.8	1.9	1.3
42 Slovakia	5.3	5.4	5.4	0.4	0.0	0.0	0.1	56.5	56.8	39.2	20.9	16.0	16.9	1.9	1.3
43 Hungary	10.4	10.0	9.8	-0.3	-0.4	0.2	0.1	65.8	68.3	30.5	21.4	20.1	23.8	1.7	1.4
44 Chile	13.2	16.6	18.6	1.6	1.0	0.1	0.0	83.3	89.0	46.7	32.5	9.6	13.5	2.6	1.9
45 Croatia	4.5	4.4	4.3	0.0	-0.2	0.7	0.0	54.0	57.8	30.1	22.1	16.6	25.6	1.5	1.4
46 Lithuania	3.7	3.4	3.1	0.2	-0.4	-0.5	-0.6	67.6	67.2	33.9	21.2	16.4	23.7	1.8	1.3
47 Antigua and Barbuda	0.1	0.1	0.1	..	..	..	..	35.4	30.3	..	..	..	..	..	..
48 Latvia	2.7	2.3	2.2	-0.3	-0.4	-1.0	-0.1	69.3	68.2	32.1	20.1	17.7	25.4	1.6	1.4
49 Argentina	32.5	39.5	44.3	1.3	1.0	0.1	0.0	87.0	92.4	50.2	38.6	15.3	16.6	2.9	2.3
50 Uruguay	3.1	3.3	3.5	0.8	0.6	-0.1	-0.3	89.0	92.5	41.7	35.4	18.7	21.8	2.5	2.1
51 Cuba	10.6	11.2	11.2	0.8	0.4	-0.2	-0.3	73.4	75.7	32.8	24.6	12.7	17.5	1.7	1.5
52 Bahamas	0.3	0.3	0.4	1.8	1.1	0.1	0.1	79.8	84.1	51.9	36.8	7.0	10.3	2.6	2.0
53 Mexico	83.4	107.5	119.7	2.2	1.4	-0.3	-0.5	71.4	77.8	67.4	42.7	7.6	10.0	3.2	2.2
54 Costa Rica	3.1	4.5	5.2	2.1	1.3	0.4	0.1	50.7	64.3	60.6	37.1	8.4	9.5	2.9	2.0
55 Libyan Arab Jamahiriya	4.4	6.2	7.7	2.0	1.9	0.0	0.1	75.7	77.9	79.7	45.9	4.7	6.6	4.1	2.7
56 Oman	1.8	2.7	3.5	3.1	1.9	0.2	0.1	66.1	71.7	81.8	46.8	3.6	4.7	6.3	3.1
57 Seychelles	0.1	0.1	0.1	..	..	..	..	49.3	55.3	..	..	..	..	..	..
58 Venezuela (Bolivarian Republic of)	19.7	27.7	33.4	2.2	1.6	0.0	0.0	84.3	94.0	65.3	45.4	6.4	8.7	3.3	2.5
59 Saudi Arabia	16.3	24.7	31.6	2.9	2.0	-0.6	0.1	76.6	82.1	75.1	49.1	4.1	4.6	5.4	3.2

Demographic trends

L

HDI rank	Total population (millions)			Rate of natural increase (%)		Net international migration rate (%)		Urban population[a] (% of total)		Child dependency ratio		Old age dependency ratio		Total fertility rate (births per woman)	
	1990	2007	2020[b]	1990 to 1995	2005 to 2010	1990 to 1995	2005 to 2010	1990	2010	1990	2010	1990	2010	1990 to 1995	2005 to 2010
60 Panama	2.4	3.3	4.0	2.0	1.6	0.1	0.1	53.9	74.8	58.8	45.0	8.4	10.4	2.9	2.6
61 Bulgaria	8.8	7.6	7.0	-0.3	-0.5	-0.8	-0.1	66.4	71.7	30.5	19.6	19.7	25.5	1.5	1.4
62 Saint Kitts and Nevis	0.0	0.1	0.1	..	..	..	..	34.6	32.4	..	..	..	..	..	..
63 Romania	23.2	21.5	20.4	0.0	-0.2	-0.5	-0.2	53.2	54.6	35.7	21.8	15.8	21.3	1.5	1.3
64 Trinidad and Tobago	1.2	1.3	1.4	1.1	0.7	-0.4	-0.3	8.5	13.9	56.8	28.3	9.2	9.5	2.1	1.6
65 Montenegro	0.6	0.6	0.6	0.7	0.2	0.5	-0.2	48.0	59.5	40.2	28.3	12.7	18.8	1.8	1.6
66 Malaysia	18.1	26.6	32.0	2.3	1.6	0.3	0.1	49.8	72.2	63.5	44.0	6.2	7.3	3.5	2.6
67 Serbia	9.6	9.8	9.8	0.4	0.0	0.9	0.0	50.4	52.4	34.6	25.9	14.3	21.1	2.0	1.6
68 Belarus	10.3	9.7	9.1	0.0	-0.5	0.0	0.0	66.0	74.3	34.8	20.4	16.1	18.6	1.7	1.3
69 Saint Lucia	0.1	0.2	0.2	1.8	1.1	-0.6	-0.1	29.3	28.0	65.4	38.3	13.4	10.1	3.2	2.0
70 Albania	3.3	3.1	3.3	1.7	0.9	-2.6	-0.5	36.4	48.0	53.0	34.0	8.6	14.4	2.8	1.9
71 Russian Federation	148.1	141.9	135.4	-0.2	-0.4	0.3	0.3	73.4	72.8	34.3	20.8	15.1	17.9	1.5	1.4
72 Macedonia (the Former Yugoslav Rep. of)	1.9	2.0	2.0	0.8	0.2	-0.3	-0.1	57.8	67.9	39.4	25.0	11.2	16.9	2.1	1.4
73 Dominica	0.1	0.1	0.1	..	..	..	..	67.7	74.6	..	..	..	..	..	..
74 Grenada	0.1	0.1	0.1	1.7	1.3	-0.9	-1.0	32.2	31.0	73.2	41.9	14.8	10.6	3.5	2.3
75 Brazil	149.6	190.1	209.1	1.6	1.0	0.0	0.0	74.8	86.5	58.5	37.7	7.4	10.2	2.6	1.9
76 Bosnia and Herzegovina	4.3	3.8	3.7	0.3	-0.1	-5.4	-0.1	39.2	48.6	34.7	21.4	8.8	19.6	1.5	1.2
77 Colombia	33.2	44.4	52.3	2.0	1.5	-0.1	-0.1	68.3	75.1	61.8	43.8	7.2	8.6	3.0	2.5
78 Peru	21.8	28.5	32.9	2.2	1.6	-0.3	-0.4	68.9	71.6	66.3	46.7	6.9	9.3	3.6	2.6
79 Turkey	56.1	73.0	83.9	1.8	1.2	0.0	0.0	59.2	69.6	60.5	39.0	6.8	8.8	2.9	2.1
80 Ecuador	10.3	13.3	15.4	2.2	1.6	-0.1	-0.5	55.1	66.9	68.5	48.8	7.4	10.6	3.4	2.6
81 Mauritius	1.1	1.3	1.4	1.5	0.7	-0.1	-0.1	43.9	42.6	43.7	31.5	7.1	10.7	2.3	1.8
82 Kazakhstan	16.5	15.4	16.7	1.1	0.9	-1.9	-0.1	56.3	58.5	50.2	34.5	9.3	10.0	2.6	2.3
83 Lebanon	3.0	4.2	4.6	1.8	0.9	1.4	-0.1	83.1	87.2	60.5	36.4	8.8	10.8	3.0	1.9
MEDIUM HUMAN DEVELOPMENT															
84 Armenia	3.5	3.1	3.2	1.1	0.7	-3.0	-0.5	67.5	63.7	47.4	29.4	8.8	16.1	2.4	1.7
85 Ukraine	51.6	46.3	42.9	-0.2	-0.6	0.0	0.0	66.8	68.1	32.3	19.7	18.3	22.1	1.6	1.3
86 Azerbaijan	7.2	8.6	9.8	1.8	1.2	-0.3	-0.1	53.7	52.2	55.7	34.4	6.9	9.5	2.9	2.2
87 Thailand	56.7	67.0	71.4	1.2	0.6	0.0	0.1	29.4	34.0	45.9	30.3	7.1	10.9	2.1	1.8
88 Iran (Islamic Republic of)	56.7	72.4	83.7	2.2	1.3	-0.4	-0.1	56.3	69.5	86.7	33.4	6.2	6.8	4.0	1.8
89 Georgia	5.5	4.4	4.0	0.6	0.0	-2.1	-1.2	55.1	52.9	37.2	24.2	14.1	20.7	2.1	1.6
90 Dominican Republic	7.4	9.8	11.5	2.3	1.7	-0.3	-0.3	55.2	70.5	66.6	49.5	6.6	9.8	3.3	2.7
91 Saint Vincent and the Grenadines	0.1	0.1	0.1	1.7	1.0	-1.5	-0.9	40.6	47.8	67.9	39.7	11.0	10.0	2.9	2.1
92 China	1,142.1 [c]	1,329.1 [c]	1,431.2[c]	1.2	0.7	0.0	0.0	27.4	44.9	42.9	27.7	8.3	11.4	2.0	1.8
93 Belize	0.2	0.3	0.4	3.1	2.1	-0.1	-0.1	47.5	52.7	82.6	56.3	7.4	6.7	4.3	2.9
94 Samoa	0.2	0.2	0.2	2.4	1.8	-1.6	-1.8	21.2	23.4	74.0	68.6	7.1	8.6	4.7	4.0
95 Maldives	0.2	0.3	0.4	2.8	1.4	0.0	0.0	25.8	40.5	94.0	39.6	5.2	6.4	5.3	2.1
96 Jordan	3.3	5.9	7.5	2.9	2.2	2.7	0.8	72.2	78.5	93.6	54.4	6.3	5.9	5.1	3.1
97 Suriname	0.4	0.5	0.6	1.5	1.2	-0.2	-0.2	68.3	75.6	53.7	44.0	7.6	9.9	2.6	2.4
98 Tunisia	8.2	10.1	11.4	1.8	1.0	-0.1	0.0	57.9	67.3	66.5	32.4	8.0	9.6	3.1	1.9
99 Tonga	0.1	0.1	0.1	2.4	2.2	-1.8	-1.7	22.7	25.3	70.1	66.0	8.0	10.3	4.5	4.0
100 Jamaica	2.4	2.7	2.8	1.8	1.2	-0.9	-0.7	49.4	53.7	61.2	45.7	12.5	12.2	2.8	2.4
101 Paraguay	4.2	6.1	7.5	2.6	1.9	-0.1	-0.1	48.7	61.5	75.9	54.7	7.4	8.4	4.3	3.1
102 Sri Lanka	17.3	19.9	21.7	1.4	1.2	-0.3	-0.3	17.2	15.1	51.1	35.7	8.9	11.4	2.5	2.3
103 Gabon	0.9	1.4	1.8	2.7	1.8	0.4	0.1	69.1	86.0	77.9	59.2	10.6	7.2	5.1	3.4
104 Algeria	25.3	33.9	40.6	2.3	1.6	0.0	-0.1	52.1	66.5	80.6	39.5	6.8	6.8	4.1	2.4
105 Philippines	62.4	88.7	109.7	2.5	2.0	-0.3	-0.2	48.8	66.4	72.6	53.8	5.8	6.9	4.1	3.1
106 El Salvador	5.3	6.1	6.6	2.3	1.4	-0.9	-0.9	49.2	61.3	75.0	51.5	8.6	12.0	3.7	2.3
107 Syrian Arab Republic	12.7	20.5	26.5	2.9	2.5	-0.1	0.8	48.9	54.9	98.9	56.1	5.4	5.2	4.9	3.3
108 Fiji	0.7	0.8	0.9	2.1	1.5	-0.9	-0.8	41.6	53.4	64.1	48.2	5.3	7.7	3.4	2.8
109 Turkmenistan	3.7	5.0	5.8	2.4	1.4	0.3	-0.1	45.1	49.5	72.6	43.4	6.8	6.2	4.0	2.5
110 Occupied Palestinian Territories	2.2	4.0	5.8	3.9	3.2	0.0	0.0	67.9	72.1	93.6	84.6	6.8	5.5	6.5	5.1
111 Indonesia	177.4	224.7	254.2	1.6	1.2	-0.1	-0.1	30.6	53.7	59.3	39.7	6.3	9.0	2.9	2.2
112 Honduras	4.9	7.2	9.1	3.1	2.3	-0.5	-0.3	40.3	48.8	88.9	62.5	6.6	7.3	4.9	3.3
113 Bolivia	6.7	9.5	11.6	2.6	2.0	-0.3	-0.2	55.6	66.5	74.0	60.2	6.8	8.0	4.8	3.5
114 Guyana	0.7	0.8	0.7	1.6	1.0	-1.3	-1.0	29.5	28.5	62.1	45.0	7.8	9.5	2.6	2.3
115 Mongolia	2.2	2.6	3.0	2.0	1.2	-1.5	-0.1	57.0	57.5	76.8	36.4	7.4	5.8	3.5	2.0
116 Viet Nam	66.2	86.1	98.0	2.2	1.2	-0.2	0.0	20.3	28.8	70.6	36.6	8.4	9.3	3.3	2.1
117 Moldova	4.4	3.7	3.4	0.4	-0.1	-0.6	-0.9	46.8	41.2	43.8	23.0	13.0	15.4	2.1	1.5
118 Equatorial Guinea	0.4	0.6	0.9	2.8	2.3	0.7	0.3	34.7	39.7	68.4	72.2	7.6	5.1	5.9	5.4

TABLE

L

HDI rank	Total population (millions)			Rate of natural increase (%)		Net international migration rate (%)		Urban population[a] (% of total)		Child dependency ratio		Old age dependency ratio		Total fertility rate (births per woman)	
	1990	2007	2020[b]	1990 to 1995	2005 to 2010	1990 to 1995	2005 to 2010	1990	2010	1990	2010	1990	2010	1990 to 1995	2005 to 2010
119 Uzbekistan	20.5	26.9	31.2	2.5	1.4	-0.3	-0.3	40.1	36.9	74.3	42.7	7.3	6.6	3.9	2.3
120 Kyrgyzstan	4.4	5.3	6.2	2.1	1.5	-1.2	-0.3	37.8	36.6	65.4	44.1	8.7	7.7	3.6	2.6
121 Cape Verde	0.4	0.5	0.6	2.9	1.9	-0.5	-0.5	44.1	61.1	97.8	58.7	9.0	6.8	4.9	2.8
122 Guatemala	8.9	13.4	18.1	3.1	2.8	-0.8	-0.3	41.1	49.5	88.5	76.8	6.6	8.2	5.5	4.2
123 Egypt	57.8	80.1	98.6	2.2	1.9	-0.2	-0.1	43.5	42.8	78.4	50.8	6.9	7.3	3.9	2.9
124 Nicaragua	4.1	5.6	6.7	2.9	2.0	-0.5	-0.7	52.3	57.3	90.4	56.6	6.2	7.5	4.5	2.8
125 Botswana	1.4	1.9	2.2	2.5	1.3	0.2	0.2	41.9	61.1	85.9	52.1	5.0	6.1	4.3	2.9
126 Vanuatu	0.1	0.2	0.3	2.9	2.5	-0.1	0.0	18.7	25.6	83.7	65.4	6.8	5.7	4.8	4.0
127 Tajikistan	5.3	6.7	8.4	2.8	2.2	-1.1	-0.6	31.7	26.5	81.4	60.6	7.2	6.0	4.9	3.5
128 Namibia	1.4	2.1	2.6	2.9	1.9	-0.2	0.0	27.7	38.0	82.6	60.7	6.3	6.1	4.9	3.4
129 South Africa	36.7	49.2	52.7	1.9	0.7	0.5	0.3	52.0	61.7	67.2	46.6	5.5	7.1	3.3	2.6
130 Morocco	24.8	31.2	36.2	2.0	1.5	-0.3	-0.3	48.4	56.7	70.6	42.1	6.8	8.1	3.7	2.4
131 Sao Tome and Principe	0.1	0.2	0.2	2.8	2.5	-0.8	-0.9	43.6	62.2	95.2	72.2	8.9	6.9	5.2	3.9
132 Bhutan	0.5	0.7	0.8	2.3	1.4	-3.8	0.3	16.4	36.8	79.2	45.8	6.1	7.5	5.4	2.7
133 Lao People's Democratic Republic	4.2	6.1	7.7	2.8	2.1	-0.1	-0.2	15.4	33.2	82.7	61.9	6.7	6.1	5.8	3.5
134 India	862.2	1,164.7	1,367.2	2.0	1.4	0.0	0.0	25.5	30.1	64.9	47.9	6.6	7.7	3.9	2.8
135 Solomon Islands	0.3	0.5	0.7	2.9	2.5	0.0	0.0	13.7	18.6	87.6	66.4	5.8	5.4	5.5	3.9
136 Congo	2.4	3.6	4.7	2.7	2.2	-0.1	-0.3	54.3	62.1	84.1	71.8	7.2	6.8	5.2	4.4
137 Cambodia	9.7	14.3	17.7	2.9	1.6	0.3	0.0	12.6	22.8	84.8	51.0	5.2	5.6	5.5	3.0
138 Myanmar	40.8	49.1	55.5	1.5	1.1	-0.1	-0.2	24.9	33.9	62.6	39.1	8.4	8.1	3.1	2.3
139 Comoros	0.4	0.6	0.8	2.5	2.6	-0.1	-0.3	27.9	28.2	91.1	64.7	5.9	5.2	5.1	4.0
140 Yemen	12.3	22.3	31.6	3.7	3.0	0.9	-0.1	20.9	31.8	111.8	79.8	4.2	4.4	7.7	5.3
141 Pakistan	115.8	173.2	226.2	2.8	2.3	-0.4	-0.2	30.6	37.0	82.1	61.7	7.0	6.9	5.7	4.0
142 Swaziland	0.9	1.2	1.4	3.1	1.4	-0.8	-0.1	22.9	25.5	97.8	67.1	5.5	5.9	5.3	3.6
143 Angola	10.7	17.6	24.5	3.0	2.6	0.2	0.1	37.1	58.5	95.3	84.5	5.2	4.7	7.1	5.8
144 Nepal	19.1	28.3	35.3	2.6	1.9	-0.1	-0.1	8.9	18.2	78.1	59.8	5.9	6.8	4.9	2.9
145 Madagascar	11.3	18.6	25.7	3.0	2.7	0.0	0.0	23.6	30.2	85.7	78.0	6.1	5.6	6.1	4.8
146 Bangladesh	115.6	157.8	185.6	2.1	1.5	-0.1	-0.1	19.8	28.1	79.8	47.4	5.6	6.1	4.0	2.4
147 Kenya	23.4	37.8	52.0	3.0	2.7	0.2	-0.1	18.2	22.2	101.2	78.5	5.6	4.8	5.6	5.0
148 Papua New Guinea	4.1	6.4	8.5	2.6	2.4	0.0	0.0	15.0	12.5	74.4	68.0	3.9	4.3	4.7	4.1
149 Haiti	7.1	9.7	11.7	2.4	1.9	-0.4	-0.3	28.5	49.6	81.3	60.2	7.2	7.3	5.2	3.5
150 Sudan	27.1	40.4	52.3	2.7	2.1	-0.1	0.1	26.6	45.2	83.1	67.0	5.7	6.4	5.8	4.2
151 Tanzania (United Republic of)	25.5	41.3	59.6	2.8	3.0	0.4	-0.1	18.9	26.4	89.5	85.8	5.2	6.0	6.1	5.6
152 Ghana	15.0	22.9	29.6	2.8	2.1	0.0	0.0	36.4	51.5	83.4	65.5	5.7	6.3	5.3	4.3
153 Cameroon	12.2	18.7	24.3	2.8	2.3	0.0	0.0	40.7	58.4	88.7	73.2	7.0	6.4	5.7	4.7
154 Mauritania	2.0	3.1	4.1	2.8	2.3	-0.1	0.1	39.7	41.4	84.5	67.5	5.2	4.6	5.7	4.5
155 Djibouti	0.6	0.8	1.0	2.7	1.8	-0.5	0.0	75.7	88.1	82.1	58.2	4.5	5.4	5.9	3.9
156 Lesotho	1.6	2.0	2.2	2.5	1.2	-1.0	-0.4	14.0	26.9	88.6	67.9	8.5	8.4	4.7	3.4
157 Uganda	17.7	30.6	46.3	3.2	3.3	0.1	-0.1	11.1	13.3	97.7	99.9	5.5	5.2	7.1	6.4
158 Nigeria	97.3	147.7	193.3	2.5	2.4	0.0	0.0	35.3	49.8	89.2	77.7	5.7	5.8	6.4	5.3
LOW HUMAN DEVELOPMENT															
159 Togo	3.9	6.3	8.4	3.0	2.5	-0.6	0.0	30.1	43.4	90.2	69.5	6.1	6.3	6.0	4.3
160 Malawi	9.5	14.4	20.5	3.3	2.8	-1.9	0.0	11.6	19.8	92.4	90.1	5.3	6.1	6.8	5.6
161 Benin	4.8	8.4	12.2	3.1	3.0	0.4	0.1	34.5	42.0	89.4	79.7	7.0	6.1	6.6	5.5
162 Timor-Leste	0.7	1.1	1.6	2.7	3.1	0.0	0.2	20.8	28.1	68.7	85.4	3.5	5.8	5.7	6.5
163 Côte d'Ivoire	12.6	20.1	27.0	2.9	2.4	0.5	-0.1	39.7	50.1	85.1	72.6	5.2	7.0	5.9	4.6
164 Zambia	7.9	12.3	16.9	2.8	2.6	0.0	-0.1	39.4	35.7	88.6	91.0	5.4	6.0	6.3	5.9
165 Eritrea	3.2	4.8	6.7	2.6	2.9	-2.3	0.2	15.8	21.6	90.7	74.1	5.1	4.5	6.1	4.7
166 Senegal	7.5	11.9	16.2	3.0	2.8	-0.2	-0.2	39.0	42.9	92.3	79.8	4.9	4.4	6.5	5.0
167 Rwanda	7.2	9.5	13.2	-0.1	2.6	-5.3	0.0	5.4	18.9	102.1	76.8	5.4	4.5	6.2	5.4
168 Gambia	0.9	1.6	2.2	2.9	2.6	0.9	0.2	38.3	58.1	79.0	76.4	5.0	5.2	6.0	5.1
169 Liberia	2.2	3.6	5.3	2.9	2.8	-5.1	1.3	45.3	61.5	87.0	78.2	5.7	5.7	6.4	5.1
170 Guinea	6.1	9.6	13.5	2.9	2.9	1.0	-0.6	28.0	35.4	85.4	78.8	6.2	6.1	6.6	5.5
171 Ethiopia	48.3	78.6	108.0	3.0	2.7	0.3	-0.1	12.6	17.6	86.5	80.5	5.5	6.0	7.0	5.4
172 Mozambique	13.5	21.9	28.5	2.4	2.3	0.9	0.0	21.1	38.4	92.7	83.0	6.4	6.2	6.1	5.1
173 Guinea-Bissau	1.0	1.5	2.1	2.3	2.4	0.4	-0.2	28.1	30.0	74.7	79.0	6.5	6.4	5.9	5.7
174 Burundi	5.7	7.8	10.3	2.5	2.1	-0.8	0.8	6.3	11.0	87.9	63.9	6.0	4.7	6.5	4.7
175 Chad	6.1	10.6	14.9	3.1	2.9	0.0	-0.1	20.8	27.6	90.7	88.4	6.7	5.5	6.6	6.2
176 Congo (Democratic Republic of the)	37.0	62.5	87.6	3.3	2.8	0.6	0.0	27.8	35.2	94.1	91.0	5.5	5.2	7.1	6.1
177 Burkina Faso	8.8	14.7	21.9	3.0	3.5	-0.3	-0.1	13.8	20.4	94.6	90.0	5.1	3.9	6.7	5.9

Demographic trends

L

HDI rank	Total population (millions)			Rate of natural increase (%)		Net international migration rate (%)		Urban population[a] (% of total)		Child dependency ratio		Old age dependency ratio		Total fertility rate (births per woman)	
	1990	2007	2020[b]	1990 to 1995	2005 to 2010	1990 to 1995	2005 to 2010	1990	2010	1990	2010	1990	2010	1990 to 1995	2005 to 2010
178 Mali	8.7	12.4	16.8	2.5	2.7	-0.6	-0.3	23.3	33.3	86.2	82.2	5.4	4.3	6.3	5.5
179 Central African Republic	2.9	4.3	5.3	2.4	1.9	0.2	0.0	36.8	38.9	81.4	72.3	7.5	6.9	5.7	4.8
180 Sierra Leone	4.1	5.4	7.3	1.8	2.4	-2.2	0.2	32.9	38.4	77.2	79.5	5.1	3.4	5.5	5.2
181 Afghanistan	12.6	26.3	39.6	2.9	2.7	4.3	0.7	18.3	24.8	89.5	88.5	4.5	4.3	8.0	6.6
182 Niger	7.9	14.1	22.9	3.3	3.9	0.0	0.0	15.4	16.7	100.7	104.7	4.1	4.1	7.8	7.1
OTHER UN MEMBER STATES															
Iraq	18.1	29.5	40.2	3.1	2.6	-0.2	-0.4	69.7	66.4	89.0	72.5	6.6	5.8	5.8	4.1
Kiribati	0.1	0.1	0.1	..	..	..	..	35.0	44.0	..	..	..	..	..	..
Korea (Democratic People's Rep. of)	20.1	23.7	24.8	1.5	0.4	0.0	0.0	58.4	63.4	37.9	30.6	6.8	14.2	2.4	1.9
Marshall Islands	0.0	0.1	0.1	..	..	..	..	65.1	71.8	..	..	..	..	..	..
Micronesia (Federated States of)	0.1	0.1	0.1	2.6	1.9	-0.4	-1.6	25.8	22.7	84.3	61.2	6.8	6.1	4.8	3.6
Monaco	0.0	0.0	0.0	..	..	..	..	100.0	100.0	..	..	..	..	..	..
Nauru	0.0	0.0	0.0	..	..	..	..	100.0	100.0	..	..	..	..	..	..
Palau	0.0	0.0	0.0	..	..	..	..	69.6	82.7	..	..	..	..	..	..
San Marino	0.0	0.0	0.0	..	..	..	..	90.4	94.3	..	..	..	..	..	..
Somalia	6.6	8.7	12.2	2.5	2.8	-2.7	-0.6	29.7	37.4	84.5	85.7	5.6	5.2	6.5	6.4
Tuvalu	0.0	0.0	0.0	..	..	..	..	40.7	50.4	..	..	..	..	..	..
Zimbabwe	10.5	12.4	15.6	2.6	1.4	-0.3	-1.1	29.0	38.3	90.3	70.0	5.8	7.3	4.8	3.5
Arab States	638.6 [T]	964.5 [T]	1,276.1 [T]	2.6 [d]	2.3 [d]	-0.1 [d]	-0.1 [d]	4.6	4.6	85.5 [d]	71.5 [d]	5.9 [d]	6.1 [d]	5.6 [d]	4.6 [d]
Central and Eastern Europe and the CIS	3,178.8 [T]	4,029.3 [T]	4,596.3 [T]	1.7 [d]	1.2 [d]	0.0 [d]	0.0 [d]	2.4	2.4	55.2 [d]	39.0 [d]	7.8 [d]	10.0 [d]	3.0 [d]	2.4 [d]
East Asia and the Pacific	720.8 [T]	730.7 [T]	732.8 [T]	0.0 [d]	-0.1 [d]	0.1 [d]	0.2 [d]	1.5	1.5	30.7 [d]	22.5 [d]	19.1 [d]	23.8 [d]	1.6 [d]	1.5 [d]
Latin America and the Caribbean	442.3 [T]	569.7 [T]	645.5 [T]	1.9 [d]	1.3 [d]	-0.1 [d]	-0.2 [d]	2.3	2.3	61.4 [d]	42.3 [d]	8.3 [d]	10.6 [d]	3.0 [d]	2.3 [d]
South Asia	282.7 [T]	341.7 [T]	383.4 [T]	0.7 [d]	0.6 [d]	0.5 [d]	0.4 [d]	2.0	2.0	32.7 [d]	29.6 [d]	18.5 [d]	19.5 [d]	2.0 [d]	2.0 [d]
Sub-Saharan Africa	26.9 [T]	34.5 [T]	40.3 [T]	1.2 [d]	1.0 [d]	0.3 [d]	0.3 [d]	2.4	2.4	41.4 [d]	37.2 [d]	14.3 [d]	16.6 [d]	2.5 [d]	2.4 [d]
OECD	1,048.6 [T]	1,189.0 [T]	1,269.7 [T]	0.6	0.4	0.2	0.2	71.8	76.8	34.6	27.7	17.5	22.1	1.9	1.8
European Union (EU27)	471.6 [T]	493.2 [T]	505.3 [T]	0.1	0.0	0.2	0.3	71.5	74.0	29.1	23.2	20.8	26.2	1.6	1.5
GCC	23.1 [T]	36.5 [T]	47.1 [T]	2.7	1.8	-0.5	0.7	78.5	82.8	70.2	43.1	3.6	3.9	5.1	2.9
Very high human development	877.3 [T]	986.5 [T]	1,051.0 [T]	0.4	0.3	0.3	0.3	73.7	78.4	29.8	25.5	19.0	24.3	1.7	1.7
Very high HD: OECD	855.4 [T]	954.9 [T]	1,013.4 [T]	0.4	0.3	0.3	0.3	73.3	78.0	29.6	25.5	19.2	24.7	1.7	1.7
Very high HD: non-OECD	22.0 [T]	31.6 [T]	37.6 [T]	1.2	0.8	0.9	1.2	88.5	89.7	40.1	26.4	10.5	12.4	2.2	1.8
High human development	784.2 [T]	918.4 [T]	996.0 [T]	1.2	0.8	-0.1	-0.1	69.4	76.5	51.4	35.0	10.6	12.7	2.5	2.0
Medium human development	3,388.5 [T]	4,380.5 [T]	5,090.6 [T]	1.8	1.3	-0.1	-0.1	30.3	41.1	61.0	44.3	7.3	8.8	3.3	2.6
Low human development	240.2 [T]	385.1 [T]	536.8 [T]	2.9	2.7	0.1	0.0	22.7	29.7	89.9	83.6	5.5	5.5	6.7	5.6
World	5,290.5 [Td]	6,670.8 [Td]	7,674.3 [Td]	1.5 [d]	1.2 [d]	0.0 [d]	0.0 [d]	2.6	2.6	53.8 [d]	41.2 [d]	10.0 [d]	11.6 [d]	3.1 [d]	2.6 [d]

NOTES

a Because data are based on national definitions of what constitutes a city or metropolitan area, cross-country comparisons should be made with caution.

b Data refer to medium variant projections.

c Population estimates include Taiwan, Province of China.

d Data are aggregates provided by original data source.

SOURCES

Columns **1–7 and 10–15:** UN (2009e).

Columns **8 and 9:** UN (2008c).

TABLE

Economy and inequality

M

HDI rank	GDP		GDP per capita				Average annual change in consumer price index (%)		Share of income or expenditure[b] (%)		Inequality measures	
	US$ billions 2007	PPP US$ billions 2007	US$ 2007	Annual growth rate at constant prices (%) 1990–2007	Highest value in the period 1980–2007 2007 PPP US$[a]	Year of highest value	1990–2007	2006–2007	Poorest 10%	Richest 10%	Richest 10% to poorest 10%[c]	Gini index[d]
VERY HIGH HUMAN DEVELOPMENT												
1 Norway	388.4	251.6	82,480	2.6	53,433	2007	2.1	0.7	3.9[e]	23.4[e]	6.1	25.8
2 Australia	821.0	733.9	39,066	2.4	34,923	2007	2.5	2.3	2.0[e]	25.4[e]	12.5	35.2
3 Iceland	20.0	11.1	64,190	2.5	35,742	2007	3.5	5.1	..	..	..	..
4 Canada	1,329.9	1,180.9	40,329	2.2	35,812	2007	2.0	2.1	2.6[e]	24.8[e]	9.4	32.6
5 Ireland	259.0	194.8	59,324	5.8	44,613	2007	3.0	4.9	2.9[e]	27.2[e]	9.4	34.3
6 Netherlands	765.8	633.9	46,750	2.1	38,694	2007	2.4	1.6	2.5[e]	22.9[e]	9.2	30.9
7 Sweden	454.3	335.8	49,662	2.3	36,712	2007	1.5	2.2	3.6[e]	22.2[e]	6.2	25.0
8 France	2,589.8	2,078.0	41,970	1.6	33,674	2007	1.6	1.5	2.8[e]	25.1[e]	9.1	32.7
9 Switzerland	424.4	307.0	56,207	0.8	40,658	2007	1.2	0.7	2.9[e]	25.9[e]	9.0	33.7
10 Japan	4,384.3	4,297.2	34,313	1.0	33,632	2007	0.2	0.1	4.8[e]	21.7[e]	4.5	24.9
11 Luxembourg	49.5	38.2	103,042	3.3	79,485	2007	2.1	2.3	3.5[e]	23.8[e]	6.8	30.8
12 Finland	244.7	182.6	46,261	2.8	34,526	2007	1.5	2.5	4.0[e]	22.6[e]	5.6	26.9
13 United States	13,751.4	13,751.4	45,592	2.0	45,592	2007	2.6	2.9	1.9[e]	29.9[e]	15.9	40.8
14 Austria	373.2	310.7	44,879	1.8	37,370	2007	2.0	2.2	3.3[e]	23.0[e]	6.9	29.1
15 Spain	1,436.9	1,416.4	32,017	2.4	31,560	2007	3.4	2.8	2.6[e]	26.6[e]	10.3	34.7
16 Denmark	311.6	197.3	57,051	1.9	36,130	2007	2.1	1.7	2.6[e]	21.3[e]	8.1	24.7
17 Belgium	452.8	371.2	42,609	1.8	34,935	2007	1.9	1.8	3.4[e]	28.1[e]	8.2	33.0
18 Italy	2,101.6	1,802.2	35,396	1.2	30,353	2007	2.9	1.8	2.3[e]	26.8[e]	11.6	36.0
19 Liechtenstein	..	..	..	..	..	..	..	..	..	..	..	..
20 New Zealand	135.7	115.6	32,086	2.1	27,336	2007	2.0	2.4	2.2[e]	27.8[e]	12.5	36.2
21 United Kingdom	2,772.0	2,143.0	45,442	2.4	35,130	2007	2.7	4.3	2.1[e]	28.5[e]	13.8	36.0
22 Germany	3,317.4	2,830.1	40,324	1.4	34,401	2007	1.7	2.1	3.2[e]	22.1[e]	6.9	28.3
23 Singapore	161.3	228.1	35,163	3.8	49,704	2007	1.2	2.1	1.9[e]	32.8[e]	17.7	42.5
24 Hong Kong, China (SAR)	207.2	293.0	29,912	2.4	42,306	2007	2.0	2.0	2.0[e]	34.9[e]	17.8	43.4
25 Greece	313.4	319.2	27,995	2.7	28,517	2007	5.9	2.9	2.5[e]	26.0[e]	10.2	34.3
26 Korea (Republic of)	969.8	1,201.8	20,014	4.5	24,801	2007	4.0	2.5	2.9[e]	22.5[e]	7.8	31.6
27 Israel	164.0	188.9	22,835	1.7	26,315	2007	5.7	0.5	2.1[e]	28.8[e]	13.4	39.2
28 Andorra	..	..	..	..	..	..	..	..	..	..	..	..
29 Slovenia	47.2	54.0	23,379	3.5	26,753[f]	2007	8.2	3.6	3.4[g]	24.6[g]	7.3	31.2
30 Brunei Darussalam	11.5[h]	19.5	30,032[h]	-0.3	83,688	1980	1.2[f]	0.1[h]	..	..	..	..
31 Kuwait	112.1	121.1[h]	42,102	1.8	47,812[f]	2006	2.0	5.5	..	..	..	..
32 Cyprus	21.3	21.2	24,895	2.5	24,789	2007	3.2	2.4	..	..	..	..
33 Qatar	52.7	56.3	64,193[h]	..	..	..	3.4	13.8	..	..	..	..
34 Portugal	222.8	241.5	20,998	1.9	22,765	2007	3.6	2.8	2.0[e]	29.8[e]	15.0	38.5
35 United Arab Emirates	163.3	226.1	38,436[h]	-0.1	101,057[f]	1980	..	..	..	..	..	..
36 Czech Republic	175.0	249.5	16,934	2.4	24,144[f]	2007	4.6	2.9	4.3[e]	22.7[e]	5.3	25.8
37 Barbados	3.0[h]	5.0[h]	10,427[h]	..	..	..	2.5	4.0	..	..	..	..
38 Malta	7.4	9.4	18,203	2.6	23,080	2007	2.7	1.3	..	..	..	..
HIGH HUMAN DEVELOPMENT												
39 Bahrain	15.8[h]	20.3[h]	21,421[h]	2.4	29,723[f]	2005	0.5	-5.5	..	..	..	..
40 Estonia	20.9	27.3	15,578	5.3	20,361	2007	10.3	6.6	2.7[g]	27.7[g]	10.4	36.0
41 Poland	422.1	609.4	11,072	4.4	15,987[f]	2007	13.6	2.4	3.0[g]	27.2[g]	9.0	34.9
42 Slovakia	75.0	108.4	13,891	3.4	20,076[f]	2007	7.3	2.8	3.1[e]	20.8[e]	6.8	25.8
43 Hungary	138.4	188.6	13,766	3.3	18,755	2007	13.4	7.9	3.5[g]	24.1[g]	6.8	30.0
44 Chile	163.9	230.3	9,878	3.7	13,880	2007	5.7	4.4	1.6[e]	41.7[e]	26.2	52.0
45 Croatia	51.3	71.1	11,559	3.0	16,027[f]	2007	32.4	2.9	3.6[g]	23.1[g]	6.4	29.0
46 Lithuania	38.3	59.3	11,356	4.1	17,575[f]	2007	11.8	5.7	2.7[g]	27.4[g]	10.3	35.8
47 Antigua and Barbuda	1.0[h]	1.6[h]	11,664[h]	1.8	19,085	2006	..	..	..	..	..	..
48 Latvia	27.2	37.3	11,930	4.7	16,377	2007	13.3	10.1	2.7[g]	27.4[g]	10.3	35.7
49 Argentina	262.5	522.9	6,644	1.5	13,238	2007	7.3	8.8	1.2[e]	37.3[e]	31.6	50.0
50 Uruguay	23.1	37.3	6,960	1.5	11,216	2007	19.7	8.1	1.7[e]	34.8[e]	20.1	46.2
51 Cuba	..	..	..	..	..	..	..	..	..	..	..	..
52 Bahamas	6.6	..	19,844	..	..	..	1.9	2.5	..	..	..	..
53 Mexico	1,022.8	1,484.9	9,715	1.6	14,104	2007	13.2	4.0	1.8[g]	37.9[g]	21.0	48.1
54 Costa Rica	26.3	48.4	5,887	2.6	10,842	2007	13.1	9.4	1.5[e]	35.5[e]	23.4	47.2
55 Libyan Arab Jamahiriya	58.3	88.4	9,405	..	..	..	1.2[f]	3.4[h]	..	..	..	..
56 Oman	35.7	56.6	14,031[h]	2.3	22,816[f]	2006	..	6.0	..	..	..	..
57 Seychelles	0.7	1.4	8,560	1.4	16,771	2000	2.5	5.3	..	..	..	..
58 Venezuela (Bolivarian Republic of)	228.1	334.1	8,299	-0.2	12,233	1980	34.3	18.7	1.7[e]	32.7[e]	18.8	43.4
59 Saudi Arabia	381.7	554.1	15,800	0.3	36,637	1980	0.5	4.2	..	..	..	..

Economy and inequality

HDI rank	GDP		GDP per capita				Average annual change in consumer price index (%)		Share of income or expenditure[b] (%)		Inequality measures	
	US$ billions 2007	PPP US$ billions 2007	US$ 2007	Annual growth rate at constant prices (%) 1990–2007	Highest value in the period 1980–2007 2007 PPP US$[a]	Year of highest value	1990–2007	2006–2007	Poorest 10%	Richest 10%	Richest 10% to poorest 10%[c]	Gini index[d]
60 Panama	19.5	38.1	5,833	2.6	11,391	2007	1.1	4.2	0.8 [e]	41.4 [e]	49.9	54.9
61 Bulgaria	39.5	86.0	5,163	2.3	11,222	2007	55.7	8.4	3.5 [g]	23.8 [g]	6.9	29.2
62 Saint Kitts and Nevis	0.5	0.7	10,795	2.8	14,481	2007	3.2	4.4	..	..	..	..
63 Romania	166.0	266.5	7,703	2.3	12,369	2007	56.4	4.8	3.3 [g]	25.3 [g]	7.6	31.5
64 Trinidad and Tobago	20.9	31.3	15,668	5.0	23,507	2007	5.2	7.9	2.1 [e]	29.9 [e]	14.4	40.3
65 Montenegro	3.5	7.0	5,804	3.8	11,699 [f]	2007	..	..	..	..	..	..
66 Malaysia	186.7	358.9	7,033	3.4	13,518	2007	2.8	2.0	2.6 [e]	28.5 [e]	11.0	37.9
67 Serbia	40.1	75.6	5,435	0.0	13,137 [f]	1990	36.4	6.4	..	..	..	..
68 Belarus	44.8	105.2	4,615	3.4	10,841 [f]	2007	114.2	8.4	3.6 [g]	22.0 [g]	6.1	27.9
69 Saint Lucia	1.0	1.6	5,834	1.3	9,786	2007	2.6	2.5	2.0 [e]	32.5 [e]	16.2	42.6
70 Albania	10.8	22.4	3,405	5.2	7,041	2007	13.0	2.9	3.2 [g]	25.9 [g]	8.0	33.0
71 Russian Federation	1,290.1	2,087.4	9,079	1.2	14,690 [f]	2007	44.4	9.0	2.6 [g]	28.4 [g]	11.0	37.5
72 Macedonia (the Former Yugoslav Rep. of)	7.7	18.5	3,767	0.4	9,096 [f]	2007	4.8	3.5	2.4 [g]	29.5 [g]	12.4	39.0
73 Dominica	0.3 [h]	0.6 [h]	..	1.4	7,893 [f]	2006	1.6	3.1	..	..	..	..
74 Grenada	0.6	0.8	5,724	2.4	7,557	2005	2.1	4.2	..	..	..	..
75 Brazil	1,313.4	1,833.0	6,855	1.2	9,567	2007	67.6	3.6	1.1 [e]	43.0 [e]	40.6	55.0
76 Bosnia and Herzegovina	15.1	29.3	4,014	11.2	7,764 [f]	2007	..	..	2.8	27.4 [g]	9.9	35.8
77 Colombia	207.8	377.7	4,724	1.2	8,587	2007	13.6	5.4	0.8	45.9 [e]	60.4	58.5
78 Peru	107.3	218.6	3,846	2.7	7,836	2007	12.5	1.8	1.5	37.9 [e]	26.1	49.6
79 Turkey	655.9	957.2	8,877	2.2	12,955	2007	56.5	8.8	1.9	33.2 [g]	17.4	43.2
80 Ecuador	44.5	99.4	3,335	1.2	7,449	2007	30.1	2.3	1.2	43.3 [e]	35.2	54.4
81 Mauritius	6.8	14.2	5,383	3.7	11,296	2007	6.2	8.8	..	..	..	..
82 Kazakhstan	104.9	168.2	6,772	3.2	10,863 [f]	2007	24.3	10.8	3.1	25.9 [g]	8.5	33.9
83 Lebanon	24.4	41.4	5,944	2.4	10,137 [f]	2004	..	..	..	..	..	..
MEDIUM HUMAN DEVELOPMENT												
84 Armenia	9.2	17.1	3,059	5.8	5,693 [f]	2007	21.1	4.4	3.7	28.9 [g]	7.9	33.8
85 Ukraine	141.2	321.5	3,035	-0.7	9,137 [f]	1989	50.6	12.8	3.8	22.5 [g]	6.0	28.2
86 Azerbaijan	31.2	67.2	3,652	2.9	7,851 [f]	2007	52.1	16.7	6.1	17.5 [g]	2.9	36.5
87 Thailand	245.4	519.2	3,844	2.9	8,135	2007	3.6	2.2	2.6	33.7 [g]	13.1	42.5
88 Iran (Islamic Republic of)	286.1	778.0	4,028	2.5	10,955	2007	20.1	17.2	2.6	29.6 [g]	11.6	38.3
89 Georgia	10.2	20.5	2,313	1.8	7,604	1985	11.4	9.2	1.9	30.6 [g]	15.9	40.8
90 Dominican Republic	36.7	65.2	3,772	3.8	6,706	2007	11.0	6.1	1.5	38.7 [e]	25.3	50.0
91 Saint Vincent and the Grenadines	0.6	0.9	4,596	3.0	7,691	2007	1.9	7.0	..	..	..	..
92 China	3,205.5	7,096.7	2,432	8.9	5,383	2007	4.4	4.8	2.4	31.4 [g]	13.2	41.5
93 Belize	1.3	2.0	4,200	2.3	6,796	2006	1.9	2.3	..	..	..	..
94 Samoa	0.5	0.8	2,894	2.9	4,467 [f]	2007	4.1	5.6	..	..	..	..
95 Maldives	1.1	1.6	3,456	5.1	5,196 [f]	2007	..	7.4	..	..	..	..
96 Jordan	15.8	28.0	2,769	2.0	4,901	2007	2.9	5.4	3.0	30.7 [g]	10.2	37.7
97 Suriname	2.2	3.6	4,896	1.8	7,813	2007	50.4	6.7	1.0	40.0 [e]	40.4	52.9
98 Tunisia	35.0	76.9	3,425	3.4	7,520	2007	3.5	3.1	2.4	31.6 [g]	13.3	40.8
99 Tonga	0.3	0.4	2,474	1.7	3,772 [f]	2006	5.7	5.9	..	..	..	..
100 Jamaica	11.4	16.3	4,272	0.6	6,587	2006	15.4	9.3	2.1	35.6 [g]	17.0	45.5
101 Paraguay	12.2	27.1	1,997	-0.3	4,631	1981	10.7	8.1	1.1	42.3 [e]	38.8	53.2
102 Sri Lanka	32.3	84.9	1,616	3.9	4,243	2007	9.6	15.8	2.9	33.3 [g]	11.7	41.1
103 Gabon	11.6	20.2	8,696	-0.7	18,600	1984	2.7	5.0	2.5	32.7 [g]	13.3	41.5
104 Algeria	135.3	262.0	3,996	1.4	7,740	2007	9.2	3.5	2.8	26.9 [g]	9.6	35.3
105 Philippines	144.1	299.4	1,639	1.7	3,406	2007	6.4	2.8	2.4	33.9 [g]	14.1	44.0
106 El Salvador	20.4	39.8	2,973	1.8	5,804	2007	5.5	4.6	1.0	37.0 [e]	38.6	49.7
107 Syrian Arab Republic	37.7	89.7	1,898	1.5	4,511	2007	4.1	3.9	..	..	..	..
108 Fiji	3.4	3.6	4,113	1.6	4,632	2006	3.0	4.8	..	..	..	..
109 Turkmenistan	12.9	22.6	2,606	..	..	..	..	..	2.5	31.8 [g]	12.9	40.8
110 Occupied Palestinian Territories	4.0	..	1,160 [h]	..	..	..	4.1 [f]	3.5	..	..	..	..
111 Indonesia	432.8	837.6	1,918	2.3	3,712	2007	12.8	6.4	3.0	32.3 [g]	10.8	39.4
112 Honduras	12.2	27.0	1,722	1.5	3,796	2007	16.2	6.9	0.7	42.2 [e]	59.4	55.3
113 Bolivia	13.1	40.0	1,379	1.3	4,206	2007	5.9	8.7	0.5	44.1 [g]	93.9	58.2
114 Guyana	1.1	2.1	1,462	2.9	2,782	2007	5.8	12.3	1.3	34.0 [e]	25.5	44.6
115 Mongolia	3.9	8.4	1,507	1.9	3,236 [f]	2007	17.2	9.0	2.9	24.9 [g]	8.6	33.0
116 Viet Nam	68.6	221.4	806	6.0	2,600 [f]	2007	4.1	8.9	3.1	29.8 [g]	9.7	37.8
117 Moldova	4.4	9.7	1,156	-1.3	4,208	1989	15.6	12.4	3.0	28.2 [g]	9.4	35.6
118 Equatorial Guinea	9.9	15.5	19,552	21.1	30,627 [f]	2007	7.6	..	..	..	..	..

HDI rank	GDP US$ billions 2007	PPP US$ billions 2007	GDP per capita US$ 2007	Annual growth rate at constant prices (%) 1990–2007	Highest value in the period 1980–2007 2007 PPP US$[a]	Year of highest value	Average annual change in consumer price index (%) 1990–2007	2006–2007	Share of income or expenditure[b] (%) Poorest 10%	Richest 10%	Inequality measures Richest 10% to poorest 10%[c]	Gini index[d]
119 Uzbekistan	22.3	65.1	830	1.2	2,425[f]	2007	..	..	2.9	29.5[g]	10.3	36.7
120 Kyrgyzstan	3.7	10.5	715	-0.4	2,652[f]	1990	11.3	10.2	3.6	25.9[g]	7.3	32.9
121 Cape Verde	1.4	1.6	2,705	3.3	3,041[f]	2007	3.5	4.4	1.9	40.6[g]	21.6	50.5
122 Guatemala	33.9	60.9	2,536	1.4	4,562	2007	8.3	6.5	1.3	42.4[e]	33.9	53.7
123 Egypt	130.5	403.7	1,729	2.5	5,349	2007	6.5	9.3	3.9	27.6[g]	7.2	32.1
124 Nicaragua	5.7	14.4	1,022	1.9	2,955	1981	..	11.1	1.4	41.8[e]	31.0	52.3
125 Botswana	12.3	25.6	6,544	4.3	13,604	2007	9.1	7.1	1.3	51.2[g]	40.0	61.0
126 Vanuatu	0.5	0.8	2,001	-0.4	3,877	1998	2.5	4.0	..	..	..	..
127 Tajikistan	3.7	11.8	551	-2.2	3,685[f]	1988	..	13.1	3.2	26.4[g]	8.2	33.6
128 Namibia	7.0	10.7	3,372	1.8	5,155	2007	..	6.7	0.6	65.0[e]	106.6	74.3
129 South Africa	283.0	466.9	5,914	1.0	9,757	2007	7.0	7.1	1.3	44.9[g]	35.1	57.8
130 Morocco	75.1	126.8	2,434	2.0	4,108	2007	2.6	2.0	2.7	33.2[g]	12.5	40.9
131 Sao Tome and Principe	0.1	0.3	916	..	..	..	..	..	..	..	..	..
132 Bhutan	1.1	3.2	1,668	5.2	4,837	2007	6.6	5.2	2.3	37.6[g]	16.3	46.8
133 Lao People's Democratic Republic	4.1	12.7	701	4.2	2,165[f]	2007	25.7	4.5	3.7	27.0[g]	7.3	32.6
134 India	1,176.9	3,096.9	1,046	4.5	2,753	2007	6.8	6.4	3.6	31.1[g]	8.6	36.8
135 Solomon Islands	0.4	0.9	784	-1.5	2,149	1995	9.5	7.7	..	..	..	..
136 Congo	7.6	13.2	2,030	-0.2	4,496	1984	5.9	2.7	2.1	37.1[g]	17.8	47.3
137 Cambodia	8.3	26.0	578	6.2	1,802[f]	2007	3.9	5.9	3.0	34.2[g]	11.5	40.7
138 Myanmar	..	41.0	..	6.8	904[f]	2005	24.6	35.0	..	..	..	..
139 Comoros	0.4	0.7	714	-0.4	1,361	1984	..	..	0.9	55.2[g]	60.6	64.3
140 Yemen	22.5	52.3	1,006	1.6	2,335[f]	2007	17.6	10.0	2.9	30.8[g]	10.6	37.7
141 Pakistan	142.9	405.6	879	1.6	2,496	2007	7.3	7.6	3.9	26.5[g]	6.7	31.2
142 Swaziland	2.9	5.5	2,521	0.9	4,789	2007	8.5[f]	5.3	1.8	40.8[g]	22.4	50.7
143 Angola	61.4	91.3	3,623	2.9	5,385[f]	2007	308.1	12.2	0.6	44.7[g]	74.6	58.6
144 Nepal	10.3	29.5	367	1.9	1,049	2007	6.5	6.1	2.7	40.4[g]	14.8	47.3
145 Madagascar	7.4	18.3	375	-0.4	1,297	1980	14.0	10.3	2.6	41.5[g]	15.9	47.2
146 Bangladesh	68.4	196.7	431	3.1	1,241	2007	5.4	9.1	4.3	26.6[g]	6.2	31.0
147 Kenya	24.2	57.9	645	0.0	1,542	2007	11.2	9.8	1.8	37.8[g]	21.3	47.7
148 Papua New Guinea	6.3	13.2	990	-0.6	2,551	1994	9.4	0.9	1.9	40.9[g]	21.5	50.9
149 Haiti	6.7	11.1	699	-2.1	2,258	1980	19.1	8.5	0.9	47.8[e]	54.4	59.5
150 Sudan	46.2	80.4	1,199	3.6	2,086	2007	35.5	8.0	..	..	..	..
151 Tanzania (United Republic of)	16.2	48.8	400	1.8	1,208[f]	2007	12.6	7.0	3.1	27.0[g]	8.9	34.6
152 Ghana	15.1	31.3	646	2.1	1,334	2007	24.0	10.7	2.0	32.8[g]	16.1	42.8
153 Cameroon	20.7	39.4	1,116	0.6	2,979	1986	4.3	0.9	2.4	35.5[g]	15.0	44.6
154 Mauritania	2.6	6.0	847	0.6	1,940	2006	6.0	7.3	2.5[g]	29.6[g]	11.6	39.0
155 Djibouti	0.8	1.7	997	-2.1	2,906[f]	1990	..	..	2.4[g]	30.9[g]	12.8	40.0
156 Lesotho	1.6	3.1	798	2.4	1,541	2007	8.2	8.0	1.0[g]	39.4[g]	39.8	52.5
157 Uganda	11.8	32.7	381	3.5	1,059[f]	2007	6.7	6.1	2.6[g]	34.1[g]	13.2	42.6
158 Nigeria	165.5	291.4	1,118	1.1	1,969	2007	21.3	5.4	2.0[g]	32.4[g]	16.3	42.9
LOW HUMAN DEVELOPMENT												
159 Togo	2.5	5.2	380	-0.2	1,147	1980	5.1	1.0	3.3[g]	27.1[g]	8.3	34.4
160 Malawi	3.6	10.6	256	0.4	800	1980	26.1	8.0	3.0[g]	31.9[g]	10.5	39.0
161 Benin	5.4	11.8	601	1.3	1,312	2007	5.0	1.3	2.9[g]	31.0[g]	10.8	38.6
162 Timor-Leste	0.4	0.8	373	..	..	..	..	10.3	2.9[g]	31.3[g]	10.8	39.5
163 Côte d'Ivoire	19.8	32.6	1,027	-0.7	2,827	1980	4.9	1.9	2.0[g]	39.6[g]	20.2	48.4
164 Zambia	11.4	16.2	953	0.1	1,660	1981	35.5	10.7	1.3[g]	38.9[g]	29.5	50.7
165 Eritrea	1.4	3.0	284	-0.7	900[f]	1997	..	..	..	..	..	..
166 Senegal	11.2	20.7	900	1.1	1,666	2007	3.3	5.9	2.5[g]	30.1[g]	11.9	39.2
167 Rwanda	3.3	8.4	343	1.1	872	1983	10.5	9.1	2.1[g]	37.8[g]	18.1	46.7
168 Gambia	0.6	2.1	377	0.3	1,225	2007	5.2[f]	2.1[h]	2.0[g]	36.9[g]	18.9	47.3
169 Liberia	0.7	1.3	198	1.9	1,910	1980	..	..	2.4[g]	30.1[g]	12.8	52.6
170 Guinea	4.6	10.7	487	1.3	1,147	2006	..	..	2.4[g]	34.4[g]	14.4	43.3
171 Ethiopia	19.4	61.6	245	1.9	779[f]	2007	4.8	17.2	4.1[g]	25.6[g]	6.3	29.8
172 Mozambique	7.8	17.1	364	4.2	802	2007	20.0	8.2	2.1[g]	39.2[g]	18.5	47.1
173 Guinea-Bissau	0.4	0.8	211	-2.6	753	1997	17.0	4.6	2.9[g]	28.0[g]	9.5	35.5
174 Burundi	1.0	2.9	115	-2.7	525	1991	12.8	8.3	4.1[g]	28.0[g]	6.8	33.3
175 Chad	7.1	15.9	658	2.4	1,555	2005	4.8	-9.0	2.6[g]	30.8[g]	11.8	39.8
176 Congo (Democratic Republic of the)	9.0	18.6	143	-4.3	794	1980	318.3	16.9	2.3[g]	34.7[g]	15.1	44.4
177 Burkina Faso	6.8	16.6	458	2.5	1,124	2007	3.8	-0.2	3.0[g]	32.4[g]	10.8	39.6

M Economy and inequality

HDI rank	GDP US$ billions 2007	GDP PPP US$ billions 2007	GDP per capita US$ 2007	GDP per capita Annual growth rate at constant prices (%) 1990–2007	GDP per capita Highest value in the period 1980–2007 2007 PPP US$[a]	Year of highest value	Average annual change in consumer price index (%) 1990–2007	2006–2007	Share of income or expenditure[b] (%) Poorest 10%	Richest 10%	Richest 10% to poorest 10%[c]	Gini index[d]
178 Mali	6.9	13.4	556	2.2	1,086	2006	3.4	1.4	2.7[g]	30.5[g]	11.2	39.0
179 Central African Republic	1.7	3.1	394	-0.8	990	1982	3.7	..	2.1[g]	33.0[g]	15.7	43.6
180 Sierra Leone	1.7	4.0	284	-0.3	855	1982	17.8	11.7	2.6[g]	33.6[g]	12.8	42.5
181 Afghanistan	8.4[h]	26.1[h]	..	..	..	..	..	17.0	..	..	..	..
182 Niger	4.2	8.9	294	-0.6	980	1980	4.0	0.1	2.3[g]	35.7[g]	15.3	43.9
OTHER UN MEMBER STATES												
Iraq	..	..	..	..	..							
Kiribati	0.1	0.1	817	2.1	1,520	2002	..	..	..	..	..	..
Korea (Democratic People's Rep. of)	..	..	..	..	..	..	..	..	..	..	..	..
Marshall Islands	0.1	..	2,559	..	..		..	..	..	..	..	..
Micronesia (Federated States of)	0.2	0.3	2,126	-0.4	3,279[f]	1993	..	..	..	..	..	..
Monaco	..	..	..	..	..		..	..	..	..	..	..
Nauru	..	..	..	..	..		..	..	..	..	..	..
Palau	0.2	..	8,148	..	..		..	..	..	..	..	..
San Marino	1.7	..	55,681	..	..		..	..	..	..	..	..
Somalia	..	..	..	..	..		..	..	..	..	..	..
Tuvalu	..	..	..	..	..		..	..	..	..	..	..
Zimbabwe	3.4	..	261[h]	..	..		105.6	..	1.8[g]	40.3[g]	22.0	50.1
Arab States	1,347.1[T]	2,285.8	..	..	..	..	..	..	..	..	..	..
Central and Eastern Europe and the CIS	3,641.3[T]	5,805.0	..	..	..	..	..	..	..	..	..	..
East Asia and the Pacific	5,661.6[T]	11,184.6	..	..	..	..	..	..	..	..	..	..
Latin America and the Caribbean	3,610.5[T]	5,576.6	..	..	..	..	..	..	..	..	..	..
South Asia	1,727.5[T]	4,622.5	..	..	..	..	..	..	..	..	..	..
Sub-Saharan Africa	804.0[T]	1,481.7	..	..	..	..	..	..	..	..	..	..
OECD	40,378.6[T]	38,543.3	..	..	..	..	..	..	..	..	..	..
European Union (EU27)	16,843.0[T]	14,811.7	..	..	..	..	..	..	..	..	..	..
GCC	761.4[T]	1,034.4	..	..	..	..	..	..	..	..	..	..
Very high human development	39,078.8[TI]	36,438.4	39,821[i]	1.8[i]	..	..	..	..	..	..	..	..
Very high HD: OECD	..[T]	35,194.8	..	..	..	..	..	..	..	..	..	..
Very high HD: non-OECD	..[T]	1,243.6	..	..	..	..	..	..	..	..	..	..
High human development	7,929.2[TI]	11,321.4	8,470[i]	2.1[i]	..	..	..	..	..	..	..	..
Medium human development	7,516.8[TI]	16,837.5	1,746[i]	4.8[i]	..	..	..	..	..	..	..	..
Low human development	147.4[TI]	312.4	380[i]	0.0[i]	..	..	..	..	..	..	..	..
World	54,583.8[TI]	64,909.7	8,257[i]	1.6[i]	..	..	..	..	..	..	..	..

NOTES

a Expressed in 2007 constant prices.

b Because the underlying household surveys differ in method and type of data collected, cross-country comparisons should be made with caution as the the distribution data are not strictly comparable across countries.

c Data show the ratio of the income or expenditure share of the richest group to that of the poorest.

d The Gini index lies between 0 and 100. A value of 0 represents absolute equality and 100 absolute inequality.

e Data refer to income shares by percentiles of the population, ranked by per capita income.

f Data refer to a period shorter than that specified.

g Data refer to expenditure shares by percentiles of the population, ranked by per capita expenditure.

h Data refer to an earlier year than that specified.

i Aggregates calculated for HDRO by the World Bank.

SOURCES

Columns 1–3 and 9–12: World Bank (2009d).

Column 4: calculated for HDRO by the World Bank based on World Bank (2009d) using the least squares method.

Columns 5 and 6: calculated based on GDP per capita (PPP US$) time series from World Bank (2009d).

Columns 7 and 8: calculated based on consumer price index data from World Bank (2009d).

TABLE

Health and education

N

HDI rank	Public expenditure on health — per capita PPP US$ 2006	Public expenditure on health — as % of total government expenditure 2006	Public expenditure on education — per pupil in primary education PPP US$ 2003–2006	Public expenditure on education — as % of total government expenditure 2000–2007	Aid allocated to social sectors[a] — as % of total aid 2007	Educational attainment levels[b] — Low: less than upper secondary 2000–2007	Educational attainment levels[b] — Medium: upper secondary or post-secondary non-tertiary 2000–2007	Educational attainment levels[b] — High: tertiary 2000–2007	Under-five mortality rate — Wealth quintile lowest 2000–2007	Under-five mortality rate — Wealth quintile highest 2000–2007	Under-five mortality rate — Educational level of mother lowest (no education) 2000–2007	Under-five mortality rate — Educational level of mother highest (secondary or higher) 2000–2007	Healthy life expectancy at birth[c] (years) 2007	Unhealthy life expectancy as a % of total life expectancy[d] 2007
VERY HIGH HUMAN DEVELOPMENT														
1 Norway	3,780	17.9	7,072	16.7	..	14.5	53.8	31.7	..	..	..	..	74	8
2 Australia	2,097	17.2	5,181	13.3	..	..	..	..	..	..	..	..	75	8
3 Iceland	2,758	18.1	7,788	18.0	..	37.4	30.3	27.6	..	..	..	..	75	8
4 Canada	2,585	17.9	..	12.5	..	23.7	38.1	38.2	..	..	..	..	75	7
5 Ireland	2,413	17.3	5,100	13.9	..	40.0	31.2	26.4	..	..	..	..	74	7
6 Netherlands	2,768	16.4	5,572	11.5	..	34.8	38.6	26.0	..	..	..	..	74	7
7 Sweden	2,533	13.4	8,415	12.9	..	20.7	51.1	27.0	..	..	..	..	75	7
8 France	2,833	16.7	5,224	10.6	..	42.6	35.9	19.8	..	..	..	..	76	6
9 Switzerland	2,598	19.6	7,811	13.0	..	21.4	52.3	26.2	..	..	..	..	76	7
10 Japan	2,067	17.7	..	9.5	..	26.1	43.9	30.0	..	..	..	..	78	6
11 Luxembourg	5,233	16.8	9,953	..	..	39.0	39.7	21.3	..	..	..	..	75	5
12 Finland	1,940	12.1	5,373	12.5	..	30.9	38.8	30.3	..	..	..	..	75	6
13 United States	3,074	19.1	..	13.7	..	14.8	49.0	36.2	..	..	..	..	72	9
14 Austria	2,729	15.5	7,596	10.9	..	26.2	57.9	15.9	..	..	..	..	74	7
15 Spain	1,732	15.3	4,800	11.0	..	58.6	17.8	23.6	..	..	..	..	76	6
16 Denmark	2,812	15.6	7,949	15.5	..	25.8	43.7	30.3	..	..	..	..	73	7
17 Belgium	2,264	13.9	6,303	12.1	..	42.3	31.0	26.8	..	..	..	..	74	7
18 Italy	2,022	14.2	6,347	9.2	..	59.5	30.4	10.1	..	..	..	..	76	6
19 Liechtenstein	..	..	..	..	..	..	..	..	..	..	..	..	..	..
20 New Zealand	1,905	18.6	4,831	15.5	..	28.7	40.1	25.9-	..	..	..	..	74	8
21 United Kingdom	2,434	16.5	5,596	12.5	..	..	..	..	..	..	..	..	73	8
22 Germany	2,548	17.6	4,837	9.7	..	21.5	57.1	21.4	..	..	..	..	75	6
23 Singapore	413	5.4	..	..	..	41.2	39.2	19.6	..	..	..	..	75	6
24 Hong Kong, China (SAR)	..	..	..	23.2	..	45.9	38.9	15.2	..	..	..	..	..	..
25 Greece	1,317	11.5	3,562	9.2	..	51.0	25.7	23.3	..	..	..	..	74	6
26 Korea (Republic of)	819	11.9	3,379	15.3	..	36.2	40.4	23.4	..	..	..	..	74	7
27 Israel	1,477	11.1	5,135	13.7	..	23.9	33.1	39.7	..	..	..	..	74	8
28 Andorra	2,054	22.7	..	..	..	48.0	34.8	16.1	..	..	..	..	76	..
29 Slovenia	1,507	13.5	5,206	12.7	..	26.4	55.5	18.1	..	..	..	..	74	5
30 Brunei Darussalam	314	5.1	..	9.1	..	..	..	..	..	..	..	..	67	13
31 Kuwait	422	4.9	2,204	12.9	..	74.4	17.3	8.3	..	..	..	..	69	11
32 Cyprus	759	6.4	..	14.5	..	41.3	33.8	24.9	..	..	..	..	71	11
33 Qatar	1,115	9.7	..	19.6	..	59.0	20.1	20.9	..	..	..	..	66	13
34 Portugal	1,494	15.5	4,908	11.3	..	77.4	11.4	11.2	..	..	..	..	73	7
35 United Arab Emirates	491	8.7	1,636	28.3	..	..	..	..	..	..	..	..	68	12
36 Czech Republic	1,309	13.6	2,242	9.5	..	14.5	73.0	12.5	..	..	..	..	72	6
37 Barbados	722	11.9	..	16.4	94.8	75.7	23.1	1.1	..	..	..	..	69	10
38 Malta	1,419	14.7	2,549	10.5	..	77.2	12.0	10.8	..	..	..	..	74	7
HIGH HUMAN DEVELOPMENT														
39 Bahrain	669	9.5	..	..	..	50.3	38.4	11.2	..	..	..	..	66	13
40 Estonia	734	11.3	2,511	14.6	..	27.9	42.3	27.5	..	..	..	..	71	3
41 Poland	636	9.9	3,155	12.7	..	..	..	..	..	..	..	..	70	7
42 Slovakia	913	13.8	2,149	10.8	..	19.2	67.6	13.2	..	..	..	..	70	6
43 Hungary	978	10.4	4,479	10.9	..	36.5	48.9	14.7	..	..	..	..	69	6
44 Chile	367	14.1	1,287	16.0	34.0	..	..	..	..	..	..	..	72	8
45 Croatia	869	13.9	2,197	10.0	72.3	40.2	45.4	13.9	..	..	..	..	70	8
46 Lithuania	728	13.3	2,166	14.7	..	23.5	50.8	25.7	..	..	..	..	68	5
47 Antigua and Barbuda	439	11.3	..	..	91.3	..	..	..	..	..	..	..	66	..
48 Latvia	615	10.2	..	14.2	..	19.7	60.0	20.3	..	..	..	..	68	6
49 Argentina	758	14.2	1,703	13.1	54.7	65.7	23.2	11.1	..	..	..	..	69	8
50 Uruguay	430	9.2	..	11.6	51.4	75.3	15.1	9.6	..	..	..	..	70	8
51 Cuba	329	10.8	..	14.2	77.5	59.6	31.0	9.4	..	..	..	..	71	10
52 Bahamas	775	13.9	..	19.7	..	28.9	70.2	0.3	..	..	..	..	68	7
53 Mexico	327	11.0	1,604	25.6	67.7	69.7	15.3	14.9	..	..	..	..	69	9
54 Costa Rica	565	21.5	1,623	20.6	26.2	64.7	18.5	15.0	..	..	..	..	71	10
55 Libyan Arab Jamahiriya	189	6.5	..	..	51.6	..	..	..	..	..	..	..	66	11
56 Oman	321	5.4	..	31.1	22.8	..	..	..	..	..	..	..	67	11
57 Seychelles	602	8.8	2,399	12.6	39.4	51.8	36.8	7.4	..	..	..	..	65	..
58 Venezuela (Bolivarian Republic of)	196	9.3	583	..	71.0	63.9	21.7	12.8	..	..	..	..	68	8
59 Saudi Arabia	468	8.7	..	27.6	78.8	65.8	19.2	14.9	..	..	..	..	64	12

Health and education

HDI rank	Public expenditure on health — per capita PPP US$ 2006	Public expenditure on health — as % of total government expenditure 2006	Public expenditure on education — per pupil in primary education PPP US$ 2003–2006	Public expenditure on education — as % of total government expenditure 2000–2007	Aid allocated to social sectors[a] — as % of total aid 2007	Educational attainment — Low: less than upper secondary 2000–2007	Educational attainment — Medium: upper secondary or post-secondary non-tertiary 2000–2007	Educational attainment — High: tertiary 2000–2007	Under-five mortality — Wealth quintile — lowest 2000–2007	Under-five mortality — Wealth quintile — highest 2000–2007	Under-five mortality — Educational level of mother — lowest (no education) 2000–2007	Under-five mortality — Educational level of mother — highest (secondary or higher) 2000–2007	Healthy life expectancy at birth[c] (years) 2007	Unhealthy life expectancy as a % of total life expectancy[d] 2007
60 Panama	495	11.5	..	8.9	47.1	66.0	23.1	10.4	..	..	..	..	68	10
61 Bulgaria	443	11.9	2,045	6.2	..	40.4	41.3	18.0	..	..	..	..	69	6
62 Saint Kitts and Nevis	403	9.5	..	12.7	58.7	..	..	..	..	..	..	..	67	..
63 Romania	433	12.4	941	8.6	..	47.3	43.6	9.0	..	..	..	..	68	6
64 Trinidad and Tobago	438	6.9	..	13.4	69.9	..	..	..	..	..	..	..	64	8
65 Montenegro	93	20.1	..	..	50.8	22.6	61.4	16.1	..	..	..	..	66	11
66 Malaysia	226	7.0	1,324	25.2	30.9	61.3	27.1	8.0	..	..	..	..	66	11
67 Serbia	373	14.3	..	..	60.6	..	..	..	..	..	..	..	66	11
68 Belarus	428	10.2	1,196	9.3	85.4	..	..	..	..	..	..	..	66	4
69 Saint Lucia	237	10.2	949	19.1	14.7	..	..	..	..	..	..	..	69	6
70 Albania	127	11.3	..	8.4	67.2	63.0	29.6	7.4	..	..	..	..	64	16
71 Russian Federation	404	10.8	..	12.9	..	..	..	..	..	..	..	..	65	2
72 Macedonia (the Former Yugoslav Rep. of)	446	16.5	..	15.6	57.4	52.2	35.6	12.2	..	..	..	..	66	11
73 Dominica	311	9.2	..	..	4.9	88.8	5.7	5.0	..	..	..	..	67	..
74 Grenada	387	9.5	766	12.9	18.4	..	..	..	..	..	..	..	62	18
75 Brazil	367	7.2	1,005	14.5	46.3	70.4	21.2	8.1	99 [e]	33 [e]	119 [e]	37 [e]	66	9
76 Bosnia and Herzegovina	454	14.0	..	..	73.2	..	..	..	..	..	..	..	68	9
77 Colombia	534	17.0	1,257	14.2	61.6	64.7	25.4	9.7	39	16	51	20	69	5
78 Peru	171	13.1	446	15.4	38.5	53.7	26.0	16.3	..	..	..	..	67	8
79 Turkey	461	16.5	1,059	..	49.9	76.8	14.7	8.5	..	..	..	..	67	7
80 Ecuador	130	7.3	..	8.0	65.4	..	..	..	..	..	..	..	66	12
81 Mauritius	292	9.2	1,205	12.7	43.8	79.2	17.7	2.6	..	..	..	..	65	10
82 Kazakhstan	214	10.4	..	12.1	32.8	29.5	56.1	14.4	..	..	..	..	60	8
83 Lebanon	285	11.3	402	9.6	33.8	..	..	..	..	..	..	..	64	11
MEDIUM HUMAN DEVELOPMENT														
84 Armenia	112	9.7	..	15.0	54.6	18.4	61.2	20.4	52	23	..	..	63	14
85 Ukraine	298	8.8	..	19.3	64.0	25.6	36.0	38.0	..	..	..	..	64	6
86 Azerbaijan	67	3.6	356	17.4	45.7	16.5	70.2	13.3	..	..	68	58	60	14
87 Thailand	223	11.3	..	25.0	36.5	..	..	..	..	..	..	..	65	5
88 Iran (Islamic Republic of)	406	9.2	927	19.5	71.7	..	..	..	..	..	..	..	62	13
89 Georgia	76	5.6	..	9.3	40.7	16.3	57.8	25.8	..	..	..	..	67	6
90 Dominican Republic	140	9.5	644	16.8	57.7	..	..	..	53	28	57	29	64	12
91 Saint Vincent and the Grenadines	289	9.3	1,227	16.1	9.3	..	..	..	..	..	..	..	66	8
92 China	144	9.9	..	..	56.4	..	..	..	..	..	..	..	68	7
93 Belize	254	10.9	846	18.1	32.6	74.2	13.6	10.9	..	..	..	..	63	17
94 Samoa	188	10.5	..	13.7	70.8	..	..	..	..	..	..	..	63	12
95 Maldives	742	14.0	..	15.0	29.7	..	..	..	..	..	..	..	64	10
96 Jordan	257	9.5	695	..	67.0	..	..	..	30	27	..	..	64	12
97 Suriname	151	8.0	..	..	15.1	..	..	..	..	..	..	..	64	7
98 Tunisia	214	6.5	1,581	20.8	52.2	..	..	..	..	..	..	..	67	9
99 Tonga	218	11.1	..	13.5	51.7	25.9	66.2	7.9	..	..	..	..	62	14
100 Jamaica	127	4.2	547	8.8	26.6	..	..	..	..	..	..	..	66	8
101 Paraguay	131	13.2	518	10.0	37.0	72.6	23.6	3.7	57 [e]	20 [e]	78 [e]	29 [e]	66	8
102 Sri Lanka	105	8.3	..	..	27.5	..	..	..	..	..	..	..	65	12
103 Gabon	198	13.9	..	..	49.6	..	..	..	93	55	112	87	53	12
104 Algeria	146	9.5	692	..	56.1	92.1	7.6	..	..	..	..	..	63	13
105 Philippines	88	6.4	418	15.2	23.1	62.6	26.4	8.4	66	21	105	29	64	11
106 El Salvador	227	15.6	478	20.0	53.6	75.6	13.8	10.6	..	..	..	..	63	12
107 Syrian Arab Republic	52	5.9	611	..	79.6	89.6	5.1	5.3	22	20	..	..	65	12
108 Fiji	199	9.1	1,143	20.0	72.5	..	..	..	..	..	..	..	64	7
109 Turkmenistan	172	14.9	..	..	79.9	..	..	..	106	70	133	88	57	12
110 Occupied Palestinian Territories	..	..	..	..	58.4	68.8	12.8	18.4	..	..	..	..	..	..
111 Indonesia	44	5.3	..	17.2	33.6	..	..	..	77	22	90	37	61	13
112 Honduras	116	15.0	..	..	47.4	..	..	..	50	20	55	20	64	11
113 Bolivia	128	11.6	435	18.1	57.3	61.6	23.8	14.0	105	32	145	48	59	10
114 Guyana	223	8.3	752	15.5	67.7	..	..	..	..	..	..	..	55	17
115 Mongolia	124	11.0	261	..	56.8	46.6	41.1	12.2	..	..	..	..	62	6
116 Viet Nam	86	6.8	..	..	34.9	..	..	..	53	16	66	29	66	11
117 Moldova	107	11.8	..	19.8	52.5	..	..	..	29	17	..	..	63	8
118 Equatorial Guinea	219	7.0	..	4.0	84.5	..	..	..	..	..	..	..	46	8

TABLE

HDI rank	Public expenditure on health		Public expenditure on education		Aid allocated to social sectors[a]	Educational attainment levels[b] (% of the population aged 25 and above)			Under-five mortality rate (per 1,000 live births)				Healthy life expectancy at birth[c] (years)	Unhealthy life expectancy as a % of total life expectancy[d]
						Low	Medium	High	Wealth quintile		Educational level of mother			
	per capita PPP US$	as % of total government expenditure	per pupil in primary education PPP US$	as % of total government expenditure	as % of total aid	less than upper secondary	upper secondary or post-secondary non-tertiary	tertiary	lowest	highest	lowest (no education)	highest (secondary or higher)		
	2006	2006	2003–2006	2000–2007	2007	2000–2007	2000–2007	2000–2007	2000–2007	2000–2007	2000–2007	2000–2007	2007	2007
119 Uzbekistan	89	8.0	..	..	69.4	..	..	..	72	42	..	..	60	11
120 Kyrgyzstan	55	8.7	..	18.6	54.4	23.0	62.1	14.9	..	..	..	..	59	13
121 Cape Verde	227	13.2	1,052	16.4	44.7	..	..	..	..	..	..	..	64	10
122 Guatemala	98	14.7	390	..	38.6	84.8	11.2	3.7	78 [e]	39 [e]	79 [e]	42 [e]	62	12
123 Egypt	129	7.3	..	12.6	28.1	..	..	..	75	25	68	31	62	11
124 Nicaragua	137	16.0	331	15.0	46.1	..	..	..	64	19	72	25	66	9
125 Botswana	487	17.8	1,158	21.0	72.2	..	..	..	..	..	..	..	48	10
126 Vanuatu	90	10.9	..	26.7	54.5	..	..	..	..	..	..	..	62	11
127 Tajikistan	16	5.5	106	18.2	53.4	21.0	68.3	10.6	..	..	..	..	57	14
128 Namibia	218	10.1	944	21.0	68.9	..	..	..	92	29	..	..	53	12
129 South Africa	364	9.9	1,383	17.4	62.8	73.0	18.1	8.9	..	..	..	..	48	7
130 Morocco	98	5.5	1,005	26.1	54.2	..	..	..	78	26	63	27	63	11
131 Sao Tome and Principe	120	12.2	..	..	49.0	..	..	..	..	..	..	..	54	17
132 Bhutan	73	7.3	..	17.2	46.8	..	..	..	..	..	..	..	56	15
133 Lao People's Democratic Republic	18	4.1	61	14.0	41.8	..	..	..	..	..	..	..	54	16
134 India	21	3.4	..	10.7	46.6	..	..	..	101	34	..	..	57	10
135 Solomon Islands	99	12.6	..	..	84.2	..	..	..	..	..	..	..	60	9
136 Congo	13	4.0	39	8.1	39.5	..	..	..	135	85	202	101	49	8
137 Cambodia	43	10.7	..	12.4	59.1	..	..	..	127	43	136	53	55	9
138 Myanmar	7	1.8	..	18.1	57.9	..	..	..	..	..	..	..	52	15
139 Comoros	19	8.0	..	24.1	68.8	..	..	..	129 [e]	87 [e]	121 [e]	75 [e]	58	11
140 Yemen	38	5.6	..	32.8	77.4	..	..	..	118	37	..	..	55	12
141 Pakistan	8	1.3	..	11.2	53.0	76.7	17.1	6.3	121	60	102	62	55	17
142 Swaziland	219	9.4	484	..	56.8	..	..	..	118	101	150	95	42	7
143 Angola	61	5.0	..	..	78.4	..	..	..	..	..	..	..	47	..
144 Nepal	24	9.2	119	14.9	51.8	..	..	..	98	47	93	32	55	17
145 Madagascar	21	9.2	57	16.4	28.6	..	..	..	142	49	149	65	53	12
146 Bangladesh	26	7.4	115	14.2	50.0	82.9	12.9	4.2	121	72	114	68	55	16
147 Kenya	51	6.1	237	17.9	54.0	..	..	..	149	91	127	63	48	10
148 Papua New Guinea	111	7.3	..	..	58.9	..	..	..	..	..	..	..	57	6
149 Haiti	65	29.8	..	..	56.0	..	..	..	125	55	123	65	55	10
150 Sudan	23	6.3	..	..	24.1	..	..	..	.. [e]	.. [e]	152 [e]	84 [e]	50	14
151 Tanzania (United Republic of)	27	13.3	..	..	31.0	98.4	0.7	0.9	137	93	160	76	45	18
152 Ghana	36	6.8	300	..	45.6	..	..	..	128	88	125	85	50	12
153 Cameroon	23	8.6	107	17.0	11.5	..	..	..	189	88	186	93	45	12
154 Mauritania	31	5.3	224	10.1	37.8	..	..	..	98	79	111	86	52	8
155 Djibouti	75	13.4	..	22.4	46.5	..	..	..	..	..	..	..	50	9
156 Lesotho	88	7.8	663	29.8	64.0	..	..	..	114	82	161	82	41	9
157 Uganda	39	10.0	110	18.3	50.8	93.5	1.6	4.8	172	108	164	91	44	15
158 Nigeria	15	3.5	..	..	38.9	..	..	..	257	79	269	107	42	12
LOW HUMAN DEVELOPMENT														
159 Togo	20	6.9	..	13.6	75.9	..	..	..	150	62	145	64	52	16
160 Malawi	51	18.0	90	..	48.4	94.8	4.7	0.5	183	111	181	86	44	16
161 Benin	25	13.1	120	17.1	51.6	85.6	12.2	2.2	151	83	143	78	50	18
162 Timor-Leste	150	16.4	..	..	72.2	..	..	..	..	..	..	..	55	9
163 Côte d'Ivoire	15	4.1	..	21.5	55.3	..	..	..	..	..	..	..	48	16
164 Zambia	29	10.8	55	14.8	57.5	..	..	..	192	92	198	121	40	10
165 Eritrea	10	4.2	99	..	56.1	..	..	..	100	65	121	59	56	5
166 Senegal	23	6.7	299	26.3	52.0	..	..	..	183	64	152	60	52	6
167 Rwanda	134	27.3	109	19.0	53.9	..	..	..	211	122	210	95	44	11
168 Gambia	33	8.7	..	8.9	72.5	..	..	..	158	72	140	66	53	5
169 Liberia	25	16.4	..	..	43.9	..	..	..	138	117	151	119	49	15
170 Guinea	14	4.7	..	25.6	53.8	..	..	..	217	113	194	92	48	16
171 Ethiopia	13	10.6	130	23.3	53.9	..	..	..	130	92	139	54	51	7
172 Mozambique	39	12.6	156	21.0	46.2	..	..	..	196	108	201	86	42	12
173 Guinea-Bissau	10	4.0	..	..	34.8	..	..	..	..	..	..	..	43	9
174 Burundi	4	2.3	132	17.7	30.8	..	..	..	..	..	..	..	43	14
175 Chad	14	9.5	54	10.1	26.1	..	..	..	176	187	200	143	40	18
176 Congo (Democratic Republic of the)	7	7.2	..	..	38.4	..	..	..	184	97	209	112	46	3
177 Burkina Faso	50	15.8	328	15.4	35.1	..	..	..	206	144	198	108	43	18

Health and education

	Public expenditure on health		Public expenditure on education		Aid allocated to social sectors[a]	Educational attainment levels[b] (% of the population aged 25 and above)			Under-five mortality rate (per 1,000 live births)				Healthy life expectancy at birth[c] (years)	Unhealthy life expectancy as a % of total life expectancy[d]
						Low	Medium	High	Wealth quintile		Educational level of mother			
HDI rank	per capita PPP US$	as % of total government expenditure	per pupil in primary education PPP US$	as % of total government expenditure	as % of total aid	less than upper secondary	upper secondary or post-secondary non-tertiary	tertiary	lowest	highest	lowest (no education)	highest (secondary or higher)		
	2006	2006	2003–2006	2000–2007	2007	2000–2007	2000–2007	2000–2007	2000–2007	2000–2007	2000–2007	2000–2007	2007	2007
178 Mali	34	12.2	183	16.8	39.6	..	..	..	233	124	223	102	43	11
179 Central African Republic	20	10.9	88	..	22.5	..	..	..	223	112	187	107	42	10
180 Sierra Leone	20	7.8	..	..	28.7	..	..	..	..	..	279	164	37	22
181 Afghanistan	8	4.4	..	..	49.0	..	..	..	..	..	..	..	36	17
182 Niger	14	10.6	178	17.6	37.4	..	..	..	206	157	222	92	45	11
OTHER UN MEMBER STATES														
Iraq	90	3.4	..	..	22.7	..	..	..	..	..	49	37	58	15
Kiribati	268	13.0	..	..	41.7	..	..	..	..	..	..	..	60	
Korea (Democratic People's Rep. of)	42	6.0	..	..	19.0	..	..	..	..	..	..	..	61	9
Marshall Islands	589	15.1	..	15.8	42.4	..	..	..	..	..	..	..	53	..
Micronesia (Federated States of)	444	18.9	..	..	42.5	..	..	..	..	..	..	..	62	9
Monaco	5,309	15.6	..	..	..	..	..	..	..	..	..	..	76	..
Nauru	444	25.0	..	..	48.5	..	..	..	..	..	..	..	57	..
Palau	1,003	16.4	..	..	11.0	..	..	..	..	..	..	..	67	..
San Marino	2,765	13.3	..	..	..	..	..	..	..	..	..	..	76	..
Somalia	8	4.2	..	..	23.8	..	..	..	..	..	..	..	46	7
Tuvalu	189	16.1	..	..	60.1	..	..	..	..	..	..	..	58	..
Zimbabwe	77	8.9	..	..	50.7	89.5	8.8	1.5	72	57	69	68	38	12

NOTES

a Refers to allocation of aid to social infrastructure and services including health, education, water and sanitation, government and civil society and other services. Out of the total, an estimated 50% is allocated to health and education. Differences in allocation of funds exist between countries.

b Percentages may not sum to 100% as those whose educational attainment levels are unknown are excluded.

c Average number of years that a person can expect to live in 'full health' by taking into account years lived in less than full health due to disease and/or injury.

d Refers to the difference between life expectancy and healthy life expectancy, expressed in percentage terms.

e Data refer to a year other than that specified.

SOURCES

Columns 1–2 and 9–13: WHO (2009).

Columns 3 and 4: UNESCO Institute for Statistics (2009c).

Column 5: OECD-DAC (2009).

Columns 6–8: UNESCO Institute for Statistics. (2008b).

Column 14: calculated based on data on healthy life expectancy from WHO (2009) and data on life expectancy from UN (2009e).

Reader's guide

Human development indicators

The human development indicators provide an assessment of country achievements in different areas of human development. Where possible the tables include data for 192 UN member states along with Hong Kong Special Administrative Region of China, and the Occupied Palestinian Territories.

In the tables, countries and areas are ranked by their human development index (HDI) value. To locate a country in the tables, refer to the *Key to countries* on the inside back cover of the Report, where countries with their HDI ranks are listed alphabetically. Most of the data in the tables are for 2007 and are those available to the Human Development Report Office (HDRO) as of 10 June 2009, unless otherwise specified.

This year the Statistical Annex begins with a series of tables A–F related to the main theme of the report—migration. They are followed by tables G–K on the human development composite indices: the HDI and its trends; the Human Poverty Index (HPI), the Gender-related Development Index (GDI) and the Gender Empowerment Measure (GEM). Finally there are three tables (L–N) on demographic trends, the economy and inequality, and education and health. Additional selected human development indicators—including time series data and regional aggregates—will be available at *http:// hdr.undp.org/en/statistics*.

All of the indicators published in the tables are available electronically and free of charge in several formats: individually, in pre-defined tables or via a query tool that allows users to design their own tables. Interactive media, including maps of all the human development indices and many of the migration-related data and selected animations, are also provided. There are also more descriptive materials such as country factsheets, as well as further technical details on how to calculate the indices. All of these materials are available in three languages: English (at *http:// hdr.undp.org/en/statistics*), French (at *http://hdr. undp.org/fr/statistiques*) and Spanish (*http://hdr. undp.org/es/estadisticas*).

Sources and definitions

HDRO is primarily a user, not a producer, of statistics. It relies on international data agencies with the mandate, resources and expertise to collect and compile international data on specific statistical indicators. Sources for all data used in compiling the indicator tables are given at the end of each table. These correspond to full references in the *Bibliography*. In order to allow replication, the source notes also show the original data components used in any calculations by HDRO. Indicators for which short, meaningful definitions can be given are included in the Report's *Definition of statistical terms and indicators*. Other relevant information appears in the notes at the end of each table. For more detailed technical information about these indicators, please consult the relevant websites of the source agencies, links to which can be found at *http:// hdr.undp.org/en/statistics*.

Comparisons over time and across editions of the Report

The HDI is an important tool for monitoring long-term trends in human development. To facilitate trend analyses across countries, the HDI is calculated at five-year intervals for the period 1980–2007. These estimates, presented in Table G, are based on a consistent methodology using the data available when the Report is prepared.

As international data agencies continually improve their data series, including updating historical data periodically, the year-to-year changes in the HDI values and rankings across editions of the Human Development Report often reflect revisions to data—both specific to a country and relative to other countries—rather than real changes in a country. In addition, occasional changes in country coverage could affect the HDI ranking of a country. For example, a country's HDI rank could drop considerably between two consecutive Reports, but when comparable revised data are used to reconstruct the HDI for recent years, the HDI rank and value may actually show an improvement.

For these reasons HDI trend analysis should not be based on data from different editions of the Report. Table G provides up-to-date HDI trends based on consistent data time series and methodology.

Inconsistencies between national and international estimates

When compiling international data series, international data agencies apply international standards and harmonization procedures to national data improve comparability across countries. When data for a country are missing, an international agency may produce an estimate if other relevant information can be used. In some cases, international data series may not incorporate the most recent national data. All these factors can lead to substantial differences between national and international estimates.

When data inconsistencies have arisen, HDRO has helped to link national and international data authorities to address these inconsistencies. In many cases this has led to better statistics becoming available. HDRO continues to advocate improving international data and plays an active role in supporting efforts to enhance data quality. It works with national agencies and international bodies to improve data consistency through more systematic reporting and monitoring of data quality.

Country groupings and aggregates

In addition to country-level data, a number of aggregates are shown in the tables. These are generally weighted averages that are calculated for the country groupings as described below. In general, an aggregate is shown for a country grouping only when data are available for at least half the countries and represent at least two-thirds of the available weight in that classification. HDRO does not impute missing data for the purpose of aggregation. Therefore, unless otherwise specified, aggregates for each classification represent only the countries for which data are available. Occasionally aggregates are totals rather than weighted averages (and are indicated by the symbol T).

The country groupings used include: human development levels (very high, high, medium and low), the world and at least one geographic grouping—either the continents (in the migration tables) or UNDP Regional Bureaux groups (in the remaining tables).

Human development classifications. All countries or areas included in the HDI are classified into one of four categories of achievement in human development. For the first time, we have introduced a new category—very high human development (with an HDI of 0.900 or above)—and throughout the Report we have referred to this group as 'developed countries'. The remaining countries are referred to as 'developing countries' and are classified into three groups: high human development (HDI value of 0.800–0.899), medium human development (HDI of 0.500–0.799) and low human development (HDI of less than 0.500). See box 1.3.

Continents To assist the analysis of migration movements, this year's HDR has classified the world into six continents: Africa, Asia, Europe, Latin America and the Caribbean, Northern America and Oceania, based on the Composition of Macro Geographical Regions compiled by the Statistical Division of the United Nations Department of Economic and Social Affairs (see *http://unstats.un.org/unsd/methods/m49/m49regin.htm*).

UNDP Regional Bureaux As in past Reports, for the majority of our tables we present the UNDP Regional Bureaux geographic groups: Arab States, Central and Eastern Europe and the Commonwealth of Independent States, East Asia and the Pacific, Latin America and the Caribbean, South Asia, and sub-Saharan Africa.

Country notes

Unless otherwise noted, data for China do not include Hong Kong Special Administrative Region of China, Macao Special Administrative Region of China, or Taiwan Province of China. Data for Sudan are often based on information collected from the northern part of the country only. While Serbia and Montenegro became two independent States in June 2006, data for the union of the two States have been used where data do not yet exist separately for the independent States. Where this is the case, a note has been included to that effect. In the migration tables, data prior to 1990 for the Czech Republic refer to the former Czechoslovakia, those for the Russian Federation refer to the former Soviet Union and those for Serbia refer to the former Republic of Yugoslavia.

Reader's guide

Symbols

A dash between two years, such as in 2005–2010 indicates that the data presented are estimates for the entire period, unless otherwise indicated. Growth rates are usually average annual rates of growth between the first and last years of the period shown.

The following symbols are used in the tables:

..	data not available
0 or **0.0**	nil or neglegible
—	not applicable
<	less than
T	total

Primary international data sources

Life expectancy at birth. The life expectancy at birth estimates are taken from *World Population Prospects 1950–2050: The 2008 Revision* (UN 2009e), the official source of UN population estimates and projections. They are prepared biennially by the United Nations Department of Economic and Social Affairs Population Division using data from national vital registration systems, population censuses and surveys.

In the 2008 Revision, countries where HIV prevalence among persons aged 15 to 49 was ever equal to or greater than one percent during 1980–2007 are considered affected by the HIV epidemic, and their mortality is projected by modelling the course of the epidemic and projecting the yearly incidence of HIV infection. Also considered among the affected countries are those where HIV prevalence has always been lower than one percent but whose population is so large that the number of people living with HIV in 2007 surpassed 500,000. These include Brazil, China, India, the Russian Federation and the United States. This brings the number of countries considered to be affected by HIV to 58.

For more details on *World Population Prospects 1950–2050: The 2008 Revision,* see *www.un.org/esa/population/unpop.htm.*

Adult literacy rate. This Report uses data on adult literacy rates from the United Nations Educational, Scientific and Cultural Organization (UNESCO) Institute for Statistics (UIS)(UNESCO Institute for Statistics 2009a) that combine direct national estimates with recent estimates based on its global age-specific literacy projections model, which was developed in 2007. The national estimates, made available through targeted efforts by UIS to collect recent literacy data from countries, are obtained from national censuses or surveys between 1995 and 2007. Where recent estimates are not available, older UIS estimates have been used.

Many developed countries, having attained high levels of literacy, no longer collect basic literacy statistics and thus are not included in the UIS data. In calculating the HDI, a literacy rate of 99.0% is assumed for these countries if they do not report adult literacy information.

Many countries estimate the number of literate people based on self-reported data. Some use educational attainment data as a proxy, but measures of school attendance or grade completion may differ. Because definitions and data collection methods vary across countries, literacy estimates should be used with caution.

The UIS, in collaboration with partner agencies, is actively pursuing an alternative methodology for generating more reliable literacy estimates, known as the Literacy Assessment and Monitoring Programme (LAMP). LAMP seeks to go beyond the current simple categories of 'literate' and 'illiterate' by providing information on a continuum of literacy skills.

Combined gross enrolment ratios in primary, secondary and tertiary education. Gross enrolment ratios are produced by the UIS (UNESCO Institute for Statistics 2009b) based on enrolment data collected from national governments (usually from administrative sources) and population data from the *World Population Prospects 1950–2050: The 2006 Revision* (UN 2007). The ratios are calculated by dividing the number of students enrolled in primary, secondary and tertiary levels of education by the total population in the theoretical age group corresponding to these levels. The theoretical age group for tertiary education is assumed to be the five-year age group immediately following the end of upper secondary school in all countries.

Combined gross enrolment ratios do not reflect the quality of educational outcomes. Even when used to capture access to educational opportunities, combined gross enrolment ratios can hide important differences among countries because of differences in the age range corresponding to a level of education and in the duration of education programmes. Grade repetition and dropout rates can also distort the data.

As currently defined, the combined gross enrolment ratio measures enrolment in the country of study and therefore excludes from the national figure students who are studying abroad. For many smaller countries, where pursuit of a tertiary education abroad is common, access to education or educational attainment of the population could be underestimated.

GDP per capita (PPP US$). GDP per capita data are provided by the World Bank and released in its World Development Indicators database. In comparing standards of living across countries, economic statistics must be converted into purchasing power parity (PPP) terms to eliminate differences in national price levels. The current estimates are based on price data from the latest round of the International Comparison Program (ICP), which was conducted in 2005 and covers a total of 146 countries and areas. For many countries not included in the ICP surveys, the World Bank derives estimates through econometric regression. For countries not covered by the World Bank, PPP estimates provided by the Penn World Tables of the University of Pennsylvania (Heston, Summers and Aten 2006) are used.

The new PPP estimates were released for the first time during 2008 and represented substantial revisions to those used in our Reports published in 2007 and earlier years that were based on the prior round of ICP surveys—conducted in the early 1990s—covering only 118 countries. The new data indicated that price levels in many countries (especially developing countries) were higher than previously thought. For 70 countries, per capita incomes were revised downwards by at least 5 percent. Many of these are in sub-Saharan Africa, including seven of the eight countries where the downward revision was at least 50 percent. By contrast, for around 60 countries there was an upward revision of at least 5 percent, including many oil-producing countries where revisions exceeded 30 percent and four countries where the values were doubled. Such massive

revisions in GDP per capita clearly affect HDI values and also HDI ranks. A halving (or doubling) of GDP per capita changes the HDI value by 0.039.

Consequently, at the end of 2008, we released a short report entitled *Human Development Indices: A statistical update 2008* explaining the reasons for this revision and its effects on the HDI and our other composite indices. More details can be found at *http://hdr.undp.org/en/ statistics/data/hdi2008.* For details on the ICP and the PPP methodology, see the ICP website at *www.worldbank.org/data/icp.*

Migration data. Migration data in this report have been sourced from different agencies.

The main source for *trends in international migrant stocks* is the Population Division of the United Nations Department for Social and Economic Affairs (UNDESA). The data are from *Trends in Total Migrant Stocks: The 2008 Revision* (UN 2009d) and are based on data from population censuses conducted between 1955 and 2008. This source provides broad data (sex and type) over time on migrants according to their countries of destination.

As far as possible, international migrants are defined as foreign-born. In countries where data on place of birth were not available, country of citizenship provided the basis for the identification of international migrants.

For data on *countries of origin (as well as destination) of the international migrant stock,* we have used the Global Migrant Origin Database (version 4) compiled by the Development Research Centre on Migration, Globalisation and Poverty based at the University of Sussex, England (Migration DRC 2007). The estimates are based national censuses conducted during the 2000 round of censuses and provide an estimate for the period 2000–2002. It is important to note that the database presents data on migrant **stocks**—i.e. the total number of migrants both by country of origin and country of destination—and not the annual (or periodic) **flows** of migrants between countries. The stocks are the cumulative effect of flows over a much longer period of time than a year and hence are generally much greater than the annual flows would be. For details see *http://www.migrationdrc.org/ research/typesofmigration/global_migrant_origin_database.html*

For more detailed data on the characteristics of *international migrants* we used the OECD Database on Immigrants in OECD Countries (OECD 2009b). This database has been compiled from data collected during the 2000 round of censuses, supplemented in some cases by data from labour force surveys. As far as possible international migrants are defined as the foreign-born, although for some countries of destination the definitions may differ slightly from those that were used by the UN Population Division. We have chosen to present results according to the countries of origin of these migrants; therefore it is not possible to make a direct comparison with the estimates from the other two sources. We have presented data on education levels and economic activity, as well as highly-skilled (tertiary) emigration rates according to the countries of origin of migrants aged 15 years and above in OECD countries.

Cross-nationally comparable data on *internal migrants* (i.e. people who move within the borders of a country) are not readily available. For this reason, during the preparation of this report we commissioned analyses from (Bell and Muhudin 2009) based on national censuses that produced comparable estimates for 24 countries of the percentage of the total population that has moved. These data have been supplemented by estimates compiled by the UN Statistics Division (UNSD) in collaboration with the Economic Commission for Latin America and the Caribbean (ECLAC 2007), which are based also on censuses and total population, as well as by World Bank data based on household surveys and the population of working age (World Bank 2009e). Because of the differences in definitions across these three sources, comparisons should be treated with caution. Where estimates were available from more than one source for a country, we have

given precedence to the estimates of Bell and Muhudin over the other two sources.

Data on *conflict-induced migration* are from several sources, depending on the type of migrant: those who have moved across international borders (refugees and asylum-seekers) and those who have moved within a country (internally displaced people). Data on refugees are from the United Nations High Commission for Refugees (UNHCR 2009b), with the exception of refugees from Palestine, who fall mainly under the mandate of United Nations Relief and Work Agency for Palestine Refugees in the Near East (UNRWA 2008). Data are compiled from various sources, including national censuses and surveys. However, routine registration, which is created to establish a legal or administrative record or to administer entitlements and deliver services, constitutes the main source of refugee data. UNHCR also provides estimates for 27 developed countries that have no dedicated registers. These estimates are based on the recognition of asylum-seekers and estimated naturalization rates over a 10-year period. The most notable challenges of this estimation method pertain to its underlying assumption that all recognised asylum seekers are indeed refugees and the harmonization of its cut-off period to 10 years. This is particularly true for the 'traditional' immigration countries where it takes less than 10 years for migrants—including refugees—to obtain citizenship. Data on *internally displaced persons* are sourced from the Internally Displaced Monitoring Centre (IDMC 2009a). They are compiled from different sources, including the United Nations Office for the Coordination of Humanitarian Affairs (OCHA), estimates from UNHCR and from national governments. Because of the difficulty in tracking IDPs, estimates are associated with high levels of uncertainty and should therefore be interpreted with caution.

Calculating the human development indices

The diagrams here summarize how the five human development indices are constructed, highlighting both their similarities and their differences.

Full details of the methods of calculation can be found at: www.hdr.undp.org/en/statistics/tn1

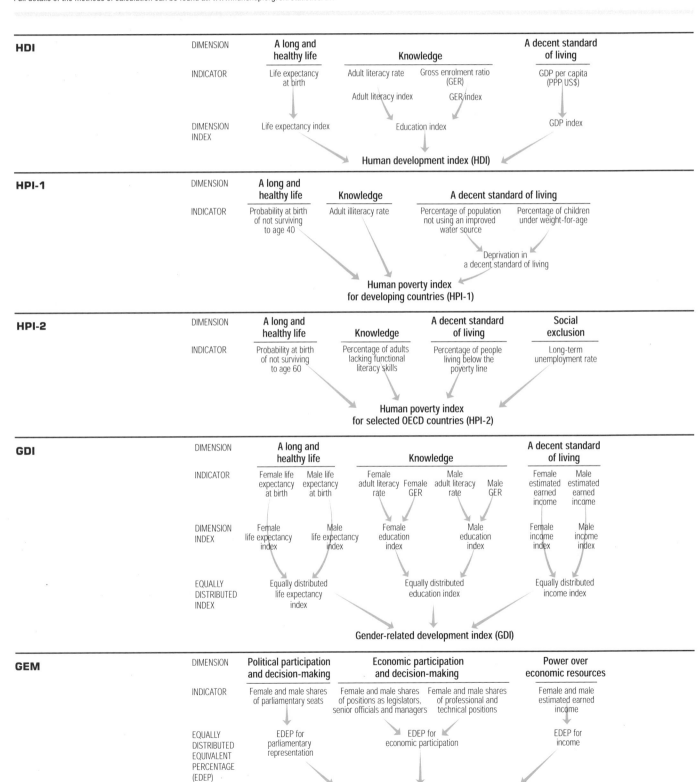

Definition of statistical terms and indicators

Asylum The grant, by a state, of protection on its territory to individuals or groups of people from another state fleeing persecution or serious danger.

Asylum seekers Individuals or groups of people who apply for *asylum* in a country other than their own. They retain the status of asylum-seeker until their applications are considered and adjudicated.

Child dependency ratio The population aged under 15 years expressed as a percentage of the population of working age (15–64 years of age).

Conflict-induced movement Human movement resulting in a change of usual place of residence in response to an ongoing or imminent violent or armed conflict that threatens lives or livelihoods.

Consumer price index, average annual change in Reflects changes in the cost to the average consumer of acquiring a standard or fixed basket of goods and services.

Country of origin The country from which an international migrant originally moves to another country, with the intention of settling temporarily or indefinitely.

Country of destination The country to which an international migrant moves, from another country, with the intention of settling temporarily or indefinitely.

Earned income (PPP US$), estimated Derived on the basis of the ratio of the female non-agricultural wage to the male non-agricultural wage, the female and male shares of the economically active population, total female and male population and total GDP (in purchasing power parity terms in US dollars; see *PPP (purchasing power parity)*. The estimated earned income is used in the calculation of both the *Gender-related Development Index and the Gender Empowerment Measure.* For details of this estimation, seehttp://hdr.undp.org/en/ technicalnote1.pdf.

Earned income, ratio of estimated female to male The ratio of estimated female earned income to estimated male earned income. See *Earned income (PPP US$), estimated.*

Economically active population (or the *labour force*) All persons aged 15 years and above who, during a given reference period, were either employed or did not have a job but were actively looking for one. See *Labour force.*

Education expenditure per pupil in primary education Public current expenditure on primary education in PPP US$ at constant 2005 prices divided by the total number of pupils enrolled in primary education.

Education expenditure as percentage of total government expenditure Total public expenditure on the education sector expressed as a percentage of total public expenditure by all levels of government.

Education index One of the three indices on which the human development index is built. It is based on the adult literacy rate and the combined gross enrolment ratio for primary, secondary and tertiary schools. See *Literacy rate, adult,* and *Enrolment ratio, gross combined, for primary, secondary and tertiary schools.*

Education levels Categorized as pre-primary (ISCED 0), primary (ISCED 1), secondary (ISCED 2 and 3), post-secondary (ISCED 4) and tertiary (ISCED 5 and 6) in accordance with the International Standard Classification of Education (ISCED).

Educational attainment Percentage distribution of population of a given age group according to the highest level of education attained or completed, with reference to education levels defined by ISCED. Typically expressed as high (ISCED 5 and 6), medium (ISCED 2, 3 and 4) and low (less than ISCED 2) levels of attainment. It is calculated by expressing the number of persons in the given age group with a particular highest level of attainment as a percentage of the total population of the same age group.

Emigrant An individual from a given country of origin (or birth) who has changed their usual country of residence to another country.

Emigration rate The stock of emigrants from a country at a particular point in time expressed as a percentage of the sum of the resident population in the country of origin and the emigrant population.

Enrolment ratio, gross combined, for primary, secondary and tertiary education The number of students enrolled in primary, secondary and tertiary levels of education, regardless of age, expressed as a percentage of the population of theoretical school age for the three levels. See *Education levels.*

Fertility rate, total The number of children that would be born to each woman if she were to live to the end of her child-bearing years and bear children at each age in accordance with prevailing age-specific fertility rates in a given year/period, for a given country, territory or geographical area.

Foreign direct investment, net inflows of Net inflows of investment to acquire a lasting management interest (10%

or more of voting stock) in an enterprise operating in an economy other than that of the investor. It is the sum of equity capital, reinvestment of earnings, other long-term capital and short-term capital.

GDP (gross domestic product) The sum of value added by all resident producers in the economy plus any product taxes (less subsidies) not included in the valuation of output. It is calculated without making deductions for depreciation of fabricated capital assets or for depletion and degradation of natural resources. 'Value added' is the net output of an industry after adding up all outputs and subtracting intermediate inputs.

GDP (US$) Gross domestic product converted to US dollars using the average official exchange rate reported by the International Monetary Fund. An alternative conversion factor is applied if the official exchange rate is judged to diverge by an exceptionally large margin from the rate effectively applied to transactions in foreign currencies and traded products. See *GDP (gross domestic product).*

GDP index One of the three indices on which the human development index is built. It is based on gross domestic product per capita (in purchasing power parity terms in US dollars; see *PPP*).

GDP per capita (PPP US$) Gross domestic product (in purchasing power parity terms in US dollars) divided by mid-year population. See *GDP (gross domestic product), PPP (purchasing power parity)* and *Population, total.*

GDP per capita (US$) Gross domestic product in US dollar terms divided by mid-year population. See *GDP (US$)* and *Population, total.*

GDP per capita annual growth rate Least squares annual growth rate, calculated from constant price GDP per capita in local currency units.

Gender empowerment measure (GEM) A composite index measuring gender inequality in three basic dimensions of empowerment—economic participation and decision-making, political participation, and decision-making and power over economic resources.

Gender-related development index (GDI) A composite index measuring average achievement in the three basic dimensions captured in the human development index—a long and healthy life, knowledge and a decent standard of living—adjusted to account for inequalities between men and women.

Gini index Measures the extent to which the distribution of income (or consumption) among individuals or households within a country deviates from a perfectly equal distribution. A Lorenz curve plots the cumulative percentages of total income received against the cumulative number of recipients, starting with the poorest individual or household. The Gini index measures the area between the Lorenz curve and a hypothetical line

of absolute equality, expressed as a percentage of the maximum area under the line. A value of 0 represents absolute equality, a value of 100 absolute inequality.

Health expenditure per capita (PPP US$) Public expenditure on health by all levels of government (in purchasing power parity US dollars), divided by the mid-year population. Health expenditure includes the provision of health services (preventive and curative), family planning activities, nutrition activities and emergency aid designated for health, but excludes the provision of water and sanitation.

Health expenditure, public as percentage of total government expenditure Public expenditure on health by all levels of government expressed as a percentage of total government spending.

Healthy life expectancy at birth Average number of years that a person can expect to live in 'full health' by taking into account years lived in less than full health due to disease and/or injury.

Human development index (HDI) A composite index measuring average achievement in three basic dimensions of human development—a long and healthy life, access to knowledge and a decent standard of living.

Human poverty index (HPI-1) A composite index measuring deprivations in the three basic dimensions captured in the human development index—a long and healthy life, access to knowledge and a decent standard of living.

Human poverty index for OECD countries (HPI-2) A composite index measuring deprivations in the three basic dimensions captured in the human development index—a long and healthy life, access to knowledge and a decent standard of living—and also capturing social exclusion.

Illiteracy rate, adult Calculated as 100 minus the adult literacy rate. See *Literacy rate, adult.*

Immigrant An individual residing in a given host country *(country of destination)* that is not their country of origin (or birth).

Income or expenditure, shares of The shares of income or expenditure (consumption) accruing to subgroups of population, based on national household surveys covering various years. Expenditure or consumption surveys produce results showing lower levels of inequality between poor and rich than do income surveys, as poor people generally consume a greater share of their income. Because data come from surveys covering different years and using different methodologies, comparisons between countries must be made with caution.

Income poverty line, population below The percentage of the population living below the specified poverty line:
US$1.25 a day and US$2 a day— at 2005 international prices adjusted for purchasing power parity;
National poverty line—the poverty line deemed appropriate for a country by its authorities. National estimates that are

Statistical terms

based on population-weighted subgroup estimates from
household surveys;

50% of median income—50% of the median adjusted
disposable household income.

Internal migration Human movement within the borders of
a country usually measured across regional, district or
municipality boundaries resulting in a change of usual
place of residence.

Internally Displaced Persons (IDPs) Individuals or groups
of people who have been forced to leave their homes or
places of usual residence, in particular as a result of or in
order to avoid the effects of armed conflict, situations of
generalized violence, violations of human rights or natural
or human-made disasters, and who have not crossed an
international border.

International migration Human movement across international
borders resulting in a change of country of usual residence.

International migrants as a percentage of the population
Estimated number of international migrants expressed as a
percentage of the total population.

International movement rate The sum of total stock of
immigrants into and emigrants from a particular country,
expressed as a percentage of the sum of that country's
resident population and its emigrant population.

Labour force All people employed (including people above a
specified age who, during the reference period, were in
paid employment, either at work, self-employed or with
a job but not at work) and unemployed (including people
above a specified age who, during the reference period,
were without work, currently available for work and actively
seeking work). See *Economically active population.*

Labour force participation rate A measure of the proportion
of a country's working-age population that engages
actively in the labour market, either by working or actively
looking for work. It is calculated by expressing the number
of persons in the labour force as a percentage of the
working-age population. The working-age population is the
population above 15 years of age (as used in this Report).
See *Labour force* and *Economically active population.*

Legislators, senior officials and managers, female
Women's share of positions defined according to the
International Standard Classification of Occupations
(ISCO-88) to include legislators, senior government
officials, traditional chiefs and heads of villages, senior
officials of special-interest organizations, corporate
managers, directors and chief executives, production and
operations department managers and other department
and general managers.

Life expectancy at birth The number of years a newborn
infant could expect to live if prevailing patterns of age-
specific mortality rates at the time of birth were to stay the
same throughout the child's life.

Life expectancy index One of the three indices on which the
human development index is built.

Literacy rate, adult The proportion of the adult population aged
15 years and older which is literate, expressed as a percentage
of the corresponding population (total or for a given sex) in a
given country, territory, or geographic area, at a specific point
in time, usually mid-year. For statistical purposes, a person is
literate who can, with understanding, both read and write a
short simple statement on their everyday life.

Medium-variant projection Population projections by the United
Nations Population Division assuming medium-fertility path,
normal mortality and normal international migration. Each
assumption implies projected trends in fertility, mortality and
net migration levels, depending on the specific demographic
characteristics and relevant policies of each country or
group of countries. In addition, for the countries highly
affected by the HIV epidemic, the impact of HIV is included
in the projection. The United Nations Population Division
also publishes low- and high-variant projections. For more
information, see *http://esa.un.org/unpp/assumptions.html.*

Migrant An individual who has changed their usual place of
residence, either by crossing an international border or
moving within their country of origin to another region,
district or municipality.

Migrant stock, annual rate of growth Estimated average
exponential growth rate of the international migrant stock
over each period indicated, expressed in percentage terms.

Migrant stock as a share of population Estimated number
of international migrants, expressed as a percentage of the
total population.

Mortality rate, under-five The probability of dying between
birth and exactly five years of age, expressed per 1,000
live births.

Natural increase, annual rate of The portion of population
growth (or decline) determined exclusively by births
and deaths.

Net international migration rate The total number of
immigrants to a country minus the number of emigrants
over a period, divided by the person-years lived by the
population of the receiving country over that period. It is
expressed as net number of migrants per 1,000 population
or as a percentage.

Official development assistance (ODA), net Disbursements
of loans made on concessional terms (net of repayments
of principal) and grants by official agencies of the members
of the Development Assistance Committee (DAC), by
multilateral institutions and by non-DAC countries to
promote economic development and welfare in countries
and territories in Part I of the DAC List of Aid Recipients.
For more details see *www.oecd.org/dac/stats/daclist.*

Official development assistance (ODA) allocated to basic social services Aid funds allocated to social infrastructure and services (including health, education, water and sanitation, government and civil society and other services) expressed as a percentage of total official development assistance (ODA).

Old age dependency ratio The population aged 65 years and above expressed as a percentage of the population of working age (15–64 years of age).

Population, annual growth rate The average annual exponential growth rate of the population for the period indicated. See *Population, total*.

Population, total The *de facto* population in a country, area or region as of 1 July of the year indicated. The *de facto* population includes those who are usually present, including visitors but excluding residents, who are temporarily absent from the country, area or region.

Population, urban The *de facto* population living in areas classified as urban according to the criteria used by each area or country. Data refer to 1 July of the year indicated. See *Population, total*.

PPP (purchasing power parity) A rate of exchange that accounts for price differences across countries, allowing international comparisons of real output and incomes. At the PPP US$ rate (as used in this Report), PPP US$1 has the same purchasing power in the domestic economy as US$1 has in the United States.

Probability at birth of not surviving to a specified age Calculated as 100 minus the probability (expressed as a percentage) of surviving to a specified age for a given cohort. See *Probability at birth of surviving to a specified age*.

Probability at birth of surviving to a specified age The probability of a newborn infant surviving to a specified age if subject to prevailing patterns of age-specific mortality rates, expressed as a percentage.

Professional and technical workers, female Women's share of positions defined according to the International Standard Classification of Occupations (ISCO-88) to include physical, mathematical and engineering science professionals (and associate professionals), life science and health professionals (and associate professionals), teaching professionals (and associate professionals) and other professionals and associate professionals.

Refugees Individuals or groups of people who have fled their country of origin because of a well-founded fear of being persecuted for reasons of race, religion, nationality, political opinion or membership of a particular social group and who cannot or do not want to return.

Remittances are earnings and material resources transferred by international migrants or refugees to recipients in their country of origin or countries in which the migrant formerly resided.

Seats in parliament held by women Seats held by women in a lower or single house and, where relevant, in an upper house or senate.

Tertiary emigration rate Total number of emigrants aged 15 years and older from a particular country with tertiary education, expressed as a percentage of the sum of all persons of the same age with tertiary education in the origin country and the emigrants population with tertiary education.

Treaties, ratification of In order to enact an international treaty, a country must ratify it, often with the approval of its legislature. Ratification implies not only an expression of interest as indicated by the signature, but also the transformation of the treaty's principles and obligations into national law.

Unemployed All people above a specified age who are not in paid employment or self-employed, but who are available for work and have taken specific steps to seek paid employment or self-employment.

Unemployment, long-term rate People above a specified age who have been unemployed for at least 12 months, expressed as a percentage of the labour force (those employed plus the unemployed). See *Unemployed* and *Labour force*.

Unemployment rate The unemployed, expressed as a percentage of the labour force (those employed plus the unemployed). See *Unemployed* and *Labour force*.

Water source, improved, population not using Calculated as 100 minus the percentage of the population using an improved water source. Improved sources include household connections, public standpipes, boreholes, protected dug wells, protected springs, and rainwater collection.

Women in government at ministerial level Includes deputy prime ministers and ministers. Prime ministers are included if they hold ministerial portfolios. Vice-presidents and heads of ministerial-level departments or agencies are also included if they exercise a ministerial function in the government structure.

Country classification

Human development categories

Very high human development
(HDI 0.900 and above)

Andorra
Australia
Austria
Barbados
Belgium
Brunei Darussalam
Canada
Cyprus
Czech Republic
Denmark
Finland
France
Germany
Greece
Hong Kong, China (SAR)
Iceland
Ireland
Israel
Italy
Japan
Korea (Republic of)
Kuwait
Liechtenstein
Luxembourg
Malta
Netherlands
New Zealand
Norway
Portugal
Qatar
Singapore
Slovenia
Spain
Sweden
Switzerland
United Arab Emirates
United Kingdom
United States
(38 countries or areas)

High human development
(HDI 0.800–0.899)

Albania
Antigua and Barbuda
Argentina
Bahamas
Bahrain
Belarus
Bosnia and Herzegovina
Brazil
Bulgaria
Chile
Colombia
Costa Rica
Croatia
Cuba
Dominica
Ecuador
Estonia
Grenada
Hungary
Kazakhstan
Latvia
Lebanon
Libyan Arab Jamahiriya
Lithuania
Macedonia (the Former Yugoslav Rep. of)
Malaysia
Mauritius
Mexico
Montenegro
Oman
Panama
Peru
Poland
Romania
Russian Federation
Saint Kitts and Nevis
Saint Lucia
Saudi Arabia
Serbia
Seychelles
Slovakia
Trinidad and Tobago
Turkey
Uruguay
Venezuela (Bolivarian Republic of)
(45 countries or areas)

Medium human development
(HDI 0.500–0.799)

Algeria
Angola
Armenia
Azerbaijan
Bangladesh
Belize
Bhutan
Bolivia
Botswana
Cambodia
Cameroon
Cape Verde
China
Comoros
Congo
Djibouti
Dominican Republic
Egypt
El Salvador
Equatorial Guinea
Fiji
Gabon
Georgia
Ghana
Guatemala
Guyana
Haiti
Honduras
India
Indonesia
Iran (Islamic Republic of)
Jamaica
Jordan
Kenya
Kyrgyzstan
Lao People's Democratic Republic
Lesotho
Madagascar
Maldives
Mauritania
Moldova
Mongolia
Morocco
Myanmar
Namibia
Nepal
Nicaragua
Nigeria
Occupied Palestinian Territories
Pakistan
Papua New Guinea
Paraguay
Philippines
Saint Vincent and the Grenadines
Samoa
Sao Tome and Principe
Solomon Islands
South Africa
Sri Lanka
Sudan
Suriname
Swaziland
Syrian Arab Republic
Tajikistan
Tanzania (United Republic of)
Thailand
Tonga
Tunisia
Turkmenistan
Uganda
Ukraine
Uzbekistan
Vanuatu
Viet Nam
Yemen
(75 countries or areas)

Low human development
(HDI below 0.500)

Afghanistan
Benin
Burkina Faso
Burundi
Central African Republic
Chad
Congo (Democratic Republic of the)
Côte d'Ivoire
Eritrea
Ethiopia
Gambia
Guinea
Guinea-Bissau
Liberia
Malawi
Mali
Mozambique
Niger
Rwanda
Senegal
Sierra Leone
Timor-Leste
Togo
Zambia
(24 countries or areas)

213

Country classification

Continents

Africa

Algeria
Angola
Benin
Botswana
Burkina Faso
Burundi
Cameroon
Cape Verde
Central African Republic
Chad
Comoros
Congo
Congo (Democratic Republic of the)
Côte d'Ivoire
Djibouti
Egypt
Equatorial Guinea
Eritrea
Ethiopia
Gabon
Gambia
Ghana
Guinea
Guinea-Bissau
Kenya
Lesotho
Liberia
Libyan Arab Jamahiriya
Madagascar
Malawi
Mali
Mauritania
Mauritius
Morocco
Mozambique
Namibia
Niger
Nigeria
Réunion
Rwanda
Saint Helena
Sao Tome and Principe
Senegal
Seychelles
Sierra Leone
Somalia
South Africa
Sudan
Swaziland
Tanzania (United Republic of)
Togo
Tunisia
Uganda
Western Sahara
Zambia
Zimbabwe
(56 countries or areas)

Asia

Afghanistan
Armenia
Azerbaijan
Bahrain
Bangladesh
Bhutan
Brunei Darussalam
Cambodia
China
Cyprus
Georgia
Hong Kong, China (SAR)
India
Indonesia
Iran (Islamic Republic of)
Iraq
Israel
Japan
Jordan
Kazakhstan
Korea (Democratic People's Rep. of)
Korea (Republic of)
Kuwait
Kyrgyzstan
Lao People's Democratic Republic
Lebanon
Macao, China (SAR)
Malaysia
Maldives
Mongolia
Myanmar
Nepal
Occupied Palestinian Territories
Oman
Pakistan
Philippines
Qatar
Saudi Arabia
Singapore
Sri Lanka
Syrian Arab Republic
Taiwan Province of China
Tajikistan
Thailand
Timor-Leste
Turkey
Turkmenistan
United Arab Emirates
Uzbekistan
Viet Nam
Yemen
(51 countries or areas)

Europe

Albania
Andorra
Austria
Belarus
Belgium
Bosnia and Herzegovina
Bulgaria
Croatia
Czech Republic
Denmark
Estonia
Faeroe Islands
Finland
France
Germany
Gibraltar
Greece
Holy See
Hungary
Iceland
Ireland
Isle of Man
Italy
Latvia
Liechtenstein
Lithuania
Luxembourg
Macedonia (the Former Yugoslav Rep. of)
Malta
Moldova
Monaco
Montenegro
Netherlands
Norway
Poland
Portugal
Romania

Country classification

Russian Federation
San Marino
Serbia
Slovakia
Slovenia
Spain
Svalbard and Jan Mayen Islands
Sweden
Switzerland
Ukraine
United Kingdom
(49 countries or areas)

Latin America and the Caribbean

Antigua and Barbuda
Argentina
Bahamas
Barbados
Belize
Bolivia
Brazil
Chile
Colombia
Costa Rica
Cuba
Dominica
Dominican Republic
Ecuador
El Salvador
Grenada
Guatemala
Guyana
Haiti
Honduras
Jamaica
Mexico
Nicaragua
Panama
Paraguay
Peru
Saint Kitts and Nevis
Saint Lucia
Saint Vincent and the Grenadines
Suriname
Trinidad and Tobago
Uruguay
Venezuela (Bolivarian Republic of)
(33 countries or areas)

Northern America

Canada
United States
(2 countries or areas)

Oceania

Australia
Fiji
Kiribati
Marshall Islands
Micronesia (Federated States of)
Nauru
New Zealand
Palau
Papua New Guinea
Samoa
Solomon Islands
Tonga
Tuvalu
Vanuatu
(14 countries or areas)

UNDP regional bureaux

Arab States

Algeria
Bahrain
Djibouti
Egypt
Iraq
Jordan
Kuwait
Lebanon
Libyan Arab Jamahiriya
Morocco
Occupied Palestinian Territories
Oman
Qatar
Saudi Arabia
Somalia
Sudan
Syrian Arab Republic
Tunisia
United Arab Emirates
Yemen
(20 countries or areas)

Central and Eastern Europe and the Commonwealth of Independent States (CIS)

Albania
Armenia
Azerbaijan
Belarus
Bosnia and Herzegovina
Bulgaria
Croatia
Cyprus
Czech Republic
Estonia
Georgia
Hungary
Kazakhstan
Kyrgyzstan
Latvia
Lithuania
Macedonia (the Former Yugoslav Rep. of))
Malta
Moldova
Montenegro
Poland

Romania
Russian Federation
Serbia
Slovakia
Slovenia
Tajikistan
Turkey
Turkmenistan
Ukraine
Uzbekistan
(31 countries or areas)

East Asia and the Pacific
Brunei Darussalam
Cambodia
China
Fiji
Hong Kong, China (SAR)
Indonesia
Kiribati
Korea (Democratic People's Republic of)
Korea (Republic of)
Lao People's Democratic Republic
Malaysia
Marshall Islands
Micronesia (Federated States of)
Mongolia
Myanmar
Nauru
Palau
Papua New Guinea
Philippines
Samoa
Singapore
Solomon Islands
Thailand
Timor-Leste
Tonga
Tuvalu
Vanuatu
Viet Nam
(28 countries or areas)

Latin America and Caribbean
Antigua and Barbuda
Argentina
Bahamas
Barbados
Belize
Bolivia
Brazil

Chile
Colombia
Costa Rica
Cuba
Dominica
Dominican Republic
Ecuador
El Salvador
Grenada
Guatemala
Guyana
Haiti
Honduras
Jamaica
Mexico
Nicaragua
Panama
Paraguay
Peru
Saint Kitts and Nevis
Saint Lucia
Saint Vincent and the Grenadines
Suriname
Trinidad and Tobago
Uruguay
Venezuela (Bolivarian Republic of)
(33 countries or areas)

Sub-Saharan Africa
Angola
Benin
Botswana
Burkina Faso
Burundi
Cameroon
Cape Verde
Central African Republic
Chad
Comoros
Congo
Congo (Democratic Republic of the)
Côte d'Ivoire
Equatorial Guinea
Eritrea
Ethiopia
Gabon
Gambia
Ghana
Guinea
Guinea-Bissau
Kenya

Lesotho
Liberia
Madagascar
Malawi
Mali
Mauritania
Mauritius
Mozambique
Namibia
Niger
Nigeria
Rwanda
Sao Tome and Principe
Senegal
Seychelles
Sierra Leone
South Africa
Swaziland
Tanzania (United Republic of)
Togo
Uganda
Zambia
Zimbabwe
(45 countries or areas)

South Asia
Afghanistan
Bangladesh
Bhutan
India
Iran (Islamic Republic of)
Maldives
Nepal
Pakistan
Sri Lanka
(9 countries or areas)

Country classification

Other country groupings

Gulf Cooperation Council (GCC)

Bahrain
Kuwait
Qatar
Oman
Saudi Arabia
United Arab Emirates
(6 countries or areas)

European Union (EU27)

Austria
Belgium
Bulgaria
Cyprus
Czech Republic
Denmark
Estonia
Finland
France
Germany
Greece
Hungary
Ireland
Italy
Latvia
Lithuania
Luxembourg
Malta
Netherlands
Poland
Portugal
Romania
Slovakia
Slovenia
Spain
Sweden
United Kingdom
(27 countries or areas)

Organisation of Economic Cooperation and Development (OECD)

Australia
Austria
Belgium
Canada
Czech Republic
Denmark
Finland
France
Germany
Greece
Hungary
Iceland
Ireland
Italy
Japan
Korea (Republic of)
Luxembourg
Mexico
Netherlands
New Zealand
Norway
Poland
Portugal
Slovakia
Spain
Sweden
Switzerland
Turkey
United Kingdom
United States
(30 countries or areas)